12/00

THE CLASSICAL WORLD

THE CLASSICAL
WORLD

An Epic History
from Homer to Hadrian

ROBIN LANE FOX

BASIC
BOOKS

A Member of the Perseus Books Group
New York

Published by Basic Books,
A Member of the Perseus Books Group

Published in the United Kingdom in 2005 by Allen Lane, the Penguin Group.

Library of Congress Cataloging-in-Publication Data

Lane Fox, Robin, 1946-
   The classical world : an epic history from Homer to Hadrian / Robin Lane Fox.
      p. cm.
   Includes bibliographical references and index.
   ISBN–13: 978–0–465–02496–4 (alk. paper)
   ISBN–10: 0–465–02496–3
1. Mediterranean Region—Civilization. 2. Civilization, Classical. 3. Civilization, Greco-
Roman. I. Title.

   DE80.L36 2006
   938—dc22

                                                                    2006020247

10 9 8 7 6 5 4 3 2 1

FOR MARTHA

Τόσσα παθούσῃ

He found his father alone in his well-ordered orchard
Digging round a plant: he was wearing a dirty tunic,
Patched and unseemly, and round his shins he had bound
Sewn leather leg-guards, keeping off scratches,
And he had gloves on his hands because of the thorns.
On his head he wore a goatskin cap, increasing his air of sorrow.
When noble, enduring Odysseus saw him
Worn by old age and with such great sadness in his heart,
He stood beneath a tall pear-tree and shed tears . . .

Odysseus returns to his father:
Homer, *Odyssey* 24.226–34

This tomb of well-sculpted metal
Covers the dead body of a great hero,
Zenodotus. But his soul is in heaven, where Orpheus is,
Where Plato is, and has found a holy seat, fit to receive a god.
For, he was a valiant cavalryman in the Emperor's service,
Famous, eloquent, god-like. In his speech
He was a copy of Socrates among the Italian people.
Leaving to his children his sound ancestral fortune,
He has died, a fit old man, leaving boundless sorrow
To his well-born friends, his city and its citizens.

Palatine Anthology 7.363,
possibly composed by Hadrian himself

CONTENTS

CONTENTS

CONTENTS

Part Six
AN IMPERIAL WORLD

LIST OF MAPS

PREFACE

I T IS A CHALLENGE to be asked to write a history of some nine hundred
years, especially when the evidence is so scattered and diverse, but it is a
challenge which I have enjoyed. I have not assumed a familiarity with the
subject but I hope that readers who do or do not have one will be drawn in
and retained by what I have had space to discuss. My hope is that they will
leave it, as I have, with a sense of how this history varied but can still be
made to hang together. I also hope that there will be parts which they will
want to pursue, especially the many which I have had to compress.

I have not followed the conventional thematic presentation of classical
civilization which discusses a topic ('a gendered world', 'getting a living')
across a thousand years in a single chapter. For theoretical reasons, I have
chosen a form with a framework of narrative. I believe that changing relations of power, sharply changed by events, changed the meaning and context of most of these themes and that these changes are lost by taking the
easy thematic short-cut. My approach is shared in contemporary areas of
medical thinking ('evidence based medicine'), the social sciences ('critical
juncture theory') and literary studies ('discourse analysis'). I owe it,
rather, to the hard old historical method of putting questions to evidence,
reading with it (not against it) in order to bring out more of what it says
and constantly retaining a sense of turning points and crucial decisions
whose results were shaped, but not predetermined, by their context.

I have had to make hard choices and say little on areas where I feel I
know most. One side of me still looks to Homer, another to the still-green
orchards near Lefkadia in Macedonia where my vaulted tomb, painted
with my three great horses, sixty-petalled roses, Bactrian dancing girls
and apparently mythical women awaits discovery by the skilled ephors of
the Greek Archaeological Service in 2056. I have chosen to give slightly
more space to narrative for one cardinal era, the years from 60 to 19 BC,
not only because they are of such significance for the role of my assumed

reader, the Emperor Hadrian. They are so dramatic, even to my post-Macedonian eye. They also attach initially to the letters of Cicero, the inexhaustible reward for all historians of the ancient world.

I am extremely grateful to Fiona Greenland for her expert help with illustrations. The jacket was the publisher's choice, but the descriptions of the illustrations are otherwise mostly mine. I am also very grateful to Stuart Proffitt for comments on the first part which forced me to go back over it, and to Elizabeth Stratford for expert copy-editing and correction. Above all, I am grateful to two former pupils who turned a manuscript into discs, Luke Streatfeild initially and especially Tamsin Cox whose skill and patience have been this book's essential support.

ROBIN LANE FOX
New College, Oxford

HADRIAN AND
THE CLASSICAL WORLD

*The following was [resolved] . . . by the council and people of the citizens
of Thyatira: to inscribe this decree on a stone stele and to place it on the
Acropolis (at Athens) so that it may [be] evident to all the Greeks how
much Thyatira has received from the greatest of kings since . . . he
(Hadrian) benefited all the Greeks in common when he summoned, as a
gift to one and all, a council from among them to the most brilliant city of
Athens, the Benefactress . . . and when, on his proposal, the [Romans] approved [this] most venerable Panhellenion [by decree] of the Senate and
individually he [gave] the tribes and the cities a share in this most honourable Council. . . .*

Inscribed decree, *c.* AD 119/20,
found at Athens, concerning Hadrian's Panhellenion

T HE 'CLASSICAL WORLD' is the world of the ancient Greeks and Romans, some forty lifetimes before our own but still able to challenge
us by a humanity shared with ours. The word 'classical' is itself of ancient
origin: it derives from the Latin word *classicus* which referred to recruits
of the 'first class', the heavy infantry in the Roman army. The 'classical',
then, is 'first class', though it is no longer heavily armoured. The Greeks
and Romans did borrow from many other cultures, Iranian, Levantine,
Egyptian or Jewish among others. Their story connects at times with these
parallel stories, but it is their own art and literature, thought, philosophy
and political life which are correctly regarded as 'first class' in their world
and ours.

In this world's long history, two periods and places have come to be
seen as particularly classical: Athens in the fifth- and fourth-century BC

is one, while the other is Rome from the first century BC to AD 14, the world of Julius Caesar and then Augustus, the first Roman emperor. The ancients themselves shared this perspective. By the time of Alexander the Great they already recognized, as we still do, that particular dramatists at Athens in the fifth century BC had written 'classic' plays. In the Hellenistic age (c. 330–30 BC) artists and architects adopted a classicizing style which looked back to the arts of the fifth century as classics. Then Rome, in the late first century BC, became a centre of classicizing art and taste, while classical Greek, especially Athenian Greek, was exalted as good taste against 'Eastern' excesses of style. Subsequent Roman emperors endorsed this classicizing taste and as time passed, added another 'classic' age: the era of the Emperor Augustus, their Empire's founding figure.

My history of the classical world begins from a pre-classical classic, the epic poet Homer whom the ancients, like all modern readers, acknowledge as simply in a class of his own. His poems are the first written Greek literature to survive. From then onwards, I shall explore how classical Greece of the fifth and fourth centuries BC evolved and what it stood for, up to four hundred years after Homer's (probable) date (c. 730 BC). I then turn to Rome and the emergence of its own classical age, from Julius Caesar to Augustus (c. 50 BC to AD 14). My history ends with the reign of Hadrian, the Roman emperor from AD 117 to 138, just before the first surviving use of the term 'classics' to describe the best authors: it is attested in the conversation of Fronto, tutor to the children of Hadrian's successor in Rome.[1]

But why choose to stop with Hadrian? One reason is that 'classical literature' ends in his reign, just as it began with Homer: in Latin, the satirical poet Juvenal is its last widely recognized representative. But this reason is rather arbitrary, formed by a canon which is hard for those to share who read forward into later authors and who approach the writers of the fourth and fifth centuries AD with an open mind. A more relevant reason is that Hadrian himself was the emperor with the most evident classicizing tastes. They are seen in his plans for the city of Athens and in many of the buildings which he patronized, and in aspects of his personal style. He himself looked back self-consciously on a classical world, although by his lifetime what we call the 'Roman world' had been pacified and greatly extended. Hadrian is a landmark, too, because he is the one emperor who acquired a first-hand view of this world, one we would dearly like to share. In the 120s and early 130s he set out on several grand tours of an Empire which extended from Britain to the Red Sea. He spent time in Athens, its classical centre. He travelled by ship and on horseback,

1. Gold aureus from Rome AD 134–8, with Hadrian (*obverse*) and a personified Egypt (*reverse*), one of his types of the provinces.

a seasoned rider in his mid-forties who revelled in local opportunities for hunting. He went far afield to lands under Roman rule which no 'classical' Athenian had ever visited. We are unusually able to follow his progress because we have the specially commissioned coins which were struck to commemorate his journeys. Even in unclassical places, they are vivid witnesses to Hadrian and his contemporaries' sense of an admired classical past.[2]

These coins show a personified image of each province of Hadrian's Roman Empire, whether or not it had had a classical age. They show unclassical Germany as a bare-breasted female warrior and unclassical Spain as a lady reclining on the ground: she holds a large olive-branch, symbol of Spain's excellent olive oil, with a rabbit beside her, Spanish rabbits being notoriously prolific. Most of Spain and all of Germany had been unknown to Greeks in the first classical age, but the fine pictures on these coins connect them to classical taste because they portray them in an elegant classicizing style. Behind Hadrian's taste and the 'Hadrianic School' of artists who designed these images lies a classical world which they themselves were acknowledging. It was based on the classical art of the Greeks four or five hundred years earlier, examples of which could be admired conveniently by Romans because previous Romans had plundered them and brought them back to their own homes and cities.

These grand tours to Greece or Egypt, the west coast of Asia or Sicily and Libya gave Hadrian the chance of a global, classical overview. He stopped at so many of the great sites of its past, but he was particularly respectful of Athens. He regarded it as a 'free' city and made it the spectacular beneficiary of his gifts, one of which was a grand 'library', with a hundred pillars of rare marble. He completed its enormous temple to the

2. Tondo originally from a Hadrianic hunting-monument, Rome. Hadrian (*second left*) and possibly Antinous (*left*) with the lion they killed in West Egypt, in September AD 130.

Olympian god Zeus which had been begun six centuries earlier but never finished. It was surely Hadrian who encouraged the new venture of an all-Greek synod, or Panhellenion, excelling even the classical Athenian states-man Pericles.[3] From all over the Greek world, delegates were to meet in Athens, and were to hold a great festival of the arts and athletics every four years. Past Athenians had been credited with Panhellenic projects, but this one was to be incomparably grand.

Those who idealize the past tend not to understand it: restoration kills it with kindness. Hadrian certainly shared the traditional pleasures of past Greek aristocrats and kings. He loved hunting as they had; he loved his horse, the gallant Borysthenes whom he honoured with verses on his death in southern Gaul;[4] above all, he loved the young male Antinous, a spectacular instance of 'Greek love'. When Antinous died prematurely, Hadrian built a new city in his honour in Egypt and encouraged his cult as a god throughout his Empire. Not even Alexander the Great had done quite so much for his lifelong male love, Hephaestion. Like Hadrian's distinctive beard, these elements of Hadrian's life were rooted in previous Greek culture. But he could never be a classical Greek himself, because so much around him had changed since the Athens of the great classics, let alone since the pre-classical Homer.

The most audible change was the spread of language. Almost a thousand years earlier, in Homer's youth, Greek had been only a spoken language without an alphabet, and was only used by people from Greece and the Aegean. Latin, too, had been only a spoken language, at home in a small part of Italy, Latium, around Rome. But Hadrian spoke and read both languages, although his family traced back on both sides to southern Spain and his father's estates lay just to the north of modern Seville, miles from Athens and Latium. Hadrian's ancestors had settled in Spain as Latin-speaking Italians, rewarded for service in the Roman army nearly three hundred years before his birth. Of Latin-speaking descent, Hadrian was not 'Spanish' in any cultural sense. He himself had been brought up in Rome and favoured the archaic style of Latin prose. Like other educated Romans, he also spoke Greek: he was even known as a 'Greekling' because his passion for Greek literature was so strong. So far from being Spanish, Hadrian was proof of the common classicizing culture which now bound together the emperor's educated class. It was based on the classical homelands of the Greek and Latin language but it extended way beyond their boundaries. As Homer never could, Hadrian could pass through Syria or Egypt speaking Greek and he could also travel far away into Britain, speaking Latin.

His classicizing mind surveyed a world of quite a different scale to Homer's. In the first classical age, Athens, at its height, had contained perhaps 300,000 residents in its Attic territory, including slaves. By Hadrian's day, the Roman Empire is estimated (no more) to have had a population of about 60 million, extending from Scotland to Spain, from Spain to Armenia. No other empire, before or since, has ruled this great span of territory, but, on our modern scale, its total population was no greater than modern Britain's. It was concentrated in patches, maybe as many as 8 million in Egypt,[5] where the river Nile and the grain harvest supported such a density, and at least a million, perhaps, in the mega-city of Rome which was also fed and supported by Egypt's harvests and its exported grain. Outside these two points, whole swathes of Hadrian's Empire were very thinly populated by our standards. Nonetheless, they required, in every province, detachments of the Roman army to keep the peace. Hadrian favoured many cities on his travels, but he also had to rule large areas which only had villages, not classicizing towns at all.

Where necessary, he ordered large stretches of walling to regulate peoples beyond the Empire, a most unclassical project. The most famous is Hadrian's Wall, in northern Britain, running from Wallsend near Newcastle westwards to Bowness. A massive barrier, it was ten feet thick and fourteen feet high, partly faced in stone with 'intercastles' every mile, two signalling turrets between them and a ditch on the north side, ten feet deep and thirty feet wide. There were other 'Hadrian's walls' too, though nowadays they are less famous. In north Africa, beyond the Aures mountains of modern Tunisia, Hadrian approved stretches of walling and ditching which were to control contacts with the nomadic peoples of the desert along a frontier of some 150 miles. In north-west Europe, in upper Germany, he well understood the danger: here, he 'shut off the barbarians by tall stakes fixed deeply into the ground and fastened together like a palisade'.[6]

Global walling had never been part of the classical past. In the age of Athens' greatness, let alone of Homer's, there had never been a single ruler like Hadrian, an emperor, nor a standing army, like Rome's, of some 500,000 soldiers throughout the Empire. In the classical age of Rome, the mid-first century BC, there had not yet been an emperor or standing army, either. Hadrian was heir to historical changes which had transformed Roman history. Hadrian respected the classical Greek and Roman past and, wherever he went, he visited great relics of it, but did he understand the context in which it had once belonged, how it had evolved and how his own role as emperor had come about?

Certainly, Hadrian was famous for a love of 'curiosities' and an exploration of them.[7] On his travels, he climbed volcanic Etna in Sicily and other conspicuous mountains; he consulted ancient oracles of the gods; he visited the tourist wonders of long-dead ancient Egypt. With a tourist's mind, he was also a cultural magpie who stored and imitated what he saw. Back in Italy, near Tivoli, he built himself an enormous, straggling villa whose features alluded explicitly to great cultural monuments of the ancient Greek past. Hadrian's villa was a vast theme-park which included buildings evocative of Alexandria and classical Athens.[8]

At this villa, after his beloved Antinous' death, he turned to writing his own autobiography. Almost nothing of it survives, but we can guess that it would have combined affectionate tributes to his male lover with a furtherance of his own urbane self-image. Hadrian was interested by philosophy and perhaps, in an Epicurean manner, he would have consoled himself against the fear of death.[9] What he would not have done was to analyse the historical changes behind all that he had seen on his travels, from Homer to classical Athens, from Alexander the Great's great Alexandria to the former splendours of Carthage (a city which he renamed Hadrianopolis after himself). Hadrian took the first emperor, Augustus, as his role-model, but he never seems to have wondered how Augustus' one-man rule had imposed itself on Rome after more than four hundred years of highly prized liberty.

This book aims to answer these questions for Hadrian and the many who are heirs to his sort of engagement, who travel in the classical world, who look at classical sites and who like to acknowledge that a 'classical age' existed, even among the competing claims of ever more cultures around the world. It is a choice of highlights and it has least to say on subjects which would have concerned Hadrian least: the range of Greek kingdoms after Alexander the Great and, above all, the years of the Roman Republic between its sack of Carthage (146 BC) and the reforms of the dictator Sulla (81/0 BC). By contrast, the Athens of Pericles and Socrates and the Rome of Caesar and Augustus claim the limelight, as 'classical' points in the past to which Hadrian attached himself.

Historians in Hadrian's own Empire were not unaware of the changes since these eras. Some of them tried to explain them, and their answers did not simply list military victories and members of Rome's imperial family. Part of the story of the classical world is the invention and development of history-writing itself. Nowadays, historians try to apply sophisticated theories to the understanding of these changes, economics and sociology, geography and ecology, theories of class and gender, the power of symbols or demographic models for populations and their age groups. In antiquity, these theories of ours were not explicit, or did not even exist. Instead, historians had favourite themes of their own, of which three were particularly prominent: freedom, justice and luxury. Our modern theories can deepen these ancient explanatory themes, but they do not entirely supplant them. I have chosen to emphasize these three because they were in the minds of the actors at the time and a part of the way in which events were seen, even when they do not suffice for our understanding of historical change.

Each of them is a flexible concept whose scope varies. Freedom, for us, entails choice and, for many people nowadays, implies autonomy or a power of independent decision. 'Autonomy' is a word invented by the ancient Greeks, but for them it had a clear political context: it began as the word for a community's self-government, a protected degree of freedom in the face of an outside power which was strong enough to infringe it. Its first surviving application to an individual is to a woman,

Antigone, in drama.[10] Freedom, too, was a political value, but it was sharpened everywhere by its opposite status, slavery. From Homer onwards, communities valued freedom in the face of enemies who would otherwise enslave them. Within a community, freedom then became a value of political constitutions: alternatives were denounced as 'slavery'. Above all, freedom was the prized status of individuals, marking them off from slaves who were to be bought and sold. But, outside slavery, in what did an individual's freedom consist? Did it require freedom of speech or freedom to worship whatever gods one chose? Was it the freedom to live as one pleased, or simply a freedom from interference? When did 'liberty' become wicked 'licence'? These questions had all been discussed by the time of Hadrian, who was hailed both as a liberator and as a god by Greeks among his subjects.

The concept of justice had been no less contested. It was claimed by rulers, including Hadrian, and even in the age of Homer it was ascribed to idealized 'just' communities. Did the gods care for it or was the hard truth that justice was not a value which shaped their dealings with mortals? What was justice, philosophers had long wondered; was it 'giving each his due' or was it receiving one's deserts, perhaps because of behaviour in a previous life? Was equality just, and if so, what sort of equality? The 'same for one and all' or a 'proportional equality', which varied according to each person's riches or social class?[11] What system guaranteed it, one of laws applied by juries of randomly chosen citizens or one of laws applied and created by a single judge, a governor perhaps or the emperor himself? Much of Hadrian's own energy was spent on judging and answering petitions, the process through which we know him best. His answers to cities and subjects in his Empire sometimes survive where recipients inscribed them on stone.[12] Others of his rulings survive in Latin collections of legal opinions. There is even a separate collection of Hadrian's own 'opinions' which were his answers to petitioners and were preserved as school exercises for translation into Greek.[13] In the classical Greek age, no Pericles or Demosthenes had answered petitions or given responses with the force of law.

Like justice and freedom, luxury was a term with a very flexible history. Where exactly does luxury begin? According to the novelist Edith Wharton, luxury is the acquisition of something which one does not need, but where do 'needs' end? For the fashion-designer Coco Chanel, luxury was a more positive value, whose opposite, she used to say, is not poverty, but vulgarity; in her view, 'luxury is not showy'. Certainly, it invites double standards. Throughout history, from Homer to Hadrian, laws were passed to limit it and thinkers saw it as soft or corrupting or even as so-cially subversive. But the range of luxury and the demands for it went on multiplying despite the voices attacking it. Around luxury we can write a history of cultural change, enhanced by archaeology which gives us proofs of its extent, whether the bits of blue lapis lazuli imported in the pre-Homeric world (by origin, all from north-east Afghanistan) or rubies in the Near East imported after Alexander (they are shown, by analysis, to have come ultimately from unknown Burma).

By the time of the classicizing Hadrian, the political freedoms of the past classical age had diminished. Justice, to our eyes, had become much less fair, but luxuries, from foods to furnishings, had proliferated. How did these changes occur and how, if at all, do they interrelate? Their set-ting had been intensely political, as the context of power and political rights changed tumultuously across the generations, to a degree which sets this era apart from the centuries of monarchy or oligarchy in so much subsequent history. If this era is studied thematically, through chapters on 'sex' or 'armies' or 'the city-state', it is reduced to a false, static unity and 'culture' is detached from its formative context, the contested, changing relations of power. So this history follows the threads of a changing story, within which its three main themes have a changing resonance. Some-times it is a history of great decisions, taken by (male) individuals but al-ways in a setting of thousands of individual lives. Some of these lives, off the 'grand narrative', are known to us from words which people inscribed on durable materials, the lives of victorious athletes or fond owners of named racehorses, the lady in Alexander the Great's home town who had a curse written out against her hoped-for lover and his preferred Thetima ('may he marry nobody except me'), or the sad owner of a piglet which had trotted by his chariot all the way down the road to Thessalonica, only to be run over at Edessa and killed in an accident at the crossroads.[14] Scores of these individuals surface yearly in newly studied Greek and Latin inscriptions whose surviving fragments stretch scholars' skills, but whose contents enhance the diversity of the ancient world. From Homer to Hadrian, our knowledge of the classical world is not standing still, and this book is an attempt to follow its highways as Hadrian, its great global traveller, never did.

PART ONE

The Archaic Greek World

In Mainland Greece, the Archaic Age was a time of extreme personal insecurity. The tiny overpopulated states were just beginning to struggle up out of the misery and impoverishment left behind by the Dorian invasions when fresh trouble arose: whole classes were ruined by the great economic crisis of the seventh century, and this in turn was followed by the great political conflicts of the sixth, which translated the economic crisis into terms of murderous class warfare . . . Nor is it accidental that in this age the doom overhanging the rich and powerful becomes so popular a theme with the poets . . .

E. R. Dodds, *The Greeks and the Irrational* (1951), 54–5

The close personal association of the upper classes at this time was a tremendous force in promoting the lightning swiftness of contemporary change; in intellectual outlook the upper classes seem scarcely to have boggled at any novelty. With remarkable openness of mind and lack of prejudice they supported the cultural expansion which underlay classical achievements and much of later western civilization. Great masses of superstition and magic trailed down into historic times from the primitive Dark Ages . . . That past, as exemplified in the epics, was not dismissed in its most fundamental aspects, but writers, artists and thinkers felt free to explore and enlarge their horizons. The proximate cause, without doubt, was the aristocratic domination of life.

Chester G. Starr, *The Economic and Social Growth*
of Early Greece, 800–500 BC (1977), 144

1

HOMERIC EPIC

So Priam spoke, and he roused in Achilles the desire to lament his father: Achilles took his hand, and pushed the old man gently away. And the two of them remembered: one wept aloud for Hector slayer of men, crouched before the feet of Achilles, but Achilles wept for his own father and then, too, for Patroclus . . .

Homer, *Iliad* 24.507–11

Travelling in Greece, Hadrian stopped at its most famous oracle, Delphi, in the year AD 125, and asked its god the most difficult question: where was Homer born and who were his parents? The ancients themselves would say, 'let us begin from Homer', and there are excellent reasons why a history of the classical world should begin with him too.

It is not that Homer belongs at the 'dawn' of the Greeks' presence in Greece or at the beginnings of the Greek language. But for us, he is a beginning because his two great epics, the *Iliad* and the *Odyssey*, are the first long texts in Greek which survive. During the eighth century BC (when most scholars date his life), we have our first evidence of the use of the Greek alphabet, the convenient system of writing in which his epic poems were preserved. The earliest example at present is dated to the 770s BC and, with small variations, this alphabet is still being used for writing modern Greek. Before Homer, much had happened in Greece and the Aegean, but for the previous four centuries nothing had been written down (except, in a small way, on Cyprus). Archaeology is our one source of knowledge about this period, a 'dark age' to us, though it was not 'dark' to those who lived in it. Archaeologists have greatly advanced what we know about it, but literacy, based on the alphabet, gives historians a new range of evidence.

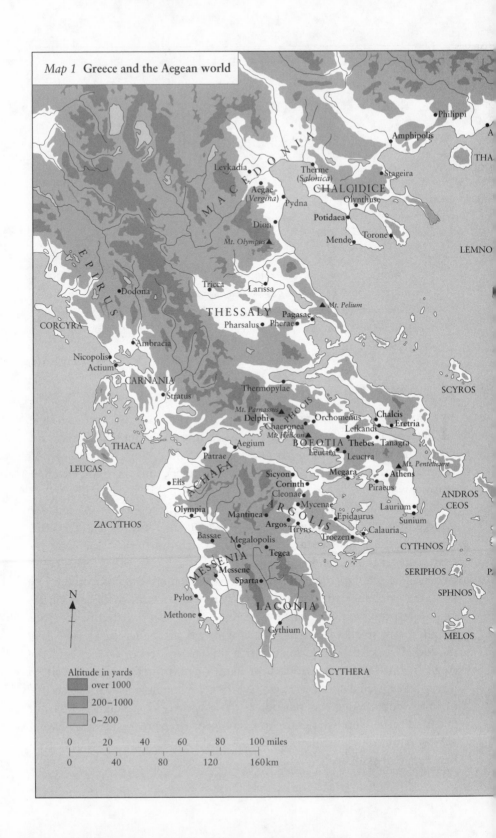

Map 1 **Greece and the Aegean world**

Philippi
Amphipolis
A
THA
MACEDONIA
Levkadia
Therme
(*Salonica*)
Stageira
CHALCIDICE
Aegae
(*Vergina*)
Pydna
Olynthus
Potidaea
Dion
Mende
Torone
Mt. Olympus ▲
LEMNO
EPIRUS
Tricca
Larissa
Dodona
THESSALY
▲ *Mt. Pelium*
Pagasae
CORCYRA
Pharsalus
Pherae
Nicopolis
Ambracia
Actium
CARNANIA
SCYROS
Stratus
Thermopylae
Mt. Parnassus ▲
Delphi
PHOCIS
Orchomenus
Chalcis
THACA
Chaeronea
Eretria
Mt. Helicon ▲
Lefkandi
Aegium
BOEOTIA
Thebes
Tanagra
LEUCAS
Patrae
Leuctra
Leuctra
▲ *Mt. Pentelicum*
ACHAEA
Sicyon
Megara
Athens
Elis
Corinth
Piraeus
Cleonae
ANDROS
CEOS
Olympia
Mycenae
Laurium
ZACYTHOS
Mantinea
ARGOLIS
Epidaurus
Sunium
Argos
Tiryns
Calauria
Bassae
Troezen
CYTHNOS
Megalopolis
Tegea
MESSENIA
Messene
SERIPHOS
P.
N
Sparta
SPHNOS
Pylos
LACONIA
Methone
MELOS
Gythium
CYTHERA

Altitude in yards
over 1000
200–1000
0–200

0   20   40   60   80   100 miles

0   40   80   120   160 km

Byzantium
Chalcedon
Perinthus

PROPONTIS

MOTHRACE

Lampsacus
Sestus
HELLESPONT
Cyzicus

ROS
Abydus

Elaeus
Sigeum
Troy

M Y S I A

R. Sangarius

Assus
Gargara

ESBOS
Mytilene
Pergamum
R. Caicus

Eresus
Pitane
L Y D I A
Cyme

SARA
Phocaea
R. Hermus

CHIOS
Erythrae
Smyrna
Sardis

Clazomenae
Teos
Colophon
R. Cayster

Lebedus

R. Meander

SAMOS
Ephesus

ICARIA
Samos

OS
Miletus
C A R I A

CONOS
Didyma

NAXOS
Myndus
Halicarnassu

AMORGOS
COS

Cnidus

L Y C I A

THERA
Ialysus
Rhodes
Xanthus

Camirus

RHODES
Lindus

P H R Y G I A

Nonetheless, Homer's poems were not histories and were not about his own times. They are about mythical heroes and their doings in and after the Trojan War which the Greeks were represented as fighting in Asia. There had certainly been a great city of Troy ('Ilion') and perhaps there really had been some such war, but Homer's Hector, Achilles and Odysseus are not historical persons. For historians, the value in these great poems is rather different: they show knowledge of a real world, their springboard from which to imagine the grander epic world of legend, and they are evidence of values which are implied as well as stated. They make us think about the values of their first Greek audiences, wherever and whoever they may have been. They also lead us on into the values and mentalities of so many people afterwards in what becomes our 'classical' world. For the two Homeric poems, the *Iliad* and the *Odyssey*, remained the supreme masterpieces. They were admired from their author's own era to Hadrian's and on to the end of antiquity, without interruption. The *Iliad*'s stories of the Trojan War, the anger of Achilles, his love for Patroclus (not openly said to be sexual) and the death of Hector are still among the most famous myths in the world, while the *Odyssey*'s tales of Odysseus' homecoming, his wife Penelope, the Cyclops, Circe and the Sirens are a lasting part of many people's early years. The *Iliad* culminates in a great moment of shared human loss and sorrow in the meeting of Achilles and old Priam whose son he has killed. The *Odyssey* is the first known representation of nostalgia, through Odysseus' longing to return home. Near its end it too brings us an encounter with pitiable old age when Odysseus comes back to his aged father Laertes, tenaciously at work among his orchard of trees, and unwilling to believe that his son is still alive.

The poems describe a world of heroes who are 'not as mortal men nowadays'. Unlike Greeks in Homer's own age, Homer's heroes wear fabulous armour, keep open company with gods in human form, use weapons of bronze (not iron, like Homer's contemporaries) and drive in chariots to battle, where they then fight on foot. When Homer describes a town, he includes a palace and a temple together, although they never coexisted in the world of the poet and his audience. He and his hearers certainly did not take his epic 'world' as essentially their own, but slightly grander. Nonetheless, its social customs and settings, particularly those in the *Odyssey*, seem to be too coherent to be the hazy invention of one poet only. An underlying reality has been upheld by comparing the poems' 'world' with more recent pre-literate societies, whether in pre-Islamic Arabia or in tribal life in Nuristan in north-east Afghanistan. There are similarities of practice, but such global comparisons are hard to control, and the more convincing method is to argue for the epics' use of reality by comparing aspects of them with Greek contexts after Homer. The comparisons here are plentiful, from customs of gift-giving which are still prominent in Herodotus' histories (c. 430 BC) to patterns of prayer or offerings to the gods which persist in Greek religious practice throughout its history or the values and ideals which shape the Greek tragic dramas composed in fifth-century Athens. As a result, to read Homer is not only to be swept away by pathos and eloquence, irony and nobility: it is to enter into a social and ethical world which was known to major Greek figures after him, whether the poet Sophocles or that great lover of Homer, Alexander the Great. In classical Athens in the late fifth century BC, the rich and politically conservative general Nicias obliged his son to learn the Homeric epics off by heart. No doubt he was one of several such learners in his social class: the heroes' noble disdain for the masses would not have been lost on such young men.

Homer, then, remained important in the classical world which came after him. Nonetheless, the Emperor Hadrian is said to have preferred an obscure scholarly poet, Antimachus (c. 400 BC), who wrote on Homer's life. By beginning with Homer we can correct Hadrian's perversity; what we cannot do is answer his question about Homer's origins.

If the god at Delphi knew the correct answer, his prophets were not giving it away. All over the Greek world, cities claimed to be the poet's birthplace, but we know nothing about his life. His epics, the *Iliad* and the *Odyssey*, were composed in an artificial, poetic dialect which suited their complex metre, the hexameter. The poems' language is rooted in the dialects known as 'east Greek', but a poet could have learned it anywhere: it was a professional aid for hexameter-poets, not an everyday sort of spoken Greek. It is more suggestive that when the *Iliad* uses everyday similes, it does sometimes refer to specific places or comparisons in the 'east Greek' world on the western coastline of Asia. These comparisons needed to be familiar to their audience. Perhaps the poet and his first audiences really did live there (in modern Turkey) or on a nearby island. Traditions connected Homer, in due course, with the island of Chios, a part of whose coastline is well described in the *Odyssey*. Other traditions connected him strongly with Smyrna (modern Izmir) across from Chios on the Asian mainland.

Homer's dates have been equally disputed. Many centuries later, when Greeks tried to date him, they put him at points which equate to our dates between c. 1200 and c. 800 BC. These dates were much too early, but we have come to know, as their Greek proponents could not, that the Homeric poems did refer back to even older sites and palaces with a history before 1200 BC. They describe ancient Troy and they refer to precise places on the island of Crete: they allude to a royal world at Mycenae or Argos in Greece, the seat of King Agamemnon. The *Iliad* gives a long and detailed 'catalogue' of the Greek towns which sent troops to Troy; it begins around Thebes in central Greece and includes several place-names unknown in the classical world. Archaeologists have recovered the remains of big walls at Troy (where excavations are enlarging our ideas of the site's extent), and palaces on Crete and at Mycenae. Recently they have found hundreds of written tablets at Thebes too. We can date these palaces way back into a 'Minoan' age (*c.* 2000–1200 BC) in Crete and a 'Mycenaean' palace-age in Greece (*c.* 1450–*c.* 1200 BC). In fact, Thebes, not Mycenae, may now turn out to have been at the centre of it.[1] In this 'Mycenaean' age Greek was being quite widely spoken and written in a syllabic script by scribes who worked in the palaces. In this period Greeks were also travelling across to Asia, but not, as far as we know, in one major military expedition. Thanks to archaeology, we are now aware of a long-lost age of splendour, but it was not an age which Homer knew in any detail. The *Iliad*'s 'catalogue' is the one exception. Even so, he only had oral stories and after five hundred years they had retained none of the social realities. A few Mycenaean details about places and objects were embedded in poetic phrases which he had inherited from illiterate predecessors. The formative years for his main heroic stories were probably *c.* 1050–850 BC, when literacy had been lost and no new Greek alphabet existed. As for the social world of his poems, it is based on an age closer to his own time (*c.* 800–750 BC): the 'world' of his epics is quite different from anything which the archaeology and scribal writing of the remote 'Mycenaean' palaces suggest.

Nowadays, scholars' dates for Homer himself vary between *c.* 800 BC and *c.* 670 BC. Most of them, myself included, would opt for *c.* 750–730 BC, and certainly before the poet Hesiod (*fl.* 710–700 BC): at least we are almost certain that the *Odyssey* was later than the *Iliad*, whose plot it presupposes. But was there one Homer or two, one for each poem? What we now read has probably been tidied up and added to in places, but at least there was a monumental poet at work. The main plot of each epic is much too coherent for them to have evolved as a sort of 'people's Homer', like a snowball over the centuries. Professional reciters, or rhapsodes, did continue to perform the poems in archaic Greece, but they certainly did not create the bulk of them. Unlike Homer, in my view, these reciters had memorized what they performed: they had learned from a text which went back to the main poet's lifetime. I do not believe that Homer himself wrote out his epic: he was, I think, a true oral poet, the heir to other illiterate poets before him. However, he was the first real 'epic' poet, the one who concentrated his very long songs on a single guiding theme. His predecessors, like his lesser followers, would have sung of one episode after another without Homer's gift for large-scale unity. We may even have the plot of one such oral poem before Homer which gives a central role to the hero Memnon from dusky Ethiopia. If he was originally in it, the earliest known Greek heroic song would be about a hero who is black.

During the eighth century the new invention, the alphabet, began to spread in the Greek world. It was not invented in order to write down Homer's great poems, but it was used (possibly by his heirs, and during his lifetime) to preserve them. They were so good that there was a future profit in a text of them. If so, much of what survives is probably the dictated version of the poet himself. The poems are very long (15,689 lines for the *Iliad*, 12,110 for the *Odyssey*), but they are unlikely to have attained this length only during his hours of dictation, undertaken to preserve them. They were also too long to be composed for performance at a banquet, as they require two or three days' listening. Arguably, they were first composed for a festival (later Greek festivals are known to have set aside several days for poetic contests, even in Hadrian's day[2]). As they survive, they do not address any one family of patrons or any one city-state. A big festival would fit this general 'Panhellenic' aspect very well: perhaps a Homer who was known to be a prize-winner was given a free run at one such festival, without rival competitors.

The two epics, the first big Greek poems, do touch already on luxury, freedom and justice. Homer does not use the later Greek word for 'luxury' (*truphe*), nor any word which disapproves of it. Rather, he enhances his grand epic world with descriptions of luxury palaces of gold, silver and bronze. He tells of wonderful silverwork from the Levant, slave-women skilled in working ivory, necklaces of amber beads, textiles and dozens of fine robes, a precious store of value. The treasures of the nobles' clothes chests have perished, but otherwise we can fit some of these luxuries (but not the fantasy palaces) to our increasing archaeological record, especially to items found in contexts of the ninth and eighth centuries BC. Homer's heroes and kings are not 'corrupted' by luxury: they fight unforgettably in mortal combat for honour, and like Odysseus they are capable of practical, everyday work with their hands. The luxuries around them are individual items of wonder. It seems that Homer and his hearers are not living in the lap of luxury 'nowadays' and taking it for granted in an effete royal world.

Individual luxuries are very attractive to the women portrayed in the poems: the amber necklaces are particularly tempting. When sold as captives, the women can be luxuries too, costing as much as twenty oxen. But in general, the poems represent women with a courtesy which is quite different from the small farmers' grudging view of women in the near-contemporary poetry of Hesiod. In the *Odyssey*, Penelope and Odysseus really do express their love as a reunited married couple; the great sorrow of Laertes, Odysseus' father, is the previous death of his wife. It is quite untrue, then, that Greeks never imagined that a man might love his wife or that 'romantic love' in the Greek world is always the love of one man for another. Homeric epic is a touching tribute to good marriage. Hesiod, too, does recognize the value of a good wife, rare though she is, but it is he, not Homer, who describes the first-created woman, Pandora, the inadvertent cause of hardship and sickness for all mortal men ever since.

Freedom is also a crucial value for the participants. Once, in a supreme moment, Hector looks forward to the time when freedom will be celebrated, the 'mixing bowl of freedom', no doubt filled with wine, will be set up and Troy will be 'free', with its enemies defeated. By contrast, there is the 'day of slavery' which takes away most of a man's powers.[3] 'Freedom', therefore, is a 'freedom from . . .': from enemies who will kill and enslave a community, and from 'slavery', the condition of absolute subjection in which men are bought and sold like objects. In Hesiod's poetry, too, slaves are assumed to be a part of the Greek farmer's way of life and a wide range of Greek words describes them. We cannot point back to a time before the classical age, when slavery, the ownership of other human beings, did not yet exist among the Greeks.

The heroes, often kings themselves, may complain about a king or leader, but they do not long to be 'free' from monarchy. They take for granted their own freedom to do much as they please before their own people. Nobles might be enslaved and sold by an enemy, but they are not worried about being 'enslaved' to another noble's will in their own community. Nor are they concerned to uphold free speech for everyone in that community or to grant an equal freedom to people outside their class. No public assembly casts votes in the epic world; no meetings occur by right, whether or not a king or noble wants to summon one. In the *Iliad*, when Odysseus rallies the Greek army he speaks gently and respectfully to the kings and 'people of eminence'. When he finds a man of the people, who is typically 'shouting', he pushes him with his staff and tells him firmly to sit down and attend to his betters. When insolent Thersites dares to insult and criticize King Agamemnon, Odysseus thumps him with his sceptre and brings out a bruise on this ugly, misshapen and unheroic free-speaker. The audience of soldiers bursts into 'sweet laughter' at the sight, although they are also 'vexed': what they are 'vexed' at is the ugly man's outspokenness and all the trouble, not at the way in which the hero has hit him.[4] The epics present the unchallengeable dominance of a heroic aristocracy. They were not composed as a reaction to a real world in which this dominance was being contested.

Nonetheless, justice is a value in its world too, exemplified by the distant 'Abioi', a 'just' people to the north of Troy to whom the god Zeus looks away for respite from the Trojan War. Paris' theft of fair Helen, Menelaus' wife, is an unjust affront to hospitality and eventually the gods will punish it. In the *Odyssey*, the gods explicitly prefer justice to human wrongdoing; in the *Iliad*, Zeus is said to send down violent autumn storms to punish 'men who use violence and give crooked rulings in the public meeting places, and drive out justice'.[5] Once only, we see a human process of justice in action, and, however we understand its action, it points to possibilities other than a hero's autocratic will. In the eighteenth book of the *Iliad*, Homer is imagining for us the wonderful scenes which the craftsman-god Hephaestus is working onto the shield for Achilles. In one part of it, two contestants are shown disputing over the 'recompense' to be made for a dead man. The people cheer them on and have to be held back by heralds. On polished seats of stone the elders sit and join in the process. 'Two talents of gold lie in the middle for whoever speaks the straightest judgement among them.'[6]

The details of this scene of justice remain mysterious and are therefore disputed. Are the contestants arguing over whether or not a price has been paid for the killing of a man? They are said to wish to reach a conclusion from a 'knowledgeable man', but what, then, are the elders doing in the process? It seems that Homer describes the elders as holding the 'sceptres of heralds': is it the elders who then rush forwards and give judgements 'one after another'? But if so, who is the 'knowledgeable' man? The people seem to be cheering on either party: are they, perhaps, the group who will decide by their shouts which elder is the 'knowledgeable' one and has given the best judgement? The contestants would then have to accept the opinion of the people's favoured speaker. He in turn would receive the 'two talents of gold' on display in the middle of the meeting.

21

There is no single king in this scene and so it reads like Homer's invention on the model of something seen in his own non-monarchical lifetime. A murder was a spectacular event, of obvious concern to people at large. The people's presence and noisy participation are certain here, in the oldest surviving scene of the giving of justice in Greek. Homer's audience would surely recognize the details, but one achievement of the next three centuries was to be the bringing of this process under written law before juries who would consist of ordinary people. As we shall see, the 'two talents' were duly removed from the middle of the proceedings, in Athens and many Greek cities and also, at least in theory, from the judicial process at Rome.

THE GREEKS' SETTLEMENTS

On these conditions an agreement was sworn by those who stayed (on Thera) and by those who sailed to found the colony (in Libya) and they invoked curses against those who would not abide by it . . . They made images of wax and burned them, calling down this curse, everyone assembled together, men, women, boys and girls: 'Whoever does not abide by this oath but transgresses it shall melt away and dissolve like these images, himself, his descendants and his property. But those who abide by the oath, those sailing to Libya and those staying on Thera, shall have good things in abundance, both themselves and their descendants.'

Oath of the settlers who founded Cyrene,
c. 630 BC (as reinscribed, *c.* 350 BC)

IN HOMER'S POEMS, the main social context for the heroes in their Greek homelands is their palaces. In Homer's lifetime, if we date him after *c.* 760 BC, no such palaces were to be found in Greece. The last buildings of such epic splendour had been the palaces of the distant 'Mycenaean' age which had come to an abrupt end *c.* 1180 BC.

There are hints, however, of a different social context, especially in the *Odyssey*: what we now call the *polis* or the 'city-' or 'citizen-state'. Exactly how and when the *polis* had arisen remains highly disputed for lack of evidence, except from such archaeology as we so far have. Some modern scholars would see it as the direct heir of the fortified strongholds of the Mycenaean age, round which (on this view) survivors regrouped and formed a new type of community. Others would see it as a later initiative, a part of a wider recovery in levels of population, riches and organization in the ninth century BC. Others would delay it even later, proposing that the very first *poleis* were founded in a new phase of settlement overseas:

faced with a new start, these settlers invented a new type of social organization, the 'city-state', beginning in Sicily in the 730s BC.

Its definition is also rather fluid, varying between a 'settlement' or a 'community', usages which are both well attested in Greek. The distinctive sense of *polis* is, in my view, a 'citizen-state'. The leader of the most recent research group to have specialized in it defines it as 'a small, highly institutionalized and self-governing community of citizens, living with their wives and children in an urban centre and its hinterland, together with two other types of people: free foreigners (often called "metics") and slaves . . . '[1] Correctly, this definition reminds us that a *polis* was not a 'city' (it could be very small) and that it was not simply a town: its population was distributed over a rural territory which might include many villages (the Athenians' territory had about a hundred and forty such villages by *c.* 500 BC). It also emphasizes people, the 'citizens', rather than their territory. Impressively, a *polis* could persist in this sense while outside its original territory: for some forty years in the fourth century BC, the men of Samos were exiled from their home island, but they still represented themselves as 'the Samians'. Or so the men did: women lived in *poleis*, and their descent from citizen-families was often important, but they were not full citizens with political rights.

If we stress the sense of the word *polis* as a community, we can follow the changing political rights of its male population: a 'citizen' in the ninth century BC certainly did not have the same rights as many enjoyed in the classical fifth century BC. The themes of 'freedom' and 'justice' play an important part in these changes. Essentially, the *polis* was a community of warriors, males who would necessarily fight for it. Again, there were changes in who fought most, and in what style: '*polis*-males' were not only warriors, nor often very war-like, but most of them did have to face the probability of a battle or two for their *polis*'s sake. In their changing styles of fighting, 'luxury' at times played a role.

In my view, *poleis* 'rose' at different times in different parts of Greece, but they certainly arose before the 730s BC and are most likely to have formed *c.* 900–750 BC. By the time of Hadrian, a thousand years later, 'city-states' of the *polis* type have been estimated to have contained about 30 million people, about half of the estimated population of the Roman Empire. The combination of a main town, a country-territory and villages remained typical, although the political rights of these elements varied over time and place. If Hadrian had ever counted, he would probably have reckoned up about 1,500 *poleis*, of which about half were in what is now Greece and Cyprus and on the western coast of Asia Minor (now

Turkey). These 750 or so were mostly city-states of the Greeks' earlier classical age. The others had been settled in lands ranging from Spain as far (with Alexander) as north-west India.

During the ninth and eighth centuries BC Greeks in Greece and the Aegean islands settled many more villages in the territories of what were increasingly identifiable *poleis*. This process was one of local settlement, not long-range migration. Then several of these *polis* centres began, from *c.* 750 BC onwards, to send settlers to yet more *poleis* overseas. Settlement overseas was an enduring aspect of Greek civilization: by Hadrian's time, as now, more Greeks lived outside poor, sparse Greece than lived in it. In the age of the Mycenaean palaces, too, Greeks had already travelled to Sicily, south Italy, Egypt and the coast of Asia, settling even on the site of Miletus.[2] Afterwards, *c.* 1170 BC, emigrants from the ending of the palace-states had gone east and settled especially on Cyprus. Later, perhaps *c.* 1100–950 BC, yet more migrants from the eastern coastline of Greece had crossed the Aegean, stopped on some of the intervening islands and then settled on the western coast of Asia Minor. These east Greeks had become resident on sites which would later be world-famous *poleis*, such as Ephesus or Miletus. Archaeology shows that one such site, Smyrna, had walls and the signs of being a *polis*, in my view, by *c.* 800 BC.

The 'Greek world', therefore, had been changing in scope quite considerably, even before Homer's lifetime. In the eighth century BC there was no country simply called 'Greece', let alone one with Greece's modern national boundaries: in Homer, the modern name of Greece, 'Hellas', refers only to one area of Thessaly. However, there was a common widely spoken Greek language which divided into only a few dialects (three are the most significant: Aeolic, Ionic and Doric): communication between differing Greek dialect-speakers was not a significant problem. Underlying each Greek *polis* there were also similar groupings, the *phulai*, which we misleadingly translate as 'tribes'. Again, their uniformity is more striking than their diversity: three particular 'tribes' existed in Doric Greek communities, four particular ones in Ionian ones. When Greeks emigrated across to settle on the coast of Asia from *c.* 1100 BC onwards it is striking that they took the precise dialect of Greek which prevailed in their former area of 'Greece' and also replicated the same 'tribes'. Modern scholars, among the ethnic confusions of our age, like to pose the question of whether a 'Greek identity' existed, and if so, when. Back in the 'dark ages' before Homer, Greeks did share similar gods and goddesses and speak a broadly similar language. Faced with our modern post-nationalist question, 'Are you Greek?', they might have hesitated,

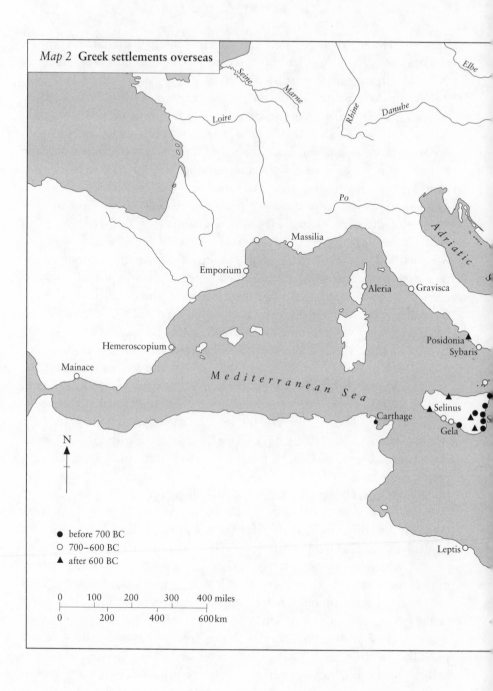

Map 2 Greek settlements overseas

Seine
Marne
Loire
Rhine
Danube
Elbe
Po
Adriatic S
Massilia
Emporium
Aleria
Gravisca
Hemeroscopium
Posidonia
Sybaris
Mainace
Mediterranean Sea
Carthage
Selinus
Gela
N

● before 700 BC
○ 700–600 BC
▲ after 600 BC

Leptis

| 0 | 100 | 200 | 300 | 400 miles |
| 0 | 200 | 400 | 600 km |

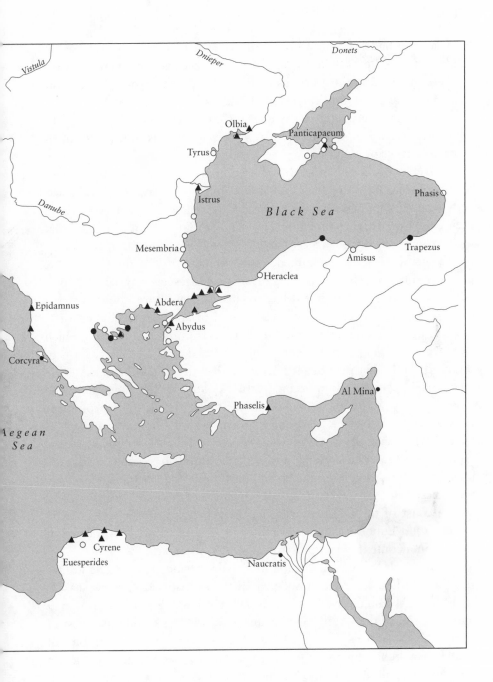

because they had probably never formulated it in such sharp terms. But fundamentally, they would say that they were, because they were aware of such common cultural features as their language and religion. Back in the Mycenaean age, eastern kingdoms did already write about 'Ahhijawa' from across the seas, surely the 'Achaeans' of a Greek world.[3] In Homer's epic, they are already 'Pan-Achaeans'; 'Greekness' is not a late, post-Homeric invention.

Between c. 900 and 780 BC, however, actual settlement by Greeks overseas is no longer evident to us. What continued was travel by Greeks, exactly what Homer describes for his hero Odysseus and his companions. In their case, they are travelling home by sea from Troy, but it is striking that they never try to establish a settlement on their way (though many Greek *poleis* in the West later claimed, quite wrongly, to be the site of one or other 'fairytale' place on their journey). Odysseus' voyage was 'pre-colonial'. Thanks to archaeology, we now know more about the real 'pre-colonial' travellers who moved around in and before Homer's lifetime. They came especially from Greek islands in the east Aegean which were temptingly close to the more civilized kingdoms of the Near East. In the ninth and eighth centuries BC, Crete, Rhodes and the Greek settlements on Cyprus were important starting points, but, to judge from the Greek pottery which accompanied these travellers, the most prominent were settlements on the island of Euboea, just off the eastern coast of Greece. The range of these Euboeans' Asian travels was forgotten by the Greeks' own later historians, and archaeologists have only recovered much of it by brilliant studies in the past forty-five years. We can now trace these Euboeans to stopping-off points along the coast of Cyprus and on the coast of the Levant, including the great city of Tyre (already by c. 920 BC): a Euboean cup has even been found in Israel, near the Sea of Galilee, in a context which probably dates to c. 900 BC.

These travels led on, once again, to actual settlements. By c. 780 BC, we can trace Euboean Greeks among the first occupants of a small seaside settlement, Al Mina in north Syria. Soon afterwards, Euboeans turn up at the other end of the Greek Mediterranean, as visitors to the east coast of Sicily and as settlers on the island of Ischia, just beyond the Bay of Naples. On Ischia, highly skilled excavation has made their settlement a focal point of modern study, but arguably, it was preceded by Euboean staging-posts on the Straits of Otranto between south-east Italy and modern Albania. Euboeans also settled on the coast of north Africa, as ancient place-names for some of the islands off modern Tunisia attest for us. Metals, especially the copper and tin which make bronze, were one magnet for these Euboean Greeks' travels both to the East and the West. In return, they brought their decorated pottery (cups, jars and plates, though not, on present evidence, any plates to the West). Perhaps they also made a profit by carrying goods from other less enterprising Greek settlements. They may also have brought wine with them, perhaps transporting it in skins. Certainly, in the fifth century BC Greek wine was imported in quantity into the Levant: in the nineteenth century AD Greek wine from Euboea, from the town of Koumi (ancient Cumae), was imported in vast quantities into Istanbul.

Sicily, Libya, Cyprus and the Levant were all points of Euboean contact before c. 750 BC, and all of them are famous points of contact for heroes who are travelling in Homer's epics. On their way west, Euboeans and other Greeks also stopped on the island of Ithaca, home of Homer's Odysseus. The Greeks' travels of the ninth to mid-eighth centuries were important, then, for some of the travel-details which Homeric poetry includes. Euboea itself was the scene for another great poetic event, c. 710 BC: the victory of the poet Hesiod (in most scholars' view, a younger poet than Homer) with a prize-poem which was probably his *Theogony* or Birth of the Gods. Appropriately for its prize-giving audience, this poem had much to say about legends which Euboeans would have picked up on their travels from peoples they met in the East. For Greeks were not travelling into empty lands in the lifetimes of Homer and Hesiod, nor were they the only travellers on the seas. Levantine people whom Greeks called 'Phoenicians' ('purple people', from their skill with a purple dye) were also criss-crossing the Mediterranean. By c. 750–720 BC these Phoenicians had gone as far west as the southern coast of Spain and even out beyond the straits of Gibraltar. Precious metals attracted them here too, especially the silver which was mined in the far West. The Phoenicians' example may even have spurred on Greeks to renewed settlement abroad, rather than just to travelling to and fro. In the mid- to late ninth century BC 'Phoenicians' from Tyre and Sidon had already settled two 'new towns' abroad, places which they called 'Qart Hadasht'. One was at the modern Larnaca beside its salt lake on the coast of Cyprus; the other 'Qart Hadasht' (which we call 'Carthage') was on Cape Bon in modern Tunisia.

Sixty years or so after the settlement of these Phoenician 'new towns', Greeks then settled on the western island of Ischia, where Levantines were also present; from there, Greek settlers moved across to the Italian coast opposite and founded Cumae, giving it a name for a *polis* already known on Euboea. From the mid–730s a spate of Greek settlements then began on the fertile eastern coast of Sicily: it marked a clear, new phase in expatriate Greek history. Meanwhile, the more distant western Mediterranean, including Spain and north Africa, was being settled by Phoenicians: there was probably a developing rivalry between Phoenicians and Greeks and by the sixth century BC, certainly, the western Mediterranean was to be kept ever more jealously as the particular sphere of Phoenicians, especially those who were settled at Carthage. Instead, Greeks settled on the south Italian coast and on the coastline of modern Albania. Back in their own Aegean orbit, they continued to settle on northern shores, on the Macedonian coast and in the Chalcidic peninsula (one of whose prongs is Mount Athos). They also travelled up into the inhospitable Black Sea, some of whose rivers were already known to Hesiod: in due course, these contacts grew into *poleis* too, probably at first on its southern coast, then up on the northern one too. North Africa and Egypt also attracted renewed Greek interest. By *c.* 630 BC, a small party of Greeks had established themselves in Libya at the wonderfully fertile site of Cyrene. In Egypt, others had already started to settle on the western arm of the Nile Delta. Within two centuries the Greek map had been transformed, especially when the first Greek settlements in a region went on to found secondary settlements there too. By 550 BC, more than sixty major Greek settlements overseas can be counted, from south-east Spain to the Crimea, almost all of which were to endure as *poleis* for centuries.

Nobody was writing a memoir or history in these years and so a study of the reasons for these settlements has to turn to much later written sources which tend to add elements of folktale and legend. Too often, they cited 'drought', a sign of divine anger, as the cause of emigration. There were also stories of chance adventures, divine intervention or even invitations to Greeks from local rulers. In more general terms, we can presume that reports of good land and easily conquerable neighbours had come back with the earlier Greek raiders and traders who had been touching on Sicily, Italy or the southern coast of the Black Sea since *c.* 770–740 BC. Back at home, their Greek communities were dominated by small aristocracies who controlled most of the land and benefited from it; indeed they needed it, if they were to graze so many of their all-important horses. In the more outward-looking Greek communities, there was probably also a rise in the population in the mid- to late eighth century. The rise need not have vastly increased the total numbers: as always, Greek families would expect many children to die (half or more of all births, on most modern estimates), whilst the surplus survivors could be exposed in most communities. At best, the exposed ones might be taken and brought up elsewhere as slaves. But there would certainly be an unequal distribution of surviving children between individual families. Less-fertile families could procure a son and heir by adoption, but even so, fertile families might still have a son or two to spare. They would not grow up to be wandering dispossessed sons: Greek families always split their inheritances formally between their sons, but the male heirs were capable of surviving informally on a family property by agreeing to share into the next generation. But a better opportunity elsewhere would certainly seem attractive to brothers in such families. There would also, as always, be a few unpopular boys among the aristocrats and a few potential troublemakers in the lower classes. When news arrived of good land abroad, it was attractive for the ruling class to choose a noble leader, collect or conscript some unwanted settlers and send them away to try their luck. We hear very occasionally of an enterprising priestess who left to help with an overseas settlement, but probably Greek women were usually left behind. In Libya and up on the Black Sea coast, it was remembered how the first Greek settlers took local women. Here, and no doubt elsewhere, the future citizens of the Greek settlements had a very mixed ethnic beginning.

Even in the 730s these overseas settlements were official ventures. The names of the Greek founders were remembered, not least because they continued to be celebrated in 'founders' festivals'. Religious rituals also accompanied the settlers' departures and arrivals. Before setting out, advice was sought from the Greek gods at one of their oracle-shrines, usually by asking if it was better and preferable to go or not: even if the venture went badly, participants would then know that the alternatives would have been worse. The most important source of advice was the god Apollo at Delphi, although the oracle there was a relatively recent cult in central Greece (no older than *c.* 800 BC). In Asia Minor, founding cities like Miletus turned to a nearer oracle, Apollo's shrine at Didyma, for similar encouragement.

Founding *poleis* left a stamp on their foundations which is often very evident to us. Founders and settlers sometimes retained reciprocal citizenship in their original communities, but even when they did not, we can often infer the origins of the main founding citizenry without any founding-legend to help us. For the personal names chosen by the settlers, the particular calendar which they adopted in their settlement, their social customs, their religious cults all reflected their place of origin. They were not the random travellers and traders of the 'pre-colonial' age, and the reasons for formally sending them off abroad were seldom commercial. On arrival, Greek settlers sometimes drove out the nearby local residents, which was hardly the action of would-be traders. We sometimes hear, too, of the formal conscription of settlers in their home city and a ban (inappropriate for traders) on their returning home for several years. In one case, 'slingers out' were appointed to wait on the shore back in the founding *polis*: they had the memorable task of slinging stones at any settlers who tried to return home.[4]

Essentially, settlement overseas headed off potential trouble at home which might lead to a demand to adjust the unequal distribution of land. In the home *polis*, a small class of nobles owned much of the available land and received 'dues' from owners of the rest of it. In a new colony, some of the humbler Greek settlers could perhaps enjoy a greater measure of freedom and a sense of a juster existence than they ever knew at home. Around a settlement, there were often some poorly defended foreigners who could be subjected and used as forced labour: these locally available slaves may have eased the demands on some of the lower-class Greeks. A new settlement also offered the chance to plan and lay out a site: some of the Greek settlements in south Italy and Sicily are our earliest evidence of Greek town planning. Temples, a regular 'gathering place' (*agora*), a shrine to the goddess Hearth and, in due course, spaces for exercise and athletics were among the hallmarks of a Greek settlement. In most of Sicily, south Italy and Libya, land for farming was definitely the settlers' aim and attraction. But by the later seventh century ever more Greeks had left to settle outposts on the Black Sea, especially on its hostile northern coast. Here, in un-Greek weather and conditions, they probably had an eye on access to local resources, including the readily exportable grain of the Crimea. Access by rivers to the interior was surely important, too, not least for the Greek settlements on the southern coast of France (*c.* 600–550 BC), including Massilia (modern Marseilles) which was not far from the mouth of the river Rhône. Further west on the coast of Spain, one new Greek settlement was openly called 'Trading Place' (Emporion, whence the modern name Ampurias). In Egypt, some of the visiting Greeks chose to settle in the Nile Delta, in a *polis* called Naucratis given to them by the reigning Pharaoh, *c.* 570 BC, who did not want them dispersed through his land. There were other Greeks who went to and fro, exchanging goods for Egypt's assets, including its grain and the soda used for washing clothes.

Some 'mother-cities' like Corinth or Miletus were prolific founders, and it surely did not escape their ruling class that selected areas were best settled with their own people or potential allies, not least so as to ensure local trade-routes and access to the sources of valuable local assets. What is impressive everywhere is the adaptability of the Greek settlers. Unlike the impractical British 'gentlemen' who settled at Jamestown on the American coast or the bickering Spaniards left by Columbus on Hispaniola, all Greeks buckled down and made a practical success, commoners and aristocrats together, like Homer's hero Odysseus and his crew. No settlement is known to have failed through incompetence.

One obvious consequence of these settlements was the spread of the Greek language and Greek literacy. The Greek alphabet actually owed its origin to Greek travel overseas: it was derived from a Greek's close study of the neighbouring Phoenicians' script in the Near East, probably c. 800–780 BC. Its inventor was one of the Euboean travellers to Cyprus, Crete or north Syria. This alphabet was then adapted by the non-Greek Phrygians in Asia and by Etruscans in Italy and used to write their own languages. As Greeks travelled with it, the result was a vastly increased spread of reading, writing and speaking Greek around the Mediterranean. Many centuries later, Hadrian was to be its beneficiary on his travels.

There was also a marked increase in known luxuries. The new Greek settlements covered many new landscapes and micro-climates which had special natural assets, richer than those in Greece. Northern Italy's plains and the steppe lands beyond the Black Sea were found to produce excellent breeds of horse. Beside the Bay of Naples, the wet land around Cumae grew superb flax which could be woven into linen and made into fine hunting-nets.[5] In Libya, at Cyrene, the settlers found an exceptionally good site for growing the saffron crocus, a most precious asset of their home island, Santorini, and one which was highly prized for dyes, scents and uses in cooking.[6] They also found a valuable plant called silphion which they traded heavily overseas. Silphion was surely related to the forms of fennel, but its exact identity continues to be disputed.[7] Conversely, there were local absentees, no silver-mines in Sicily, no olive trees in the northern Black Sea, no salt, either, in the water of the southern Black Sea's coastline. Local specialities and local deficiencies encouraged trade-links between settlements, not just with their mother-city but also in important networks between one another.

Where there was a rich soil, watered with good rivers, several of the new settlements flourished famously. The luxury of Acragas (modern Agrigento) in south-eastern Sicily became famous and at its height (c. 420 BC) was said to be supported by nearly 200,000 immigrant non-citizens.[8] Its Greek residents became celebrated for their 'luxurious' fishponds, swans and pet songbirds. Most famous of all was the Greek settlement at Sybaris in southern Italy, founded c. 720 BC and increasingly prosperous until its destruction *c.* 510 BC. The word 'Sybarite' is still proverbial for a lover of luxury. Up to 500,000 people have been suggested as a possible population for Sybaris' fertile site at its peak (*c.* 550 BC): if so, the place dwarfed Sparta or Attica on which most historians of archaic Greece now concentrate.[9] Wonderful stories were later told of its Greek citizens' refinement, so as to explain their destruction. The Sybarites are said to have banned cockerels because they disturbed their sleep; they invented chamber pots and took them along to their drinking-parties; they gave prizes for cookery; they taught cavalry-horses to dance to the flute (a possible circus-trick); the Greek Sybarites are the people who invented what we call the Turkish bath.

Seen from the locals' side, the first Greeks had rather less that was novel and desirable to bring to their settlements, except for poetry, painted pottery, athletics and their convenient alphabet. Inevitably, they wanted olives for their diet and so very often they brought olive oil to a region for the first time. They also wanted wine, but quite often it had preceded them. Through the Etruscans' earlier contact with France's south coast, the first wine to be drunk in France was 'Italian'. In the mid-fifth century, however, a Greek at the Cap d'Antibes inscribed two verses on a black stone shaped like a penis: 'I am Mister Pleaser, the servant of the holy goddess Aphrodite.'[10] The first person in France to record himself as a great lover is therefore a Greek.

Meetings with so many non-Greeks, from Spain to the Crimea, can only have helped to sharpen the settlers' existing sense of their Greekness. They also had a strong sense of kinship with the distant Greek *poleis* which had founded them. By *c.* 650 BC we first encounter the word 'Panhellenes', 'all Greeks together'; by *c.* 570 Greek visitors to Naucratis in the Nile Delta had a special temple, a Greek 'Hellenion'. Across the Mediterranean, settlement had helped to reinforce the settlers' underlying Greek identity. Within it, of course, local Greek pride remained very strong. When Hadrian visited the Greek settlement of Cyrene in north Africa, he flattered the citizens by referring to their connection with ancient Sparta and to the oracles from the god Apollo which had guided the first settlers.[11] The oracles by then were seven and a half centuries old, and the Spartan connection was supposedly very much older still. But the citizens still prized them: the widened Greek world was patterned with these tales of kinship and affinity, within the sense of Greekness which the settlers and their parent *poleis* shared.

3

ARISTOCRATS

Happy is the man who has dear children and sound horses and hunting hounds and a friend abroad . . .

Solon, F23 (West)

In rams and donkeys and horses, Cyrnus, we look for noble thorough-breds, and anyone wants to breed from noble parents. But a noble man is not concerned if he marries the ignoble daughter of an ignoble father so long as he gives plenty of money with her.

Theognis (c. 600–570 BC), lines 183–6

AT HOME IN WHAT WE CALL GREECE, the mother-cities of these set-tlements were not 'state-less' societies. Already in the eighth century these home-grown *poleis* had magistrates and ruling councils who could enforce and co-ordinate a foreign settlement. They could also impose fines and tithes, agree treaties and declare wars. But the men who ruled them were drawn from a very small class: their cliques had aristocratic names, like the Eupatrids, the noble caste of the Athenians, or the Bacchi-ads, the dominant family at Corinth. Their social attitudes and style of life were the dominant image of power in their world: they even shaped Greeks' ideas of their gods. On Mount Olympus, Homer's gods regard mortal men much as aristocrats, in Homer's world, regard their social in-feriors. As Greeks' moral thinking changed, so did their ideas of their gods, but the cultural pursuits of the first aristocrats persisted for cen-turies. In many aspects of his life, even the Emperor Hadrian was still the heir to them, a thousand years later.

The word 'aristocracy' is of Greek origin, but does not occur in our surviving Greek texts until the fifth century BC: perhaps it was coined then, as an answer to common 'democracy'. But, as often in Greek history, the absence of a general word for something is certainly not evidence that the thing did not exist. In Homer's poems, particular Greek leaders are already 'the best' (*aristoi*) by family and breeding. In many Greek city-states, the ruling families had the names of exclusive kin ('Neleids' or 'Penthelids') and in Attica, the name of the ruling caste, the 'Eupatrids', meant 'of good fathers'. Aristocrats differ from others, including the merely rich, by their noble descent from other aristocrats. In the eighth and seventh centuries these clans and castes were certainly aristocratic, even before the word 'aristocracy' was in use.

In any society, particularly a pre-scientific one, noble families are at risk from infertility. In the Greek city-states, adoption was permissible, a crucial social fiction, and, as riches spread into non-noble hands, marriage to a non-noble rich bride could re-establish the fortunes of a noble line. So a nobility could maintain itself sufficiently across the generations. But so far, nothing found in the archaeology of archaic Greece confirms the existence of whole families in Greece with a long record of persisting noble splendour. The existence, therefore, of true aristocrats in eighth-century Greece has been questioned by some modern historians who rely on 'material evidence': were the Greek communities, perhaps, more egalitarian between *c.* 850 and *c.* 720 BC, led by only temporary 'big men' or local 'chiefs'? However, archaeology is not the best guide to this sort of question, and the aristocrat's splendour lay in goods which would not survive for posterity, in textiles, in metals which might be melted down and reused and, above all, in horses.

The older, more persuasive view among historians is that in the aftermath of the age of 'Mycenaean' kings or during the disorders of what we call the early 'dark age' (*c.* 1100–900 BC) particular families in mainland Greece established themselves with greater holdings of land in the former territories of their kings and princes. These families may have been powerful under the previous kingship, or even the descendants of its royal line. Those who maintained their power pointed back to their ancestry and sometimes traced it to a god or hero. They also controlled particular cults of the gods in their community's territory and passed the priesthoods of these gods down their direct family line. They were not a 'sacred caste': landowning was their basic distinction and the priesthoods were only another one. As and where *poleis* or city-states formed, these superior families dominated them. By *c.* 750 BC those who owned the most land and held such priesthoods were described as the 'best' or the 'good' or the well-born (hence the 'Eupatrids'). In most Greek communities, the aristocratic families, or *gene*, stood at the head of groups of social inferiors, pyramids of dependence of which the best known are 'brotherhoods', or 'phratries'. These phratries were not a new eighth-century invention, but into them the male members (in my view, all members) of the early Greek citizen-bodies were grouped. Those who were not noble or 'good' were simply 'bad' or 'wicked'. From an early date, Greek aristocrats invented a frank vocabulary of social incorrectness.

The life of an aristocrat involved prowess and display, but it also brought duties and responsibilities. It was the nobility who decided on all wars and treaties and led the fighting. Nowadays, we think of aristocrats as amateurs, but there was nothing amateurish about early Greek aristocrats in action. They were champion fighters in war and expected a due reward of the booty and prizes. Homer's heroes fight on foot in memorable, stylized duels with swords and 'long-shadowing' spears. Real aristocrats might also fight such 'battles of champions', but, unlike Homer's heroes, they also fought from their beloved horses. They rode them without stirrups or heavy leather saddles (at most, they sat on padded horse-blankets) and the horses were not even shod, although the dry climate helped to toughen their hoofs. Literary and artistic evidence for early Greek cavalry is so scarce that some modern historians have doubted its existence. But many hundreds of horses are attested in later literary texts for some of the early Greek city-states, and they were not kept solely for competitions or for use in farming: there was no efficient horse-collar which would allow horses to pull heavy loads. On horseback, a nobleman could scatter and pursue the ill-armoured groups of lower-class foot followers whom his noble opponents brought to war. Noblewomen, by contrast, never rode at all. They were priestesses, objects of competition (if they were rich and pretty) and mothers, without any political power.

In city-states beside the sea, nobles also had a close relationship with the bigger ships. They owned them, surely; perhaps in their youth they sometimes fought or went raiding with a crew of social dependants. It is a subject on which, as yet, we lack clear information. However, already in the eighth century, we see scenes of warships rowed by two levels of oarsmen on some of the fine pottery painted in Attica, fit for noble owners. Warships would probably be a nobleman's responsibility, and were coordinated by magistrates even in early city-states (the *naukraroi*). In due course they developed into the supreme Greek warship, the trireme, propelled by three levels of oars and armoured with a metal ram on its prow.

Phoenician warships probably showed the Greeks the way here, and in my view they had shown it by the late eighth century BC (the great historian Thucydides thought so too, although many modern scholars adjust his dating to refer to the late seventh century, or even the sixth). Triremes were not merchant-ships (no Greek state had a 'merchant navy'). They could travel up to seven knots an hour and as we shall see, conditions aboard them were awesome. As crews constantly needed water, they tended to stay close to coastlines, but even so they could cover 130 (even 180) sea miles in a long day. Nobles have left us an image of themselves as horse-lovers, but in Corinth or Euboea or islands like Chios and Samos they were lords with an eye for the sea.

In peacetime a nobleman was expected to arbitrate disputes and pronounce justice. At the start of his poem the *Theogony*, Hesiod gives us an idea of such an aristocrat in action (*c.* 710 BC). He speaks 'gentle words'; he persuades, and 'mild words' flow from his mouth. He gives 'straight justice' with 'discrimination' and can put an end to a 'great dispute' with 'knowing skill'. In another poem, however, the *Works and Days*, Hesiod chides these same nobles for 'devouring gifts' as bribes.[1] But the ideals are important too: persuasion, insight and a degree of gentleness, before disputants who have caused and suffered damage. Without written laws, even more depended on the nobleman's own judgement, or lack of it: 'gifts' were a frequent means of influencing it.

These godlike judges were revered, but they did not receive godlike honours themselves: rather, they presided over the rites and offerings to their community's gods. Their priesthoods did not require any special religious knowledge. The priest would say a prayer in public when an animal was being sacrificed to a god, but another assistant would kill the beast on his behalf. There was no special training, and so noblemen's wives and daughters might serve as priestesses too. A priest or priestess, often finely dressed, would then allot the all-important meat to people present at the sacrifice. Except for a kill during hunting, a religious sacrifice was the main occasion when a Greek ate meat. The priest also retained the animals' hides and skins, a valuable privilege as they were the community's main source of leather.

Aristocrats also monopolized the magistracies of their communities. In Corinth, the Bacchiads monopolized all these jobs; in rural Elis, Aristotle later recalled, 'the citizen-body was small in number and very few of them ever became councillors, because there were only ninety of them, and the election was limited to a few dynasties'.[2] In Attica, the region we know best, magistracies were limited to members of the noble Eupatrid caste.

There were nine such magistracies, and a nobleman could probably aspire to all but the top magistracy in sequence, holding each one for a year at a time. After holding office, an Athenian nobleman then became a lifelong member of the prestigious council, the Areopagus. Political life in their city-state's council and its public meeting place was the lifeblood of most aristocrats' existence: there is a fine tribute to it by the noble poet Alcaeus, who was missing it during a time of rustic exile *c.* 600 BC.

Rhetoric did not yet exist as a formal theory, but leaders certainly had to speak effectively in public. Already in Homer, the gift of speaking well was admired in a nobleman, in an Odysseus, for instance, from whom words would pour in public 'thick and fast as snowflakes'. Some of the finest speeches in all Greek literature are in pre-rhetorical Homer.[3] Judging and speaking were not the limits of an aristocrat's accomplishments. He was also brought up to dance, to sing and to play music, especially on the *aulos*, an instrument like the modern oboe. He learned to ride, still without stirrups, and to use his sword and spear, but he could also compose verses and cap a neighbour's wit at a party. He was accomplished in ways in which his modern critics tend not to be. But even in peacetime most of the outlets for these accomplishments were combative and competitive. Typically, an aristocrat would be a huntsman, adept at killing hares especially, and also foxes, deer and wild boar. Some of his hunting was conducted on horseback, but hare-hunting was often on foot as the hares were chased with hounds into carefully laid nets. Slaves assisted the netting, but young noblemen indulged in the chase personally. The pursuit was fun, and if wild boars were the prey, they could be dangerous, so prowess was highly respected.

The physically fit aristocrat also competed in athletics, aristocracy's supreme legacy to Western civilization. The researches of later Greek scholars fixed the start of their Olympic Games in what we calculate as 776 BC, and we can certainly think of them as blossoming during the eighth century, while being wary of too precise a starting-date. For a while, the Olympics were mostly contested by competitors from nearby states in southern Greece (the Peloponnese), but by *c.* 600 BC their scope had become 'Pan-Greek', a status they retained for nearly a thousand years. Women, however, were not allowed to watch the Olympics where men competed in the nude (they did have their own little 'games', separately conducted in honour of the goddess Hera). The basic male events were running, boxing, throwing and wrestling. Almost no holds were barred, and boxing was carried out with thongs around the wrist, although not with the spiked gloves which Roman cruelty later introduced.

3. A pentathlete doing the long jump with hand-held weights. Amphora of the Tyrrhenian group, *c.* 540 BC.

Victors would inflict severe wounds, especially in the 'all-in-victory' (*pankration*) where kicking was only one part of the violent repertoire. There was nothing effete about the contestants, noble or not. They smashed teeth, limbs, ears and bones, occasionally to the point of death. 'Gentlemanly' is entirely the wrong description.

These sports and games are an aristocratic legacy for three reasons. The athletic events were probably never confined to aristocratic entrants, but aristocrats (as in Homer's description of games) certainly set the standards and were more likely to win in the early years: they had the most leisure in which to train and the greatest resources to pay for a healthy diet. More importantly, aristocrats patronized athletic contests at fellow aristocrats' funerals, thereby supporting an infrastructure of local games on which the Olympics rested. Above all, nobles dominated the most spectacular Olympic events, those which they themselves had invented: horse racing and chariot racing. These events spread the fame of the major games far and wide: Greek aristocrats are the founding heroes of the hippodrome and the racecourse, legacies as enduring as 'democracy' or 'tragedy'. Noblemen owned the best horses, although they tended to hire skilled depen-

4. A sexually aroused older male fondles a young, probably pre-pubic, boy in a gym or wrestling space (*palaestra*). Brygos painter, Athens, *c.* 480 BC.

dants to drive and ride them: one of the neglected heroes of Greek history is the horse Pherenicus who won at three major sets of games during an amazing twelve-year span (from the 480s into the 470s BC).

This culture of prowess and trophies had links, too, to the life of love. The most freely expressed love was for a youth of the same sex, not least because the exercise for athletics was naked and promoted admiration for, and close contact with, nude male bodies. For the nobly born were not just the 'best' or the 'good', they were the 'fair', the beautiful (*kaloi*), in an explicit monopoly of good looks. To 'look good' was to 'be good'. In due course, male beauty contests became a feature of local games, at Athens or at Tanagra in Boeotia, where the winning boy was allowed to carry a living ram on his shoulders around the city's walls in honour of the god Hermes the Ram-Bearer. Boys were most 'pleasing', as Homer noted, in early adolescence when the first soft hair appeared on their cheeks. On painted pottery this supreme beauty was often commemorated: an older bearded man would be shown courting a boy of this age, touching him up or having sex with him between his young thighs. Even

41

5. Hunter, wearing the typical *petasos*-hat, with his spears and hound, *c.* 510-500 BC, Edinburgh painter, Athens.

in this culture of *ephebo-philia* (love for the adolescent male), the naked athletic ideal left its imprint. As sculptures would soon exemplify, particularly beautiful young men were those with an athletically fit figure: broad shoulders, tight narrow waists, prominent buttocks and firm thighs. There was no romantic cult of the girlish or the pale, frail intellectual: on painted pottery, girls' anatomy was usually represented with boyish lines. Exceptionally muscly boxers or wrestlers would be too chunky to be very desirable, but the ideal was the fit pentathlete, skilled in all departments, including the throwing of the javelin.

The context for this sexual activity is that boys, in most city-states, were not being formally educated beyond the age of fourteen: rather, they exercised and competed, teeming with hormones, in the wrestling-rings for naked men or in due course in special 'gyms', the gymnasiums which archaic Greek aristocracies have also bequeathed to modern Western imitators. Older men watched and sighed at all this young beauty in the dust-clouds. When they courted it, they were not engaging in a macho proof of their virility, in which 'honour' and 'masculinity' were to be shown by forcing and penetrating a lesser man, rather than being penetrated themselves. As usual, the practical details of lovemaking are concealed from us, but it is only a modern prejudice to link them with 'Mediterranean' values of 'honour' and 'shame'. There were links, often tender ones, between sexual desire and the culture of gift-giving and physical prowess. On painted pottery, especially in the sixth century BC, we see scenes of an older man, a hunter, bringing hares, deer and other trophies from the field to his young loved one. Here, hunting and love-gifts go together. Typically the older man would court an adolescent: a competitive culture of pursuit and gift-giving pitted men, not against an 'inferior' lover, but against one another in rivalry for a lovely young boy's favours. Not for nothing were so many political quarrels traced back by later anecdotes to quarrels over a boy-lover. Participants were not usually one-way 'homosexuals': the Greeks did not have a notion of a 'homosexual nature'. Nor were they only a counter-culture. Most participants would marry and have sexual relations with a wife, or slave-girls and courtesans: they simply had them, at times, with males too. Courtship of a noble heiress might also set noble suitors against each other, as they competed for her father's favour (and fortune). But homoerotic courtship was more fleeting and thus kept recurring in a man's life: its changes and chances were publicly proclaimed, a favourite subject for poetry. At their parties, men did not sit and listen to poems in praise of their wives or married love.

Hunting, courtship and athletics are not arts which leave solid archaeological survivals. Instead, the main relics of aristocratic life are fragments of its painted pottery which was cast in many specialized shapes and styles. The setting for so much of this pottery was the stylized drinking-party, or *symposion*, held by male diners after dinner. Arguably, its origins go back into the mid-eighth century BC.[4] At the *symposion*, male aristocrats reclined in parties of a dozen or so on couches. They mixed water into their wine and drank from cups with short 'stems', allowing them to slip them between their fingers and swirl wine and water together. Civilized parties also included poetry and songs and games of riddles or the capping of one another's words. Free women were excluded, but there was music from the slave-girls who played the *kithara*, or lyre.

Despite being mixed with water, wine led to drunkenness and sex was always near the surface. One reason, indeed, for changing from sitting at tables to reclining on couches was said to be the greater ease for sex on a sofa during the evening. The height of a symposiast's skill became the game of *kottabos*, most famous in Sicily, in which reclining male players would flick drops of wine at a cup hung on a stick or peg. They are even believed to have exclaimed, while flicking, that 'so-and-so is beautiful', naming their own or a widely admired male pin-up. During the party, male guests might touch up one another; female courtesans might join in,

6. A slave-girl entertains male symposiasts with music: red-figure *krater*, or mixing-bowl, fourth century BC.

and on one view the winner in contests or at *kottabos* was given one of the musical slave-girls as a sexual prize.[5]

The male *symposion* was one part of the accomplished web of a noble-man's life: it was not the key to it all. Like the giving of justice, it is a re-minder that not all aristocratic life was ruthlessly competitive (or 'agonal', from *agon*, the Greek word for a contest), as if the only aim was to defeat and humiliate rivals. Good counsel, good manners and compan-ionship were every bit as valued as the more 'combative' virtues: the aris-tocratic ideal was rounded, and many-sided. In our more generous moments, we think of aristocrats nowadays as above competition and too naturally grand to worry about petty titles or sordid gain. We think of them as unworldly, and perhaps best at planning a model estate. Land-scape gardening, or any gardening at all, is not the recorded interest of early Greek aristocrats. In Attica, the 'estates' of the nobles were ranked in the highest class if they were no more than about fifty acres.[6] Else-where, in spacious Thessaly perhaps, a nobleman might own rather more, farming it with lowly serfs, but estates of a thousand acres or more, like a modern duke's, were most unlikely even there. Nonetheless, noblemen's riches existed to be spent and displayed, especially on the widely seen splendour of their marriage-feasts and funerals. Aristocrats also used finely made objects to mark out their graves: at first they used big, decorated pottery vessels and then, from the later seventh century BC, sculpted statues and reliefs. By then Greek craftsmen had learned from renewed contact with Egypt the art of making big sculptures in stone of the human form: for their aristocratic patrons, they began to innovate in representing the balance and proportion of human figures. Sculptures thus became another noble mark of status. They were put up for the 'special dead', for athletic victors or for womenfolk who had served in the cults of one of the divinities. Inscriptions helped to personalize these statues and to attach names to them even if they were statues of women. However, the statues of athletes were statues of famed individuals and so they were sometimes personalized directly as quasi-portraits. 'Portraiture,' the great cultural historian of ancient Greece, Jacob Burckhardt, observed, 'in this case, begins by and large with the whole, necessarily naked figure and it never again had such an origin anywhere in the world. The athlete forms an artistic genre before there is any such thing as a statuary of statesmen or warriors, to say nothing of poets.'[7]

This increasing luxury was not a cause of decadence among the upper class. Rather, it encouraged emulation and it certainly did not exclude the pursuit of gain. No aristocrat, it is true, would ever wish to be a full-time 'businessman'. Daily traders, like craftsmen, were lucidly despised as vulgar by Greek authors with an upper-class bias: for one thing, they realized, they tell lies. In later Greek history, the known traders are almost all non-citizens of their communities, and the upper classes are certainly not among them. However, the chance of riches was too good to miss. Even the aristocrats had young sons who were fit and able to lead a temporary raiding (or 'trading') party in a ship abroad: seen from the other side, these bold ventures were as much about piracy as boring commerce. Although no nobleman was 'in' trade, he could always profit 'from' trade by using slave-agents and social dependants to deploy his ships, exchange his farms' surplus and barter overseas for metals and fine materials.[8] On these commodities yet more of the nobles' display at home was based. For display, not canny giving, was a noble's primary use of riches: in their upper class, gifts were not calculated solely to prompt gifts in return. At funerals or weddings, within families or before a grateful community, noblemen gave grandly, without always thinking of the 'reciprocity' which Hesiod, at a lower social level, urged on shrewd small farmers. Even in Homer's poems, one noble's gift is promptly 'exchanged' with another's only twice. Rather, the nobles' display of riches and gifts intensified competition, as the 'best' had to keep up with the 'best' of them. Those who simply lived on rents and agricultural dues were not likely to be the 'best' for very long in many parts of the Greek world.

4

THE IMMORTAL GODS

There is the virgin Justice, too, daughter of Zeus, respected and
revered among the gods who hold Olympus.
And when anyone scorns her by his crooked speech and harms her, at
once she sits by her father Zeus the son of Cronos
And tells him the unjust purposes of men so that the people pay for
the follies of the noble princes . . .

Hesiod, Works and Days 256–61

Anaxippus asks Zeus Naos and Dione about male offspring from his wife
Philista . . . by praying to which of the gods might I fare best and most
well?

Oracular question, inscribed on lead at Dodona

I N HOMER'S POEMS, the dominant image is that there is no life beyond the grave. In the world below, the 'souls' of the heroes live a
shadowy life, fluttering like bats, but in the main lines of the epics they
have no power to influence events on earth and none, certainly, to rise
from the dead. This superb view of man's condition heightens the
poignancy of a hero's life. We are what we do; fame, won in life, is our
immortality. Until Achilles cremates his dear Patroclus, the dead man cannot cross over finally into the house of Hades. So Patroclus' spirit appears
to Achilles by night, asking for the last rites: 'give me your hand, I beg
you in sadness: for I will never come back again from Hades once you
have given me my due of fire'.[1] Achilles reaches out with his hands, but
Patroclus is gone 'like smoke': Achilles never sees him again.

Few, if any, aristocrats shared this poetic view of death which so greatly enhanced the pathos of the epics and their legendary choices. All over Greece, they honoured rather different local heroes, in the belief that their anger and favour still worked locally in the world: this cult was logically inconsistent with the predominant view in Homer's poetry which, therefore, did not inspire it. For themselves, many of the nobles may have expected rather more than a bat-like afterlife of shadows, a life, perhaps, in the 'Elysian fields' at the far ends of the earth with some of the games and contests which they had known in life or, if not, perhaps some punishment (at least for their enemies) for wrongs done here on earth. Homeric life was 'this-worldly', but in one corner of their minds few Greeks in the seventh and sixth centuries BC would have been quite as certain as a Homeric hero that it was all there was.

In the early sixth century BC a post-Homeric hymn imagines for us how the gods enjoy the 'lyre and song' up on Mount Olympus. All the Muses, we learn, 'sing antiphonally with their fair voices of the immortal gifts of the gods and the sufferings of mortal men, all those which men have from the immortal gods as they live witlessly and helplessly and cannot find a cure for death or a defence against old age'.[2] So much for 'justice' or 'love' in heaven: life is as it is, and the gods simply like to hear it contrasted with their own immortal ease, much as aristocrats on earth might listen to songs of the toils of the lower classes.

It is, again, a magnificently hard image, but one, also, which Greeks would not quite so readily sustain throughout their own 'witless' lives. Greeks were polytheists, accepting that many gods existed. Homer's poems had said most about twelve gods (Dionysus and Demeter having the least mention), but the 'twelve' on Olympus were a poetic convention, and in real life there were hundreds more. Titles and adjectives linked gods with a particular place or function (Zeus Eleutherios, of freedom, or Apollo Delios, from the island of Delos) and brought them especially close to local worshippers: in Attica, at least ten 'varieties' of Athena are attested. Outside the Homeric circle, there were gods who were even closer, the sort of gods we find in the local cult-calendars of Attic villages or the gods of crops and farms for the ordinary man. In grave-mounds and special places, there were also the un-Homeric heroes, the semi-divine figures whose potential anger was so unpredictable: hundreds of these heroes existed in Attica alone, and Athenians maintained due relations with them. For, at all levels of a community, all Greek social groups looked to particular gods or heroes, whether the hunting-groups in Macedonia who looked to 'Heracles the hunter' or the phratries in Attica who looked to a local god or hero, to 'Zeus Phratrios' or Ajax or simply the 'hero by the salt-deposits'. Gods and heroes were bound up with the social infrastructure as well as with the land and citadels of each city-state. On the streets and outside the houses of many Greek cities (Athens is the best known) there were stone pillars, or 'herms', with a god's head on top and erect male private parts lower down. They were probably a warning, to keep off bad things ('watch out, or you will be penetrated').[3] As time passed, educated minds regarded them as rather ridiculous, and so groups of clever young things smashed off the herms' parts on one famous night in 415 BC, probably so as to scare the simpler classes into feeling that the gods would oppose their forthcoming naval campaign to Sicily. In fact, the simpler classes turned on the arrogant 'herm-smashers' and put them on trial.

The gods, on the whole, were imagined as more kindly than cruel, though their cruelty could be spectacular. Their justice was most divine when it was most random, sending a punishment many years later for the misdeed of a previous family member. For the gods did have their values too: they expected oaths to be observed, strangers to be respected and their shrines not to be polluted. When a spectacular misfortune occurred, Greeks tended to look back to the gods and the past for an explanation, a way of making sense of the world which never died out among most of them in the course of their later classical history. In the poetry and oracles of the archaic age, this belief in divine punishment is particularly prominent, but even then people were not oppressed by holy dread. For most of the time their religiousness was passive, ticking over with a few of the usual offerings and no undue anxiety. Only in a crisis, whether personal or collective, did it become active, and then belief in divine justice across the years or generations was one way of making sense of grave misfortune. Until such a crisis, 'act first, explain later' was one way of keeping it all in perspective; another was to try to win a god over before risking an adventure. If it failed, the god might have been the wrong one, or unwilling, this time, to 'get involved'.

These gods and heroes were not simply up in heaven, enjoying the Muses' gloating over human suffering. Greek life was lived with a sense of their potential presence, in the clamour of storms or the stresses of sickness, in the dust-clouds of battle or on distant hillsides, especially in the midday sun. 'Not to everyone', Homer had said, 'do the gods appear', but they were most freely accessible at night, in dreams. For, as the painted sculptures multiplied, Greeks saw around them the representations of gods crowding their public spaces: at night, the images, fixed by their craftsmen, then seemed to 'stand beside' them as 'manifest helpers'. The choral hymns, the poems, the stories of childhood, the talk at festivals all helped this nightly converse. They referred so often to the gods and their earthly appearances and their doings in the flexible stories, or *muthoi*, which we rather grandly call 'myth'. Like the nobles, most of the gods of these statues and stories stood for shining beauty and grace: 'they were marvellous figures; their deeds and their loves were as fascinating as those of film stars.'[4] Like superstars, gods and goddesses were said to have made love occasionally to mere mortals, never better than Poseidon, who swept his girl away in the folds of a purple wave.[5] Like film stars, gods might love a boy (as Zeus loved Ganymede, or Apollo the hapless Hyacinthus) and their female lovers were not always virgins. Unlike film stars, gods always made their lady pregnant. If a god made love to her twice in succession, she had twins. But she was also commanded not to 'kiss and tell'.[6]

The potential presence of these gods was keenly felt on festival days when their statues came out from the temples which were built to be their houses. On other days visitors might find a temple unlocked and go in to contemplate a god's statue. What visitors did not do was sit inside and participate with a priest in a service. There was no polytheist Church, no special training or theological essentials for being a 'priest' or a 'priestess'. There were no sacred scriptures in the main cults: religious texts were a distinguishing mark of the minority, 'secret' cults. The core of polytheism was the paying of honours to the gods in the hope of favours or of appeasing and averting divine anger. The honours might be cakes or first-fruits or libations of wine or honey. Above all, they were offerings of animals, killed for the occasion on altars, whether birds, sheep, piglets (costing about 3 drachmas) or the most expensive, cattle (costing '90 drachmas').[7] There were 'gods below the earth', for whom blood and libations would be poured out onto the ground and the animal totally burned (the origin of our word 'holocaust'). Or there were the Olympians and the gods 'above' with whom the animal's meat would be shared. The gods enjoyed the smoke and mostly received the fat and bones (although Aphrodite did not like pigs, except in semi-Greek Aspendus). The mortals cannily ate the meat themselves.

These 'sacrifices' emphasized the line between mortals and immortals and although anyone might offer a victim, they were most frequent in cults paid by social groups, especially by the city-state or community. Each city-state had a calendar of yearly festivals which varied from place to place, but everywhere the dead, the crops and human fertility were the unpredictables whose well-being underlay much of this cultic activity. Citizens did not have to attend the rites, but a priest or priestess did, and there would often be meat or little gifts for the crowds on the day. Particular festivals were focused on women, too. In the Attic calendar, the Thesmophoria (widespread in the Greek world) was celebrated by respectable married women only, in honour of Demeter and the Maiden (Persephone). They spent three days with their priestesses which ranged from a sacrifice of piglets to a day, at least, of fasting while sitting on mats on the hard ground and a day of celebration on which the women offered sacrifice in honour of 'fair Birth'. Sexual abstinence was required before and after the festival. At the Haloa, by contrast, Attic women carried models of male and female private parts, while cakes of a similar shape were set before them and priestesses (it was said) whispered to them to commit adultery. Outside the civic calendar, women also sometimes celebrated an exotic festival for young Adonis, the gorgeous beloved of Aphrodite. The rites involved some hasty gardening in flowerpots, bare-breasted lamentation and a sense, it seems, that divine Adonis was the ideal lover whom these 'desperate housewives' failed to find in their typical Greek husband.

A recurrent feature of these festivals was a suspension of 'normal time' and social rules, either by briefly inverting the usual reality (the 'world turned upside down') or by enforcing an exceptional routine. Inversion and exceptionalism were most visible in the cults of the rampaging Dionysus, the god of wine, growth and life-giving forces. Dionysus was often represented in feminine dress himself, as an asexual being among his female maenads and the half-bestial satyrs who were so very over-sexed. We should not deny the revelry and 'altered states' in Dionysus' real-life cult or limit the women participants merely to dancing, as if only the men drank the wine. Drinking, ecstatic dancing and (in Macedonia) snake-handling were indeed practised by women: sometimes they worshipped Dionysus in 'wild' nature, even up on the mountains. Nonetheless, worshippers of either sex probably never ripped up living animals (let alone a slave) in real life as opposed to myths or drama. Dionysus was included among the civic cults of city-states, even though his worship was especially conducted by women: their 'wild' worship projected the image that women were 'wild' and 'irrational' (their laments at funerals, women's business, gave a similar impression). Then, as the cult ended, the brief festival-time of release was over, and so the controlled norms of sound everyday behaviour (guided by men) were reasserted: as the festival showed, these 'irrational' women really needed a sober-minded man. But Dionysus, though long known in Greece, remained potentially exotic.

Myths therefore characterized him as a foreign invader from barbarian, 'irrational' lands, from Thrace or Lydia or even India (where Alexander the Great and his soldiers later believed that they had discovered real traces of him). In fact, Dionysus was not an intruder at all, or somehow 'younger' than the sober, rational Olympians. He was an old member of the total Greek pantheon, but his wildness was accommodated by these myths and imagery of 'eastern' luxury.

Rituals with these sorts of contrasting references ran through each city-state's calendar and, in that sense, 'religion' was intertwined with 'politics': increasingly, citizens voted funds for the cults, or chose their priests by lot or election or passed decrees to keep the sanctuaries orderly. It was not, conversely, that 'politics' were somehow always 'religious' or that laws were really 'sacred'. For the *polis* was not a religious community organized simply for cult or the worship of the dead: it was a community of citizens whose political meetings were prefaced by prayers or religious honours but whose debates, decisions and conflicts were quite independently political, about contested human ends and means. The gods were appealed to, rather, as 'helpers'. Throughout this book, the Greek city-states and armies must be thought of as carrying out repeated honours for these 'helpers', occasions which brought crowds together, suspended public business and even delayed soldiers on the march: there were almost no known atheists. Citizens had to accept that the civic gods existed (only a very few philosophers seemed not to), but otherwise the main limit was only that they must not worship some weird god who denied that the other gods were gods needing worship too. Until the Greeks met Jews or Christians, this exclusive sort of god was not an issue. 'Freedom of worship', therefore, was not a freedom for which Greeks fought and died amongst themselves. Nor was religious 'tolerance' an issue in their struggles. As polytheists, the Greeks accepted many gods, and the gods which they met abroad were usually worshipped and understood as their own gods in yet another local form. The only major attempts to ban 'private' cults were in the pages of that political revisionist, the philosopher Plato. Like the rest of his horrible ideal city, they were ignored by every other Greek in real life.

Nor was Greek religion simply '*polis*-religion'. Beside the calendar of public cults, families observed their domestic cults on their own properties (especially to Zeus 'of property') and in their households (in Alexandria in Egypt, the 'good *daemon*' or snake was to prove very popular). Families would also worship together, led by their father, as we can see on sculpted votive-reliefs which show them paying their vows. For beside the public cults there was a flourishing culture of personal vows to the gods by individuals, whether in hope of, or thanks for, a favour. Individuals 'vowed' sacrifices, statues or even temples, let alone the little clay and terracotta statues that turn up by the thousand in excavations of sanctuaries, especially in some of the shrines of the western Greeks. These vows were made for worldly ends, for conception, childbirth or success in love, for victory or profit and especially for recovery from sickness: gods were widely represented as healers, even by educated doctors. The god who received a vow did not have to be a god of a civic cult. Hesiod's poetry contains a lavish tribute to the powers and functions of the goddess Hecate whom his family had perhaps met on their travels:[8] a cult of Hecate is not known then or later in the region of his Boeotian *polis*. The idea of a 'vow' paid for a favour could quite easily slip over into a 'curse' made for the favour of doing harm to somebody else, a rival in love or at the games or even in democratic politics. Curses also followed precise rituals, but although they were sinister, they too were trying to bring the gods to bear on a personal interest much as a vow or a conventional prayer did.

Prayers do often stress the hope of reciprocity which underlay so much of the giving between Greeks, except (in my view) between aristocrats. The pattern was taken for granted in earthly social relations and so it was projected onto heaven: 'If I ever gave you a pleasing sacrifice, Zeus, please give me'... The aim was not bribery but the continuance of relations with a divine superior who, like a social superior, might sometimes (not always) intervene. Worshippers never knew when he would, and when not.

But they did have a chance of discovering what the gods' commands and wishes were. Experts would watch the flight of birds and interpret any unusual omens or the tangled entrails of an animal when sacrificed. In such contexts, the will of the gods might be discoverable. Again, many of the decisions of individuals throughout the classical world would have been preceded by prayers or divination. The gods were not only spectators or 'listening' gods: they also communicated, albeit very obliquely.

Outside one's dreams, these communications were most accessible at particular sanctuaries, above all at the oracular shrines where prophets and prophetesses 'spoke' for the gods. In the eighth century the reputation of the most famous, at Delphi, became established: its priesthood were later described as immigrant Cretans, a tradition which I accept, at least until a Sacred War there, *c.* 590 BC, may have expelled them.[9] On a few favourable days a priestess would respond at Delphi on the gods' behalf to the questions put by visitors. She usually became inspired, perhaps after drinking toxic fresh honey and chewing 'daphne' (it may be wrong to translate this plant as non-toxic 'laurel').[10] The responses were then given as prose or hexameter verse (with the help of priests), but, Apollo being the god he was, they were very often ambiguous or perplexing. So, human intelligence was needed, and frequently, the god only said 'it would be better if . . . '. However bad it proved, the alternatives would then be known to be even worse.

In the aristocratic age, oracular sites flourished in the Greek world, not just Delphi but Dodona in north-western Greece or Didyma and Claros on the western coast of Asia, among many others. Much of the business might be the everyday anxieties of individuals: whom to marry, whom to blame, how to have children. But these sanctuaries also offered an external sanction for major civic decisions, a stamp of divine approval which would reassure and exculpate the small, fractious ruling class of a community who submitted a question. In due course, democracy would tend to provide its own fully authoritative stamp anyway. Then, too, oracles would be a community's resort when coping with questions of innovation in a cult or fears of unusual divine anger: they allowed a god to speak out on matters which were the gods' own affairs. In the age of aristocracy they were also a support for proposed new settlements abroad or major changes in the political order. In turn, the outcomes of these ventures enhanced their reputation: 'at the beginning it is surely true that colonization was far more responsible for the success of Delphi than Delphi for the success of colonization.'[11]

TYRANTS AND LAWGIVERS

What I said I would do, I did with the help of the gods and I did not do anything else heedlessly—nor did it please me [to do] by force anything which a tyranny would do, nor that the 'good men and true' should have equal shares with the 'bad' in their rich land . . .

Solon, F 34 (West)

AMONG THEIR SPLENDOUR, aristocrats did have an idea of a 'just city'. Already, Hesiod's poetry had imagined one for them, not a theoretical and utopian sort of place, but a city of 'straight judgements'[1] where peace rules and famine is absent. In it, the nobles would naturally rule, taking their freedom for granted. They did not write about this freedom in the few poems and inscriptions which survive because within their living memory they had not set themselves free and asserted it by taking power away from a previous king. Nor was a politically active lower class threatening to limit their freedom or subject them. The one slavery they feared was enslavement by an enemy in war, a danger to them as individuals and also to their communities as a whole.

Nonetheless, in the 650s BC the political monopoly of the aristocratic cliques began to be broken. The world's first 'age of revolution' began in Greece at Corinth and spread to Corinth's nearby communities.[2] Aristocrats could be described as 'monarchs' (*mounarchoi*), but from the 650s a single ruler sometimes replaced them, a true 'monarch' in our sense of the word. Greek contemporaries called the new monarch a *turannos*, or 'tyrant', and for more than a century, these 'tyrannies' flourished in many Greek communities. They have left us some spectacular stories about their behaviour, the first surviving Greek gossip, and some significant relics of Greek architecture, bits of their huge stone temples. One of the biggest, to

Olympian Zeus in Athens, was so huge that it was only completed by Hadrian, six and a half centuries after its beginnings *c.* 515 BC.

What Hadrian did not know was that *turannos* was a word which Greeks had adapted from the foreign Lydians in western Asia. There, in the 680s, a usurper, Gyges, had dared to kill the long-established line of Lydian kings. The gods did not punish him, and Gyges even consulted the Greek oracle at Delphi for advice. Within thirty years Greeks were applying a word of Lydian origin to similar usurping rulers who had taken power in states on their own Greek mainland.

Why, though, did the aristocrats' monopoly ever break up? It has to be relevant that in the early seventh century, certainly by *c.* 670 BC, we have evidence of a famous change in Greek military tactics, to the long-lasting 'hoplite' style. 'Hoplite' infantrymen adopted a large shield, about three feet across, which was held by a double grip inside its rim and could protect the warrior's left side from his chin down to his knees. In a massed line, the overlapping shield of each warrior's neighbour helped to protect his right side and thus freed his right hand to use a thrusting-spear or a short sword at close range. Metal helmets and a metal or padded linen breastplate gave body-protection, as did metal greaves on the legs, at first an optional extra; they allowed a close-packed line to stand firm against enemy arrows and missiles. New styles of warfare developed against the previous style of warfare and, crucially, the prevailing Greek style of cavalry could not charge down this heavy-armoured line of infantry so long as the ranks stood firm. Noble horsemen became peripheral and henceforward were most useful in giving pursuit when the heavy infantry broke before their hoplite opponents. So too, noble champions and their individual duels diminished: they were no longer the main focus of most of the battles fought on foot.

In this change of infantry tactics, the crucial item was a double grip, positioned inside the shield, which allowed a warrior to hold such a big item of protection on one arm. Sufficient evidence links its introduction on the Greek mainland with Argos, where the new-style fighters were admired as the champion Greek 'stings of war'.[3] However, the new shield-grip and several items of armour may have begun earlier in western Asia as the equipment of non-Greek Carians and the neighbouring Ionian Greeks who served the Lydian rulers as infantry. Gyges may even have been the military leader of such soldiers. Among the Argives, too, the adoption of 'hoplite' tactics is convincingly ascribed to an individual, the former King Pheidon. An individual was needed for the innovation, because no aristocracy would have voluntarily introduced a new style of fighting which so obviously undermined its own aristocratic power. Pheidon of Argos, c. 670 BC, was a near-contemporary of Gyges and probably copied the eastern example. Once the Argives fought as hoplites, neighbours in Greece had no choice but to follow suit; similar constraints would later force the use of firearms on the reluctant military class of the Ottoman Turks.

The new hoplite tactics had social consequences which we can compare with the adoption of the thrusting-spear and massed line by the mighty Shaka Zulu in southern Africa only 150 years ago. They did not create a separate social order, 'the army': the new hoplites were the citizenry who mustered on call to take up arms. But now the smaller landowners among them could club together with weapons and a formation of their own so as to defend their property or ravage others' without depending on aristocratic champions. They were not a new class, but an old class made newly class-conscious. For the new tactics were certainly a change to 'safety in numbers'. The solid metal helmet greatly restricts a warrior's view from side to side. The big shield, with its double grip, is also a very clumsy object to manoeuvre in single combat outside a formation. Reconstructions of this weaponry do persuade me that the new tactics required quite a big, solid formation for the armour to be effective. The first vase paintings which show hoplites do sometimes show them with one or two throwing-spears too: perhaps, at first, the front ranks used such missiles, but in my view they are only shown as an artistic convention. For the next three centuries, however, the massed hoplite line would be the dominant Greek form of battle by land. Its participants, the citizens, would exercise in their athletic gyms and wrestling-grounds, but, except in Sparta, their military training on parade grounds would be very limited. For the front ranks, nonetheless, a battle was a fearsome experience, culminating in 'pushing and shoving' (ôthismos) against the enemy's opposed hoplite line (the details of a hoplite battle are nowhere fully described and so its usual course remains disputed).

Obviously, these new tactics had implications for a state's structure of force and power. We cannot say that 'wherever there were hoplites, then there were tyrants and a break in aristocratic rule'. What we can infer is that without this military change there would have been no tyrants at all. Nobody would have dared to kill off their community's main fighting force, the nobility. Hoplites, therefore, were a necessary precondition of Greek tyranny, but they were not a sufficient one.

An accompanying cause of change was the increasing division and disorder among the aristocrats themselves. Aristocracies were notoriously vulnerable to faction. Why should one noble family give way to another, if noblemen in theory were all of a similar splendour? As life and leisure developed in the urban centres with their wrestling-grounds and council meetings and rooms for lengthy drinking-parties, there was increased scope for insults between competitive noble cliques and for resentful disappointment among those who had been denied an honour or a particular magistracy. As in medieval Italian towns, the rise of urban living promoted closer daily contacts between noble families, with a resulting rise in violence and faction. Nobles were free to say whatever they wanted, with no fixed laws as yet against slander or physical abuse. Even their male parties, or *symposia*, were intensified by the intoxicating, though watered, wine, and were heated by the recitation of poems of personal praise and blame. In the evenings groups of young party-goers would form into drunken revels, or *kômoi*, like those for the god Dionysus. They would go off to find slave-prostitutes (*hetairai*) or even to serenade a desirable boy or lady outside the bolted doors of a house. Poems accompanied these noisy outings too, and brawls and quarrels could easily erupt along the way. Nobles formed groups of close 'companions', or *hetaireiai*, who dined and idled together, solid in their contempt for other *hetaireiai* in their city-state. Each noble family could also call on their loyal inferiors, members of the phratries which their clans dominated; these 'brotherhoods' would often be located round a noble family's residences in the country-territory of their *polis*.

In the more accessible Greek communities, which were open to the sea, these sources of social tension were compounded by an economic effect of the ever-increasing Greek settlements overseas. Exchanges between Greek communities multiplied, both between the new settlements and between a settlement and its 'home' community. Most of the gains from the increased trading and raiding went first to the aristocrats who were usually the backers of such ventures. As a result, ever more fine luxuries and items of distinction entered into the social circuit. Some of the finest came from localized sources of supply abroad (ivory, flax or silver), while others were devised by craftsmen for the increased buying-power in their city-state's upper class. New levels of luxury and display were highly divisive. No nobleman could afford to be seen as less magnificent than other noblemen for very long. At weddings or funerals, his family's splendour was on public view and the more 'luxurious' the other nobles became, the more he must strive to keep up with them.

As faction and social competition intensified, the older ideal of a 'peer group' of nobles splintered into violence and disorder. This faction had wider consequences. Lowly citizens still looked to their noblemen for just judgements and wise arbitration, but faction and personal enmities would distort a nobleman's conduct of public office or his verbal dispensation of justice. To keep up with his peers, he might also impose harsher terms on his local dependants and on those who turned to him for loans or help with a temporary crisis.

There was also a slight diffusion of riches. Aristocrats could not continue to monopolize the gains from foreign trading or to contain the effects of their own magnificent spending. In turn, they created new rivals to their own pre-eminence. As they spent freely to enhance their prestige, their spending passed down through the social pyramid by the 'multiplier effect' familiar to modern economists. Not only did non-nobles also engage in trade: the nobles' demands enriched owners of skilled slave-craftsmen or the suppliers of precious new 'luxuries'. As the nobles' spending diversified, non-noble rich men began to emerge, perhaps a few dozen families at first in each community, and certainly not a commercial 'middle class'. But if they, too, could prosper by their own skill, why could they not hold a prestigious civic magistracy as well as anyone in the noble caste?

Sixty years earlier Hesiod had exhorted his local nobles not to give crooked judgements for fear that the god Zeus would send a thunderbolt against the entire community. Homer had described the storms of autumn as the gods' punishment for violence and crooked rulings in the public meeting-space (*agora*). But now that military tactics were changing, repeated injustices and factional disorder could be met by human means. After a particular outrage, a fellow aristocrat, perhaps a commander in war, could urge the citizenry to take up the new style of 'hoplite' arms, eject their most troublesome aristocrats and install himself as their ruler instead. He would stop faction, 'set things to rights' and preside over high society's spiralling competition. Tyrants, therefore, are the first rulers known to have passed laws to limit competitive luxury. The main reason was not that the costs of such luxury would be better diverted to public use for the community's good. Luxury was divisive in the upper class and a threat, too, to the tyrant's own pre-eminence.

'Undeserved' office in the community was also a source of grievance and disruption. There were not many jobs of any distinction in an archaic Greek community but as riches filtered downwards, there were more people who thought themselves competent to hold them. Disappointed candidates, as always, were one source of trouble and excluded but confident 'new men' were another. So tyrants opened up high offices in the community and the ruling council to more families, including rich and able non-nobles. They became the arbiters of much social honour and preferment and also, ultimately, of civil judgements. Meanwhile, political elections to magistracies could be quietly fudged into 'selections'. At home, troublesome rivals had to be killed or exiled, but abroad, tyrants were wary of gratuitous border-wars against other tyrants: they brought the risk of military failure.

In short, tyrants helped to stop spiralling ambition and faction by an ultimate act of ambitious faction: their own coup. Usually, it involved bloodshed, and, as tyrants regarded their rule as the inheritable asset of their family, their dominance passed on to a second generation. Inevitably, some of these heirs were much less discreet or able than their fathers. Amazing stories circulated about Periander, the second tyrant of Corinth (how he made love to his wife's corpse, how he threw brothel-keepers into the sea), or Phalaris in Sicily (how he roasted his enemies in a big bull of bronze: the story was probably inspired by one of the tyrant's surviving bronze sculptures). Tyranny had a basic illegitimacy, and observant citizens were well aware of its drawbacks. Within decades of the first tyrants some of the Greek communities were already trying to find an alternative way of resolving tensions. Their preferred option was the use of law, prescribed by contemporary lawgivers.

Among the aristocrats, there had already been individual lawgivers, but the social and political crisis of the mid-seventh to sixth centuries BC gave them a new scope. From Dreros, on Crete, we have our earliest inscribed Greek law (probably c. 650 BC). It limited unduly prolonged tenure of the main civic magistracy, just the sort of 'disorder' which might result in a tyranny. In Athens, in the 620s, faction-fighting broke out after the foiled coup of a would-be tyrant acting with foreign backing. To restore social harmony, laws were set out and displayed in writing by the Athenian nobleman Draco, of harsh 'Draconian' fame. In 594 BC, again at Athens, a tyranny was within easy reach of Solon, another aristocrat. However, Solon preferred to 'call the people together',[4] as the chief elected magistrate of that year, and then to write down wide-ranging laws which regulated anything from boundary disputes to excessive display at weddings and funerals, provocative insults of a man's dead ancestors and the due sacrifices in the year's religious calendar.

Solon is the best-known and most admirable lawgiver in early Greece. He was also a poet and he defended his reforms in vigorous verse. To Solon, we owe the first surviving statement that the conflict leading to tyranny was 'slavery': freedom, therefore, was a value for citizens to prize and fight for, not just against foreign enemies, but also within their own community.[5] Tyranny sharpened men's sense of what they had lost. To avoid it, Solon installed a second council beside the nobles' monopoly of the Areopagus council, and opened magistracies to the rich in Attica as well as to the nobly born. Famously, he abolished the 'dues' which had been payable to noble overlords by lesser landowners throughout Attica. In return for a noble's 'protection', landowners had been paying one-sixth of their harvest; the non-nobles did own the land in question and could buy and sell it, but the 'charge' remained attached to the land, whoever bought it. Graphically, Solon describes in verse how he set the 'black earth' free by uprooting the markers on which this ancient 'due' was recorded.[6] The earth, too, had been 'previously enslaved': now, thanks to Solon, it was free.

These 'dues' had probably been exacted by the nobles in Attica since the turbulent years of the 'dark ages'. By 594 BC many who paid them were the new hoplite-soldiers and so they no longer depended on their nobles for their military safety. The payments had become unjust, and even the nobles acquiesced in their ending. For them, the crucial point was that Solon had not gone on to redistribute lands from the rich to the poor: the nobles' own properties were left intact. What he did do was to ban the bad practice of creditors who demanded their debtor's free person as security for his debts. Most of these debts would be small and short-term, but they brought the debtor the accompanying risk of default, real or alleged: there was no idea of 'collateral' and as the security (a person) was so much more valuable, it was tempting for a creditor to foreclose unjustly. Debts thus led to the unacceptable enslavement of one Athenian by another. Solon also enlarged the process of justice by extending the right to prosecute offenders to third parties outside the particular crime. Solon promoted 'active citizenship', while believing in abstract, impersonal justice which was sustained by written law, not by his personal tyranny.

Earlier scholars of this period, who were familiar with the Old Testament prophets in Israel, ascribed this Greek concern with 'justice' and 'fair play' to Greece's prophetic centre, the Delphic oracle. Prophetic Delphi, it was believed, inspired this new 'rule of law' and the moral revulsion from tyranny. In fact, Solon probably joined a 'Sacred War' in order to rid Delphic Apollo of a priesthood which was declared to be unjust and too partisan. Lawgivers like Solon did not claim divine inspiration or the gift of prophecy from the gods. Rather, they addressed social crises in the belief that human laws would avert them and that by giving up some of their interests, the protagonists could cohere in a new, sustainable order.

Solon's legislation had a scope and detail which certainly qualify it as a 'code'. We can compare it with our best-attested collection of laws for an early Greek community, those which were publicly inscribed in the Cretan city of Gortyn, *c.* 450 BC.[7] Some of these laws were new or recent, but others were much older, contemporary with Solon's. They had not grown up year by year, as if each year's magistrates routinely added to the laws which they inherited: in Greek city-states, the annual magistrates did not publish their year's judgements as a body of laws when they left office. They had surely been collected up into a single text by a public decision. In Gortyn, special 'law commissioners' had, in my view, been appointed to collect up existing laws and publish whatever they could find.

These Cretan laws address vexed questions of inheritance which also concerned Solon in Attica: bequests are a source of social inequality and potential tension, especially within an upper class. Throughout, the laws' penalties for offences vary hugely according to social class. If a free man raped a household slave, he had to pay a fine about a hundred times smaller than the fine for a slave who raped a free person. The laws at Gortyn accepted the existence of semi-free 'serfs' (called *woikeis*) and in-feriors (*apetairoi*) who were excluded from the dining-groups of the free citizens.[8] The codification of these laws did not bring freedom or equality for everyone who came within their scope.

Solon, too, accepted and upheld the distinctions of social class. How-ever, all Athenians were declared free by him, and the legitimate slaves in Attica would henceforward be foreigners only. What, though, of relations between the Athenian 'people' and the new 'upper class' of nobles and rich men which Solon had recognized? Solon denied the hopes of those Athenians who wanted 'equal shares' in the land of Attica and a redistrib-ution of property. The 'people', or *dēmos*, he tells us, did have its 'leaders', but they were probably not drawn from the very poor, as if they were en-gaged in a straight class-conflict with the rich. They are more likely to have been lesser landowners, men from the newly armed hoplites, the sort of people who had supported a tyrant elsewhere. Traditionally, even be-fore Solon the citizens of Attica had been categorized as those who owned a horse, those who owned a 'yoke' of two oxen and those (the *thētes*) who owned neither but worked for others. The Attic hoplites were the oxen-owners, people with lands from about 'seven acres and two cows' up to about twelve to fifteen acres.[9] They were, by modern standards, very small freeholders. Solon freed such people from paying an outdated 'due' to the nobles, but he did not redistribute land or assets to them or give the lowest classes (the *thētes*) a full share in political power. It was not appropriate, he considered, to their station.

Like tyrants, therefore, lawgivers were not the active promoters of a unified lower class. They restored 'order' and 'justice', but the dominant culture in their communities remained the culture pursued by aristocrats. During the continuing age of tyrannies in Greece, the scope for noble, competitive glory actually increased. By 570 BC four further great festivals of athletic games existed to rival the Olympics. The Pythian Games at Delphi began in 590 as a gymnastic contest financed by war-booty, probably from the recent Sacred War; they then included a famous musical contest too. The Isthmian Games (in 582) probably celebrated the ending of tyranny in Corinth. The surviving tyrant in nearby Sicyon then rivalled them by founding local Pythian Games of his own (also in 582); his enemies in nearby Cleonae, helped by the men of Argos, then founded Nemean Games too (in 573). All across the Greek world, a culture of the 'celebrity' began, not a culture of great warriors but one of great sportsmen, poets and musicians. By contrast, there are no 'celebrities' in the world described in the Old Testament or in the Near Eastern monarchies. For their athletes, the Greeks invented the victory parade, our 'red carpet'. Cities welcomed and rewarded their returning victors, and fine stories were told about these celebrities' prowess and then their sad decline (from old age, not narcotics). The all-in wrestler, Timanthes, would prove himself daily by drawing a huge bow, but when he fell out of practice, he could no longer do it and there was nothing left but suicide. And yet he killed himself, it was said, on a bonfire, like the great hero of wrestling, Heracles.[10]

Victors in these games were proclaimed in the names of their home cities. Audiences from all over the Greek world heard their moment of glory, and it was mortifying for a city's tyrant that he could not command such success for himself. It was a young man's business, and the aristocratic poets dwelt on the short-lived glories of youth. It was also beset with risks, but risks were something which no nobleman professed to fear. In politics or in war, at the games or on the seas, there was a constant flow of winners and losers in the archaic age. In a temple on his home island of Lesbos, the lawgiver Pittacus, a 'wise man', was said to have dedicated a ladder, symbol of life's inevitable ups and downs of fortune.[11]

The families of tyrants did have one advantage: they controlled much greater revenues than almost any other noble rival in their community. The same tyrants who legislated against disruptive luxury could afford to build grand temples in the newly devised styles of stone architecture, copied from Egypt. Not all of their temples were sound projects: one of the biggest, on Samos, was begun, but never finished, on very unstable ground. But at Corinth or Athens, the tyrants' temples and buildings are the earliest which still impress us. In suitably placed city-states, tyrants also developed that earlier invention, the trireme, and built bigger fleets. Naval service, in due course, would add to the morale and shared sense of identity of their citizenry. While regulating extravagant weddings, tyrants also held the most magnificent contests among suitors for their own daughters in marriage. Unlike some of the aristocrats, they were not known for writing poetry, but they did patronize poets and artists and their own cities' festivals. They kept striving to outdo each other in the style of the old aristocrats, whose motto was 'anything you can do, I can do better'. To be secure, tyrants needed to outshine the nobles among whom they still lived; this pre-eminence was more important to them than fostering 'civic identity' for non-noble members of their city-states. Before tyrants existed, aristocrats had already patronized poets, craftsmen and the naval adventures of trading and raiding. While lacking a popular pro-gramme, tyrants strove to achieve even more of the same. As a result, the first era of political revolution was not the era of a new 'people's culture': rather, the aristocrats' values outlived their political monopoly.

6

SPARTA

He was capable, too, of convincing everyone with him that 'Clearchus must be obeyed'. He used to do it by being hard: he was gloomy in appearance, harsh in voice, and he used to punish severely, sometimes in anger so that there were times when even he was sorry afterwards. He used to punish on principle, for he used to think that there was no good in an unpunished army . . . In danger, the troops were willing to obey him wholeheartedly and they would choose no one else to command them, for his gloominess then seemed to be brightness and his hardness . . . to be a saving grace. But when they were out of danger . . . many of them would desert him . . . for he had no charm . . . and they regarded him as boys regard a schoolmaster.

Xenophon, *Anabasis* 2.6.9–11, on Clearchus the Spartan

IN THE SEVENTH CENTURY BC FREEDOM, justice and luxury were indeed active agents of political change. The pursuit of 'luxury' really did divide Greek communities' upper classes, and it was not an irrelevant moralizing which caused laws to be passed to limit it. The political exclusion of non-nobles and the biased settling of disputes led to a demand for impersonal justice which is best seen in Solon's reforms and their underlying values. Solon also stood for freedom, in the sense of freedom from the 'slavery' of a tyrant and the 'enslavement' of paying 'dues' as a citizen to a superior. After his reforms all Athenian citizens were assured legally of freedom from one another's harassment. They could bring lawsuits, even as a third party, against anyone who behaved violently and abusively (showing *hubris*) and they were forbidden to make a fellow citizen into a slave. By law, they were granted a crucial 'freedom from . . .' superiors as arrogant as the *Iliad*'s Odysseus.

It is, however, in Sparta of this period that freedom, justice and luxury brought about the greatest changes. For centuries, the Spartans' lives would be conditioned by the results. In winter 125 Hadrian himself visited Sparta and is said to have praised 'Spartan values'.[1] Like other tourists, he witnessed the games and festivals of the Spartan young men and would have watched the brutal whipping of the young male runners who took part. It was still a most peculiar place with a famous past, but he and his contemporaries had no true idea of how and why 'Spartan values' had originated. Sparta's secrecy is notoriously hard to penetrate because legends about Sparta, a 'Spartan mirage', colour almost all of our surviving evidence, from the early fourth century BC onwards. An idealized Sparta has been the most influential of all utopias in history, and has influenced generations of political thinkers, from Plato through Thomas More to Rousseau.

Unlike most other Greek communities, ancient Sparta retained kingship, but unlike all known ancient states (except the Khazars by the Black Sea in the eighth century AD) she had not one king but two at the same time. These kings had religious duties, duties which other Greek states parcelled out among priests: they led the army in war and when they died they were given a highly reverential burial. The villages from which Sparta was made up were odd too: throughout their history they were unwalled. Nobody in future times, the historian Thucydides remarked, would ever infer Sparta's power from her insignificant physical remains. Her political order spanned a wide range of unusual statuses. There were Spartiate 'Equals', 'Inferiors', people called *mothakes*, and the 'Dwellers Around' (*perioikoi*, who lived in outlying towns in Sparta, not the main villages). There were also the helots ('captives') who were owned by the community; they worked the land and gave half of their produce to the Spartiates, but could not be bought or sold like slaves elsewhere. Helots ranked for ancient theorists, too, as people 'between slave and free'. As for Spartan children, the boys of Spartiate (citizen-Spartan) families underwent a fearsome compulsory training from the age of seven. There were many oddities in Sparta which puzzled outsiders. Several Spartiate brothers might end up sharing one wife (in my view because she was an heiress); girls, too, would be trained in running, wrestling and other sports, some of which were undertaken naked (arguably to prepare them to be mothers of fit, healthy children). All male Spartiates dined in communal groups or messes and ate simple food including a notorious black broth. Respect for superiors and fellow Spartans' opinions was integral to these messes' social values.

Adult Spartiates prized brief utterances and vivid, verbal images. Even those who could write a few words saw no need to write at length or use books for self-enrichment. Their restricted code of speech went with a strongly conservative and ordered society. Above all else, the system was shaped to train soldiers, so much so that a Spartan's failure in battle was quite often followed by his suicide. It is understandable that archaeology in archaic Sparta has recovered thousands of little lead figurines of hoplite warriors, bronze figurines of female dancers who are holding their skirts (or 'mini-chitons') above the knee, and large reliefs in limestone, showing small figures approaching big seated persons, evidently heroes who were worshipped. The male warriors and the female dancers point to Spartans' education, while the reliefs show Spartans' extreme reverence for the gods and heroes, which was famous even in antiquity. But some of the Greek gods were not prominent among them: Spartan men are not known to have had a cult of Dionysus. The god of drunk, disorderly release was the very opposite of masculine Spartan control.

Spartan society was never static, and the ancients were wrong to ascribe its entire constitution to one single early lawgiver, Lycurgus. When they tried, many years later, to date people in the distant past with a formal chronology, they gave Lycurgus dates which equate to c. 800–770 BC. However, his very existence is now rightly doubted. Most of the laws which reformed Spartan society had occurred, I believe, by c.640 BC and were intended to address the basic issues of freedom, justice and luxury which underlay the rise of tyrants and lawgivers elsewhere in the contemporary Greek world.

In the late eighth century the Spartans, under their two kings, did not follow other Greeks and embark on a series of overseas settlements. Instead, they incorporated a fifth village, Amyclae, into their existing four, the *obai*. They also took in exiles from the coastal settlement, Asine, of their great rival and near-neighbour Argos. They then conquered lands of Messenia, their independent Greek neighbour, which was separated from western Sparta by a high intervening range of mountains. The Spartan kings then allotted these conquered lands to their own warrior-citizens. This allotment was selective and unequal and it was probably the unrest which it caused that led to the Spartans' one overseas settlement, Tarentum in southern Italy (modern Taranto), supposedly in 706 BC. Later legend ascribed it, wrongly, to the promiscuity of women in Sparta during their husbands' absence in war: when the men returned, it was said, they had to expel the resulting bastard children.

7. Marble statue of a god or hero, found on the Spartan acropolis. The sides of the helmet are decorated with male rams. Late fifth century BC.

These moves outside their home villages were varied and, no doubt, therefore controversial; arguably, it was in the wake of them that the Spartan kings sought the approval of the Delphic oracle for a constitutional reform. Its thirty-eight words (preserved later by Aristotle) are known as the 'Great Rhetra' (or 'pronouncement') but they are highly obscure, and their interpretation is disputed. Certainly they recognize the formal existence of a council of older men who are later known as the Gerousia. This council, made up of men over sixty, was given the formal role of preparing business to be put to 'the people': this formal role of preparatory committee work has rightly been described as a major contribution to the techniques of government.[2] Proposals were then to be put to the 'people', and, on the likeliest interpretation of the text, the 'people's' sovereign right was defined as the right to say 'yes' or 'no' to them. If members of the 'people' spoke on anything other than the proposal before them, the elders' council had the right to 'set aside' and simply submit their original motion for decision (even in antiquity, the translation of these Greek words was hard to understand, but in my view 'setting aside' in this archaic Greek meant 'asking opinions').[3]

The 'people', or *demos*, were the Spartan citizens, male only. As a body they appear to have been given final power or *kratos*, a first anticipation of what we later encounter as the single word *demo-kratia* ('democracy').

However, this popular power depended on the prior decisions of a council of elders and two kings, and it was exercised only in the deferential context of a soldiers' assembly. Was this political freedom a concession to a Spartan people who had just changed over to the new massed hoplite army tactics and were newly able to defend themselves in war? In my view, the political change in Sparta came before the military change to a hoplite style. It is better ascribed to the results of Sparta's major oddity, the existence of two kings. In the disputes of the previous decades, from *c.* 730 to 705, the kings and their supporters might well divide on contentious decisions and fail to agree. In Homer's *Iliad*, such a dispute between two great kingly heroes, Agamemnon and Achilles, is irreconcilable and is played out before the Greeks' army: it comes before the soldiers only because King Agamemnon lets it spill over into their presence. In Sparta, however, the political reforms required decisions to be put to the citizenry by right, in regular public meetings held at formally defined intervals. This political reform encouraged *eunomia*, the orderly conduct of citizens under the law. *Eunomia* was not a new Spartan word or an abstract word for a new constitution.[4] It was already used by Homer: the reformed Spartan state allowed an old ideal to flourish.

Nonetheless, a century or so before Solon the Spartans had invented what we would call political rights for a citizen body, and their citizens were free men because they exercised them. Their sense of freedom was sharpened by two local contrasts, one with the oppressed helots, the other with the inhabitants of outlying towns who were classed as *perioikoi*. *Perioikoi* later fought in the Spartan army, practised arts and crafts and constructed and manned ships for Spartan use. But they could not vote or attend Spartan meetings. It does not sound very 'just' to us, but in the 670s Sparta was already being complimented by a visiting poet, Terpander, as a place where 'the spear of young men flourishes, as does the clear Muse and Justice in the wide streets'.[5] In due course, justice became the business of yet more Spartan magistrates and specially convened judges. Popular magistrates, the ephors, served for a year and spent days judging Spartan citizens' cases, including cases of civil contract. The kings' judicial powers were more limited, but were most far-reaching on military campaigns. Otherwise, capital cases went to the elderly council. Even a king could be put on trial in Sparta, but only before the ephors, the council and the other king. What never developed in Sparta was the big popular jury, chosen by lot from ordinary citizens, as at Athens. Spartan justice was never 'democratic', nor were Spartan magistrates or councillors ever held 'accountable' by a formal process as a matter of principle during or after their public service. Wrongdoers were occasionally brought to trial, but the lack of obligatory 'accountability' was a major contrast with the Athenians where the principle became very widely extended.

It was between *c.* 680 and 660 that the Spartan army made the change to the new hoplite style of fighting, not least in order to oppose their 'hoplite' neighbours, the Argives. In 669, however, the Argives won a major victory over the Spartans and in the 650s, the Spartans' conquered land of Messenia rose in a revolt. Gruesome poems by the Spartan poet Tyrtaeus urge the Spartan troops on to greater effort in the war to recover Messenia: they continued to be sung by Spartan soldiers on the march in many subsequent campaigns.

By the late 640s, neighbouring Messenia had been finally conquered by the Spartan army and its entire land became available for allotment to the victors. The Spartans were now well aware of the new style of 'tyranny' which had become established in Corinth and elsewhere to the north of them since the 650s; they surely knew of the conflict and bloodshed which it had caused. As masters of Greek Messenia, the Spartans could not possibly risk such a turbulent tyranny in Sparta too, and so they addressed the social rivalries and competitive 'injustice' which were likely to bring it about. Social and economic reforms were therefore introduced within the existing political framework of their previous Great Rhetra. In my view, then, the major social laws were approved as early as *c.* 640 and were conceived as a genuine Spartan 'alternative to tyranny'. Its authors were then conflated into the legendary lawgiver Lycurgus and their names forgotten; nonetheless, they are the first comprehensive lawgivers in early Greece.

These laws obliged all Spartan males to undergo the training which equipped them as soldiers and citizens. For the first time ever, education was made compulsory for an entire social class. Aged seven, boys were taken from their families and obliged to train barefoot, sleep outdoors or on hard pallets, and 'steal' as an adventurous duty. They had to eat truly austere 'Spartan' food. They progressed through clearly defined age groups which were under the authority of older 'prefects'. At each stage, there was selection and competition. Aged twenty, a small corps was selected to be the 'Knights' (*hippeis*) in the kings' bodyguard; those who were not selected were encouraged to fight and make trial of those who were, a process which was repeated annually. These Knights were not at all the cavalry-*hippeis* of other Greek states: a socially superior cavalry would have been contrary to the Spartan ideal of a solid 'peer group'. Instead, they were the picked group of 300 who guarded the kings and fought as first-choice troops. The Knights, then, were surely the '300 champions' who fought with 300 picked Argives in a celebrated contest in 546, and, above all, the Knights were the world-famous 300 who fought against the entire Persian army at Thermopylae in 480 BC. Each year, the five oldest surviving members of the Knights became 'Benefactors'. These Benefactors were not active financial donors, like benefactors in other Greek cities: they were police officers whose duty was to oversee conduct in and outside the city. Horses, alas, were not at all a part of the Spartan Knights' life.

Young males of citizen birth were elected into a common 'mess', or dining-club, by existing members, although a single contrary vote could exclude a candidate. Once elected, all members had to meet the expense and demands of their common table. Sexual affairs were frequent in this male society, but they were not required by law or imposed as a fixed stage of a citizen's initiation into full manhood. Young members of the 'messes' were encouraged to roam the countryside, both in order to hunt to supply the common table and to check on the subservient helots. They had orders to kill any troublemakers: in due course, the yearly Spartan magistrates, the ephors, would declare war annually on the helots, so that any killing of them would be 'justified'.

Adult Spartan males were obliged to marry, probably in their mid-twenties, and were expected to father children, the future warriors, and to sustain them in turn through their long education. Their brides would be younger women of citizen parentage, perhaps aged eighteen or so, who were trained in the running, dancing and other sports. Marriages were occasions when the sexes had unusually disparate roles. The male made as if to seize the female from her family; then her family attendants would cut her hair short to mark her change of status and help her to put on a man's cloak and sandals. She waited in an ill-lit room for her long-haired husband to come and consummate the union, evidently with the minimum disturbance to his homoerotic expectations and mess-life among men. The aim was to produce a healthy male child: ancient sources, written by non-Spartans, claimed that weak and deformed Spartan babies were exposed as a matter of principle.

This coherent system trained males as citizen-soldiers in an openly entitled 'peer group'. The system was not a survival from an earlier, tribal past: it was deliberately imposed and extended so as to head off the contemporary danger of tyranny. When outsiders tried to explain the self-styled Spartan 'Equals' (the *homoioi*), they found the precise nature of their 'equality' problematic. They alleged that all the plots of land in

8. Bronze figurine of a Spartan girl, from the rim of a
bronze vessel. Her robe, cut away off the shoulder,
suggests she is dancing. Late sixth century BC.

Sparta and Messenia belonged to the state and that private possessions
were forbidden between true 'Equals'. State-owned land did indeed exist,
but perhaps only in the Spartan homeland, and the probability is that
once, and once only, equally sized allotments had been given out as
'starter-plots' to each male warrior-citizen after the conquest of Messenia
in the 640s. These plots, however, could be bought, sold and bequeathed,
unlike the 'state-owned land'. By an important loophole, property left to
a daughter could pass outside the family on the girl's marriage. Inevitably,
girls with property were married off to the most propertied suitors and
then, the doubly propertied young couple would try not to rear too many
children between whom their newly gained economic superiority would
have to be divided. Consequently, land-holdings were concentrated into
fewer hands by a familiar narrowing of inheritance. This process was one
which other Greek states, including the Athenians, tried to regulate strin-
gently. It eventually contributed to a decline in the number of Spartan
citizen-males who were able to pay their way through the messes and the
education. Some 9,000 Spartiate 'Equals' are said to have existed when

the system began (*c.* 640 BC). By *c.* 330 the numbers of Spartiates had shrunk to less than 1,000: infertility was not the cause of the decline.

The core of the Spartans' austere system was adopted so as to enable a fully 'hoplite' citizenry to persist in Sparta without the accompanying risk of a coup by an aspiring tyrant. Ruthlessly, the system aimed to limit divisive luxury, to a degree which intrigued later political theorists, especially Rousseau. The Spartans took an extreme route to the aim of social cohesion which was being addressed by the piecemeal laws against extravagance passed by tyrants and lawgivers elsewhere.

What had seemed precautionary and 'modern' in the 640s persisted at Sparta and came to seem especially archaic and curious to later outsiders. Items like the Spartan use of iron weights had not been peculiar in the 640s, before coinage even existed, but they became very odd from *c.* 520 BC onwards when coinage began to be used widely by other city-states in Greece. Despite the fantasies of later political theorists (whether Karl Marx or the Nazi publicists), Sparta never became a totally collectivist state. In fact, the vagaries of private ownership continued and before too long 'all Spartiates were equal, but some were more equal than others'. From the mid-sixth century onwards, we can point to a rich Spartan minority who owned hugely expensive teams of chariot-horses. From the 450s onwards, during years of persistent war and crisis, superior members of the 'peer group' are recorded as winning glittering individual prizes with horses and chariots at Olympia and elsewhere. As a retort, King Agesilaus II is said to have encouraged his sister to finance a winning entry at Olympia in order to teach the Spartiates that chariot-victories were an unmanly business.

The Spartans remained, nonetheless, free of tyrants and the disruptive bloodshed which would have broken their hold on conquered Messenia. The Spartans still enjoyed festivals for the gods, competitions (even in horse racing) and fine occasions for singing and choral dancing: their young girls sang and danced to a haunting Maidens' Song (composed by the visiting poet Alcman, *c.* 610 BC), and, at their shrine of Artemis, finds of clay masks imply that males engaged in ritual dancing too, wearing 'young' masks or 'old' ugly masks in a performance the nature of which escapes us. To Aristotle, nonetheless, Spartan society appeared like an army camp, and indeed he was right. Back in *c.* 700 BC, in my view, Spartan males had first acquired their right of political decision, but not because they were a newly empowered hoplite soldiery. Some fifty years later, however, they were exercising this right in a social structure which had become focused on military success before all else. The competitions, even the female dancing, were designed to promote fit and hyper-ambitious participants: mockery was one of the great reinforcing social instruments in Sparta, including (we are told) the mocking of helots who were made to tramp around absurdly when drunk.

What endured was the novelty of the Spartans' permanently trained, professional army of hoplites, far superior to the lightly trained occasional hoplites, the citizens of all other Greek states. For centuries, they marched in ranks, dressed in their purple cloaks, to the sound of pipers and the martial poems of Tyrtaeus. Their neighbour, Argos, had been so prominent in Homer and, as the seat of King Agamemnon, might have been expected to dominate southern Greece. But the Spartans hit back with their professionally trained army and a constitution which continued to adapt itself after their occasional grand blunders. The Argives had no such system. The kingdoms of the Near East also lacked a solid trained infantry of their own and in the 550s BC, when they cast around for trained and heavily armoured foot soldiers, it was to distant Sparta that they turned. Gifts to woo a Spartan military alliance were sent from rich King Croesus in Lydia, while the Pharaoh in Egypt sent a heavily woven linen breastplate, a real wonder, including gold thread and figured embroidery, each thread being made of 360 separate strands (a sister-piece was sent to Athena's temple at Lindos on the island of Rhodes; it had the same density, as was verified by the studious Roman governor, Mucianus, in *c.* AD 69: he claimed to have counted 365 strands per thread in its fragments, perhaps miscounting one for each day of the year).[6] These gifts beckoned Sparta to an altogether less fettered and archaizing world, the settlements of Ionian Greeks on the islands of the Aegean and mainland Asia Minor.

THE EASTERN GREEKS

My heart has become heavy, my legs do not carry me
Which once were swift to dance, like young fawns.
I often bemoan this, but what can I do?
Be ageless? That, a mortal cannot become.
For, they said of Tithonus that Dawn, with her pink arms,
Was once smitten with love and took him off to the ends of the earth
As he was fair and young—but in time, grey old age seized him
Though he had a wife who was immortal . . .

Sappho, Cologne Papyrus, first published and restored in 2004

Apatorios to Leanax . . . I have had my goods plundered by Heracleides
son of Eotheris. It is in your power to see that I do not lose the goods. For
I said the goods are yours and Menon said that you entrusted them to him
. . . and he also said that the goods in my possession are yours. So, if you
present the documents written on hides (probably, leather) to Heracleides
and Thathaie, your goods [will be recovered . . . ?] . . .

A Greek letter written in Ionic script on lead by Apatorios
(an Ionian name) c. 500 BC and found up at Olbia, the site of
a Milesian Greek settlement on the northern coast of the
Black Sea (to date, only five other Greek letters on lead, datable
c. 540–500 BC, are known; this one was first published in 2004)

ACROSS THE AEGEAN, on the coast of western Asia and the nearby islands, the eastern Greeks have strong claims to be the cultural leaders
of the archaic Greek world. Many modern histories of Greece do not give
that impression: the Greeks of Ionia have even been classed as 'followers',

not leaders. One reason is that their sites have been much less explored by archaeology and, as they often lie in modern Turkey, they have been less at the centre for modern 'philhellenes' and their embassies and schools based in Athens.

In my view, Ionia and the eastern Greeks in the eighth to sixth centuries would have made mainland Greece seem decidedly drab and unsophisticated. Their use of language was far superior. In poetry, they had produced some of Homer's oral forerunners (or so his traditional dialect suggests) and almost certainly Homer himself. They had exported the poetic genre of elegy back to Greece and invented many of the metres and genres of lyric poetry too. The metres used by two island geniuses, the noble Alcaeus and the lady-poet Sappho, gave a new rhythm and polish to lyrics, as the poets of Rome and, later, England tried to imitate in their 'Sapphic' and 'Alcaic' stanzas. When texts began to be written down in prose (c. 520 BC), it was the Ionian Greek dialect which showed the way. Ionians also have their own fine tribute in Greek poetry, by the unknown author of the Hymn to Apollo on Delos (arguably, c. 670–650 BC), who was probably an Ionian himself. In their long, trailing robes, he tells us, Ionians would come with their 'children and modest wives' and commemorate Apollo, with their 'boxing and dancing and song' at one of their competitions on Delos.[1] 'Anyone who met them, then, when they were gathered together, would say they were immortal and would never grow old,' and 'he would delight his heart while gazing at their men and fair-girdled women, at their swift ships and many possessions'. At that time, the Athenians would have been a much less impressive sight, let alone the Spartans. It is the most beautiful tribute; the Ionian visits to Delos are a poetic picture which still delights our mind's eye.

Not that these eastern Greeks were soft. On the mainland, the broad plains of Asia were very well suited to cavalry and it was there, in the seventh and sixth centuries, that some of the finest Greek horsemen could be seen. On land, Ionian 'men of bronze', hoplites therefore, had already been helping in Egypt by c. 665: eastern Greeks were the first to adopt the new tactics and the 'hoplite revolution'.[2] They were surely on the forefront of trireme-warfare too. The earliest surviving use of the word happens to be east Greek in the 540s BC, and although islanders kept on using the older 'fifty-oared' vessels, the numbers and skill of Ionian triremes (353 in all) which appear in 499 BC cannot have emerged from only a few decades' experience.

Off the battlefield, eastern Greeks lived elegantly too, unless they were at the bottom of the social pyramid. Their luxury was famous and their scent and finely woven robes were so fine that they were said to have 'softened' their morals. In some of their cities (we know specifically about Colophon, on the Asian coast), a thousand or more male Ionians would go to their public meeting place, dressed in long, sumptuous purple robes. Men did their hair up into a topknot and used golden brooches on their dress; among women it is probably no accident that the most famous courtesans of the era were eastern Greeks. Even their food was more interesting. The climate, so hot to us, was envied, and after contact with the nearby kingdom of Lydia they had figs worth exporting, chestnuts worth boiling and a much whiter variety of onion. By *c.* 600 BC, they even had peach trees, as the find of a peach-stone at Hera's shrine on Samos has now proved: peaches had come west all the way from China, far earlier than was previously thought. Through Near Eastern contact they developed their own elegantly decorated 'Ionic' order of architecture with prettily rounded capitals. They also developed coinage, initially a Lydian invention. Previously, Greek city-states had been using measured quantities of metal as a standard of value. Coinage merely cut them down into more convenient shapes, and at first it was struck not as everyday small change but from a precious mixture of gold and silver (known as electrum). City-states had their own varying weight-standards which inhibited coinage's prompt adoption as an inter-state money supply. It developed into a convenience, but it did not single-handedly change Greek economic horizons.

In the early sixth century BC the most remarkable east Greek voice was not a trireme-rower or a coin-striker: it was Sappho's. She is the one female in the archaic Greek world whom we can still read in her own words, unrivalled until the poetess Erinna in the fourth century BC, who is also known only through fragments. Sappho is the unique early Greek witness to love and desire between women, the namesake of modern lesbians (she lived on the island of Lesbos). Only fragments of her poetry survive, although another one, lamenting old age, was discovered and published from papyrus as recently as 2004. More may reappear, but what we have implies a fascinating context. Women come and go from Sappho's presence, while Sappho expresses love for them and intense regret at their departure, especially for Anactoria who has left Lesbos to 'shine' among the Lydians. What social context is Sappho assuming? Ancient sources, and many moderns, made her into a schoolmistress with female pupils. It is more likely that she was a poetess in a well-connected household (she is credited with a daughter) who shared songs, dances and poetry with other young ladies and female visitors to Lesbos. Some of her poetry might be for formal choral performance; some of it, certainly, was for weddings; the 'lesbian' part of it was surely performed for women, not necessarily at a religious festival. As the poems show, one or other lady would then leave Sappho's company, for marriage or perhaps to follow a husband. But Sappho is the great poetess of desire, of the 'fluttering heart' and its physical symptoms and the bitter-sweetness of love. There is more to this language than close friendship; she really desires these ladies, Anactoria or Gongyla or Atthis, and she expresses desire with fine analogies from the natural world. Sappho is the most sharp-eyed poetess of flowers: she describes a young bride as having 'a bosom like a violet', not a bruised purple violet but the milky-white violet which is native to her island, a 'Lesbian pansy' with petals the colour of fine female skin.[3]

Sappho and her ladies' comings and goings are not so easily imaginable in an Athens regulated by Solon or in a reformed Sparta where no Spartan lady 'married out'. But her brother, too, had travelled far (he loved a famous Greek prostitute in Egypt) and compared with most Athenians, let alone Boeotians, many eastern Greeks had seen much more of the world. Their main reason for travel was trade, and the supposed 'barrier' between trading and landowning in Greek city-states was paper-thin among the eastern Greeks' upper classes: they were particularly aware of the scope for gain overseas and the need for securing desirable imports from the varying landscapes and non-Greek societies around them. In the criss-crossing networks of their Aegean islands it is hard to believe that the day-to-day business of trade and exchange was eschewed on social grounds by all male members of the landowning class. From the mid-seventh century onwards (at the latest), the Milesians pioneered dozens of settlements along the southern and northern coasts of the Black Sea, going up into the Crimea for access (surely) to its abundant grain and resources. From c. 630 BC onwards, Milesians were prominent, too, in renewed Greek contact with grain-rich Egypt. By c. 600 BC, eastern Greeks from the promontory of Phocaea had settled in the western Mediterranean, establishing Massilia (Marseilles) near the mouth of the river Rhône. They also touched on southern Spain, so rich in silver, and skirted along the coast of north Africa. By c. 550–520 BC eastern Greeks were familiar with the non-Mediterranean societies of the Scythian nomads (beyond the Black Sea), Egypt along the Nile and the curious tribes of north Africa. These three points, Scythia, Egypt and Libya, would remain fixed points of contrast with the Greeks' own way of life for eastern Greek authors in the fifth century. But they had been discovered and made into a talking point by Ionian traders and settlers long before. One eastern Greek traveller, Aristeas, had even journeyed far off into the steppes of central Asia and described what he saw in a poem. He imagined how ships and the sea would have seemed to a Scythian nomad if he had sent a 'letter' home.[4]

It is not then surprising that the first Greek attempt to draw a map of the world was a Milesian's. Anaximander (c. 530 BC) showed the continents of Asia and Europe as equal in size and surrounded by an outer Ocean. Another Milesian, the learned aristocrat Hecataeus, improved it (c. 500 BC) and wrote a *Circuit of the Earth* which set out its known place-names: surviving quotations from his work allow us to follow information gained from Ionian sea-travellers along the coasts of north Africa and southern Spain. Travel was not their only contact with foreign barbarians. In the western Mediterranean, increasingly from the 540s onwards, Etruscans and Carthaginians fought hard to contain eastern Greeks' attempted settlements in their area. In Asia, meanwhile, the east Greek cities had been constantly threatened by foreign warriors, by nomads from the north (the Cimmerians, during the mid-seventh century), by the rich kings of Lydia, including Gyges (c. 685–645 BC) and Croesus (c. 560–546 BC), and finally by the Persians who emerged from further east in the mid-sixth century BC. In 546, the great Persian king, Cyrus, conquered Lydia and his generals took over the east Greek cities in Asia. They would control them for most of the next two hundred years.

The simple tough life of the Persian tribesmen became contrasted with the luxury, the purple dress and softness of the eastern Greeks, and in due course the contrast was cited to explain the Greeks' defeat by these barbarians. One city, however, made treaties both with the Lydians and Persians and prospered from them: Miletus, whose nearby oracle of Apollo at Didyma was remembered for speaking the 'entire truth' to the conquering Persian King Cyrus. It is in Miletus, during the years of the city's special treaties with eastern kings (c. 580–500 BC), that we first hear of a new Greek innovation: philosophy. Some of it also qualifies as the world's first scientific thought.

We hear of Thales the Milesian who predicted an eclipse of the sun correctly to 585 BC, of Anaximenes who traced all things to the simple element of air, and of Anaximander who proposed an amazing theory of human and animal origins. Life, he argued, began in a watery element and as the world began to dry up, land animals developed. As man needed prolonged nursing, the first men were born in prickly coatings from fish-like parents, and these coatings protected them for a long while. These thinkers did not conduct experiments or randomized trials. They did not reason from repeated observations. Their claim to be scientists rests on their attempts at a general explanation of aspects of the universe without appealing to gods and myths. No other thinkers had attempted such theories anywhere else, and for the first time we can apply tests of formal logic to the sequence of their arguments. Why did they occur then, and why there?

Thales' predictions of the eclipse surely rested on existing astronomical records which had been kept for centuries by Babylonians. Thales himself travelled to Egypt; conquest then brought Iranians into western Asia. When the Ephesian thinker, Heraclitus (*c.* 500 BC), proposed an underlying 'strife' behind the apparent unity of the world, his ideas perhaps owed something to theories of cosmic 'strife' which would have been current among Persians in Ionia who followed the prophet Zoroaster's religious teaching. Contact with 'eastern' thinking was a precious stimulus for these intelligent Greeks in Asia. But so also was travel and their own observation. It may seem absurd when Thales is reported to have said that 'all is water', but his own city, Miletus, lies beside the eddying river Maeander which has continued to deposit so much silt there that the city is now several miles from the coast. In Egypt's Nile Delta, Thales could see and observe exactly the same process: water creating a land mass. Everyday analogies from cooking and the making of pottery may underlie other Greek thinkers' attempts at explaining the world.

Travel alone was not enough to create 'science'. These thinkers also lived in communities which were held together by impersonal laws. As a result, they tended to explain the universe by underlying law too, and metaphors of 'justice' and 'requital' were sometimes important in their account of change. It is too vague, though, to ascribe the 'birth of scientific thought' to the existence among Greeks of the citizen-community, or *polis*. The first thinkers did not argue their theories before the common man in these communities. They did, however, react to each other's opinions as known through books. Crucially, such free reaction was possible because the Greek communities were not ruled by kings and the priesthoods in them had a restricted non-dogmatic role. They were sharply different from the kings and priests to be found in the older kingdoms of the Near East. These early Greek thinkers were not atheists (one of them, Xenophanes, even argued for 'one God', supreme, it seems, among many), but their theories of the universe were not religious theories, either. They were not the sort of thing which could arise in societies where priests propounded 'wisdom' on such matters and kings had to be flattered and obeyed.

It is probably in the eastern Greek world that we should locate the most widely cited and endorsed of all Greek prose texts: the so-called 'Hippocratic Oath'.[5] Doctors still contest, or appeal to, its principles, but within Greek medicine it was only the 'oath' of a minority of practitioners. There is no reason to ascribe it to the great Hippocrates, the most famous early Greek teacher of medicine who is linked to the east Greek island of Cos. Like Hippocrates himself (probably an early to mid-fifth-century doctor), its date is unknown, but its morals and ideals have been upheld for centuries as a tribute to 'Greek science'. As a 'charter text', what it says is sometimes misrepresented by those who appeal to it. It is even cited in support by those who disapprove of euthanasia. What it actually requires is that doctors swear not to assist poisoners, rather than not to assist those who wish to be helped to die. Most modern doctors still admire the clause against the sexual harassment of patients, women as well as men, although the Greek oath also protected the persons of slaves; most doctors are less keen on the oath not to give a pessary to a woman 'to assist an abortion'. The clauses swearing to share one's livelihood with one's teacher in medicine and not to repeat gossip heard in the course of everyday life, outside professional hours, disqualify even the most admiring modern doctors from the halo of the Hippocratic Oath's observance.

Nowadays the most vivid material survivals from the eastern Greek world happen to be from the Greek West. In a much later text, we happen to have a description of an amazing robe, dyed with purple and made for one Alcisthenes, a man of luxurious Sybaris, who lived in southern Italy.[6] Some six yards long, it showed woven images of two palaces in the East, Susa and Persepolis, the ceremonial seat of the Persian king. It must have been made in the later sixth century (Alcisthenes' home city-state of Sybaris was destroyed in 510 BC), but it survived to have a long history, eventually selling for a vast sum to a Sicilian tyrant and then ending up in Carthage. As Greek gods were part of its design, its origin was certainly Greek. The answer must be that it was made in Miletus, the greatest of east Greek cities, and was commissioned by a man from Sybaris, the western city in Italy with which Miletus had a very special relationship. The text which describes it is a glimpse of the wide horizons spanned by its artist, a man of Miletus who knew about the Persians' great palaces so many miles to the east, who drew the first Greek sketch of Persepolis, quite soon after the palaces there were being built, and who then sold the result to a western Greek in Italy, miles from the Persian Empire but within the orbit of Miletus too.

In the 540s, when Persian armies conquered western Asia, the Greek citizens of little Phocaea decided to escape. They put on board ship their women and children and the statues and all the dedications from their temples 'except', the historian Herodotus tells us, 'for bronze or stone or paintings'.[7] Then they sailed west. It is in the West in the following decades that we can still catch a last echo of their east Greek style of painting. It survives at Tarquinia on the west coast of Italy about sixty miles north of Rome; here, Etruscan nobles were buried in impressive tombs like underground houses, their walls plastered and then painted with figured designs. In the late seventh century Tarquinia was the Etruscan place of origin of Tarquinius Priscus, who moved south to rule Rome as a king, as did his descendants. From c. 540 BC the style of the nobles' tomb paintings shows that Tarquinia had received able Greek artists from the east Greek world. Their style is evident in painted masterpieces which conform to the taste of their Etruscan patrons: these Greek migrants painted scenes of the hunting of ducks, banqueting and sports, exquisite echoes of their east Greek talent in a West which adapted and admired it.

TOWARDS DEMOCRACY

*Histiaeus of Miletus held the opposite view: 'as of now,' he said, 'it is be-
cause of King Darius that each one of us is the tyrant of his city-state. If
Darius' power is destroyed, I will not be able to go on ruling the Milesians, nor will any of you anywhere else, for each of the city-states will
prefer to be democracies rather than tyrannies.'*

Herodotus, 4.137, on events at a bridge
across the Danube, *c.* 513 BC

WHEN THE PERSIAN KING CYRUS and his commanders reached the
western coast of Asia Minor as the new conquerors in 546 BC, the
Spartans sent him a messenger by boat, carrying a 'proclamation' (another Spartan 'Great Rhetra'). They told him 'not to damage any city-
state on Greek land because they would not allow it'.[1] For Sparta, there
was a clear line between Asia and Greece (surely including the Aegean),
and the latter's freedom was their concern.

In Greece, the years from 546 to *c.* 520 were to be the supreme years of
Spartan power. Her warriors had already defeated their powerful neighbours in southern Greece, the men of Argos and Arcadia, and forced the
defeated cities of Arcadia to swear an oath to 'follow wherever the Spartans lead'.[2] In battle, the trained Spartan soldiers had been heartened by
the presence among them of the great mythical hero Orestes, son of
Agamemnon. In the 560s BC his enormous bones were believed to have
been discovered in Arcadia by a very prestigious Spartan who transferred
them to Sparta, bringing the hero's power with them. The hero's bones
were probably the bones of a big prehistoric animal which the Spartans,
like other Greeks, misunderstood as the remains of one of their race of superhuman heroes ('Orestesaurus Rex').

It also helped the Spartans that during the sixth century BC tyrannies came to an end in most of Greece. In many city-states, the sons or grandsons of the first tyrants proved even harsher or more objectionable than their predecessors and were remembered in some spectacular anecdotes, the best of which concerned their sex life. Periander, tyrant of Corinth, was even said to have insulted a boy-lover by asking him if he was pregnant by him yet. The brittle, competitive culture of homoerotic love was indeed one source of insult and revenge, but it was not the only cause of turmoil. Tyrants had seized power at a time of faction in the noble ruling classes, after the military hoplite reform had changed the balance of power between nobles and non-nobles. Two or three generations later this military change had settled down and the former noble families could at least unite in wanting the tyrants out. Spartan soldiers were a convenient ally with whom to overturn a tyranny which had lost its point. Sparta was believed to have the most stable 'alternative to tyranny'[3] in her social and political system, the nature of which, however, outsiders did not really understand. Spartans, therefore, were frequently invited in by discontented nobles to help put a tyranny down. Sparta 'the liberator' ranged far and wide in Greece. With one eye on Persian ambition in the Aegean and a close connection with her distant kin at Cyrene ('Black Sparta') in north Africa, from 550 to c. 510 Spartans did indeed have a wider interest in the Mediterranean. When one of their kings, Dorieus, was forced to leave Sparta (c. 514 BC), he set off first to Libya with supporting troops, then later to south Italy and Sicily where he died trying to conquer the northwestern, Phoenician end of the island.

Tyrannies had been resented as 'slavery' by their discontented citizens and their removal was therefore celebrated as 'freedom'. When tyranny ended on the island of Samos (c. 522) a cult of 'Zeus of Freedom' was instituted, a type of cult which was to have a long history. Freedom, here, meant freedom of the citizenry from arbitrary misrule. For, within a *polis*, the value of freedom had not been forced to the male citizens' attention by unfree slaves or women, protesting at what they did not have. It had become prominent thanks to the experience of the political '*polis*-males' under 'enslaving' tyrannies which had overstayed their welcome. Nonetheless, even under a tyranny, the magistrates and procedures of a city-state were not suspended. Important principles of subsequent free Greek, even democratic, political life went back, by origin, to the aristocratic-tyrannical age of the seventh and sixth centuries BC. Tenure of a civil magistracy was limited in duration by law: retiring magistrates were to be scrutinized, albeit rather cursorily, when their office ended. Legal procedures also developed and

9. *(Left)* Reconstruction of the so-called 'Peplos Kore' from Athens, a 'Maiden in a Robe'. Most Greek marble statues were painted brightly. Original *c.* 530 BC.

10. *(Right)* Reconstruction of the grave-stele of Aristion by Aristocles. Original *c.* 510 BC, found at Marathon in Attica. Aristion was possibly the famous sculptor from Paros.

there was already a public use of the 'lot', in some states, to select office-holders. The names which entered the ballot for office were pre-selected, no doubt with a tyrant's approval. Between *c.* 650 and *c.* 520 BC there was a continuing growth of 'the state'. Under the subsequent democracies, these procedures were to be extended and applied by the male citizenry as a whole. But they were not introduced into a void, as if tyrants and nobles had ruled autocratically.

Nor were tyrannies the only form of government outside Sparta. Throughout the sixth century BC they continued to be replaced or avoided; and it was still a period of active Greek political experiment in the male citizen-bodies. Some of the Greek communities (such as Corinth or Cyrene) changed the number and names of their 'tribes'; there and elsewhere, more broadly based constitutions replaced tyrants. In Cyrene, *c.* 560 BC, the powers of the ruling kings were curbed by a lawgiver, invited in from Greece; the reform did not cause bloodshed. In the 520s, after a time of internal turmoil in Miletus, foreign arbitrators even gave political power to those of the citizens who had the tidiest farms. By the end of the century new political terms had begun to be coined. City-states started to insist on *autonomia*, or self-government, a degree of political freedom which left them to run their own internal affairs, their courts, elections and local decisions. Quite where this degree of freedom began and ended would be constantly contested and redefined during subsequent centuries. By origin, the demand had arisen only because there were now outside powers strong enough to infringe it. In absolute terms, it was a city-state's second best to total freedom, which included freedom in foreign policy. *Autonomia* is first cited in surviving sources as the concern of eastern Greek communities when confronted with the much greater power of the Persian kings. The context would well suit the idea's invention.

Besides *autonomia*, citizens within a community would also claim *isonomia*, perhaps best rendered as 'legal equality', leaving open whether it was equality under the law, or equality in administering the law. This term is first ascribed to political proposals which followed the ending of tyranny on the island of Samos, *c.* 522 BC. Again, this context fits the idea well, suggesting that *isonomia* was a word for freedom after the re-sented 'slavery' of tyranny. The main force of the word was probably equal justice for all citizens after the favouritism and personal whim of tyrants; it was not necessarily democratic, but could become so. For, the years of tyrannies had often weakened the power of local noblemen. In several city-states, some of the nobles had been exiled and in their ab-sence, or their curtailment, the 'people' (*dēmos*) had had good reason to learn to manage local disputes on their own behalf. By the mid-sixth cen-tury there had been signs, too, of an obstinate solidarity in some city-states among people who were not noble or rich. In Megara, *c.* 560 BC, the 'people' were even said to have forced creditors to repay all interest-payments to their debtors. But who, exactly, were the 'people'? Those farmers with small (perhaps tidy) properties? Those who fought as hop-lites? The word did not necessarily refer to the entire male citizenry, in-cluding the lower classes.

In 510 one of the last major tyrannies in Greece was ended, the rule of the Peisistratids in Athens. During the previous six years attacks by noble Athenian families had weakened the second generation of this tyrant fam-ily's control. By bribing the priestess at Delphi, exiled Athenian nobles then obtained oracles from 'Apollo' which urged the Spartans to inter-vene and finish the tyranny off. In 510 BC they succeeded, at the second attempt. The Athenians now had to run themselves very differently.

For two years their noble families continued to compete within the sur-viving shell of Solon's constitution: in an anti-tyrannical mood, they seem to have agreed to a law that in future, no Athenian citizen could be tortured. It was symptomatic of a new sense of 'freedom'. The aristocratic Alcmeonid clan had been noble pioneers in the expulsion of the Athenians' tyrants, but in spring 508 BC they failed to win the supreme magistracy for one of their own number. Something drastic was needed if they were to regain favour, and so it was probably in July or August, when their rival came into office, that their most experienced elder statesman, Cleisthenes, proposed from the floor of a public meeting that the constitution should be changed and that, in all things, the sovereign power should rest with the entire adult male citizenry. It was a spectacular moment, the first known proposal of democracy, the lasting example of the Athenians to the world.

Like St Paul, Cleisthenes knew from inside the system which he so cleverly subverted: he himself had been the Athenians' chief magistrate under the tyrants, seventeen years before. What he proposed was a new role and composition for some very familiar Athenian entities. In his speech, he probably referred to a council and an assembly (both of which had functioned, at times together, since Solon), to tribes and 'demes' (Attica's small villages and townships, already totalling some 140) and to 'thirds' or so-called *trittyes* (entities which had long been familiar in Attica's organization). At a local level, he proposed something new; locally elected officials to be called 'demarchs' ('deme governors') would preside over local meetings in the village-demes and replace the time-honoured roles of the local noblemen. Cleisthenes' proposal was that the male citizens should go off and register themselves in a 'deme' locally, and then they would find themselves allotted deme by deme to one of thirty new 'thirds' which, in turn, would connect them to one of ten newly named tribes. The numbers of tribes and 'thirds' were to be increased (to a 'decimal system') but the core of it all seemed wonderfully clear and straightforward. Until this moment, the highest clique in Attica had been the ex-magistrates who made up the revered Areopagus council and served on it for the rest of their lives. They could only look on and listen helplessly to Cleisthenes' populist speech. In 508 BC almost all of them were politically discredited men, former magistrates who had been 'selected' in previous decades by the hated tyrants. Their main concern was to avoid being exiled for their past.

Cleisthenes' proposals were excitingly new. Since Solon's reforms, a second public council (other than the Areopagus) had helped to run the Athenians' business and had sometimes brought items after discussion to a wider assembly of citizens. We know nothing about this council's powers or membership, but it is most unlikely that almost everything which it discussed went on to the assembly as a matter of course. Henceforward, Cleisthenes' idea was that every major public decision must go to a popular assembly by rights. The one inscribed decree of the Athenians which survives within decades of 508 BC begins bluntly: 'it seemed good to the people'. In future, too, the council was to be chosen from all male citizens over the age of thirty and no restrictions of class or property are attested as limiting membership of it. In the later Athenian democracy, a man could serve on the council only twice in his lifetime, and in my view this rule, too, was enacted in 508 BC. In an adult citizenry with perhaps 25,000 men over the age of thirty, almost everyone could now expect a year on the council in his own lifetime. The implications were obvious, and like his audience Cleisthenes could see them.

So could his main opponent, the year's leading magistrate, Isagoras. He promptly summoned the Spartans to intervene, whereupon Cleisthenes artfully withdrew from Attica. The Spartans invaded, and Isagoras gave them a list of a further 700 families who were duly exiled. This listing is a fascinating example of the detailed knowledge which one aristocratic clique might have about the others, its rivals. The aim was for the Spartan invaders to install Isagoras and his partisans as a narrow pro-Spartan oligarchy, but the existing Athenian council members (400 of them as prescribed by Solon) resisted vigorously. The Spartans and Isagoras resorted to occupying the Acropolis, whereupon the other Athenians, 'agreeing with the council' (though some dispute this translation of the Greek),[4] joined in and besieged them. Resistance had now caught on among the citizenry, and when the Spartan invaders surrendered there was no stopping the progress of Cleisthenes' proposals, the origin of the incident. The outrage of the Spartan invasion made them seem all the more desirable. By the early spring Cleisthenes was back in Attica and the proposed reforms could be voted through and carried out. There was now a much finer alternative to tyranny than Sparta's system. The word 'democracy' happens not to be attested in any surviving Greek text before the mid–460s, but it was a very simple one to have coined on the spot.

The Athenian version counted on a very strong willingness of all citizens to participate. In 508 less than a fifth of the citizenry lived in Athens 'city': many of them had to walk in and lodge with friends if they were to serve and attend meetings. For one-tenth of the year a fraction of the council, the Athenians' most visible 'presiding' body, would even be kept in the city on permanent alert. Yet a council of 500 continued to be manned yearly without difficulty. Assemblies, at least four a month, would meet in the city too, though they were expected to number more

than 6,000 for important business. In due course, procedures to scruti-
nize all new council members both before and after holding office became established beside the 'scrutiny', still rather cursory, of magistrates.
After *c.* 460 BC an Athenian who served for a year on the council would
expect to hear the brief 'vetting' of 509 separate participants in public affairs. As a great modern historian of their democracy, M. H. Hansen, has
observed, 'to our way of thinking it must have been deadly boring; that
the Athenians went through it year after year for centuries shows that
their attitude to this sort of routine must have been quite different from
ours. They evidently enjoyed participation in their political institutions as
a value in itself.'[5]

After nearly forty years of tyranny, and after centuries of aristocratic
domination, this keenness was not surprising. Between 510 and 508
Athenians had feared above all a return to the noble faction-fighting
which had brought them such bloodshed in the 560s and 550s. Now,
there were to be no bureaucrats, no detested 'ministries', not even any
specialized lawyers: *l'état, c'est nous*, all adult male Athenian citizens. To
modern eyes, there were still conspicuous exclusions: 'all citizens' did not
mean 'all residents'. Non-Athenian residents (the *metoikoi*, or metics,
meaning those living away from their home), inhuman objects of property
(the many slaves) and the unreasoning second sex (women) were excluded
without question or hesitation. These exclusions were universal in the political systems of Greek states. But what was new was that every male citizen was included equally. From now on, a male citizen might find himself
on the council, appointed by lot to a minor magistracy or standing,
thrillingly, in a mass meeting, waiting to vote or even (if brave) to speak
on the fundamental topics of life, on whether or not to go to war, on who
should pay what, on who should be honoured or excluded. On controversial questions, he would raise his hand to vote and be counted. In Sparta,
when choosing magistrates, the assembled Spartiates would merely be
asked to shout in favour of each candidate, and the 'authorities' would
decide for which one they had shouted loudest. Even Aristotle considered
this a childish game show. Among the Athenians, each male citizen
counted for one and no more than one, the simple porter or goatherd beside the smart aristocrat. By having to choose and to be seen to have chosen, people soon learn to think and to take up informed positions. The
results were anything but mob-rule.

The danger, rather, was that a leader of a frustrated option might try
to rush a proposal through the assembly a second time and refuse to accept defeat. Brilliantly, Cleisthenes proposed that once a year Athenians

should vote whether they wanted to hold an 'ostracism'. If so, with more than 6,000 people present, they could cast a bit of broken pottery (an *ostrakon*) inscribed with the name of any citizen-candidate they proposed, in the hope that he would attract the most potsherds and thus be sent off into exile, to cool off for the next ten years. He would leave knowing that a majority had been against him, thereby ruling out his hope of a counter-coup; when he returned he would be 'yesterday's man'. Ostracism was a purely political process in intention and execution: it did not derive from religious beliefs or some need to expel 'pollution' or a 'scapegoat'. Political through and through, it became a crucial safety valve during the next seventy years or so of Athenian politics. It also presupposed that a high proportion of the Athenians could read or could at least find somebody to read for them. However, the ability to read, in many societies, does not require the separate skill of writing. Thus we hear stories of potsherds being written out in batches for voters to take up: our increasingly large volume of surviving *ostraka* do show that some of them were written by the same hand breaking up one and the same pot. This organization does not necessarily point to cheating or a manipulation of the ignorant. People who did not write could still read what they held. The surviving bits of pottery contain some wonderfully rude comments against individual rotters which appeal to personal prejudice and the scandal in the news-headlines of the time. Some of them even have witty drawings on them too. There is nothing similar, of course, in Persia, Egypt, Carthage or any monarchy.

With two minor interruptions, this democracy persisted among the Athenians and evolved for more than a hundred and eighty years. In our terms, it was remarkably direct. It was not at all a 'representative democracy' which elected local representatives either to 'represent' their constituents or their own careers and prejudices. Its whole concern was to limit power-blocs or over-assertive cliques, to achieve fragmentation, not representation. In many moderns' opinion, use of the lot was the hallmark of Athenian democracy; in fact, Cleisthenes is not known to have extended random allotment in any new way. As a Greek practice, use of the lot had a long pre-democratic history anyway, not least as a way of allotting shared inheritances fairly between brothers. Nor were property qualifications abolished for the democracy's senior magistrates: they were to be elected, but only from propertied candidates. So far as we know, there was to be no pay yet, either, for them or for council members. But what mattered was that they served only for a year and that they were not a 'government' with a 'mandate' of their own devising. Power lay with the assembly, and in that assembly each male citizen counted for one, and one only.

To our eyes, this democracy was more just than any previous constitution in the world. Nonetheless, the administration of justice was left unchanged: cases were still heard and tried by magistrates, with only a possibility of a secondary appeal on a few charges to a wider, popular body. Cleisthenes certainly did not base his proposals on judicial reform or new law courts. To modern outsiders, then, how 'just' is it all? Slaves continued to be widely used; women were politically excluded; immigrants were separately categorized and were not able to claim citizenship in virtue of a few years' residence in Attica. The point, rather, is that throughout the ancient world, even the gift of equal votes to all male citizens, to peasants as well as noblemen, was almost unparalleled (it did exist, though, in Sparta) and the combination with it of a popular, rotating council and an assembly with almost total power to enact or reject proposals was unprecedented, as far as we know.

On present evidence, the Athenians were the first to take this democratic leap. No well-informed contemporary source implies that any other Greek city already had such a system. In south Italy, nonetheless, archaeologists have proposed the Greek city of Metapontum as a forerunner. In c. 550 BC a large circular building was constructed here, with space for some 8,000 people. Surveys have suggested that the city's territory was indeed divided into equal lots, perhaps of this approximate number. In due course, the houses along the city's streets were built to a similar, repetitive style and size. Perhaps Metapontum had had 'equal' government of some sort before 510 BC, an extended oligarchy maybe, but we do not know that the owners of its land were the entire citizenry nor that the circular building was used for political meetings, let alone for equal voting by every male, peasants included. It is not the proof of a democracy before Athens.

Unlike many Greek citizens, especially those overseas, Athenians had one great asset: they had lived for centuries in the same territory. Their local social groupings and local cults gave them an unusually strong infrastructure and a sense of community on which Cleisthenes capitalized. He did not attack private property or redistribute riches. Perhaps his particular 'clan' gained a degree of advantage from the detailed local arrangements of citizens into new tribes, but it was an advantage in a new and changed arena. Cleisthenes brought a new justice, an equal vote for every male citizen, and the blessings of a new freedom, political participation.

Justice was also applied to the local units of community life, the many demes, who were duly influenced by the centre's new system.

Alarmed, the Athenians' non-democratic neighbours tried to invade and kill off the new democratic system, but the newly inspired citizenry beat them back on two fronts at once. Their victories were seen, rightly, as a triumph for a freedom which they all shared: freedom of speech.[6] There was no limit now, in principle, on who could serve in the new council or speak in the assembly. The 'freedom' at stake was not a freedom from state interference or a freedom from harassment by social superiors or unchecked magistrates. It was not a reserved area, merely protected by 'civil rights'. Since Solon, in 594 BC, their superiors' licence to enslave ordinary Athenians had been abolished anyway. Instead, male Athenians now had the one right which really mattered, an individual vote on every major public issue. Their new freedom was a 'freedom to . . . ', worth fighting for. From their battles in self-defence they returned with hundreds of prisoners for lucrative ransom and rich plots of land: 4,000 such plots were divided from land taken from the cavalry-classes of hostile Euboea, once the champions of early Greek overseas ventures. These gains were hugely rich and probably given to the poorer Athenians, a further bonus of new democracy; the fetters of the prisoners were displayed for years on Athens' Acropolis. Athenians who died in these first 'democratic' battles may even have been honoured with a new privilege, burial in a new public cemetery. But it had been a hard battle, and, in order to find allies in these years of crisis, the newly democratic Athenians even sent envoys out east to the Persian governor at Sardis. Better a distant Persian, they thought, than a Spartan-style oligarchy. When their ambassadors agreed to submit to the Persian king and offer the symbolic 'earth and water', the Athenians in their democratic assembly held them 'greatly culpable' and rejected them.[7] Fifteen years later, their new democratic freedom would be severely tested by those very Persian helpers whom they had sought.

THE PERSIAN WARS

When they had finished dining, they had begun the drinking and the Persian [Attaginus] said as follows to the Greek, a man from Orchomenus, who was sharing a couch with him. 'Since you are my companion at table and we have shared in the same libations, I want to leave you with a memorial of what I think, so that you may have foreknowledge and be able to decide what is to your own advantage. You see these Persians dining here and the army which is camped up by the river: in a short while, out of all these people you will see only a few left alive.' As the Persian said this, he shed copious tears . . . Then he said, 'My friend, no man can turn aside what must come about from God . . . Nobody wants to heed even those who say what is trustworthy. Many of us Persians know this but we follow, bound by necessity. This is the most hateful anguish of all among men, to understand much and to prevail in nothing.'

Herodotus, 9.16, on the Persian–Theban
drinking-party before the battle of Plataea (479 BC)

WHEN THE SIXTH CENTURY BC BEGAN, the Persians were living in a trivial kingdom south-east of modern Shiraz in Fars in Iran. It is most unlikely that any Greek, Egyptian, Jew or Levantine had ever heard of them. They had contacts with the more civilized court at Susa, seat of the Elamite kings on their western borders, but their own society was tribal, their riches still mainly in their flocks. At his accession, their king would drink sour milk and chew the leaves of the terebinth tree. No Persian bothered to learn to read or write. Their values were much more straightforward: tell the truth, ride a horse and shoot arrows.

Between the 550s and 520s the Persians overran the entire Near East from Egypt to the river Oxus. They profited from discontent in several of

11. Footguards of the Persian king, with pointed hats of Scythian style. From Persepolis, fourth century BC.

the major neighbouring kingdoms, the total absence of a popular nationalist opposition and their own hardy style of warfare with bow and spear on foot and horseback. Susa, Sardis, Babylon and Memphis fell to invaders who had never even seen a city, let alone cities of such splendour. In 530 their great King Cyrus died in an aggressive war against a tribal army out east in central Asia beyond the river Oxus. The Greek historian Herodotus claimed to know at least seven Persian versions of Cyrus' death, but the one which he chose to tell had none of the others' solemnity. Cyrus' opponent, he wrote, the tribal queen Tomyris, had taunted him for being 'insatiable for blood'.[1] When he attacked her army and was killed, she proved her point by filling a bag with blood, hunting for King Cyrus' corpse and stuffing its head into the bag to give it more of the blood it had craved.

The Persians, like the Greeks, worshipped many gods, except for a small minority who respected the dualist teachings of their reforming prophet Zoroaster (of uncertain date, but perhaps *c.* 550–520 BC). Wherever they went, they worshipped the local gods of the land, not through 'tolerance' but through prudence. On conquering Babylon in 539, King Cyrus was approached by many groups of petitioners who wanted favours for cults which the previous Babylonian rulers had harmed. Among them was a group of exiles from the Near East who asked for leave to rebuild a temple to their favoured god in their homeland and to restore its cult-objects. These petitioners were Jews, deported to Babylon about fifty years earlier. Cyrus gave them permission, as we can still read at the start of the biblical Book of Ezra, and so these Jews returned home to Judaea to honour their particular god, Yahweh. In due course they developed in their homeland the Temple-cult which would remain central to Jewish worship for nearly six centuries. Like the Greeks, who ignored Judaea, Cyrus had no idea of the momentous implication of his decision, one among many which he made in Babylon. His favour gave Yahweh's devoted supporters the upper hand among their own fellow Jews in Judaea, without which 'God' might have remained the cult of a minority.

In western Asia, too, Cyrus' generals were open to approaches from prominent petitioners. They included Greeks from the east Greek city-states who were offering surrender and sometimes, like the exiled Jews, bringing favourable oracles from their local gods. Persians had no idea of citizenship or political freedom. Unlike the Greeks, they had never lived through a military hoplite reform and towns were simply not their sort of thing. Cyrus is said to have described the *agora*, or 'market-place', in Greek cities as a place where people met to tell lies and cheat each other.[2] Noble Persians preferred their country 'towers' and parks ('paradises', the origin of our word) where they could plant trees and hunt wild animals on horseback (on their sealstones, we see them spearing foxes, outrageously, with a sort of three-pronged trident).

'Luxury' was widely invoked to explain their conquering progress. The Greek cities of Asia were said to have gone soft because they indulged in too much scent and finery and therefore capitulated to hardy Persian warriors. In fact, there was brave local resistance: 'luxury' was irrelevant to the Greek defeat and the Persians outmatched the Greeks in Asia with their manpower and the art, learned in the Near East, of heaping mounds against city-walls so as to overtop them. Some of the eastern Greeks fled westwards to escape the whole ghastly conquest. They were not being unwisely 'Hellenocentric', as multi-cultural critics might nowadays suspect. The conquering Persians settled some of their faraway subjects as garrison-troops and colonists so as to hold down Asia; tribesmen from the Caspian Sea were drafted west to new settlements with names like 'Cyrus' Plain' or 'Darius' Village'. Persians had no tradition of provincial government and they inflicted the most savage penalties on suspected enemies. In his public record of his accession, their King Darius publicized vast, precise numbers of the 'opponents' to his own usurpation, including the number of nobles whom he had had impaled. Persian methods of punishment were utterly beastly, including physical mutilation of 'rebels' by cutting off their nose and ears.

Nonetheless, the king did profess to be a fine dispenser of justice. 'I am a friend to right,' proclaimed King Darius in his 'official version' of his reign. 'I am not a friend to wrong. It is not my wish that the weak man should have wrong done to him by the mighty . . . nor that the mighty man should have wrong done to him by the weak.'³ The king was also not overcome by anger: 'I am not hot-tempered. Whatever develops in my anger, I keep firmly under control by my thoughts. I rule firmly over my own [impulse].' The trouble was that practice was rather different: 'justice' was decided by what was in the king's interest. There was no new 'Persian law' imposed on all of his growing Empire. At most, local laws were assembled in a province and then applied to it alone as the 'king's law'. In *c.* 512/1, after a campaign beyond the Black Sea, the Persian King Darius came down to Sardis and took up his seat in the suburb of the city: requests and petitions were then made to him personally, not least by insecure tyrants from the eastern Greeks' cities. It was a cardinal moment in Greek history, the first time that a ruling king of an entire Greek region (Ionia) was accessible and sitting in judgement within reach of ambitious Greek petitioners. Not only did some of Darius' rulings for Greek sanctuaries live on for centuries in their local keeping; his presence is the first instance of the giving of justice by petition and royal response, a pattern which was to become entrenched, some one hundred and sixty years later, with the rise of the kings of Macedon. It would then prevail for centuries with the establishment of Roman emperors.

As conquerors, the Persians took tribute from all of Asia, piling up uncoined bullion in their distant royal palaces. They also took land locally for their own provincial estates. Conquest, in turn, was believed to have brought luxury to the Persians and to have corrupted these hardy sons of an austere home kingdom. Having no court-culture, the Persians certainly borrowed from peoples whom they conquered. Their kings started to wear splendid robes and cosmetics and to be protected by court-ushers, symbols which were taken over from their predecessors, the kings of the Medes in Iran. According to Herodotus, the Greeks taught the Persians pederasty, in the palace maybe, or in those erotic hot beds, the army and navy, where Greeks were recruited: physical beauty may account for the rise of particular Greek favourites at the Persian court. But sex and luxury did not sap ambition. The truly missing link among

Persians was political freedom, a Greek value which Persian kings increasingly threatened.

The Persians' favoured solution for the Greek cities in Asia was to rule them through a friendly tyrant or a small clique: true to their values, Persians often gave them power as a reward for 'services rendered' to the king's interests. By *c.* 510 BC Darius I had even gained the submission of the king of the Macedonians in the north of Greece beyond Mount Olympus. Further pressure on Greece would probably have occurred anyway, as each Persian king would have tried to win renown and extend his dominions. It was hastened, however, by a clear sequence of 'tit for tat'. In 499 BC Greeks in western Asia rebelled against the Persian rule which they had endured for nearly fifty years. The rebellion has become known as the 'Ionian Revolt', although it called on the bravery of other Greeks in Asia besides the Ionians and also involved some of the minor kings on Cyprus. It was supported, too, by the valiant non-Greek Carians in southwest Asia. Two of the most prominent Greek leaders in the revolt were probably playing a double game, at best, and keeping a sharp eye on the possibility of a career in Persian service and a place high up in its graduated system of rewards in kind. But in most of the Ionian cities, most citizens wanted something else when given half a chance: democracy, as in Athens for the past nine years. The continuing revolt and its battles would root this desire even more strongly among the main Greek participants.

When the revolt began, the Greek participants met in common council at the Ionians' central religious shrine (the Panionion on Mount Mycale, the promontory opposite Samos). Their unity was very fragile and in due course there were some conspicuous Greek 'neutrals' in the area, including the important city of Ephesus. Within five years, the full Persian fleet, manned by skilled Levantines, proved far too strong in open combat for the Greeks' rowers and their triremes. On Cyprus, too, there were strong examples of anti-Persian, pro-Greek loyalty, but no lasting success. It is on this island that the main relics of the revolt are still to be seen, the impressive siege-mound which Persian troops piled up in order to take the walls of the royal city of Paphos and the great buried tomb at Kourion which probably belonged, like its excavated 'treasure', to one of the main participants, King Stesanor, who treacherously deserted the rebels' cause.

Initially, this uprising among the eastern Greeks received support from two mainland Greek communities, Eretria on Euboea and Athens. The Athenians paraded the strength of their 'kinship' with the first Greek settlers in Ionia, and sent ships with a commander called Melanthus (evoking the name of the Ionian hero Melanthius). When the revolt was crushed in 494 BC, Persian revenge against Athens and Eretria was inevitable. It came in two waves, the second bigger than the first (5 million men, in later Greek tradition) and provoked five crucial battles: Marathon (490), where the Athenians beat the Persian raiders on land in Attica; Thermopylae (480), where the 300 brave Spartans tried to hold the pass into central Greece against a full Persian invasion, perhaps of 250,000 men; Salamis (480), where Athenian and Corinthian crews distinguished themselves in the biggest naval engagement known in all ancient history; Plataea (479), where Spartan hoplite infantry were crucial in the defeat of Persia's remaining land-army on Greek soil; Mycale (479), where a Spartan and an Athenian commander won a final victory off the Asian coast having followed the Persian fleet across the Aegean.

For the big sea-battles, the Athenians accepted a near-total mobilization. Their fleet of triremes had only multiplied in size three years before, thanks to their wise use of a new silver-strike in their Attic mines. Into these recently built ships, tens of thousands of Athenians now packed themselves (200 to a trireme), willing to risk all in the heat, sweat and chaos of ramming-battles against the experienced Phoenician fleet. We cannot really imagine how intense and transforming this experience was. Even the reconstruction of one trireme has taken years of scholarly skill and dispute and it is still unexplained how the rowers could be guided and kept to an overall plan in the din of battle. The modern reconstructed trireme used loudspeakers because 'the length of the hull . . . and 170 sound-absorbing human bodies . . . meant that calls at maximum volume reached at most one third of the way down the ship'. Otherwise, the best method was found to be the humming of a well-known tune by all crew-members: 'unfortunately, there is no clear evidence that the ancient Greek ever hummed in our sense, either at sea or ashore.'[4]

It was unfortunate, but not culpable, for a naval enterprise that the Persian participants in the main invasions could not swim. It was downright stupid that King Xerxes did not cut off the grain-ships which he met sailing to Greece from the Black Sea or that he did not send ships ahead to seize Cythera, the island off Sparta from which the Spartans themselves could have been attacked. With hindsight, both of these errors were recognized by the Greeks who knew their potential danger. Only a small proportion of the 'Persian' invasion was actually Persian. Their cavalry was excellent, but the main army was recruited from their subjects and was at its best when engaging in vast projects of forced labour. For three years, a canal more than half a mile long was dug through Mount Athos to assist the Persians' advance into Greece. The workmen were driven on by whips, under the skilled planning of Phoenicians, and their surviving handiwork has recently been surveyed and verified on site. A remarkable bridge of boats and rope, woven from flax, was intertwined to ferry the Persian king's troops across the Hellespont. In both 490 and 480 horses were transported by sea in boats, a use of 'floating horseboxes' which is said to have been invented by Greeks from Samos.

In 490, it was said, the brave Athenians at Marathon were the 'first who held out when they saw [Oriental] Median costume, and people wearing it: until then, the very name of the "Medes" was a terror for Greeks to hear'.[5] Even the Greek Herodotus (author of these words) could respect the 'spirit and impulse' of the Persians, the equal of the Greeks' own; what they lacked, he thought, was good armour, know-how and expertise (*sophia*). Certainly, the heavy-armoured solid ranks of the Greek hoplites proved crucial on land. At Marathon, the Athenian hoplites proved to have been the first to attack 'at the run', across a mile (or so they said). At Plataea, in 479, the solid Spartiates were decisive against the lightly armoured Persians who rushed on them in fatally small groups. The fine Persian cavalry had horses which were proved by experience to be even faster than the Thessalian horses, the pride of many Greek racecourses. Their riders sometimes wore heavy suits of metal, but again they could not charge down a hoplite formation which stood firm. Nor could the famed Persian archers break through so much metal armour. The Spartan hoplites could even move backwards in formation, as if retreating: at Plataea, the manoeuvre was critical. At Thermopylae, their 300 used it less formally in the narrow pass and ended by grappling and biting the barbarians with their teeth. At Marathon, the Athenian 'run' was surely a fearsome shock tactic too, plunging the Persians into hoplite battle as an American historian, Victor Hanson, has tried to visualize it: 'the awful thud of forceful impact at the combined rate of ten miles an hour ... the unusual size and bowl-like shape of the Greek hoplite shield helping to create a feeling of absolute protection in the last seconds of the run ... Any man who stumbled or fell wounded was in danger of being ground up as the men in the rear lumbered forward, blinded by dust and the press of bodies.'[6] But that horror was what Greek citizenship and political freedom could sustain.

Despite a cluster of Greek deserters and traitors, many of the Greek states did agree, in 481 BC, on a common 'Hellenic Alliance' whose representatives would meet at Corinth to decide major matters of war. During the invasion Greek 'expertise' included some very artful tricks, none more so than those of Themistocles, the Athenian politician. When the Persian fleet was anchored off Euboea in September 480 BC he had messages inscribed on the rocks urging their east Greek contingents to desert (he assumed, therefore, that some of them were literate). At Salamis, for the crucial naval battle in late September 480, he sent a false message to the Persian king with his children's tutor Sicinnus, implying that the Greek fleet was about to try to break out of the narrow Bay. The tutor Sicinnus was a slave, possibly a bilingual slave from Asia, and he had three effects. He persuaded the Persians to divide their fleet into four, two parts of which went off to block irrelevant exits in the Bay. He kept the Persian crews at their oars all night, in case the Greeks tried a night-time escape: by dawn, they were exhausted. He also influenced the heavier Persian warships to move up into the narrowest entry to the Bay in the morning, expecting to find most of the Greeks gone. In fact, they were all there and broke the Persians' left wing, catching them in the narrows where their superior numbers were no help to them. Themistocles' trick was the ultimate cause of the Greek victory.

If the Persians had won in Greece, Greek freedom would have been curbed and with it, the political, artistic, dramatic and philosophical progress which has been a beacon to Western civilization. Satraps would have ruled Greece and dispensed personal justice; a few Greek traitors and collaborators would have flourished, and, at most, Persians might have dined on sofas and encouraged and watched the Greeks' athletic games, although their kings would never have risked competing in them for fear of losing, and, for good Persians, naked exercise (though titillating) was shameful and out of the question. In 480 brave Greeks and their families died for freedom not slavery. Posterity has remembered several of them, Pytheas from the island of Aegina who died in a sea-battle from so many wounds that even the enemy kept his corpse on board their ship to honour it, or Aristodemus of Sparta who survived alone from the glorious Spartan band of 300 'Knights' at Thermopylae and then, out of shame, fought way beyond the line with frenzied bravery so as to acquit himself, next year, at Plataea. To commemorate the victories, a column of three entwined serpents, made of bronze, was set up at Delphi to the god Apollo and was inscribed with the names of thirty-one grateful Greek states. Among them, the Spartans at Plataea and the Athenians deserved a particular praise. In 490 the Athenians had won the first round of battle against the Persian invasion at Marathon. In winter 481/0 they acted on their dire decision to evacuate their city and left it, with their dogs swimming beside them. In their absence they saw a great Persian sacrilege, the burning and ruin of the temples on their Acropolis. For two consecutive harvests they were out of their own territory, but nonetheless they ignored offers of terms from the Persian king and continued to fight heartily at Salamis, Plataea and Mycale. The Delphic oracle, by contrast, took the Persian side, and then had to invent stories of its 'divine' protection in order to explain why the Persian invaders, its friends, had not sacked it.

The battle was for Greek freedom, but the contrasts of justice and luxury were woven into memories of it. Persians were capable of a terrible ruthlessness, decapitating and impaling corpses, having young boys castrated and, in Xerxes' case, ordering an attempted 'draft dodger' of a father to be flayed. The father's skin was then stretched as a covering on the very seat from which he had once given justice. Greek values of restraint, modesty and justice were affronted by these anecdotes. The invaders' finery made an equally profound impression and was remembered in some vivid episodes. One Persian cavalryman had armour entirely made of gold; Persian cavalry-horses ate from mangers made of solid bronze, too; the Greek concubine of a Persian nobleman dressed herself and all her maids in gold jewellery in order to win pardon from the Greek commander after the defeat at Plataea. An astounding quantity of gold and silver objects, including wonderful clothing, was taken as spoils in the battle. Some of it was stolen by the Spartans' helot-serfs, but some was still being found in the nearby fields many years later. Just once, in 479, the young Spartan commander Pausanias ordered the captive cooks of King Xerxes to prepare a magnificent Oriental dinner and set it out for his guests in the former royal tent. He then ordered a Spartan meal to be prepared too and served in all its sparseness beside the Persian one. Among the king's lavish silver and gold furniture, Pausanias is then said to have told his Greek guests how silly the king had been to come so far, when he had so much, in order to invade a Greece which had almost nothing.

The costumes, the jewellery, the gold which the Greeks observed were classed as soft and 'effeminate'. In subsequent Athenian art, in vase painting and in the theatre, barbarian Orientals were indeed represented in these 'Oriental' terms. But this representation was not a new Greek 'invention' of the barbarian, in the wake of victory. Greeks abroad in the West and East had already anticipated it, beginning with Homer's description of a 'barbarian-speaking' Carian who was dressed in gold 'like a girl' (*barbaros* referred to the alien 'bar-bar' sound of non-Greek speech).[7] Rather, old stereotypes were reinforced by the Greeks' amazing triumph. The barbarian losers were presented as 'slaves' to one master, their king (Persian kings did indeed refer to their subjects as their 'inferiors', a word which Greeks translated as 'slaves'). By contrast, the free Greeks were hardened by their poor land. The Spartans, Xerxes was said to have been told, were free men who knew only one master, their law.

The ultimate victors were the Greek gods and semi-divine heroes. They seemed to be present in the awful tumult of battle; their very multiplicity kept up morale. If prayers and sacrifices to one of the gods proved ineffective, there was always another one to try hopefully instead. Persians, by contrast, included Zoroastrians who believed in two warring powers, one good, one evil, and when things went badly, the evil one, Ahriman, would seem unstoppable. Victory monuments to the Greek gods were built at the great Greek athletic centres, Olympia, Delphi and the Isthmus. In a fine celebration after the victory of 479, the Spartan king Pausanias, a warrior in his early thirties, sacrificed to Zeus Eleutherios, 'Zeus of Freedom', in the main *agora* of brave little Plataea. It is the most touching victory-celebration in all ancient history.

Evidence of the wars continues to reappear, with more, no doubt, to be found. In 1959 a reinscribed text of what appears to be Themistocles' proposal for the evacuation of Athens in 481/0 was found on a stone at the ancient site of Troezen: it was itself a later copy, evidence of the event's continuing fame.[8] In 1971 another inscribed text was found at Plataea whose citizens had helped the Athenians at Marathon in 490 and had witnessed Pausanias' great sacrifice after the nearby battle in 479. This text testified to a cult some two centuries later of 'Zeus the Liberator and the Concord of the Greeks' and to an athletic contest which the Greeks were still celebrating 'for the brave men who fought against the barbarians for the liberty of the Greeks'.[9] 'Freedom' games remained popular, and for us the 'tombs' and the 'heroes' have acquired more meaning. In 1992 parts of a celebratory poem by the great poet Simonides were recovered from a piece of papyrus: they compare Pausanias, the Spartan commander at Plataea, with the hero Achilles, the star of Homer's Trojan War against barbarians.[10] In Athens, during the 1990s, yet more fragments of an inscribed text which was set up to honour the valiant dead at Marathon were recovered during building work. A further inscription now shows that they belonged to a special cenotaph in the heart of Athens which was set up like the one at Marathon to honour the Athenian dead.[11] For centuries, Athenians continued to honour both monuments; their famous Funeral Speeches began to be recited by a picked orator at the city cenotaph.

Six centuries after the event, Greeks who presided over the cults at Plataea were also priests of the cult of the Emperor Hadrian 'the Panhellene'. Greek freedom had changed, but the fame of the great days of 480 lived on under the Roman Empire. They owed their preservation, above all, to the *Histories* of Herodotus, the author who preserves for us the stories, values and turning points in the Greek triumph. At dawn on the awesome September day of Salamis it was Themistocles, he tells us, who made the best speech. 'Throughout, he contrasted what is noble with what is ignoble, and told them, in everything which concerns man's nature and predicament, to choose the nobler part.'[12] King Xerxes was remembered for no such speech, and freedom, we may be sure, was at the heart of the choice Themistocles offered. It was a crucial reason why the Greeks won.

THE WESTERN GREEKS

Grant O son of Cronos, that the battle-cry of the Carthaginians and the
Etruscans may stay quietly at home . . . Such were their losses when they
were vanquished by the ruler of the Syracusans, who threw their young
men into the sea from their ships, drawing Greece from heavy slavery . . .

Pindar, *Pythian* 1.71–5 (470 BC)

A (Roman) citizen is not to bury a dead man in the city. He is not to do
more than this: he is not to smooth the funeral pyre with a trowel. Women
are not to lacerate their cheeks or to hold a wake for a funeral . . . Nor is
a Roman citizen to add gold. But, for anyone whose teeth have been
joined with gold, if he buries or burns it with the dead man, it shall be
done without his being liable.

Table X, of the Twelve Tables at Rome (451/0 BC)

T HE PERSIAN THREAT to Greek freedom was matched by another in
the western Mediterranean. Greek settlements here had multiplied
since their beginnings in east Sicily in the later eighth century BC, but in
480, the year of Salamis, the Greek sector of Sicily was invaded by a vast
barbarian army, led by Carthaginians. The impulse for it came partly
from a Greek initiative. A recently ousted Greek ruler on the island, together with his brother-in-law, had appealed for help to Carthaginian
friends. The Carthaginians needed little encouragement. Not long before, the Greek ruler of Syracuse, Gelon, had been trying to persuade the
Greeks in Greece to join him in attacking the Carthaginian sector of
Sicily. He had even promised them renewed trading opportunities, a
clear call to a Greek war with a commercial motive. But there was also a

Persian dimension. In 480 the Persians were said to be urging Carthage to attack Sicily and to keep its Greeks from helping Greece itself. Carthage had a connection with the Persian campaign because she was the colony of Tyre in the Levant, and Tyrian sailors were serving loyally in the Persian fleet against Greece.

In reply, an army of 300,000 barbarians are said to have swarmed into the island, but the Greeks in Sicily won a tremendous victory on their north coast, at Himera. Gelon of Syracuse was credited with an ingenious stratagem, Themistocles' equal, which deceived the Carthaginian commanders by intercepting a letter of help to them. In defeat, the Carthaginian general Hamilcar died, possibly by throwing himself onto the fire during a religious sacrifice, and Greek freedom was saved. Justly, the poet Pindar described the victory as 'drawing Greece from heavy slavery': it imposed slavery on the barbarian participants instead.[1] Hordes of them were distributed as captives to Greek cities on Sicily. At Acragas (Agrigento), it was said that many of the citizens acquired up to 500 prisoners each as their personal slaves. The slaves were used to quarry stone and to work on big temples to the gods: Acragas completed a gigantic temple of Zeus (whose debris is still visible). As so often in ancient history, the acquisition of quantities of captives or fugitives in war was the most effective transformation of a local economy. In the West, barbarian slavery assisted new levels of Greek splendour and luxury.

Twice in his life the Emperor Hadrian visited Sicily, on the first occasion climbing volcanic Mount Etna to see the sunrise which was 'said to be like a rainbow'.[2] By then many Greeks had been there before him, not least the poet Pindar who had composed a wonderfully sonorous ode for Hieron the Greek tyrant, founder of a new city of Etna in the 470s. The poem reveals a first-hand awareness, surely Pindar's own, of Etna and its slopes during an eruption. By Hadrian's day Sicily had had more than three centuries of Roman rule, and he would have had no clear idea of the island's turbulent past.

The western Greeks' dynamics were complex. Phoenician-Carthaginians had settled in western Sicily at least since the early eighth century BC. Earlier migrants to the island continued to occupy parts of it, especially the Sicels in the interior; since the eighth century Greeks had also settled in the east and south, especially near the coastline. The two sectors were not segregated; Carthaginians lived in Sicilian Greek cities, just as Sicilian Greeks lived across the sea in Carthage. The Greek islanders' main networks lay not with Africa, but with yet more Greek cities, those which

12. Painting on the inner surface of the coffin-lid of the 'Tomb of the Diver', found in 1968 about a mile south of Paestum. Four other paintings of scenes from a symposium decorated the inner sides: the young boy dives, holding his head awkwardly, from a plinth of uncertain significance. Like the symposium scenes, the scene surely refers to worldly life, perhaps to something in the dead man's earlier life, rather than symbolizing his dive out into the 'unknown' space of the underworld, a favoured but fanciful interpretation. Painting on white stucco surface.

had been settled on the nearby Aeolian islands and in southern Italy. In due course this region became known as 'Great Greece', Magna Graecia.

It certainly had a 'New World' grandeur and extravagance: the great modern Sicilian novelist Lampedusa called Sicily the America of antiquity. Already in the mid-sixth century BC Greek cities had ostentatious temples to the Greek gods, as we can see at Selinus in south-west Sicily: half-cut columns still lie in the big stone-quarries, several miles from the acropolis to which they were pulled on huge wooden rollers. In Sicily, as a pupil of Plato later observed, the Greeks even ate two major meals a day.[3] Pindar's fine poems for Sicilian patrons celebrate the rich farmland on the island, the crops and flocks, as well as the recent grand buildings. Pindar evokes the blossoming townscape of Camarina, in 456 BC, where 'a soaring forest of solid dwellings' was helping to bring 'the people of the city from helplessness into daylight'.[4] There was also very lucrative trade, not least

13. Small terracotta plaque from Locri, in the Greek West. A young woman handles a folded cloth at a decorated chest, beneath a mirror, a wool-basket, a flask and cup, c. 470–450 BC.

from the Sicilian coast to barbarian Carthage. By land and sea, many Sicilian landowners had the best of both worlds.

Since their first foundations in the 730s BC the Greek settlers had gone on to found yet more settlements as they gained in confidence. These sub-colonies lay on excellent farmland too, great swathes of it (about a hundred and fifty square miles) at Selinus in the south-west. The greatest modern historian of the western Greeks, T. J. Dunbabin, who was himself a New Zealander, has compared these settlers with 'the almost complete cultural dependence . . . on which the colonials most pride themselves'.[5] Were they simply creating more of the same?

The main lines of their history down to c. 460 are already familiar from mainland Greece. There had been wars between western Greek cities and also wars between the Greeks and the many non-Greeks on the is-land. There had been no new 'Western' military inventions and no really new political experiments: there was no common Sicilian Greek council or festival. The most pan-Siciliote occasions must have been their horse races but we do not even know where the big meetings were held. On the mainland Greek model, there were citizen-armies of armoured hoplites and excellent cavalrymen (horses proliferated in the good river-lands, as only in Thessaly back in Greece). There were tyrants, and eventually there were democracies to replace them. The main difference was the timescale. The grandest Sicilian tyrants emerged in Syracuse and Gela c. 505 BC

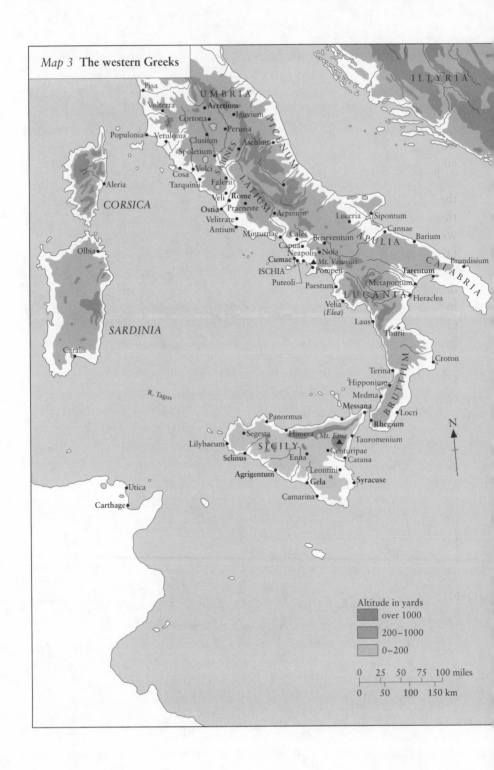

Map 3 The western Greeks

ILLYRIA

UMBRIA
Pisa
Volterra
Arretium
Cortona
Iguvium
Populonia
Vetulonia
Perusia
PICENUM
Clusium
Asculum
Spoletium
Cosa
Volci
SABINES
LATIUM
Tarquinii
Faleri
Aleria
Veii
Rome
CORSICA
Ostia
Praeneste
Arpinum
Luceria
Sipontum
Velitrae
Antium
Minturnae
Cales
Cannae
Capua
Beneventum
APULIA
Barium
Olbia
Neapolis
Nola
Cumae
Mt. Vesuvius
CALABRIA
ISCHIA
Pompeii
Tarentum
Brundisium
Puteoli
Paestum
Metapontum
SARDINIA
Velia
(Elea)
LUCANIA
Heraclea
Laus
Thurii
Caralis
Croton
R. Tagus
Terina
Hipponium
Medma
Panormus
Messana
BRUTTIUM
Segesta
Himera
Mt. Etna
Locri
Lilybaeum
Tauromenium
Rhegium
SICILY
Centuripae
N
Selinus
Enna
Catana
Agrigentum
Leontini
Utica
Gela
Syracuse
Carthage
Camarina

Altitude in yards
over 1000
200–1000
0–200

0   25   50   75   100 miles
0   50   100   150 km

(when the Athenians had just adopted democracy). Democracies replaced Western tyrants quite often, but not until the 460s (in Asia Minor, democracy had already been motivating the eastern Greeks to revolt by *c.* 500). From Sicily, we now have inscribed evidence of the reforms by which the newly strengthened city-state of Camarina adapted its social units *c.* 460 BC, but the reform was some fifty years later than Cleisthenes' somewhat similar reforms in Attica.[6]

In religion, too, the western Greeks were traditional. They honoured the same Greek gods and connected themselves to similar myths. A few of them have left some clear evidence for beliefs about life in the underworld, and until recently these speculations were loosely called 'Orphic' (after Orpheus, who escaped the underworld) and were thought to be a western Greek innovation. New evidence has shown that they were not distinctively Western but were widespread in Greece too. An important inscription, dated *c.* 450 BC, gives us some of the flavour of everyday religiosity in the big Greek settlement at Selinus: it sets out ways in which people can purify themselves from a hostile spirit-presence, whether seen or heard, by sacrificing a full-grown sheep and following other rituals.[7] It shows no sign of a 'Western enlightenment', and is not a response to a rare crisis.

The Greek cities in the West had been settled 'top down', by land-distributions from their leaders to their settlers. This style of settlement rested on less of an infrastructure of villages and nuclei in the countryside than many 'bottom up' settlements in old Greece: in the Sicilian city-territories, rich and absentee landowners may have been more frequent. Yet, this pattern was not the prime cause of political turmoil. As in old Greece, the dynamics for it were faction among a competitive upper class and greater riches in a few new hands, combined with changes in military tactics and continuing popular resentment of corrupt justice. The West's tyrants were no more 'populist' than the upper classes whom they dominated: the rulers of Syracuse were said to regard the common people as an 'unfit object of cohabitation'.

Of course, in such a wide network of so many Greeks, there were also a few innovations. Sicilian Greeks invented the after-dinner game of *kottabos*, or wine-flicking: they began a limited form of comic drama; they were credited with a special type of cart, forerunner of the painted festival and wedding carts in later Sicilian life and opera.[8] To judge from vase paintings, women in 'Great Greece' may have worn more transparent clothing than women in Greece itself, although neither wore what we call underpants.

These innovations were not a new type of culture, but they were part of a confident and self-assertive one. Western Greeks increasingly amassed their own prized deeds and memories. They showed them off in old Greece, but not as Greece's obsequious poor relations. In the eighth and seventh centuries dedications from Italy and the Greek West were already quite conspicuous at the great sanctuary of Olympia. They included weaponry, probably to thank the gods for victories won by western Greeks over their fellow Greeks or the surrounding non-Greeks. In the sixth century BC a prominent terrace at Delphi became the setting for an array of lavish 'treasury' buildings: five out of the ten 'treasuries' had been paid for by western Greeks. Westerners also proved to be great racehorse-owners and competitors on the Greek athletic circuit. It was, then, no novelty when the tyrant-rulers of Sicilian Greek cities dedicated helmets, tripods and statues at Olympia and Delphi in the 470s. They, too, were showing off their victories in games and their prowess in battle against barbarians. This same Western self-confidence greeted the mainland Greek envoys who arrived to seek help in the crisis of the Persian invasion of 480. The ruler of Syracuse demanded the command of the entire Greek force against Persia as his condition of acceptance. The Athenian envoys cited their role in Homer's Trojan War and refused him. It was an effective retort, because at that remote time the Sicilian Greek cities had not even existed.

Seen from old Greece and the Aegean, the West was simply a convenient refuge for a 'new start' when all else failed. Losers in old Greece's headlong political upheavals went west to found or take over a community. Greek refugees from the Persian conquest of Ionia took their gift for philosophy to south Italy and founded a settlement, Elea (about forty miles south of Paestum), which became famous for its subtle approach to questions of truth and knowledge. In the Bay of Naples, c. 521 BC, aristocratic refugees from Samos founded a place called 'Just Government' in explicit contrast to their tyranny at home (it later became the important port of Puteoli). Followers of the philosopher Pythagoras had preceded them, c. 530 BC, in south Italy, especially at Croton. Nonetheless, not every migrant was as just as the admirable Cadmus, who came to Sicily having renounced his tyranny on the island of Cos 'out of justice'.[9] In c. 514 one of the two Spartan kings, Dorieus, was ousted by his brother and arrived in the West with a small band of adventurers. First, they tried to help in an inter-city battle in south Italy; then they invaded the Carthaginian end of Sicily in the belief that they were 'reclaiming the heritage of the hero Heracles'. Dorieus died and a few of his followers withdrew to the south coast where they founded a consolation prize, another 'Heraclea', on the site, however, of an existing Greek city-state.

As these Greek exiles arrived and the existing Greeks in the West remained confident, neighbouring non-Greeks were not left in peace. In *c.* 570 the Greek settlers at Cyrene in Libya won a spectacular victory over Libyans and Egyptians and cleared the way for a further wave of Greek settlement in north Africa. However, in *c.* 560 the non-Greeks then won something of their own back and thereafter, the Greeks in the West did not carry all before them. From *c.* 560 to *c.* 510 attempts at further western Greek settlements failed, on Corsica, in western Sicily and close to Phoenician settlement in northern Libya. In the West, there were few entirely empty spaces for people to fill up. Carthage, too, had grown in confidence in the centuries since her foundation from the Levant: in the late sixth century Carthage's surviving treaty with Rome shows Carthage trying to limit Romans' access to her coastlines. The western Greeks, therefore, remained only one 'ethnicity' in a wider crowd. Like others, they travelled up the west coast of Italy, but the sanctuaries outside the coastal settlements there were already being frequented by quite other visitors and traders: Phoenicians and Etruscans were prominent, and these peoples were already concerned with their own inter-relations.

For the sixth century BC was a particular age of splendour for the ruling families in Etruscan settlements. As at Tarquinia, they liked to drink from painted Greek pottery, to patronize Greek sculptors and painters and even to imitate the Greek style of hoplites and, probably, cavalrymen. But they were not passive debtors to the Greeks so much as self-aware choosers and adaptors of what they were offered. They were also aggressive. In the Bay of Naples, in the 470s, the Greek 'tyrants' of Syracuse had to intervene to protect the local Greek cities from a major barbarian invasion, headed by Etruscans. Soon afterwards Sicilian Greeks helped in the founding of a local 'New City' (called Neapolis, modern Naples). Its regular layout of streets is still visible, even in the jungle of the modern city. 'New City' was not so very far south of another famous site, Rome: how far, if at all, was the future 'eternal city' integrated into this western Greek melting pot around her?

The early history of Rome remains a vivid arena of dispute, scepticism and scholarly ingenuity. The Latin sources have obviously been elaborated, or invented, many centuries later and so modern scholars rely heavily on local archaeology. On questions of political change and ethnic variety, its evidence is often ambiguous or irrelevant. What we need to stress here is that from the eighth century BC, the age of Homer onwards,

Rome was not an odd community, isolated from surrounding fashions. Archaeological finds do show that Levantine 'Phoenicians' and Greeks (probably Euboeans) had visited the site up the river Tiber. For the Romans were not sufficiently supplied to remain quietly inland: it has been brilliantly observed that Rome had no nearby source of that animal and human necessity, salt. Salt-fields, the only ones in west Italy, lay at the river Tiber's mouth on the north bank. In due course a 'salt road' (the Via Salaria) ran down from Rome and Ostia was founded at the river-mouth, traditionally in the mid-seventh century BC, no doubt with an eye on the salt-assets.[10] Up at Rome, meanwhile, the local huts were being replaced by houses; there was a public space, or 'Forum', which was paved; by c. 620 BC archaeologists detect an 'urban transformation', in which the cultural influence of Etruscans was extremely important, accompanied by migrants from Etruscan towns. Then (as strong tradition said) it was followed by the rule of a sequence of Etruscan kings, the Tarquins (traditionally, 616–509 BC).

Western Greek visitors to the Roman community in this period would have found a society which was not wholly unfamiliar. Until the late sixth century BC it was being ruled by kings, although their line was not hereditary. Clans (or *gentes*) and 'tribes' organized society, with thirty local units (*curiae*) which a Greek might assume to be like his city's brotherhoods, or phratries. During the sixth and early fifth centuries the social organization also changed in ways which are broadly familiar from Greek communities. The number of Rome's tribes was increased and the army was reorganized. At the end of the sixth century kingship was overthrown (like tyrannies in the Greek world) and annual magistrates assumed the leadership of the resulting state. Within decades there was to be popular agitation over indebtedness and access to land; concessions had to be made to what Greeks would call the *dēmos*, or 'people'. In the 450s there was even the publication of a body of laws (Rome's famous Twelve Tables), just as laws were sometimes published in early Greek city-states. The Roman laws included a ban on intermarriage between the noble patricians and non-patricians (many Greek aristocrats would have applauded). They addressed the problems of debt and adoption, marriage and inheritance which were important in Greek communities too. According to these laws, badly deformed children should be rapidly killed (Spartans would have agreed), but what was unique (as Greeks later observed) was the exceptional power granted to the male head of a Roman household over all its members, including children. So long as a Roman father lived, his sons had no right to own anything: they could simply be killed by their father, the *paterfamilias*. This extreme power for the father was evaded in practice, but it remained an important element in later Roman respect for tradition.

In the stories which were told later about this period, Rome's connections with the wider world were drawn even closer. The last three kings of Rome were said to have begun (in 616 BC) with a migrant, Tarquinius, from the Etruscan city of Tarquinia: his father had been an aristocrat from Greek Corinth. This Greek, Demaratus, had been ejected by the first tyranny at Corinth (*c.* 657) and obliged to seek a new life in Italy. The second of Rome's Etruscan kings was the celebrated Servius Tullius (in tradition, 578–535 BC) who became remembered for a lowly origin (the son of a slave), and a special relationship with the gods; he was probably an Etruscan warrior, called Mastarna in Etruscan. It was he who introduced a fundamental reform of the tribes and connected 'centuries' of the Roman people to their public assembly. Servius' reforms had a definite similarity to those of the early Greek reformers who had changed the structure of 'tribes' in their city-states during the sixth century BC. Even the first publication of Roman law was connected to the Greeks. Ambassadors are said in later tradition to have been sent out from Rome in the late 450s to study the laws of Greek cities, specifically those of Athens, the 'laws of Solon'.[11] Certainly, the Twelve Tables' word for 'punishment' (*poena*) was derived from Greek (*poinē*); the reason was not, surely, contact with Athens, but Roman contact with some of the newer Greek communities in south Italy. It was, however, a particular Roman precision to specify that a debtor who defaulted when owing debts to several people should be divided into pieces and distributed to each of his creditors.

By *c.* 500 BC the Roman community numbered probably about 35,000 male citizens, and its territorial control already extended southwards as far as Terracina, on the coast about forty miles from Rome. Although its male citizenry was probably bigger than contemporary Attica's, culturally it was still a humble place onto which a strong rejection of 'luxury' was only later projected by legends. But values of 'freedom' and 'justice' were prominent. The reforms of Servius were admired by later Romans as a source of 'freedom': at the time the most urgently desired freedom was surely freedom from the monarchical rule of a king. Freedom from kings continued to be the political value of all noble Romans, long after the ending of monarchy. Roman nobles, not the people, deposed the last tyrannical 'king' in 510/9 BC, at a time when aristocrats in most Greek cities had already deposed their tyrants.

What followed, however, was a decidedly popular demand for justice. In 494 BC, probably during a military levy, some of the common people (the plebs) are said to have decamped to a hill outside Rome and 'seceded' from their superiors at a moment when their help was needed as soldiers. One of their concerns was protection against the abuse and physical oppression of the powerful, the sort of abuse which, a hundred years earlier, had been curbed by Solon in Attica. Defence of these interests was therefore assigned to a new type of magistrate, to be known as 'tribunes of the plebs'. On hearing of an individual's 'cry for help' these sacrosanct officials could now physically interpose themselves between the aggrieved citizen and his oppressor. In later tradition, the burdens of debts and dues were also said to have been resented at this time, and demands for a distribution of land followed. In broad terms, these demands, too, would have been familiar to Greek observers. In the 450s the collection and publication of the laws met a further demand for justice, which arose as much from Rome's ruling class as from their social inferiors. At Athens, in the 620s, the publication of the first Athenian written laws can be traced to similar social pressure.

In early Rome, then, we can detect some of the dynamic which had precipitated changes in parts of early Greece too. Of course, the Romans spoke their own 'barbarian' Latin, worshipped their own gods and went their own way without Greek guides. If Romans really did ever visit Athens to inspect their law-code, the Athenians certainly left no record. Rome was of no interest to them. What interests us, however, is the Athens which these Romans were supposed to have visited.

PART TWO

The Classical Greek World

AMONG THE GREEKS, individuals determined to stand out from all others were characteristic, and the concept of personal power became paramount; depending on circumstances, they ranged from the most devoted servants of the polis to those who committed the greatest crimes against it. This polis itself, with its mistrust and its narrow ideas of equality on the one hand, and its high expectation of integrity (*aretē*) from individuals on the other, drove gifted men to follow this course, which might lead them to reckless greed and possibly to megalomania. Even Sparta, which tried to contain potentially many-sided individuals within the strict bounds of their usefulness to the State, only succeeded in producing a breed of ruthless hypocrites; as early as the sixth century there is the terrible Cleomenes, then in the fifth, Pausanias, and finally Lysander. It is debatable whether this development was beneficial for the poleis, and whether in any case it was avoidable; but as a result the Greek world makes the impression of an immense wealth of genius both for good and evil.

Jacob Burckhardt, *Greek Civilization*
(1898, translated by Sheila Stern, 1988)

'ETERNAL VIGILANCE IS the price of liberty.' No doubt, but like all truisms, this one offers little practical guidance. Vigilance against whom? One answer is to rest one's defence on public apathy, on the politician as hero. I have tried to argue that this is a way of preserving liberty by castrating it, that there is more hope in a return to the classical concept of governance as a continued effort in mass education. There will still be mistakes, tragedies, trials for impiety, but there may also be a return from widespread alienation to a genuine sense of community. The conviction of Socrates is not the whole story of freedom in Athens.

M. I. Finley, *Democracy Ancient
and Modern* (1973), 102–3

CONQUEST AND EMPIRE

'I shall not revolt against the people of the Athenians either by guile or by trick of any kind, either by word or deed. Nor shall I follow anyone in revolt and if anyone does revolt, I shall denounce him to the Athenians. I shall pay to the Athenians the tribute which I persuade them (to assess) and as an ally I shall be the best and truest possible. I shall help the people of the Athenians and defend them if anyone does injury to the people of the Athenians, and I shall obey the people of the Athenians.' This oath shall be taken by adult Chalcidians, all without exception. Whoever does not take this oath is to lose his citizen-rights and his property shall be confiscated.

Athenian treaty with Chalcis, 446/5 BC

For Megacles, son of Hippocrates and his horse as well . . .

**Inscribed potsherd, cast against noble Megacles at Athens
(Cerameicus, Ostrakon 3015, first published in 1994)**

Megacles, son of Hippocrates.

**With a drawing of a fox on the run. Another such potsherd.
The fox (alopex) is the voter's own allusion to Megacles' deme
(Alopeke) and his 'bushy-tailed' duplicity, foxiness being associated
with treachery and pro-Persian sympathies. So, Megacles
must run far away . . . (Cerameicus, Ostrakon 3815)**

THE GREEK VICTORIES OVER barbarian Persians and Carthaginians were certainly related to the three major themes of this book. Both the Carthaginians and the Persians displayed far more riches and 'luxury' than the Greeks in the city-states. They set out to destroy Greek political freedom and if victorious they would have substituted their own justice. But luxury was not the main reason why their armies failed. Freedom, rather, was the crucial value in the Greek victories, and its absence as a motivating force was a crucial reason for the failure of the Persians' army and the Carthaginians' mercenary force. The Greeks' military innovations were important, too, the metal-armoured hoplites, especially the Spartans', and the newly built Athenian ships. But they, too, were connected with underlying values. In the 650s BC the introduction of hoplites had become connected with a demand for justice which the tyrants and law-givers then addressed. The supreme source of hoplites was the Spartans' system and initially it, too, addressed the stresses caused by luxury and the need to stay 'free' from tyranny.

A different theme, to be repeated in the later rise of Macedon, was the luckily timed discovery of a source of precious metal: the silver in Attica. In Sicily, there was no local source of silver, but the Sicilians did not win by building a new fleet. The Athenians did, and the silver was crucial: new supplies of precious metal, newly mined or taken through conquest, are important in the power-relations of ancient states. They made states rich, far more so than a rise in their manufacturing or any export-led growth. But mining-strikes had to be exploited, and here the Athenians' supply of slaves was crucial: they enabled the metal to be mined quickly. The ships, once built, then had to be rowed with commitment and here, too, the Athenians' distinctive class-structure was important. All their citizens, the lower classes included, were willing to combine and fight for their re-cently acquired democratic freedom. The Spartans, lacking democracy, could never have mobilized such numbers of committed citizens. By con-trast, several of the Greek communities which were under aristocracies or broader oligarchies treacherously took the Persian side. There were ex-ceptions, not least the Corinthians, but one reason why Greeks 'Medized' was that the noble Persians seemed more congenial than the risk of a hos-tile democracy emerging at home.

Class, then, played a relevant part in the Greek victories, along with a material windfall (the silver) and no end of good luck (the weather at sea). There were also, of course, the Greeks' values and the resulting ambitions of their citizens. For the Greek victories over barbarian invaders were fol-lowed up quite differently in the West and East. In the West, the defeated

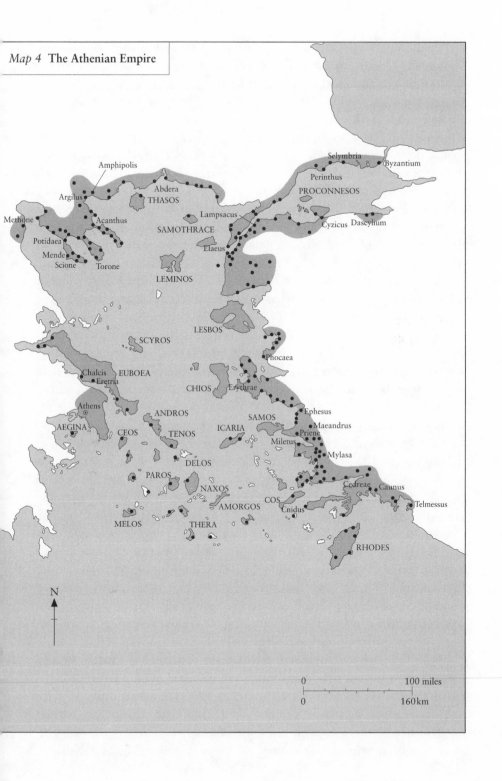

Map 4 The Athenian Empire

Amphipolis
Abdera
THASOS
Argilus
Acanthus
Methone
Potidaea
Mende
Scione
Torone
LEMINOS
SAMOTHRACE
Lampsacus
Elaeus
Selymbria
Byzantium
Perinthus
PROCONNESOS
Cyzicus
Dascylium
LESBOS
SCYROS
Phocaea
Chalcis
EUBOEA
Eretria
CHIOS
Erythrae
Athens
ANDROS
SAMOS
Ephesus
AEGINA
CEOS
TENOS
ICARIA
Maeandrus
Priene
Miletus
Mylasa
DELOS
PAROS
NAXOS
Cedreae
Caunus
COS
AMORGOS
Cnidus
Telmessus
MELOS
THERA
RHODES

N

0   100 miles
0   160km

Carthaginians were left alone with their own sphere of 'domination' (*epikrateia*) in western Sicily. There was no attempt by the Sicilian Greeks to take revenge in north Africa on Carthage herself. In the East, the Greeks went on the offensive. The Hellenic Alliance had sworn oaths of alliance in the dark days of the Persian advance and it was now enlarged and launched into a 'Hellenic War', the sequel to the 'Persian War'.

The declared aim was to punish the Persians for their acts of sacrilege in Greece (the burning of temples, especially at Athens) and to liberate fellow Greeks in the East who were still under Persian rule. At first, nobody could have assumed that the Persians would not soon return for revenge of their own. It required another Greek victory in 469 BC at the mouth of the river Eurymedon on the south coast of Asia (now the Gulf of Antalya) to deter a big Oriental fleet which was intended to regain the sea for the Persian king. Liberation of the eastern Greeks was also patchy. Some of the Greek city-states in Asia were still in the Persian king's gift as late as the mid–460s. Liberation did, however, make a difference when it happened: many of the eastern Greeks were freed from tyrants and satrapal rule in return for a modest yearly payment to the Greek allies' Treasury. There were also persistent attempts to free Cyprus, where Greek rulers were sympathetic to them, but Phoenicians were still embedded in the 'New Town' of Kition on the south-east coast of the island. These attempts began heroically in 478, but during a later one in 459 BC the allied Greek forces were diverted by a request for help from a rebel ruler in nearby Egypt. If Egypt could be detached from the Persian Empire, it would be a spectacular gain, not least for the mainland Greeks' grain-supply and economy. In fact, the large Greek expedition to Egypt failed dismally after a five-year campaign. In 450 one final attempt to free Cyprus failed too and the island was then ceded to the Persian king in return for an agreement that Persian ships would not enter the Aegean and that the Greek cities in Asia would no longer be tribute-paying and under Persian rule. This 'peace' was fragile, but it was a significant gain nonetheless. The east Greek city-states now paid tribute yearly to the Athenians instead of to the Persian king, but they were free, at least in theory, from Persian political interventions.

In the Greek West, the Greeks' trouncing of Carthage's forces in 480 was followed by a decade of splendour, not for democracy but for Sicily's Greek tyrants. Their major tyrant-families intermarried, and so the main political tensions were those between the tyrants' family members: we can see evidence of them even in the most famous surviving work of art in their honour, the bronze Charioteer at Delphi. Significantly, its dedicatory inscription by one brother was changed and replaced by another brother's name. In mainland Greece, however, the years of 'punishment' for Persia coincided with a real political choice, the continuing split between two opposed styles of Greek life: the harsh oligarchy of Sparta's military peer group and the increasingly confident democracy of the Athenians. Feebly, the Spartans presented the governments which they favoured in their allied cities as 'iso-cracy' ('equal rule'), a response to the Athenians' proud and very different 'democracy'.[1] To placate their allies, since c. 506 BC the Spartan kings had had to agree to discuss all proposed allied wars in a joint synod.

Against the Persians in Greece, nonetheless, the two powers had sunk their differences. From 478 to 462 the Athenians then led the Hellenic Alliance by sea, the Spartans by land, as the Spartans lacked any trained fleet and any coinage with which to pay one. They could hardly risk recruiting their helot-serfs as fighting oarsmen. On many fronts, they ran into severe problems. Their kings were brought to trial in Sparta after military failures or complaints about their policies. Even the young regent Pausanias, hero of the Persian Wars, was dismissed and put on trial. Within the Spartans' southern Greek orbit, there was continuing opposition among the Arcadians on their doorstep; democracy began to infect important allies in the Peloponnese; in 465 a major revolt broke out among the Spartans' dependent helots. They were not alone. In the West, in the late 460s, the Greek cities also confronted a major war against non-Greek Sicels who lived beside them near Mount Etna. It persisted until 440 and created a Sicel hero, the leader Ducetius, who founded a lasting settlement, Kale Akte (Fair Coastline). But unlike the Sicels, Sparta's helots were oppressed fellow Greeks, and so the long Spartan serf-war was the more dangerous of the two. After three years, under the terms of the Hellenic Alliance, the Spartans summoned Athenians to help them, because they valued their general Cimon's skills in siege-warfare. The summons was a turning point. Before long, in Sparta, Athenian soldiers realized the uncomfortable truth, that the Spartans, supposedly their fellow liberators, were suppressing their neighbouring Messenian Greeks. Many of them had never realized this truth about a 'helot'. The Spartans then dismissed their Athenian helpers because they feared their audacity and capacity for causing a revolution. This cardinal rebuff broke up the Hellenic Alliance and soon led to war in Greece between 'the Athenians and their allies', as the old League became, and 'the Spartans and their allies', what we now call the 'Peloponnesian League'. On their return, the Athenians ostracized the pro-Spartan Cimon, adopted reforms which further entrenched democratic principles in their constitution and accepted alliance with the Spartans' allies, the Megarians, and a traditional Spartan enemy (Argos). For some fourteen years war would persist between the Athenians and, in particular, Sparta's allies, the oligarchic Corinthians.

While a helot revolt was going on in their own land, these years were desperate for the Spartans. They could seldom help their allies, even when they were in dire need. There were also Spartan fears that the Athenians would influence control of the Delphic shrine and once again manipulate the priestess of Apollo into giving them favourable oracles. Eventually, Spartan counter-attacks in central Greece became possible and in 446 a peace for thirty years was sworn between the Athenians, Spartans and their respective allies. Ominously, one wing of opinion in Sparta was still dissatisfied, and the young king and an adviser who were responsible for the peace settlement had to go into exile.

In Athens, by contrast, these decades saw a new dynamism. The arts of painting, drawing and sculpture had already begun to change at Athens before the Persians' invasion and sack of the city in 480. The move to a severe, classical style was not interrupted by this shock, and in the post-war years of victory its exponents enjoyed major new commissions. So, too, tragic dramas had been performed before 480 but it is to the following decades that we can trace our knowledge of complete plays, the masterpieces of Aeschylus (his *Persians* was put on in 472). Politically, the years after the great victory at Marathon in 490 also showed a new polarization. In the 480s Cleisthenes' device of ostracism began to be used by the people against prominent nobles. On many of the surviving bits of potsherd, candidates were accused of 'Medism', or favouring Persia, which the events of 490 had made into such an unambiguous crime. In 487 access to the Athenians' yearly magistracy, or archonship, was widened (among other duties, an archon would preside over ostracisms and the important counting of their 'votes'). In 486 comic dramas became part of the public festivals: in due course they made fun of personal and political targets, a sign (like the personalized *ostraka*) of increasing democratic freedom.

Behind this political ferment there were real contrasts of political outlook and political choices which members of the Athenian upper class confronted. The ostracisms were symptomatic of a changing political culture. On the one side were those who merely 'found themselves living under a democracy', well-born men who valued athletic prowess and military skill, who prized the all-Greek arena of the Olympic Games, who talked airily of 'all Greeks together' with their noble friends in other cities and who saw artists and monuments as sources of personal glory, while thinking that they could still fix things politically by their own prestige before a deferential audience. In Athens in the 470s the champion of such men was Cimon, son of the great Miltiades, the general who had done the most to help the Athenians to win at Marathon. Cimon's world was the older world of all-Greek glory which did not care unduly for most of the Greeks before whom it shone. It is the world which we meet most splendidly in the victory odes of the poet Pindar who so often composed poems for men of Cimon's class. 'I am grieved', Pindar wrote in his poem for the ultimate Athenian aristocrat Megacles, 'that envy requites fair deeds'.[2] Megacles' four-horsed chariot had won in the games at Delphi, yet the people at Athens had just ostracized Megacles from their midst for ten years.

On the other side were well-born men who had seen, since Cleisthenes, how the popular tide was sure to run in a new democratic age. Political influence could not be fixed with a few like-minded friends and judicious intermarriages in the upper class: it must be earned and accountable before a public audience of equals. The Spartans, hostile to their Greek helots' freedom, must be curbed and mistrusted. Nebulous all-Greek, 'Panhellenic' rhetoric was a poor second to the Athenians' democratic freedom. Themistocles, the great victor at Salamis, was perhaps the quickest to see how the future might develop, not least because he had visited Sparta on a 'victory tour' in 479 BC: the Spartans gave him 'the most beautiful chariot' and escorted him back on the road home, but dark thoughts about his hosts surely gathered in his mind as the prize 'car' rolled northwards.[3] Ostracized in the late 470s, he went south across the Isthmus again and helped to provoke political dissent among some of the Spartans' allies: then in *c.* 466/5 he was forced to flee Greece, finally taking refuge in western Asia by courtesy of his former enemy, the Persian king.

Back at Athens, his mantle passed to others who were willing to challenge the old guard's supremacy, to curb the revered Areopagus council and to put open and accountable government more freely in the people's hands. In 463/2, when Cimon returned humbled from his rejection as helper of the Spartans against their helots, further democratic freedoms were approved in the Athenian assembly. They marked significant changes in the process of justice. Outgoing magistrates were now to be vetted by the big public council, not the cosier Areopagus, most of whom would be sympathetic members of their class. Magistrates were no longer to have a primary power of judgement in Athenian lawsuits. From now on they had to pass them after a first hearing to one of the panels of public jurors whose members were usually to number several hundreds, chosen yearly from 6,000 of the Athenian citizenry. It was an unprecedented victory for popular, impersonal justice. Henceforward, to be an active Athenian was to be willing to sit and listen, and sometimes barrack, as a juryman while orators on either side pleaded civil or criminal cases for hours on end. 'Lawyers' were out of the question.

These changes to a yet more popular style of government and justice were highly distasteful to the old-fashioned minority in Attica. In 458/7, while a Spartan army was nearby, a small disaffected group of Athenians even attempted to betray their city to the enemy. Spring 458 was the occasion of our great surviving trilogy of tragic dramas, Aeschylus' *Oresteia*. In the final play, Aeschylus includes an implicit comment on the recent curbing of the Areopagus, approving of it (in my view) but also implying 'enough is enough'. Significantly for spring 458, he also includes a plea for civil strife to stay away from the Athenians.

While the Hellenic Alliance had set about freeing the eastern Greeks, Athenian power benefited greatly in the generation from c. 490 to c. 440. In 479 strong defensive walls were quickly built up to protect the city and link it to the sea. The Spartans, such poor besiegers, would soon regret their existence. Then, the 'all-Greek' campaigns against the barbarians continued to capture points on the map which were precious for Athenian economic interests, above all for the supply of grain which was being imported into Attica by sea-routes from Egypt and especially from the Crimea in the northern Black Sea. At first, the allies (in my view, including the Athenians) paid tribute into a common Treasury, but in the mid–450s this Treasury was moved to Athens for 'security' reasons. What had been joint payments for a war effort became tribute paid from allies only: it persisted after the fragile 'peace' had been agreed with the Persian king in 450/49. From the start, defection by Greek allies had been forbidden as contrary to their Hellenic Alliance's oaths. It occurred nonetheless, and from the 440s onwards the Athenians' suppression was increasingly represented as 'subjection' or even 'servitude'. In a vivid use of metaphor, the Athenians' allies in the war of liberation were said to have become 'slaves' of the Athenians' leading power. At first their delegates had met and voted in common meetings; by the 440s, at the latest, these meetings had ceased.

The greatest beneficiaries of this growing power were the Athenians themselves. From many sources, a richer style of life became available in their city. One, importantly, was treasure captured from the Persians in

480/79. Major Oriental trophies found their way into the Athenian Treasury, including Xerxes' travelling throne. Despite the hostile comments on Persian 'softness' and excessive splendour, well-off Athenians responded to the styles of dress and metalwork, fine textiles and precious armour which they saw in the prizes taken from the Persian invaders. Soft, comfortable shoes even became known at Athens as 'Persian' slippers. The greatest beneficiaries were Greek horses. The invading Persians had brought the rich 'Median grass', or lucerne, with them into Greece in 490 (it was said) with Darius' army:[4] seeds, perhaps, came in with their cavalry's fodder. This fine 'blue grass' from the horse-studs back in Media then became a food-crop for horses on rich Greek soil.

Other new sources of luxury were imports by sea, which were assisted now by the Athenians' growing naval power abroad. It was not that the Athenians took direct control of overseas sources of supply, like imperial 'colonies': rather, their growing city-population and its centrality became the obvious magnet for traders who were exporting the good things in life. Carpets and cushions came in from Carthage, fish from the Hellespont and excellent figs from Rhodes; all sorts of delicacies arrived for sale, including quantities of slaves for use down the Attic silver-mines, in the citizens' households and even on the smaller farms. The houses of the Athenian rich were magnificent and finely decorated in this era. Sadly, none survive, but we can form some idea of their interior paintings from scenes on Athenian painted pottery. In public, extreme distinctions of dress may have been moderated, at least the distinctions between the dress of the upper class and that of others. But from *c.* 460 onwards there was not a general abandonment of stylish living by the upper class in an age of enhanced democracy.[5]

In Syracuse, the introduction and abuse of a form of 'ostracism' in the 450s was said to have caused upper-class dignitaries to withdraw into private luxury. In Athens, it did nothing of the sort. Even before democracy began in 508, the rich citizens had been liable to expensive services, or 'liturgies' (*leitourgiai*), which paid for parts of the state's naval force, for the festival-displays and the training of the choruses for theatrical plays. On these 'voluntary' contributions, much of Athenian cultural splendour depended. As the Athenians' cultural life developed under the democracy, there was ever more prestige and honour to be won by paying up as a liturgist. The rich, therefore, took a deep civic pride in their increasingly pre-eminent city, whatever they thought of its constitution: peer-pressure impelled them to give generously to the liturgies and not to disgrace their families or their own fame by a poor show. Anyone who tried to dodge their turn as a liturgist would be resented by his own class. In these cultural displays, the rich enjoyed the glory which 'mob-rule' had diluted in the political assembly. Even the ostracized Athenians remained keen to return and have another chance to shine in the city-state which, basically, they loved.

By the 440s alliances existed between the Athenians and more than two hundred other Greek communities and constituted the most powerful 'empire' yet known in Greek history. In contemporary texts, we hear most about its 'enslavement' of its members and its arrogance, yet arguably it assured more Greek freedom and justice than it ever removed. Most of its member-states had their own internal conflicts developing between the options of democratic and oligarchic rule. The Athenians never intervened unasked to impose or export a democracy onto a stable allied state. Instead, they and the democrats among their subject-allies knew that Athenian power was the people's most solid support for popular rule. The tribute paid to Athens was low and adjustable and, in an allied democracy, most of it would be voted to be paid by the local rich anyway. Even after the fragile peace of 449 BC the threat from Persia and her western satraps was far from dead. Athenian ships, meanwhile, prevented piracy on the seas and promised anti-Persian defence in a crisis, all for a relatively low yearly payment. Allied supporters of Athens were protected by a right of legal appeal against any major sentences imposed on them at home; they could demand a hearing at Athens, just as Athenians, meanwhile, could transfer cases involving an ally and themselves to their own law courts. The Athenian courts did not always side with Athenian suitors: compared with a small allied city's system of justice, the big popular Athenian juries were incorruptible and increasingly experienced.

Through such 'empire', Athenian power, finance and public splendour were transformed: reserves of tribute piled up in the city and it was because of them that the people could vote to rebuild the ruined temples on their Acropolis with the greatest splendour. From 449 onwards a brand new Parthenon temple was joined by an imposing entrance-gate, yet more temples and some stunningly big and precious statues of the goddess Athena: they made the hilltop the artistic wonder of the world. They are the defining monuments of 'classical art', and even though they were built with allied tribute, there were surely allied visitors who marvelled at what had been made with a bit of their money. There would also, as nowadays, be grumblers and pessimists, but in antiquity even they would remember that the alternatives for the member-states of the Athenian alliance were the likelihood of Persian revenge or a brutal coup by their city's oligarchic fringe. An ally's worst enemy was most often another ally, a local oligarch or a long-hated ally in a city-state nearby. For most people in most places, obedience to Athens was the better alternative available to them. The Athenians themselves had few illusions. They, too, could profit individually, not least by acquiring land in their allied states, an intrusion which was later widely (not always justly) resented. Quite openly, their leading politicians endorsed the view that their Empire was 'like a tyranny'.[6] So, in one sense it was, as it tended to curb the allies' most prominent individuals and to favour the people's rule instead. But the 'tyranny' also offered fair trials to its friends, freedom from Persia and freedom, too, from the plottings of oligarchic cliques who had the money and skill to overthrow their fellow citizens' free political rights.

12

A CHANGING
GREEK CULTURAL WORLD

Then, there is something which some people find amazing: in every area,
the Athenians assign more to the wicked and the poor and the populists
than to the Good. In this way, they are actually preserving the democracy.
In every land on earth, the Best are opposed to democracy . . .

The 'Old Oligarch', 1.4 (probably in 425 BC)

T HE YEARS FROM THE 450s to the 420s are cardinal years in the cultural history of ancient Greece. Tragedy flowered in the theatre at
Athens, as we can follow in the dramas of the three great surviving tragedians (Aeschylus, Sophocles and Euripides). Athenian comedy followed
suit, combining music and dance with jokes on political subjects. The
Athenian art of this period is the supreme example of 'classical art'. In
sculpture and vase painting, the human form has an idealized realism; the
proportions are finer, the poses more confident. The art in this period
does not stand still, but the best of it has a contemplative naturalism
which exists only in antiquity in Greek culture, and only elsewhere because of it. 'Classical art' is not always 'severe' or 'austere', labels which
are suited only to a fraction of the art of the 'classical' era and are mostly
applied because the surviving sculptures have lost their painted colour.

Since the Persian Wars there was also remarkable intellectual progress
in a Greek world free of barbarian invaders. It was not even predomi-
nantly at Athens or from Athenian-born thinkers. In the Greek West, philosophy's 'way of truth', with implications for language and reality, was
explored by Parmenides in a poem of obscure, but profound, imagery. He
raised sceptical problems about reality which were then addressed by two
thinkers, Democritus and Leucippus, who postulated indivisible particles

('atoms', the origin of our word); they even argued that these atoms moved in empty spaces and by their collisions came together to form bigger objects. More mundanely, the symptoms and progress of diseases were described with careful observation in a book of medical *Epidemics*, composed between *c.* 475 and 466 BC.[1] It contains an exact description of mumps, including its familiar effect on young males, as observed on the island of Thasos (females were not so readily infected, a fact which says much for the absence of close contact between the sexes there at a young age). Mathematics also found their first theoretical exponent, Hippocrates of Chios. In Athens, the architectural plan of the Parthenon temple combined exact ratios between its parts and its whole with subtle adjustments for the visual effects of regularity. In the 440s, perhaps first in 'east Greece', unknown thinkers invented political theory and pursued the abstract avenues which it opened. Above all, a new type of prose-writing began, 'enquiry' (*historiē*) into the past, what we now know as history.

Unlike writers about the past in Near Eastern societies (including the writers of Hebrew scriptures), the first surviving exponent of 'history' wrote overtly in the first person, weighing evidence and expressing his own opinions. Herodotus was born in the 490s and was busy with his great enquiry into the conflicts of Greeks and Persians at least until the early 420s BC. He was born not in Athens but in south-west Asia, at Halicarnassus, where Greek and non-Greek cultures coexisted under the wavering control of the Persian Empire. He was well born, with literary relations in his family. He is credited with political action against a tyrant in his home city, followed by exile abroad. Eventually he settled in Thurii in south Italy, a city whose foundation in the late 440s was organized on the former site of luxurious Sybaris by the Athenians. In the Greek world, historians were so often to be exiles, cut off from the daily exercise of politics and power which was so much more interesting than writing a book.

Herodotus set out to explain and to celebrate the great events of the Persian Wars against the Greeks. The enterprise led him on long digressions, both literary and personal. He travelled widely to 'enquire' and, if possible, find the truth. He went to Libya, Egypt, northern and southern Greece and even east into Babylon. He did not know any foreign languages and of course he had no convenient reference books with numbered dates which would place events in different countries side by side. He noted quite a variety of inscribed objects and monuments during his travels, but he did not always describe every detail of them correctly and he did not engage in searches for locally preserved documents. Nonetheless, he came across several written sources, including what he took to be a 'list' of Xerxes' great invading army in 480. His main evidence was oral, what people in different places told him when he questioned them. Out of it he devised a story, but he was not simply another raconteur. Here and there, he used existing written sources, particularly the work (now lost to us) of his great predecessor, Hecataeus of Miletus, who was more inclined to 'geographic' detail than to political 'history'. He also seems to have used the poem of Aristeas, the Greek who had travelled into Central Asia *c.* 600 BC. Herodotus was explicitly critical of many of the oral stories which he himself reported from his oral sources but could not endorse.

Herodotus brought strong, personal interpretations to the complex sources he interrelated. The great themes of freedom, justice and luxury are very prominent in his 'enquiry': he shared the Greek view of the battles of 480/79 between Greeks and Persians as battles for freedom and for a life under the impersonal, just rule of law, and it is his history, above all, which has immortalized them in that light. The final speech in his 'enquiry' dwells on the contrasts between the hardy, impoverished Persians who had embarked on an age of conquest and the 'soft' luxury of peoples who live in the 'soft' plains and become others' subjects. Particular themes were evident to him in human life: that 'pride goes before a fall' and that extreme good fortune leads to a debacle, that truly outrageous behaviour often gets its deserts, or retribution, that human affairs are very unstable, that the customs of different societies differ and that some, but not all, of our cherished behaviour is therefore relative to the society in which we happen to live. These beliefs are still valid in our own world.

However, Herodotus also accepted that the gods are active in human affairs and that, through oracles, they speak truly to men. Dreams and visions are very important for individuals in his history: he knows that some of his contemporaries refuse to accept the truth of oracles, but he is most indignant at their refusal. He accepts, as oracles did too, that the gods may punish a descendant for the deeds of an ancestor. This belief in 'hereditary guilt' is most centrally associated with the idea of an 'archaic age' ('archaic' otherwise being an art-historical term for the sculptures and paintings before the more 'human' classical style of the 490s onwards). 'Retribution', therefore, and 'inevitability' are still independent forces in Herodotus' way of writing and thinking. But they coexist with a dense range of human motives, including spite and covetousness of which he is a connoisseur. Herodotus can also relate a community's development to its physical setting, its laws and customs and its rising population. But he thinks more readily in individual, human terms.

The results are amazing in their range and human variety. Like eastern Greek settlers and travellers in the previous century, Herodotus accepts that Libya, Egypt and the world of the Scythian nomads are the extreme points of contrast with the world of the Greeks. He digresses on all three, while returning, justly, to his main theme of the Persian expansion which touched on these peoples too. He is interested in so much in other cultures, in their marriage-practices, in questions of health and diet, religious rites and styles of burial. In Egypt, especially, he reasons with cogency from his evidence, though he tends to see the Egyptian world as a polar opposite to Greece and thus misunderstands it. As we have lost so much other east Greek debating and writing conducted *c.* 480–460, we have to compare him with later writers, thereby making him seem more 'modern' than he probably seemed to his contemporaries. His religious outlook and language would suggest otherwise. So, too, would his politics, for Herodotus sympathized with the passing 'Panhellenic' world of an international Greek upper class, Cimon and his like. To them, the enemies were treachery, spontaneous violence and the lower classes: the wars between Greek states since the 460s were a profoundly regrettable outcome. Admiring liberty, Herodotus was not an uncritical democrat: the Spartans are frequently seen in a favourable light in his 'enquiries'.

Naturally, Herodotus visited Athens, probably in or just before 438/7 (to judge from a comment about the entrance-way to their Acropolis). He is even said to have received an enormous cash prize for his *Histories*, as voted by the Assembly. He talked with important Athenians, but he was already in his mid-fifties. By the early 430s abstract theorizing about power and inter-state relations was current in the city among members of the younger generation, but it was not Herodotus' way of looking on the world. Nor was the new subject of political theory, although Herodotus had picked up one example of it, a clever 'debate' among Persians about the merits of alternative constitutions, including democracy, set in 522 BC; it was a witty fake, but old Herodotus believed it.[2] This new, hard cleverness underlies an accelerating change in the intellectual and cultural outlook of the big names in Athens.

The victories over the Persians, then the years of expanding empire had helped to root Athenians' self-confidence and trust in their democracy. How far, then, was the culture of the Athens which Herodotus visited a democratic culture, shaped by the equalities of a political system based on equal popular voting? It was certainly not a level, egalitarian society. Culturally, it was still a place where the upper class enjoyed their hunting and cultivated their sexual advances with gifts and protestations

14. A wreathed young boy, perhaps not a slave, fills his party-cup, or *kylix*, with watered wine from the mixing-bowl. Attic red-figure cup, Cage painter *c.* 490 BC.

to the ever-fickle young boys. Hunting scenes and hunters' 'love gifts' happen to disappear from Athenian painted pottery after *c.* 470, but this change is only a fact about a taste in pottery decoration; it is not evidence for a new caution and a lack of openness about these old aristocratic pursuits. In the evenings socially select groups of males still dined and drank luxuriously in their 'men's rooms' and sang the aristocratic anti-populist songs of the past. Were these old-style *symposia*, though, on the defensive in the new age of 'mob-rule'? A much-discussed group of Attic drinking-cups, dated to the early fifth century, shows paintings of men wearing ef-feminate dress, apparently as cross-dressers. They have been interpreted as a reflection of an upper-class social life which had adopted this trans-vestite style as a symptom of 'anxiety', now that its own supremacy was under stress. But 'anxiety' was not obviously the mood of Athenian aris-tocrats at the time. Taking the long view, they believed they needed only to wait until their political hour dawned again. Militarily, meanwhile, they were indispensable members of the cavalry which even the most committed democrats were about to increase sixfold and honour with provisions for a public 'insurance-repayment' on any registered horse

15. Upper half of the 'Riace Bronze' statue, Warrior A, evidently a hero, who held a shield. Fine classical work, arguably Athenian, *c.* 460 BC. Shipwrecked, and thus preserved, off southern Italy.

which an upper-class warrior lost in battle. Probably, the cross-dressing simply portrays revels in honour of Dionysus.

On other cups, we see the young differently, as owners of exotic cheetahs and hunting leopards. These superior young shockers were not 'anxious': even in the democratic age, the cultural life of the theatre and the festivals still depended on the spending of their male upper class. In Attica's social infrastructure, too, not so much had changed since the aristocrats of the sixth century BC. If Herodotus had asked a male Athenian who he was, he would have named his father and his deme, as Cleisthenes' reforms had emphasized. But he would also have named his 'phratry', or 'brotherhood', as in the older times, and only then, if at all, his membership of one of the democracy's new ten tribes. Even under the democracy, aristocratic families retained a significant power of veto on candidates for inclusion in 'brotherhoods'.

In the early 430s Herodotus would have talked to young Athenians of noble birth, people who still styled themselves the 'good' as opposed to the vulgar 'bad'. Not so very far below the surface, these people hoped that one day democracy would simply go away, but from the 470s to the

430s conquest abroad and the huge increase in the numbers and tribute of Athens' allies helped meanwhile to compensate for their discontent. The gains of Empire blurred class-tension for both the rich and the poor. Empire brought new land-holdings and revenues abroad for both classes of Athenian, and, as the rich well knew, it was on the poor and their hard days as oarsmen that this Empire's safety rested meanwhile. Vital though the cavalry might be against the Theban 'pigs' and their horsemen or scattered Spartan ravagers of the land, horses, as Homer's *Odyssey* remarked, were no use on islands overseas. For the 'island empire', what mattered was the trireme. Fleets of a hundred ships or more were now a commonplace in most years. Although some of the rowers were hired foreigners, the bulk were lower-class Athenians who had amassed years of practice beyond any possible enemy's. On midsummer expeditions these rowers were far tougher than anyone nowadays. Their modern re-creators had to drink about two pints of water for each hour of rowing (the modern oarsmen of a trireme would thus need nearly two tons of water in a ten-hour day, and yet an ancient trireme could not carry a big water supply). 'Almost all the water consumed', writes the modern trireme's mastermind, 'was sweated off, with the rowers feeling relatively little need to urinate. Much of this sweat dripped onto the lowest row, making life particularly unpleasant for them. The smell in the hold became so unpleasant that it had to be washed out with sea water at least once every four days (but ancient Athenians may have been more tolerant).' The body must evaporate fluid to stay cool and so 'ventilation is an absolute necessity, but it is barely adequate for the lower of the three rows'.[3] None of the noble 'fine and fair' would have lasted in this heat for long. Those who did were the Empire's ultimate sanction, and it was no use calling them a 'naval mob' and expecting them not to vote when they came home.

For us, the most distinctive fact about the Athenian culture Herodotus visited is that it was a slave-society. Some 55,000 adult male citizens owned some 80,000–120,000 other human beings, 'objects' whom they could buy and sell. These slaves (almost all non-Greeks) were central to the Athenians' economy, working in the silver-mines (often down appallingly narrow tunnels) and also in agriculture where contemporary comedies present them to us as a normal part of quite modest Athenian families' property. The prices of untrained slaves appear to have been low, because supply was abundant, from war or raids on barbarian Thrace or inland Asia Minor. Cheap slavery was a major support to the class-distinctions and the purchasing-power for luxuries among the better-off Athenians. However, Herodotus would not have remarked unduly on this

16. A rare Athenian representation of a slave, ugly, chained at the ankles and collecting stones. Attic black-figure, *c.* 490–480 BC.

fact of life. Slaves were *andrapoda*, 'man-footed beasts'; they were ubiquitous in the Greek communities into whom Herodotus enquired. He never queried the justice of this fact.

To many of us, the absence of political participation for citizen-women would also be striking. The Athenians were typical among Greeks in ensuring that women could not vote; women could not even give evidence in a law court in their own person. Among the Athenians, their capacity to buy or sell was exceptionally limited; their choice in marriage was not entirely free and, essentially, they were in the power of their male 'guardian', or *kyrios*. These rules were for women's 'protection' (although modern women look on them from a different perspective). On a longer view, it is a real question how far an everyday Athenian woman's status differed from a slave's. Unlike a slave, she could never escape her condition. She did, however, bring a returnable dowry with her, whereas slaves were bought for a non-returnable price. A woman's relative degree of 'freedom' depended greatly on her social class by birth or marriage. Humble women did work visibly in the fields (they had their own harvesting-songs and there were women called *poastriai*, who were grass-cutters and perhaps weeders),[4] but, as in many modern societies, the visibility of women out-doors was not at all a sign of social equality. They did not sit outdoors at leisure, drink in a shop or hang around in public spaces, any more than the hard-working Berber women in modern Morocco who work in the fields, return home through the village and cook, weave and cope with children indoors. In Attica, respectable households in any case kept their women indoors, to dreary tasks like weaving and spinning. 'Shopping' was left to slaves, although a free woman might go out to fetch water from a public spring: we hear of a 'women's *agora*', or market-area, but it was a market where a man could buy a woman, as a slave and sex-object. When Pericles told Athenian war-widows in his great Funeral Speech 'not to prove inferior to their nature' and to be talked about as little as possi-ble, he was not being idiosyncratic. Respectable Athenian women did have important roles as priestesses in some of the Athenian cults of the gods. But the political limits were absolute. They did not belong to a phratry, although their fathers did want them to be married off to an Athenian citizen-husband. Since 451, therefore, a man's Athenian citizen-ship depended on having both a citizen-father and a mother of citizen-birth too. But this new requirement did not bring women a new freedom of action. It simply ensured that Athenians' daughters were seldom 'mar-ried out' to foreigners or left as spinsters, a burden on their brothers and fathers. In public, a married Athenian woman was still only called 'the wife of . . . '; to use her own name would imply she was a prostitute.

In the late 340s we find an Athenian orator reminding a citizen-jury that 'we have "courtesans" [*hetairai*] for pleasure, prostitutes for every-day attention to our bodies and wives for the production of children legit-imately and for being a trustworthy guardian of the contents of our household'.[5] Unlike some of his modern readers (in England, not France), the jurors were expected to take him literally. Some husbands did, of course, love their wives, but the orator Lysias (a foreign resident) loved his *hetaira* enough to have her initiated into the Eleusinian mystery-cult for her own good beyond the grave (it was, nonetheless, considered a mark of a 'complaining man' to wonder, when a *hetaira* kissed him, if she was kissing him sincerely, from the heart). Those Athenian males who could afford all three types of woman would have agreed with the orator in question, while adding that in youth (and, perhaps, still), they had young boys for competitive pursuit, idealization and quick sexual pleas-ure without the risk of a baby. They never met an educated Athenian woman, because no women were taught in an Athenian school with the boys. No Athenian women joined in the all-male discussions of philosophers and their pupils. A few women did learn to read and write; *hetairai* could pick up more, but only like many Edwardian aristocratic ladies, by listening to male talk at parties. Only the most eccentric philosophers, like Pythagoras in the Greek West, were credited with having female pupils as regular hearers. Like vegetarianism, it was a sign that they were dotty.

Outside Athens, by contrast, Herodotus' *Histories* are full of stories of active women, wise or vengeful, but their setting is usually in a monarchical (or 'tyrannical') family world. In the different setting of a democratic community, the restrictions on Athenian citizen-women would surely have impressed him, as they were such a contrast with the Spartan women whom, as a visitor, he would have seen dancing naked. Among the male Athenian citizens, Herodotus would have noted the time given freely to democratic business, to assemblies (about four times a month), to the yearly council (up to twice in a lifetime) and to jury-service (for those on the yearly list of 6,000 volunteers). He did not think especially highly of the wisdom of a democratic crowd, but he would have had to respect the citizens' dedication. When he visited, the Athenians' Acropolis was being lavishly rebuilt with the support of the annual tribute received from their allies. Yet publicly elected committees were supervising all these public works and upholding the details of financial accountability on which the democracy insisted. Nothing so thorough and public would have been going on in his own Halicarnassus or in aristocratic Thessaly.

Nonetheless, the architecture and the sculpture were not celebrations of democracy. A strengthened sense of political freedom underpinned their artists' reasoned vision, but it did not provoke 'political sculptors': there were no representations of mass-meetings or 'crowd solidarity'. The Parthenon's fine sculpted frieze did not celebrate democracy. It showed elements of a festival-procession which had begun long before Cleisthenes: it included the mythical hero, Erichthonius, and, on one modern view, one section showed the sacrifice of the legendary king's daughters to save the city in war. From the late 420s onwards they were joined by the supporting figures on the re-built Erechtheion temple, a famous image of classical Athens. But arguably, these figures represent women pouring libations to the dead Cecrops, the Athenians' legendary king, whose tomb lay below them.

The religious life of the city also ran in largely pre-democratic channels. The Athenians, like all Greeks, had no weekend holidays (they did not even observe weeks), but they did have a calendar packed with religious festivals. By the 430s there were some 120 days of potential celebrations (the 'festival city', critics complained).[6] Many of these days were long-established occasions and, in many cases, the families who provided the priests and priestesses were still the noble families of the pre-democratic past. Few of these jobs were filled by election or use of the lot. However, every Athenian male, female or slave could be initiated into the secret religious 'mysteries' at the nearby shrine of Eleusis, a rite which offered the promise of a happier afterlife beyond the grave. Yet this most inclusive feature of Athenian life went back long before the democracy too.

Democracy had, however, made two clear cultural marks: in oratory and in drama. The big meetings of the assembly and the new law courts with their big juries gave a new scope for subtle oratory, both civic and forensic. Nothing like it is known from a non-democratic Greek state, although unfortunately we have no surviving Athenian example, first-hand, until 399 BC. In the wake of the Persian Wars, there had also begun the practice of a glorious Funeral Speech which was spoken by a picked orator in praise of the war-dead and their city. The best-known of such speeches is the one ascribed to Pericles in winter 431/0 BC. We do not know of this sort of speech in a non-democratic state, either.

The relations between democracy and tragic drama have been much emphasized in recent cultural studies, but they are not at all direct. Indeed, the judges for the dramatic contests were now chosen by lot (to avoid bribery), but choice by lot was not exclusive to democrats. This theatre would be more 'democratic' if all citizens were receiving a state subsidy to enable them to buy theatre tickets, but the beginnings of this eventual Athenian practice are still disputed (in my view, the 440s are likely) and on any view, even the most optimistic, the free tickets only began when tragedies had been flourishing for some fifty years. Even when tickets were on offer, it is not at all certain that women could attend the performances too. But even if this eventual subsidy helped to broaden the social class of audiences, drama was not therefore 'democratic' by nature or unimaginable except as a democratic creation. The main festival for the god Dionysus had been introduced under the tyrants in the 530s BC and had begun with a simple programme of song and dance. No doubt it would have expanded under any form of government, even to the point (attained in the democratic era) when about a thousand male citizens sang and danced in the choral events each year. Probably, there would have been tragedies anyway under a different political system: they were, after all, dramas which explored the moral and religious conflicts not in everyday plots but in mythical tales from the 'royal' past. Certainly, Attic tragedy flourished perfectly well when it was composed or performed for non-democratic audiences abroad. If the Athenians had opted for an oligarchy of (say) 6,000 citizens in 508, surely they would have been enough of an audience to encourage dramatic contests ('democratic' audiences were probably often no more than 15,000 anyway, not all of whom were always citizens).

Herodotus would have seen these dramatic contests prefaced by religious sacrifices and by the display of imperial tribute which was brought to Athens by allied tribute-bearers. These 'extras' were appropriate items on the programme because the occasion was so big and public, the biggest Athenian meeting in the entire year. But the plays which followed were not therefore religious rituals or expositions or explorations of democratic or imperial ideology. Set in the mythical royal past, they explored issues of family and community, sexual relations, religion and the temper of heroes. They moved their audiences, as their minds and emotions ranged over the extreme moral events in the plays and the complex singing and dancing of their chorus. But they were not confirming, or questioning, a 'democratic ethos' in their spectators or instilling a lesson in civic duties, like a long 'Marseillaise'. The tragedies which survive could perfectly well have been composed and performed before an oligarchy of richer Athenians only. Tragedy's presentation of divine and human nature, especially the nature of great heroes, was wonderfully bleak and awesome. It deeply moved audiences and enlarged their horizons, but, two days later, had it not all been pigeonholed and worn off?

One possible link with democracy, however, lies in a formal aspect of some of the surviving tragedies. Since the 460s, in a democratic law court, Athenian orators debated the rights and wrongs of a case before citizen-jurors. In tragedies, a long debating scene then developed in the middle of the play (the *agon*), in which characters debated a case before the citizen-audiences, many of whom were jurors on holiday. This form had surely developed at such length in drama in response to the citizen-spectators' own law-court experience. Otherwise, there was only one truly democratic art-form: political comedy. In it, prominent Athenian politicians were hilariously satirized and attacked. It would certainly not have arisen in a restricted and wary oligarchy, and when democracy was checked by Macedonian generals, after 322, dramatists close to the resulting oligarchy preferred to put on plays which were harmless, depersonalized 'situation comedies'.

For us, Athenian democratic comedy is dominated by its one surviving genius, Aristophanes (active from the 420s to the 380s), but his own comments, and those of others, suggest that the plays of his older rival Cratinus are some of the saddest losses in all ancient literature. Aristophanes' humour ranges from brilliant puns and wordplay through crude and sexual allusions (some of which are still being recovered) to fantasy, parody, jokes about drama itself and brilliant, but merciless, personal invective and satire. His plays' combination of witty obscenity and sweet, agitated choral song is unique in all surviving drama. It is through him that we can best share the scale of the Athenians' admirable self-awareness. They have a marvellous ability to enter into hilarious thought-experiments about gender-roles and male and female relations (the plots were even more hilarious when every part was played by male actors). They also have a complete callousness about slaves or about the battiness of philosophers (there is a really aggressive note in Aristophanes' famous comedy, the *Clouds*, about Socrates and his influence).

The plots of Aristophanes' comedies probably arose from specific news stories or public statements of the moment which are now lost to us, rather than from the sort of concern with abstract 'issues' which is familiar to us in the modern satires by Brecht. The surviving plays, nonetheless, span anything from a fond hope for peace during war to a sex-strike by women in order to bring it about, and a classic attempt to find and bring back the best dramatic poet from beyond the grave. Like Aristophanes, other contemporary comic dramatists were capable of almost any hilarious subversion. In 423 BC, old Cratinus' play the *Wine Flask* showed himself married to Comedy as his wife, but Comedy was wanting a divorce as Cratinus cared more for being drunk than he did for her.[7] This promising self-parody has sadly not survived for us in any more detail. In 421 Eupolis even staged a comedy whose chorus was divided into two halves, the rich and the poor, while the plot satirized a leading popular politician as the eunuch-slave of the Athenian people, presented as his 'Persian' master.[8] The mercurial minds of Athenians in this era could subvert and enjoy almost any fact of social and political life: freedom is, above all, democratic, and the proof that it exists is whether or not an Aristophanes is politically and culturally possible. He is the true symptom of a 'classical' age.

If Herodotus had been in Athens in spring 438 BC, he would have appreciated Euripides' enchanting drama the *Alcestis*, which was first performed in that year. He would readily have entered into its presentation of the dilemmas and devotion of a mythical king and queen, conducted under the kind patronage of Apollo. No doubt he would also have laughed at the year's salacious comedies, although one side of him would have been telling himself that they went much too far. From his own 'enquiries', however, he would remember how he knew dozens of much more recent tragic 'dramas', reported to him as real-life conflicts between fathers, sons and wives all over the world, between gods and mortals, between people like the Lydian King Gyges or the blinded shepherd Euenius in north-west Greece, or Hermotimus the Chiote who had avenged his own awful castration with a similar act against his castrator and the cruel man's sons. Outside Athens, there were so many real Greek tales in the recent past which contained the germ of real-life tragedies. Lacking Herodotus' wide researches, the Athenians found this germ and darkened and deepened it, but only in the world of legendary myths.

13

PERICLES AND ATHENS

Only Athens, among city-states of our day, is superior to the reports of her when she comes to the test; she alone causes no indignation in any enemy who comes against her, such are those from whom he suffers damage; nor is she blamed by those who are her subjects, as if they are being ruled by those who are unworthy to rule. Our power has great testimonies to it and is not without witness, so we will be admired both by those of our own time and those to come. We do not need Homer to praise us nor anyone else whose poetry pleases for a moment, whereas the truth will damage the impression the poet gives of the facts. For we have compelled all the land and the sea to be accessible to our daring and everywhere we have, together, set memorials of our successes and our failures.

Pericles, in the Funeral Speech of 431/0,
according to Thucydides, 2.41.2–3

FROM THE 450S UNTIL 429 the most famous Athenian politician was Pericles, so much so that this era is often known nowadays as the age of 'Periclean Athens'. The Emperor Hadrian was well aware of Pericles' example. Among his special favours for Athens, Hadrian may even have modelled his 'Panhellenic' role for the city on a project which biographers had ascribed to Pericles himself. Pericles has continued to inspire the modern world. In 1915, during the war with Germany, buses in London displayed a translation of the fine words on freedom which were ascribed to Pericles' famous Funeral Speech.

The real Pericles is more elusive. He was born in the mid–490s to a noble father, Xanthippus, and a mother of the noble, but controversial, Alcmeonid lineage. As a young man, he was shaped by two particular changes: the Athenians' new prominence, won by their role in defeating the Persian invasions, and the growing confidence of their democracy since Cleisthenes' reforms in 508 BC. Athenians, Pericles saw, were special, as even their fellow Greeks conceded, sometimes grudgingly. Democracy was now the well-founded setting for a politician's career and it was a fantasy of the 'good' to believe that it would disappear. It was in Pericles' youth, in the 480s, that popular activity had intensified, with the spate of ostracisms proving that the Athenian people could now vote to expel even the most noble individuals from their assemblies. In 489 Pericles' father had already exploited popular opinion by prosecuting no less a hero than Miltiades, the great victor of Marathon, before a popular court. In their assemblies, as Cleisthenes intended, the majority voting of the people was now the judge of what should happen. Someone, therefore, who could win the people's trust would be far more effective than an old-fashioned aristocrat, however brave he might be in war and athletics and however well connected in the wider Greek world.

Such trust would only be won by public speaking, proposing policies to the assembly which appealed and were then found to succeed. Political successes had not started to depend on the written word and its dissemination. Admittedly, the decrees passed by the assembly were displayed prominently on whitened boards in the public *agora* so that 'anyone who wished' could look at them. More Athenians could read, in my view, than could write, but it is likely that most of the assembly-voters had never troubled to read a literary text. Somebody could be found to read a decree on display and recite it for the less able, but if Pericles had tried to campaign by issuing written manifestos, he would have missed most of his political voters: at Athens, political writings were left to theorists and oligarchic sympathizers who were not in the political mainstream. The circulation of book-scrolls, the scenes of reading and writing on Athenian vases, the texts of the orally performed masterpieces which we now read and admire are evidence of the literate habits of only a small educated minority.[1] Political culture was oral.

The two lessons of Pericles' youth, the pre-eminence of Athens and the public role of each adult Athenian male, were to shape his political vision. Our supreme evidence for his words and deeds lies in the histories of his admiring younger contemporary, Thucydides (born *c.* 460–455 BC). Thucydides revered Pericles' oratory, his cool applied intelligence, his immunity to bribes and corruption and his ability (the young Thucydides thought) to control and lead the fickle people so that politics among the Athenians 'were becoming the rule of one man'.[2] In Thucydides' eyes, it also helped that Pericles was 'one of us', an aristocrat who was a brave and able general. But Thucydides did not go unchallenged and the views of Plato the philosopher proved more powerful, though written a generation after Pericles' death.

No democrat himself, Plato insisted that Pericles had been a flattering 'demagogue' who had misled the Athenians and corrupted them. He could not be exempted from the blame for the Athenians' eventual defeat by the Spartans in the ensuing Peloponnesian War. Later authors tried to reconcile these opposing views by claiming that Pericles had begun as a 'demagogue', as Plato complained, but had then attained the Olympian pre-eminence which the young Thucydides so admired. The most suggestive personal memoir of Pericles survives from a non-Athenian contemporary, the amiable Ion of Chios. On meeting Pericles, Ion found his company 'insolent and extremely conceited and there was considerable disdain and contempt for others mixed in his arrogant manners'.[3] Other famous Athenians, including the dramatist Sophocles, were much more to Ion's taste.

Pericles, we may infer, knew that he was gifted with no ordinary aims and responsibilities. He was said to be a single-minded politician who would walk only down the street which led from his house to the city's political centre. He is also said to have avoided social occasions if possible: popular politics were a serious, full-time business. His best friends included visiting intellectuals, people like Damon the musical theorist or the philosopher Anaxagoras who enraged the common man by claiming that the 'divine' sun was only a lump of burning matter. If Pericles relaxed, it was not with his wife, whom he divorced amicably, but with his famous mistress, Aspasia, who had come over from elegant east Greek Miletus. We hear of Aspasia as a wise authority on the pitfalls of matchmaking between couples or on the secrets of being a good 'wife'. The comic poets in Athens had a field day, claiming that she coaxed Pericles into various foreign wars, that she taught him oratory and philosophy, that she procured girls for him, that she ran a brothel on the side and even, in a mock trial–scene, that she was guilty of 'impiety' against the gods. Posterity has liked to imagine her running a salon of good taste and intelligent talk, but actually we know nothing about her. With delicious malice, Plato later credited her with an eloquent 'Funeral Speech' of her own, in praise of Athens.[4] Wickedly, he was making fun of the real Funeral Speeches by Pericles, one of which had been immortalized by Thucydides' *Histories*. At least we can say that Pericles did love the woman. He is the first man in history who is said to have always given his lady friend a passionate kiss on his way out to work in the morning and another on his return

17. A pensive goddess Athena contemplates what is probably a grave monument, perhaps inscribed with names of Athenian casualties in war. Fine classical marble relief, Athens Acropolis, *c.* 460 BC.

home each evening.[5] No source connects him with any homoerotic interest in boys.

Pericles' sons were thick and undistinguished, the home-life was nothing special, so what was 'Periclean' about what we call Periclean Athens? Pericles was elected as a general, and in the 430s he was elected year after year: he was, however, only one of a board of ten. He held no special position and his public achievements had to depend on his oratory in the big public assemblies. It is clear that he was only one voice among a much wider group of important leaders, some of whom advised some of his same policies. He could never decide something and impose it, as a modern Prime Minister does on his Cabinet. Nonetheless, there is a distinctive thread in what we know of the Athenians in the later 450s until *c.* 430. It is Pericles, surely, who put it into words and helped people to opt for what they had dimly wanted and would never have expressed so clearly.

In their foreign policy, Athenians were (arguably) not just Pericleans. Like Pericles himself, they were loyal heirs of Themistocles. Peace was agreed with the Persian king in 450/49 BC, as the older Themistocles would have approved; so, too, approaches from potential allies in the Greek West were acted on in the 440s and 430s and an Athenian general

was even briefly active in Naples: there are hints, no more, that Themistocles, too, was interested in the scope of the Greek West. In Greece, Pericles was remembered for a truly Themistoclean remark: 'already I see war
bearing down from the Peloponnese.'[6] The Spartans, he meant, were the
enemy and for the remark to have any point he must have uttered it long
before the fateful war which began in 431. If Athenian expansion meanwhile upset Sparta's allies in the northern Peloponnese, so be it. As
Themistocles' example had shown, there was scope for subverting their
pro-Spartan governments and even for bringing them over to Athens'
side. Pericles had lived through the slow war in Greece against the Spartans and their allies between 460 and 446. It would have convinced him
of the scope for sheltering the Athenians behind their impregnable Long
Walls, Themistocles' creation, and resisting Spartan land-invasions. They
could survive there through their naval supremacy, Themistocles' legacy,
and with it they could always import food. If they were allied to a friendly
neighbouring Megara, they could anyway block Sparta's easy access into
Athenian territory: they could 'win through' without a pitched battle. If
Spartans did try to ravage Attica, cavalry would be turned on them to
drive them off. The Periclean years see a sixfold increase in cavalry numbers and the new 'insurance' scheme for their horses.[7] Pericles was not a
lower-class bigot.

Pericles' firm, reasoned insistence on this strategy went with something
new and more profound than Themistocles' opportunism on the international scene. When a noble Athenian colleague, Callias, pulled off the
coup of a peace-agreement with Persia in 449, Pericles replied by summoning a Greek congress to Athens to discuss the rebuilding of Athens'
ruined temples, the offering of new sacrifices to the gods and the free and
peaceful use of the seas. The implication was that the Athenians' allies
would continue to pay tribute to the Athenians for these ends, in a continuing Hellenic League which would have Athens at its centre. Predictably, Sparta refused to attend, but in 449 the new temples did start to
be built on Athens' Acropolis, financed by her allies' continuing payments. The peace with Persia was presented as a 'victory', and so the
Athenians' previous oath never to rebuild their ruined shrines was over-
taken by a new building-programme. For Pericles, Athens was the great
centre of the free Greek world and was deservedly the ruler of so many
Greek allies. He was impressively hard-headed about the need to retain
the Athenians' alliance, or 'Empire'. All attempted revolts were repressed:
even her subjects, he says in Thucydides' memories of him, agreed that
they were being ruled by 'people who were not unworthy to do so'.[8]

Athenians should 'love' their city and its power. Athens was remarkable for its new beauty, for the character of its inhabitants and their exceptional grace, skill and mutual tolerance (slaves, after all, were simply objects). With varying degrees of probability, we can ascribe to Pericles a scattered range of proposals for his fellow Athenians' benefit. From c. 448 BC onwards Athenian settlers were sent out to new settlements or to land-holdings in the territories of Athenian subjects: the policy was probably Pericles'. Most of the settlers were drawn from the poorest classes and by renting out their new land abroad they were raised to a better standard of living. Since the early 450s Athenians who served on the many juries in the city's law courts were paid a small daily fee for doing so: this state-pay is a Periclean proposal. In due course, all Athenians would be given the sum needed to buy their 'tickets' for the dramas and events at Athens' major city-festivals: it is disputed, but in my view probable, that Pericles was responsible.

The definition of Athenian citizenship was also tightened on his advice. It was Pericles' own proposal that only the children of an Athenian citizen-father and an Athenian mother would be Athenian citizens themselves. This law of Pericles was prospective, applying to children born from 451 BC onwards, and so it was popular enough to be voted in by the existing citizenry. Probably, as we have seen, its main aim was to encourage Athenian men to take Athenian brides, and the topic was more urgent when so many Athenians were receiving new plots of land to rent or cultivate abroad. Families, Pericles realized, did not want to be left with unmarried daughters while their males took foreign wives: the tighter requirements of citizenship would also keep up the Athenians' sense of group identity.

Through all of these innovations runs a principled belief that the citizens of Athens are special, that each adult male is capable of responsible political duties, that they should be rewarded for their role, and that the arts help to honour the gods and to civilize their beneficiaries. Pericles himself served prominently on the commission to oversee the splendid new buildings on the Acropolis. He was a close friend of the great sculptor Pheidias and he was identified with the proper conduct of the building-programme. Under his general guidance, the robe which young Athenian girls wove for the goddess Athena was transferred to her new 'house', the Parthenon, where it would hang as a huge backcloth behind Pheidias' enormous new statue of the goddess.[9] Just below the Acropolis, Pericles also proposed the building of a special Odeon, supported on a forest of columns. It became a venue for musical contests in the great festivals, although comic poets alleged that it was a conceit, modelled on the captured tent of the Persian King Xerxes.

Between *c.* 560 and 510 the Athenian tyrants had had a vision of a grander Athens; now for the first time, we find a vision for Athenian citizens. No previous Athenian politician, not even Cleisthenes, is known to have associated with philosophers and intellectuals. Unlike previous aristocrats, Pericles asked for no poems or texts in his honour: he did not even try to inscribe his name on what were seen as the entire citizenry's buildings. He had an idea of a new community, enhanced by power and by the equal participation of male Athenians. His intellectual contacts extended to Protagoras the philosopher who was invited, posterity said, to write the laws for the new settlement which was sent out to Thurii in south Italy under Pericles' guidance. In music or political theory, in the use of oratory and sheer reason, Pericles applied a new intellectual clarity. It was the outcome of the Athenians' new prominence in his lifetime, which drew talented and intelligent experts to his city, attracted by its new power and rewards. He and his friends did not believe in that old archaic bogey, the gods' willingness to punish them for a distant ancestor's misdeeds. They had a new classical clarity.

In this company, the random 'anger' of the gods was not a convincing 'explanation of misfortune': descendants would not be considered liable for their ancestors' crimes. This clearer understanding of responsibility is for us a hallmark of the change from an archaic to a classical age. At Athens, Pericles and his friends had such understanding, and the important point for our sense of a change is that a few people had it at all, not that most other people in 'classical Greece' still entertained the older archaic ideas. In the Greek West, at Selinus, citizens still feared 'avenging spirits' in their midst; at Cyrene, they believed a legend of the 'wrath' of Apollo which accounted for the city's foundation and they bothered about rituals to cope with their fears of pollution. At Locri, citizens were still sending a group of their virgin daughters yearly to Troy so as to atone for a 'wrong' perpetrated by their ancestors in the mythical age of the heroes.[10] The Periclean age was not an age of general Greek enlightenment, but it was an age when intellectuals and their enlightened thinking first flourished around a like-minded political leader.

We hear some of it still in Pericles' Funeral Speech for 430 BC, which Thucydides presents in his own words while claiming to keep 'as close as possible' to the 'gist of what was actually said'. Behind Pericles' fine claims, we can also catch an answer to contemporary critics. 'We are lovers of beauty, yes, but without extravagance; we are lovers of wisdom, yes, but without being soft.' In our democracy, any man can contribute, whatever his background, but Athenians are tolerant of fellow Athenians' private ways and do not resent them if they act for personal pleasure. Freedom pervades both political and private life, but it is a freedom under the law. Athenian liberty is not 'licence'. The man, however, who refuses to participate in public life is 'useless'.[11] As for women, they have no such participation. The speech ends with a brief mention of 'womanly virtue' for those who are now widows. They should be 'celebrated as little as possible for virtue or reproach among men', keeping out of attention as modestly as possible. For them 'great is the glory if they are not worse than their existing nature', with the implication, therefore, that their nature is not the best anyway. He is giving 'a purely negative injunction not to fall short of an innate limitation'. Here, as elsewhere, Pericles put into words what his citizen-hearers, but not many of his modern readers, accepted anyway. For males, the ideal is not 'public splendour, private squalor'. It is no disgrace to be poor, but it is a disgrace not to try to escape being poor in the first place. Throughout the 430s, the comic poets of Athens and the rival politicians tried to satirize and even to prosecute Pericles, Aspasia and his intellectual and artistic friends. The 'Olympian' Pericles, the comedians alleged, was under the sway of his mistress: he started the war with Sparta—why not?—to avoid scandal: his head, even, was 'squill-shaped'.[12] As a 'squill', in the ancient Greek flora, was a flower with a rounded, smooth bulb, the meaning is that Pericles had a round, prematurely bald head. He was said to wear a military helmet very often in public, perhaps to hide his baldness as much as to evoke his constant service as a general. The comic satire and the prosecutions are evidence of the freedom for which Pericles spoke so wonderfully. The public loved the poets' 'tabloid' humour, but it is Pericles' vision which has outlived theirs.

14

THE PELOPONNESIAN WAR

The [five] Spartan judges considered that their original question would be right, whether they had had anything good from them in the war . . . so they took each one [of the Plataeans] aside and asked them the same thing again, whether they had done the Spartans and their allies any good in the war, and when they could not say that they had, they took them off and killed them, and they made not a single exception.

Thucydides, 3.68.1, as the siege of Plataea ended in 427 BC

D URING THE LAST THREE DECADES of the fifth century BC the Athenians and the Spartans, with their respective allies, were at war again with one another. This war, known as the 'Peloponnesian War', may seem clear evidence of the ancient Greeks' political failure. More than twenty years of fighting, with seven years' 'uneasy truce' in the middle, killed tens of thousands of Greeks (perhaps half of the Athenian male population), destroyed homes and trees and cost large sums of money and manpower. The war was only resolved by help given by the Persian king to the Spartans which required, in return, the abandonment of all the Greek cities in Asia again to the Persian sphere. War, observers themselves said, increased human cruelty. There were spectacular acts of ferocity on either side, including the killing of prisoners by Spartan commanders and the massacre, after due warning, of the island population of Melos by the Athenians because the islanders had refused to join their Empire. The theme of freedom was sadly prominent throughout. It was promised initially to the Athenians' 'enslaved' allies by Spartan rhetoric, but it was grossly betrayed by the outcome. The eastern Greeks in Asia were handed over to the Persian king as tribute-paying subjects, while communities in the Aegean found themselves under the rule of hideous pro-Spartan juntas, the decarchies or the 'rule of ten' pro-Spartan men.

This war and all its ferocity were not driven by religion or nationalism: there were no crusades and there was no genocide. There were, however, real principles at stake, rather than killing for killing's sake. At first sight, the conflict appears to be one only of power. The war arose from the continuing expansion of the Athenians' power, especially as it turned in more detail to opportunities in Sicily and the Greek West. During the 430s these foreign ambitions increasingly alarmed Sparta's important ally Corinth, the mother-city of the dominant state in Sicily, Syracuse. Corinth also had important colonies on the coast of north-west Greece, which lay on the natural route for warships to the West. Against this background of anxiety, the Corinthians were in no mood to give Athenian ambitions the benefit of any doubt. Suspicions intensified during a diplomatic clash over the Corinthian colony Corcyra (modern Corfu). Unless the Spartans would go to war against Athenian interventions, Corinthian envoys threatened to desert the Spartans' alliance, an act which would expose the Peloponnese to a much greater risk of subversion and the consequent breaking of the Spartans' hold on it. A chain of events unfolded, in which the Athenians did not technically break the prevailing treaty, sworn in 446, with the Spartans and their allies. But without Athenian ambitions outside this treaty's area, the pressure for war would not have arisen at this point. The final flashpoint was Corinth's neighbour Megara, an ally of the Spartans. The Athenians issued a decree with commercial intent against her, banning Megarians from walking in to Athens' market-place or sailing into the harbours of her many allies. The aim, surely, was to destabilize the Megarians' ruling oligarchy indirectly, without actually declaring war. If the Megarians could be turned into a democracy, they might become allies of the Athenians. The recent wars between 460 and 446 had shown what a vital strategic ally they could be, as they could block their mountain-passes against Spartan invaders and close the natural route for invasions of Attica.

More than five hundred years later the Emperor Hadrian still met memories of this famous feud. On visiting Megara, he found that, only recently in his reign, the Megarians had been refusing to allow Athenians and their families, ancestral enemies, into their houses. Behind these territorial conflicts lay something more fundamental, the complete difference of lifestyle, culture and mentality between Pericles' Athenians and the Spartans to whom Megara in that era had been aligned. Hadrian would have needed reminding how in the 430s classical Spartans had continued to crush and occupy their Greek neighbour, Messenia, and to maintain the harsh way of life which had been imposed by their lawgivers since the seventh century BC. Around Sparta's vulnerable territories, her kings and elders worked to maintain a cordon of loyal oligarchies, in which a relatively few citizens ruled firmly over all others and denied them political rights. Athens, by contrast, was the great democracy, the seat of a culture which could be said to be the 'education of Greece'. The thinking, the theatre, the arts, the varied lifestyle which we still admire were all Athenian or based in Athens. The Spartans did not trust it, fearing it would infiltrate and overthrow the protective cordon of allies on which their own way of life depended. If only the few oligarchs who ruled her northern Peloponnesian allies, especially Corinth, could have had the nerve to desert Sparta and join the Athenian allies, their fellow seafarers. Forty years later brave democrats were indeed active among the Spartans' Isthmian allies, even in Corinth. Together with the Athenians, they could have mounted an unstoppable expedition to Sicily, south Italy and beyond. With the Greeks of Sicily as their allies, they could then have attacked the furthest point of Athenian ambitions, Carthage. Carthage's dependence on hired troops would probably have failed her; the Greek community in Carthage would have helped the Greek allies, and Carthage, the richest, most powerful alternative to the Greek way of life in the Mediterranean, would have submitted. Athenian values, democracy and prosperity would have blossomed all the way from north Africa to the Black Sea. Eminent Athenians would have found a new outlet abroad for their talents. The flamboyant aristocrat Alcibiades, the suspect hero of Athenian audiences, would have fitted well as the governor of Athenian Carthage, among the gold, the girls and the city's famous carpets.

By contrast, the years of war became a dull, damaging stalemate. In 431 BC Greek opinion had expected a swift Athenian surrender, but the Athenians, on Pericles' advice, retreated behind their city's Long Walls which were far too strong for the Spartans' poor grasp of siege-warfare. Pericles had talked of 'winning through', but a man of his intelligence had surely more than a plan for survival in mind. The Athenians' fleet was some three hundred warships strong and was still brilliantly manned and trained (even if a few slave-'attendants' sometimes rowed too). It continued to dominate the sea, to assist imports of food into the city and to maintain security among the Athenians' allies. The Spartans' naval skills, by contrast, were minimal and they lacked the money to build and maintain first-class ships. They had helot-serfs, but no free lower-class citizens to serve as rowers. Their supreme strength lay in traditional hoplite war-

18. Marble relief of Athenian cavalryman, his gaze fixed on his fallen enemy. Possibly a reference to the first cavalry battle in the Peloponnesian War, *c.* 431–430 BC. If so, Pericles's Funeral Speech was spoken over the dead, including this warrior.

fare by land, conducted by their superb infantry who marched in step to music, still chanting the repulsive verses of the poet Tyrtaeus, with their purple cloaks still fluttering in the wind.

Pericles' strategy involved letting the Spartans do what little they could, while Athenians continued to put pressure on the crucial Megarians and Corinthians. If one or both would defect to the Athenian side, perhaps as a democracy, the Spartans would be blocked from Attica. Meanwhile, the Spartans' successes in subverting Athenian allies remained limited, not least because the Spartans' own system and the harshness of most of the Spartan commanders were such a grim alternative. The Spartans' main impact lay in their yearly invasion of Attica when they cut down the local trees and burned the land. Nobody could beat them in a pitched battle, but the Athenians denied them one, merely harassing their raiders and foragers with their recently enlarged cavalry. Sparta's allies could not stay long in Attica: they lacked a workforce of helots at home, and so they needed to return to gather in their own harvest with their own hands.

Pericles had not provoked war, but because he had a rational strategy for seeing off the Spartans, he had urged the Athenians not to give in to the pre-war diplomatic pressure. His reasoning was faultless, but it was ruined by pure chance. The Athenians became infected by an unforeseen plague (probably, typhus) and Pericles was one of the many victims. Straining for pre-eminence, his followers proposed an increasingly active strategy, including an un-Periclean first venture to Sicily, a source of grain for Corinth and Spartan allies. Even so, Athenian failures did not undermine the basic model of Periclean planning: the Spartans could not win, and so they agreed to a truce in 421 BC which left them with no real gain and no popularity among their allies. The events of the war give a fascinating glimpse of the weaknesses in Spartan culture and society. The numbers of Spartiate soldiers were already declining and the outlying 'Dwellers Around' were being used to fill up infantry units which had previously been for Spartans only. The Spartan state was financially feeble (she still refused to strike coins) and at sea, her commanders were incompetent. In 425 a genuine Spartan cavalry was introduced, but it was not a success. Once outside Sparta, most of the Spartan governors were detestable men, trained to be harsh, not tactful, with a tendency to homoerotic affairs with their subjects and excessive use of the military baton. No Greek army marched without a strong sense of the gods as onlookers and guides, but the Spartans were exceptionally conscious of them. Like every Greek army, they respected the possible wrath of 'gods and local heroes', but they respected them in a more prominent way. They had a heightened sense of these gods' anger and their 'punishment' of any Spartans who transgressed them. It was not just that 'behind a Spartan army there trotted a mixed herd of sacrificial animals, ready for use to test the will of the gods at any time'. Before crossing Sparta's borders, Spartans were distinctive in their practice of offering 'crossing-sacrifices' and would even withdraw if the omens proved unfavourable. Like other field commanders, Spartan kings and generals could sometimes treat the gods, the omens and the yearly calendar of religious festivals as flexible factors, whose rules could be bent or evaded. But they became very conscious of such manipulations if events proved their decisions wrong. More than those of their Athenian opponents, Spartans' activities were limited by fear of the gods.

In 415 BC, six years after an initial peace, the Athenians accepted a request from some of the Sicilian Greeks and other allies on the island and dispatched a huge armada, hoping to dominate the West. The venture came close to success, but was foiled above all by the skill and horsepower of their main Sicilian enemy, Syracuse. The Athenians had failed to send horses in boats or sufficient cavalry to oppose such a horse-rich enemy. A year later the expedition ended in a total disaster for the Athenians and their navy. Even so, the Spartans were very slow to profit from this unexpected gift. In September 411 they had their best chance of victory when an Athenian fleet was defeated off nearby Euboea and the Athenians in the city were deeply split by an anti-democratic coup. Yet the Spartans went away without pressing their advantage. The next year they were offering peace, an offer which they are said to have repeated five years later.

Among the Spartans, the war's final years, from 411 to 404, were distinguished by continuing naval incompetence and the careers of some of the harshest thugs in Greek history, the dour Clearchus and the ruthless Lysander. Among the Athenians, despite the Sicilian fiasco and the brutal coup of 411, they were years, amazingly, of extreme cultural vigour. The tense early months of 411 saw two of Aristophanes' comic masterpieces, the *Lysistrata* and the *Women at the Thesmophoria*, both playing hilariously with gender-roles (and the latter with Euripides the tragedian). Responding to the 'new music' in Athenian taste, Euripides took the tragic chorus to new extremes and put on one of his masterpieces, too, a brutal reworking of the Orestes myth. He then withdrew to Macedon and composed his finest play, the *Bacchae* with its tale of resistance, then submission to the god Dionysus' power. Sculptors back in the city carved a classical masterpiece too, the victory-figures and the procession of cattle for sacrifice on the parapet of the recently completed temple to Athena, goddess of victory.[1] Above all, the elderly Sophocles, battered by an unwilling role in the coup of 411, staged his two finest plays, though in his eighties: the *Philoctetes*, with its theme of deception, and the heroic *Oedipus at Colonus*, the tragedy which best conveys the awesomeness of the 'heroic temper'. The citizens remained polarized, between oligarchic sympathizers and determined democrats but the tensions did not disintegrate their master-artists' skills.

The Spartans' eventual victory in 404 BC owed much to the Persians' funding for their fleet and to the harsh and aggressive tactics of their newly emergent leader, Lysander. It was also assisted by the extreme behaviour of the Athenians, who had exiled and executed most of their best generals in politically motivated proceedings. In 404 the Athenians' 'second squad' of commanders lost a naval battle up at the Hellespont and exposed the sea-route on which the city's grain imports relied. The Athenians had to surrender their fleet, breach their Long Walls and accept a narrow oligarchy, backed by Spartan support. Their neighbours in Thebes and Corinth are said to have pressed for the complete destruction of the city.

More than twenty years of intermittent war had seen at most five major engagements. However, there had been more than a hundred lesser encounters all over the Greek world. Almost every region had memories of dire days and nights when their freedom had stood in the balance and parties of local men had braved all for safety and survival. All around Greece, sweaty rowers, horsemen (still without stirrups) or even divers had stretched their human endurance to its limits. A rash of local victory-monuments, or trophies, commemorated minor successes of the war's early years, but on a long view, this scrappy stalemate would never have loomed so large in our awareness of Greek antiquity. Without one great asset, we might have struggled to reconstruct it from inscriptions (whose dating sometimes depends on fragile assumptions about the particular style in which they are cut on stone) and oblique references in Athenian comedy. It is of lasting human significance because of its surviving historian, the aristocratic Athenian Thucydides, whose work, unfinished at his death, extends down to 411 BC.

Thucydides had been nobly born in *c.* 460–455 BC and was linked by family to Cimon, the political antithesis of Pericles. Nonetheless, Pericles became his hero and ideal leader, the dominant voice in Athens when the young Thucydides could begin to attend assemblies for himself. In the late 440s Pericles' pre-eminence appeared to have cowed the potential excesses of the democracy which he addressed. It was a 'golden age', therefore, in the young man's eyes: by birth, sympathy and intellect Thucydides was no democrat. He wrote with contempt of Pericles' most populist successors (men who were 'most aggressive', hiding their misdeeds by prolonging the war, or simply 'wicked'). His own political preference was for a restrictive oligarchy which eliminated more than half of the Athenian male voters ('the best constitution the Athenians had, at least in my time').[2] The ignorance, quarrelling and incompetence of the 'people', he argued, were root causes of the failure of the campaign in Sicily. Others, more fairly, might have blamed the feeble dithering of its main general, Nicias. But Nicias, for Thucydides, was 'one of us', a rich man, though not a noble, and was remembered later as someone 'who never did anything populist in his life'.[3] From Thucydides, Nicias receives a glowing last tribute, which refutes the usual pattern whereby the historian praises men of achievement, rather than those who failed but had good intentions.

Thucydides prized accuracy, 'exactness' in the newly fashionable Greek word for it. When compiling information he was admirably aware of the problems of false memory and the need for 'laborious investigation'.[4] He had thought carefully, too, about the problems of establishing a chronology. Above all, he removed the gods as explanations of the course of events. In his mid-twenties he could well have heard a lecture by the older 'enquirer', Herodotus, or even met him on his visit to Athens. His predecessor would have struck him as naïve, uncritical and (no doubt) superstitious. There is no sign that he wrote with Herodotus' 'enquiry' prominently in his mind. It was not so much a model as (in his view) a muddle. Admirably self-confident, Thucydides saw his own very different approach as his means of writing a 'possession for all time'.

Dreams and omens, the simple wisdom of 'wise advisers', the belief that those who go too far get a just revenge and a divine retribution: Thucydides excluded all these Herodotean staples, just as he excluded explanations in terms of curses and divine causes. He had nothing to do with the 'archaic' belief that people may suffer for their ancestors' misdeeds: on an occasion when Herodotus saw divine justice working itself out, Thucydides never even mentioned it and gave a political explanation only.[5] He favoured a new and penetrating realism. The gap between expectation and outcome, intention and event fascinated him. So did the bitter relations between justice and self-interest, the facts of power and the values of decency. He was well aware of the difference between truth and rhetorical pleading. What men professed publicly, he knew, was not what they practised. The Spartans began by promising 'liberation' to the Greek world, and then betrayed the value of freedom. Thucydides was no cynic, not a person who always imputes a selfish and unworthy motive to participants. Rather, he was a realist, having learned the hard lesson that in inter-state relations, powers simply rule where they can, a fact of life which others, professing justice, obscure or ignore at their peril. 'Ethical foreign policy', he realized, is a vain irrelevance.

His *Histories*, therefore, are the most penetrating account of freedom and justice and the practical limits on both in the cut and thrust of life. Luxury concerned him less: he could accept that an individual might combine public astuteness and success with private dissolution and an excessive lifestyle. He saw this possibility exemplified by his colourful friend Alcibiades at Athens during the one truly valuable phase (411–407) of Alcibiades' long public career. It was Thucydides' explicit aim to teach his readers, but his lesson was not just how to cope with a military problem or a challenge in a battle. Thucydides admired practical wisdom, the clever improvisations of a political genius like Themistocles or the long sight and (arguable) steadiness of a Pericles. Such qualities, and their exemplars, were to be emulated. But he also wished to lay bare, through speech and action, the amoral reality of inter-state politics, the verbal distortions of diplomatic speakers and factional leaders, and the terrifying violence which political revolution unleashes 'as long as human nature stays the same'. His diagnosis is still only too recognizable.

He died, probably in the early 390s BC, before finishing his history: it breaks off in 411 BC, not with the defeat of 404 to which it looks forward. The stages of composition of even the eight books we have remind us that it was not written in one single sweep: we must allow for eventual adjustments in his point of view. Nonetheless, we can see from what survives, unfinished, that his presentation of the bleak facts of life in factional politics and inter-state relations was not itself bleak or inhumane. He gives a brilliant description of the lethal plague which beset Athens from 430 onwards, and it is a masterpiece of observation. Above all, it is unmarked by reference to divine causation, although even his keenest Greek admirers later adduced such explanations for similar epidemics in their own histories. At the same time, he gives an account of the participants' own psychology and human suffering which is written with a victim's understanding: Thucydides merely tells us, with noble restraint, that he, too, had suffered this plague. His human analysis is so much more penetrating than the day-by-day case notes of the external symptoms of sicknesses which were compiled by the most 'scientific' of the Greek writers on medicine. So, too, his analysis of factional strife is written with a heartfelt pity for the plight of those caught between the extremists. He expresses real regret for the values of simple decency. Through speeches, as much as through his narrative's angle of vision, Thucydides brings out the strength of participants' feelings and sufferings, and encourages us to understand what it was like to be one of them at the time. We need to grasp the way the world is, he is telling us; but implicitly, that way is distressing, even regrettable. The master of realism is also well aware of its emotionally upsetting context.

The ancients themselves acknowledged Thucydides as the pinnacle of history-writing, harsh and difficult though his style seemed. Some thirty years younger than Herodotus, he belonged to a generation which had seen no technological revolution, no sudden change in its geography or material life. Yet his way of presenting his contemporaries belonged, intellectually, to a completely different mental universe. Like Herodotus and so many Greek historians, he wrote in exile from his home city, but not before he had listened, argued and learned from debates in Greece's most powerful city-state and had himself served briefly as one of its generals.

He was formed and steeled at the centre of power in Athens, in a climate where political theory was being taught for the first time, where generalizations about human psychology were the talk of his class and where power, and its exercise, were questions of passionate concern. Athens was his New York, whereas Thurii was Herodotus' Buenos Aires. In his *Histories*, Thucydides claimed to have kept 'as close as possible to the general gist of what was actually said' when he gave the speeches of selected contemporaries. Frequently mistranslated here, Thucydides is disavowing word-for-word accuracy, but he is claiming, nonetheless, to have kept as close to the reality as he possibly could. The implication is that, often, he has kept very close indeed. The style of these speeches at times may be Thucydides' own, but his gallery of speakers allows us to hear the voices of a new articulate realism, the style of the generation which was his own singular context. Through them, and his underlying insight, the Peloponnesian War remains the most instructive war in human history.

15

SOCRATES

We went in and found Socrates just released from his chains and his wife Xanthippe—you know her—holding his little son and sitting beside him. When Xanthippe saw us, she cried out and said the sort of things which women usually do say, 'Socrates, this is the last time that your friends will ever speak to you, or you to them.' Socrates looked up at Crito and said, 'Crito, let somebody take her off home.'

Plato, *Phaedo* 60A

But now is the time to depart, for me to die, for you to live, but which of us is going to the better business is unclear to all, except God.

Plato's 'Socrates' to his jury: *Apology* 42A

IN A TRIBUTE TO CLASSICAL ATHENS, Hadrian's villa included a 'Lyceum', an imitation of the shrine in which the most famous of all Athenians had taught and conversed. He was neither rich nor handsome. He never wrote a book and he never received a prize. He was described by the Delphic oracle as the wisest man in Greece, but wise, it was said, because he knew his own ignorance. His style of teaching appears to have been by question and answer, through which he exposed his participants' contradictory beliefs. He inspired at least two Athenian comedies at his expense, a cluster of texts on his supposed 'Conversations', posthumous allegations that he had been a bigamist and a series of recollections by the sober, though artful, Athenian Xenophon to show that he had whole-heartedly worshipped the gods and had been opposed to sex with boys. Above all, he inspired the writings of his pupil Plato. Through them he shaped the entire future of Western philosophy.

In spring 399, however, a large jury of Athenians condemned him to death. Socrates, the prosecution claimed, 'does not acknowledge the gods which the city acknowledges'; he introduces new 'divinities'; he 'corrupts the young'.[1] After a month in prison, he died from a cup of hemlock. The condemnation of a chubby, quizzical seventy-year-old who had been teaching in Athens for some forty years is a reminder that the world's most thorough democracy was not liberal, tolerant or committed to personal freedom on every issue.

Socrates was born at Athens in *c.* 470 BC into a humble family, the son of a stonemason and a mother, it was said, who was a sturdy midwife. He was strikingly ugly, with a snub nose, a paunch, big lips and protruding eyes which swivelled as he spoke. He was wonderfully scruffy, wearing a worn-out cloak and sometimes not troubling to wear shoes. His priorities lay elsewhere, and he was said to become rapt in intellectual concentration, oblivious of his surroundings. He was married, nonetheless, to Xanthippe and, according to Xenophon, she was awfully difficult. 'I want to keep company with the human race and so I have acquired her,' he makes Socrates say, 'for if I can put up with her, I will easily get on with all the rest of mankind.'[2] He had three sons, none of whom came to anything special. He also proved his resilience and courage by serving on at least three Athenian campaigns abroad as an infantryman, in one of which he saved the life of the city's controversial 'golden boy', the young and noble Alcibiades. In his later years he served on the council at a critical moment and opposed a ferocious proposal to condemn the Athenians' generals in a single block vote. To be serving on the council he had had to be appointed by lot: he was willing, then, to take his turn in a democracy, although, in discussions, he regarded the random lot as a stupid device with which to run a state. Two years later, after a brutal political coup in the city, he bravely opposed another outrageous order, to arrest a resident foreigner and cause his death. Ever the loyal citizen, Socrates made no attempt to escape when he himself was awaiting death in prison under the restored democracy.

One of his effects is to leave us with a 'Socratic problem'. Evidence about him is tendentious in two ways. It is either hostile and satirical, or it is defensive and idealizing in the hands of his pupils Plato and Xenophon. If Socrates was modestly born and took no fees, how ever did he live, while questioning all comers (but especially noble young men) day after day? We do not know, but like other scruffy academics he liked a good dinner-party and was said to have a strong head for wine. He also liked beautiful, well-born young men: did they pay for him, or did he find

some source of income which his admirers have hidden from us? His followers included two pupils who took contrary views on luxury. One opposed it, and focused on the 'ascetic', shoeless Socrates, whereas the other
endorsed 'pleasure' as the supreme good, like the Socrates who enjoyed a
smart dinner table. Centuries later, the Christian St Augustine noted
Socrates' contradictory 'effect' in this respect. It seems that he liked a
good evening, enriched by upper-class Athenian splendour, but it was not
his ambition or his measure of his own worth.

Socrates enquired above all into questions of values and ethics. Justice
and its advantages were no doubt one such question and Socrates would
seek a clear definition of the concepts at issue, in order to help sort out
disputed cases. He did not teach religiously assured 'values', but he did
argue from premises. It was later believed, wrongly, that he claimed to
know nothing, except that he knew nothing at all. Instead, he said that he
lacked wisdom. Unlike an expert in carpentry or shoe-making, he had no
body of knowledge which he could pass on systematically and prove in
practice. He knew some things, but he did not know a system. This questioning was so important because others in Athens claimed to have found
such knowledge on so many exciting new subjects.

Socrates was remembered, especially by Plato, for his irony or mock
modesty. Importantly, he practised it as one among a wider group of intellectuals. Since the 440s Athens had become a magnet for visiting
thinkers and foreign teachers who transformed the horizons of the city's
young: by the 420s it is correct to talk of a generation gap here between
fathers and sons. It was not an absolute gap, because some of the old listened to the new thinking, too, but it marked a real, perceptible change
in Athenians' ways of reasoning and arguing. Some of these thinkers
taught the art of speaking; some of them had radical views about the
gods, even claiming that they were man's creations for social reasons.
They continued to teach astronomy, geometry and the sciences which
had been first broached in Ionia; Hippias, whom Plato mocks, even
worked on the chronology of the past. They also distinguished what was
'natural' from what was 'conventional', thereby raising a fundamental
question in human ethics and societies: Protagoras argued, according to
Plato, that some conventions might actually be natural, because man is a
social animal by nature. For those in their charmed circle, lectures by
these people were thrilling. Plato's dialogue the *Protagoras* catches the
excitement of one such visit by these great men. Hearers had swarmed
into the exclusive home of the rich aristocrat, Callias, and had slept over
in every corner in order to hear the lectures.

Thinkers are always good for a laugh and in 423 BC two separate Athenian comedies picked on Socrates. The best known, Aristophanes' *Clouds*, satirizes him as a sophist who teaches new gods with names like Chaos or Swirl, and who denies that thunder and lightning are instruments of Zeus' punishment. He runs a 'Thinking Shop' and teaches fee-paying pupils how to make unjust arguments prevail over just ones. His scientific eccentricities mean that the usual gods are no longer his 'common currency'. His pupils learn amoral behaviour. They cheat, behave unjustly and beat up their elderly fathers. One father, in conclusion, urges that the 'Thinking Shop' should be burned down. 'Why did you insult the gods,' he asks, 'and inspect the moon's backside? Chase them, beat them, pelt them for a hundred reasons but most of all for remembering how they "wronged the gods".'[3]

Aristophanes appears to have dined in Socrates' company and bantered with him. Social acquaintance, however, can go with private ridicule and disgust, especially when one of the guests is an intellectual. Perhaps some of Aristophanes' hearers and readers were as sophisticated as some of his modern scholars and somehow took the extreme aggression of the aggrieved father in this play as another joke. But most of them took it, surely, at face value.

These attacks had a wider context. In the 430s an Athenian decree had been passed which appears to have made impiety a criminal offence for 'those who do not acknowledge the divine' and who (perhaps) 'teach about things on high'.[4] The democracy did not tolerate atheism, but it took a crisis or some political manoeuvring to make it a major issue in the law courts. In 415 BC, just before the ill-fated Athenian expedition to Sicily had sailed off, organized groups of wreckers smashed the erect phalluses off the herms on Athenian streets. Fearing a political coup, the people prosecuted the suspects and uncovered even more who had profaned the Athenians' cherished cult of the Eleusinian Mysteries in their private houses. The guilty parties included well-born young men, often in their mid-twenties or thirties, who had probably enjoyed the intellectuals' teaching. The most spectacular profaner of the Mysteries was the gifted Alcibiades, nobly born, lisping, handsome and a bold and envied presence on the political scene. He was also Socrates' most celebrated pupil and was widely believed to be one of his lovers.

In spring 399 the case against Socrates was 'impiety' and the charges against him reflected the satire in Aristophanes' play. He was said to be introducing 'new gods', which was not an offence in itself, but only if the 'new' gods excluded worship of the traditional gods of the city's cults.

Socrates' supposed scientific divinities were said to do just this, and he was also known to appeal to a guiding 'inner divinity', which stopped him from some things, according to Plato, and gave positive orders too, according to Xenophon. Atheism, implicitly, was the consequence, and Socrates also 'corrupted the young'.

To our minds, 'corruption' suggests sexual harassment. Such harassment was obviously an issue in Socrates' reputation, although Aristophanes ignored it. Both Plato and Xenophon protest too much against its existence. Xenophon's Socrates admits that he is 'always in love with someone',[5] but deplores homosexual acts: he rebukes an Athenian who is about to engage in one, and criticizes him for behaving like a piglet which is rubbing itself against a stone. Plato's Socrates admits to being set on fire by catching a glimpse of a lovely boy's body under his tunic. Plato also acquits him, too emphatically, of having sex with Alcibiades: Alcibiades wanted it, Plato tells us, but Socrates supposedly slept chastely in his arms. Socrates' social life is teeming with homoerotic lovers and their passions: one rare item in his personal knowledge was certainly the god of love.

To the Athenian jury in 399 BC, what mattered most was Socrates' moral effect on his most famous pupils. By rejecting the accepted gods, was he not encouraging grossly amoral behaviour? Here recent events were against him. His beloved Alcibiades had behaved outrageously at Athens' expense, even deserting to the Spartans. His darling Charmides had ended up as one of the abominable Ten who had terrorized Athens in the final stages of a Spartan-backed coup at the end of the war. Sweet, flaxen-haired Critias had been unspeakably awful, the mastermind behind the Thirty Tyrants who had started the rot and had cost many innocent Athenian lives.

In spring 399 an amnesty forbade political charges based on these dreadful events. Socrates was accused of other things, but his prosecutors will have cited the bad company he kept: it seemed to be the supreme proof of his amoral, irreligious influence. One prosecutor, Meletus, had just pursued a charge for impiety against Andocides, another unpopular aristocrat: he is probably the speaker of a surviving speech for the prosecution of this case which is filled with notable religious bigotry. The manoeuvring escapes us, but Meletus then helped to prosecute Socrates. It was not that Socrates had ever taught tyranny or the political philosophy of a junta: if he thought use of the lot silly, he could still tolerate it or reconcile this view with his continuing to participate in the democracy. His best-known friends were already corrupted before he met them; they had been spoiled by their birth and family position, and Socrates was only culpable in so far as he did not convert them. The legal form of his trial left the jurors to choose between either party's proposed sentence. The prosecution proposed death, and if Socrates had proposed exile or a big fine, he would have saved himself. He did not, because he knew the trial was unjust and a mockery of his life. To Plato we owe the sublime speech of defence which he himself had never troubled to make. In it, 'Socrates' anticipates an afterlife spent discussing philosophy with pupils in the next world. It was indeed his mission, and as the afterlife will be eternal, he will, logically, be spared the risk of tutorial fatigue and boredom.

16

FIGHTING FOR
FREEDOM AND JUSTICE

Proclamations such as these are to be made from time to time so as to scare and deter conspirators. The free population and the harvest-crops are to be brought into the city, and anyone who wishes may lead away or carry off from the countryside without penalty the goods of anyone who disobeys . . . There are to be no private gatherings anywhere whatsoever, neither by day or night, but those which are really necessary may be held in the town-hall or the council or any other public place. No soothsayer is to sacrifice in private without a magistrate. Men shall not dine together in a common mess, but each must dine in their own houses, except for a wedding or a funeral-feast and even these they must notify in advance to the magistrates.

Aeneas, on measures during
attack by invaders, 10.3–5 (late 350s BC)

THE FORTY YEARS OR SO which followed the Spartans' unlikely victory over the Athenians are a kaleidoscope of wars, ever-changing alliances and brief bouts of supremacy for one or other major power in Greece. But behind the apparent confusion, the ideals of justice and freedom were still passionately defended and variously interpreted. There were local gains, too, in the loss of supremacy by any one great power. Outside Sparta and Athens, citizens of other Greek communities once again became prominent.

Culturally, the concentration of thought, theatre and the arts in one great city, Athens, was weakened when her power and finances ceased to be exceptional after 404 BC. Perhaps half of her male citizenry was dead (down to around 25,000 by 403 BC, not the 50,000 or more of the 440s), but her cultural legacy did not die too. Beyond Athens, it continued to spread because it was still the 'education of Greece', as Pericles had called it. Sculptors who had worked on the great building-programme of the Athenian Acropolis migrated to dynastic patrons elsewhere and took their tricks of the trade with them. Upper-class houses in Attica had been decorated with fine wall paintings but, as their patrons went into eclipse, a new school of painters emerged in their wake in Sicyon, a Peloponnesian town which had been out of the limelight for nearly two centuries. Theatres, an Athenian invention, were to be found all over the Greek world and would stage the recent Athenian masterpieces as part of their repertoire. Admiration for the top actors would be shared by the new dynasts of the age, the rulers in Sicily and the kings up in Macedon.

There were also new centres of success and prosperity. In the north of Greece, on the Chalcidic peninsula (near modern Mount Athos), a powerful League began to prosper around its leader, Olynthus, the city whose town plan and levels of comfort and luxury are the best known to us in Greek history: King Philip, father of Alexander the Great, flattened the city in 348 BC, thereby preserving it for archaeologists as a Greek precursor of Pompeii. Like many other towns in the Greek world, it was laid out on a formally planned pattern. A regular grid-plan with regular blocks of houses was not an Athenian invention, nor was it necessarily the creation or reflection of a democracy: it had existed in western Greek cities like Selinus or Metapontum since the mid-sixth century. At Olynthus, it originated in the 430s, but it may have owed something to a recent innovator from whom Athens, too, had recently benefited. In the 440s and 430s areas behind the Athenians' port, the Piraeus, had been redesigned: the *agora* there, especially, had been devised by the flamboyant Hippodamus, a visitor from Miletus. Hippodamus was a theorist, a social utopian and a planner who believed in 'zones' and divisions in a city's layout; he was invited to work on the town plan of the Athens-led settlement out at Thurii in 443 BC. He could be particularly influential because he wrote a text on his theories. Certainly, archaeologists have uncovered a regular grid-plan on Rhodes where Hippodamus is said to have worked. Such plans did go on to characterize many fourth-century cities: one is most evident at little Priene in western Asia which was refounded in the 340s and 330s. Hippodamus' work for Athens was probably important for their adoption, especially if his 'book' discussed the principles: Athens was not, however, responsible for their wider adoption.

The ending of the Athenians' empire also diluted Athens' attraction for visiting intellectuals. Here too she was important, but no longer central.

19. Gravestone
of Sosias and
Kephisodorus:
two citizen-hoplites
shake hands; a man
in a priestly tunic at
left. Athens, *c.* 410 BC.

While Plato, mostly in Athens, idealized the recent advances in maths, the
greatest mathematician and astronomer arose in a town which had been a
backwater, Eudoxus from Cnidus in Asia Minor. In Athens itself, the most
popular options were rhetoric, the art of speaking and writing, or philosophy. For many years, pupils from all over the Greek world came to
Athens to study with the literary teacher Isocrates. However, his prose
style suffered from his detachment from active political life; even now his
works have a tediously predictable rhythm when analysed by computers.
Isocrates attacked his intellectual superiors, the philosophers who studied
with Plato. There was a real 'war' of higher education, but Plato, then
Aristotle, were the winners, as we shall see.

Politically, the major event of the first decades of the fourth century
was the renewal of brutal dominance by the Spartans, to be followed by
the welcome collapse of their main power-base. At the end of the fifth
century, Lysander the Spartan had already posed severe questions about
the scope for an individual's pre-eminence in the Spartans' so-called peer
group. He had challenged the system's opposition to luxury and the import of foreign riches: it was in connection with Spartan ideals that the

enfeebling effects of 'luxury' were most widely discussed in this period. 'Softness' and personal extravagance were seen as social vices in the eyes of contemporary moralists. They characterized despots (the princes of the kingdoms on Cyprus were particularly 'bad' examples) and undermined hardy warrior societies (the weaknesses of the fourth-century Persian Empire were therefore traced rather superficially to 'luxury').

Through the spoils and victories of the late fifth century, hundreds of silver talents arrived into a Sparta whose ideals were still strongly opposed to incorporating them. Other hoards of silver were detained, or directed, by Lysander himself. Lysander did not succumb to luxury personally; rather, he was a masterly briber and corrupter of others. From 406 BC he devised his own shocking versions of 'freedom' and 'justice' for Greek communities. They involved the subjection of whole cities to decarchies, or cliques of ten men who were fiercely pro-Spartan and anti-democratic. The result was an 'uncountable slaughter of populist democrats in the cities': what would Lysander do to a defeated Athens? It was said that he proposed the enslavement of the entire population, while a Theban, the hateful Erianthus, even demanded that Athens should be dug up and Attica turned into a sheep-farm. Both Thebes and Corinth pressed for Athens' destruction.

In the last years of the great war, Sparta had been assisted from 407 BC onwards by a Persian prince, the young Cyrus. No sooner was the war ended than she had to help this Cyrus in an outright attempt at fratricide, his campaign to murder his brother Artaxerxes, the legitimate new king of the Persians. Cyrus failed and was killed in Mesopotamia in autumn 401, while charging into battle on his hard-mouthed horse Pasakas. As a result, Sparta was regarded as the prime Greek enemy by the surviving Persian king. She soon had problems, too, in Greece. In 403 Sparta had finally agreed terms with the surviving Athenian democrats, but her continued dominance quickly alienated the Corinthians and the Thebans. So they began a war against her in alliance with the very Athenians whom the two of them had recently tried to annihilate; the allies were helped with ships and money by the anti-Spartan Persian king. At least this war killed off Lysander, who died in battle in late summer 395 in central Greece. His ambitions had scared even his fellow Spartans. After his death his supposed plans for reforming Sparta's kingship were said to have been found in his house. They were too persuasive, it was said, for their finder, King Agesilaus, to dare to read them out, so they were destroyed. This riveting story had implications for all parties who were involved in it.[1]

In this renewed war, the Athenians depended on the crucial support of the Persian king, but as their fortunes revived they began to trouble his territories in Asia too. In the late 390s the Athenians began to play for very high stakes: they assisted rebels on Cyprus and in Egypt as if to repeat the ambitions in Asia which they had held in their heyday in the 450s. To regain Persian favour, the Spartans agreed to turn Cyprus and the Greek cities in Asia back to the Persian king: the result was a Spartan–Persian agreement, the motive for the more general 'King's Peace' of 386 BC. After this grave betrayal of Greek freedom, the Spartans set about a brutal abuse of the principle of 'autonomy' which had been offered in the King's peace-terms in Greece. 'Autonomy' was a sort of freedom, but as always, a freedom within limits: it still presupposed an external power strong enough to infringe it. The Spartans promptly lived up to this definition. They broke up the city of their unreliable Arcadian neighbours, the Mantineans, while claiming that 'autonomy' required it to be split into villages.

During the next fifteen years the wisdom of the great historians was proved right. Herodotus' old belief in 'pride before a fall' was promptly confirmed by Sparta's eclipse, as was Thucydides' shrewd perception that in inter-state relations, 'justice' is the plea of the weak when they lack the power to enforce their own interest. Despite the King's Peace of 386, the Spartans condoned gratuitous raids on Thebes and Athens. They also went northwards, by request, on an expedition to restore the endangered king of the Macedonians. Each move would return to haunt them. In 379 the Thebans threw out the garrison which the Spartans had imposed on them and turned democratic and fiercely anti-Spartan instead. By spring 377 the weakened Athenians were pleading justice and inviting Greek allies to join a new anti-Spartan 'Confederacy' which would avoid the perceived grievances of the Athenians' years of 'Empire'. The 'Confederacy' was a great success, and within two years more than seventy allies had joined it. As for the Macedonian king, his rule was restored, thanks to Sparta, but forty years later, first King Philip of Macedon, then Alexander the Great would be explicitly anti-Spartan; their diplomacy and campaigning would isolate Sparta even more in Greece. With hindsight, the Spartans ought to have ignored the Macedonians' pleas.

No city-state in Greece wanted war for war's sake, and the Spartans' dominance caused their own downfall. A raid on the Piraeus had outraged Athens in the 370s and Spartan troops continued, too, to challenge a hostile Thebes, who was expanding meanwhile within her own confederacy of neighbours. In 371 the turning point came. After trying to stop the Thebans' local expansion yet again, the Spartans lost a cardinal land battle at Leuctra against a deeply packed Theban line. Their king was caught with his cavalry in front of his infantry, condemning the Spartans to their worst ever defeat. People said later that the gods and omens had been against Sparta and that the battle had been fought near a site where Spartan soldiers had raped young virgin sisters in the legendary past.[2] If so, the rape victims took a fine revenge.

The consequences were pursued immediately by citizens in the southern Greek communities which Sparta had terrorized for centuries. In winter 370 the able Theban general Epaminondas was invited across the Isthmus and was able to realize the long-held dream of Sparta's enemies by invading the Spartan homeland itself. Two great goods came out of Sparta's defeat. The Messenians, their Greek neighbours, could at last regroup themselves as a free Greek community, a status which they had been denied for some three hundred and fifty years. Their days of serfdom, or helotage, were over and to emphasize it they built stupendous defensive walls, assets which Spartans had always detested. The Arcadians, meanwhile, resolved on the building of a new 'Great City' (Megalopolis) into which the surrounding villages were forcibly merged. There were local protesters, but the 'Great City' became the centre of another long-held dream, an 'Arcadian League'. The Arcadians had been seeking one for at least a hundred and fifty years. The separate towns of Arcadia were all to join it, although local rivalries and factions beset its foundation. The League was to have a big Assembly (the 'Myriad', probably including all male Arcadian citizens); Arcadian oligarchs, so long supported by Sparta, were most unhappy with it. For six years the League was a democratic force, maintaining a big army (the 'Select') from its member-cities' funds. After 370 Spartan power was severely damaged by it, to the greater freedom and justice of most of her long-suffering Greek neighbours.

Fittingly, Epaminondas was commemorated in the Arcadia which he had helped to free. It was there that his tomb was admired by the Emperor Hadrian on his tour through southern Greece. Near Mantinea, Hadrian saw a pillar engraved with a serpent and learned that it honoured Epaminondas' noble family: he was descended from the legendary sons of the dragon's teeth with which Thebes' mythical founder, Cadmus, was supposed to have sown the city's fields. No doubt the boy-loving Hadrian also appreciated the nearby tomb: it commemorated Epaminondas' boy-lover. Perhaps he also discovered that Epaminondas' victories had been helped by a famous homoerotic unit, the Thebans' 'Sacred Band' of 300 infantry-men who were bound together by homoerotic pairing. The merits of 'gays in the army' had been discussed by Greeks at least since the time of Socrates.[3] They had also been exemplified individually in the Spartans' own ranks. But the Sacred Band made sex between males a necessity.

What Hadrian did not understand was that the Thebans and Epaminondas were not the ideal champions whom Greek freedom and justice might have hoped for. The Thebans were not allowed by other Greeks to forget that their ancestors had cravenly taken the Persian side in the invasion of 480 BC. On their own doorstep, they had recently de-stroyed one Greek city (Plataea, in 373) and then damaged three more, all within her Confederacy. They were hardly more palatable to the Atheni-ans than the old enemy, the Spartans, and they had the disadvantage of being much nearer to the Athenian frontier. After much hesitation, the Athenians set aside old prejudice, allied themselves with Sparta in 369 BC and used this alliance as a counterweight to the Thebans throughout the 360s. Their rivalry was played out in the north (including Macedon, a source of ship-timber), the Aegean (where a Theban fleet tried to support oligarchic opposition to Athens) and in southern Greece. In 362 a big bat-tle at Mantinea saw Epaminondas' death and no clear-cut winner, leaving 'confusion and indecision' in Greek affairs.[4]

These decades may seem a melancholy failure, in which Greeks could not unite despite their awareness of their shared gods, their shared language and a common ethnicity. Yet there were valid obsta-cles to unity, and the urge for peace was not gone. Repeatedly, settle-ments of Greek affairs were attempted, at first with the backing of the Persian king. The king, Artaxerxes II, had his own reasons for wanting peace: he needed Greeks to be free to serve him as mercenaries in his attempts to reconquer rebellious Egypt. When the king's proposals be-came too partisan, there were attempts at forming a 'Common Peace' among Greeks without him. There was also a continuing faith in arbi-tration as a solution to Greek communities' long-standing disputes. However, valuable territory was often at issue in these conflicts, as was the greater freedom (for male citizens) of a democratic life. For democ-racy shared financial burdens more equitably between citizens: it meant that all male citizens were consulted before being committed to a war. Under an oligarchy the laws might be said to be 'equal' for all citizens, but under a democracy, they were more likely to be equitably applied. When the Spartans' oligarchic stranglehold broke up in southern

Greece, democracy was realized in Arcadia, offered in Achaea and feared once again in Corinth. There was no question of it being discredited or in retreat in the fourth century. Political theorists did discuss the merits of a 'mixed' constitution, as if elements of an aristocracy, an oligarchy and a democracy could somehow be blended into the best of all three. These theories were quite impractical (a state is either completely democratic, or not at all) and made no mark on real life. True democracy still aroused the strongest political passions among actual citizen-bodies. In Argos in the 370s, existing democrats indulged in a fearful act of 'Clubbing' during which they attacked the rich in the city and left 1,200 citizens dead in civil conflict. Nearly a hundred and fifty years after Cleisthenes had proposed democracy in order to avoid renewed faction-fighting, democracy was being propelled by open conflict between classes. For in this period there was a real class-struggle within the citizen-bodies. It was not a struggle between citizens and slaves. It was one between poor citizens and the rich. Poorer citizens used democracy against the rich, but a real desire for justice impelled these fights, not just greed or simple revenge.

Among such mayhem, respect for the gods might seem to be on the wane. In the fourth century Greek sculptors took the bold step of representing goddesses as topless or naked females; oaths were broken bewilderingly on the inter-state stage. After so much theatre about the mythical past, were the myths really so believable? But in fact, the traditional gods were still assumed to be as active in the fray as ever. They received vows and sacrifices before battle, and afterwards they still took a share of the spoils. Far and wide they still gave oracles, even though the Delphic shrine of Apollo had been ruined by fire and earthquake in 373 BC. There was not a growing disbelief; there was flexibility, as ever, in manoeuvring human actions and decisions within their divine framework. As ever, omens from the gods were variously interpreted and although the festival-seasons were often a time of truce, it was nothing new when they were exploited by Greek generals. A temple's treasures were supposed to be sacrosanct, but nonetheless they could be 'borrowed' on loan to finance a war, just as Periclean Athens had 'borrowed' from the goddess Athena to finance the great war. None of this casuistry was a new godlessness: rather, it presupposed that the old divine framework was still valid. So far from becoming pretty legends, the myths and the distant heroes continued to be advanced as compelling diplomatic claims and as sound reasons for alliances between Greek states.

To an outside eye, what changed most from the 370s on was the apparent eclipsing of a single *polis*, or community, as the focus of political life. For, on the surface, these decades appear to be an era of Leagues and Confederacies, something which Hadrian would have understood, as he later promoted Leagues again in Greece. Before and after Leuctra the Spartans relied on the support of their 'Peloponnesian alliance' whose members were mostly ruled by convenient oligarchies. From 377 onwards the Athenians led their large new Confederacy of allies against Sparta. In the 370s the Thebans managed to dominate the votes on the inner council of the long-proven Boeotian Confederacy; in the 360s they perhaps imitated the Athenians and began a new 'League' for their allies outside Boeotia. The Spartans' decline in the 360s led to the new League in Arcadia and also to other confederacies in Achaea and Aetolia; the longer-standing Leagues in Thessaly and even in Epirus in north-west Greece become visible or more prominent in our evidence. Together, these Leagues refute the temptation to see this era as a proof of the menace of little warring Greek city-states. As genuine confederacies, most of these alliances were made up of a central decision-making body and separate decision-making communities. In Arcadia, the Assembly of the 'Myriad' met in its special building (the 'Thersilion') and chose magistrates from the member-communities who, initially, paid the costs of the League's 'Select' military force. Athenians, by contrast, discussed or voted on proposals which were passed to their existing city-assembly by a separate 'parliament', made up of delegates from their allies. The representative councils of these confederacies were all rather different from the democratic practice of one vote, one adult male in a single city-assembly.

Nonetheless, they were not superstates which marked the end of the *polis* as a political unit. Like the Athenian assembly, the assemblies of the Arcadian or Boeotian member-cities continued to meet and take decisions too. They continued to fear internal faction or the attack of a fellow confederate member, not least one by the ever-aggressive Thebans. The same mainstays of Greek political life continued vigorously: civic oaths and civic magistracies, debates about new citizens and debates about financial contributions to be paid by individuals. In 363, after only six years of existence, the unity of the Arcadian League fractured on the decision of some of its magistrates to pay the League army by 'borrowing' funds from Olympia, rather than by exacting payments from the member-states.

Through the ancients' own narrative histories, we continue to know this era for the names of famous individuals, Epaminondas the Theban or Jason the Thessalian (active there until 370 BC) or Agesilaus the Spartan king. But it is quite wrong to see these men as signs of a new age of individualism. Each of them held office in their home communities and remained locally accountable to them. 'Community' was not breaking down before a drift into superstates or a new era of great men. The struggle, at bottom, was still about freedom and justice and their interpretation, without an Athens rich enough to support the majority view or a Sparta strong enough to suppress it in her own interest.

WOMEN AND CHILDREN

When a woman's womb moves up towards her head and suffocation oc-curs there, her head becomes heavy . . . One symptom is that the woman says that the veins in her nose and beneath her eyes are hurting her and she becomes sleepy and when this condition is improved, she foams at the mouth.

You should wash her all over with hot water and if she does not im-prove, with cold . . . Rub her head with the scent of roses and use sweet-scented fumigations beneath her vagina, but foully scented ones at her nose. She should eat cabbage and drink cabbage-juice.

Hippocratic doctor, *Diseases of Women* 2.126 (fourth century BC)

When a husband and wife are at odds with one another, they are much more likely to be reconciled for the sake of their children than to detest the children they have had together because of the wrongs they have done to one another.

Demosthenes, speech against Boeotus, 39.23 (348 BC)

WOMEN AND CHILDREN were not exempted from the wars in the fourth-century Greek world. When their city was taken by siege, their fate was to be killed or sold into slavery. There was no mercy during an invasion for non-combatants, either. In 364 BC the Thebans simply en-slaved and sold all the women and children whom they captured in little Orchomenus. We can well see why city-states would try to send off their women and children (and livestock) to a place of safety during war: in 431 BC, the Plataeans evacuated their women, children and non-combatants to Athens before the siege which is so vividly described by Thucydides.

20. A baby learns to crawl as its parents, surely, look on. Athenian red-figure jug, *pelike, c.* 430–420 BC.

Spartans apart, a love of children and an affectionate family life were prominent, in my view, in Greek city-states. Extreme modern theories that parental calculation prevailed and that there was a reluctance to invest love in children who were so likely to die young are refuted by the images, texts and dramas of our best sources, those from fifth- and fourth-century Athens. Representations of a child and a parent are shown (admittedly, rarely) on painted Attic pottery from the late fifth century BC onwards. There is a loving poignancy to many of the Attic grave-reliefs and the inscriptions for children who have died young. It is hard to miss the force of the painting on a white-figured Athenian oil flask, to be set at the tomb, which shows pathos and parental love in its scene of a young child in the boat of the waiting ferryman of the underworld, the child holding out its hands to a fondly gazing mother on the far bank.[1] There are images of a mother looking on at a young baby wriggling happily in its high chair or of a child crawling towards its mother, watched (in my view, with pleasure) by a man, surely its father, as it sets off on its course. These scenes, and others, imply a public who enjoyed children. They were not only mothers: fathers are represented too, never better than in the character-sketches of the wry philosopher Theophrastus of Athens, who describes how the 'obsequious man' is a man who plays excessively with other people's children, while the 'talkative man' is so endlessly talkative that his children, even, will call to him to come at bedtime and talk to them so that they will fall asleep. Of course individuals varied, as nowadays. When Aristophanes represents Dicaeopolis, his cussed rustic of an Athenian, taking a sexual interest in his own daughter, he is meaning that we should laugh at the man's ghastliness. Publicly, too, fathers were expected to be much more than unloving absentees. The orator Aeschines could attack the orator Demosthenes before an Athenian jury for his supposed callousness about his daughter's death: 'the man who hates children,' he goes on, 'the bad father, would never be a trustworthy leader of the people.'[2] There were assumptions, here, which an orator could exploit.

In Athenian citizen-households, the father decided if a new-born child was to live: he would run round the hearth carrying it on the fifth day of its life, in a ceremony called the Amphidromia. On the tenth day the child would usually be named. Aristotle remarks that parents waited for ten days because so many children died meanwhile. Modern estimates of the average losses tend to be high, as high as half of all babies born. Nonetheless, in some Greek states (but not all), exposure of unwanted children was freely practised. The exposed ones might sometimes be picked up by others and brought up as slaves, and so cast-offs tended to be exposed in public places, as if hoping to be 'found': girls were more frequently exposed than boys.

Like other social transitions, the stages of an Athenian child's life can be attached to Athenian festivals. In their third year, children attended a day of February's Anthesteria festival. They had their first taste of wine, and we still have some of the drinking-mugs, with children shown on them, which marked the occasion. For citizen-born boys, the focus then became the autumn festival of the phratries, or 'brotherhoods', which would enrol them in due course as citizens. Fathers would take them along to be introduced to members (and to show that they were legitimate, not sons by a slave-girl). There would be a sacrifice, called the 'lesser', when the boy was perhaps only five or six, and then one for the cutting of his hair, when the boy was eighteen and old enough to be a full citizen. Contacts with the phratry were therefore spread out across the boy's years of change in childhood.

Bastards, obviously, were known to pose problems, of which children born to two citizens out of wedlock were the least. If the mother was mar-

21. White-ground oil-flask, showing a female, playing as a Muse, captioned with the word 'Helicon', signifying the muses' mountain. Achilles painter, *c.* 440–430 BC.

ried to somebody else, she would probably pass off such a child as her husband's; if not, she would abort it. In a slave-society, however, masters or their sons were also quite likely to father a child on a slave-girl; if the child was not aborted, it would be left to follow its mother's status and be a slave. The complications were greater if a citizen-male fathered a child on a metic or non-citizen foreigner. If the mother was a prostitute, she would be expected to abort it (it would ruin her future livelihood). Otherwise, the child would surely become a metic too. For bastards, with one citizen-parent, were not members of a phratry nor were they eligible for Athenian citizenship. They are said, however, to have had a particular 'gym' for their exercise, connected with the shrine of Heracles at Cynosarges outside the city-gate. Comic poets made fun of this site and have probably complicated our evidence for it. Heracles was a 'bastard', too, fathered by Zeus on a mortal mother.[3]

Whether bastards or not, girls were not presented to phratries: they would never be full citizens. A few of them, however, could look forward to a role as a servant of the gods. Here, the most prestigious were the *arrhephoroi*, up to four citizen-born girls between the ages of seven and eleven who lived on the Acropolis, served the civic goddess Athena and probably helped to weave her great ceremonial robe. Ritually, the girls played at ball and then went to and fro with mysterious baskets on their heads to a shrine of Aphrodite in the garden below, approached by a tunnel. This rite was only for a very few, whereas all young girls of citizen-birth (probably) engaged for a while in a splendid rite of transition known as the *arkteia*. Between the ages of five and ten, they would play at being 'bears', possibly to symbolize their wild immature nature, which was to be tamed in due course by men and marriage. Little cups, dedicated to Artemis, give us an impression of this ritual: the young girls are shown running naked, while a bear is sketched too. A main centre of the rite was Artemis' temple at Brauron in east Attica, the site which has left us the visual evidence, although the details are so uncertain.

Four or five years after playing at 'bears' Athenian girls would be married. Girls were not formally educated in schools (in the classical period, at least) and any reading which they picked up would be learned in a household, from mothers (perhaps) or, in richer households, from literate slaves: girls might go to each other's houses for the sake of it. Boys, however, would be educated, usually beginning at seven and going on at least to fourteen; their teaching included writing, reading (including the reading of poets) and music and athletics. The city-state did not provide teachers, but small fee-paying schools were probably a familiar feature throughout Attica. Richer families maintained slave-tutors too. In due course, young men would marry, but marriage for men tends to be recommended at quite a late age, between twenty-five and thirty. Until then, young men could satisfy their hormones by using slave-prostitutes, who charged all sorts of prices (a woman bending over is implied, in a comic scene, to be the cheapest position, whereas a 'woman on top' was the most expensive[4]). They could try slave-girls in their father's households, or a more permanent slave-courtesan (or a share in one); they also had one another. On painted pottery the dominant image of male sex is still sex between an older man and a young, scarcely pubertal boy. The implication is that boys would first submit to male sex, but then grow up and do it to others. But male sex between boys of the same age was surely also frequent.

For Athenian citizen-women, who married young, life in a well-off household was sheltered and protected. The '*polis*-males' had their 'men's room' for their drinking-parties; women had their 'women's quarters' where they spent much time with the children and female slaves. Certainly, nothing had relaxed for Athenian women in the fourth century. They were still under the guardianship of their nearest male relative (their important *kyrios*) throughout their lives; their marriages and remarriages were governed by strict rules of family inheritance, while their economic dealings were limited to contracts up to the simple value of a bushel of barley. In my view (and that of some arguable ancient sources), they could attend the theatre-festivals, but they were never actresses playing the female parts.

However, women in Attica were a broad and varied category. There were not just the many widowed and remarried women: divorce was possible, both for the male and female partner. There was also the majority of citizen-wives, the poor who had to work. Inside their houses, respectable Athenian women would engage in spinning wool or supervise the wet-nurse to whom many of them handed their babies. They would often wear a veil, a thin one, to judge from the many Greek words for such a covering, although the veil could be pulled up or to one side. In the lower classes, however, women worked outside, came out onto the streets and were not confined.

Beside the citizens, too, there was the world of the *hetaira*, or courtesan. It is not one to be romanticized, as *hetairai* were usually slaves. From around 340 BC we have our single most vivid insight into its undergrowth, a speech delivered to an Athenian jury against the activities and family of a former practitioner, Neaera. It shows us how men might buy shares in a *hetaira* and use her by turns (*hetairai* were mostly slaves); similar contracts were also struck for young rent-boys. We should enjoy, but discount, the speech's more disreputable stories, especially the one about group sex at a dinner-party in a temple-sanctuary in south-east Attica. The more important items of the context are that the Athenian speaker names Neaera openly (a good Athenian wife was always the 'wife of . . . ', in speech) and that this extremely twisted and manipulated case was being brought against a woman who was well over fifty years old and bore no resemblance to the unbridled 'tart' of its innuendoes. It was all a male prosecutor's attempt to humiliate a political male rival who was associated with her.

Even in fourth-century Athens, we have no first-hand surviving evidence of conversations between husband and wife. Like children, wives were certainly loved by Athenian husbands, and the more scandalous *demi-monde* which is evoked against Neaera must not be taken as the norm. Other sources tell us how it was bad form to frequent 'courtesans' when married, let alone to keep one in the matrimonial home. What we do not know is the tone of male–female relations in Athenian households: were upper-class wives really so submissive as idealizing male texts imply?

22. The 'Lady in Blue', one of five painted terra-cotta 'Tanagra' figurines from a tomb just north of Tanagra, central Greece. The lady with her fan, robe and covered head is perhaps a courtesan. *c.* 330–300 BC.

There is also the problem of how typical these women were of other Greek city-states, except for the contrarian Spartans. At Locris, in south Italy, women were said to have held real power and to have passed inheritances down the female line (in my view, this ancient 'mirage' is most unlikely). In the mid-third century BC a traveller in Greece describes how women at Thebes were veiled, so much so that only their eyes were visible: we even have examples of this attire, in a few of the terracotta figurines of women, known as 'Tanagras', some of which were found at Thebes.[5] Had a similar style been imposed on women by the male 'Boeotian pigs' (the Athenians' name for them) already in the fourth century BC? The Athenians' strict insistence on a citizen's birth from two citizen-born parents was very important for their sense of cohesion and civic identity, but it, too, was not the norm in most other Greek city-states. Up in the north of

Greece, there are mothers who look even less 'Athenian'. In the Molossian kingdom in Epirus, two fourth-century decrees actually bestow citizenship on a woman: perhaps a monarchy had different criteria.[6] In its neighbour, the Macedonian kingdom, the relations of wives, husbands and children had a much more dramatic character.

The Macedonian kings were polygamous and, as we shall see, their history would be coloured for centuries by the consequences. In the 390s the ruling king, Amyntas III, took a second wife, Eurydice. She was alleged, at least, to have attempted to kill her husband and to have cohabited with her own daughter's husband. She was also credited with killing two of her three sons.[7] These extreme stories do at least point to the potential tensions in a polygamous royal family, whether all, part or none of them is justified. But her third son, certainly, lived in the world in which they circulated. He was Philip, the future king of Macedon and father of Alexander. Family tensions were as much a part of his formation as of his son's, and they were carried to most un-Athenian lengths, matched only on the Athenians' tragic stage.

PHILIP OF MACEDON

Philip despised those who were of an orderly character and took care of their own property, but he praised and honoured those who were extravagant and spent their lives in playing dice and drinking . . . Were not some of them shaven and smooth-skinned even when they were adult men, while others dared to mount one another and have sex even though they had beards? They used to take around two or three male prostitutes each, and themselves give the same services to others. Justly, then, would someone suppose them to be 'courtesans' not 'court-Companions' . . .

Theopompus F225 B (Jacoby), after his time at Philip's Pella

DOWN TO THE 350s there were many changes in inter-state relations in Greece, but no great surprise emerged from an unforeseen corner. Within twenty years, however, the freedom of the Greeks would have a new master, a king of Macedon, who ruled beyond Mount Olympus in the north of Greece. The unexpected dominance of Macedon would far exceed that of Periclean Athens and would persist for more than a hundred and seventy years.

Its beginnings were most inauspicious. Its founder, Philip, entered the stage aged twenty or so as the regent for an even younger prince. His elder brother had been killed in battle (not, as rumour said, by his mother) and his kingdom was being overrun by barbarians from the north-west. Greek city-states to the south had seen it all before: murders in the Macedonian royal family, a disputed succession to the throne, oaths sworn and broken by harassed kings. There had been brief flashes of power, but during more than two centuries not a single king of Macedon had died peacefully in old age. Nonetheless, after more than twenty years in power, the new Macedonian leader, King Philip, could now marshal a highly trained army, including many Thessalians and other Greeks, and win a decisive victory over the major Greek city-states, including Athens. By 338 BC his power extended from the river Danube to southern Greece. He then imposed a highly restrictive peace on his Greek 'allies'. He even began an invasion of the Persian Empire. His making of a new Macedon was antiquity's most rapid and remarkable feat of power-building.

In the fourth century BC Macedon centred on a lowland palace and capital, Pella, but it was a patchwork of little kingdoms whose own ruling houses had at times followed their own line. Hostile Greeks to the south had sometimes called its kings 'barbarian' and the 'Macedonian speech' of its ordinary people was very difficult for many southern Greeks to understand. The 'Macedonians' did sometimes distinguish themselves, even in official lists, from 'Hellenes'.[1] However, the royal house claimed descent from Argos and traced back their arrival to *c.* 650 BC, as if they had fled north from the coming age of tyrants and hoplite warfare in Greece. That claim is rather dubious, but in *c.* 500 BC their king Alexander I had been allowed, after careful screening, to compete in the Olympic Games, which were confined to Greeks only. What, then, was the truth? Were Macedonians Greeks?

In the past thirty years, ever more evidence has been found of Macedonians' patronage of fine Greek arts and crafts. Texts had already told us how their fifth-century kings had settled Greek exiles in their kingdom. They also patronized great Greek poets like Pindar and Euripides and hired the great painters of the day: we can now add the master-sculptor, Callimachus, to the list after recent archaeological finds. Certainly, the Macedonian kings and courtiers wished to be seen as Greeks. Patronage does not make a patron into a Greek, but there has also been renewed study of Macedonian personal names, the month-names in the Macedonian calendar, and some of the odd words preserved from 'Macedonian dialect'. A growing number of personal inscriptions have been found in fourth-century contexts; they begin to allow us to connect the 'Macedonian dialect' to the Greek which was current in north-western Greece. One of the earliest Greek inscriptions in Macedon, recently found, is a curse written for or by a woman at Pella who invokes the gods against that perpetual human phenomenon, a man who had proved to be a love-rat.[2]

The 'perceived common ancestor' of the kingdom was the legendary Makedon whom Greek genealogy accepted as a son of the Greek god Zeus. At their original capital and dynastic centre, Aigai (modern Vergina), the kings even held local Olympics, a festival in honour of Zeus. Near their kingdom's southern border at Dion they held a musical and

23. Wall painting from the earliest tomb excavated under the Great Mound at Vergina (Aigai), the Macedonian dynastic centre: the god Pluto abducts Persephone to the underworld, *c.* 340 BC.

cultural festival for the Muses.[3] Within the kingdoms, even the kings had sometimes intermarried with non-Greek 'barbarians': Philip's own mother is said, perhaps rightly, to have been one. But the dominant culture and language of the kings and their nobles was certainly Greek.

Philip's own upbringing had a double element. As a young man he was sent as a hostage to Thebes, the dominant military power in Greek affairs. A leading Theban general is said to have been his male lover. Yet Philip also spent time as a hostage in barbarian Illyria. He himself favoured Greek artists, actors and orators, although his mother is said to have learned to read and write only in middle age; we have recently found Greek inscriptions, beautifully carved in her name, at the Macedonians' dynastic centre, Aigai. But Philip also kept company with barbarian kings and allies, people who responded to extravagant shows of prowess and generosity. In this company, it was customary to reward a barbarian ally who cut off an enemy's head in battle with the gift of a gold cup: 'heads for cups' had never been the classical Greek way.[4] Some of Macedon's own traditions were also decidedly primitive. In the past, a man could not wear a belt unless he had killed an enemy in battle. In Philip's day, he could not recline at dinner until he had killed a wild boar while out hunting. Like previous kings, but unlike contemporary Greeks, Philip was polygamous. Within three years, he had four 'wives' in his palace and ended up with seven, three of whom were non-Greek barbarians. One of them, Audata, became famous as a warrior in battle and taught martial arts to her brave daughter Cynnane. Philip played one wife off against another, much as, publicly, he played off the major Greek powers. His final infatuation, the young Macedonian Cleopatra (also called Eurydice), split the royal family and arguably cost Philip his life. The sensational finds of painted tombs in the royal burial ground at Aigai include a double royal tomb, certainly Philip's, in which his cremated remains and a young woman's, perhaps queen Cleopatra's, were laid. Greek outsiders, including the historian Theopompus, a contemporary visitor, told lurid stories of revenge about this burial ground: in the recently found tombs, we now have the basis of fact from which these unchecked rumours developed.

The self-image of the kings and nobles was Greek, but they could also distinguish themselves as 'Macedonians', a view which their successes strengthened. Ambassadors from all over Greece came increasingly to Philip's Pella and the Athenian delegates did recognize his exceptional style. By then Philip had lost an eye during a siege, one of the many wounds, including broken collarbones, which his strong physique survived in twenty years. Yet his Athenian visitors remarked on his handsome looks, his excellent memory, his hospitality and his talent at his drinking-sessions. Philip had an educated charm, combined with great bravery in battle and an impulsive generosity. They were apt gifts for a court-life which retained its wilder side. It was probably in Macedon that the poet Euripides had written his dramatic masterpiece, the *Bacchae*, on the god Dionysus. At court, the staging of this tragedy must have had a raw resonance, not least because Philip's main wife, Olympias, was said to handle live snakes (we now have evidence of local women worshipping Dionysus, implied by a leaf of gold, inscribed with a girl's name and buried with her at Pella).[5] At dinner, Philip was also said to toast his guests with wine in great drinking-horns, which were probably modelled on the horns of oxen from the European steppes. There were also tales of women dancing on the table, whips and unsavoury Greek exiles urging on the evening's revelry.

Publicly, Philip was favoured by the difficulties of his elderly neighbours. The ageing barbarian kings around him opted for peace with him and then bequeathed divided kingdoms to their weakened heirs: Philip could conquer these heirs one by one. First in Thessaly, then in central Greece, Philip was also invited south to take sides in the political divisions of Greek communities. In his first three years he followed the traditional ambitions of previous Macedonian kings, as befitted a young prince who was ruling as a regent among hardened older nobles. Then, in one magnificent year (356 BC), he became father to a son (Alexander), routed a coalition of barbarian enemies and captured a nearby Greek city-state (Potidaea). He also won a prestigious victory with his racehorse at the Olympic Games, and signalled his own status by striking silver coins showing himself with a hand upraised, on horseback. He even founded a new town, named after himself, the famous Philippi beside the river Nestus to which he had advanced Macedon's eastern frontier.

Further conflicts in Greece then brought him into central Greece and to the symbolic 'rescue' of the threatened Delphic oracle. Here, Philip profited by invitations from Greeks with wars of their own. After a rebuff in nearby Euboea in 357 BC the Thebans had started a gratuitous war against the local Phocians who were long-standing friends of Athens. When the Phocians resisted and borrowed treasure from Delphi, the Thebans labelled them 'temple-robbers' and gained Thessaly, an old enemy of Phocis, as an ally in a war on 'sacrilege'. Having started the war the Thebans could not finish it. They ended by inviting their former hostage, King Philip, to come south and help them out. The request was to prove disastrous for Greek freedom. In spring 352 BC Philip's victories in central Greece won him immense support from Thessaly's traditionalists who even appointed him 'ruler' of their League: Thessaly's revenues were at his disposal, and the greatest gain was her cavalry, which numbered thousands. Fighting in their diamond-shaped formations, Thessalian cavalrymen would loyally follow Philip and his son Alexander, until Alexander dismissed them in 329 BC at the faraway river Oxus in central Asia.

Backed by Thessaly, Philip won a 'Sacred War' against Phocis' 'sacrilege', as if he was fighting on behalf of Apollo: Phocis' captive mercenaries were drowned in the sea, to mark them out as polluting enemies. In 346 Philip then swore a peace and alliance with the Athenians, while promising them vague 'benefits': realists in the city were not deceived. This peace should not be understood as Philip's intended base for a permanent settlement with the Greek city-states. Rather, it would contain affairs in Greece for him while he engaged on massive campaigns into barbarian Illyria (perhaps as far as modern Dubrovnik) and then into Thrace (modern Bulgaria), right up to the river Danube. Meanwhile, before the Greek city-states, his envoys continued to profess his willingness to heed their grievances; professions of 'friendship' and 'benefits' were classic weapons in Philip's diplomatic armoury. At the same time, from summer 343 to 341 approaches from discontented factions in Greek cities were rewarded with money, arms and even mercenaries. All the while Philip encouraged the notion that in southern Greece, he would curb the feared and hated Spartans. Sparta's neighbours, therefore, hesitated to join any opposition to him, because they feared a Spartan revival even more than this untried Macedonian 'ally'.

After major campaigns in Thrace on his eastern borders from 342 onwards, Philip was brought back into central Greece by local political quarrelling in 339/8. Alarmingly, his previous ally, the Thebans, had finally broken their alignment and turned to the Athenians; since 346 Philip's cautious retention of several forts near Thermopylae had helped to disillusion Theban opinion and in 340 his attack on a Theban ally, Byzantium, had hardened opinion against him. All along, a Theban–Athenian alliance was the outcome which Philip had feared. However, at the battle of Chaeronea, in August 338, he won his most famous victory, 'fatal to liberty', over the combined Theban and Athenian troops.

The diplomacy and conflicts of these years 348–338 have an enduring fascination and their consequences were a turning point for Greek civic life and its setting, Greek freedom. After his victory in 338 Philip ostentatiously respected Athens (the city still had the impregnable Long Walls) but was much harsher to Thebes. War was then declared on the Persian Empire which had been Philip's long-term aim at least since the late 350s. Supposedly, this war was to 'punish the Persian wrongs of 480', especially the burning of Athens' temples, and to 'free' the Greek cities in Asia. In 338/7, Philip imposed a peace and alliance, offering 'freedom', on his Greek allies prior to going east, although many of them were reluctant, or sceptical, about his true aims.

For his Asian campaign, Philip's publicity cleverly recalled the history of the great Panhellenic years from 478 to 465; he formed a second 'Hellenic Alliance' which was based, like its predecessor, at Corinth. This time, Sparta was excluded, much to the glee of her enemies in southern Greece. In their eyes, Philip's supervised 'freedom' was far preferable to the risk of a Spartan resurgence. From an Athenian viewpoint, this sort of local calculation was close to treachery. For Philip's Hellenic Alliance was far harsher than the one in the 470s which Athens had led by sea and Sparta by land. In the member-cities, changes to the political system and the radical menaces of a redistribution of land and an abolition of debts were strictly prohibited. A council of deputies was to arbitrate disputes

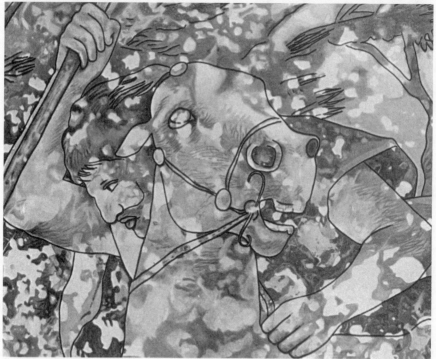

24. *(Top)* From the hunt-painting on the façade of the double royal tomb at Vergina, correctly ascribed to King Philip II. Details of rider identified as young Alexander.

25. *(Bottom)* Detail of the older King Philip, matching his own coin-portraits, as he attacks a lion with the young Royal Pages whom he instituted.

26. Reconstruction of a section of the hunt-painting on the tomb: young Alexander, after killing a boar, rides to the lion being attacked by King Philip and the Pages. Similar in style, perhaps the same artist, as Plate 34. 336/5 BC.

between member-states, thus enshrining in a sworn treaty the old Greek practice of public arbitration. But there were also to be people 'appointed for the common safety', a carefully vague euphemism for Philip's own men: probably, they were his generals and the army which he left in Greece.[6] Rebel states, meanwhile, were to be punished at the Macedonian leader's own whim.

Throughout, Philip's remarkable successes in Greece had owed much to bluff and promises, artfully dressed up as diplomacy. He addressed letters repeatedly to the Athenians which were full of vague promises, misleading self-justification and, eventually, tendentious history. Never before had one Greek state communicated so much to another by unsolicited communiqués. Behind the fine words, Philip increasingly had the greater manpower; he had widened Macedon's frontiers, and so he drew on the resources of a newly united kingdom whose military numbers were so much greater than that of the Athenians. He also multiplied the kingdom's horsepower by settling Macedonians, his future cavalrymen, on lush new pastures in the wetlands which he conquered on his eastern border. He even improved the strength of his warhorses by bringing new breeding-stock back to his kingdom's stables. By the end of his reign his cavalry (charging with long lances) numbered more than 5,000, more than five times greater than the numbers which are attested at its beginning. On his north-western and eastern borders, Philip also annexed accessible mines of gold and silver. Archaeologically, finds in Macedon are conspicuous even before Philip's reign for their quantity of gold objects, a luxury which far exceeds the gold found elsewhere in Greece. The new mines intensified this splendour and transformed the kingdom's economic base. Their effects were soon seen in Philip's superb coinage, as for the first time, gold pieces circulated from a Greek monarch. They proved to be one of Philip's lasting memorials: they lived on in second-hand copies among European barbarians and continued to be used long after his death as far west as Gaul.

Philip's other memorials were his new towns and his changes to the social and military order of the Macedonians. Various 'towns of Philip' were founded on the kingdom's borders, the forerunners of his son's Alexandrias. A cluster of them lay on river-sites in modern Bulgaria where Plovdiv still commemorates Philip's name. The new towns strengthened his frontiers and conquests, while new units, based on a new social order, bound his newly balanced army closer to the king. A large unit of 3,000 'Royal Shield-bearers', Philip's invention, linked a trained unit of 'Royal Foot Companions' to the enlarged Companion Cavalry who rode on the wings of the flexible army-line. These new titles of distinction honoured recruits in the royal service and although their units were still led by their local nobles, they were now trained and merged into a single royal force. The Foot Companions' symbol was the long pike, or *sarissa*, which was made from cornel wood and weighted with a butt-spike; held by two hands, it extended to a length of more than sixteen feet. Philip had plainly thought hard about military tactics and so he devised a new model army which was an unusually varied and balanced unity.

Remarkably, Philip bound this new army to himself as king without surrendering any of the monarchy's powers. Neighbouring kings, by contrast, had become restricted by fixed councils and magistrates; Philip remained an autocrat who was swept along by his success and his ability to make gifts and to bestow grants of conquered land on his soldiers. A Macedonian king had to be a man of prowess and achievement. His people were solidly loyal to monarchy (it lasted far longer than Athens' democracy), but at any time his nobles might well prefer another king for the job. Behind the charm and the diplomacy, Philip had to be a great warrior and a great hunter, a generous giver and a great drinker. These sides to a man were what formed a Macedonian leader and what the court admired. So Philip fought personally in the front line and after battle would lead a tireless pursuit on horseback against the enemy's fugitive leaders. His other known skills can even be illustrated now by archaeology. On the double royal tomb at Vergina, a superb painting shows scenes of hunting in which he, his young Royal Pages and (surely) Alexander attack a lion (lions still lived in and near his Macedon). Even the hunting-dogs are shown with terrifying jaws. Deer, bears and boar are all repre-sented as the Macedonians' prey, face to face. The superb ceremonial shield and couch in Philip's tomb-chamber were also decorated with vig-orous scenes of hunting on horseback. The grave-goods included a gold arrow-case of a type known in barbarian Scythia: it was a gift to Philip, no doubt, like the gifts he himself liked to give. An array of silver drinking-cups and big jugs and containers, often beautifully decorated, attest the prominence of bold drinking in the parties, on couches, in Philip's palace rooms.

Philip gained loyalty by excelling at all these arts. Within Macedon, he had advisers, especially his Companion nobles, but there was no formal 'constitution': within the kingdom, it was still he as king who dispensed personal justice, in answer to appeals and petitions. This pattern of per-sonal justice would become prominent in the next three centuries under succeeding monarchies; then it would be practised for more than five cen-turies by subsequent Roman emperors. But it became conspicuous for the first time in Greece with King Philip. The Emperor Hadrian perhaps heard the story which is reported about an old woman who approached him on his travels: she was petitioning for justice, only to be told by Hadrian 'don't bother me'. 'And don't you be king, then,' she retorted, whereupon Hadrian did bother to hear her case.[7] What Hadrian would not know was that this story had been told of several previous rulers who were also dispensing personal justice. Aptly, the earliest of whom it was told was Philip, king of Macedon.

19

THE TWO PHILOSOPHERS

Plato used to call Aristotle 'the foal'. What did he mean by that name?
Plainly, it was known that foals kick their mothers when they have had
enough milk.

Aelian (*c.* AD 210), *Varia Historia* 4.9

Aristotle accuses the old philosophers who thought that philosophy had
been perfected by their own efforts and says that they were either very
stupid or very vain, but that he himself could see that, as great advances
had been made in such a few years, philosophy would be completely fin-
ished in a short while.

Cicero, *Tusculan Disputations* 3.28.69

PHILIP WAS TO BE ONE of the two great founders in the classical world (the other being Octavian–Augustus), but his career coincided with the two who were certainly its greatest thinkers: Plato and his pupil, Aristotle. Plato ended by teaching at Athens in the surrounds of a hero-shrine, the Academy (the origin of our word, 'academic'); those who heard him do not seem to have paid or usually to have heard him behind closed doors. Aristotle taught in the surrounds of a shrine once favoured by Socrates, the Lyceum. His followers became known as the Peripatetics (from the Greek word for a colonnaded walk). Both schools persisted for another eight hundred years and their founders' thought then revived again in Europe. In my Oxford college, Aristotle's thinking has been taught and studied continuously for more than 625 years.

Both of them associated with the most powerful Greek dynasts of their age. Plato visited Sicily to lecture and converse with two successive

194

tyrants at Syracuse, both called Dionysius, father and son. A book of his teaching was then published, purportedly by the younger Dionysius, which Plato's followers promptly disowned. After studying with Plato in Athens, Aristotle lived for a while at the court of a dynast, Hermeias, in north-west Asia Minor, who had created a circle of 'philosophic' companions and was eulogized by his visitor in an extravagant hymn. He then travelled to Macedon where his father had been a doctor at court. In 343/2 BC he had been chosen to teach Philip's son, Alexander, the world's most wide-ranging mind teaching the world's greatest conqueror-to-be. When Alexander became king Aristotle returned to teach in Athens for another thirteen years.

Plato was the older philosopher, born in 427 BC and living until he was nearly eighty in 348 BC. He was also the greater writer, in my view the greatest prose-writer in all world literature. He was born into the Athenian upper class and was not too young for those of his same background who hoped, indeed plotted, that democracy would one day go away. He was a star pupil of Socrates, whose questioning about ethical terms, the possibility of knowledge and self-knowledge powerfully influenced the younger Plato's early dialogues. Socrates' execution and the experience of majority voting ('mob-rule') did not win Plato over to be a democrat. A democracy, he later wrote, is a 'charming, anarchic and many-sided constitution' which bestows a 'sort of equality on the equal and the unequal alike': Plato detested it.[1]

It was not only in politics that he went against the current of his fellow citizens. His philosophy was founded on a radical contrast between the worlds of appearance (real to us) and 'reality', knowable only to a philosopher who has prepared and trained for more than fifteen years. Plato and his pupils did perhaps engage in classifications of the natural world (the best evidence is only a comedy, sending them up) but they were not really empiricists. What they were most encouraged to admire were the newish sciences of mathematics and astronomy (although Plato himself made no lasting contributions to either of them, as opposed to their appreciation). Plato argued that the soul is separate from the human body, that it enters the body with knowledge from a previous existence which we can then 'recall', that there are punishments, and a renewed existence, for souls after bodily death. Famously, he proposed the existence of 'Forms', culminating in an enigmatic 'Form of the Good', on which he taught but never published a coherent account. These Forms are thought of as the ideal types which are the essence of the objects (beds, dogs, even horses) and qualities (justice, goodness, wisdom) in the world which we wrongly call 'real'. Like universals to particulars, they represent the good-ness or 'dog-ness' which is instantiated in our world.

Plato also returned repeatedly to questions of knowledge, belief and explanation. What is it to 'know' something? Does it presuppose knowl-edge of its definition? What is the difference between knowledge and a be-lief which is true? What is the moral value of self-knowledge and is it really knowledge if it is not of an object beyond the subject? Is virtue like one of the crafts which expert craftsmen know how to follow? These and other questions, greatly refined, underlie some of the writings which philosophers continue to find the most challenging in all his thought, cul-minating in his late masterpieces, the *Theaetetus* and the *Sophist*. Even the difficult theory of Forms was to come under Plato's own criticism, es-pecially in his remarkable *Parmenides* where he criticizes it as leading to an infinite regress and propounds his celebrated 'third-man' argument. In the earlier dialogues, especially, Plato hides his own exposition behind his deliberately chosen dialogue form. Keen young opponents are shown ar-guing with Plato's version of Socrates who confounds them, sometimes with arguments which strike us as very feeble. On one view, Plato is delib-erately exercising his dialogue's readers by making them engage with ar-guments whose own validity he is not personally endorsing. This process helps us to tone up our minds, preparing us for future progress. Certainly, Plato does not present his speakers' views as his own. The use of the dia-logue form and the long evolution of his writings across some forty years make it wrong to turn their ideas into one system and call it 'Platonic'. In antiquity later readers did so, claiming that they were not adding any-thing new. Their neo-Platonism was radically untrue to much that Plato had discussed.

In the later dialogues, the questioning and provoking Socrates fades away, taking his artful irony with him. The Socratic method becomes a long disquisition by Socrates (or a main speaker) to which a pulverized dialogue-partner can only answer tamely, 'How not, O Socrates?' Plato does allow some unusual views to be expounded, nonetheless. In his ideal republic, women are to share in the system of education. In his late work, the *Laws*, punishment is not just to be a retribution or a deterrent, but it is to be curative in certain circumstances too. But this same Plato can ex-press entirely derogatory views about women's inferior irrationality; in his earlier works, he is relatively positive about pederasty, but in his *Laws* he is the first known Greek author to describe homosexual male relations as contrary to nature ('Plato the homophobe');[2] he is adamant that those who spread atheist views need correction and if they are spreading them cynically and deceptively, they must be put to death. The Plato who so brilliantly turned his tutor Socrates into an eloquent martyr by writing the posthumous *Apology* for him ended up by propounding laws that would have sent Socrates off to a correction-centre.[3]

Plato's writings return often to a central theme, how the 'best' can rule and therefore bring justice to a state. Although he was such a contrary voice to his contemporaries, the question was urgent in his own day. The city-states and Leagues of his lifetime were torn by social conflicts and wars over dominance; these became particularly acute in the Sicily which he had visited, after the fall of his hosts, the two despotic tyrants. For Plato, political 'freedom' was not a central concern. He disapproved of 'freedom to live as you please', which he would equate with 'licence', the insatiable pursuit of pleasure and the characteristics of mob-rule. His ideal states in the *Republic* or the *Laws* were designed to give people the best possible life and to make them better. The liberal idea of limiting those states' interference with their citizens' lives would not concern him. To obey their laws was necessarily to be made good.

Luxury, however, was another matter. As some of his pupils quickly emphasized, its prevalence in Sicily struck Plato and led him to insist on the necessity of living modestly. One side of Socrates' image, after all, was a Socratic indifference to pleasure or hardship. This theme was strongly emphasized by Plato who transposed it to the life of political communities. In the *Republic*, the misguided (but rather attractive) 'inflamed' community is one which is given over to luxury, and is afflicted with it as if it is a disease. The luxury of sofas, incense and prostitutes turns it away from the pursuit of justice based on self-control. There is an enduring puritanical streak in Plato's thinking.

Justice remains absolutely central to it. In his earlier works, Socrates tends to question a young participant on what exactly is courage, say, or piety or knowledge. Quite often, the resulting mental gymnastics reach no conclusion: we do, however, learn that justice is soundness of mind which results, in turn, from self-knowledge and helps us to maintain virtuous relations with others. In the *Republic*, the nature of justice then becomes the major question. The answer digresses through ten books, ending in a magnificent myth to answer the hard question of why we should be just at all. Ascribed to a mysterious 'Er, the Armenian', it describes what befalls the soul after death and how it is allotted its next human life after being judged for the previous one. This myth answers beautifully but quite implausibly the question 'What are the rewards of justice?' rather than of an injustice which hopes to go unpunished. The *Republic*'s general definition of justice is related to its complex idea that there is a three-part nature in the soul, matched, in turn, by the three-part nature of the ideal state. Justice results when each part co-operates with the others for its own good and for the good of the whole.

The trouble is that Plato's ideal communities strike readers as potentially most unjust. In the *Republic*, the assumption is that the best community will be ruled by the best who are duly educated and selected for their responsibility. There are to be three classes: the workers, the warriors and the philosophic rulers. Citizens will be selected for each, but only the rulers will be put through a very long process of philosophical education which leads to the point where they will know the Forms and the supreme Form of the Good. Without any check or accountability or majority voting, they will then simply rule everyone else. Later in life, in his *Laws*, Plato does accept that even the rulers may need some laws which they themselves must obey. However, the problem then is that the laws which his long dialogue constructs are so dictatorial and repressive that no sane Greek contemporary would accept for one moment that this community is the 'just' one in which he should live. The *Republic*, with fine regrets, had already banished artists, poets and even the 'deceiving' Homer. It had proposed that all goods should be held in common, including women (Aristophanes had made wonderful fun of this notion way back in the 390s, in my view because he had heard a very early report of Plato's emerging views on the subject). The *Laws* then multiplied the repression by proposing a Nocturnal Council (imitated, however, in Renaissance Venice) and threatening uses of religion to deter citizens from having sex.

Plato's pupil, Aristotle, was born in Stageira in northern Greece in 384 BC, more than forty years after Plato; he lived until 322 BC. While shaped by Plato and sharing several approaches with him, he was much more of an empirical thinker, a brilliant classifier and categorizer and much more alert to everyday accepted wisdom which needed intellectual support, not demolition. He persistently stressed the existence of exceptions and particular cases as opposed to all-embracing generalizations. Ever the empiricist, he ranged widely and even when set beside Plato's, his mind has the most amazing range in history. Philosophers admire him for his system of logic, including his discussion of 'subject' and 'predicate'; and his outstanding writings on ethics. Some of his central ideas are now superseded, his views on perception, say, or the pervasive 'purposiveness' in biology, while others are certainly over-played, his distinction between the 'potential' and the 'actual', his four different types of cause or his elusive views on substances. But the discrimination and guiding use of inference with which he discusses them are immensely rewarding.

Yet Aristotle was not only a pure philosopher. His theoretical interests extended to political theory, to poetry, especially drama, to the constitutions, even, of 158 different Greek states, a massive undertaking which surely drew on research teams of his pupils. He wrote on the weather, *On Colonies* (for his pupil, Alexander), on the parts of animals, or on rhetoric. He even compiled chronological lists of victors in the major Greek games. His range was prodigious. His treatises on individual subjects do not follow the deductive methods of his most abstract treatises on logic, but the underlying approach is that all these forms of knowledge can, when understood, be brought as far as appropriate under logical and axiomatic reasoning.

Aristotle is capable of some reassuringly mundane or inaccurate beliefs, nonetheless. He considers that a work of art gives pleasure when it resembles the object depicted: he has a rather straightforward view of a good drama, which should have items like a mistake (not a 'moral flaw'), a reversal of fortune and a recognition at its core. He would intensely dislike Pinter and Beckett, but he would much like the modern definition of a good novel as 'what happens next?' He was much too trusting in the apparently genuine documents which he used in the one of his 'Constitutions', that of the Athenians, which we know best: they tended to be fakes. His theories of change and of the desirable 'mean' between two extremes distorted his views of early Greek history. Like Plato, he saw the political conflicts of the archaic past in horizontal terms, as conflicts between classes: Plato and he had seen such conflicts played out in contemporary Sicily. In the past a vertical model of conflict between powerful men, backed by their dependants, would usually have been more appropriate. But even his mistakes are intriguing. Like Plato, he believed in a previous lost era of civilization: for Plato the imaginary 'Atlantis', for Aristotle, too, a world before a great flood. Rain, he believed, had washed away an old civilization in the plains, but a few survivors had lived on in the mountains and preserved the 'ancient wisdom'. Being simple people, shepherds and the like, they had gradually distorted it into myths.[4] If Aristotle had met a modern shepherd or forester, he would have had to accept that the 'ancient wisdom' was sexist and racist. But he also believed that such a great flood would happen again.

For non-philosophers, the most remarkable of his works are those on biology and natural history. These masterpieces of observation are rooted in the years before he went to Macedon, especially the years which he spent on the island of Lesbos. Aristotle's physiology is not always on the right lines, and although he has an idea of a hierarchy of natural kinds, he has no idea of evolution. But his fieldwork and classification are breathtaking, ranging from a superb account of the life cycle of a mosquito to a brilliant attempt to understand an octopus (including the use of its tentacles for sex) and some shrewd observations about elephants. These observations were improved by the Macedonian conquests of Asia, except that he did not understand the size of an elephant's penis or its usual lifespan. Of course there are some quaint inferences: men with long penises, Aristotle believed, are less fertile because their sperm 'cools' as it has further to travel. But throughout, there is a superb range of empirical thinking. The sperm of Ethiopians, he insists, is not black, as some Greeks presumed, a fact which makes us wonder how he himself had established it.[5]

Aristotle is less interested in the possible effects of luxury than in the futility of making money for its own sake. For him, a good, happy life is the 'activity of the soul in accordance with excellence', with sufficient 'external goods', but no more. Freedom concerns him in his writings on the ideal state, and he is certainly less authoritarian in this respect than Plato. Although he presents extreme democracy as a reprehensible attempt to be free to live as one pleases, a caricature of its principles, he accepts the good principle that citizens should rule and be ruled in turn. He does see that a state should be a partnership, common to all citizens, but because of his low opinion of the uneducated and property-less masses, including tradesmen, he opts for a constitution which includes farmers and soldiers but not all the poorer citizens in its territory. He was too strongly attracted by the idea of a 'mixed' constitution, an unrealizable ideal of mere theorists, and he also believed that a constitution which fell between two opposed extremes would be fairer because it stood midway as the 'mean' between them. He underestimated the justice, stability and sound sense of the democratic Athenians among whom he lived, but at least he did not deviate from it as unattractively as Plato and his proposed alternative.

Notoriously, he had views on slaves and women. Unnamed thinkers, probably in Socrates' Athens, had denied that slavery was in 'accordance with nature': Aristotle disagreed. There were 'slaves by nature', he believed, who were incapable of foresight, deliberation or practical wisdom. At times he even writes as if they are animals. Most of the slaves whom Aristotle saw in Athens, western Asia or Macedon would have been non-Greek 'barbarians', whom he regarded as inferior by nature: he says explicitly that the existence of natural slaves can be proved both by theory and by experience.[6] His views about natural slavery caused his own arguments serious problems on many counts, but they were not just a passing consequence of his theories on ruling or the household. What he saw in his own experience seemed to require them, just as his perceptions of women accounted for his view that they are defective versions of the rational '*polis*-male': what he saw were uneducated, irrational beings, who would typically lament in public. Although women have a trace of a power of reason, it is very feeble and 'without authority'.[7] For barbarians and women, therefore, freedom is a wholly inappropriate state.

For Aristotle, justice is the very nature of virtue and like Plato, his ethics and political theory are centrally concerned with it. Typically, Aristotle distinguishes several types of it, and although, oddly, he says nothing about criminal justice, he is explicitly concerned with notions of 'equality' and fairness. If the rulers of a state are unjust to those they rule, the result, he sees, will be civil strife. We have an equal claim to justice, but justice is not necessarily a claim to receive an equal amount. For Aristotle, a 'distributive' type of justice allots justice in accordance with the recipient's 'worth': this notion of proportionate justice is not at all the notion of a justice which distributes equal shares for all citizens, the justice which sustained Athenian democracy.

I N PLATO'S *Republic*, the participant, Adeimantus, complains to Socrates that philosophers are mostly weird or even wicked, and even the best of them are rendered useless in government. Plato and Aristotle had scores of pupils and listeners: did their teaching have a practical, political impact? The point here is not that Plato's *Laws* are completely impractical and that no state could possibly survive them, not even a little one with no more than Plato's ideal number of 5,040 land-holding citizens. Rather, Plato did try, we are told, to apply his philosophy to the reform of a real state by his visits, three in all, to the ruling tyrants in Sicily. His experience of the harsh elder tyrant Dionysius surely shaped his striking portrait of the insatiable 'tyrannical' man in his subsequent work, the *Republic*. His project, we are told, was that the state should be ruled by the 'best laws': the exceptional luxury of the Syracusan citizens should be curbed and the ruler, the Syracusan tyrant, must adopt philosophy like one of Plato's philosopher-kings. We know of these efforts from the remarkable *Seventh Letter* which is manifestly a fiction ascribed to Plato, but was surely written by a pupil soon after Plato's death. It is clearly apologetic, as it attempts to explain Plato's repeated visits to this brutal tyranny and to credit him with high hopes of the notorious Dion, uncle to the younger of the two tyrants. Supposedly, Dion was at first won over to Plato's reforming project, only to be led astray by undesirable friends. The fact was that Dion also ruled harshly when he had power in the 350s, that he murdered a political contemporary (which the *Letter* glosses over), that he probably used Plato in the hope of saving his own property from the tyrants' confiscation and that he was murdered by a particularly frightful Athenian who had also, wondrously, been a listener to Plato in the Academy. There was no philosopher-king here in the making.

Nonetheless, the will to apply and reform was certainly there in Plato, and we must do justice to his interest in laws and his detestation of tyranny. Later sources credit him with many pupils who were asked, as he was, to help in drawing up laws for city-states: there is no evidence that any of them really did so. Several of them are also credited with actions against reigning tyrants, even with killing them. This involvement may be true. Two of Plato's former hearers did assassinate Cotys, the despotic king of Thrace, in 359 BC and six years later another is said to have killed Clearchus, a remarkable Greek tyrant at Heraclea on the south shore of the Black Sea.[8] Aristotle's pupil Callisthenes was also believed to have encouraged a plot against the 'tyrannical' Alexander. There are several stories of such involvement, but the Academy did not urge political murders and we do not know how far any philosophic principles inflamed these various people. They may have done, but not at Plato's direction.

The more difficult legacy comes after Plato's death. We have a repulsive letter ascribed to Speusippus, his successor at the Academy, which is addressed to King Philip of Macedon and which smoothly assures Philip that his forceful conquest of so much of Greek city-territory in the north is simply the reclaiming of 'his own', his heritage, as is proven by some highly dubious references to the ancient Greek myths. This letter picks up contemporary diplomatic issues and is very well informed: it reads like a genuine flattery of the greatest enemy to Greek freedom in the years 343–342 BC. It is a major warning against allowing a philosopher near foreign affairs.

A Platonist pupil, we are told, had also helped Philip to establish his rule in Macedon before his accession. We know nothing more of it, but we do know that in 322 BC, when the Athenians' democracy was at the mercy of Alexander's victorious Macedonian Successors, the Athenians chose the head of the Platonist Academy, Xenocrates, to go as one of their ambassadors to plead for a lenient treatment of their city-state: Xenocrates was a resident foreigner, not even a citizen. He was a landmark, the first of many future philosophers to be used on embassies (previously, Athenians had preferred to send theatre actors). The choice was surely made because the Academy stood so high in the respect of the Macedonian 'tyrants'; Alexander himself had favoured Xenocrates, who had addressed four books *On Kingship* to him, although, sadly, they do not survive.

Similar involvement was even more obviously true of Aristotle. He lived at court in Macedon from 342 to 335 BC and he taught Alexander. Before he arrived King Philip had flattened his home town of Stageira, but the tradition that Aristotle did get the king to agree to its rebuilding now seems more likely, as archaeologists have proved there was some rebuilding on the site in Philip's reign, albeit on a smaller area. Perhaps Aristotle did also later receive funds and materials for his researches from the far-ranging Alexander. His visit, then, was not an entirely fruitless stay with the kings.

Aristotle also developed close links with Philip's senior general, Antipater, and probably with his family. We have a text of his will, of which Antipater is to be an executor. He even wrote a work called *Justified Claims*, probably to help with the claims of the Greek states in the Peloponnese after the Spartan-led rebellion which Antipater crushed there in 331/0 BC. When Alexander died and the Athenians rebelled against the Macedonians, we can see why Aristotle, the friend of top Macedonians, was forced to leave the city: he was accused, tendentiously, of impiety, and so he left, saying that he wished to save the Athenians from 'sinning twice against philosophy' (the first sin was condemning Socrates). He is also reported as saying he became 'fonder of the myths as he became alone'.[9]

He had some role, surely, in the continuing curiosity of Alexander about the Asia which he was conquering, but his main role appears to be in passing on his awful sense of geography. Aristotle believed that the edge of the world was visible from what we call the Hindu Kush mountains in Afghanistan: like many, Aristotle confused them with the distant Caucasus. He also reasoned that the river Indus ran neatly round to Egypt and that modern Morocco is quite close to India, on the grounds that both lands have elephants. This view of the world can only have strengthened the young Alexander's resolve to conquer to the edge of it. For Aristotle, our world lies at the centre of the universe, and the assertions of astronomers are consistent with that view.[10]

His real political influence followed after his death. Plato's admiration for the stars in the heavens, the universe and a supreme God were to be taken up in subsequent philosophy: they make him the father of a distinctive strand in Hellenistic religion. Aristotle's followers, rather, were to carry forward the systematic study of laws and constitutions. Their advice may well have been very important for the first ruling Ptolemies in Egypt's Alexandria, especially what they could say about a Library, a Museum and royal laws. Certainly, Aristotle's 158 local Constitutions influenced one of the major Alexandrian poets, Callimachus. But the most immediate impact came from a pupil of one of Aristotle's own former pupils, the Athenian Demetrius from Phaleron. In 317 BC the Macedonians put down the Athenians' attempt at a revived democracy and instead supported this Demetrius as the head of a restrictive oligarchy. The poor were disenfranchised and the rich were spared the expense, in future, of liturgies; Demetrius passed laws to limit luxury in funerary monuments and approved the appointment of 'inspectors of women', surely so as to curb female extravagance, including the city's notorious prostitution. Quite probably, his motives were ethical, formed by Aristotelian values of moderation and restraint. He was then attacked, inevitably, for his own luxury, including the supposed use of make-up and blond hair-dye and the acceptance of statues in his own honour ('360', it was alleged). His friends included other pupils of Aristotle, and he was most urbane in defending his own elegant and gentlemanly habits.[11] His rule lasted ten years, until 307 BC, but when it fell and democracy returned, the Athenians ecstatically celebrated their liberation. Freedom was back, and one Sophocles promptly proposed that philosophers should be banned in future from teaching in the city unless they were licensed by the democracy.[12] The Athenians did relent, but the proposal was eloquent. Democrats detested these philosopher-friends of kings and tyrants and their unbearable notions of an ideal state.

FOURTH-CENTURY ATHENIANS

*He is just the man to buy a little ladder for the pet jackdaw which he
keeps indoors and to make a bronze shield which the jackdaw can carry
as it hops on the ladder. When he has sacrificed an ox, he nails up the
skull straight opposite the entrance to his house and ties it round with
long ribbons so that people who go in can see that he has sacrificed an ox.
And when he has processed with the cavalrymen, he gives everything else
to his slave to take home, but throws back his cloak over his shoulder and
walks round the agora in spurs. And when his little Maltese dog dies, he
makes a monument for it and having put up a little grave-marker he inscribes on it, '[Barker (Kelados)], a Maltan . . . '*

Theophrastus, caricaturing the Man of Petty Ambition
with Athenian detail, *Characters* 21 (*c.* 330–310 BC)

T HE NEAREST TO AN IDEAL STATE in the classical world was not the
state of Plato or Aristotle: it was the Athenians', their contemporaries. To us, it is far from ideal as it was still a slave-society, using perhaps some 80,000 fellow humans as objects. But the philosophers' ideal
states also took slavery for granted, although Plato in his *Laws* was the
first to consider that the existence of slavery might corrupt slave-owning
masters.

Nonetheless, fourth-century Athens has been severely misjudged. It
has been seen as decadent, after the Periclean years of glory, apathetic, in
the face of Macedon, and immoral, even, in its continuing attachment to
power over other Greek city-states. For Jacob Burckhardt, it was the
symptom of a wider political decline. 'Everywhere,' he wrote, 'democracy nourished a tremendous degree of ill-will'; in his view, the results
were visible in 'private contempt' for the public authorities, general

27. Grave monument of husband and wife, Thraseas and Euandria, watched by a young slave girl. Attica, *c.* 350–340 BC.

mockery (Burckhardt disliked personalized comedy), lawbreaking, excessive praising of the glories of the past and the frequency with which the sons of prominent men turned out to be so much worse than their fathers.[1]

Certainly, there were fewer Athenians. The losses in the long war had reduced the citizenry by up to a half, perhaps to only 25,000 adult males by 403 BC. Numbers recovered to around 30,000 adult males in the fourth century, but were still far short of the 50,000 which we estimate for the 440s. Finances were greatly down, too. The biggest change in fourth-century Attica was that the revenues from the former Empire were gone: they had amounted to more than 1,000 talents a year in its later phases. The 'contributions' of the member-states of the Athenians' revived Confederacy (from 377 BC onwards) were smaller and much less in total. So, too, the official valuation of the visible property of rich taxpayers in Attica had fallen. The working estimate had probably been around 10,000 talents by 430 BC. In 378 it was just below 6,000.

Nonetheless, the slimmed-down citizenry maintained an admirable stability in this age of surrounding civic violence and revolution. Fourth-century Athenians did not forget the two dreadful oligarchic coups in their state, briefly in 411 and again in 404/3 BC: grandfathers still passed stories of them on to the young in the 350s. Oligarchy became, in my view, nothing more than a theoretical possibility for a few, ignored theorists: twice bitten, Athenians were for ever shy, even those from upper-class families who would have favoured oligarchy in the fifth century. One reason why their proclaimed Confederacy was such a success, with over seventy members for its first twelve years or so, was that the Athenians were the true democrats, proven by nearly a hundred and fifty years. They were other democrats' increasingly self-proclaimed friends.

The social and religious infrastructure of the city-state was still intact. The calendar of festivals continued undiminished, the setting for an Athenian's social year: there was no 'religious crisis', least of all one provoked by Socrates' scepticism. Citizenship still depended on a mother and father of pure citizen descent and exceptions for foreigners were still extremely rare. Even on their tombstones, the inscriptions for Attic citizens maintained a simple restraint. The phratries still received (and verified) the young male citizens; the demes maintained their local assemblies and festivals and linked citizens, as Cleisthenes intended, to one of the ten tribes. As the population changed irregularly, the numbers of yearly councillors each deme was to choose were adjusted to keep pace. What did not change was a family's deme-membership (reflected in their name, their 'demotic'): in the 330s BC it still reflected their ancestors' place of enrolment back in 508 BC. The laws of family inheritance remained unaltered, just as Solon had first had them written down. The restraints on an Athenian 'heiress's' free marriage were never relaxed, although comic dramatists made such fun in the later fourth century BC of the preposterous circumstances which extreme cases could bring about.

The best-known fourth-century Athenian gives us a sense, indirectly, of this cohesive society and its values. Apollodorus (born c. 394 BC) was the son of the immigrant metic Pasion, an ex-slave who had won the very rare gift of Athenian citizenship for his role as a banker to many of the big names in fourth-century Athens, and above all for his great benefactions to the state. To his contemporaries, Apollodorus remained preposterous, as a whole cluster of Athenian speeches for and against him testify. They show the Athenians' sensitivity to Greek when spoken with an accent, to boastfulness, to *arrivistes* who were publicly too prominent. A whole industry of 'winding up' the litigious Apollodorus developed, as he took on lawsuit after lawsuit in the manner of a newcomer who is touchy about his newly gained status. In reply, there were fellow Athenians who never left him alone. 'The mouse has tasted pitch,' they even joked about him, alluding to the story of a mouse who fell into a wine jar but found the contents (like Apollodorus' citizenship) less palatable than expected.[2]

The Athenians of his era were not a 'face-to-face' society where almost everyone knew each other: 30,000 adult males were far too many for that. But what they all liked to hear were praises of themselves as special, a 'cut above'. In the orators' speeches to juries and assemblies, the male citizens as a whole attract the language once used of the noble aristocrats. They are now the 'fine and fair'.[3] The one self-made politician whom we know in his own words, the orator Aeschines, is notably careful to associate his family with noble pursuits, the cavalry and so forth, before an Athenian jury. In such company, Apollodorus, the son of an ex-slave, was a hilarious figure of fun.

For there was no popular culture, breaking through with the loss of empire and destroying the cultural forms of the fifth century's golden years. Rather, most of that culture had begun with the nobles and filtered downwards, gaining comedy (the one non-noble extra) and tragedy (it so happened) on the way. The great athletic contests were still prized in Attica and were watched during the nobles' invention, the festival of the Panathenaia (founded by them in the 560s BC). All classes enjoyed cock-fighting and it is probably only by chance that we now hear less about the noble sport of hunting hares and boar. Fine drinking-parties persisted, the stylish *symposia*, in houses with a smart 'men's room' in which to hold them. It was only for want of space and money that poorer Athenians drank in bars and drinking-shops around the town.

Culturally, nonetheless, where are the great names in the theatre and the arts? The question is a misleading one, because so much already existed and what continued is mostly lost to us. Fourth-century Athenians lived, as some of us still do, in the happy shadow of great architecture: they were not therefore 'shadows' themselves. The city-state still had its superb classical temples and statues on the Acropolis and outside in Attica. The place had not been sacked, nor (despite the Thebans) ploughed up. If Athenian religious building falls away, one good reason is that the Athenians already had the finest temples in the world. Stylish houses certainly did not die out, as archaeologists increasingly emphasize. In the 380s painted pottery in the old style does die out, but the result is not an artistic collapse: the terracottas of women, the famous 'Tanagras', then begin at Athens, where the genre possibly originated. In the late 370s we first know of a sculptor who copies a fifth-century statue (Cephisodotus' Peace, copying aspects of a work by the great Pheidias), but there was nothing dead about a tradition which could then produce the great Praxiteles (Cephisodotus' son). The fifth century BC had produced the 'ideal type' of male nude beauty; in the fourth century Praxiteles produced what became the 'ideal type' of the female nude: small breasts, wide hips, an oval face and in general, a body-type which was well covered and not a skinny modern aberration. Praxiteles' most famous work in this style was the naked Aphrodite which he sculpted for Cnidus, so erotically beautiful, it was said, that male spectators tried to make love to it. Hadrian had a replica of it in his garden, in an outlying temple where it occupied a similar circular shrine.

Below the Acropolis, the Theatre of Dionysus was still unscathed and even in the years of extreme financial shortage the payments for theatre tickets continued for every Athenian citizen. In 386 BC an older tragedy was indeed put on again by the tragic actors at the Dionysia festival, and in the 330s the three great fifth-century tragedians were honoured with statues in a refurbishment of the Athenian theatre. Great plays from the fifth century are freely quoted to juries by the orators of the 350s onwards. But revivals did not mean a new age of sterility. The same people who quoted the classics still longed for the honour of a chorus-provider's prize. The most conspicuous such monuments survive in Athens from the 320s, just before these liturgies' abolition.

What obscures our view is that all the continuing flood of new tragedies has been lost: they did not pass into the small canon which was later imposed in Alexandria. There were surely some excellent new pieces, as Aristotle certainly thought, quoting two now lost to us, the *Lynceus* and the *Alcmeon*. The guiding force was probably Euripides, but the influence of Plato and especially Aristotle may have been important from the 350s on. One of the most admired tragedians was Theodectes, a migrant to Athens who was friendly with the philosophers; surely his treatment of character and moralizing speeches will have shown their effects. There were even a few history dramas, not just for living patrons outside Athens, but also within the city if (as I believe) Moschion wrote for the fourth-century stage. His works include a *Themistocles* and a tragedy about the death of Thessaly's best-known tyrant, Jason. This event in 370 BC would be a very odd choice for a dramatist of a much later era.

The 'decline of tragedy', then, is only a fact about our lack of evidence. In comedy, the usual view of a lull of about sixty years (380–320 BC) is also mistaken. Already at the end of Aristophanes' long career, the comic chorus was on the way out; not all of his comedy was still robustly personalized, but the genre was in no way shutting down. Scores of comedies went on being composed, although they are known to us only in fragments. Comedy's re-emergence with Menander in the late 320s is only apparent. Two long-lived authors, among others, refute it: Antiphanes (active *c.* 385–*c.* 332 BC) and Alexis (active *c.* 355–275 BC) were each credited with more than two hundred and forty plays, and the latter was admired into Roman times. It is simply that we have none of them nowadays. Their younger heir, Menander, then becomes the master of unpolitical 'situation' comedy with a pleasant feeling for character and dramatic settings. His comedies are evidence, among much else, that young Athenian males and females of citizen families would fall romantically in love and decide to marry even without their parents' encouragement. In his comedies, unlike Aristophanes', there are no homoerotic jokes or affairs. In my view, this 'good taste' reflects Menander's own Athenian friendships and political inclination: Menander became linked with Aristotle's pupil, Theophrastus, and then with the oligarchic Demetrius in whose dominance (317–307 BC) his plays flourished. There was no lasting ban on personalized political comedy, but these 'enlightened' superior people disliked it (like Jacob Burckhardt). So Menander was more tasteful (homoerotic affairs continued, of course, but jokes about them and sodomy were simply too coarse). One contemporary, Timocles, did continue to write personalized political jokes, but he seems to have supported the Macedonians' dominance, and so the targets of his jokes were acceptable to the governing class.

The fourth-century democracy was not at all in retreat, until the Macedonians ended it forcibly in 322 BC. After the awful oligarchic coups in the late fifth century, the people voted to entrench it even further. Pay for attending the assembly (some forty days a year) was introduced for all citizens, even in the dark financial days of the mid–390s; the pay for jurymen and council-service continued unassailably (though unlike assembly-pay neither was increased). The total pay for state service probably came to about a hundred talents by the 340s, a sum spread widely among participants rather than supporting a small group of professional civil servants. There was also a democratic concern about the methods of adopting new laws. Eventually, the agreed procedure was to appoint a panel of 'law commissioners' to make a recommendation on a particular topic. But their recommendations came back to the people's assembly and had to be voted on to have any force. There was no loss of 'popular sovereignty'. After the brusque malpractice of the reforming oligarchs, there was a sharpened awareness of the difference between a 'law' and a mere 'decree' as resolved at a public meeting. This awareness could be exploited against political enemies. The older political check of ostracism had disappeared since *c.* 417 BC (when Alcibiades had artfully distorted the result of one), and instead, orators' proposals were increasingly exposed to lawsuits for 'illegality'. However, the procedure for such suits had existed in the late fifth century, and once again they were not a surrender of popular 'sovereignty'. These cases were heard in the popular courts by random panels of citizen-jurors. They were not the objects of a separate Supreme Court.

In the end, the people of Attica were still the only sovereign body, meeting in their assembly in the belief that 'the people can do whatever seems good to it'. Their meetings were not ignorant occasions. Practice increased a citizen's political discernment, and to judge from surviving orators' speeches, or references to them, a whole body of complex foreign diplomacy would be brought to the assembly for a decision. There was no 'government', no continuing group who 'ran' the place: the councillors still changed yearly, and their 'recommendations' had to be voted in by all the people. Since the death of Pericles a division had already become apparent between the military generals and the most prominent political orators. In the fourth century this division becomes even clearer, as does the Athenians' propensity to prosecute generals who failed them on expeditions abroad. The people were highly suspicious of malpractice, and so their generals realized that they were well advised to work with a political orator who would champion them at home.

These political orators owed their pre-eminence to speaking and persuading. 'Those who engage in politics' begin to be referred to as an identifiable group, but they were not paid to do so by the state. They would take 'gifts' for their services, a difficult line to sustain when the accepting of 'gifts against the interests of the state' could be prosecuted as bribery. Some of them became known for particular specialities. Demosthenes, for instance, for his views on policy towards Macedon and the North: he maintained contacts and sources of information up in these areas which kept him well informed.[4] Some speakers made particular sense about finance or the West or the corn-imports, but the crucial skill remained the same: to be persuasive in the assembly and to establish credibility for what was proposed as one's own decree. It was necessary for orators to have active friends and contacts, not least on each year's council, as the council set the assembly's agenda. It could also help, surely, to have good contacts with deme officials locally who might encourage citizens to come and vote. But without good speaking and a record of successful persuasion, an orator was soon a nobody. There was no new expertise, no specialized technology which only 'those in politics' had mastered. They sometimes had more information, but above all, they were the ones who spoke with success.

This talent prevailed even though financial circumstances marked the biggest change from Pericles' days. In the fifth century BC no need had been felt for a budget each year: the imperial revenues were usually more than enough. In the fourth century a yearly division of revenues was introduced, and authorized by law; under it, particular funds received moneys for particular purposes, 'military' or 'festival' (from the mid–350s the latter was voted by law to be the recipient of any yearly surplus too). After this law of the mid–350s supervisors of this 'theoric fund' did have particular importance, and in the 330s the fund was to be headed by a commissioner, elected for five years: the Athenians thus came near to having a financial Chancellor.[5]

Without previous levels of tribute, particular value attached to the income from rents on state property (including mines), indirect taxes (including taxes on imports and resident foreigners) and fines (always a temptation). These sums covered the state's basic running costs, but in a time of continuing wars capital levies became more common on the defined group of richer citizens who were liable for them: they fell on 'visible property' and had to be paid in cash, nonetheless. Even if they were imposed at only 5 per cent of a citizen's assets and were not imposed annually, they still had to be funded, and after several such years they would certainly stretch a payer's resources. The full range of liturgies continued too and were met by the rich: excluding the variable number of military liturgies, there were between 100 and 120 such 'services' to be met in a year.[6] There was no income tax, let alone surtax, but the richer Athenians were not given an easy time, especially in the difficult decades of the 390s, 380s, 360s and 350s. In 378, the collection of the capital levies was reformed, with the introduction of syndicates whose richer members had to pay up in advance. Pre-payment was quite a burden for them, as was the need to recoup the sums from the less rich members. Nonetheless, the military crises of the 350s and 340s saw a conspicuous number of 'voluntary donations', too, made over and above the levies of tax. Proposed in assemblies, they were met by voluntary 'donors' who gained honour before their fellow citizens by volunteering.[7] The civic spirit of the richer Athenians was certainly not dead, and they cannot be 'blamed' for Athens' failure to defeat Macedon.

The social profile of the citizenry was not drastically changed, either: 'bourgeois' or 'middle-class' are still quite inappropriate terms for it. There was still a rich upper class, whether we assess it by the 800–1,000 men who were capable of serving as cavalrymen, or by those sufficient to put forward 1,200 members a year for the considerable cost of 'commanding' a trireme. Those liable for the capital levies were not, in my view, as few as these groups: the net was thrown wider, catching perhaps 3,000–4,000 people, including the estates of orphans.[8] To judge from the imposed oligarchies of 322 and 317 BC, there were another 8,000–9,000 citizens with enough land and property to rank as hoplite-soldiers, owning anything from about fifteen acres down to the minimal 'seven acres and two cows'. In 403 BC, at the end of the war, 5,000 Athenians were believed to be without any land at all. Probably the number of the landless did reduce as the city-state recovered, but what did not change was the general pattern of land-holdings in Attica. Small freeholdings (to our modern eyes, very small ones) remained the rule. The biggest known fourth-century estates are still only about 70–100 acres, although a rich man might own several such farms at once.

Within the richest group, there was the usual fastidiousness and interest in visible distinctions, and we know most about them because orators and comedies make such fun of them. A man might travel in a smart chariot pulled by white horses, groom himself too fussily or even keep an Ethiopian slave and a pet monkey. Smart drinking-parties still went on, where one or two self-important people now had their 'personal assistants' or 'parasites' (*parasitos* meant a man 'beside you at table').[9] In the late fourth century comic poets made great fun of these obsequious attendants who smoothed and flattered their way to a living but were surely an amusing exception. There was also a continuing polemic against 'luxuries', against the eating of rare fish, the search for the best imported fruit, the use of the smartest metal drinking-cups. This polemic slipped into polemics about dissipation, about spending too much on scent, or on the city's demanding courtesans, or on gambling. This sort of selfishness and lack of control could then be used against the credibility of a political orator.

On a wider view, the behaviour is not a very pronounced sort of luxury, least of all when compared with the new age of Macedonian conquerors or the stories of the various kings on Cyprus. Even so, how did the richer Athenians assure their rather limited riches? Land-holdings, though often scattered, were the main source of it, in a state where there was no inheritance tax, no income tax and no worrying inflation. As the liturgies and capital levies had to be paid for in cash, this land would need to be farmed quite intensively with crops which could be sold for coin. There was no 'subsistence farming', and at all social levels coinage was in widespread use.[10] At busy seasons hired labour would be brought in to back up the owners' basic workforce, the ever-present slaves. For there was no retreat from slave-owning in fourth-century Attica and, as before, most of the slaves were foreign imports. Manufacturing was also based on slaves, who were almost always working in small units. It is not that the Athenian economy was suffering from foreign 'copies' of Athenian goods, like Far Eastern copies of modern European luxuries. That impression is misleadingly given by archaeology's great survivor, painted pottery. Attic styles are indeed copied, but painted pottery was of marginal importance to the Athenian economy.

What mattered, above all, was the mining of silver and the export of olive oil. The silver-mines were the state's property, but citizens took on leases and then worked them for profit, usually with wretched slaves. By the early 360s the number of known mining leases had fallen away somewhat, a sign, perhaps, of temporary economic caution among Athenian lessors, but the fall was then reversed in the next three decades (to the benefit of the state, which received payments for the leases). What never fell was the export of olive oil, a main Athenian item of exchange for the wheat which shippers (not all of them Athenian) brought in bulk from Egypt and especially from the Crimea (which also sent hides for leather and shoe-making). The soil of Attica was good for growing poor barley, but very seldom good for wheat. This big import trade was largely paid for by exports of olive oil (olive trees could not grow round most of the northern Black Sea) and probably by raw silver too, exported as bullion from the mines.

Richer Athenians did rent out property too, and their income from rents remained an important element in their yearly revenues, not least because the resident foreigners, or metics, could not own land or houses in Attica and had to rent where they lived. The rich did also engage in moneylending, although most of their fellow Athenians' borrowing was small-scale and short-term. Above all, many of them took on the bigger risks of maritime loans which were made to a shipper or trader so as to finance his cargo or his ship. Returns here could be very high, at least 30 per cent for the duration of a voyage, but so were the risks: if the ship sank, the lenders lost everything. These loans were not a new Athenian speciality: surely they went back by origin into the archaic age. But they were important for many rich Athenians' revenues. Any one ship or cargo might be the security for a number of different loans, advanced by different individuals. They were a genuine speculation on commerce which enabled the shippers and traders to pass on risk and increase their scale of operation. They have nothing to do with 'insurance' as we understand it: there was no concept of a premium in them, to be paid in advance to insure a bigger loss. Like many modern investors, the lenders were taking part of a total risk in the hope of a big return. In my view, there were links between most of the prominent Athenians and characters from the port, the Piraeus, and its 'shipping world'. But it was bad form for a citizen to boast about them socially and so the evidence is very oblique.[11]

Without the Empire's tribute and the services which the days of Empire encouraged, how did the city as a whole and the poorer majority survive without discontent? From the mid–360s the main answer was simple: once again, Athenian citizens had taken over land in another city-state. In the mid–360s they had begun by expelling pro-Persian 'traitors' off the Aegean island of Samos; they then returned, here and elsewhere, to take yet more of the farmland for Athenian citizens. The beneficiaries could either reside on this new bonus or rent it out. By the mid–340s the 'Athenians on Samos', as we know from a recently found inscription, maintained a half-sized rotating council of 250, implying that the populace there numbered many thousands.[12] In the 350s orators back home had said in the city's assembly that 'they recognize what is just as much as any other man, but owing to the poverty of the masses they are compelled to be rather more unjust in their treatment of the city-states'.[13] Samos was an example.

For their allies (the Samians perhaps not being one), those same Athenians had forsworn in 377 BC the taking of land for settlements abroad. In the kaleidoscopic foreign politics of the fourth century Athenians had had to make hard choices: in the 390s they had to make alliances with hated Thebes and Corinth and then, after the Thebans' victories, an alliance in 369 BC with the Spartans, the old enemy. In 357 BC the Athenians' own confederate allies would rebel against them too. But the origins of this rebellion are not recoverable (was much of it provoked by dissident oligarchs in allied states?) and even after peace returned the Athenians' Confederacy did not fall apart. Once the Spartan menace of the 370s had been tamed, the Confederacy's main aim had been satisfied. But it continued to exist, and the wrongs were certainly not all on the Athenian side. In the mid–360s the Thebans took the crucial harbour-town of Oropus on Attica's borders. Justifiably, the Athenians appealed for allied help under their treaty so as to recover it. None came, and it was left to Philip to restore the place to them after his victory in 338 BC.

28. Copy of the lifesize marble statue by Polyeuctus to honour the democratic orator Demosthenes in 280 BC at Athens, forty-two years after his death.

In difficult years, the Athenian citizenry thus retained stability and their own democratic system. In what survives from the Athenian orators, there is only one text which addresses the citizens as if the rich and the poor have differing sources of discontent: it occurs in Demosthenes' Fourth Philippic (probably composed c. 340 BC), but it concentrates on the rich's discontent against payments to maintain the poor and their (justified) dislike of attempts to divert their property for the poorer citizens' use.[14] The latter, it seems, is a grumble against vexatious prosecutors, the hated 'sycophants' in Attica who would denounce a fellow citizen in the hope of receiving part of his property if their case was proved. But 'sycophants' had been hated in the Periclean age, too; they were not a new phenomenon (there was no public prosecution service in Attica), and in the fourth century they were still checked by the risk of penalties if the cases which they brought were heavily defeated in court.

The good Athenian, meanwhile, was expected to arbitrate any disputes put to him by his fellow citizens: arbitration was often informally sought and carried out, and it was an accepted way to keep a dispute out of a law court. If a citizen was rich enough, he was also expected to contribute to liturgies, to voluntary 'donations' and to collections in a time of need for other fellow citizens. Orators dramatised exceptional cases, and their speeches should not mislead us about the solid backbone of thoughtfulness, co-operation and civic spirit which made fourth-century Athenians as 'classical' as their much-praised ancestors.

What has most blotted their reputation is an undeserved charge of apathy, even of cowardice. Again, it derives from surviving speeches of the orators, which so often castigate their hearers and exhort them to war, to the point where we might think the hearers had lost their previous spirit. They had not; war and finance, rather, had changed. Distant naval campaigns were needed to safeguard Athenian interests, but there was not the money to pay Athenian crews properly. For long absences, hired mercenaries were preferred anyway, to be funded by whatever means their generals abroad could contrive. At critical points, nonetheless, Athenian soldiers would still turn out to risk their lives, in 359 BC in Macedon, in spring 352 against Philip at Thermopylae, in 348 in Euboea and in the north and in 338 against Philip (almost successfully) for the vital battle of Chaeronea. These expeditions are not directly the subject of major surviving speeches on foreign policy, but they are proofs of Athenians' civic commitment.

Among these speeches, the masterpieces are by Demosthenes, the greatest of Athenian orators. Though slow to wake up to Philip's menace, Demosthenes was then his most effective Athenian opponent, from c. 350 BC to his own brave death in 322. At intervals, the situation was better suited to peace and compromise, as Demosthenes well realized. But the best option (as, arguably, he had long recognized) was for Athenians and Thebans to stand together against the encroaching Macedonians. When this alliance eventually came, Demosthenes' oratory continued, we may be sure, to inspire it. Philip won, but Demosthenes' speeches on the need to defend freedom against a king whom, increasingly, he saw as the enemy of democracy, were a victory too. Philip's biography was never written in antiquity, but for more than a thousand years Demosthenes' speeches were to be the texts which men imitated, copied and knew by heart.

PART THREE

Hellenistic Worlds

THE RECONSTRUCTION AND transformation of the bureaucratic system of the East, according to a general plan and with a definite purpose, must be recognized as one of the most astonishing achievements of the Greek genius, and as evidence of its flexibility and adaptability.

> M. I. Rostovtzeff, *The Social and Economic History of the Hellenistic World*, volume II (1941), 1080

SOME HISTORIANS HAVE WRITTEN of the equilibrium established by the early Ptolemies. The phrase will serve if analysed as follows: Egypt was a country of, say, seven million Egyptians and 100,000 immigrants. The latter class could not expect to maintain a claim to an equal, much less to a larger, share of the products unless they contributed (or were considered to contribute) a qualitatively much more important share. To create the illusion was the task of statesmanship. (Ptolemy I) Soter, and more surprisingly (Ptolemy III) Euergetes, succeeded in the task. (Ptolemy II) Philadelphus had every advantage in his favour, but pressed his successes too hard and frittered away his assets. After the battle of Raphia in 217 BC followed sterile stalemate.

> Sir Eric Turner, in *The Cambridge Ancient History*, volume VII part 1 (1984, 2nd edn.), 167

ALEXANDER THE GREAT

When King Darius sent him a letter asking him to accept 10,000 talents in return for the prisoners, all the land west of the river Euphrates, one of his daughters in marriage and friendship and alliance, Alexander put the terms to his companions. 'If I were Alexander,' Parmenion said, 'I would accept these terms.' 'And so would I,' said Alexander, 'if I were Parmenion.'

Plutarch, *Life of Alexander* 29.4

THE RISE OF MACEDON MARKED the end of the classical age by curtailing Greek freedom and placing kings and their courtiers at the centre of power and the city-states' public affairs. Luxury, increased by conquest, now characterized the new ruling class and the big showy style of so much of their post-classical 'Hellenistic' art. Philip's 'Hellenic Alliance' did proclaim the 'freedom' and the 'autonomy' of its members. It did also impinge on the conduct of justice: disputes between city-states were to be referred to arbitration, and, by a 'letter', the king could 'advise' the judicial treatment of 'traitors'. But freedom and justice are not the explanation of his Macedon's success. Philip and his men were not really fighting for Greek freedom: it was proclaimed as a means to an end, the advancement of their own power.

Philip's rise is better explained by his military innovations, his personal skill as an absolute king and once again, by conquest and access to new sources of precious metal, the two great agents of economic growth in antiquity. By conquest, Philip increased his sources of military manpower and changed the social profile of his kingdom. Macedonians were settled on rich land taken from the free Greek cities on his eastern borders; they could then sustain horses and become his new cavalrymen. War captives were brought back into Macedon as slaves, a labour-force for the newly developed mines and, surely, for farms whose owners could then be re-cruited as a professional standing army, available throughout the year. There was also, as we shall see later at Rome, a motivating set of values. A Macedonian king grew up to admire glory won in war, as did his fol-lowers. If he won it, he continued to enjoy their support. In this post-Homeric world, there was no question of ruling by being peaceful. The more a king conquered, the more secure his personal kingship became, and the more his resources for yet more conquest.

These values were to be realized by Philip's most famous memorial, his son Alexander the Great, who took the dynamic of glory, gain and con-quest to unprecedented lengths. Born in July 356, Alexander succeeded his murdered father in 336; five years later, aged twenty-five, he had con-quered the great armies of the Persian king in Asia and had taken over the palaces and treasures of the Persian Empire which were more than two hundred years old. Incomparably richer than anyone known in previous Greek history, he pressed eastwards into India, bound for the Outer Ocean, so he believed, which encircled the world. Nobody from Greece had ever seen India and, like his tutor Aristotle, Alexander underesti-mated its vast size and population. Like conquistadors, his troops entered the kingdoms of an unknown Indian world. They believed they were fol-lowing the trail of the god Dionysus and the hero Heracles. They saw ele-phants and Brahmins, but they only heard of people who lived up in the high mountains, our Himalayas, and ran with their feet turned back-wards. These people could not survive at low altitudes, they believed, and so they could not be brought into camp: Alexander's troops were the first westerners to hear of the fabled yeti, the Abominable Snowman of these mountain-peaks. Forty years earlier, their fathers had been the playthings of warring Athens and Thebes.

Aristotle, Alexander's tutor, had believed that the edge of the world lay just beyond the Hindu Kush mountains. In the pouring rains of a mon-soon, Alexander's troops refused to press far into India and investigate, not least because they were hearing reports of a massive unknown Indian kingdom which lay beyond them on the river Ganges. Alexander had to return, although he was now leading an army of more than 120,000 men, the biggest such force in Western history, the majority of whom were Indi-ans, Iranians and barbarians, recently his enemies. At the mouth of the river Indus, in what is now Pakistan, he did manage to sacrifice to Outer Ocean as if at the southern edge of the world. It was a second-best, and he marched back towards Babylon, where he died less than two years later, aged thirty-two years and ten months. He was not poisoned, but perhaps he had caught malaria in the previous weeks. Inevitably, his officers blamed one another, or even the pupils of Aristotle, for having poisoned him, starting these rumours against one another in their struggle for his succession.

Like Alexander, the Emperor Hadrian also made a dedication to Outer Ocean, but his was made in the north of the world, at the mouth of the river Tyne in Britain, which Alexander never knew. Hadrian visited Alexander's great city, Alexandria in Egypt, and our best surviving narrative of Alexander's campaigns was written by one of Hadrian's provincial governors, Arrian, a keen hunting man, like his hero. If he wished, Hadrian could certainly have found out much more about Alexander than we can, as many more histories were surviving in his day than in ours.

As a general, Alexander remained globally famous, but his conquests were essentially won with the army which Philip had created. His favourite battle-tactic was already Philip's: an angled charge with the cavalry from one wing, drawing the enemy sideways to cover it, then a turn inwards in pointed formation towards the enemy's centre, which this manoeuvre had unbalanced. It was followed up by the infantry in the centre, armed with the long pike, or *sarissa*, which was swished up and down like the quills, observers said, of a terrifying porcupine. Alexander's crack troops were Philip's Shield-bearers, hardened infantry who savaged the Indian armies and their elephants, even when many of them, Philip's recruits, were already over sixty years old. They survived Alexander, and remained the world's most lethal troopers, a refutation of our modern ideas of 'old age'. Even the plan to invade Asia was Philip's own, as were the Greek experts in artillery who added torsion-power to the stone-throwing catapults and designed ever bigger machinery and siege towers for the assaults on city-walls.

Unlike Philip, Alexander interpreted 'Asia' to mean the world to its (supposed) eastern edge, not simply all or part of the Persian Empire. On the way east, unlike Philip, he was a supremely successful besieger. He never lost a battle and his minor campaigns were masterpieces of audacity and hardly credible stamina. He was lethal up an Indian mountain-peak or alone in a Lebanese forest. He led his men from the front, although this inspiring habit nearly killed him in 325 BC when he jumped down off a city-wall in India single-handedly into a terrified crowd of Indian archers. He took the island city of Tyre by building a mole across the sea; he flattened the rebellious city of Thebes, Philip's uneasy ally, and sold the inhabitants into slavery (as Philip had done to many Greek cities in the north). In one spectacular evening, encouraged by wine, women and

29. Legendary Alexander at the Last Judgement with Indian Porus, Cyrus the Persian and Nebuchadnezzar the Babylonian, two hundred years his senior. From Kastoria, in his home Macedonia. Late Byzantine wall painting, fourteenth century AD.

song, he and his men burned the Persians' ceremonial capital, Persepolis, to the ground. Yet he was also extraordinarily canny. He could trick opponents by a series of stratagems; he was a master of what military theorists now teach as 'dynamic manoeuvres'; he could split his forces and co-ordinate them in a planned campaign. He was cool enough to take huge risks, but intelligent enough to adapt them to the weak points of his ever-changing enemies. He also helped his progress by an appropriate political 'spin'. Philip had given his Asian invasion an artful presentation as a campaign of revenge; Alexander publicized a 'dossier' of letters exchanged with the Persian king Darius in which he 'justified' his aggression in terms of previous Persian aggression and interference. After three years as the avenger of Persian outrages, he then recycled himself as the respectful heir of Cyrus, the first great Persian king. Behind the spin, he had been determined to rule and retain his conquests in Asia from the very start.

Alexander's bold, impulsive nature owed much to his extreme youth. It was enhanced, however, by two singular supports. His father Philip had given him a good Greek education, shared with the young sons of Macedonian nobles, Philip's newly formed corps of Royal Pages, who became Alexander's supporting officers. The pupil of Aristotle, Alexander read Greek texts, staged Greek dramas to entertain his army across Asia and shared his men's fascination with the new world around them which seemed at times to recall the old myths of the Greeks. But he also modelled himself on the supreme hero of Homer's epics, Achilles. He ran naked to the supposed site of Achilles' tomb at Troy, while his male lover, Hephaestion, crowned the tomb of Achilles's beloved Patroclus. He placed his copy of Homer's *Iliad*, annotated by Aristotle, in the most precious casket captured from the Persian king. When the Athenians sent him an ambassador called Achilles, he granted them their request. In Alexander, Homer found his most avid over-interpreter.

In Macedonian society, this personal rivalry with a Homeric hero was not entirely misplaced. The king ruled by prowess among his Companions and, as Philip had shown, he had to bestow gifts and strive for personal esteem; the heroic world of Homer's epics was not so remote from Macedonian values. Like a very special hero, Alexander also came to believe that he was the begotten child of a god. Again, there were Greek precedents, in the Spartan royal family, in the ruling family at Syracuse and even, admirers said, in Plato the philosopher, the 'begotten son of Apollo'.[1] Alexander publicized this personal claim after his visit to an oracle in the Siwah oasis on the borders of Libya and Egypt. Its god, Ammon, had often been consulted by Greeks before him and was understood to be Zeus; its priest greeted Alexander, Egypt's new ruler, as 'son of Zeus'. It was said that his mother Olympias had already hinted that Alexander's father was more than human, a view which her eventual quarrels with Philip may have reinforced in her. Certainly, Alexander prized his divine sonship. He also honoured the god when he reached, as second-best, the 'Outer' Indian Ocean: his sacrifices here were announced as being 'in accordance with Ammon's oracular words'.[2] It seems, then, that at Siwah in 332/1, he had already asked the god which gods to honour when he reached the Ocean, the edge of the world. When he asked the question, aged twenty-four, he had not yet defeated the Persians' grand army. The question says much for his priorities and for the self-confidence which helped to realize them.

The role-model of a hero and the parentage of a god supported Alexander's innate energy and boundless ambition. No doubt his edgy relationship with his own father, Philip, also accentuated his own endless wish to excel. The result was a conquest which changed the horizons of the Greek world. As a result, the army and military style of the Persian kings were

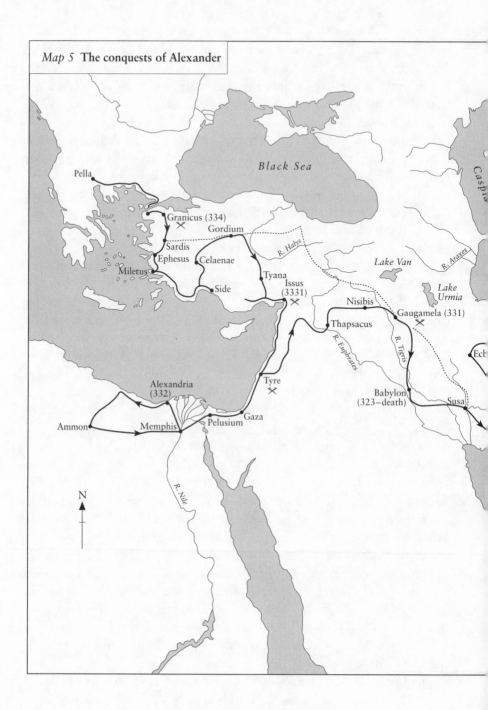

Map 5 The conquests of Alexander

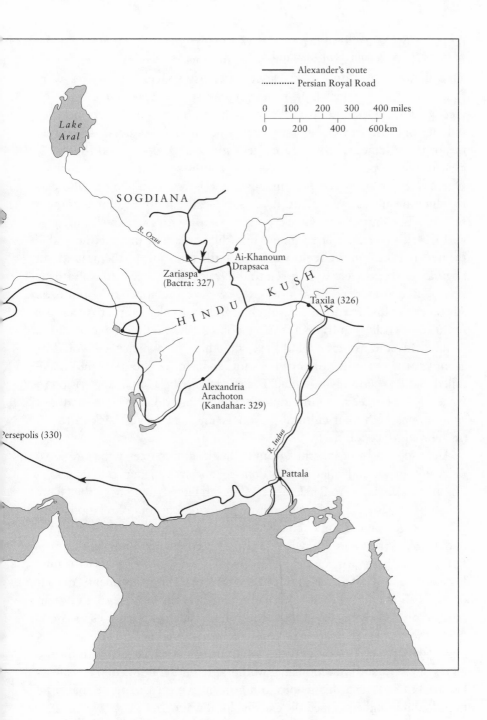

replaced by Macedonian training and troops, as first mapped out by Philip. The festivals and ideals of Persian kingship were replaced by the Macedonians' personal royal style. At least sixteen new cities were founded by Alexander at promising points across Asia, while tradition credited him, questionably, with many more. These cities were not just military outposts, a type of settlement which he also founded. They were meant to be famous, to their founder's glory, and to that end they were placed, where possible, near accessible routes for trade and exchange. One city commemorated Alexander's noble horse, Bucephalas, who carried him for more than seventeen years; typically, another commemorated his dog. The cities, with Greek settlers, were centres of Greek language and Greek entertainments, including athletic games and the inevitable theatre. But local non-Greeks were also settled in some of them. Once, in Sogdia, rebel prisoners were given to the residents of a new Alexandria as slaves, but elsewhere local non-Greeks were included as volunteers. Alexander's close friend, his admiral Nearchus, explained that Alexander founded townships in Iran so that the nomads should become 'cultivators of the fields and as they would have something for which they would be anxious, they would not do one another harm'.[3] The plan may have failed, but it is certainly not anachronistic to ascribe a 'civilizing' vision to some of Alexander's foundations. Previous Macedonian kings had had similar aims with their cultural patronage and new towns back in rough uncivilized Macedon itself.

Alexander had also inherited from Philip the aim of freeing the Greeks of Asia. Within a year, he had largely done so, and was encouraging democracies as the alternative to Persian-backed oligarchies. Tribute from the Greek cities was abolished, a unique favour in these cities' history of relations with greater powers. Freedom, in consequence, became equated with democracy in the Greek city-states. Elsewhere, in non-Greek Asia, in Babylon or Egypt or Cyprus or Sidon, Alexander could capitalize on recent grievances against Persian rule and offer 'freedom', in the sense of self-government ('autonomy') as an alternative. But he also inherited here the Persian king's system of taxation and claims to ultimate control. Outside the territories of Greek cities, the 'land', as one of his early rulings proclaimed, 'I recognize as mine'.[4] His governors oversaw it, while troops were kept strictly in the hands of Greek and Macedonian governors. Tribute continued to be paid as before, but in return, his troops and governors kept the peace (or so he hoped) and in India stopped the existing local wars.

In Asia, therefore, there was a real increase of freedom for most of the Greek cities, but for other people there was peace after slaughter and a subtle change of master: in Arabia or in India, no less than in Greek Asia, Alexander did persuade himself, at least, that he was granting 'autonomy', even to non-Greeks. In Greece, meanwhile, Philip's well-armoured peace between the Greek allies remained in force. Those Greeks who sought justice under its terms could turn, as always, to local arbitrators or to the courts of their home city-states: in theory there was no limit to the penalties, except exile, which these local courts could impose. To settle disputes between Greek cities, the League in Greece might also appoint arbitrators. 'Justice', therefore, had a new framework in Greece, although the freedom of local 'leagues' and city-states was restricted by it. In Asia, meanwhile, Greek cities continued to operate their own courts, but there was always the possibility of sending an embassy to the king himself for a higher ruling. Alexander had not put the eastern Greek cities into his father's Hellenic Alliance. He personally had freed them, and after constitutional upheavals in such cities he himself might prescribe a new political settlement by letter. In summer 334, he implied to the restored democracy on the island of Chios that he personally would read through their proposed new law-code so as to check that nothing in it was contrary to their democratic future. In these cities, the question of exiles and their peaceful restoration remained the object of his personal intervention; he even specified, by letter, that their cases should be judged by jurors using a 'secret ballot'. Inevitably, within the local framework of a 'free' city's laws, Alexander's own edicts by letter did acquire an irresistible power.

Outside the Greek cities, aggrieved parties throughout Asia could appeal to a local governor or to one of Alexander's underlings in the hope of an enforceable ruling. They might even gain access to the king himself and aspire to a judgement in their favour (they would need an interpreter to present the case). In Asia, therefore, justice remained at the dispensation of a king's local officials, as before. There were no judicial reforms or new constitutions for his non-Greek subjects, but here and there (where a tradition of local laws existed) Alexander did publicize a return to pre-Persian rulings.

His conquests also multiplied the scope for gain and luxury beyond any Greek's wildest dreams. Whereas Philip's income had hardly sufficed to mount an invasion of Asia, Alexander's allowed him the most lavish displays in Greek history. Ten thousand talents, about ten times the yearly income of Pericles' Athens, were expended on a single celebration, a royal wedding or banquet. His Companions dined on couches with silver feet; individual officers were said to own fine hunting-nets a mile or more in length; even the staid elderly officer, Polyperchon, one of Philip's men,

30. Tomb painting at Agios Athanasios (probably Chalastra) near Thessalonica, showing Macedonian males processing with torches and drinking vessels, dining, and standing as infantrymen. Arguably *c.* 320-310 BC.

was said to dance in a saffron cloak and slippers.[5] Drink had always flowed freely at the Macedonian court, and it came to flow very freely in Alexander's later years. There were nights when Alexander sat up drinking until dawn. At the funeral celebrations of an Indian wise man at his court, the winner in a drinking contest drained several gallons, while the runners-up included several Indians, who died in the aftermath. When Alexander married two more brides from the Persian royal houses near the end of his life, the occasion was celebrated with lavish gifts and his audience-tent was enlarged into the most magnificent marquee. Even the big curtain-poles were made of gold.

At his death, Alexander was planning further conquests in Arabia (whose scale he perhaps underestimated) and then possibly a march into the West against Carthage and north Africa. His aims, of course, are disputed, but in my view he had decided early on to march to the eastern edge of the world; when he was denied it, he went down to what he thought was a southern edge (the Indian Ocean); at his death he was exploring a possible northern edge (the Caspian Sea) and surely, therefore, thinking of conquering to the western edge (the Atlantic Ocean). His 'geography' was only slightly less mistaken than Aristotle's, but it set his ambitions.

What was his sexual nature? He was not a one-way homosexual. During eleven years on the march, he married the Bactrian Roxane and two Persian brides, taking three wives as opposed to Philip's seven. He also fathered a child on another Persian mistress, and perhaps one on an Indian chieftain, and was said in court gossip to have slept for twelve days with a visiting 'Queen of the Amazons' near the Caspian Sea. Since early boyhood he had also loved Hephaestion, whose death before his own drove him to extreme grief. Plainly, there was a homoerotic sexual element to his love for his 'Patroclus', but their love was more than just sex. In Asia, Alexander also had sex with a Persian court-eunuch, Bagoas, who joined him in 330 and was made one of the ship-captains, the only foreigner, when Alexander's fleet turned for home down the river Indus in 326. The fairest modern label for his sex-life is 'bisexual': Philip was said to have behaved likewise, and homoerotic sex was part of the lifestyle of his Royal Pages. As in contemporary Athens, so in Macedon a sexual love for a boy was something which a man could profess openly, without discredit. We do not know what his accompanying Indians thought of it.

As a passionate man, Alexander had his drunken moments and his outbursts of rage; they culminated in the dark evening in late 328 BC when he personally killed one of his father's veteran Companions, Cleitus, at a party. His life was emphatically not lived without moral blots and stains; his ambition also killed tens of thousands of Indians who refused to surrender and be his subjects rather than subjects of their existing kings, and his army plundered the goods and supplies of countless families in order to feed themselves as they crossed Asia. However, after the initial conquest, further looting and violence were not Alexander's idea of ruling his subjects. He had a magic which was personally exercised for the troops who loved him, and we must do justice to it too, and the accompanying extravagance of his youth. Such were his feats, his benefactions and his capacity for favours that some of the Greek cities spontaneously offered him 'honours equal to those for the gods'. Sometimes they were offered in admiration or gratitude, at other times as hopeful flattery. Benefaction, in the sense of material favours, was central to Greek ideas of a god; Alexander was as capable of it as almost any Olympian god, while his prowess, as far as India, rivalled most Olympians' known deeds. There had been divine cults previously for Greek men of power and achievement, but they only became an established practice among Greeks because of Alexander's exceptional prowess. But he himself knew very well that he was mortal, and he continued to honour the immortal gods and to obey their oracles. His own religious life remained traditional, rooted in Greek practice and precedent.

Above all, Alexander had an emotional bond with his men, maintained through storm and desert, wounds and hardship and the many moments when he and his commanders had no idea where they were on the map. They had marched on foot against vastly bigger armies and they had seen deserts, cities, mountains and elephants which none had ever imagined in his youth. Some of them had ridden without stirrups and without saddles, forming into pointed formations for the sudden shock of battle-charge, those moments of 'all or nothing' which are the moments for glory, to be won at the expense of enemies and sustained, for years, with ever-enlarging stories. When Alexander lay dying, 'his soldiers longed to see him, some of them so as to see him alive, others because . . . they thought his death was being concealed from them by his bodyguards. Most of them were driven to see Alexander by grief and longing for their king. As the army processed past him, he was unable to speak, but he gestured to each of them, lifting his head with difficulty and signalling to them with his eyes.'[6] Like us, they were left unsure exactly what their king had in mind.

ALEXANDER'S
EARLY SUCCESSORS

When Seleucus saw that his troops were terrified, he kept on encouraging them, telling them that it was not fitting for men who had campaigned with Alexander and been promoted by him for their courage to rely solely on power and money. They should use experience and clever understanding, the means by which Alexander, too, had accomplished his great and universally admired deeds . . . Alexander had stood beside him in a dream and clearly signified about the future leadership which he was destined to attain as time went by . . .

Diodorus, 19.90, as Seleucus rides off to Babylon (312 BC)

I T WAS ON 10 JUNE 323 that Alexander died in Babylon. By a remarkable chance, we have the clay tablet on which a Babylonian scribe recorded the event in a day-by-day record of the heavens: 'The King died,' he noted. 'Clouds . . . '[1]

None of the surviving Greek or Roman sources mentions the clouds. Instead, they dwell on the bonfire of personal ambition which the unexpected death of the king ignited. Alexander left no designated heir, but his Bactrian wife, Roxane, was already six months pregnant. He had a half-brother, Philip Arrhidaeus, who was also in his thirties, but this son of King Philip and a Thessalian mother was half-witted. Already there were the makings of a stupendous struggle. The unborn baby would be half-barbarian and, like the defective Arrhidaeus, it would need guardians to exercise real power in its name.

The first struggle, therefore, was for the 'guardianship' of the royal line. But which line? From 330 BC onwards, young Alexander had practised the 'inclusion' of Persians and other Iranians into positions of honour around him and eventually even into the inner, world-conquering units of his Macedonian army. He had married the Bactrian Roxane; he had loved the eunuch Bagoas; he had had 30,000 Iranian boys trained in Macedonian weaponry and entitled them his 'Successors'; in one spectacular ceremony, he had even married off ninety-two of his Macedonian officers to Iranian brides (arranging that any children of his and Hephaestion's brides should be cousins); at the same moment he had given presents to no less than 10,000 of his troops who had already 'married' Asian women too. This inclusion had gone way beyond a mere recruitment into supporting units so as to keep up his army's manpower. It put barbarians into the great Companion cavalry and made a few of them Companion nobles. Alexander did not need to do this. It was a principle of the king, the recruitment of 'Alexander's men', irrespective of origin, ethnicity and background, into an inclusive court and army of the future: 'Zeus', he was remembered as saying, 'is the father of all men,' as in Homer, 'but he makes the best particularly his own.'[2] So, now, did Alexander, in an 'empire of the best'. Some of his Macedonians, the older ones especially, hated the policy. They had no wish to fraternize with people they had once tried to kill. As soon as he was dead, this hatred erupted.

Others were more flexible, his younger and closer friends and his cavalrymen, who could accommodate any able fellow lover of horses: they were willing to wait for Roxane's unborn son. Meanwhile, the older Macedonians and the veteran infantry, united by their thick Macedonian Greek dialect, agitated for a Macedonian heir, a son of King Philip, even if he was mentally unsound. There were riots, followed by a compromise: Roxane's child would share the kingship with the half-wit, Philip Arrhidaeus. The most prominent advocate of the settlement was Alexander's trusted Perdiccas, a noble Macedonian of royal highland descent. After Hephaestion's death, Perdiccas was the man whom Alexander had appointed to be his next 'chiliarch', or second-in-command, with the charge of the most respected unit of cavalry. He was (later) said to have been given Alexander's ring by Alexander himself and even to have received the job of caring for Roxane. On such matters, propaganda proliferated.

Within five days of Alexander's death, the former Persian queen mother had starved herself to death, lamenting (men said) the loss of Alexander: only eight years before, he had been her son's sworn enemy. Amongst Macedonians, there was a complication. Alexander had sent their respected general Craterus back to Macedonia with 10,000 elderly Macedonian veterans whom he had dismissed. Craterus was strongly conservative and was no friend to 'inclusion'. Alexander had ordered him to 'take care of the freedom of the Greeks', a reminder of how that old ideal had now been diluted.[3] He was also to replace the elderly Antipater who had been commander in Greece in Alexander's absence.

What orders from Alexander might Craterus invent or claim for himself? There was no precedent or system in Macedonian society for dealing with such a crisis. The early death of a childless king had left a vacuum, and somehow the gaps must be filled in. Titles of honour could be quickly invented to placate the senior figures, 'guardian' or 'overseer' or 'chiliarch' (in the sense of 'deputy'). At Babylon, Perdiccas also claimed to have found Alexander's 'Last Plans'. He presented them to the troops, surely intending them to be cancelled: it is quite likely that he and his aides, including the artful Greek secretary Eumenes, had invented them in an evening of frantic improvisation. They were made to include fantastic building projects; one was a temple at Troy, another, a vast mound as 'big as a pyramid' in Philip's honour in Macedon. Plans for Western conquest were added, stretching on through Carthage and beyond. The aim, surely, was that the troops should listen respectfully but reject them. The likes of Craterus could not then appeal to different 'plans' and claim that they were empowered by them. But would the troops be sure to reject even this much? So another vast plan was included: 'transfers of population' between Europe and Asia, so as to bring them into harmony by 'intermarriage and assimilation'.[4] From a king who had stood up for inclusion, this plan was just credible: the Macedonians, 'Asia-sceptics', dreaded it, and rejected the 'plans', as intended.

Roxane's baby, born in September, was a boy (Alexander IV). Meanwhile, Perdiccas took the lead in Asia with Antipater, now in his seventies, a 'rotten thread' in Macedonia.[5] Within twenty-two years, Alexander's kingdom would have fragmented among quite other generals: his lifelong friend Ptolemy, in Egypt; his infantry commander Seleucus, in Asia; his bodyguard, Lysimachus, in Thrace and north-west Asia; Antipater's impetuous son, Cassander, in Macedon (as Alexander's companion at Babylon, Cassander was alleged, even, to have helped to have him 'poisoned'). For a while, other major competitors led troops and played for high stakes: the big, burly Antigonus, one-eyed, with a booming voice, the veteran who had commanded in western Asia throughout Alexander's march east; his flamboyant son, Demetrius, 'brave as a hero and beautiful as a god, of such majesty that strangers followed him merely to gaze';[6] the artful Eumenes, no Macedonian himself, but a literate Odysseus of a Greek who had been Alexander's secretary. Until 281 BC wars were waged incessantly between the major participants and their followers.

31. Portrait bust of Demetrius the Besieger, the most flamboyant of Alexander's successors, showing small bull's horns, attributes of the god Dionysus. Cast of the Roman replica, Herculaneum.

The first of the long-term winners to show his hand was Ptolemy. He had known Alexander well since childhood; he had even been appointed as his food-taster (obviously a highly responsible job, in a world of poisons). At Babylon, he received rich Egypt as his governorship, but he entrenched himself there by conquests in the West (in Libya) and then by invading Cyprus. His weakest frontier lay in the East, causing him to invade Syria repeatedly in a pattern of 'Syrian wars' which would preoccupy his successors for a hundred years and more. Ptolemy was to found the dynasty, the Ptolemies, which ruled Egypt for three hundred years. One of his most artful moves was to seize Alexander's dead body when Perdiccas sent it home from Babylon on a magnificently decorated funeral carriage. One story is that Ptolemy cheated his pursuers by substituting a sham corpse: they must have chased him, and so perhaps some such trick is historical.

At first, Ptolemy kept Alexander's body in the old Egyptian capital at Memphis. Later, it was moved down the Nile to Alexandria where a subsequent king, Ptolemy IV, built a magnificent mausoleum, the *Sēma*, for Alexander and the other dead Ptolemies. Rumours that Alexander's tomb has been found continue to attract publicity, but they would have to involve the rediscovery of a huge dynastic monument under the built-up centre of Alexandria. As for his body, it continued to be displayed there to visitors, including the first Roman emperor Augustus, who laid flowers (in 30 BC) on the coffin's glass lid. It was said, perhaps rhetorically, to be still on display in c. AD 380, but there is no specific reference to a visit to it after one in AD 215.[7] The tomb and the corpse were almost certainly destroyed in one or other great city-riot in Alexandria.

For seventeen years, the competing 'successors' avoided the title of king, but then Alexander's little son died (in 310) and his own tantalizing sister Cleopatra died too (in 308 BC). Antigonus was the only successor with that royal necessity, a promising son, Demetrius: after a fine victory by the young man, he first took the title of king, knowing that now he had a worthy heir. His rivals then followed suit, including Ptolemy in Egypt, though the scribes in Egypt waited until 305 to describe him as Pharaoh-king too. Ptolemy had to fight hard to survive, first against Perdiccas, then against Antigonus and his son. Since 311, he too had posed as a champion of the 'freedom of the Greeks': most of all the successors, he needed Greeks for his armies and his new Egypt. His plea for freedom, however, was not a committed plea for democracy.

In Greece, meanwhile, many of the Greeks had anticipated him. On news of Alexander's death, they had risen in revolt, summoning Greeks to 'freedom' from the Macedonian 'barbarians' in a way which reversed the spin of Alexander's own invasion of Asia. Despite some valiant successes, they were crippled by defeats at sea, leading to the Athenians' capitulation. In 322 BC, after more than a hundred and eighty years, the Athenians' democracy was ended by a conqueror, Antipater. Political rights were confined to those Athenians who had moderate property or more; the lowest classes were to be exported to the wilds of Thrace.

Only the changing power-struggles of the Successors allowed Athenian democrats to restore their system, briefly in 318, more lastingly in 307. 'Freedom' would remain a much-publicized slogan for Greeks, but it was now a slogan for the competing Macedonian generals to offer. As under Philip and Alexander, it depended on concessions from a powerful overlord. Such concessions continued to be made, however, either to destabilize a rival general or else to secure Greece (and thereby, Macedon) and attract Greek settlers and recruits out into the new dynasties in Asia. There was, then, room for manoeuvre for the Greek city-states, but not for full liberty: since 338 BC, under Philip, the Athenians no longer controlled the vital sea-route for their grain-imports from the Black Sea.

32. Portrait bust of Seleucus I, Alexander's commander of the Royal Shield-bearers and eventual Successor in Asia. Cast of the Roman replica, Herculaneum.

In Asia, the wars had two unusual patterns: an absence of local nationalism and a general respect for continuing kingship and legality, even when the 'kings' were a half-wit and a child. Remarkably, none of the people in Asia rose in rebellion during the fights for the succession. Asian recruits even continued to serve copiously in the Macedonians' own competing armies. Meanwhile, the two 'compromise kings', Philip III and Alexander IV, continued to be recognized in public inscriptions in the Greek cities, in Babylonia and in Egypt; the various royal treasuries continued to be guarded punctiliously and made available only to those with royal letters; a royal coinage and a royal calendar (numbering the years by their reigns) continued to prevail, at least until Philip the half-wit was killed in autumn 317 BC and then young Alexander IV (with Roxane) in 310 BC.

Why were there no national revolts? At first, Alexander had reappointed those Iranian governors who surrendered to him. In his absence in India, some of them then revolted, but other Iranians helped to capture and surrender them. There was no national solidarity, and the Macedonians had the monopoly of trained military force. Perceptions of the con-

33. Silver plate with gilding: a goddess, perhaps Cybele, drawn by lions to an altar. From the Greek city at Ai Khanum, Afghanistan, *c.* 300 BC.

quest also varied according to class. For many of their subjects, the Macedonians' victory had meant very little change. Tribute continued to be demanded; local collectors still gathered it. Even when land was given to new beneficiaries, it still had to be worked by the same local workers. Why, then, revolt for more of the same, under a new or old name? Alexander's conquests in India were lost after twenty years, but not because of local nationalism: his emerging general, Seleucus, exchanged them with Chandragupta, a newly emerged Indian military leader from the south, and then for the massive price of 500 war-elephants. His conquests in Bactria survived in Graeco-Macedonian hands for more than a hundred and fifty years. In Babylonia, so densely populated, Seleucus himself could profit from good memories of the previous governorship which he had held since the 320s: in 312 BC he reinstated himself with a core force of only a few hundred horsemen after a bold gallop back from Syria. All over Asia, non-Greek subjects acquiesced in Macedonian rule or preferred to profit by joining their new masters.

Not only were these masters hardened soldiers: they were prepared to fight massively against each other. From King Philip's reforms onwards, the Macedonians refute so many of the popular stereotypes about soldiers and the human condition. They fought loyally although they had no votes, no 'republican' freedom to inspire them. In the chaos after Alexander's death, they did start to express approval for one or other leader in their military assemblies, and so consultation of them became a customary necessity. They did not, however, gain any democratic liberty, or even seek it. Nor did they want to retire from the army; Alexander's best Macedonians in India were often over sixty, but they fought on for another ten years, still terrorizing their opponents. After his death they were prepared to fight fellow Macedonians, especially if attacking younger Macedonians from the 'new intake' who had never served the great Alexander. In the absence of a true hereditary king as general, these veterans served whoever could pay them and protect the goods and baggage (including women) which represented their personal riches on the move. At first, endorsement by the two compromise kings did help the competing generals to win them over, but then the kings were killed off and in the end Alexander's successors were just military men, no more. They were a generation of 'lucky *condottieri*',[8] whereas Philip and Alexander had been truly dynastic kings of the Macedonian people.

Alexander's own memory and style, therefore, did matter to his would-be heirs. Naturally, they continued the style of his army and tactics, including his one innovation in Greek warfare, use of the elephant. So far as there was an 'arms race', it was only to create ever bigger versions of the same machines as Alexander's, the ships or siege-engines: in 306 young Demetrius could even mobilize fabulous siege-towers, 120 feet high, against the walls of Rhodes (the city survived the siege, nonetheless). By 318 war-elephants, even, were being used against city-walls in Arcadia in Greece: an Indian expert taught the Greek defenders how to conceal spiked planks in the ground before their walls so that the soft undersides of the elephants' feet became impaled. In Syria, Ptolemy then repeated the trick in a pitched battle six years later.

For seven years the prominent career of the non-Macedonian Eumenes showed what an aspiring leader needed to represent in the wake of Alexander. Although he was also a secretary, Eumenes was a wily general; though a Greek, he was not above being drunk (like a good Macedonian) for a night in his army-camp. How ever could such a non-Macedonian lead hardened Macedonian troops? Eumenes had problems with their dialect, but he did know how to make a point to them, by telling them a simple fable about a lion, the sort of story last recorded in our history books in the archaic world of the speeches in Herodotus' 'enquiries'.

34. Reconstruction of a painting of a Macedonian lion- and boar-hunt, set in Asia. Alexander rides in to rescue what may be Lysimachus, a future Successor. Perhaps first painted perhaps in *c.* 332/1 BC, and copied later in the mosaic.

Lacking Macedonian roots, it was crucial that Eumenes did have letters of royal Macedonian approval from the compromise kings. These letters allowed him to claim money: they even made the famous veteran 'Silver Shields' follow him, because he was validated as the kings' man. When some of the big names from Alexander's past joined him, he artfully persuaded these uneasy 'equals' to agree to meet in a tent containing the dead Alexander's throne. His sceptre was placed on it; they all revered Alexander as a god and when they took counsel, they felt as if a 'god was leading them on'. Six years after Alexander's death, they could still unite in his unseen presence.

Eumenes' tactics were only a part of a wider imitation of the famous king. Alexander's great multi-racial banquets were imitated in Persia; his Successors were said to imitate his voice or even the way he held his head. The least powerful of them, Lysimachus, was the one who eventually issued the most idealized portrait of a godlike young Alexander on his silver coins. Like Alexander, himself a passionate hunter, the Successors paraded their hunting prowess, claiming to be true 'lion kings':

Perdiccas was even said to have taken a lioness's cubs from her den bare-handed. Like Alexander, the Successors received local cults from hopeful or grateful Greek cities, without actually demanding their own worship as gods. As Seleucus' power in Asia grew, he claimed to have been acknowledged by a great Greek oracle as the begotten son of a god, like Alexander: the god was Apollo, the oracle the shrine at Didyma near Miletus. His Iranian queen, Apama, was encouraged to be a benefactress of the site which thus gained its enormous temple, the biggest and finest surviving monument of the early Hellenistic world.[9]

By 302 BC there were five competing kings, but a year later they were reduced to four when Seleucus defeated the elderly Antigonus and killed him. India had by now been given away, but the rest of Alexander's territories stayed under Greek rule. In 281 BC, after more years of struggle, the four kings became three when Seleucus, an Alexander-survivor, killed off Lysimachus, one of Alexander's bodyguards, at an old site of Persian military settlement, 'Cyrus' Plain', in western Asia. From 281 BC until the clashes with Rome, Alexander's Greek world remained split into the resulting three kingdoms: the Seleucid kings in Asia (without India), the Ptolemies in Egypt and the Antigonids in Macedon, bound by garrisons and treaties to the city-states and 'leagues' in Greece. On a long view, the split was not so very new. The previous empire, the Persians', had had recurrent problems in retaining Egypt. They had a loose hold on India and had never conquered Greece. The Successors' three-way split, then, was already visible in the early years of the fourth century BC.

During the years of the dynasts' rivalry, one social group did gain greater prominence: royal and well-born women. Alexander's sister Cleopatra was soon widowed, a prize for the aspiring Successors; until 316, his mother Olympias was still at large in her home kingdom; his niece Adea (Philip's granddaughter), when she was aged only sixteen, proved to have a spirit and public audacity worthy of her military mother. But there were other great women, too, outside the royal house. Antipater's daughter Phila won a good name for charitable actions and sound sense, although she had to endure a marriage to the younger playboy Demetrius. One of the least promising of Alexander's arranged Oriental marriages had been the union of Darius' Persian niece, Amestris, with the staunch Macedonian 'Asia-sceptic' Craterus. He died soon afterwards, having ignored her, but she then married the dynast of a Greek city on the Black Sea and ended, by origin a royal Persian, as the ruler of the city-state.

The honours, not unfittingly, went to Olympias. Brought back to Macedon in 317, she protected her son's half-Bactrian child, Roxane's boy, and attacked the vigorous young Adea who was by now the wife of the half-witted Philip III. In autumn 317 Olympias offered a truly theatrical choice of death to Adea (a dagger, a noose or poison), but within a year she herself had to surrender to her enemies after the most fearful siege in the coastal town of Pydna. It took the relatives of her previous victims to murder her: no less than two hundred soldiers, sent for the purpose, had refused the task 'out of respect for her royal rank'. Her death was worthy of Greek tragedy's over-powering Queen Clytemnestra. But even this tragic drama was excelled on Cyprus by the awesome Axiothea, the queen of Paphos. In Paphos' palace, in 312 BC, she made each one of her daughters kill herself before finally taking her own life, rather than fall into the hands of Ptolemy's agents.

In Greece during these years, we hear of prominent courtesans, heirs to the top 'mistresses' of Alexander's own court. None was more famous than the mature Lamia, whose doings with Athens' liberating prince Demetrius remained a topic of witty scandal and comic theatre. In Athens, some of the courtesans are said to have been hearers of the affable philospher Epicurus; we even know of portraits of two distinguished Greek poetesses, Myrto and Anyte. But these women were of minimal public impact compared with the feminine rivals who were active inside the Successors' own palaces.

When praising the Ptolemies, the poet Theocritus cited the quality of being a 'good lover' (*erōtikos*).[10] It was different to being a good husband. In almost every Successor family, the kings not only fell repeatedly in love; they actually married a second woman, or more, and fathered more sets of children. Marriage to Cleopatra, his seventh wife, had been the cause of King Philip's murder back in 336, but even so, Alexander left three Iranian wives at his death: Roxane, the new 'queen mother', was said to have been very quick to poison one of the other two brides. In the Successors' families, 'second-wife syndrome' then became rampant, as if no lessons had been learned from the Macedonian past. Ptolemy married one of Antipater's daughters, but then fell in love with one of her Macedonian attendants and married her too: this younger wife's sons became the more favoured sons in Ptolemy's priorities, causing a serious dynastic quarrel with the older children. Lysimachus repeated the same mistake and killed his eldest son by one wife after foolishly marrying another. This family chaos undermined his rule and helped to bring Seleucus against him. Cassander did no better, and Seleucus only escaped trouble by sharing his kingdom with his son in his lifetime and conceding one of his wives to him: the boy, it was said, was lovesick for her. One-eyed Antigonus was the only steady man in marriage, but his son Demetrius made up for him by his two marriages and his prodigal liaisons with star Greek courtesans. A hunting prince, he never killed a lion, but he did make love to a famous prostitute called 'Lioness' (the name of a sexual position, too).

In the great Athenian tragic dramas which these Macedonians must have watched, there were scenes of noble suicide in royal families split by infidelities and second marriages. In the Successors' families, what had once been myth came true. The new age of kingship threw women into prominence on an unstable royal stage: fact became even more chilling than dramatic fiction.

23

LIFE IN THE BIG CITIES

For a slave who has hit a free man. If a male slave or a female slave hits a
free man or a free woman, they shall be whipped with not less than 100
strokes of the lash . . . Blows exchanged between free persons. If a free man
or a free woman hits a free man or free woman, starting an unjust attack,
they shall pay 100 drachmas without assessment if they lose the suit at law.

Laws in Alexandria, *c.* **250 BC,**
***Dikaiomata* lines 196 ff., 203 ff.**

Timanthes engraved this star-like lapis lazuli
   This Persian semi-precious stone containing gold
For Demylus; in exchange for a tender kiss the dark-haired
   Nicaea of Cos re[ceived it as a lovely] gift.

Poseidippus of Pella, 5 (Austin-Bastiniani),
first published from papyrus in 2001

THE CENTURIES AFTER ALEXANDER, from 323 to 30 BC, are known as
the 'Hellenistic' age. In modern usage the word first referred to the
extension of Greek language and culture to non-Greeks in the East, resulting in its unclassical mixing and implicit dilution. In fact, such extension had gone on long before Alexander, occurring round many Greek
overseas settlements, let alone on the island of Cyprus. The more distinctive feature of the age is the multiplication of Greek-speaking kings and
royal courts, combined with a new surge in city foundations. Here Greek
language and culture remained dominant, although some of the new adherents were still bilingual. The kings, their governors and settlers were
not men with a religious mission: as prudent polytheists they sometimes

worshipped existing local gods. But they did also 'improve' whole areas of the near East, bringing the Greek cultural life which they wanted and cultivating land, especially in Egypt, which had been under-exploited before. In our post-colonial age, modern historians are now wary of imposing a 'colonial' interpretation on their actions. We need to be wary, but some of the kings and settlers, including Alexander and his courtiers, did have an orientalising attitude to Asia and regarded it as inefficient or under-utilised. It is not wrong to credit them, too, with a belief in the splendour and civilizing power of their Greek culture. Macedonian kings, since Alexander I, had taken a similar view of it in their own rough home kingdom.

As Alexander's conquests settled down, the three main 'Successor' kingdoms built on his example as a city-founder. His Successors in Asia, the Seleucids, settled dozens of new cities and towns, above all in Syria and Mesopotamia. In Egypt, the Ptolemies added only one city (Ptolemais) but they made his Alexandria the greatest city of the age. In Macedonia and old Greece, the Antigonids also founded yet more cities: the most intriguing is the 'City of Heaven' (Uranopolis) which was founded by Antipater's son Alexarchus, who is said to have compared himself with the sun and sent a letter in a made-up language to his brother Cassander's new city nearby.[1] Like us, they must have been baffled by it.

Hadrian was residing in just such a great 'new city', the Seleucids' Antioch in Syria, when he heard the news of his accession. Like its founder, Seleucus, he climbed the imposing Jebel-Aqra mountain, the 'Mount Sion' of ancient paganism, which towers above it. Although he continued to favour Antioch and gave it funds for a smart new set of baths, he also visited Alexandria in Egypt and enjoyed it much more. He even honoured aspects of this city in the water-garden of his villa in Italy. Like the Successor kings, Hadrian also founded cities in the eastern provinces of his empire. One of them commemorated one of his spectacular hunts; another, 'Antinoopolis' in Egypt, commemorated his boyfriend Antinous, who had died nearby while still young.

The continuities here are very strong, for Alexander would have sympathized: he himself founded a city in memory of his dog and would surely have founded such a place for his lover, Hephaestion. Like Hadrian, Alexander and the Successors also founded military colonies in the East. Unlike the Roman colonies of Hadrian's predecessors, their colonies were not sites for retired soldiers. Instead, their colonies' land-holding families remained liable to military service. Initially they were not very numerous. The best-known such colony is Dura, on the river Euphrates, for which a maximum population of 6,000 has been proposed at its peak. Recent surveys, however, have shown that its first population was very much smaller.[2]

The new cities in Asia were vastly greater places from the start. Alexandria in Egypt soon contained more than 100,000 people and by the second century BC it may have risen to more than 300,000. Antioch in north Syria and Seleucia on the Tigris were also enormous. Life in these places was on a different scale to classical Athens, even in the age of Pericles. To put them in context, we can compare the former 'Great City', Megalopolis in old Greece which had been founded so triumphantly in the 360s against a weakened Sparta. In 318, just after Alexander's death, it had only 15,000 men fit for military service, including slaves and foreign residents.[3] The Successor kings' standing armies were so much bigger, and their numbers were swelled by mercenaries and by colonists on call-up. Armies of 60,000 or more foot soldiers were widely deployed, despite the acute problems of supplies and the transporting of their soldiers' all-important personal baggage, often including women. Military life remained at the level exemplified by Alexander. It stayed fairly true to his and Philip's basic units and formations, but the siege-machinery, fortifications, warships and victory-monuments all grew in size and complexity. The war-elephant, encountered by Alexander, became a regular terror in the Successors' armies. Above all, the kings in Greece, western Asia and the Levant continued to launch big war-fleets, maintaining their standards of 'gigantism' in the Aegean.

With the help of these Alexander-style armies, the Successor kings held down the lands of the old Persian Empire and extracted a high level of tribute. War was essential to a Successor king's image (ten of the Seleucid kings died on campaign). In turn, it yielded highly valuable booty and was a major element in the kings' economies, combining with their yearly taxation to support a level of royal luxury far beyond anything which Greeks, even in Sicily, had previously seen. Whereas observers had previously blamed luxury for the fall of this or that city in the eastern or western Greek world, luxury was now used publicly as a statement of royal power. This use is a sign of the end of the fifth and fourth centuries' classical age.

The Successor kings kept vast war-fleets in their harbours, but in Egypt, the kings themselves had fantastically luxurious boats, real floating palaces which excelled any modern Nile cruiser. They had mines which were worked by slaves, and they themselves enjoyed many of Asia's new precious stones, on which Theophrastus, Aristotle's pupil, wrote a work

Map 6 The Hellenistic world

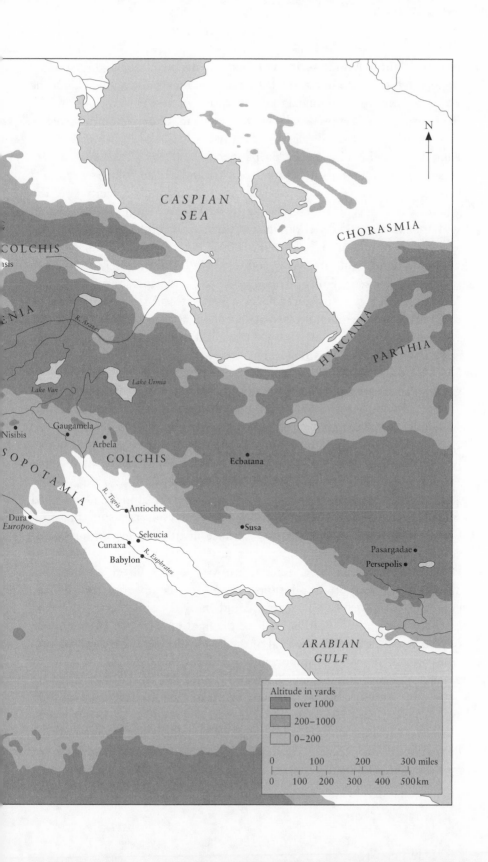

N

CASPIAN
SEA

CHORASMIA

COLCHIS

isis

ENIA

HYRCANIA

PARTHIA

R. Araxes

Lake Urmia

Lake Van

Nisibis

Gaugamela

Arbela

COLCHIS

Ecbatana

SOPOTAMIA

R. Tigris

Dura
Europos

Antiochea

Seleucia

Susa

Cunaxa

R. Euphrates

Pasargadae

Babylon

Persepolis

ARABIAN
GULF

Altitude in yards

over 1000

200–1000

0–200

0   100   200   300 miles

0   100   200   300   400   500 km

of classification. Macedonian ladies had always liked oils and scents (big pottery jars for them have now been found in their palace-towns), but the Ptolemaic queens encouraged the preparation of new perfumes, for which the court became renowned. The most amazing luxury of all occurred at the celebration of the Ptolemies' family festival, the Ptolemaia, which King Ptolemy II held in Egypt, probably in winter 275/4.[4] A fantastic procession of wild animals, tableaux, treasure and armed soldiers processed through the streets of Alexandria and then through the city stadium where seated spectators could admire it. The occasion was associated with the gods, especially Dionysus with whom the Ptolemies linked themselves. It also honoured the dead Ptolemy I, the friend of Alexander, who was now being honoured as a god too. The tableaux included a huge winepress, worked by men dressed as satyrs, and a personified statue of Mount Nysa, Dionysus' birthplace, which sat and stood up automatically: there were women dressed as maenads with ivy in their snaky hair. About 25,000 gallons of wine were poured out for the crowds on the streets, while birds, dressed with ribbons, were released for them to catch and take home, no doubt for dinner. A pole, 180 feet high, displayed a gigantic phallus and more than two thousand men tugged floats which included allusions to the Ptolemies' Greek dependencies abroad and to Alexander in the context of his Indian conquests. A parade of animals included a white bear and a two-horned rhinoceros, all of which were displayed, but not killed. Models of the morning and the evening star evoked the passage of time; 57,000 soldiers marched at the end.

Among his many shows and festivals, not even Alexander had arranged such a spectacle. There were no distinctively Egyptian tableaux, but non-Greeks could join in the occasion because it did not rely on an understanding of Greek. What Egyptians saw was a massive statement of power and splendour, linked to images of Greek gods. Greek visitors from abroad would pick up the allusions to Dionysus' complex mythology, but everyone, whatever their language, could enjoy the extravagance and the free gifts and engage with the scale of the final march-past. Huge crowns of gold were displayed on several of the floats and were joined by the precious crowns donated by important Greek visitors. These donations went towards the cost of a display which showed off the power and generosity of a ruling family who could afford to make their streets run with milk and wine. Perhaps there were royal festivals of a similar scale in Antioch too, but Alexandria certainly set the standard. Like Alexander, the Ptolemies built the most luxurious dining-rooms and filled them with far more couches and furniture than had ever graced a classical Greek dinner-party. Egypt's cut flowers were famous all the year round: a single dinner-party in the 250s BC was adorned with three hundred wreaths of flowers.[5] King Ptolemy II even decorated the pillared colonnades around his dining-room with paintings which referred to the theatre and to great dinner-parties known in myth.

Alexandria's golden years were placed by contemporaries in the mid–240s, a period of 'fair weather'. By then the city had become extraordinarily impressive. There were straight streets (later said to be up to fifty yards wide) which ran in a rectangular plan, oriented to catch the prevailing wind. The quarters were named after letters of the alphabet ('B' and 'D' became the main Jewish quarters). The main street ran on past green awnings to no less than three interrelated harbours. The kings had magnificent palaces on the coastline; its erosion later buried their remains under the sea, but they have begun to be revisited by underwater archaeologists. On an islet by the harbour there was an acknowledged 'wonder of the world', the gigantic lighthouse, or Pharos. Recent explorations have located its massive blocks on the seabed and proved that two colossal statues of a Ptolemy and his queen in the style of Egypt's Pharaohs stood at the base of the monument. Throughout the city, such bits of ancient Egyptian statuary were re-erected as decoration. The lighthouse was dedicated not by a Ptolemy but by an immigrant Greek courtier, Sostratos, who was rich enough to pay for it. Stories were told of the fire-beacon which blazed on top of it and even of the mirror which reflected its light, but nobody has yet reconstructed the upper levels definitively.

This wonder of a lighthouse was obviously very necessary: shipwrecks have been located on the nearby seabed. The royal palaces housed two less mundane marvels: a 'Museum' and a huge library. The Greek tyrants of the past had competed for artists and poets, and one of them, Polycrates of Samos, was credited with a special library of books. In Alexandria, these ideas were encouraged by intellectual fashion, especially by Demetrius the Athenian, the immigrant follower of Aristotle; Aristotle himself had had a grand library and had founded a religious society for his pupils' studies. These Aristotelian examples now found a new grand patron. The Ptolemies used libraries to amass all the Greek texts in existence. They forced visitors who arrived with scrolls to surrender them for copying and they even kidnapped the Athenians' master-copies of their great tragedies. The biggest library, located in their palace, was said to have grown to nearly 500,000 volumes. Scholars gave it a catalogue, and although the texts were not for public consultation, a second library, in the temple of the god Serapis, was smaller and perhaps more accessible.

Old and new Greek texts made Alexandria, the city of so many disparate Greeks, into the powerhouse of all Greek culture. Like the royal processions, the texts enhanced the kings' power and prestige. The rival great cities, therefore, joined in the library race. There was a major library in the Seleucids' capital, Antioch. Recently, a fragment of a philosophy dialogue, based on Plato, was discovered on parchment in the remains of the Greek city at Ai Khanum, up by the river Oxus in modern Afghanistan; the room which contained it may perhaps have been a palace library too.[6] In the second century BC the rival kings at Pergamum, in western Asia, founded a major library of their own. The Pergamene kings competed with the Ptolemies and when their rivals tried to deny them Egyptian papyrus for their texts, they took to using parchment, made from animal skins, instead. Ultimately, Hadrian was heir to this Hellenistic habit. He was a great donor of libraries, not least to Athens where his library's grand plan is still visible.

Demand, inevitably, encouraged fakes, like the faking of several 'antiquities' for the huge buying power of today's Getty Museum in America. In Alexandria, the kings also maintained a building whose contents were the real thing, a scholarly 'society of the Muses', the world's first Museum. Its assets were humans, not antiques. Important Greek scholars were attracted by the pay, the offer of free meals and access to the nearby library. In due course, they edited and tidied up the texts of the Greek classics, including Homer's epics. They included some lively and erudite poets, the immensely learned Eratosthenes who calculated the circumference of the earth, almost correctly, and the mathematical genius Euclid. Euclid's famous book of *Elements* set out definitions, mostly Euclid's own, 'postulates' and axioms and proved them by penetrating arguments which built on each other, stage by stage. They are still admired for their method. Unfortunately, less is known of Aristarchus, an astronomer from Samos. His work on the 'size and distance of the sun and moon' survives, but his greatest claim to fame is his theory that the sun is the centre of the universe and the earth goes round it in circular motion. This brilliant new idea became controversial, but it was perhaps only aired as a possibility, not as an 'axiom' admitting of proof. In the early to mid-third century BC such men justify Alexandria's reputation as a centre of scholarship and science.

In the third century BC Greek medicine also made its greatest progress, owing it to two Greek immigrants in the kings' big cities. In Antioch, Erasistratus examined the valves of the heart and theorized that 'breath' passed through the arteries. In Alexandria, Herophilus made amazing

35. South façade of the court of Tomb I in the Moustapha Pasha necropolis, Alexandria. The painting showed Macedonian cavalrymen and standing ladies, *c.* 280–260 BC.

progress in discovering the nerves, ventricles in the brain, ovaries (though he did not understand their purpose) and much else, while writing admirably about the pulse. The Ptolemies are said to have helped this great leap of knowledge by making condemned prisoners available not just for dissection but for vivisection too. The doctors' brief access to living anatomy bore a cruel, but valuable, fruit. Egyptian medicine, by contrast, had tended to trace all diseases to that root of evil, the backside.

Hadrian, too, visited the Museum in Alexandria: typically, he insisted on asking the inmates questions which they could not possibly answer. The presence of scholars had dignified the Ptolemies' public image, but then too the relationship between kings and 'talent' had not been easy. Conspicuously, Alexandria produced no historians and in the shadow of its royal family, it produced almost no philosophers, either. Instead, the Ptolemies attracted witty gossip and were given graphic nicknames by their Greek subjects. They certainly had their oddities, as we can still see from the portraits on the vessels of faience which were used in their cult. As their great modern connoisseuse has pointed out, they show us 'generals, scholars, predatory and patient wives, nervous girls, debauchers, compulsive eaters, savage slayers. Such, we realize, were the Ptolemies and we feel that we would recognize them still on the colonnaded streets of Alexandria.'[7] Their 'luxury' made them unmistakable. Some of the kings were reckoned to be excessively fat, so much so that a tunic had to flatter them; two men, serving as walking sticks, had to support one of them when he set foot on the ground. But even the fat kings could be ruthless. In 145 BC the obese Ptolemy VIII turned on the Greek intellectuals in the city, persecuted them and drove these bright sparks out of Alexandria. Independent minds are never truly safe with a king.

In this context, freedom did not have the scope of the freedom which classical Athenians had known. The kings maintained courtiers and favourites who depended on them. In the 190s, after a military crisis, they resorted to an old Macedonian habit and extended ever more 'titles of distinction' to their entourage in order to flatter them. In the first years of Alexandria the Greek citizens did begin by having a political council and an assembly. So did Egypt's other new city, Ptolemais. But Alexandria's council was then abolished, probably in the mid-second century BC, and its assembly never included all the city's male residents. In Ptolemais, in the 240s BC, we hear of 'disorderly behaviour' in public meetings, especially during elections to office. As a result, the presiding magistrate's hold on public business was strengthened. In Alexandria, meanwhile, the city had an 'overseer'; the citizens were enrolled in demes, as in Attica, but the demes' names honoured the Ptolemies and their god Dionysus. From the 270s BC onwards, the royal family was honoured with a dynastic religious cult: it was a useful bond for the many courtiers who came to the king from so many different Greek communities. Alexandria's non-citizen population, including the Egyptians, did not even have the Greek citizens' limited degree of political freedom. From 203 BC onwards the city's Egyptians took part in uprisings under Ptolemaic rule, so much so that the 'savagery' of the Egyptian 'mob' became notorious to Greek outsiders. But these rebellions were often for or against a particular prince in the Ptolemaic house. Freedom was not even a promise for the Egyptians, and their 'mob' did not riot to get it; rather, they rioted within a royal system which they accepted.[8]

Justice was arguably more accessible, both to Greek and non-Greek. The Alexandrians had courts of law in their city, and these courts did serve all residents, not just the restricted ranks of the Greek citizenry. We know something of their recognized body of laws, including the laws on perjury and on sales: they are related to laws which are known in older

Greek cities, including Athens. Here, too, Aristotle's pupils and their re-searches may have helped Ptolemy I to draw up a new code. But the kings could also proclaim other laws by edict, and this 'law' then took prece-dence over the city code. Beside the city-courts there were royal officials who also dispensed justice according to their own lights.

Outside Alexandria, in Egypt proper, courts of Greek or Egyptian law were available both to Greeks and to Egyptians, and it was up to them which type of law they chose to use. But here, too, the king's edicts took precedence over all other rulings: as a result, there was the possibility of acquiring a judgement issued by the king himself or by one of his officials which would have greater authority than a local court's decision. It is in Ptolemaic Egypt, therefore, that we have the best evidence for the change which Macedonian royal dominance, since Philip, had brought about in the previously classical Greek world, the giving of justice by an individ-ual's response and its soliciting by individuals' written petitions. Surviving petitions on papyrus extend to the most intimate problems of family life, even to such a case as the ungrateful foster-daughter who had grossly neg-lected her mother, the petitioner. According to her mother, she had taken up with a boyfriend, the 'bugger' (literally), and was ceasing to honour the promises she had made on her mother's behalf.[9] These vivid petitions were addressed to the king himself, but usually they went no further than to the officials who were in charge of each district of Egypt. The excep-tions were those which could be forced on the king's attention while he travelled on one of his tours round Egypt's temples and townships. On these expensive occasions, as both sides realized, the king was exposed to the hazards of a royal progress. In October 103 BC we find a Ptolemy telling his local commander at Memphis to be sure to see that the 'amnesty' which he has recently proclaimed is in force before he himself arrives. Otherwise, people will go on pestering him with their existing grievances.[10] Justice had begun to depend on access, but access was not to be had for the asking.

TAXES AND TECHNOLOGIES

To King Ptolemy: greetings from Philotas son of Pyrsous, holder of a military allotment in the great town of Apollo. As there are frequent droughts on the land, now and utterly so, I want, king, to inform you of a machine from which you will sustain no harm, but the land will be saved. For three years the river (Nile) has not risen, so the drought will bring such a famine . . . But within fifty days of sowing there will immediately follow a plentiful year's harvest throughout the whole Thebaid.

**Edfou Papyrus number 8, perhaps *c.* 250 BC,
whose author asks for travelling expenses to show off
his new wonder (a water-lifting pump?)**

There is nobody who could see these unfortunate wretches and not pity them for their excessive distress. No sympathy or respite is shown to anyone, not to the sick, the maimed, the aged or a woman's weakness. But all of them are forced by physical blows to persist at their labours until they die from maltreatment in their forced necessity.

**Agatharchides (*c.* 170–50 BC), description of the
slaves in the Ptolemies' southern gold mines**

THE WARS, FLEETS AND CITY-BUILDING of the Hellenistic kings involved huge quantities of raw materials, shaped and transported with remarkable skill. Royal armies fed and deployed 60,000 men or more on either side, numbers which are vastly bigger than those in Western battles in post-classical times until France in the seventeenth century. Often they included elephants, which intrepid hunters sought out for the Ptolemies on the east coast of Africa, naming their stopping places in the 'Region of

36. The most distant known Ionic Greek column-capital: from the big temple at Takht-i-Sangin on the further bank of the Oxus, in Tadjikistan, *c.* 300–280 BC.

the Elephant Hunters', its harbours, cliffs, and guard-posts. Sieges were conducted with even bigger towers and wheeled machines which ranged up to 180 feet in height. Kings patronized military engineers, Diades the man who 'besieged Tyre and other cities with Alexander', or the amazing Archimedes at King Hiero II's court in Sicily. Surely this world was capable of a high level of technology?

Off the battlefield, however, there were striking gaps. The pulling power of horses was still blocked by the lack of a horse-collar which did not pull on the horse's throat and stop him breathing. No text, word or monument indicates the existence of a wheelbarrow. Sea-transport was relatively quick and ever cheaper in bulk as the cargoes of merchant-ships increased up to 500 tons by the Roman period. But it remained cheaper to transport heavy goods in bulk from one end of the Mediterranean to the other than to haul them without a river-way for seventy miles inland.

In one view, 'attitudes are the key to the blockage',[1] the literary prejudices of a governing Greek class who regarded applied technology as vulgar, while the abundant existence of slaves made the reduction of labour

37. Aerial view of the most remote Greek city, at Ai Khanum, Afghanistan, by the rivers Oxus and Kokcha, probably an Alexandria by origin. The lower city area has been devastated by plundering during the recent wars.

costs irrelevant. Big property owners might like athletics, horse racing and the theatre, but surely they were detached from grubby production and trade, the business of their slave-bailiffs and agents while they dined, enjoyed poetry and polished themselves for sex in the city?

Gentlemanly prejudice was certainly eloquent among those who wrote well. Plato scorned applied mathematics, and Plutarch (c. AD 100) claimed that Archimedes left no texts on applied engineering because he considered it 'ignoble and vulgar' beside purely theoretical study.[2] But many attitudes were possible in ancient society and men do not always practice what they or others preach. Significantly, we do not know the names of most of the inventors of machines or techniques which the evidence attests for us. But Archimedes, one exception, may have seen things differently to Plato and Plutarch.

There was no explicit concept of 'growth' as a good in itself year in, year out, and patchy technologies might take a while, perhaps too long, to speed through the diverse kingdoms into which the 'classical' world was now dividing. In itself, however, slavery did not foster technological disdain or stagnation. Slaves were widely available in the age of wars and non-Greeks without citizen rights could be forced very hard. Labour

38. Painting of drunken Silenus, with a similar big 'griffin' drinking horn to the one in plate 30. From a marble tomb-bed found at Potidaea, south-east Macedonia, late fourth century BC.

costs, then, were not a serious issue, but output was still worth increasing, to turn into cash and spend on a royal court, an army or an educated life. In the American South, slavery did not stop slave-owners from investing in new technologies. Slaves might make innovations too: shorthand and a system of heating vaulted bathhouses were among those credited to them in the early Roman Empire.[3]

Country life was not a barrier to innovations, either. Techniques of milling grain and pressing olives developed importantly, though anonymously. The size and scale of millstones had already progressed by the fifth century BC in Greece, greatly improving the flow of ground flour. Grinding by pairs of rounded stones was then introduced, probably in the third century BC, including the turning of the stones by use of a crankshaft, pivot and handle. Olive presses also developed from simple flat beds with stone rollers to a rotary principle attested before 350 BC. These changes began from a very low base of slow labour, but they directly increased food production. They interrelated with an increasing population, and from the Hellenistic age onwards the ability to sustain more people concentrated in bigger cities. Breeding-stocks of animals were also selected, accounting for the improved bone and muscle of the horses which are shown on Macedonian coinage across nearly two centuries (King Philip must have kept studs and selected and guarded the good stallions).

Greeks even introduced Egypt to a better breed of pig. New varieties of fruit were named, selected and increased by grafting. The Roman Pliny (c. AD 70) knew dozens of different types of pear, plum or apple and regarded grafting as at its peak because 'men have now tried everything'.[4] Anonymous ingenuity could transform an entire industry here. Roses were selected so as to flower twice a year, thereby doubling the crops for the cut-flower and petal trade and the big luxury demand for scent. Twice-flowering roses resulted from a deliberate crossing with the 'phoenician' rose species. It is still abundant in the wild on the south coast of Turkey, ancient Cilicia, where its value may have been recognized quite early by Levantine settlers, not Greeks.

After Alexander, Greek rulers confronted unfamiliar non-Mediterranean landscapes which they had a motive to improve. They wanted as much tax as possible for the luxurious court-splendour which partly justified their royal status, and for the armies which conducted their mutual wars. Into Egypt, the Macedonian rulers introduced tax-farming, whereby the collection of a particular tax was bid for in advance by contractors. The successful bidder had guaranteed to pay the sum he bid, but was free to collect more (or less) as he could. The system suited rulers who needed an assured revenue from taxes which had an unpredictable yearly yield.

Such taxes were very common in Hellenistic Egypt because the Ptolemies raised revenues by a multiplicity of individual charges, applied to particular types of asset and transaction. There was a salt tax on each adult man or woman, an oil tax, a tax on nitron-soda (essential for cleaning clothes) and dozens of others. Customs dues were levied on goods being moved between administrative districts of the country, the 'nomes', and even across the line between Upper (southern) and Lower Egypt. Import taxes were imposed at many points of entry into Egypt, at harbours on the Nile Delta or at the southern frontier into Nubia. Known customs rates are as high as 25 or even 50 per cent, and another tax, the 'Gate Toll', was applied to imports which were brought on to Alexandria. Only the Ptolemies' coins were acceptable inside Egypt, and so visitors needed to change their money for re-minting at rates which naturally suited the rulers. There was even an export tax too, showing that 'a short sighted concept of immediate profit to the state dominated all aspects of trade'.[5]

As the kings had monopolies on several essential commodities, it might even seem that the high taxes on imports were intended to encourage buying of the kings' locally produced goods instead. But scholars' older view of Hellenistic Egypt as a 'command economy', directed by centralized targets and taxes, is certainly wrong. New readings of the difficult papyrus texts and more awareness of those written in the Egyptian language, not Greek, have changed the emphasis. The kings owned much land and leased much too, to tenants for rent and to military colonists in return for service. They also taxed the land's produce (up to half of the year's yield). However, they did not own everything. Temples retained plenty of land, and private land continued to change hands, as we see very well from non-Greek documents in Upper Egypt. There were no yearly targets for production, set by central bureaucrats. Lists of lands under cultivation were indeed compiled locally and sent up the chain of command. Crops to be cultivated were also partly prescribed, but the realities of cultivation on the ground could be quite different. The emphasis has shifted from a 'totalitarian' system to one which was trying to boss and list but which was subject quite often to the gaps between bureaucrats' lists and wishes and what small farmers, the cultivators, would actually do.

Much of the king's yearly revenues were still paid in kind: the payers of harvest taxes would have to take grain personally to state granaries. In the Persian period, we know from a newly read papyrus that there were already customs dues on imports to the Nile Delta. There had also been censuses in Egypt and no doubt the individual taxes on many items were traditional. But under the Ptolemies there were even greater changes. Taxes were now being 'farmed' to contractors. The salt tax was new (it probably had a Macedonian precedent) and was payable both by men and women and only in cash. From the 260s on, the tax on orchards and vineyards took a 'portion' (up to one-sixth) of the crop value for the novel purpose of a cult of the reigning Ptolemy's sister as a god (she was also his wife). Most of this tax was also to be paid in cash. Coinage was thus greatly extended into Egyptian life, even rural life: in Egypt as a whole, its use had probably been minimal during the Persian period. The settlement of individual soldiers on plots of land was a novelty too, up to fifty acres going to each cavalryman. Above all, there was the great new presence of Alexandria which drew in crops, textiles and objects from the Egyptian countryside. More trade was said, very plausibly, to pass into the city from the hinterland to which it was linked by canals and the Nile than came into the city's harbours from the Mediterranean.

It was in the interest of the kings to improve cultivation and to increase taxable output. They were not passive heirs to an 'age-old' Egypt where they merely replaced the Persian rulers. Their attempted changes did not all work, and meanwhile the long-proven Egyptian ways of the farmers went on too, especially in the south. But there was also a new attempt at

39. Big column-capitals, removed from Ai Khanum in Afghanistan, site of the Greek city, by origin (probably) an Alexandria on the river Oxus. Reused since 1980 in this nearby tea-house.

40. Foot of a colossal Greek statue, surely of a god, from the Greek city at Ai Khanum, Afghanistan, c. 250–150 BC.

41. Silver tetradrachm, *c.* 310–305 BC, showing Alexander, struck for Ptolemy I, his friend, historian and commander.

'development' both in the south and above all in the Fayyum, only some 250 miles south of Alexandria. In the far south, the kings made a military campaign into lower Nubia possibly in the 260s and then retained and exploited the very rich local gold-mines. In the 260s and 250s the Fayyum became a major 'development region', as we shall see, with a smart new town (Philadelphia), a big lake to help to irrigate it and allotments of several thousand acres to important friends and courtiers who tried to farm there intensively. It is here that we have most of our evidence for the use of metal tools and ploughs, novelties in Egyptian farming. New crops were also tried out, to the scepticism of the Egyptian workers. A new type of summer wheat did catch on, allowing a precious second harvest where watering was possible. The wheat flour for bread then changed throughout Egypt.

The aims and scale of these particular changes were vast: did they cause technological innovations? In Alexandria's scholarly museum, the thinkers were working on the power of compressed air (pneumatics), a new type of force pump and even a limited use of steam power which they applied to some amusing toys. However, renewed study of their technical texts has shown that new water-lifting devices, powered by animals or water power, were also devised in the third century BC, greatly improving the possible techniques of irrigation. They would be valuable in the new Fayyum farmlands where water needed 'lifting' from the main lake and canals so as to sustain a double harvest. There may even have been water- and animal-powered pounding of grain, exploiting the rotating axles and 'cams' which were certainly invented and applied to Alexandrian toy machines. There is no evidence, as yet, for a Ptolemaic watermill or for extensive water power in the washing, extraction and pounding of the

42. Indo-Greek silver tetradrachm, *c.* 170–145 BC, with bust of King Eucratides the Great, ruler and conqueror in Bactria, Sogdia and north-west India long after Alexander.

43. Indo-Greek silver tetradrachm, *c.* 150–135 BC, with bust of Menander, a truly great conqueror from Bactria through India to the river Ganges: he was remembered in Buddhist tradition.

Ptolemies' gold. Instead, we have a vivid account of the slaves in their gold-mines, written by the able courtier Agatharchides (*c.* 170–150 BC). Throughout, he stresses the hard labour of individual men and women, war captives and criminals who were working naked in intense heat 'until they die in their maltreatment among their forced necessity'. Men and boys would wear their lamps on their heads down the mines' rock-tunnels, but the technologies were muscles and whips.

'Stagnation' is not the right description for the future of such technology as did exist. At some point before the mid-first century BC, watermills were applied to grind flour in the Greek world: we first know of them in a neat poem, celebrating that the slave-girls can now sleep on peacefully as the Nymphs are running the job mechanically.[6] Watermills (but not, so far, windmills) continued to spread through the provinces of the Roman Empire, ever more being found archaeologically, with no 'decline' in the later Empire of the fourth century AD. The huge Roman mine workings in north-west Spain did use slaves too, but a good case now exists for the use of applied water power in the washing and crushing of the ores. Windmills are still unattested and the supreme siege-machine, the trebuchet, was yet to filter westwards from China. But the supposed 'blockage' of technology under Roman and late Roman rule is not borne out on the ground.

The ancients, who achieved so much, did not achieve an 'Industrial Revolution'. One simple answer for their failure has been given: their inability to cast big metal boilers so as to make industrial use of steam power. But the absence of 'the industrial' did not mean the absence of applied technologies, used regionally but nonetheless effectively. By *c.* AD 200 there was at last an improved type of horse-collar, known to us in northern Gaul under Roman rule. It was locally exploited, admittedly, but it did allow a horse to pull loads without being throttled.[7]

THE NEW WORLD

In India, Megasthenes says, the Brahmans do not share their philosophy
with the wives they marry, in order that if the women are wicked they
may not communicate any of their unpermitted secrets to the profane
public, and if the women are serious they will not promptly abandon their
husbands. For nobody who considers with disdain pleasure or hard work,
life and death too, is willing to be subjected to another person. A serious
man and a serious woman, however, are people like that . . .

Megasthenes (who visited India, *c.* 320–300 BC), as quoted in
Strabo, *Geography* 15.1.59

For a long while, the house of my ancestors flourished
Until the unopposable force of the three Fates ruined it . . .
So I, Sophytos . . . of the family of Naratos . . .
Received money, which can multiply, from another and left my home
Resolved never to return, until I had gained the highest pile of riches.
That is why, going for trade to many cities, I gained a vast fortune,
    without damage.
Much praised, I have now returned to my land after countless years
And my return was a joy to my friends . . .
At once I rebuilt the decayed house of my fathers
With new funds, bigger and better . . .

From the Greek verse-inscription of Sophytos, son of Naratos
(a non-Greek name), on his *stele* at Kandahar,
c. 135 BC (first published in 2004)

AFTER ALEXANDER, THE GREEK LANGUAGE was the language of power all the way from Cyrene in north Africa to the Oxus and the Punjab in north-west India. It was the main language of culture, and not only in big Alexandria. In what is now Afghanistan, on the banks of the river Oxus, Greek settlers put down roots and developed the big city at Ai Khanum. The first settlers here had probably included veterans whom Alexander dismissed in 329/8 BC. One of the them may have been the very man, Cineas, who was commemorated with a hero-shrine inside the city. It was then inscribed with moral precepts which were attributed to the former Seven Wise Men of Greece. They had been brought all the way from Delphi by one Clearchus, surely the man known as a pupil of Aristotle. The Greek gods received cult from the new settlers in some very distant landscapes, but there was no attempt to impose them on non-Greek subjects. The polytheist Greeks made something, too, of gods which they found in Asia already, identifying them with Heracles, their hero, or giving them a familiar feature: they added Macedonian hats to one of Asia's favourite votive-figures, the potent male rider on his potent horse.[1]

Within the former Persian Empire, a wide horizon had already been spanned by Aramaic, the language used by secretaries all the way from Egypt to India. This separate horizon did not close with Alexander's conquests: Aramaic literature continued to have a broad perspective, some of which survives in many Christian Bibles' books of Jewish stories, composed in the new Greek age. Greeks, however, were more keen to understand their vast new world. With Alexander, they measured its roads and then put up 'distance-markers' along them. They sought out its mines and noted their potential; they observed its new flora and fruits: one type of wheat in the East was said to have been so strong that when Macedonians ate it they burst apart.[2] Despite these local observations, Alexander and his staff had usually underestimated Asia's size and, quite often, Alexander had been lost. How far east did India really go? Was the Caspian Sea a landlocked lake? These questions began to be explored in the decades after his death, when the most remarkable journey of all was made westwards, beyond Alexander's conquests. Pytheas, a Greek from Marseilles, travelled north past the Bay of Biscay, explored the coast of Britain and commented on a thick 'lung' which confronted him: it was probably a fog-bank in the northern latitudes.[3] Pytheas was aware of the latest Greek astronomy, and went very far north, as his calculations prove; he probably went north-east to Norway, rather than north-west to uninhabited Iceland. He wrote up his travels, but their careful observations seemed incredible to many later critics. Pytheas had seen a world which Alexander had never even imagined.

It would be quite wrong to think that Greeks in the long-established Greek cities were disoriented by these new horizons or by the royal courts and kingdoms which were so much grander than their own citizen-bodies. The decades after Alexander's death are a fertile era in Greek thought and culture which grow directly out of the previous classical age. Comedy returns to view for us in the romantic 'sitcom' tales of family life composed by the Athenian Menander. At Athens, too, philosophy developed three new schools, the last three of importance in ancient history. In one of them, Epicurus discussed profound questions of perception, ethical aims and sensations: his 'School of the Garden' was not at all the pleasure-seeking Epicurean centre of later legend. Zeno, from Cyprus, wrote on the ideal state, on norms of conduct and the nature of knowledge and obligation: his 'School of the Colonnade' (or *Stoa*) became known as the Stoics. Pyrrho contested the very grounds of knowledge and certainty and founded the Sceptics. For each of these philosophers, freedom was an individual's freedom, from fear or passion or deception: it was not a freedom to vote as one citizen in a free democracy.

It was later said that Pyrrho had accompanied Alexander and, after seeing so much, had concluded that nothing could be known at all. In fact, these philosophies were reacting not to Alexander, but to previous philosophers, especially the challenge of Plato. Zeno's ideal state answered Plato's horrible utopia; Epicurus engaged with the pre-existing scepticism of fourth-century Greek thinkers. The new thinkers were not propounding a new global state or a new emphasis on private withdrawal and ethical relativism in a new multi-cultural world. For, all around them, the Greek civic communities were still vigorous. The new foundations in Asia were not filled with rootless settlers, lost in a new landscape. What we know of them suggests that the citizens sustained their unity through the familiar Greek practices of intermarriage with one another or with the particular compatriots of their own civic subgroup. Family structures held firm, and old and new city-states were not pulled apart by some new 'Hellenistic individualism' or cosmopolitan ethos. Admittedly, they now had to cope with royal edicts and the threat of royal armies or unreliable royal 'friends'. But the citizens did not lose their strong sense of community and local political engagement. They attended their exclusive gymnasiums, whether in Macedonia or Syria or Egypt, social centres which were the citizens' privilege. 'Gyms' were no longer only centres of naked exercise. Here, the young were given lectures and cultural events. The gymnasium was a focus of civic life, passing on Greek values and learning. Beyond these training-centres, civic festivals and games continued. In the third century BC artistic and athletic festivals multiplied in the Greek and Asian Greek cities (except, curiously, in Syria). Again, these occasions brought city-states together for traditional Greek pursuits, celebrating Greek values.

What Greeks in the city-states lacked was a level of personal luxury comparable to the royal society around the kings. We have a marvellous letter written from Macedon, perhaps *c.* 300 BC, where the Macedonian author Hippolochus says he had just been at a wedding-feast.[4] He describes for an Athenian reader the dazzling display of silver and gold, the female musicians ('to me they looked stark naked, but some said they were wearing tunics'), the female fire-eaters and jugglers (also naked), the huge helpings of wild boar and the activities of a grandson of one of Alexander's heavy-drinking courtiers (his nanny's son) who also drank massively and was rewarded with a cup of gold. The twenty guests received astoundingly valuable presents. 'You think yourself happy,' the author tells his friend in Athens, 'listening to the propositions of [Aristotle's pupil] Theophrastus and eating wild thyme and those fine bread rolls. But we have taken away a fortune from a single dinner and are looking for houses, farms or slaves to buy with the proceeds.'

In the recipient's same Athens, we can draw a similar contrast around a basic pleasure of life: gardening. Between *c.* 310 and 290 BC the Theophrastus whom this letter mentioned so honourably wrote the two texts which qualify him as the father of botany. Theophrastus had heard reports from Alexander's soldiers; he had read the first historians' books about Alexander's conquests and their strange flora, but he also knew stories about trees in Sicily and south Italy and had even picked up details about the varying habitats of trees in Latium, near Rome.[5] He had no idea of the chemical properties of soil or the sexual reproduction of plants, the aspect which is the basis of their modern classification. But he did observe plants very closely, and they were not just dried specimens, or plants reported by friends and previous writers. Theophrastus gave an exact account of the cherry's flowers and fruits which depended on prolonged observation across the seasons. He discriminated between the habits of wild and cultivated pears. He must have studied these subjects in his own garden, which he later bequeathed in his will, specifying it as his resting place. Theophrastus is the first man to have literally buried himself in the garden. He even cultivated dandelions, correctly observing their seed-heads but finding them 'bitter and unfit for eating'.[6]

In Egypt, within twenty-five years of his death, we can enter into a very different world of planting and gardening, organized by a grandee, Apollonius, the 'finance minister' of King Ptolemy II. Apollonius was one of a group of the king's beneficiaries who were given personal estates of nearly 7,000 acres each in the Fayyum, a sandy area about 250 miles south of Alexandria. Nearby, Ptolemy II had founded a new town, Philadelphia, with a rectangular plan, a theatre and a civic gymnasium. All around, the Fayyum was vastly cultivated, irrigated and improved by new proprietors during the 260s and 250s. Apollonius' estate-manager was another Greek immigrant into Egypt, Zenon, and his surviving papers take us into the domineering and insatiable world of a 'projects-man' who has turned his energies to changing nature. Letters from Apollonius order the planting of thousands of vines on his estates, some of which were grafted stock. Donkeys were to cart these plants down to the Fayyum for Zenon's attention, although the local Egyptians were mocking the Greek newcomers' ignorance of their hallowed ways of doing things. Once, the gardeners on the Fayyum estate threatened to run away and abandon them. But Apollonius was unstoppable: from a second estate at the old Egyptian capital of Memphis, many cuttings of olive trees, apricots and other fruits were ordered to be sent to Zenon at the Fayyum property. The Greek presence in Egypt transformed the scale of vine-growing in the country (previously Egyptians drank beer). Good olive trees, a Greek necessity, were also unavailable in Egypt, and so oil-bearing plants were cultivated to supplement the gap, including the oily seeds of the opium poppy: opium poppies enjoyed a short-lived phase of mass production on Apollonius' estate, but not, it seems, as narcotics. To decorate his park, there were to be second-rate wild olives (they would be sent to Zenon by the thousand), laurel bushes and masses of conifers; there were to be roses, too, for scent-making, garlands and ornament. Other 'seven-thousand-acre' Greek owners were doing likewise, and yet slow delivery, artificially irrigated soil and the risks of salt and sand endangered their massive experiment in new-style farming. Within twenty-five years Apollonius' grand estate had reverted to the kings, its ultimate freeholders, and the mass poppy-crops vanished. The experiments in luxurious agriculture became fragmented and went the way of other grand gardening-schemes in history.

Among Zenon's own papers, nonetheless, we find evidence of his literary taste, including a fine copy of Euripides' tragedy of the young hunting man, Hippolytus. Zenon himself wrote clear and thoughtful Greek and was always searching for the apt expression; he loved dogs and the irrepressible sport of a gentleman, hunting. One of his favourite dogs was praised in two poems for saving him from a wild boar: his letters refer to gazelle-hunters who came and went in his life. While the Hellenistic kings continued to vaunt their prowess on the hunting-field, out east at Kandahar another expatriate Greek left verses and a monument in praise of a dog of his who had bravely killed a wild prey. Among these new landscapes and their new 'big game', the noble sport of heroes became the beloved recreation of common men in the public eye.[7]

Naturally, these Greeks abroad observed the new and unusual peoples around them. Herodotus had anticipated them here, and Alexander's own generals and staff had already been quick to record the oddities they observed in Indian society. There was a constant tension in this sort of writing. Was the distant East a society to be idealized, as Egypt had been idealized by Plato and the rhetorical Isocrates? After Alexander, legendary Greek utopias continued to be fathered on faraway places, whether in the North, East or on islands in the southern 'Ocean'. Or was the East to be observed, researched and understood? Few if any of those who wrote on the new world learned anything of its languages, but they did go and look, and either they or their informants were able to communicate a little with one another in Greek.

In Bactria and north-east Iran, many of the new Greek settlers proved to be tenacious even when they found that Alexander's death was not their cue to return home to Greece. Up at Ai Khanum, near the river Oxus, settlers continued to use the Macedonian calendar for more than a hundred and fifty years; in Iran, the old city of Susa was given a new Macedonian name; lines from Euripides, the same few, were copied out as a school-exercise both in Egypt and Armenia. In Egypt, the Ptolemies spoke Macedonian Greek, but not Egyptian, and encouraged Greek school teachers by exempting them from their tax on salt and other Greek speakers by another small tax-break: their government relied on Greek. Yet scholars' old idea of a blinkered Greek attitude to the 'East', close to apartheid, is too extreme. The Ptolemies and Seleucids never forgot their Macedonian origins, but in Egypt it was not possible to rule in the narrow strip of territory south of Alexandria without a certain openness to the long-established local culture. After all, the Egyptians' big temples and priesthoods were still active. In the Seleucid kingdom, from Syria to eastern Iran, there was much more space, and the upper ranks of the court, army and governorships remained overwhelmingly in Greek hands. In Mesopotamia, however, the Seleucid kings did take on some of the ancient royal titles and profess a respect for some of the local temples: Alexander had already done the same. Overall, though, there was no new 'multi-cultural' openness about the Seleucids' style of monarchy. In Iran, Alexander had ended the Persians' complex system of food-rations and court-customs and the Seleucids never tried to bring them back. In Egypt, by contrast, a lively ideal of Egyptian kingship did survive with the local priesthood. It associated the ruling Pharaoh with eternal well-being and the ordered fertility of the land. Arguably, the Ptolemies did address this Egyptian culture which they found to be running in parallel to their own. They themselves were open to one or two Egyptian traditions, and it has been argued, perhaps correctly, that the Ptolemies imitated the ancient practice of the Pharaohs and subsidized doctors, free to all patients, by levying a special 'doctors' tax'. In Greek cities elsewhere, the council might interview and appoint a 'civic doctor', but all of his patients then had to pay him. There was no concern outside Egypt for subsidized 'national health'.

In Egypt, the central role of Egyptian culture in the world's civilization was emphasized very early by a most remarkable Greek mind, Hecataeus, an immigrant to Egypt from Abdera, who arrived in the early years of Ptolemy I. While following Herodotus, Hecataeus claimed to have exceeded his great predecessor and to have consulted actual Egyptian records. His descriptions of ancient Pharaonic buildings are notably precise and his accounts of ancient Egyptian laws and customs are not always fictional. He even praised the ancient Pharaohs for their obedience to law and justice and their moderation of personal luxury. The prejudice in him shows through when he praises them for having kept craftsmen out of political life: Hecataeus' view of old Egypt was not at all the view of a democrat.[8]

Hecataeus is also a witness, probably the first in Greek, to a new discovery: the Jews. After Alexander's death, Ptolemy's troops had encountered Jews during their campaigns in Syria, and Hecataeus presents them as an offshoot of Egyptian civilization. They had merely been corrupted, he thought, by their ill-advised lawgiver Moses. Yet his picture is not a hostile or anti-Semitic one. When describing their idealized priestly society, Hecataeus appears to allude to a sentence in the biblical book of Deuteronomy. Within a hundred years, his successors in Alexandria would not be so tolerant: some of their literature marks the beginning of Western anti-Semitism.

To the east, meanwhile, the great new fascination was India. During their invasion of 327–325 BC, Alexander's officers had seen and noted so much which Greeks had never previously encountered. In their histories, they described Indian dress, Indian cotton, the broad banyan trees and the elephants. At this level, they were capable of exact observation. But when they tried to explain Indian societies or teachings, they were hampered by their ignorance of the language and the stereotypes they brought with them. One Indian wise man did follow Alexander's army and is also said to have lectured to them: we may even have evidence of his teaching on the stars and seasons. The officers called him by the name 'Calanos', but it was not his true Indian name. They gave it to him for the word of greeting (*kalē*) which he liked to utter. Some of them thought it was an Indian word, but he is much more likely to have been showing off his one bit of Greek ('*kalē*', for 'very nice'). So, he acquired the name of 'Mr Nicely'.[9]

On the slightest evidence, traces were 'discovered' locally of an invasion of India by the gods Dionysus and Heracles. Fanciful Greek minds also saw traces of an idealized Sparta in the customs of some of the Indian kingdoms. Others, more bluntly, explained things by their own male sexism. Some of the Indians were found to practise suttee (the burning of a man's wives with him on a funeral pyre). The invaders ascribed it to the infidelity and wickedness of Indian wives. Indian men were seen to marry much younger women, and so these women, they presumed, would soon want to poison their ageing husband and go off with a younger lover. Suttee, therefore, was the husband's deterrent: if a husband was poisoned, his wife would be burned to death with him. So the women were kept in check. The explanation is probably the free invention of men with Alexander, without any Indian supporting story.[10]

Soon after Alexander's death, yet more of India was visited by an intrepid Greek envoy, Megasthenes. He, too, combined observation with idealizing theory. He did visit the Indian royal city of Palimbothra on the river Ganges, a site which had eluded even Alexander, and he gave a credible account of its appearance, wooden architecture and all. He also distinguished seven orders of Indian society which were sustained by close intermarriage. He was presumably trying to describe the Indian castes. He made them seven (not four, the usual number) because he was influenced by his knowledge of Herodotus who had supposed there to be seven classes in ancient Egypt. Megasthenes also wrote about someone called 'Boudyas', a companion, he believed, of Dionysus when he invaded India, and later a king. He had heard, surely, of Buddha and misunderstood him. He does, however, describe some of the Indians' funerary customs, but not the big Buddhist stupas which were to become so famous. Perhaps we should trust him, and conclude that stupas did not yet exist.

By the end of the fourth century BC Alexander's conquests in India had been given away to the warrior Chandragupta. Yet the horizon which he had opened did not shut. A literate Greek-speaking population still existed in the Alexandrias and the Successors' cities which lay in the territories near the Punjab. For their sake, the Indian king Asoka had his royal Buddhist edicts translated into Greek and inscribed in the mid-third century BC in this region. Asoka could also name all the Hellenistic Greek kings as far west as Libya and refer to 'the world, my children'.[11] From the 240s onwards, the Successor rulers in Bactria became independent Greek kings, and in due course, they took up Alexander's example and conquered again in north-west India. Under their remarkable king Menander (c. 150–130 BC), they went even further east than Alexander, conquered more Indian territory and reached the river Ganges. Greek sculptures had begun to influence the newly devised Indian representations of Buddha: King Menander himself, a strikingly handsome man, was remembered in Buddhist tradition and may even have become a Buddhist.

As in Egypt, Greek authors on India described a foreign world mostly in terms of the Greek customs, myths and laws which they knew at home. It was not so much imperialism as a rather heartening belief, implicit in Homer, that, in general, these other people were really quite like Greeks. Greeks did not persecute them or try to 'cleanse' them as lesser beings. In early 323 BC embassies had come to Alexander in Babylon, including, some said, ambassadors from the Romans. However, Alexander's court historians appear to have ignored these Roman visitors. So far as Rome was even discussed by Greek contemporaries, it tended to be seen as a 'Greek city', one more point of Greek contact along the western coast of Italy.[12] The most important people of the future, therefore, could have been investigated by Alexander's early followers, but were understood the least.

ROME REACHES OUT

Lucius Veratius was an extremely wicked man of immense brutality. He used to consider it very amusing to slap the face of a free man with the palm of his hand. A slave used to follow him, carrying a purse full of small change and whenever he had slapped someone, he would order twenty-five small coins (asses) to be counted out, as prescribed by the Twelve Tables. As a result, the praetors later decided that this law in the Tables was obsolete and defunct, and declared by edict that they would appoint assessors to estimate personal damages instead.

Favorinus (*c.* AD 120–50), in Aulus Gellius, *Attic Nights* 20.1.13,
on a change in the early law-code of Rome

WE LEFT ROME IN 451 BC at the time of its early laws, the Twelve Tables, and looked at it mainly in the context of the surrounding Etruscans and western Greeks. The site of Rome had long been inhabited, but, like so many of the towns in the Greek-speaking world, by the fifth century BC Rome traced her origin back to a founding hero. In fact, she looked back to both a founder and a visitor, and they were a remarkable contrast. One was Romulus, who was believed to have been suckled by a she-wolf and brought up by the wife of a simple shepherd. As a 'once and future king' he began as an outcast, a type of story which is quite frequent for founders and leaders in many societies. In due course, Romulus killed his brother Remus, a less usual turn to the story.

Alternatively, Rome was credited with a visit from the wandering Trojan hero Aeneas, who arrived in Italy and founded nearby Lavinium after the sack of Troy. Aeneas was well known in Greek poetry, including Homer, but his connection with Rome is not attested for us before *c.* 400 BC. By then it was part of a wider Western trend. Non-Greek cities in south Italy and Sicily also claimed similar links with travelling Trojans. These Trojan claims were a useful way for non-Greek outsiders to connect with the respected myths of the Greek world. For the Romans, the 'Trojan connection' was developed through Aeneas' son and was to prove very useful when they began to have dealings with Greeks in Greece and Asia.[1]

Wolf's milk, exile and fratricide were an unusual ancestry. But they went with something very important: an exceptionally generous asylum policy. Romulus was supposed to have declared his new Rome to be an asylum centre for all comers. In Athens, myths and dramas presented the Athenian hero Theseus as kind to strangers too, but at Rome the kindness went with a most un-Athenian readiness to grant citizenship to outsiders. The citizenship was even granted to Romans' slaves when they were formally freed by their citizen-masters. Freeing became frequent in Roman households (less so on Roman farms), but there was a hard-headed reason for much of it. Many slaves paid for their freedom and continued to pay or help their masters when freed. For masters, therefore, it was more sensible to free slaves after a while than to maintain them as an ageing asset. The community also benefited: children born to slaves when freed were available for recruitment as Roman legionary soldiers. From this abundant source, Rome's military manpower thus grew far beyond the armies of Athens' or Sparta's tightly limited citizenry.

Nonetheless, it was slow to bear fruit. From the 450s (when the laws of Rome's Twelve Tables were published) until the 350s Romans evidently had had to confront a whole series of difficulties. There were recurrent political tensions in their citizenry; years of bad harvests beset them; many of their Latin neighbours renewed hostilities. The late fifth century was a time of widespread migrations by other peoples in Italy, especially those who descended from the inland Apennine mountains. They entered the plains and the fertile western coast of Italy and blocked Rome's expansion in that direction. The best-known of these migrants are the Samnites in south Italy: their warriors on horseback were honoured by stylized tomb paintings, well preserved in the area of Paestum in southern Italy.[2]

For a century or so, from 460 to 360 BC, there were fewer than ten years in all when the Romans were not at war. Their darkest hour was c. 390 BC, when Gauls (ultimately from southern France) came south into Italy and raided Rome itself. Legends later multiplied around this event, but it had been big enough to be noticed by Greeks, including Aristotle.[3] The most famous story is that the raiding Gauls were dislodged from

Rome's revered Capitol hill when they caused the sacred geese of the goddess Juno to cackle in the night. The brave Manlius was alerted and drove the enemy off. Actually, the Gauls' looting may have continued without interruption. Holy objects from Rome's religious cults were escorted for safety to the nearby Etruscan town of Caere (modern Cerveteri) in the company of the six Vestal Virgins, the distinctive young servants of Rome's virgin goddess Vesta (Hearth). It was this retreat, not the geese, which became known to Aristotle in Greece. The day of Rome's worst defeat by the Gauls, 18 July, remained a day of ill omen and no business in the Roman calendar.

After this crisis, a Greek visitor in the 370s, the age of Plato, would have found Rome a rambling muddle. Later the Romans explained the absence of any town plan as due to their hasty rebuilding after Rome's sack by the Gauls. In fact, it was endemic. Unlike Alexandria, Rome was never planned by a king or lawgiver. Instead, it evolved untidily, both in politics and architecture. The expulsion of the kings in the late sixth century had led to the immediate founding of the Republic and the dividing of the king's powers among magistrates. They were to hold office for a year and, in most historians' opinion, the most important of them were to be two consuls, serving as colleagues. Arguably, the consulship was not formally confined to patrician nobles, but initially patricians almost always held it. Much depends on how much trust we can put in the later lists of consuls, or *fasti*, but even so it seems clear that there were periods of irregularity, especially in the eighty years or so after the Twelve Tables. Quite often, two consulships were not filled.

Beyond the small group of ex-consuls, there were many other Roman citizens to consider, both in the town area and in its dependent countryside. Politically, the position of half of them is easily summed up. As in the Greek world, half of the city of Rome, the women, could not vote or hold political office. Unlike Athenian women, they were not even able to be priestesses of the gods, unless they were one of the six Vestal Virgins. While their father or grandfather lived women were legally (like sons) in his 'power', and when he died they were put promptly (unlike sons) under the guardianship of their male next of kin. As perhaps more than half of Roman women aged twenty did not have fathers or grandfathers still alive (on a likely average), most adult women would be under guardianship. When they married, the predominant form of marriage conveyed them like children into the 'hand' of their husband. But even when 'guarded' they could own or inherit property (although they could not dispose of it without their guardian's consent). When married, they could

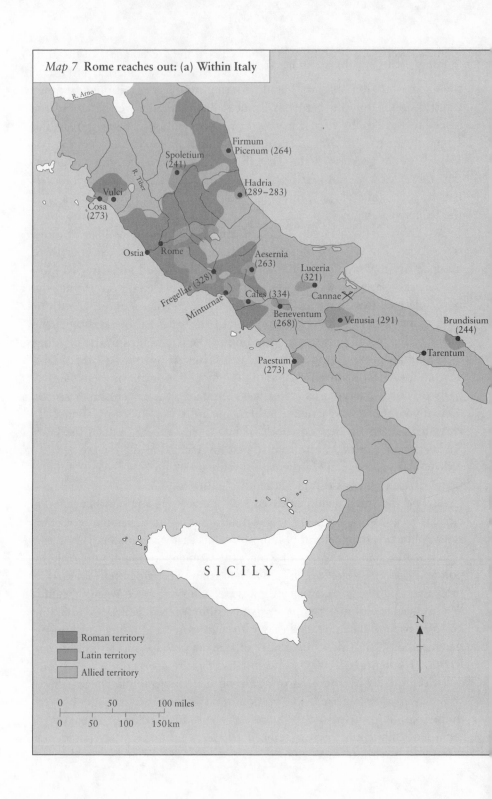

Map 7 **Rome reaches out: (a) Within Italy**

R. Arno

Firmum
Picenum (264)

Spoletium
(241)

Hadria
(289–283)

Vulci

R. Tiber

Cosa
(273)

Ostia

Rome

Aesernia
(263)

Luceria
(321)

Fregellae (328)

Cales (334)

Cannae

Minturnae

Beneventum
(268)

Venusia (291)

Brundisium
(244)

Paestum
(273)

Tarentum

SICILY

N

Roman territory

Latin territory

Allied territory

0   50   100 miles

0   50   100   150 km

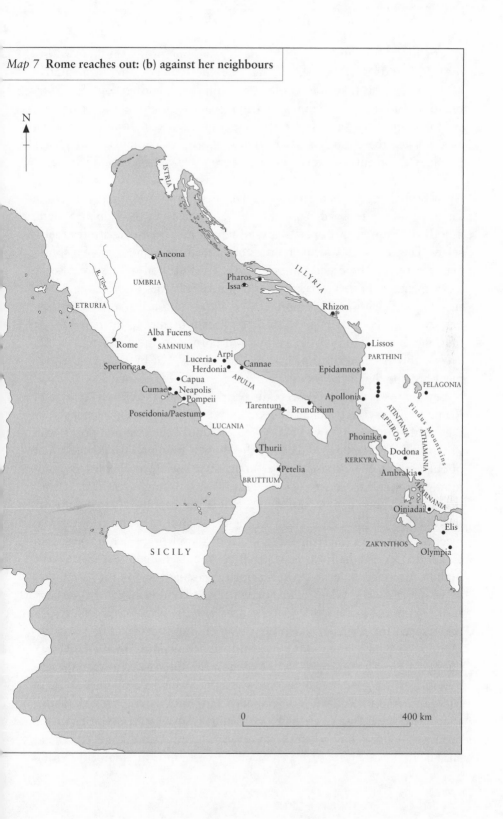

Map 7 **Rome reaches out: (b) against her neighbours**

N

ISTRIA

R. Tiber

UMBRIA

Ancona

ILLYRIA

Pharos
Issa

Rhizon

ETRURIA

Alba Fucens

Lissos

PARTHINI

Rome

SAMNIUM

Sperloriga

Luceria
Arpi

Cannae

Epidamnos

PELAGONIA

Herdonia

APULIA

Capua

Cumae

Neapolis

Pompeii

Apollonia

Tarentum

Brundisium

Poseidonia/Paestum

Pindus Mountains

LUCANIA

ATINTANIA

ATHAMANIA

EPEIROS

Phoinike

Dodona

Thurii

KERKYRA

Petelia

Ambrakia

BRUTTIUM

AKARNANIA

Oiniadai

Elis

ZAKYNTHOS

SICILY

Olympia

0   400 km

inherit from their husband on his death, like one of his children. Moreover, husbands were often away fighting and women were authoritative both within their own households and with their children. The legal formalities seem to exclude almost any independent action on their part, and yet the legends of the early Republic (perhaps reflecting domestic reality, especially in the upper class) are rich in stories of courageous or chaste heroines. Politically, however, women were irrelevant on the public stage.

Here the most important people were the small male clique of senators. Most probably, they had served as advisers to Rome's kings and after the kings' expulsion their advisory council had lived on as the Roman Senate, a body of distinguished men, many of whom had been magistrates themselves. They could advise the holders of public offices and resolve disputes between them. The crucial question was whether non-nobles were to be made members of this Senate or not. As in Greek cities of the seventh century BC, the question became increasingly acute, until it was agreed, c. 300 BC, that the 'best men' should be selected by merit, not by birth. At first, the 'best' would mostly be the well-born, nonetheless. Senators had presumably been enrolled at first by the consuls, but by c. 310 BC enrolment became the job of the two annually appointed censors.

Beyond the Senate, there were the people at large, the citizens on whom Rome's military activity depended. There were particular reasons why they could not be overawed and relied on, unlike their contemporaries in Philip and Alexander's Macedon, the 'Foot Companions'. Rome's first popular strike, or secession, in 494 BC had not been forgotten by the common people and there were ample reasons why it might recur: debt continued to tie poor people harshly to their social superiors, but politically they had scope (though not much) for manoeuvre. For the citizenry did meet in assemblies (including a 'council of the plebs' which no patrician could attend). Formally, at least, each adult citizen-male did have a vote in these meetings, and the citizen-majority was sovereign in the assemblies which passed laws. What the majority decided became a law, without any further checks on a law's legality and its relation to existing statutes; in this respect, the Romans' assembly was even more capable of instant legislation than the contemporary assembly in democratic Athens. However, the assemblies were organized as if the prime aim was to exclude the 'tyranny' of the crowd. The assembly of the 'tribes' mainly met so as to pass laws, and by 332 BC it was divided into twenty-nine 'tribes', or districts. The system was one of block-voting, and when a majority of the twenty-nine tribes had voted the same way the others did not even vote at all. Such votes as were given went only to establish the majority within each tribal 'block'. As these 'blocks' were of very different sizes, many more voters might have voted against a law than for it, and yet by a majority of 'blocks' the law would go through.

The other main assembly, the 'centuriate assembly', was most important for electing most of the magistrates and for judging certain trials. Its organization was even more cleverly weighted against a lower-class majority. Those without property were bunched into only one century (out of a total of 193) and, yet again, would very seldom vote. The richest, including the cavalry, voted first and their centuries' majority votes usually sufficed for a majority. Such changes as there ever were to this unprecedented system were only changes of detail.

Each type of assembly could only be summoned and presided over by a magistrate. Nobody else could speak, and until the later second century BC voters voted visibly and could therefore be intimidated by 'canvassers'. The 'tribal' assembly gave most blocks of votes to people outside the city, with the inevitable result, no doubt intended, that only the reliable and richer citizens who could come into Rome would vote at all. These assemblies were complicated bodies and certainly assumed that 'the people' were sovereign. But that sovereignty was so cleverly contained that only a few modern historians would insist on calling it democratic, quite apart from the hierarchical social context (and clever bribery) within which votes were exercised at all.

There was, however, a glimmer of popular sovereignty and rights here. The 'people' did elect magistrates, including the tribunes who could veto unacceptable proposals put to a public meeting. The tribunes were not necessarily populist, but there was scope to be so if they dared to use it. There was also a brute fact of life: the Senate could not legislate. It could pass advisory decisions (*consulta*) and for a while it either did or could vet any decision which was to go to an assembly and be made into a law. But the senators were not 'the government' nor was public business consigned for a matter of years to any representative body of delegates or magistrates, chosen from their number. As the Romans had not adopted a constitution from a lawgiver, it is we who look for their 'constitution' in what was a bundle of evolving customs, traditions and precedents. At the heart of their practice, there was a two-headed beast, as some of them later characterized it: the venerable senators and the (formally) sovereign plebs.

At first, the tensions were contained within a sharply stratified social order. Nonetheless, they were there, and as a result the years from the mid-fifth to the mid-fourth centuries are rightly described by historians as Rome's 'struggle of the orders'. It was not carried on as an extreme struggle of the poor against the rich: there were no demands by the poor to redistribute private property, as in some of the contemporary Greek cities in nearby Sicily. There is a constant risk of believing the much later traditions which were projected back into this period from later times of crisis and are overwhelmingly our main type of evidence. However, it does seem that the main struggle over land was simply over the 'public land' which was being annexed by conquest from Rome's neighbours. Rich Romans used this land, but it was not strictly theirs. Should this use be restricted for other Romans' benefit?

More immediately important were struggles over debt and the related issues of 'freedom'. The demand was not, as in the Greek world, to abolish existing debts. It was rather to regulate the ways in which debtors were treated and to check the harassment of poor men by their social superiors. Far more than at democratic Athens, 'freedom' was valued at Rome in a negative sense, as 'freedom from' interference. Among the senators the most prized freedom was the 'freedom from' monarchy or tyranny, the one-man rule against which the Roman Republic had developed. Among the people, the most prized 'freedom' was 'freedom from' unchecked harassment by superior persons like senators. But there was also a stubborn sense of Roman citizens' 'freedom to . . . ', freedom to legislate, freedom to judge cases of treason and freedom to elect magistrates. These 'freedoms' were embedded in the assemblies which had existed before the Republic took over from the rule of kings.

There was scope for struggle on each of these points, but the most likely dangers lay with initiatives from within the upper class. A prominent Roman might break rank with his own class and, in order to be dominant, appeal for support to the lower orders. Manlius, the hero against the Gauls, was accused of such a tyrannical tactic. As riches were never static within only a few families, there was also tension in the upper levels of society over the distribution of privileges: within the growing ranks of the rich, who was to be eligible for magistracies and the Senate? Gradually, the noble patricians gave ground in order to preserve a united ruling class, but not because the poor as a class rose against them on this issue.

Historians formerly tended to see the struggling Rome of this era as out of touch with the main Greek world. Nowadays, the opposite is emphasized, with good reason. Indeed, there were acute food shortages, but they caused Romans to look outwards and send envoys to south Italy and Greek Sicily. There were wars with the migrant Gauls and others, but in 396 BC the spoils of a Roman victory over nearby Veii were sent to Greece to be dedicated at Delphi: the intermediary was Massilia (Marseilles), an important western Greek contact of Rome who had her own 'treasury' already on the site.[4] In the 340s this same Delphic oracle was said to have been consulted by Romans in their own right and to have told them to put statues of two famous Greeks, the 'wisest' and the 'best', on their designated space for public meetings. The wisest Greek was Pythagoras (well known in south Italy and Tarentum), and the bravest Greek was Alcibiades the Athenian aristocrat (known for his actions in Sicily and at Thurii in south Italy).[5] Thenceforward, the images of these two Greeks are said to have looked down on Roman public business.

In the 320s the wars of Alexander and of the Successors were marginal to the Romans, although they did probably send an embassy to the great man in Babylon. Much more important were their dealings with Carthage. Since the late sixth century a series of treaties had regulated the two powers' access to one another's spheres of interest. These treaties prove that 'struggling' Romans were certainly not cut off from interest in north Africa, either.[6]

Each of these foreign outlets (south Italy, Sicily, Carthage and mainland Greece) were to attract Roman troops within a single lifetime, in a remarkable burst between the 280s and the 220s BC. But the prelude was remarkable too. Between the 360s and the 280s the Romans sorted out most of their political tensions and became dominant among the Latins who surrounded them. They also extended their power into the rich hinterland of the Bay of Naples (from 343 onwards) and even to Naples itself (in 326). A setback at the Caudine Forks (321 BC) against a Samnite ambush was promptly avenged (320 BC). In 295 they won a huge battle up at Sentinum in Umbria which confirmed their growing power to the north. The battle was even mentioned by a distant Greek historian, Duris of Samos.[7]

This surge up and down Italy occurred in what was the single lifespan of the Macedonian Ptolemy, friend of Alexander and founder of the royal line in Egypt. Ptolemy is most unlikely to have even mentioned Rome in his history of Alexander: the great Greek minds in his contemporary Alexandria were moving on a totally different level to that of the Romans. The Roman expansion was the work of people who had no literature and as yet, no formal art of oratory. At Rome, Homer was still unknown and Aristotle would have been completely unintelligible. The great arts of the most classical Greeks, thinking, drawing and democratic voting, were not talents of the Romans. Nonetheless, plain blunt Romans reformed their army and gave up their 'hoplite' style of tactics, arguably in the 340s–330s, the years of further concessions by the noble patricians to the non-nobles.[8] They also broke up the political league of their Latin neighbours and imposed settlements on its member-states one by one.

This decade (348–338 BC) is therefore of crucial importance to ancient history. In Macedonia, King Philip, Alexander's father, was balancing and training a new Macedonian army with a new type of tactics. In Italy, Romans were also undertaking a military revolution. It resulted in three main ranks of infantry being combined in a flexible formation and being equipped with heavy throwing-spears and swords. The two resulting types of army would dominate the East and West respectively, before clashing decisively in the 190s BC; the Romans' greater flexibility won the encounter, and the tactics of this time remained the backbone of her world-conquering armies for centuries. In 338 BC, a cardinal year, Philip had conquered the Athenians and their Greek allies and then imposed a 'peace and alliance' which marked a decisive limit on political freedom in Greece. In this same year, Rome imposed long-lasting settlements among the neighbouring Latins. She did the same elsewhere in Italy, in the towns then and later who submitted to her. The various grades of citizenship which she offered to these Italian towns were also to have a long, important future. They became a blueprint from which the Romans' relations with towns throughout their Western Empire later developed.

These years of Roman struggle occurred outside the course of politics in the Greek world, but the major themes of justice and luxury were as prominent in Romans' public life as 'freedom'. The older Roman framework of public justice had been relatively simple. Much was left to self-help and privately initiated prosecution, but according to the Twelve Tables (in 451 BC), a few major crimes, including murder and theft, would also be prosecuted before one of the magistrates.[9] In 367 BC a major change was made to the magistrates available. A separate 'praetor' was introduced besides the two consuls. Thereafter Roman praetors became major overseers of justice. Their edicts while holding office were to have a fundamental impact on Roman law; praetors did not legislate, but they did grant legal actions for a far wider body of civil cases than the Tables had specified. Successive praetors took over previous praetors' edicts which thus grew by gradual additions; the edicts filled in gaps in the civil law, becoming the 'Roman equity' of later legal thinking.

Within this growing framework, Roman justice was still heavily conditioned by social relations and by wide discrepancies of social class. In the 320s one major oppression of the poor, debt-bondage, was at least brought under legal restraints. The status itself did not disappear (as it had in

Athens since Solon's reforms in 594 BC), but henceforward a Roman creditor could put a defaulting borrower into bondage only after obtaining a
judgement in court. Citizens, meanwhile, did have one major resort against
physical harassment and the blatant use of force by a social superior. Inside
Rome itself, they could 'appeal' or call out, by the famous Roman right of
provocatio.[10] This right had begun as an informal cry for help which any
citizen might make to the public at large. It acquired a new focus when
tribunes of the people were established in 494 BC. These officers had the
right to interpose their persons between a bully and his victim if a citizen
'called' on them inside the city; the tribunes had been declared 'sacrosanct'
by oath and could not be harassed without the wrong to them being
avenged. By *c.* 300 BC the practice of appeal became formalized further in
law. It became a 'wicked crime' for someone to execute a citizen who had
appealed for justice. However, no actual penalty is prescribed in our surviving evidence for anyone who was so wicked, nor were beatings or other
types of harassment outlawed.

Among the people, this right of 'calling out', or appeal, was a corner-
stone of freedom. Among the senators, 'freedom' had a further connota-
tion: equality within their own peer group. This ideal was sustained by a
very strong tradition of the rejection of luxury. Great Roman leaders of
the past were idealized as simple farmers, men like Cincinnatus (the
namesake of modern Cincinnati) who left his plough only briefly in order
to serve as Rome's dictator. Curius Dentatus (a consul four times, with
three triumphs) lived simply in a little cottage and was believed to have
rejected offers of gold from the Samnites (who were idealized as a hardy,
simple people too). Curius' cottage continued to be revered, and a special
'Meadow' near Rome commemorated Cincinnatus.[11] Roman women were
also supposed to behave with restraint and here too examples upheld values, in a typically Roman fashion. Continuing tales were told of the virgin
Tarpeia who had been seduced by the sight of the gold bracelets on
Rome's enemies, the Sabines.[12] In early days a Roman wife was said to be
forbidden even to drink wine. One Roman woman who tried to steal the
keys to the wine cellar was actually said to have been clubbed to death by
her husband, a cautionary tale to the others.

This ideal of austerity did not exclude the use of slave-labour by its exemplary heroes and their heirs. Such labour was freely available at Rome,
because captives in war and defaulting debtors became enslaved and were
readily available for the richer Romans' use. As in Athens, there was
never a Roman 'golden age' before slavery. Slave-owning was not, then,
seen as unbridled luxury; rather, 'luxury' was ascribed to rival cities in

Italy, south of slave-owning Rome, where it was cited as their undoing. The most effete were said to be Capua (near Naples), a city of Etruscan origin, and Tarentum (modern Taranto), the bastard child of her austere founder, Sparta. These cities' love of scents, baths and ornaments was said to have sapped their capacity to resist or to take wise political decisions. In fact, each city marked an important staging-point on Rome's advance southwards down Italy. In 343 Capua's appeal to Rome first brought Roman troops into the immensely fertile land behind Naples. In 284 Rome's attack on Tarentum ended by entrenching her power among the Greek cities of southern Italy.

During this advance through Italy Roman power was not without attractions for the upper classes in the towns along her route. Men in the upper class who feared their own lower classes were much more ready to team up with these apparently sound conservative leaders in Rome. In 343 such people in Capua threw themselves on Rome's decision by opting for voluntary surrender (or *deditio*).[13] Roman troops entered the city and in the following year, an outburst of discontent among Rome's occupying garrison was blamed on the 'corrupting' luxury of 'soft' Capua. In fact, the discontent probably had political roots too. At Rome, it led on to further concessions to the plebs by their Roman superiors: one good reason for giving them was that the commoners were needed as working soldiers.

In the 280s yet more local rivalries drew Rome even further into the south of Italy. In the south, Greek cities of considerable size and cultural distinction still regarded themselves here as 'Great Greece', but they had continued to be beset by non-Greek barbarian peoples and by deep-seated rivalries between each other. Rome did not hesitate to accept a request for help from distant Thurii, Herodotus' former refuge and the Greek city which had been founded by Pericles' Athenians. Thurii's immediate enemies were the non-Greek Lucanians, but a friendship with Thurii traditionally caused the hostility of another Greek city, Tarentum, further north. Tarentum, an ancient Spartan foundation, was by now a rich and cultured democracy.

Siding with Thurii, Rome then turned against Tarentum and justified herself later with a concerted campaign of historical spin. When Roman envoys arrived in Tarentum they were said to have been mocked before an assembly in the city's theatre. One citizen, Philonides, was even said to have excreted on the Roman envoy and to have made fun of his barbaric Latin.[14] To the Tarentines, the Romans seemed like illegal troublemakers. Some of their ships had been infringing a previous agreement that they would not sail beyond a specified point on Italy's south-east coast. For there was a long diplomatic history here in the Greek-speaking south. Fifty years before the Roman incident Tarentum had summoned the brother-in-law of Alexander the Great to help her cause locally (c. 334–331 BC) and the coastal agreement in question may go back to his short-lived intervention.[15]

Instead, Rome pleaded an 'insult' by Tarentum and attacked her. Armed intervention in the south required willing soldiers and, once again, we find that important political concessions had recently been made at Rome to the common people from whom the soldiers would be drawn. Shortly before the involvement with Thurii, it was enacted that decisions of the Roman people's assembly were to be binding on all the people, nobles included. The senators, moreover, would no longer be able to vet decisions of the assemblies before agreeing to adopt them.

This fateful rule, the Hortensian Law, was passed with a background of continuing resentment by debtors and probably did not seem an unduly dangerous concession in the eyes of the governing class at the time. From the 340s onwards magistracies at Rome had progressively been opened to non-nobles, and so a broader class of former office-holders had been gradually built up. As these same office-holders became senators, a like-minded governing class had been formed from the nobles and the rich newcomers. In the eyes of this class, there was not too much danger in giving 'popular' decisions the form of law. The 'tribal' assembly which approved them was heavily weighted against the city-dwelling poor, the majority. It only met when magistrates summoned it, and only voted when they put proposals to it. The magistrates were usually reliable members of the governing class.

Spurred on nonetheless, Roman soldiers would fight decisively against old, civilized Tarentum. Their ally, 'Athenian' Thurii, was no longer a democracy, whereas their enemy, 'Spartan' Tarentum, was now the democracy instead. The age-old rivalry of Sparta and Athens was thus played out again, but this time in the presence of Romans, and Roman troops proved to be the decisive military force.

THE PEACE OF THE GODS

*When the Roman legate arrives at the frontier . . . he covers his head with
a band of wool and says, 'Hear, Jupiter: hear, boundaries of this people;
let the divine law hear. I am the official herald of the Roman people; I
come lawfully and piously commissioned; let there be trust in my words.'
Then he sets out his demands and calls on Jupiter as a witness. 'If I unjustly and impiously demand that these men and these goods be surrendered to me, then let me never be a full citizen of my fatherland.' He
recites these words when he crosses the boundary, again to the first person
he meets, again when proceeding through the town gate and again when
he enters the market-place . . . If his demands are not met, at the end of
thirty-three days . . . he declares war as follows: 'Hear, Jupiter and you
too, Janus Quirinus and all you gods of heaven and you gods of earth and
you gods below, hear! I call you to witness that this people [naming them]
is unjust and does not render just reparation. But we will consult the elders in our fatherland about these things, as to how we may requite what is
our due.'*

Livy, 1.32.6, on the Romans' early ritual for declaring war

ROMANS' EVER CLOSER ENCOUNTERS with the Greek world were
not to be a simple meeting of minds. Romans regarded Greeks as essentially frivolous, people who talked too much and were too clever by
half. They were duplicitous, and quite unreliable with money, especially
their own public funds. Among the Greeks, free male citizens had sexual relations with one another; Roman males were only supposed to do so with
male slaves and non-Roman inferiors. Greeks even exercised and competed
at games in the nude. Greeks' tunics left the body free, whereas Romans
were wrapped up in their solemn, inhibiting togas. Greek drinking-parties,

or *symposia*, were also very different. Romans gave dinners at which the food was the central item and free-born women, including wives, were present. At Greek parties, the only women were slave-girls and the point was to drink wine after dinner: the free-born guests were all men, and sex was a possibility, with a slave-girl or with one another. During the third century BC a new Latin word was coined, *pergraecari*, to 'have a thoroughly Greek time': it meant the lazy feasting and debauching which Greek drinking-parties encouraged. Romans' conversation was prosaic and factual: 'repeating Greek verses was for a Roman something like telling dirty stories.'[1]

Greeks loved beauty and (except the Spartans) brains. They also loved their invention, celebrities. None of these distinctions was a hallmark of the Romans' ancestors. They stood for solid, serious 'gravity', *gravitas*, which Cicero regarded as a Roman particularity.[2] When the traditionalist Cato wrote his history of the origins of Italy, he was so opposed to celebrities that he left out all the major players' personal names. Our first long surviving appraisal of Roman customs by a Greek visitor, the historian Polybius (writing *c.* 150 BC), emphasizes the solemnity of two special Roman features. At funerals of prominent Romans, the dead man was brought into the Forum and a fine memorial speech was spoken before an admiring crowd. Families brought with him the lifelike wax funerary masks of their dead relations which were set on robes of honour or worn by participating actors. These masks were a privilege given to men who had held one of the higher magistracies and made them publicly 'known' or *nobiles* (our 'nobles'). Crowds gazed on the splendour of these family processions and then a wax mask of the dead man was added to the masks which the family kept in their halls. They were an encouragement, Polybius rightly believed, to the young family members to rival their ancestors in glory.[3]

The other distinctive feature, he thought, was Roman religion. It was so much more elaborate and more prominent in public and private life than in any other society. Polybius believed that the Roman upper classes had emphasized it so as to terrorize the lower classes with religious fear. Roman nobles would not have seen religion in that detached way. For them, their religious rites honoured and appeased the gods so as to maintain the all-important 'peace of the gods' and avert their anger. They were kept up as the proven tradition of their ancestors, a tradition which had worked across the ages and could not be lightly abandoned. It kept Rome and the Romans safe. Ancestral tradition had 'authority', an element in Roman religiousness which has been argued to be still surviving in the 'authority' of tradition in the Roman Catholic Church.

Greek religion teemed with stories, or 'myths', about the gods, but the Romans' own myths had been very few during their earlier history. Art, especially statues, shaped the Greeks' ideas of their superhuman gods, but the learned Roman scholar Varro reckoned that there had been no Roman statues of their gods until as late as *c.* 570 BC. Nonetheless, many underlying principles of Roman religion were similar to the Greeks' own. Like the Greeks, the Romans were polytheists who worshipped many different gods. Important divinities had Latin names (Jupiter, Juno, Mars or Minerva), but they could be equated with Greek ones easily enough (Zeus, Hera, Ares, Athena). There were also many other gods, as if anything which might go wrong had a divine power to explain it: diseases of the crops ('Robigo', or blight) or the opening and shutting of doors (Janus, in various aspects). Yet, behind the big gods of Greek literature, similar divinities can be found in the calendars of the local demes, or villages, in classical Attica.

As in a Greek city, the main aim of religious cult was to aid worldly success, not to save citizens from sin. Romans' own ideas of a future life were as shadowy and ghostly as those of the Greeks with which they later enhanced them. The purpose of religious worship was honour and appeasement, pursued by pouring libations, giving animals or offering firstfruits at country altars. In Virgil's superb poem of country life, the *Georgics*, we glimpse the simplest of all offerings, garlands of 'Michaelmas daisies' on turf altars.[4] As in Greece, the main act of public religious cult was the killing of an animal, parts of whose meat were eaten afterwards. Priests attended, but in Rome they were almost always male priests and, distinctively, their heads were covered during the ceremony. As in Greece, too, there was an active art of divination so as to infer the gods' will. The entrails of sacrificed animals, the flight of birds, omens and oddities were all studied closely. At Rome, these arts were especially technical, because of the Etruscans' legacy to Roman culture. On military campaigns or before public meetings, a presiding magistrate would 'take the *auspices*', or look for signs of the gods' wishes, and a priestly augur would be consulted too. Romans were particularly concerned by 'prodigies', odd things and events which seemed to be signs of the gods' communication. A prodigy might be a deformed child at birth, a mole (reportedly) with teeth or an apparent shower of blood from heaven. Soothsayers and a priest stood by to list prodigies and interpret them.

Divination, then, was particularly elaborate at Rome and bad omens could be used even to interrupt a public assembly. On their way through Italy in the fourth and third centuries BC, Roman commanders would have paid close attention for any signs from the gods that relations with them were amiss. When Romans became aware of Greek philosophical theories a few of them did begin to reflect on the validity of this pseudo-science: there were a very few sceptics, including Cicero, but even Cicero was delighted to be chosen to be an augur and to uphold tradition, although the thinking half of his personality knew that divination was false. Every important Roman, whether Sulla, Pompey or Augustus, lived with a sense of the potential presence of the gods. In the 50s and 40s Julius Caesar's career was punctuated by omens, by escaping animals who were about to be sacrificed (twice in the Civil Wars, in 49 and 48) and by animals whose entrails were defective (in Spain, in 45, and in February 44, a month before his murder). He reinterpreted some of these signs so as to encourage his troops, but he never denied that they were signs.

Omens and prodigies warned of the gods' ill-will; the public calendar of cults aimed to avert evil and encourage safety, fertility and prosperity. As in classical Athens, an individual's personal religion was unimportant for the public rites: the rites, however, assured each individual Roman's well-being as a member of the community. Again as in Greece, there were no holy books or scriptures: the gods' 'due', or *ius divinum*, was passed on largely by oral tradition. Male priests attended the major rituals and, to Greek eyes, were organized in unusually specialized 'colleges'. The main female officials were the six Vestal Virgins, attached to the cult of Vesta, the goddess of the Hearth, whom they served for many years as virgins (though free, eventually, to move on and marry). As in the Greek cities, Roman festivals included processions, or *pompae* (whence Christians' 'pomp of the Devil'), and elaborate prayers and hymns. Romans' respect for tradition meant that if a priest made a mistake while reciting a traditional Latin prayer the rite was invalid and had to be repeated all over again.

As in Greece, there was a lively accompanying culture of individuals' vows, made to a god in hope of, or thanks for, a favour. Unlike the Greeks, Romans sometimes picked on human beings as the object which they vowed to offer. A general might 'vow' his enemies to the gods of the underworld (this rite was used in the siege of Carthage in 146 BC). On rare occasions he even vowed himself on behalf of his soldiers in battle. Stories were told of three such vows by Decius Mus and then by his descendants, all in the third century BC. Later, an ordinary soldier was said to be permissible as a substitute.[5]

In their households and on their farms, families would also pay religious cults to the 'gods in a small way', gods of crossroads or boundaries or gods of the inner recesses of the household (the *penates*); the powerful father of the household conducted the rites. Publicly and in households, there were also rites for the dead and their unseen ghosts. None of this worship would have surprised a Greek, and as time passed, Roman religion had more and more of a Greek imprint anyway. For its evolution reflected the influences on the city which we have traced since the seventh century BC: the age of kings, including the Etruscan kings; the change to a Republic; the role of the plebs, or commoners; the ever-growing contact with the Greek world, especially the Greek cities of Italy and Sicily. The single most important temple in Rome, Jupiter's on the Capitol, dated back to the last years of the kings. Unlike the last tyrants in Athens and their temple of Zeus, the kings had actually finished building it. In 496 BC, after the kingship had ended, an important temple to the agrarian Ceres, with Liber (Bacchus) and Libera, was founded: the cult was surely influenced by the cults of Demeter and Dionysus in Greek cities in Italy. It was adopted as a religious centre by the plebs.

There was, then, never a time when Roman cults were static. Things changed, new temples arrived and, in a crisis, a new cult might be sanctioned by another 'foreign' import, the oracular Sibylline Books. This collection of written Greek oracles had entered Rome, tradition said, under the Etruscan kings. Yet beside these additions to tradition, the Romans' calendar of yearly festivals retained obvious roots in the military and agricultural year, even when the calendar-months had fallen far out of line with the underlying seasons. In March the god of war and youth, Mars, was especially honoured, as befitted the month which had marked the new military year. One distinctive March rite was the prolonged dancing of twelve young patrician nobles, chosen from those with living parents, who served as the Salii, or dancing priests. They wore distinctive dress, including red cloaks and conical helmets, and danced through the city on a traditional route, carrying twelve ancient bronze shields which were said to be modelled on a prototype fallen from heaven. Each night, they stopped at a special house and ate a sumptuous dinner. Their entire ritual lasted for more than three weeks.

On 14 March there was a fine horse race on Rome's Field of Mars, balanced by another race in October, the month when soldiers would clean their weapons and put them away for the winter. On 15 October chariots raced in the Field of Mars and one of the winning horses (on the near side of the chariot) was sacrificed to the god. Its tail was cut off and hurried to the 'royal house' in the Forum so that its blood would drip on the hearth's sacred ashes. On the following 21 April these bloodied ashes were mixed with the ashes of cremated unborn calves and thrown onto ceremonial fires at another festival, the Parilia. The horse's head, meanwhile, had been cut off: two of the main districts of Rome competed for it, before nailing it (it seems) to the outside of the 'royal house' in the Forum.[6]

This rite of the October Horse spanned both war and agricultural fertility, according to Roman interpreters. Nonetheless, it would have struck many Greeks as barbaric. They would have been surprised, too, by mid-February's Lupercalia, when two teams of young men met at the Lupercal cave on the Palatine hill, associated with the she-wolf who had suckled Romulus and Remus. They sacrificed a goat and a dog and had the blood rubbed on their foreheads. They feasted and drank heavily in the cave and then ran out, naked except for goatskins, following an ancient route along the Palatine hill. They would whip anyone they met with the goatskin, a rite which was thought to promote fertility. It survived, nonetheless, for centuries, becoming famous with Mark Antony in the month before Julius Caesar's murder and living on, remarkably, until AD 494 in Christian Rome, when the Pope replaced it with the festival of the Purification of the Virgin.

In the public calendar, there were plenty of such festivals, festivals for the dead in February (the Parentalia, especially for the aged dead), or a 'carnival' festival in December, the Saturnalia, when social roles were briefly reversed and slave-masters would wait on their domestic slaves in their households. Greek cities, too, had these types of festival, just as they had festivals of release and merriment. At Rome, the main such feast was Flora's in April. Then goats and hares, highly sexed animals, were let loose on the last day of the accompanying games. Sex and fertility were part of the ritual's reference, and by the time of Julius Caesar striptease shows were being staged, too, on theatre stages in the city.[7]

Traditionalism was the overwhelming self-image of Roman public religion, but the festival of Flora is an instance of the scope, nonetheless, for additions and innovations. The festival gained a week of games only in 238 BC during a time of famine: they were sanctioned by the Sibylline Books. These books contained Greek oracular verses, supposedly spoken by a prophetic female Sibyl, and were kept by a board of fifteen respectable Romans. Plainly, the prophecies were Greek by origin, but they gave a divine sanction to the Romans' religious innovation. In 399 BC they had encouraged the adoption of a type of 'heavenly banquet', known in the Greek world, whereby statues of the gods were arranged for a feast on couches. In the 290s, during famine, they backed the introduction to Rome of the Greeks' god of healing, Aesculapius. In times of crisis, therefore, the Books would tend to add yet more Greek cults to the core of Roman tradition.

Wars, naturally, were under the care of the gods, and they were treated by Romans in two distinctive ways, at their end and at their beginning. With the Senate's permission, a victorious general could be granted a 'triumph', whereby he would be allowed, uniquely, to bring his troops and booty across the sacred city-boundary and into Rome. His face was painted red for the day, like Jupiter on the Capitol; he held a sceptre and wore special dress. His troops were allowed to shout obscenities and rude remarks at him, while a slave (it was said) stood by his shoulder and whispered to him, 'Remember, you are a man.' The ceremony crossed normal social boundaries in a single day of 'festival time': just for one 'red-carpet' moment, the triumphing Roman was like a god (or, some said, like a king). He ascended the Capitol and left his wreaths of laurel in Jupiter's lap. His name was then entered in honour into the public records. The generals who went south against Tarentum would certainly be hoping for a triumph. They also believed that their war was 'justified'. For, one of the priestly colleges, the *fetiales*, would have declared it according to rites which were believed to go back into the mid-seventh century BC. The Romans, this rite showed, did not fight except in 'self-defence': the fetial priests would traditionally send an envoy to throw a spear into the enemy's territory. At Tarentum, sufficient 'insults' were reported in the Roman tradition to 'justify' self-defence. When Tarentum was helped by King Pyrrhus from Greece, his territory was too far for an envoy to be sent all the way to cast the spear into it. So a prisoner taken from him was said to have been made to buy land at Rome so that the priests could declare a 'just war' on this nearby territory instead.[8]

In the Greek world, concern for a 'justified' war had long been current, whether with the Spartans or Alexander the Great or the philosopher Aristotle. Romans were not the inventors of the doctrine of the just war: they were merely more punctilious and ceremonious about it. Their publicity was that their successes in war confirmed that the gods were indeed on their side. They would soon assert as much to the Greek cities in their conquering path. But first the gods had to cope with Tarentum's rightful opposition.

LIBERATION IN THE SOUTH

The Roman embassy was led by Gaius Fabricius ... to whom Pyrrhus was privately disposed to be kind, and so he tried to persuade him to accept gold ... But Fabricius refused ... and so on the next day, wanting to terrify him as he had never seen an elephant, Pyrrhus ordered the biggest of his beasts to be set just behind them while they conversed, with only a curtain drawn across. When a signal was given, the curtain was drawn and the elephant suddenly raised its trunk, held it over Fabricius' head and let out a terrifying, harsh cry. But Fabricius turned round calmly and said to Pyrrhus with a smile: 'Yesterday, your gold did not sway me; today, this beast of yours does not sway me, either.'

Plutarch, *Life of Pyrrhus* 20

ROME'S ATTACK ON THE CITY-STATE of Tarentum turned out to be a military milestone. In self-defence, the men of Tarentum appealed for help to a Greek adventurer across the Adriatic Sea, for the third time in recent history. In the late 330s they had turned to Alexander the Great's brother-in-law and in 302 to an adventurous Spartan king. Now they appealed to King Pyrrhus in Epirus in north-western Greece. In spring 280 he crossed into south Italy and confronted the Romans for the first time with troops who had been trained in the world-conquering tactics of Alexander the Great. He also brought another of Alexander's novelties: war-elephants. No Italian had ever seen an elephant before. Pyrrhus' herd were real 'Indians', direct descendants of Alexander's, and he had taken them over in Macedon.

Through Tarentum—the child of Sparta—Rome and the Hellenistic world thus met face to face. But King Pyrrhus was also a throwback; he was the last great rival of Homer's heroes in Greek history. Like Alexander, he matched himself with Achilles, his ancestor, and set off to fight a new Trojan War against the Romans of 'Trojan' descent. Pyrrhus shone in the front line of battle in his silver armour and crowned helmet (silver armour was later copied, a classical allusion, for the great fighter of the Italian Renaissance, the duke of Urbino, in the fifteenth century). He enjoyed single combat and claimed that once, with a single swipe, he hacked a savage Mamertine mercenary in half. But he was not just a lout. He wrote a book on tactics and a book of memoirs and was later admired for his siegecraft and diplomacy. Nowadays, the Carthaginian general Hannibal is remembered as the famous user of war-elephants. In fact, Pyrrhus used them in far more settings, including Italy, throughout his career. In the West, he, not Hannibal, is the true 'elephant-king'.

When Pyrrhus reached Italy in 280 BC, he was already thirty-nine, seven years older than Alexander at his death. Discontented non-Greek peoples in southern Italy started to join him and, after a bloody victory against Roman troops near Tarentum's colony, Heraclea, he even dashed north towards Rome and sent a trusted Greek diplomat, Cineas, to offer terms to the Roman Senate. It was a great meeting. The elderly Cineas had once studied with the master-orator, Demosthenes. For the first time Roman senators heard a real Athens-trained speaker, but, in order to understand him, they surely had to have an interpreter as very few of them knew a word of Greek. In turn, Cineas was struck by his majestic audience (the Senate, he thought, was a council of kings). He was refused bluntly, but he is also said to have reported that the Roman people were like a many-headed monster whose numbers would keep on being replenished.[1] Many such comments were attributed later to Cineas by Romans who liked this connection with Greece, but if this one is true, Cineas, pupil of Demosthenes, was a shrewder judge of Roman manpower than of the Roman constitution.

After this refusal Pyrrhus won a second hard victory in 279 in Apulia, in which his elephants played a major role. Only when a Roman foot soldier hacked the trunk off one are the Romans said to have realized that 'the beasts were mortal'.[2] Nonetheless, they still terrified the enemy cavalry. The Romans are said to have mounted long spears on wagons to poke them away and to have tried to throw fire against the beasts from a height. Once again, the casualties on both sides were very heavy: 'another such victory,' Pyrrhus is said to have remarked, 'and we shall be lost'[3] (whence our saying, 'a Pyrrhic victory').

In 278 BC Pyrrhus faced a choice: either to turn back to Macedon where recent events gave him a new hope of the throne, or else to turn to

Sicily, in keeping with his former marriage to a Syracusan of dynastic family. While continuing to protect Tarentum, he chose to go south into Sicily. In Italy, he had been promising 'freedom' from Rome to the Greek cities, although they were wary about accepting it. In Sicily, he now promised 'freedom' from the Carthaginians, perhaps with a new joint Sicilian–south Italian kingdom of his own in mind. For three years he showed no more of a commitment to real freedom than any true Hellenistic king and failed in his hopes. On his return journey to Italy he lost several of his war-elephants and although he won a third victory against Rome at Beneventum in 275, it was another bloody encounter, with heavy losses on his own side. In this victory, too, the elephants played a big part, until a mother-elephant ran riot to protect its calf (the pair of them are perhaps commemorated in art on a contemporary plate found in Campania). The Romans are said to have terrified the elephants by setting pigs among them, squealing because the Romans covered them in fat and set them on fire. So Pyrrhus left a garrison at Tarentum and withdrew back to Greece. He ended up fighting first in Macedon, then in Sparta and Argos. In Macedon, he replenished his elephants by a victory over the king, Antigonus, and then took them down to southern Greece. While his elephants blocked the gates of Argos in 272 BC, he was stunned by a roof-tile (thrown by the mother of an Argive opponent) and was decapitated. His head was brought to the king of Macedon who rebuked its bearer, his son, and wept with a truly Homeric sense of his past losses. It was a typical show of sympathy between Hellenistic princes. Pyrrhus' head and body were buried, but his big toe survived, a sign (men said) of its divine quality.

When Pyrrhus left Sicily, he is said to have described it as the 'future wrestling-ground for Rome and Carthage'.[4] At first, Rome and Carthage had reasserted their old alliance in the face of the new invader. Within fifteen years they would be locked in war, as Pyrrhus had predicted. On and off it was to last for more than sixty years.

After Pyrrhus had left, Rome first received a remarkable new approach, from Ptolemy II, king of Egypt. Rome's victory had impressed him, perhaps because he had helped Pyrrhus in Epirus when the war began. Now he made a friendship, sealed with splendid gifts. As Rome was becoming more intertwined with affairs in the wider Greek world, events in the West increasingly interested Greek historians. The elderly Greek Hieronymus of Cardia, a hardened veteran of Alexander's Successors, digressed on the early history of Rome in his major work on the wars of Alexander's followers. He included Pyrrhus, his western battles and his death, presumably basing them on Pyrrhus' memoirs. In Athens, the exiled Sicilian Timaeus also wrote on Pyrrhus and claimed that the two cities of Rome and Carthage had been founded in the same year (which he calculated as 814/3). He was completely wrong, but the claim arose from an awareness that their twin histories were about to collide, at the expense of the old Greek West.

The Romans followed up Pyrrhus' departure by bringing the remaining Greek cities in the south of Italy into line. In 277 the town of Locri had struck silver coins on which 'Good Faith' (the Roman *fides*) was shown crowning the seated figure of Rome. In return, Locri would expect Roman trust and protection. In fact, the days of a free 'Great Greece' in south Italy were to be over. In 273, a colony was settled at 'Paestum', transforming the once Greek site. In 272 the Romans retook control of troublesome Tarentum. In 264 they found a pretext for a further step. Some barbarian Mamertine soldiers had seized the Greek town of Messina on the Sicilian straits, and then, very artfully, appealed to Carthage (who sent a garrison) and to Rome's 'good faith': they appealed for help from Rome against the many enemies, especially the Syracusan Greeks, whom they had made in Sicily. Despite misgivings in the Senate, the Romans accepted the Mamertine appeal and crossed into Sicily for the first time.

This momentous act of aggression brought them an important ally and an even greater enemy. The ally was the Sicilian Greek Hiero, who had recently established himself as king of Syracuse. At first Hiero spoke the necessary truth: 'the Romans', he said, 'were publicizing the words "good faith", but they certainly should not shield murderers like the Mamertines who totally despised "good faith" and were utterly godless'. By starting a war to help them, the Romans were 'showing the world that they used "pity for those in danger" as a cover for their own greed'. In truth, 'they desired all Sicily'.[5] The rights, or wrongs, of this crucial war, the 'First Punic War', have never been better put. Within a year, however, Hiero changed sides to Rome and stayed loyal to her for nearly fifty years. He could show his Roman visitors a level of royal luxury which they were certainly not supposed to covet. Its crowning glory was a pleasure-boat, called the *Syracusan*, which Hiero sent to his allies, the Ptolemies in Egypt. On the Nile, the Ptolemies' royal cruisers resembled floating palaces, but Hiero excelled them with a gigantic show-boat on three levels. It contained a gymnasium, green gardens, stables, and mosaic floors which illustrated the whole of Homer's *Iliad*. It could only be winched down to the sea by a special invention of the great Archimedes, the king's retained Greek engineer.

By invading Sicily, Rome gained a new enemy, Carthage. Carthage had long had designs on all of Sicily, but since her failed armadas against the Sicilian Greeks in 480 (and again in 410 BC) she had not pressed them. Meanwhile she had continued to develop economically and politically in north Africa. She had a long-standing presence in southern Spain, an area which was very rich in metals; she had developed an increasingly strong presence in her north African hinterland where the richer Carthaginians farmed estates with slaves; as before she continued to control north-western Sicily and metal-rich Sardinia too. For troops, she relied heavily on the mercenaries whom she hired in north Africa with her surplus riches: she pursued a real 'privatization' of warfare. But mercenaries were always a possible source of trouble and might well prefer their individual generals to the Carthaginian state. The Carthaginians' constitution had evolved a series of councils and magistracies which served as checks and balances against a coup by any one individual, even if backed by hired troops. Aristotle, even, had admired the system. By the 260s many of Carthage's leading citizens were educated men. One of them wrote an excellent long work on agriculture (Romans later translated it from Punic into Latin). Another described (surely correctly) the amazing journey of Hanno the Carthaginian and his fleet (perhaps *c.* 400 BC) out into the Atlantic, down the west coast of Africa and on past Senegal. Here was an adventure beyond any Roman's horizon, including a meeting with a tribe of hairy 'women' near the African shore whom Hanno's men named 'gorillas' (the origin of our name for the animal).[6]

Lying near to Greek Sicily, Carthage had always had a big Greek community too. Her rich households were famous for their fine carpets, their gold and their luxury, but they were also open to Greek design. They displayed ornamental Greek sculptures for owners who sometimes had a Greek education: it is not surprising that in the next generation the young Hannibal had a Greek tutor and was attended on his march by a Greek historian. Carthaginian 'cruelty' and 'treachery' were legendary among her enemies, at times unfairly. However, Greeks did also observe, correctly, that Carthaginians preserved the old Levantine practice of child-sacrifice to the gods, especially in times of crisis. The archaeology of Carthaginian burial grounds supports their observation, although it is probably only a Greek elaboration that music was played while the small children were being killed so as to drown the cries of their mothers.[7]

The First Punic War developed from Rome's illegal entry into Sicily and lasted from 264 to 241. It was the longest continuous war in classical history. In Carthage, Rome's wolf-children met a worthy match, and both sides were innovative. After watching Pyrrhus in Sicily the Carthaginians had added a new weapon to their army: the forest elephant, which was still native along parts of north Africa (including, as Aristotle knew, Morocco). As the First Punic War centred on Sicily, the Romans, too, were obliged to take a bold step: they built their first major fleet. It relied on the help of Greek and south Italian allies (and a captured Carthaginian warship, it was said, as a model), and when built it owed much to coastal Italians' command and experience. In 256, therefore, Roman generals were already confident enough to risk the four days' journey over open sea and invade Carthage's north African territory. But the venture failed, partly because the Carthaginians had a Spartan expert as their military adviser. Rome's general was the famous Marcus Regulus whom Carthage captured, but it is only a legend, propagated by his descendants, that his captors sent him back to negotiate at Rome where he advised against any concessions and then went back to Carthage for a heroic inevitable death. Actually, Regulus was killed locally and his widow tortured two Carthaginian prisoners in revenge.[8]

The long war had important economic consequences. In Sicily and Carthage, Roman armies took slaves by the ten thousand, more than they ever took in Italy. They even enslaved the entire population of luxurious Greek Acragas (Agrigento). Many of these captives were then sold, but as Acragas was soon repopulated, fellow Greeks had probably ransomed the city's former citizens in order to save them. However, many of Acragas' other slaves were surely taken back to Italy, as were many of the captives from Carthage, to be the booty of rich Romans. Most of these slaves had already worked on the land and so they would farm for Romans too. They increased Rome's ability to send so many free soldiers (otherwise essential farm-workers) so regularly overseas. Already slave-users, the richer Romans were certainly now a slave-society.

By contrast, Carthage lost the war after a big Roman naval victory in 242/1 and was fined a huge sum. She was obliged to evacuate Sicily (after five hundred years on parts of it) and was left to fight a bitter war back in Africa against the foreign African mercenaries on whom her army depended. Crushing peace-terms usually encourage revenge, all the more so when the Romans then coolly seized the valuable Carthaginian dependency of Sardinia in the 230s while Carthage's mercenary war was ending. In response, members of one prominent Carthaginian family, the Barcids, set off for Spain with troops and war-elephants to recover some of Carthage's lost prestige and no doubt to see how far success might go. On leaving, the father is said to have made his nine-year-old son take an oath at an altar 'never to be a friend to the Romans'.⁹ So much for Carthaginian 'perfidy': the son, Hannibal, never betrayed what his father made him swear.

For nearly twenty years (from 237 to 219) this Carthaginian force engaged in conquests in southern Spain. Two new towns were founded there, a New Carthage (now Cartagena) and a Fair Cliff (perhaps modern Alicante). In 226, however, a Roman delegation arrived and bluntly told the Carthaginian commander 'not to cross the river Ebro' which lay on the route north-eastwards from Spain to the Pyrenees and ultimately, therefore, in the direction of Italy. But just as in Sicily in 264, the Romans now followed up their agreement by accepting an appeal from the far 'Carthaginian' side of the Ebro. Here, a turbulent faction in the non-Greek city of Saguntum called on their 'good faith' against pro-Carthaginian enemies. The Romans accepted the appeal and caused no end of spin and whitewash by later Roman historians who were concerned to put an unjust Rome in the right. From Hannibal's perspective, Rome's behaviour was an unlicensed interference in territory which was his. It was made in order to support a group who had harassed good friends of Carthage inside a city which was not rightfully Rome's at all. So he set about besieging Saguntum.

Rome was not exactly free for a big new battle. She had been having serious problems with turbulent Gallic tribesmen in north Italy and in 219 was far from secure on that front. She was also concerned with an intervention she was making across the Adriatic into Greece. However, these distractions did not make her hesitate in the West. A few cautionary voices were sounded in the Senate, but, in response to Hannibal's siege of Saguntum, Roman ambassadors were sent to Carthage. They could not speak Punic but one of them was competent in the other language of Carthage's senators, Greek. 'We bring you peace or war,' said Fabius (who was from a Greek-speaking family), and he formed a fold in his toga with one hand; 'choose which you prefer.'¹⁰ From the Carthaginians' perspective, what business was it of the Romans if one of their generals in Spain attacked a city on behalf of pro-Carthaginian friends while he was not bound by any contrary treaty? So the Carthaginians told the envoy to choose instead. Fabius smoothed out the fold in his toga and shook out war.

HANNIBAL AND ROME

One of Hannibal's friends, known as the 'Gladiator', remarked that as far as he could see there was only one way by which they could manage to reach Italy. Hannibal asked him to explain, and the 'Gladiator' replied that they must teach the army to eat human flesh and become used to it. Hannibal could not refute the boldness or the practicality of this idea, but he could not persuade himself or his friends to accept it.

Polybius, 9.24

THE RESULTING SECOND PUNIC WAR with Carthage, from 218 to 202, strained Rome to the very limit, wracked Italy and ended by transforming Rome's resources, range and ambitions. To us, the hero is Hannibal, twenty-nine years old at the outset, who astonished the Romans by crossing the Alps and offering 'freedom' yet again, but this time to Italians throughout the peninsula. No wonder his name was evoked later by Napoleon during a similar transalpine campaign to 'liberate' Italy. Yet Hannibal was also remembered for destroying 400 towns and costing 300,000 Italian lives. His supreme victory at Cannae killed 48,000 enemy troops and is still studied in Western military academies. The rate of killing during the battle has been estimated at 500 lives a minute.[1] But even so, he did not win the war. The greater heroes turned out to be Roman: the noble Fabius Maximus, who turned defeat gradually into victory by a campaign of painful delay and devastation, and the brilliant young Scipio who ended by invading Africa and winning a last great battle near Zama in 202.

Had Hannibal's father talked to his son of crossing the Alps one day and avenging the previous war (and the loss of Sardinia) on a startled Rome? Perhaps, and perhaps Romans were right to be nervous, especially as north Italy below the Alps was so troubled with the Gallic tribesmen. But even then, Rome was miles away and the territories which she controlled totalled some 15,000 square miles. After the many conquests and treaties which she had made in Italy since the 340s, her adult male citizens now numbered more than 270,000, increased by particular Italian communities. From other communities she could draw on Italians as allies too. These Italians' treaties with Rome did not require them to pay tribute, but did oblige them to send and pay soldiers for Rome's wars. Rome's allied Italian manpower was more than 600,000, on top of her own ever-increasing citizenry. The heady days of the 390s, when a few Gauls could migrate south and seize Rome's Capitol, belonged to another era: Rome's potential soldiery was enormous, far bigger than the 30,000–50,000 citizens of classical Athens' days of dominance.

During the previous twenty years, the preceding Carthaginian conquests in Spain had been a slow business. Nonetheless, it was from Spain that Rome's greatest opponent emerged: the young Hannibal crossed the river Ebro in June 218 BC with 40,000 troops and thirty-seven elephants, only a fraction of the Carthaginian commanders' herd. He then crossed the Pyrenees and by mid-August he had also crossed the broad river Rhône north of Avignon by ferrying the elephants across on camouflaged rafts (although some of them panicked and swam). His troops were vastly fewer than Rome's potential manpower, and as he headed northwards up the Rhône's far bank, the watching Roman general, Scipio, cannot have given him much chance of reaching Italy at all. The Alps towered in his way, but Hannibal turned east and took them on, probably crossing Mont Cenis (arguably by the Savine Coche pass, around 7,500 feet high) in late October.

Up in the Alps, he was later said to have used hot vinegar to split open rocks which blocked his path (where, though, would he have found enough firewood to heat up enough vinegar?). The elephants must have helped to clear the way and certainly scared off the hostile local tribesmen. When he came down into the plains above Turin he had only 20,000 infantry and 6,000 cavalry; none of the elephants had yet died. Although his army was already halved, he still won a first skirmish against Roman troops by the river Po. He followed it up in late December with a crushing victory over a Roman consul and army at the river Trebbia (near Piacenza). A key to his success here was the doubling of his army with recruits from the anti-Roman Gauls in north Italy. They had at first hesitated to join him, but they were encouraged by his initial success and his terror tactics towards those who had refused.

With this army of hired Africans, Spaniards and Gauls, Hannibal was wary of a plot against his life, and in camp he is said to have worn different wigs in order to disguise himself.² Disguise would have been difficult because he lost an eye while travelling through marshlands around the river Arno. By then he had also lost almost all his elephants: only seven survived the cold winter and Hannibal, the most famous 'elephant-general', never used them decisively in Italy. However, the few (perhaps only one) who soldiered on were still a symbol: Italian towns on his route struck coins showing an elephant, even an Indian elephant (attended by a negro): perhaps Hannibal had acquired it from trade with the Ptolemies. If so, it is antiquity's great traveller, from Egypt to Italy. It may be the one called the 'Syrian', remembered as the bravest in battle. It had only one unbroken tusk: did one-eyed Hannibal ride it? In June 217, at Lake Trasimene in Etruria, his one eye was still clear-sighted: he took advantage of misty weather and outwitted another Roman consul and a bigger army.

Hannibal's crack troops were his cavalry, of which he had many thousands. His Numidians, from north Africa, were brilliant horsemen, able to direct their horses without any bridles by their clever use of a neck-rein. They had a flexibility which mounted Romans and Italians could not match. It is, then, for horses that Hannibal's march should be famous: when he pushed on to reach the eastern coast of Italy he reconditioned his horses there with the contents of the local cellars: he bathed them in old Italian wine, a vintage tonic for their coats.³ Personally, Hannibal was not a drinker and his only luxury was the food he had to consume. He had also left his Iberian wife back in Cadiz. Not until three years later, when he was in south Apulia at Salapia, is he known to have succumbed to an Italian woman, and she was a prostitute.⁴

In August 216 Hannibal won his supreme victory at Cannae in southeast Italy by pitting what were now some 50,000 troops against a much bigger Roman army which was probably about 87,000 strong. Once again, his mobile cavalry and ingenious battle-order proved unbeatable. After a day of slaughter, a Carthaginian, Maharbal, is said to have urged Hannibal to hurry straight to Rome, 250 miles away, where he could be 'dining on the Capitol after four days'.⁵ It would have been an amazing multi-ethnic dinner-party above the Forum, but Hannibal hung back. Instead, he won successes in the south, above all when he detached the powerful state of Capua from Rome's alliance. His troops then wintered in the town which had so long been famous for its luxury, including a council-chamber called 'the White House', a big scent-market and a tempting line in women and soft bedding. Moralists later said that this winter in Capua corrupted him, but oft-cited 'luxury' was not really the root of his problems.

Fundamentally, they were political. On entering Italy Hannibal had proclaimed freedom. His quarrel, he said, was not with Italy but with Rome. Italian prisoners were courteously dismissed. Just as he had hoped to profit from Rome's Gallic enemies north of the Po (in what is now, but was not then, 'north Italy'), so he hoped to detach Rome's many differing allies and dependencies throughout Italy. His brother Mago was sent down into the south to activate Pyrrhus' former stamping ground and liberate the Greek cities too. Attempts were to be made on all the Roman gains of the fourth and third centuries BC, including Naples and Tarentum. An alliance was even struck with King Philip V of Macedon over in northern Greece. Hannibal was certainly not acting as a lone adventurer without the approval of the Carthaginian government in Africa: in 215 they did manage to send him some more elephants across to southern Italy. His treaty with Philip makes his official support clear. Nor was he aiming to flatten Rome. She was to be left with a role, but without a confederacy, as if history could be turned back two hundred years. Hence, in part, Hannibal's refusal to hurry from Cannae straight to Rome's Capitol hill.

If Hannibal had succeeded, history until Hadrian's lifetime would have been completely different. Hannibal knew about Pyrrhus; he could read and speak Greek and Greek historians accompanied him. Nonetheless, did he simply repeat Pyrrhus' mistakes? Pyrrhus had been called a brilliant dice-thrower who could not exploit the results; Hannibal, too, was said to know how to win, but not how to use a victory. Actually, Hannibal had more in his favour. Unlike Pyrrhus, he had the full support of an established home government with the capacity to reinforce him, both from Africa and Spain. His victories were not 'Pyrrhic': they were crushingly one-sided triumphs. Neither Pyrrhus nor Hannibal made decisive use of their elephants, but Hannibal was a cavalry-king, the great Alexander's equal. Whereas Pyrrhus was a Homeric Achilles in combat, Hannibal was a consummate trickster, more of an Odysseus. He was a master of ambushes, of cunning battle-plans and false letters. He even tied blazing sticks to the horns of two thousand oxen and herded them away from his army by night so as to mislead his enemy about the 'lights' and line of his troops on the move. Like Pyrrhus, he came within a few miles of Rome (in 211, on a diversionary march northwards) but ultimately, like that of Pyrrhus, his was yet another 'liberation betrayed'. Even in the south, there were Greek city-states which never fully took his side.

For this hesitation, there were good reasons. Whatever Hannibal's personal culture, his troops were mostly random barbarians with little charm for the wary, civilized Greeks or for Rome's most favoured Latins. What would 'freedom' really mean when offered by a wild Gaul or a Carthaginian oligarch? The more Hannibal had to wait around, the more he devastated the countryside, while his own reprisals in captured cities could be dreadfully harsh. Above all, southern Spain had been blocked off from Italy by shrewd, long-term Roman generalship. Right from the start, in 217, the two elder Scipios, Rome's generals in Spain, had realized that they must keep troops on the coast there to block more troops from reaching Hannibal. If Hannibal had galloped to Rome after Cannae, there would have been the obstacles of the city's walls, many Roman survivors and some robust street fighting. But could he not have succeeded, like the Gauls in the 390s and without the treacherous geese?

On the Roman side, awesome prodigies were recorded for 218 and 217, as if the gods were communicating trouble: a six-month-old child called out 'triumph' in Rome; in Italian towns the sun seemed to be fighting the moon and shields were seen in the sky.[6] Nonetheless, as Cineas was said to have predicted, the many-headed monster could regenerate and struggle on. In Italy alone, 100,000 citizen troops were put in the field in the year after Cannae, besides those in Spain and those already on board a scattered fleet of 150 big ships. It was a fantastic effort. In 214 the Roman commander, a Gracchus, recruited at least 8,000 slaves and took them down to Beneventum, formerly the scene of a 'Pyrrhic' victory. This time, he won decisively against the Carthaginians and slaughtered many of them, whereupon the grateful Beneventans feasted his troops at tables which they set out in the streets. Gracchus freed the slaves and had the scene painted, showing his slave-soldiers wearing caps or white bandannas, and then dedicated this remarkable work of art in Rome's temple to Liberty.[7]

To confront the crisis, exceptional religious rites were carried out. As in the 220s, a pair of Greeks and a pair of Gauls were buried alive in the Cattle Market (Forum Boarium) in the centre of Rome. Human sacrifice was not the Roman way, so they were left to die naturally. Divine reinforcements were also brought in, Venus from the Carthaginian sector in Sicily and in 204 the 'Great Mother' (Cybele) and her black stone from Pergamum in Asia (her cult turned out to be wilder than the Romans expected, with exotic chants and self-castrated priests). Women were active too, particularly in hymns and processions to Juno in the later stages of the war: Juno was identified with the Carthaginian goddess Astarte and the honours to her would help to win her over to the Roman side.[8]

Rome's financial spirit was also not broken. The city, when war began, no longer conformed to its ideal of austerity. Already shops selling luxuries clustered round the Forum, a distinctive element of Roman life whose townsmen were so very much a 'nation of shopkeepers'. After Cannae, however, Rome's women gave up their jewellery so that it could be melted down for the war effort (in north Africa, women had done the same, but they were African women helping the mercenaries' revolt against Carthage). Roman citizens' tax was doubled and rich Romans even agreed to man warships at their own expense. In the crisis, a new silver coin, the *denarius*, was introduced; it would remain a part of Rome's coinage for centuries. Of course, there was still scope for fraud by those who contracted to supply armies in the field, but there was also a real 'Dunkirk spirit'. The Senate even refused to ransom Roman prisoners from Hannibal, including noblemen, because the money paid over would strengthen him.

In 215, while reinforcements for Hannibal (including elephants) could still be shipped over from north Africa, Rome's chances of long-term victory were slim. In the south of Italy, most of Tarentum had now turned to Carthage, no doubt with memories of Rome's harsh conduct to her since the 280s. Most importantly, King Hiero had died in Sicily and Syracuse had defected from Rome. But from 214 BC onwards the Roman fleet held enough of the Italian coast to block any more foreign support from reaching their enemies. From now on, Roman control of the sea proved crucial, both in Italy and in Spain. By land, meanwhile, Fabius insisted on a strategy of devastating the crops and avoiding battles on Hannibal's terms. The Carthaginians began to be bottled up.

For the Romans, the year 212/1 was a turning point. In Spain, their generals, the two elder Scipios, were killed in a setback, but their son and nephew, the younger Publius Scipio, leapt over the usual political career and was promptly made commander while still in his mid-twenties. He proved to be a bold genius, adored by his troops and also (men said) by the gods. In Italy, meanwhile, the able Fulvius Flaccus recaptured Capua and punished it ferociously. Above all, in Sicily the hard and proven general Claudius Marcellus attacked rebellious Syracuse. It could not even be saved by the skills of Archimedes, the famous Sicilian Greek engineer; it is only a legend that he built giant mirrors so as to burn up the attacking Roman ships. As at Capua, the Romans sacked the place with a stunning brutality. Shiploads of precious Greek art-works were transported back to Rome. For the first time, a great Greek city suffered the brutality of the she-wolf's Roman kinsmen on the rampage, although Marcellus was said to have tried to moderate them.[9]

Hannibal was still capable of effective ambushes and as late as 208 both the Roman consuls were killed in action at either end of Italy. In summer 207 one of his brothers did at last manage to bring reinforcements (and fresh elephants) into Italy from Spain. However, his dispatches were intercepted and he was defeated by a swift Roman counter-action up the east coast of Italy, encountering him at the river Metaurus in Umbria. It was the Carthaginians' last chance and without more reinforcements Hannibal became only a long-running sore on Italy's toe. In 205 the young Scipio crossed to Sicily, trained up a cavalry corps and then boldly sailed over to Africa in 204. During his campaign in Spain he had struck up a friendship with a most useful prince in north Africa, Masinissa the Numidian. Like Hiero in Sicily, Masinissa would give support to Rome for some fifty years. On African soil, his cavalry proved crucial allies and in 202 Hannibal (now back from south Italy) was decisively beaten. He had assembled eighty African elephants, but, like those of Pyrrhus, they ended by stampeding and doing more harm to their own side than to Rome's, even though Hannibal's father had pioneered a method of hammering spikes into the skulls of any beasts who went wild and began to charge their own supporters.

Both in Carthage and in Rome, the politics of the war and the generals had not gone smoothly. Hannibal always had enemies, and at Rome, the system had had to show a saving flexibility. For the 'struggle of the orders' had not vanished with the defeat of Pyrrhus. In principle, the people's decisions at Rome were now binding and there were ambitious senators who were ready to push this system in a more 'populist' direction. Nonetheless, Roman 'traditions' proved adaptable enough in the face of a crisis. Slaves were enlisted as troops; one dictator, then an unprecedented two at once, were appointed; when the conservative Fabius overruled an elected candidate to the consulship by citing improprieties in the religious context, he was allowed (just this once) to replace him with the man he wanted. Even the great Scipio jumped straight into his command of an army after only one lowly public job and then found himself being hailed as 'king' by his troops in Spain (a true Roman, he refused). To the Greek historian Polybius, the Roman 'constitution' appeared with hindsight to be in its best condition at the time of the disaster at Cannae. On closer inspection, it was still riddled with the contradictions of its evolution. It was rescued by its flexibility and its overall ability to absorb and to make exceptions.

The effects of the Hannibalic War have been much discussed by modern historians, but they left a lasting impact on Italy. None of Rome's closest dependencies, her Latin towns, went over to Hannibal, despite a bout of war-weariness at Rome's endless calls on their levies of troops. As elsewhere, the local upper classes preferred the known support and protection of Rome to the prospect of freedom for their own lower classes, especially when backed by savage Gauls and Carthaginians. In south Italy, defection to Carthage had been most evident, but Rome took a very fierce revenge. Hannibal's long presence in the south had already burdened the local harvests and led to much devastation. In reply, Rome confiscated considerable territory as public land. The local peasantry suffered huge losses in many areas, or fled to the towns. Rich Romans would then farm this new public land with slaves, their fruits of military conquest. In parts of the south, 'Hannibal's legacy' probably did amount to a long-term change in farming and land-use; the use of flocks and herds increased over the planting of arable crops, and these herds were tended by slaves, not free peasants.[10]

On Carthage's side, defeat required her to hand over her war-elephants and to promise never to train any more: they disappear from her army, while the survivors went up to Rome to grace young Scipio's spectacular triumph. The loss of the war did not lead to Carthage's total urban decline, but obliged her to make much bigger payments to the victor, Rome. It also made Hannibal into history's first global warrior. For more than thirty years, he had been out of Carthage, fighting in Spain, the Alps, then Italy. Rome's final terms for Carthage did not enforce his personal surrender; the Carthaginian political system continued and Hannibal held office as a reforming magistrate. Not until six years later was he driven out of Carthage, this time by his Carthaginian enemies. Supposedly, he was being too populist. He headed east, where he served with Rome's next major opponent, the Seleucid King Antiochus III in Asia Minor and in Greece. After a detour to Syria, he ended up, first in Armenia, then in Bithynia (north-west Turkey), two places where he was credited with designing and helping to found new towns. Eventually, aged sixty-seven, he was poisoned at the Bithynian court because of its courtiers' fears of reprisals from a Roman embassy. He was found to have built himself a fort with seven underground tunnels, a real bunker for Rome's ablest opponent. He had not taken plunder and riches for himself. Similarly, when his conqueror Scipio died his house was found to be a simple, turreted fort with a set of old-fashioned baths.[11] The two of them had been worthy opponents, and Hannibal's memory continued to haunt Rome. Years later, in the 90s AD, a Roman senator was said to be hoarding maps of the world and the speeches of great kings and generals, and maintaining two household slaves whom he had named Hannibal and Mago.[12] It was enough for the suspicious Roman emperor to have him executed.

DIPLOMACY AND DOMINANCE

As a superior power is naturally disposed to press ever harder on its sub-ordinates, is it in our interest to work with the impulses of our masters and not to make any obstacle, so that very soon indeed we experience even harder commands—or is the opposite our interest, to wrestle with them, as far as we can, and to hold out to the point where we are completely [exhausted] . . . and by reminding them of these things, we can put a check on their impulse and to a degree curb the harshness of their authority, especially as up to now, at least . . . the Romans do set more store on observing oaths and treaties and good faith towards their allies?

Philopoimen, in Polybius, 24.13

THE ROMAN MAGISTRATES and commanders in these epic years were men with military life in their bones. They all underwent ten years of military service before they were eligible for office. Every magistrate was a horseman, capable of serving his fatherland on horseback on a horse which was underwritten and maintained by public funds. In the age of kings, the cost of the Roman cavalry-horses' maintenance had been levied, magnificently, from Roman widows and unmarried women. In the Republic, orphans were made liable too. The idea of state-maintained horses had been copied from Greek city-states. Romans like the Scipios or the Fabii were hardened riders, a necessity in Roman republican life which our modern studies of their oratory and political programmes incline to overlook.

These mounted warriors were not deterred by Italy's surrounding seas: the Adriatic had already been crossed by Roman armies before Hannibal invaded. His first victories then coincided with important business in Greece and Asia, the world of Alexander's successors. The year 217 saw action on all fronts. In Italy, Hannibal won his devastating victory at Lake Trasimene, but in Asia, King Ptolemy IV and a newly trained army (including Egyptian infantry) won a fine victory at Raphia, to the south-west of Gaza, against the Seleucid army led by King Antiochus III. In Greece, in late summer 217, Greek envoys then met to discuss a continuing war between Greek states. At the time, the Ptolemies were at the forefront of the news after their mid-June victory. One speaker warned, nonetheless, of Rome, 'the cloud in the West'.[1] Within thirty years, this Roman 'cloud' would have burst decisively over Greece and the Seleucids' empire in western Asia. The Ptolemies, by contrast, would have lost their many forts and bases across the Mediterranean and would be further weakened by revolts within Egypt itself.

The Romans' eastward push into Greece and Asia was most remarkable. They had had a friendship with the Ptolemies since the 270s, in the aftermath of Pyrrhus, but they did not send armies into Greece for that reason. Rather, since the 280s they had settled colonies on the eastern coast of Italy and so, naturally, the Adriatic Sea had become an area of activity for the settlers and their associates. On the other side of the sea lay Illyrian tribes with a long history of raiding. By the 230s they had formed themselves into a more coherent kingdom and so complaints about Illyrian 'piracy' could be referred to a recognized authority there. In 229 Roman troops were sent across the Adriatic to uphold such complaints from Italian traders. Romans were also acting once again on an appeal to them from Greek petitioners, this time from Greeks on the intervening Adriatic island of Issa.[2]

After a quick campaign, the commanding consuls were granted a triumph. The news of Roman victories against the 'barbarian' Illyrians was then carefully publicized among the watching Greek states, including Athens. A second 'Illyrian' war followed which tidied up threads from the first and brought Rome more directly into contact with the then king of Macedon, young Philip V. In 215 Romans found that this King Philip had been offering his alliance to none other than Hannibal, with the possibility of Macedonian reinforcements in Italy. That discovery was enough to guarantee that a Roman war in Greece would eventually be resumed.

There was ample scope for interference. For a hundred years Greek city-states had remained under the control of the Macedonian kings. There had been periods of war, in which some of them, including Athens, fought for 'freedom', but these ventures had usually been helped by a rival Macedonian king, including the Ptolemies in Egypt. Macedonian rule remained in place, drawing revenues from those under it and relying on its garrisons at important points in Greece, as first instituted by Philip II. Within this general framework, power-politics had continued in directions which a Demosthenes or a fourth-century diplomat would readily understand. The 'leagues' of that era had gained in strength, especially the Aetolian League in western Greece and the Achaean League, which was now focused on Sicyon in the northern Peloponnese. Within the city-states, there were continuing factional splits between leaders favouring democracy and those favouring oligarchy. In the 220s the longest-running terror in Greek history had returned, a reformed and newly aggressive Sparta under able kings, first Agis, then Cleomenes. The prospect of renewed Spartan rule was enough to turn the Achaean League back to an alignment with the Macedonian king and to give a new twist to a war with the other Greek power-blocs.

The Romans, then, could side with one or other league, respond to one or other faction in the divided city-states or even challenge the Macedonian kings directly. For the time being they were preoccupied with Hannibal in Italy and their next moves in Greece were blunt and ill-judged. In 212/11 they agreed an alliance with the Aetolians in central Greece, the dominant power at Delphi but the least civilized element in all the political divisions in Greece. There was no question of Rome offering 'freedom' or even liberation to Greeks under Macedon or anyone else. The Aetolians were to keep any cities taken in war, while Romans would take any movable booty, including quantities of slaves. Other Greeks regarded this sort of robbers' deal as barbarous and alien.[3]

For more than ten years Hannibal and Spain distracted the Romans, but in 200 they were free once more, so they returned to Greece in force. They would have returned anyway, but they could point to the useful fact that King Philip of Macedon had meanwhile been attacking friends of Rome in the east Aegean. By autumn 200 the Athenians had joined Rome's side (they would stay loyal for more than a hundred years), and in 197 the flexible lines of the Roman legionaries, with 2,000 Roman cavalry, won a good victory over Philip's traditional Macedonian formations at Cynoscephalae in Thessaly. It was now in Rome's power to announce a settlement of Greek affairs. The hit-and-run style of the earlier treaty with Aetolia had been abandoned and no favour was being shown to its Aetolian partners, despite their help with cavalry at Cynoscephalae: they remained very pained by their rejection. Instead, the Roman commander, Flamininus, declared the 'freedom of the Greeks'. It was not just a freedom within which key points in Greece would continue to be garrisoned (this limited 'freedom' was familiar since Philip II in the 330s). It was a

44. Silver tetradrachm from Sardis, *c.* 213–190 BC, with head of the Seleucid King Antiochus III, defeated by Rome in 189 BC.

freedom for those key points too. Flamininus had an unusual feel for Greeks' interests. The announcement was made at the Isthmian Games in 196 and was greeted with such thunderous Greek applause, people said, that birds dropped dead from the sky.[4]

Even so, the Romans' horizons were not confined to the Greeks in Greece. They had already begun to make public references to the status of Greek cities in Asia and Europe who were under royal Seleucid rule. Artfully, they presented themselves here too as if they were intervening on behalf of friends. For there were fellow 'Trojans' in Asia around the site of Troy, and further south Romans had their long-standing 'friends', the Ptolemies. The Ptolemies had recently lost a whole cluster of their overseas Greek bases in western Asia; they were even alleged to be at risk from a 'secret pact' between King Philip of Macedon and the Seleucid King Antiochus III. To foster their image the Romans publicized their conviction that, as their successes were proving, the gods were on their side and their foreign campaigns were justified.

In 192 the disgruntled Aetolians invited the alarmed King Antiochus to cross over from Asia into Greece with an army. Nonetheless, the Romans had already decided on a direct campaign against him, to be taken east into his own historic territories. First they won a clever victory at the historic site of Thermopylae in Greece and forced Antiochus back into Asia. In winter 190/89 their legionaries then won the final battle at Magnesia in western Asia. The territory of Seleucid kings here was 'liberated' after a hundred and fifty years of Greek rule since Alexander the Great, a 'liberator' too. But much of it was promptly given over to friends of Rome, in the south to the islanders of Rhodes, in the north-west to King Eumenes, who was based in his royal city of Pergamum. The interests of the Ptolemies were bluntly dropped from consideration.

The Romans, meanwhile, received the immense sum of 15,000 talents, to be paid in instalments. Carthage, too, was still paying them yearly sums and the 15,000 talents did not even include the copious booty from Asia. Their public finances were transformed. At the same time, their economic strength was helped by a simultaneous increase in the numbers of Romans established up and down Italy. The years from 200 to 170 saw a surge of new Roman colonies in Italy which extended up into rich northern farmland near the river Po. It has been estimated that as many as 100,000 settlers were sent out to take up to a million acres of land; great Italian sites like modern Parma or Bologna began their 'Roman' history in these years.[5] The settlements were an outlet for poorer Roman citizens, who were a possible source of social tension at Rome. Once again it was a classic transformation of an ancient economy, in which war multiplied income and assets, and land-settlements changed the conquering state's social profile.

After Rome's victories in Greece, justice, of a sort, followed for Greeks in the new age of publicly declared 'freedom'. The Roman Senate and Roman commanders found that they were now a frequent resort for appeals from Greek states for impartial justice and territorial arbitration in their own internal disputes. Romans repeatedly heard these requests, but when they reached decisions, quite often they departed from what had seemed to be their previous inclinations. This inconsistency suited the Romans' new policy of profiting from Greek weaknesses and internal strife. One after another, their former Greek friends and beneficiaries became disgruntled at Romans' answers to them: Rhodes, King Eumenes of Pergamum and eventually the important Achaean League in the Peloponnese. Ominously, individual Romans began to be remembered for outbursts of 'anger' when dealing with Greeks and their business.[6] There was a further shift of sympathy. Until the late third century BC democracies had been relatively widespread in the Greek cities. After 196 Romans favoured their avowed friends in the cities and reckoned that these individuals would best advance their interests against an unreliable populace. These friends were usually the richer citizens who stood for 'order', not popular rule. It is no coincidence that increasingly dominant big 'benefactors' emerge in many of the Greek city-states, as the checks and balances of the democracies began to be set aside, first in the more recently founded Greek city-states, then in the older 'mother-cities' in Greece.[7] Romans combined the role of 'policemen of the Mediterranean world' with an awareness that they were now the most powerful force and could act more or less as they thought fit. Then, too, it was a dangerous combination for their 'allies' abroad and those around them.

Between 168 and 146 Roman power was forcefully exercised against remaining 'enemies', the king of Macedon (Perseus in 168), the Seleucid king in the Near East (Antiochus IV in 165), tribes on the Dalmatian coast (156) and both the Achaean League in Greece and the remaining territory of Carthage in north Africa (146 BC). The most important of these engagements was the defeat of the Macedonians, ending the power which they had enjoyed for nearly two centuries. In 179 the kingship had passed to Perseus, a prince in his mid-thirties, whose flare and energy quickly perturbed Roman onlookers. He married a princess from the Seleucid royal house in Asia. He proclaimed favourable terms for debtors in Greece and revived the appeal of Macedon for the many Greeks whom Roman actions had increasingly helped to impoverish. Roman suspicions of him mounted during the 170s, culminating in their decision for war late in 172. One final Roman embassy only misled Perseus and delayed his preparations by suggesting, duplicitously, that he might win a settlement at Rome. Even some of the Romans criticized this cynical diplomacy.

During the next two years, Roman commanders in Greece behaved no more commendably. Greek opinion had to be smoothed over before a big Roman army arrived in 168 with the consul, Aemilius Paullus, descendant of the very consul whom Hannibal had destroyed at Cannae. On the south-east coast of Macedon, the two powers met for battle in the cramped mountainous country by mount Olympus. Perseus' army was nearly as big as Alexander's at Gaugamela, but a Roman detachment succeeded in a brilliant flanking movement through two mountain passes to the west, dislodging two Macedonian garrisons and suddenly threatening Perseus' army with encirclement. This crucial manoeuvre was led by the son-in-law of the great Scipio: he later enhanced his success in his written account of the action.

Perseus retreated, but as Aemilius Paullus pushed after him, he was surprised to find the Macedonian army drawn up once more in a narrow plain south of Pydna. His subordinates wanted an immediate attack, but Aemilius delayed, sizing up his opponents: he would later say at dinners in Rome that the Macedonian phalanx, bristling with its long spears, was 'the most terrifying thing' he had seen in his life. Battle began on June 22, the day after an eclipse of the moon, and the Romans almost lost the field in the first central assault. The phalanx's long pikes pierced their infantry's shields and drove their centre back, but its traditional weakness then showed during the follow-up onto rough ground. Its ranks began to break, allowing the Roman infantrymen to penetrate the formation and deploy their longer swords against the short daggers which phalanx-soldiers used at close quarters. The killing was furious, accounting for 20,000 Macedonians, we are told. Meanwhile the Macedonians' cavalry-charges down the wings failed, partly because of the Romans' elephants, partly because their own elephants were truncated by a Roman anti-elephant corps.

Perseus fled, but was duly captured and brought before Aemilius who lectured him before his young Romans on the instability of fortune in terms which Herodotus would have approved. The Macedonian palaces were plundered, yielding a huge quantity of ivory tusks, which remind us how elephants had long been kept in the once-marshy plain around Pella. Perseus and his children were taken back to Rome and made to process as humble captives in the triumph which marked the end of Macedonian royal power: Aemilius Paullus took the contents of the royal Greek library. The kingdom had been split into its four underlying districts, but the Macedonians were not used to even a slight degree of democracy. Before long they rebelled under one more royal pretender.

The following years, from 168 to 146, were regarded by a sharp Greek observer, the historian Polybius, as real 'times of trouble'.[8] Certainly, the Romans showed no quarter to those whom they declared to be enemies. In 149 they announced their decision to dismember the long-established Achaean League in Greece, and in 146 they duly did so and destroyed the ancient city of Corinth. In the same year, they utterly destroyed what remained of Carthage (its years of paying reparations had recently ended). Already in 168 their victor at Pydna, Aemilius Paullus, had taken fearful reprisals against the peoples of Epirus in north-west Greece, who had aided adjacent Macedon. The Senate ruled that seventy towns in Epirus were to be plundered and, as a result, as many as 150,000 people were brutally sold into slavery. Masses of Greek works of art were also shipped back to Rome with huge quantities of gold and silver objects. After that horror, it is hard to accept that Rome somehow deteriorated.[9]

Within seventy years, from the disaster at Cannae in 216 to the ruination of Carthage in 146, the Romans had become the one superpower in the Mediterranean. The results are instructive. Romans now expected 'obedience' to orders which they issued of their own accord; Roman commanders were used to exercising 'command' (*imperium*) as magistrates at Rome. When they declared war (as in 156 BC) they were careful to give out a 'just' pretext for public consumption, although the real reasons lay elsewhere. By following these pretexts, modern historians have sometimes argued that Rome was only drawn step by step into Greek affairs, that her attacks were usually in self-defence and that, as she did not immediately form her conquests into new provinces, she began with no fixed aim of exploiting them. Fascinating problems of chronology and evidence can be brought against this interpretation, quite apart from the reported views of contemporaries. They also overlook important elements in the Roman mentality and the interrelated complex of glory and gain in Roman society; there was an urge among aspiring commanders to live up to family-ancestors who had aspired to the same achievements, and the goals were booty and a public triumph. It is more cogent to credit Romans with bold designs and decreasing scruples about duplicity and frank aggression in attaining them. Some of the Romans did pick out a 'new-style wisdom' among their politicians in the 170s BC which involved telling outright lies and assuming that 'might is right'.[10] Arguably, the 'new wisdom' was only an intensification of pre-existing practice. Rome's success in Greece and western Asia rested above all on her vastly superior manpower and the flexible military tactics which had been adopted before the 320s and had already been proven against Carthage. Her behaviour to her enemies in Greece in these grim years is less of a surprise to those who begin by studying her previous behaviour in Greek Sicily in 212/11. To exploit her conquests, she did not need to class them into territorially defined provinces. Her dominance could be less direct, even if we hesitate to call much of it an outright 'empire' as yet, in our understanding of the word.

PART FOUR

The Roman Republic

ROME, FROM THE THIRD to the second century before our era, was the most aristocratically governed city that existed in Italy or Greece . . . If the Senate was obliged to manage the multitude on domestic questions, it was absolute master so far as concerned foreign affairs. It was the Senate that received ambassadors, that concluded alliances, that distributed the provinces and the legions, that ratified the acts of the generals, that determined the conditions allowed to the conquered—all acts which everywhere else belonged to the popular assembly. Foreigners, in their relations with Rome, had therefore nothing to do with the people. The Senate alone spoke, and the idea was held out that the people had no power. This was the opinion which a Greek expressed to Flamininus, 'In your country,' he said, 'riches alone govern, and everything else submits to them.'

N. D. Fustel de Coulanges, *The Ancient City*
(1864, English translation 1956)

I REITERATE THAT IN THIS SYSTEM (the Roman political system of the late Republic), public office could only be gained by direct election in which all (adult male) citizens, including freed slaves, had the right to vote, and all legislation was by definition the subject of direct popular voting. That being so, it is difficult to see why the Roman Republic should not deserve serious consideration not just as one type of ancient city-state, but as one of a relatively small group of historical examples of political systems that might deserve the label 'democracy'.

Fergus Millar, *The Crowd in
Rome in the Late Republic* (2002)

LUXURY AND LICENCE

'I have neither a building nor a vase nor a costly robe nor a high-priced slave or slave-girl. If there is something I have to use, I use it. If there is not, I do without. Anyone may use and enjoy what is theirs, and that is fine by me.' But then Cato goes on, 'They blame me because I do without so many things. But I blame them because they are unable to do without.'

Cato the Censor, in Aulus Gellius, *Attic Nights* 13.24

THE ROMANS' CONQUESTS IN ITALY, then in Greece, were due partly to their military skill and values, partly to their superior and ever-increasing manpower and their appeal to local upper classes or factions within them. Obedience to Rome seemed the lesser of political evils to people whose standing and property were at risk from their own lower classes or from surrounding barbarian enemies. 'Freedom', by contrast, was late to emerge as a Roman offer to states in Greece.

As Romans and Greeks were thrown into new, closer relationships, a conflict of cultures was necessarily involved. Greeks evidently interpreted offers of 'freedom' in a spirit which Romans, expecting loyalty and obligation, did not. At Rome, meanwhile, increasing exposure to Greek customs greatly enlivened 'traditional' Roman life. By *c.* 200 BC there were quite a few senators who would have spoken and understood Greek: some modern historians reckon that as many as half were capable of it, though, in my view, that is an overestimate. Rome had been exposed to Greek artists, Greek cults and Greek-speakers for centuries now and her conquests in south Italy had long brought her up against Greek culture. But there are many levels of knowing a language and many degrees of what we call 'Hellenization'. Owning Greek objects and Greek slaves is one thing; thinking in Greek and admiring the heart of Greek culture (wherever we place it) is another.

Certainly, Greek culture had started to make a transforming mark on Latin. From the 240s the Latin language had begun to acquire its own literature, directly modelled on Greek (beginning with the *Odyssey*).[1] The first Latin authors reflect the results of Rome's military progress southwards through Italy and beyond: the first Latin playwrights come from the Greek-speaking south including Tarentum; the first historian, the senator Fabius Pictor, was moved to write a history in order to explain the war with Carthage, and he wrote it in Greek, purely for a Greek audience. The great Latin comic dramatist Plautus originated from central Italy (Umbria) and also followed Greek models. Above all, the first Latin epic poet, Ennius, came from the toe of Italy and spoke two languages besides Latin. He wrote in erudite Greek poetic forms and produced a remarkable epic poem, the *Annals*, which ran from the Trojan War to the triumph of his Roman senatorial patron, Fulvius Nobilior. The triumph was given to Nobilior for conquering Rome's former allies, the Greeks of Aetolia. Ennius could no doubt elaborate on the triumph's occurrence a thousand years after the supposed fall of Troy, which was dated with misplaced learning to the 1180s BC.[2]

Nonetheless, this poetic literature was all in Latin. The most widely enjoyed, Plautus' comedies, had a strong Latin tone in their settings, even their food, and their roles for freed slaves, which were much more pronounced than in Greece. What sort of 'Greekness' would a Roman senator most relate to? Not to the classical Greekness of an Athenian democrat, philosophizing about difficult questions of knowledge and necessity, accepting equal votes from the peasantry and sighing for the beauty of a young male athlete. Nor to the splendour of a Hellenistic king: Roman ideals could relate more readily to the Spartan ideals of austerity and a 'peer group', but their own formation and pursuit of riches were not at all those of a good Spartiate. There was no neat overlap with any one sort of Greek life. What mattered in Rome's so-called 'Hellenization' was the social and moral context in which Greek ways were received: Romans could collect art, poets and skilled slaves, but they were not made into true Greeks merely by being philhellenes, any more than the francophile Russian nobles of Tolstoy's *War and Peace* were fundamentally French. In Roman circles, the master-exponents of Greekness were kept socially in their place. Greek poets became only the clients of the Roman rich; the 'talent' from the Greek world brought yet more skills, arts and luxuries to Rome, but they arrived as slaves and war-captives. In this respect, the Roman triumph over Macedon in 167 was seen as a turning point which brought anything from Greek musicians to Greek cooks and skilled prostitutes into Roman society. After the 160s the utilitarian brothels of Plautus' plays (*c.* 200 BC) would have seemed a poor second to the skills of the new Greek-style courtesans at Rome. Homoerotic 'Greek' sex became more fashionable for Romans, although it was still not to be conducted between free citizens. These years of cultural awakening are fascinating because the new Roman context imposed such challenges on the immigrant Greek artists. In February 166, at games for a victory over the Illyrians, famous Greek flute-players and a chorus of dancers were put up on a temporary stage in the Roman circus. As their artistic routine seemed boring to the Roman spectators, they were told to liven it up by starting a mock battle. The chorus split into two and obliged, whereupon four boxers climbed up onto the stage with trumpeters and horn-players. The waiting tragic actors, brought from Greece, had to change their performance, so much so that the Greek historian Polybius, probably one of the crowd, could not even bring himself to describe it for his serious Greek readership.[3]

Inevitably, the new fashions and new imports activated traditional Roman fears of 'luxury'. Several laws to limit it are attested within fifty years, although they were not the first in Roman history. They fitted with deeper Roman attitudes. Austerity and parsimony were admired in the stories which were told about the receding seventh to fourth centuries BC. Roman fathers were expected to emulate them and educate their sons in restrained conduct. The censors, two magistrates, had acquired the duty of supervising public morals: when the lists of Roman citizens were periodically drawn up, they could place a 'black mark' against anyone whose behaviour had been disgraceful. In the new age of eastern conquest there was so much more to reprehend. 'Luxury' was attacked as 'Asian' and 'eastern', picking up the old stereotypes applied by Greek thinkers and historians from Herodotus onwards. But there was also truth in the stereotypes. The art and architecture, metalwork and cultural skills of the Macedonian and 'Asian' Greek monarchies were vastly more advanced than the crude levels of art and culture which had prevailed at Rome before the 180s. There was also the continuing example of the Ptolemies in Egypt, the luxury of whose kings had a quality of Dionysiac fantasy and royal splendour. At Rome, so hostile to one-man rule, such extravagance was wholly unacceptable.

Laws against luxury were not imposed in this period by the people's assemblies so as to curb an extravagant upper class. Rather, members of the

Senate (not all of them) brought the proposals forward.[4] One often-feared luxury was the excessive entertaining of guests at public banquets. It was indulgent, but it was also a way in which Roman holders of public positions could court too many supporters. Laws also tried to limit the consumption of excessive imports. Of course the laws were contested, or merely ignored, but they belonged in a wider context of concerns. The triumphs from the 180s onwards were occasions for big public feasts, and, as we shall see, for novel 'spectator sports' which provoked rivals' concerns: three times, between 187 and 179, senators tried to limit the money spent on circus-games. They also tried to ban the import of animals for 'hunting' in the arena: a populist tribune frustrated them. Laws also tried to limit bribery and to regulate the stages at which men could hold public offices. Like this political opportunism, luxury could intensify competition within the upper class at a time of exploding opportunities. The crisis of the aristocracies in the Greek city-states during the seventh and sixth centuries BC was being replayed at Rome, but with weapons of a vastly greater scale.

The supreme Roman voice against luxury and the accompanying tensions was the famous Cato the Elder, fragments of whose Latin writings survive. Cato emphasized his 'parsimony and austerity' and his years of working the land among its 'Sabine' stones.[5] But he was certainly no peasant or spokesman for poor farmers: he was from a well-off Italian family. Beginning in 217, Cato's career ran on into 149, peaking in 184 when he served as censor and showed a famous severity even to some of the Roman senators. Posterity would uphold him as the strictest of all traditional Romans, but Cato's traditionalism was the conservatism of an *arriviste*, a new man made good. The style of his household became legendary. Cato would sometimes retreat to the simple cottage which had formerly been used by the austere, exemplary Curius. There, his wife would suckle children of their slaves so that they would imbibe loyalty to the master with her milk; plain plates and cups were the dinner-service (not the silver and gold cups acquired in new shapes in Greece) and Cato had the unpleasant habit of turning sick or old slaves loose so as not to be a burden to his estate.[6] Cato was not opposed to making money: it was a virtue, he believed, for someone to increase his inherited estate.[7] Nor did he abhor trade, though he did think it horribly risky. What he loathed was moneylending because it was an 'unnatural' and infamous pursuit.[8] He also feared the political effects of ill-gotten gains abroad. For that reason, he spoke against those senators who in 167 BC wished to attack Rome's former ally, the island of Rhodes.[9]

It was not that Cato had any fondness at all for Greeks as Greeks. Memorably, his speeches and writings attacked their intellectual pursuits, their philosophy, their poetry and their doctors. They were the 'most wretched and unruly race',[10] championing nakedness and frivolity; their doctors were conspiring to kill off the 'barbarian' Romans. Romans' fashion for Greek examples, Cato said, was disgraceful, especially as Romans and Italians had heroes in their own past who were just as great. Cato's complaints reflected Rome's increased wave of Greek contact. When the Athenians sent leaders of their philosophy schools to Rome on an embassy in 155 BC, one of them, the sceptic Carneades, pleaded on one day for justice in politics, on the next day for injustice. Cato was so disgusted that he wanted the philosophers to leave Rome at once and return to corrupt their own youth, not the youth at Rome.

Nonetheless, Rome's youth had been very much taken with these Greeks' cleverness. What Cato opposed was a rapidly rising tide, and he himself had been buoyed up, of course, on its groundswell. He had studied in Athens: his work *On Agriculture* drew on Greek sources, as did his work *Origins*, on the beginnings of Italy's peoples and places. He had profited from a basic Greek framework, but nonetheless he detested its frills and excessive cleverness. There was also a one-sidedness in his attitude to Carthage. Cato had served in the Hannibalic War and, when the Carthaginians ceased paying their indemnity for defeat (in 151), there was debate at Rome on what to do to them next. Cato, the Hannibalic veteran, was for destroying Carthage totally. He even emphasized the danger by exhibiting a fresh fig in the Senate which had 'just' been picked in Carthage, as if the place was forty-five minutes away from Rome.[11] But his policy of destruction was feared for a reason which ought to have swayed him: if Rome was left with no foreign enemy to fear, would not 'luxury' and softness proliferate even more? Nonetheless, Carthage was destroyed.

These sorts of contradiction continued to be posed to traditional Roman ways of thinking by the spread of Roman power abroad. Friendly Greek cities instituted cults of Rome as a goddess and even approached Roman magistrates as if they were like the courtiers or princes whom they knew in their own Greek world of kings. Such personal honours ran flatly against the freedom and equality which the senatorial class prized among its members. As Romans became more imperious, their own social structure was even played back to them by a reluctant subordinate, King Prusias of Bithynia.[12] In the 170s Roman envoys came to Prusias' court in north-west Asia, but he cleverly parodied the realities of the situation by dressing and presenting himself as a freed ex-slave, a truly Roman sort of dependant. 'You see your freedman, myself,' he told them, 'who wishes to gratify you in everything and imitate what happens among you.' Prusias then travelled to Rome and, brilliantly, went a stage further on entering the Senate. 'Hail, saviour gods,' he greeted them while grovelling in adoration both to the threshold and to the senior senators inside the building. He seemed so utterly despicable that he was given a friendly response. Arguably, the laugh was with Prusias who was ironically parodying the self-image of his arrogant new Roman masters.

Rebuffs received from Rome could even touch off secondary culture-clashes farther afield. In spring 168 the Seleucid King Antiochus IV at last broke into the rival territory of Egypt's Ptolemies, only to be confronted and halted there by an imperious Roman envoy. Obliged to withdraw, Antiochus staged a festival of his own in Antioch, in deliberate rivalry of the Roman generals' contemporary celebrations of their victory over Macedon. In the new Roman fashion, Antiochus staged a show of wild beasts in combat, but then baffled his guests by waiting on them personally in an ostentatious show of affability during his gigantic royal banquet.[13] A year later, he stopped in Judaea, where he heeded the request of a faction of Jews in Jerusalem; they wished to subdue their opponents and adopt Greek customs while abandoning traditional Jewish practices. Antiochus supported them, as if to work off his anger after his recent rebuff in Egypt by Rome.[14] The result was a nationalist uprising by outraged fellow Jews and a bitter war (the 'Maccabean Revolt'). It resulted in a newly powerful Jewish state and a new theology of martyrdom for those Jews who died in the course of it. They were said to have gone directly to Paradise, the first mention of this historically fertile idea.[15]

Above all, a culture-clash was lived out by the man to whom we owe so much of our knowledge of Rome's advance from 220 to 146, the last of the great Greek historians, Polybius, a Greek from Megalopolis. He was born into a prominent political family in the Achaean League, but in 167 he was deported to Rome with a thousand others, as a hostage suspected of hostility to the Romans. While a hostage, he befriended important Romans, including the young Scipios (hunting was one important bond with them). Later he travelled widely in Spain and the West, even down the coast of west Africa. Yet again, a fine Greek history was to be written by an exile. Polybius' original plan was to write a history down to 167 BC but he prolonged it because he lived to see the 'troubled times' of Rome's years of domination.[16] He himself played a part in them, by assisting in the very settlement which was imposed by Rome on Greece in 146

45. Silver denarius, Rome, showing a scene of voting. 113 or 112 BC.

BC, after the ruthless destruction of Corinth. Polybius had a difficult role to explain: he had been a 'fellow traveller' and a participator in Roman actions which otherwise he would be expected to have opposed.

Polybius is the historian in antiquity with the most explicit view of what historians should be and do. While attacking his predecessors (much to the benefit of our knowledge of them) he emphasizes the value of 'pragmatic history'.[17] It is the history of events and actions as they affect cities, peoples and individuals, and it must be written by a 'pragmatic' individual, someone who travels to the sites in question, interviews participants and personally studies documents. Polybius is the declared enemy of library-worms like his learned predecessor Timaeus. There is much of Thucydides in his aims, except that, once again, Thucydides' exclusion of the gods as an explanation of history proved to be too austere for an admirer's simpler mind. In Polybius' view, the defeats of the kings of Macedon and Antiochus IV in one and the same year (168) were a revenge for their predecessors' beastly decision to combine in a pact in c. 200 BC and meddle against Ptolemy V of Egypt, a child-king at the time. Thucydides would have enjoyed pointing out that this 'revenge' was only a coincidence and that the 'pact' which it supposedly avenged was almost certainly a fiction publicized by the Romans.

Nonetheless, Polybius searches for explanations of change and is explicit about formulating them. Admittedly, what he makes explicit is less penetrating than what is implicit in Thucydides. It also confronts us in his turgid sort of polytechnic Greek. But his vision across the entire Mediterranean, from Spain to Syria, is wholly to his credit and his accounts of other peoples, landscapes, myths and resources are a fine testimony to a Hellenistic Greek mind.

His observations of the Romans are particularly important. Here, at last, survive the impressions of an educated Greek who lived at Rome, learned a little Latin and formed friendships with individual upper-class

Romans during these fascinating years. In Polybius' histories, Greek speakers do castigate Romans and their behaviour as 'barbarian'.[18] They are not just 'barbarians' because they are foreign speakers. Polybius also presents Roman customs as foreign, 'theirs', not 'our' Greek way. Romans could be exceptionally savage: 'one can often see,' Polybius wrote, 'in cities taken by the Romans not only the bodies of human beings but dogs cut in half and the severed limbs of other animals.'[19] But Romans were deliberate in their ruthlessness, unlike the stereotype of the 'irrational' barbarian, someone who combined savagery and panic. When comparing Romans with peoples other than Greeks, Polybius does not call them barbarians at all.

Most suggestively, he shares perceptions of contemporary Roman behaviour which were expressed by stern Cato. For Polybius, too, most Romans were madly keen to make money, just as Cato's complaints and maxims confirm. Through his Greek education, Polybius prized restraint, patriotism and austere self-control, qualities which were supported by his distorted image of ancient Sparta. In his Roman context, Cato trumpeted the same values. The two men knew each other personally, but the similarity of their professed values was not the result of Polybius' greater intelligence shaping what Cato thought. It was the result of a similar outlook, independently formed. A bridge between their shared values was their fondness for the simple Greek of the classical Athenian, Xenophon, the enemy of luxury, the admirer of bravery and military prowess and the champion of 'moral' life, including the common bond of hunting.

For Polybius, too, the year 167 was a turning point because of the new wave of 'luxury' which the conquests in Greece released into Rome. The young, he complained, would now pay 'more than a talent' for a boy-lover; similarly, Cato warned the Roman people that they would 'see the change for the worse' in their constitution when 'good-looking boys were being sold for more than the price of fields'.[20] Polybius and Cato shared a disapproval of the new 'luxury' and a view that it would contribute to political decline: in his histories, Polybius is concerned to give the gist, where possible, of what his speakers actually said. But unlike Cato, Polybius had a predictive, explanatory theory, the idea that one constitution follows another in a necessary cyclical pattern which is repeated through time. In the year of Cannae, Polybius believed that the Roman constitution had been at its peak. It was not a 'mixed' constitution in his view, one which was blended from the differing elements of oligarchy, democracy and so forth. Rather, it was in an oligarchic phase, but held in balance by elements of monarchy and democracy which served as checks against change and degeneration.[21] According to Polybius' theory, such change would inevitably occur, linked to changes in the citizens' 'customs' and behaviour: oligarchy would change to democracy, democracy to degenerate mob-rule and then back to monarchy, the starting point. Polybius continued writing as a very old man: he was said to have died aged eighty-two, in the mid–120s therefore, from a fall off a horse. His simple theory of Rome's constitutional elements owed more to his Greek education and its framework than to the Roman reality. Were the Roman consuls really so 'king-like' and where was a democratic role for the 'people' in a full-blooded Greek sense? Like a Greek in India, he allowed his theory to distort his understanding of what he saw and heard. But his predictions were to have a particular resonance in the next hundred years for the Rome which he knew as a resident.

TURBULENCE AT
HOME AND ABROAD

*Someone cut off the head of Gaius Gracchus, we are told, and was carry-
ing it, but a friend of Opimius took it off him: he was called Septimuleius.
At the beginning of the fighting a proclamation had been made that anyone who brought in Gaius' head . . . would receive its equal weight in
gold. So Septimuleius stuck Gaius' head on a spear and brought it in to
Opimius, and when it was placed on the scales it weighed in at seventeen
and two-thirds pounds, for Septimuleius had shown himself a scoundrel
in this too and had acted like a rascal: he had taken out Gracchus' brain
and filled the head with lead.*

Plutarch, Life of Gaius Gracchus 17

*Sulla's memorial stands on the Campus Martius and the inscription on it,
they say, is one he wrote himself, and the gist of it is that 'none of his
friends surpassed him in doing good and none of his enemies in doing
harm'.*

Plutarch, Life of Sulla 38

WITH CARTHAGE DESTROYED and Greece cowed, we might have
expected the Romans to settle down to a steady domination of the
Mediterranean. They had removed kings from Macedon for ever; their
conquests in western Asia had left a large hole in the largest Hellenistic
empire, that of the Seleucids. They had intrigued decisively in the affairs
of the Ptolemaic kings in Egypt: in 155 the young Ptolemy VIII had even
drawn up a will bequeathing the entire kingdom to Rome if he failed to
produce a legitimate heir. As he was still hardly thirty years old, the 'be-

46. Silver denarius, Rome: Sulla triumphing in a four-horse chariot, 82 BC.

quest' was rather hypothetical, and was probably meant only to scare his enemies in Egypt. But it was the first example of a practice which would have a significant future and which later worked to Rome's benefit. The main problem in view was still Spain: in the late 150s a series of campaigns were needed here against insurgents.

A system of control over Rome's conquests was also forming. During the second century BC Romans developed their rule over conquered peoples by sending out magistrates as governors with standing armies to help them. These individuals became focal points for their subjects' petitions and disputes. As always, many cases gravitated to a new source of justice which had suddenly become accessible in their midst. On the other side, however, the individual governors saw new possibilities of enrichment, and their misconduct was still very loosely regulated. Until the 120s the most they might suffer for 'rapacity' ('extortion') was a ruling that they should repay what they had taken. The new scope for gain abroad would have crucial implications for individuals' capacity to compete for pre-eminence back at Rome.

Most Roman warfare abroad in the third and second centuries BC had already had economic motives: one obvious result of victory for Roman individuals was ever more slaves and plunder. There was also subsequent access (albeit sometimes through active middlemen) to land, moneylending and assets overseas. Collectively, too, Romans began to receive regular yearly tribute from their conquests. It had begun in Sicily, from 210 onwards, where they had taken over the taxation of previous kings. Then annual tribute was imposed in Spain in the 190s; payments were spread to Greece, Asia and north Africa. After 167 the newly won control of Macedon and its rich mines enabled Romans to abolish the direct tax which had previously been levied on individual Roman citizens in Rome and Italy (the indirect taxes continued). No single uniform system of tax was imposed as yet on all provinces, but from 146 onwards Rome's subjects in north Africa are known to have had to pay a tax on 'land' and also a poll tax. Those two taxes would become the mainstays of Roman taxation in the early Empire: they were mainstays under Hadrian too.

This new financial strength was confirmed by receipts of booty, fines and war-reparations: surely these gains would allow the Romans to sort out some of their social injustices at home? In fact, the years from 146 to 80 BC were to see outbursts of extreme social and political tension in Rome and Italy. The historian Sallust later looked back on the year 146 as the start of a wave of 'disturbances and riots', combined with corruption.[1] The removal of the external fear of Carthage (he thought) had made things worse. It is also important that the settlement of new colonies in Italy had all but ceased since the 170s: poorer citizens were no longer being sent off from Rome to a new home.

From the later vantage point of the Emperor Hadrian, the tensions of these years would have seemed only a prelude to others which were even more important, the emergence of Pompey and Julius Caesar in the 70s and 60s, the resulting Civil War and the eventual ending of the free Republic. The later crises therefore will feature at more length here, but for historians, these forerunners (as we now see them) are a fascinating kaleidoscope. Political combinations which would later prove so dangerous are already in evidence, and yet are somehow surmounted. Conquering generals started to enjoy prolonged commands abroad and to link up with tribunes in Rome so as to protect their interests at home. In 147 BC the charismatic Scipio Aemilianus was elected directly to a consulship without any previous job as a magistrate and was then elected to a second consulship, of dubious legality. Populists started to take proposals directly to the people to turn them straight into law without approval from the Senate; in reply, political reformers were killed by senatorial opponents in the centre of Rome. In the 80s there was to be civil war for the first time in Italy and a disgruntled patrician would actually march on Rome.

During these decades of intense manoeuvring at Rome itself, there was nonetheless a continuing fight to retain and extend Rome's conquests overseas. Wars continued bitterly in Spain; they then erupted in north Africa and in Gaul. In 88 the bold King Mithridates of Pontus (on the south coast of the Black Sea) made as if to avenge the appalling Roman misdeeds in Greece and Asia Minor during the previous century by beginning a war against them and killing (it was said) more than 80,000 Romans in Asia in the first bout, a magnificent reprisal. Nearer home, a slave-society's worst nightmare came true: big slave-revolts and slave-wars broke out, persisting from 138 to 132 and again from 104 to 101.

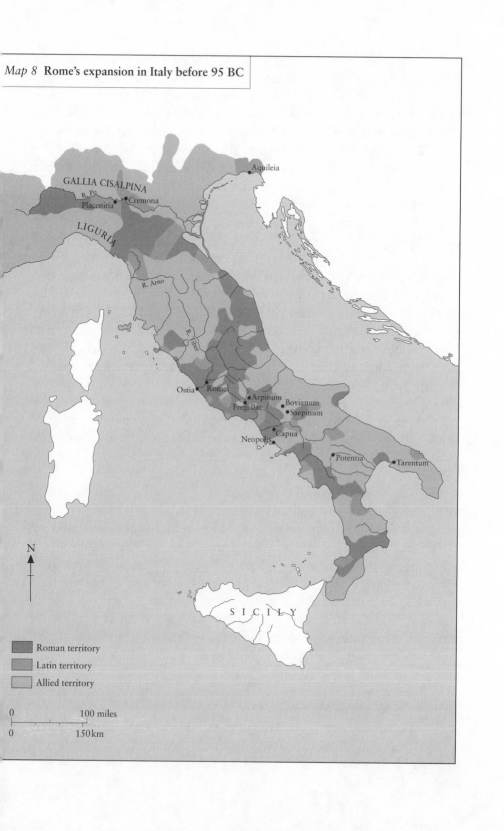

Map 8 Rome's expansion in Italy before 95 BC

GALLIA CISALPINA

R. Po

Placenitia • Cremona

LIGURIA

Aquileia

R. Arno

R. Tiber

Ostia • Rome

Arpinum

Fregellae

Bovianum

Saepinum

Neopolis

Capua

Potentia

Tarentum

N

SICILY

Roman territory

Latin territory

Allied territory

0   100 miles

0   150 km

Their major cause was the intensified use of slave-labour in Sicily and the Italian south, a delayed result of 'Hannibal's legacy'. Above all, Rome's own heartland, her Italian allies, then rose up in war against her from 91 to 89 BC. They even declared their own 'Italy' and their own senate. They struck coins which showed a sexually aroused bull goring a Roman she-wolf.[2] Interpretation of their aims in this Social War varies, but the Romans' refusal to give them Roman citizenship (aired, but then withdrawn in 95) was crucial. Renewed offers of it did, surely, hasten the war's end.

Freedom and justice were conspicuously involved in all of this turbulence. 'Freedom' was a rallying-cry of the rebellious Italians; in order to curb Mithridates, freedom was proclaimed by the Romans for the nearby Cappadocians in Asia. Mithridates, by contrast, was seen by Greeks (including Athens) as their 'liberator' from Rome. In the political struggles at Rome, the two-headed nature of the Roman constitution and the differing ideas of liberty of its social orders also began to be exploited. On a populist view, one aspect of freedom was the freedom of the people to pass laws without consultation of the Senate. On this view, the 'people' were even free to decide about areas which senators had traditionally reserved for their own decision: finance, the composition of courts and juries, the allotment of commands abroad, the ways in which corrupt senatorial Roman governors abroad should be regulated. A clear, populist approach began to be pursued which ignored this senatorial 'tradition' and created its own heroes; those politicians who exemplified it became objects of cult, even, among a loyal plebs long after their death.

One result of this populist approach was a reform in the method of voting at Rome. Secret ballots were introduced, first for elections (139 BC), then for public non-capital trials (137 BC) and then for legislation (131/0 BC). Deliberately, they reduced the scope for intimidation of the voters: they did not eliminate it, because voters still processed up narrow ramps in order to cast their votes, and 'canvassers' could threaten them and try to inspect what each voter had written as he passed up the queue before voting. Eventually, the ramps were broadened, so as to make the intimidation of individuals more difficult. In the Greek world, at Athens and elsewhere, secret ballots had been the accepted practice for particular types of trial, but the extension of them to votes on law-making is a Roman innovation. Descendants of the reformers would even illustrate the changes in images on their coin-types.

These changes were the prelude to even more serious 'populist' turbulence. The major figures in it were Tiberius Gracchus (in 133) and then his remarkable brother, Gaius. They had a noble ancestry, but the problem which first stirred Tiberius appears to have been the poverty and apparent depopulation of Italy: in addressing it he was not only thinking of a shortage of soldiers. As a result, he proposed a reallotment of public land in Italy. Rich landowners were no longer to be allowed to encroach on it for their own purposes: a basic limit of about 350 acres for each landowner (with maybe 150 acres more for each son) would release a significant amount of land in Italy for redistribution by commissioners to rural landless peasants. The new lots, which ranged up to twenty acres, were not to be bought and sold by recipients. The proposals and the issues here were not new, but they were enthusiastically received by many countryfolk outside Rome. They were also very fiercely opposed by traditional senators. As an elected tribune, Tiberius took them directly to the people's assemblies and then invoked the sovereignty of the people in order to depose a fellow tribune who tried to veto what he was proposing. This last argument was quite unprecedented, although Tiberius could have cited an ancestor, the consul of 238 BC, who had built the temple to 'Jupiter Liberty' (now known as 'Liberty') on the popular hill, the Aventine. His clash with his colleagues was followed by the lucky coincidence of a bequest to Rome of the kingdom of Pergamum. Tiberius referred this financial matter to the people for their decision, too, with the proposal that some of the funds be directed to help his new settlers. Traditional senators regarded financial decisions as the Senate's. On top of it all, Tiberius then proposed to stand as tribune for a second year, with even bigger plans for reform. Led by the Pontifex Maximus, his senatorial enemies had him killed on the very Capitol hill. Tiberius (they said) had been aiming to be a king; he had the 'purple robe and diadem' of the king of Pergamum in his house; he had pointed to his forehead while on the Capitol as if to want a diadem on his head.[3] His killer, Scipio Nasica, was a liberator acting for freedom.

This allegation was a monstrous distortion: Tiberius was no king and if he pointed at his head, it was to show that his life was in danger. His brother Gaius was the greater political genius. Naturally, Tiberius' murder grated on him, as with others: in 125 Liberty appears on the coins of two Romans, descendants of legislators who had helped to protect it. Gaius then became elected as tribune (in 123 and 122) and proposed the most far-ranging legislation in senators' living memory. It covered almost every popular grievance. It saw to monthly distributions of grain at a subsidized price to the people; it set up new courts to try cases of extortion in which none of the jurors would be senators and voting would be by secret ballot: it proposed mixed juries in other courts, too, with a preponderance of the non-senatorial rich (the 'knights', *equites*, in the sense of those capable of serving as cavalry). Before 123 BC, we must remember, the judges and advisers on all major criminal and civil cases had been senators only. Gaius capped his major reform of Roman justice by legislating that no Roman citizen should be sentenced to death 'without the bidding of the Roman people'. This law directly addressed the senators' lynching of his brother, Tiberius. This widening of the juries was detestable to senators and their dignity, but it was upheld by its proponents as 'equal liberty'. Gaius also provided for the privatizing of tax-collection in the rich province of Asia, by handing it over to the bids of companies who could collect the taxes (and their own profit), thereby ensuring that a known revenue would always be assured in advance of collection. He even resumed land-settlements for the poor by proposing Roman colonies overseas (including one on the site of ruined Carthage). In 125 one of the consuls had talked of giving Roman citizenship to Italian allies: the previously loyal Latin colony of Fregellae had revolted, as if in frustration, and had been all but destroyed. In the aftermath of this crisis, Gaius Gracchus seems to have proposed giving the Roman citizenship to all the peoples of Italy (precise details are disputed), but to have allowed those who might want to keep their local independence to opt for particular privileges only.

In most of his laws, there was a considered response to injustice and abuse; Gaius Gracchus was later said to have described himself as putting a 'dagger in the ribs of the Senate'.[4] A close reading of his best-known law, the law on 'extortion', has helped to tone down extreme views of his radicalism: responsibilities were being given to the new equestrian jurors, too, who would have to exercise them in full public view.[5] But in principle, judgement in this court was to be the job of non-senators, to whom the people, not the Senate, had devolved the task. That slight to senatorial pre-eminence was most fiercely resented. In the political turmoil which continued after Gaius' two years as tribune, he and his supporters (up to 3,000 of them) were callously murdered. The senators simply declared an emergency and urged the consuls to see that the republic was defended and 'came to no harm'. This measure is now known by the modern name of the 'last decree': it was a brazen innovation, a measure by senators to suppress those who could be regarded (by themselves) as public enemies. In the next sixty years it was to claim some of the most notable populists as its victims. One of Gaius' attackers, the consul Opimius, was acquitted when put on trial after the event.

Nonetheless, the two Gracchi had set a populist example which was not forgotten. Both of them received cult as gods from their admirers after their death and the spot where they died was regarded as sacred. Against them, the more 'traditional' senators now stood forward as self-styled 'good men', or the 'best' (*optimates*). Badly stung, they were explicitly hostile to change, to challenges to the Senate's pre-eminence, to ideas that questions of finance or senatorial privilege (and much else) could be taken directly to an assembly of the people and be turned into legislation without any consultation, and prior approval, of the senators. 'Traditionalists' is one translation of their elastic catch-word *optimates*. They were never organized into a party, but, from the Gracchi on, there was a real division of political approaches among prominent Romans. It polarized their political methods and professed ideals.

Gaius would not have been altogether surprised that the 'knights' (or *equites*) to whom he gave new responsibilities proved not entirely admirable in exercising them. But the next personal challenge to the senatorial nobility came from an ambitious military man, not from a comparable reformer. Gaius Marius, a non-noble, rose to an unprecedented series of consulships (five in a row, from 104 to 100). He took his cue from charges that the senatorial commanders, 'good men', were proving highly incompetent in fighting a war in north Africa. He ended it, not without luck, and then won impressive victories in 102 and 101 against two feared tribes who had migrated south from the area of Jutland into southern Gaul (Provence) and north Italy. To win these wars, Marius trained his troops very hard: he had already begun to recruit legionaries for the first time from all classes of Roman citizens, whether or not they had property. This change was to prove a milestone in the social impact of service in the Roman armies. From now on, many military recruits would have much more to fight for and much less to return to. The innovation was to have revolutionary results in the next fifty years, although Marius, in his emergency, had certainly not foreseen them.

Marius was a 'people's hero' rather than a reforming populist, and by his exploits he won a degree of acceptance among Rome's top families despite his non-senatorial birth. Back at Rome, the Gracchi's mantle of reform fell, rather, to the clever Saturninus, a tribune in the year 100. He began by combining with Marius but then took to proposing yet more popular laws and thereby losing the great military man's support. Saturninus was eventually killed in the centre of Rome with Marius' connivance: again, a populist's legislation ended in murder. Yet even so, political turmoil did not become anarchy. In the same year as this crisis, we know from inscriptional evidence that detailed, carefully considered laws were being passed by the people's assembly so as to continue to regulate extortion and to prescribe details of Roman governors' conduct abroad.

In 91 BC came the Social War against the allied Italians, and then the war in 88 against vengeful Mithridates in Asia. These represented crises of a much greater order. Marius, not untypically, had opposed a recently revived proposal to enfranchise the Italians. In his late sixties, he then intrigued to try to take over the command of the war in Asia. Instead, the 'good men', the traditionalist senators, let it go to a formidable figure from the old patrician nobility, Cornelius Sulla. Sulla had served as an officer in the past under Marius; he was known for a somewhat dissolute lifestyle, but as he also had the backing of the family who most hated Marius, he was an obvious choice for the 'traditionalists' to support. Crucially, his appointment was overturned by a populist tribune, Sulpicius, who took the matter of the command to the people's assembly and had Marius appointed to it instead. It was a shocking blow to Sulla's esteem and an intolerable intrusion into a type of decision which senators had typically regarded as theirs to make. With awesome disdain, Sulla relied on his troops' loyalty and turned round and marched on Rome. He then settled his scores with his enemies, including the tribune Sulpicius who was killed in office.

This behaviour was a bitter taste of civil war. Sulla escaped the consequences only by setting off for Greece to cope with Mithridates' war, his original assignation. In Greece, even Athens had broken with Rome and taken Mithridates' side after a time of political turbulence in the city. Sulla earned the distinction of being the one man in history to attack both Rome and Athens when he sacked the Piraeus and parts of the main city. At Rome, his enemy Cornelius Cinna became consul for 87 and outlawed him. Nonetheless, Sulla headed on to Asia where he ended by making a rather feeble peace with Mithridates in 85. To meet his costs, he continued to ravage the Asian Greek cities in his path.

Back in Rome, Cinna died, whereupon Sulla rebelled and marched promptly back into Italy for a second, more serious bout of civil war. Again, he showed extreme severity to his enemies (including to some of the newly enfranchised Italians), but nonetheless he won a decisive victory at the very Colline gate of Rome. It was a real breakdown of the Republic; with our hindsight it is a foretaste of the 40s BC and is the point at which histories of the 'Roman revolution' ought to begin. Nonetheless, after his victory, Sulla had himself approved as a dictator with the task of 'settling the state'.

The laws which he then executed were detailed and not always extreme, but the most important of them were resoundingly traditionalist. Freedom and justice were at the heart of them. In the interests of justice, Sulla did increase the number of standing jury-courts, adding at least seven more, but he did away with Gaius Gracchus' 'equal liberty' by handing the juries back to senators only. He increased the number of senators from 300 to 600 (the increase was made up from his supporters), but he also regulated the lower ranks of a man's career towards the consulship: the likes of a Marius, rising directly to the top job, would now be illegal. The censors' powers to choose senators were also checked: anyone who held a junior magistracy, a quaestorship, would now automatically become a senator.

Above all, Sulla settled his veteran soldiers, so loyal in his years of rebellion, on plots of land confiscated in Italy; the sites of Fiesole and Pompeii were among those settled with new Sullan colonies. And, wonder of wonders, he neutered the populists' weapon, the tribunate, which had been turned against his own original command in Asia. He ruled that tribunes could not go on to hold other prestigious magistracies; ambitious men would therefore avoid the position. He even took away the tribunes' power to veto (and probably, propose) legislation in the people's assemblies. Arguably, he did not also give the Senate the formal right to vet all proposed laws in advance. But even so, his was a stunning political reaction.

Sulla's lesser reforms were neither extreme nor ill-considered. He passed laws which limited the freedom of commanders outside Italy, and these persisted for decades. So did his establishment of a civil court to hear cases of 'injury', which was defined as assault or violent entry into private property. By these courts, the minimal framework of justice in the old Twelve Tables was filled out. Sulla had thought carefully about details which were ill-organized. Having turned the populist clock back, he then gave up his powers as dictator and in 80, unexpectedly took up the consulship instead. He had realized a conservative vision, as if the likes of Gaius Gracchus had never existed. Having done so, he retired, whereupon he died in 79 of disease, leaving his 'restoration' to be immediately contested. His funeral was a public one, the first known for a Roman citizen: a vast procession accompanied his body to the Forum where an orator spoke out on Sulla's deeds. Actors wore the family's masks; 2,000 crowns of gold were said to have been donated; his statue was carved from the precious wood of a spice tree.[6] Thirty-five years later this funeral would be excelled for the next dictator, Sulla's only superior.

Sulla, the dissolute young man, had ended by legislating against disruptive luxury. What mattered more, though, was his stunning example: an outright defence of his own 'dignity', backed by veteran soldiers loyal to him and a long list of killings of enemies and confiscations of their property in Italy. From this short sharp revolution, whole fortunes changed hands, often passing to Sulla's decidedly unsavoury agents. Sulla himself stressed his personal favour from the gods (especially Venus, whom he encountered in the town, as yet little known, of Aphrodisias in Asia Minor). He had also been told by an eastern prophet that he would achieve greatness and die at the height of his good fortune. The prophecy was one more reason why, mission accomplished, this bloodstained dictator resigned and let the 'good men' in the Senate get on with what he had put back into their hands.

POMPEY'S TRIUMPHS

Gnaeus Pompeius Imperator, having ended thirty years of war, defeated, killed or subjected 12,183,000 men, sunk or captured 846 ships, brought under Roman protection 1,538 towns and fortified settlements and subjected the lands from the Sea of Azov to the Red Sea, fulfilled his vow to the goddess Minerva according to his merit.

Pompey's inscription on his temple to Minerva,
vowed in September 62 BC

SULLA'S REACTION was not exactly based on consensus. However, it took ten years of impassioned political dispute before its most controversial elements were dismantled. Those disputes, as always, took place in open air in the Roman Forum, supported by the space for elections, the 'Campus Martius', outside the formal 'boundary' of the city. The Forum was less than a square half-mile of ground and it had already seen seething political turmoil, but the next thirty years would bring contests whose highlights were more dramatic than those on any comparable political playing field in the world. If the statues of wise Pythagoras and brave Alcibiades still looked down on the space for Romans' public assemblies, it was the spirit of Alcibiades, the treacherous but charming Athenian aristocrat, which was most in tune with events.

Throughout the 70s the senators did not make distinguished use of the liberty which Sulla had handed to them. Sulla's senators, after all, were mostly his own appointments, whereas previous senators, the most traditionalist ones, had been killed off by him as his opponents. If he hoped that the many members of his enlarged Senate would be honest judges of the few senatorial commanders, because they themselves would never win such high office, he was mistaken. Allegations of corruption and collusion

47. Portrait head of Pompey, an imperial Roman copy, combining the realism of small
eyes and expression with a hairstyle recalling the great Alexander's.

proliferated. He had given back too much to men unworthy of administering it: there was also his own bad example of force, violence and a
march on Rome. But already by the 70s the Republic had survived so
much that to those in the Forum at the time, whose views we must represent, its death was not at all inevitable.

Not that the turmoil was confined to Rome and the Forum. In Italy,
Sulla's land-grants to his veteran soldiers were promptly contested by
existing landowners and neighbours. Those ex-soldiers who settled on
their small plots did not always find farming to their taste or ability,
even if they had been recruited originally from rural life: they, too, began
to take on debts (Cicero blamed their 'luxury'). In 77, with Sulla only
dead for a year, the ex-consul Aemilius Lepidus marched south with
troops against Rome when the senators tried to summon him back from
his large provincial command. Lepidus had combined commands in bits
of Gaul on either side of the Alps, a precedent on which Julius Caesar's
career would later thrive so dangerously. But Lepidus' troops were not
so effective.

Out in Spain, meanwhile, a former supporter of Marius, the talented knight Sertorius, maintained an open rebellion against the Sullan supremacy. He had his own alternative senate and a readiness to recruit able Spanish talent and encourage them to learn Latin and Roman ways. Opponents of the Sullan supremacy in Rome could now escape to the West. When Sertorius' hold was eventually broken in 73, his Roman conqueror Pompey tactfully burned Sertorius' letters from important people in Rome without (so he said) even reading them.

Born in September 106, Pompey was only in his thirties but self-evidently a military man to be reckoned with. His background was not altogether encouraging. His father, Pompeius Strabo, had held the consulship in 89 BC and had fought fiercely against Italian rebels in the north during the Social War. But his career was then marred by duplicity and a strong suspicion that he had tried to collude with the rebel leader, Cinna, whom he was supposed to be fighting. He died of disease, but his body was thrown into the mud during his funeral: he was also accused of a ferocious greed for money. His son, Pompey, was to learn his lessons early: the need for financial backing and for popularity, but also the scope for dissimulation and the unprincipled use of troops who would become their leader's own personal army.

As yet, Pompey's pre-eminence lay in the future. It was much more worrying that in 73, back in Italy, seventy-four slave-gladiators escaped from their barracks at Capua and started by making a stand on the nearby slopes of Mount Vesuvius near Naples. Their leader was Spartacus, a Thracian who had previously fought in the Roman army. Before long he had attracted more than 70,000 slaves and herdsmen from southern Italy. Spartacus was a real hero, big, brave and great-hearted. His followers' aim was not to attack slavery (before long, they took on slaves themselves) but to free themselves, preferably after heavy plundering. In 72 Spartacus' men defeated both Roman consuls, but in the next year their terrifying revolt (perhaps now 150,000 strong) was put down by no fewer than ten legions. It reflected on the poor rural conditions and the extensive slave-labour which was current in much of south Italy, intensified by 'Hannibal's legacy'. And in the same year as Spartacus, King Mithridates was at war again in Asia. He had been provoked by the Romans' acquisition of the nearby kingdom of Bithynia in Asia Minor. It would be ten years before he too was finally beaten.

Rural discontent, an ex-consul marching on Rome with an army, a huge slave war and these big wars in Spain and Asia (Sertorius and Mithridates even linked up briefly): nonetheless, the senatorial supremacy survived. Not until 75 was any of the political neutering of the tribunate reversed and not until 70 were its final elements removed by law. Ten years is a long time, and yet the total male citizenry was increasing hugely meanwhile, swollen by the recently enfranchised Italians. Some 910,000 adult citizen-males were registered in the census of 69, about three times as many as in the 130s. The composition of the citizenry had also changed markedly. Even in Rome, very few of the citizens had any ancestral link with Roman voters of the fourth or third centuries BC; outside Rome, they now had none. The new citizens were distributed between the river Po in the north and the toe of Italy in the south, and, in principle, every single one of these adult males had a vote in the assemblies at Rome, whether or not they owned any property.[1] If the lower-class majority of this huge Italy-wide 'electorate' had asserted itself at Rome, or if even the urban part of it had rioted in unison in the city, surely those populist symbols, the tribunes, would have been restored much sooner?

The answer is that very few, if any, of the lower classes throughout Italy ever voted or visited at all. Distance deterred many of them, hundreds of miles away from Rome, and the wondrous voting-system neutered the rest of them. Those at hand in the city were clustered into only four of what were now the thirty-five 'tribes' in the assembly which passed the laws. A majority among the tribes decided a motion, and it was still the block-vote within each tribe which decided its overall vote. Seldom, if ever, would all 'tribes' vote, and a majority of the total votes cast still decided nothing (the 'block-vote' system stopped a pure majority of votes from being decisive). In the thirty-one other 'rustic' tribes, the voters present in Rome would tend to be the good men and true of the local propertied classes, although we are unsure quite how many poor rustic Italians might also have migrated into Rome and tried to subsist there. Above all, there was the context of such assemblies: they had no prearranged calendar throughout the year; only a magistrate could put a proposal; as always nobody in the audiences could speak, or propose an alternative.

We do hear of harangues at public meetings other than assemblies, great speeches to crowds in the Forum, public notices, pictures, even, to influence opinion: but who were this 'people' or 'crowd'? In the city, so many freedmen were still heavily obliged to their patrons. Small shopkeepers and the entire service-industry depended on the magnificence of their superiors; clients and hangers-on would go by arrangement to a great man's household in the early mornings to pay their respects (and probably be told to turn up if he or a friend was going to harangue 'the people' from a vantage point in the Forum that day). Any lower-class immigrants from Italy would be part of this layer of social dependence. Proposed legislation was posted weeks in advance, giving time for opponents and supporters to contact like-minded men of influence in and outside the city and mobilize enough of them in enough of the thirty-one 'rustic' voting tribes. There was ample time, too, for 'canvassing' and for its counterpart, organized bribery, to suit the rich.[2] Humble voters went along with it and expected their betters to give them presents in return for 'correct' voting. In 70 we first find the relevant officers, the 'distributors' (*divisores*), in action before an electoral assembly meeting even took place. They were now coming to the houses of individual candidates in order to receive the loot in advance. It was to be distributed before the electoral meeting and before just enough voting, but no more, took place.

This context does not mean that political life was all fixed in one direction, harmoniously agreed by the upper class. Within that class there were the clear alternative political approaches, 'populist' or 'traditionalist', to which important men remained true and constant over time. They became known for them, even though they did not acquire or maintain them in organized political 'parties'. Nor were most of the elections and legislation prearranged by a few powerful families on simple family or factional lines. Oratory and its impact really mattered before potential voters, as did a speaker's popular 'esteem': there was an important interplay between the political leaders and the local crowds in the Forum before whom they performed. But money and 'generosity' mattered more. Sulla's rules on office-holding had intensified competition by those lower down on the ladder for what were still the very few top jobs, and as a result there was an even greater pressure on the keen careerists: twenty candidates competed yearly for only eight praetorships, the next step on the way up. In the race for office, they had to borrow huge sums (usually from fellow politicians) so as to make a grand show at an early stage. It helped them if they bought a fine house, preferably on the Palatine hill or the Sacred Way within a few hundred yards of the Forum's centre, and standards expected of such houses had soared since the 140s. The next hope was to be appointed to a juicy province, squeeze it and repay the debts. Abroad, a man could win military honour and return to a magnificent public triumph, with a celebratory banquet and games to follow, financed by the provincials' losses. The shows and feasting would increase his following and he would hope for the highest honour of a consulship and then another even greater command. The expenses were becoming far higher, the risks ever greater, but the roars of applause and

the intoxication of being seen to be so great were the very lifeblood of aspiring great men. The ideal great man would combine military skill with
oratory and money: if not, orators would have to be bribed to speak for
him, and the money borrowed.

In Sulla's aftermath, therefore, liberty, justice and luxury were never
more vigorously invoked and contested. Speakers, whether populist or
not, could appeal to the liberties of the distant past to support their arguments, and in 73 one of the tribunes was Macer, himself a historian. A
later version of a speech by him probably reflects his line of argument.[3]
Wanting to restore the tribunes' powers, he gave a stirring call to 'liberty'.
Sulla's settlement, he insisted, was really 'wicked slavery'; the people
should not be fobbed off by the token distributions of grain, recently reintroduced (at a low price, admittedly, but probably for only about 40,000
free citizens, a fraction of Rome's current total). The wars of noble senators, Macer insisted, depended on the people as soldiers: let the senators
fight alone, in Spain or Asia, with only the masks of their former ancestors to help them. But Macer's speech also complained of the people's apathy. Outside public meetings, they seemed to forget about 'liberty'. That
fact, too, is relevant; democratic Athenians, by contrast, did not forget.
And despite Macer, the plebs continued to fight as soldiers. For many, it
was a better life than struggling on as a small farmer in Italy, risking slavery for debt to a canny rich neighbour.

As for justice, the senators made a fine abuse of the monopoly of the
jury-courts. Without the check of non-senatorial jurors, corruption became even more prevalent: Sulla had promoted new men to be senators
and they were even more prone to bribery, as they needed funds for the
vast expense of being in the senatorial order. Both in Rome and in the
provinces, magistrates exempted themselves or their friends from the very
rules which they enunciated in their 'edicts'. Senatorial governors were
blatantly extortionate and in general they could be 'shamefully' luxurious. As 'chief priest' in 70 BC, the noble Metellus gave an amazing dinner
of three courses, with ten dishes each, including seven rare types of
seafood and 'sow's udders' (banned by law). The famous orator Horten-
sius was attacked for dining on roast peacocks and watering his plane
trees with wine.[4] The able general Lucullus had such an extravagant villa
that a picture of it was displayed to the people when his enemies were trying to get him replaced in his command. In due course, Lucullus even introduced the cherry tree from Asia and his 'gardens' (more of a park)
became the envy of fellow Romans.[5] Both men were accused of the ultimate extravagance, maintaining exotic fishponds.

This private luxury was particularly controversial at a time when the few subsidized corn-distributions were not adequate to meet the poor's needs and the price and availability of grain was being squeezed by pirates in the Mediterranean. Nor was the charge of 'luxury' simply a slogan. After the restoration of the tribunes' power in 70 no less than sixty-four senators were expelled as 'unworthy' from the Senate by the newly approved censors. Sulla's purges had left too much room for these second-raters, but would even better men have held out against the temptations of a decade of senatorial 'liberty'? In late 69 BC extravagance was limited by law once again. The slogans of the moment were clean provincial government, no favouritism by magistrates and a restrained private life. They were reactions exploited by the rival 'populist' politicians.

In the year 70 BC the last of the tribunes' former powers were restored by a notable pair of consuls. One of them, Crassus, was of noble family but had already made himself extremely rich, no doubt by profiteering during Sulla's confiscations. He was also distinguished by military commands, not least against Spartacus: it was he who had 'decimated' his own reluctant troops (executing one man in ten) and had then crucified 6,000 of the slave-rebels along the main road back to Rome. For the purposes of a consulship, he had managed to suspend his dislike of his colleague, the emergent Pompey. It was very intense. At the end of the Spartacus War, Pompey had returned to Italy and helped to defeat some of the slave-fugitives. Nonetheless, it was he, not Crassus, who was voted the full glory of a triumph, partly because of his victories elsewhere on Rome's behalf. Crassus had had to make do with a mere ovation. In the 50s the two of them would be thrown together again by their respective needs, but their personal relations were never easy. For the moment, Crassus marked his successes by giving a tremendous series of feasts for the people.

Nonetheless, the star was Pompey, who added two weeks of games to the celebrations. He had already been voted one triumph (in his midtwenties) and yet, amazingly, he was still not even a senator: he was the son of a respected consul, but personally he had remained a knight. When about to take up his consulship, he had had to have a little book on senatorial procedure written for him by the scholarly Varro. It was not that he was wholly uneducated. He knew Greek; he had an interest in Latin vocabulary and grammar; he would later respect a great Greek scholar by having his symbols of office lowered in the learned man's presence; he once freed a slave without any payment because of the man's intelligence. But he was not very bright. Pompey was married five times in his life; one of them was for a political marriage, made with a woman who was already pregnant by another man. But he only divorced twice: his last young wife was dear to him, the remarkable Cornelia, who studied mathematics and philosophy and ranks as one of the late Republic's educated upper-class young ladies. Pompey was also remembered fondly by his former mistress, a courtesan called Flora: she said that he had never made love with her without sinking his teeth into her and leaving toothmarks.[6]

Outside the bedroom, Pompey's supreme skill was military command. He had brought privately raised troops to help Sulla, but his brutality against his fellow Romans was to be vividly recalled more than twenty years later as the acts of a 'teenage hangman'.[7] He had then been made into a commander against Sulla's enemies in Sicily and north Africa. It was in Africa that his troops had acclaimed him (in his mid-twenties) as 'Great'. With his open, boyish looks and brushed-back hair, young Pompey did have a look of the real 'great' Alexander, though it is only visible to his fans. When Sulla died in early 78, Pompey at first supported Lepidus' renewed populism, but he won even more fame by helping to defeat Lepidus when he marched on Rome. Then Pompey left for Spain in order to defeat Sertorius too. It took him six years of hard fighting and he commemorated it with a trophy in the Pyrenees, topped by his own statue and inscribed to say that he had conquered no less than 876 cities. The result was a second triumph, on 29 December 71, the consulship for 70 and popularity in that year for restoring the tribunes' powers. Aged thirty-six, Pompey had already veered artfully from one political line to another, while proving to be Rome's supreme general of the moment.

His consulship was not followed by a provincial command. He remained in Rome, but in due course he was voted two controversial commands by legislation taken to the people. The first, in 67 BC, was against the Mediterranean pirates, for which he received a massive fleet and powers equal to the provincial governors: he polished off the job in only three months, greatly to the people's gratitude. Meanwhile, the traditional senators' choice, Lucullus, was failing to finish off the war in Asia against Mithridates. Lucullus had shown diplomatic skill and had even penetrated Armenia, but enemies of his 'traditional' style emphasized his scandalous luxury and his slow progress and had Pompey sent out to replace him: he was 'sent down from heaven', Cicero even said.[8] The war took Pompey, too, four years, and even then King Mithridates had to kill himself (his famous book on cures for poisons was translated into Latin on Pompey's orders). As the war had spread through connected kings in Asia, Pompey went on south to win victories in Syria, the Lebanon and, in

63 BC, in Judaea. There, the leaders of the Jews were split between two rival candidates for the High Priesthood; first one, then the other invited Pompey to help them, and eventually he settled down to besiege the Temple Mount in Jerusalem. He then entered the Holy of Holies of the Temple itself, a shocking profanation in Jewish eyes. The Jews' territories were reduced, taxed and brought, decisively, under Roman control.

In Asia, Pompey showed a shrewd eye for durable diplomacy and for workable local kingdoms.[9] His conquests of the mid–60s mark the beginning of the 'Roman Near East' and once again transformed the Romans' public finances. Tribute received from abroad was nearly doubled and the booty and chances for investment were enormous. But Egypt remained for the taking, complex, alien but uniquely rich in grain and gold. It would haunt the next thirty-five years.

Two triumphs before the age of forty were bad enough for envious contemporaries. At the first one, Pompey was said to have tried to drive a chariot pulled by elephants through the city gate, only to find that the gate was too narrow.[10] A third triumph, at the expense of the respected Lucullus, would be alarming and intolerable. It was a cardinal tradition of the Republic that no one man should dominate it, and the traditionalist senators were duly mobilized against the returning Pompey. In January 62 a proposal made in his absence to appoint him to settle unrest in Italy was stopped only when the leading young 'traditionalist', Cato, vetoed it as tribune. Armed soldiers had been brought to see the bill through, but a fellow tribune put his hand over the mouth of the proposer and refused to allow him to finish speaking when he tried to recite his proposal before the assembly by heart. Yet this Cato was the young man so renowned for his integrity and entrenched conservative principles: generally, said Cicero, he behaved as if he was living in 'the ideal republic of Plato, not the cesspit of Romulus'.[11] Cato was the great-grandson of stern old Cato the Elder, but he too could play in the dirt when his Republic was threatened. Nonetheless, Pompey was voted days of grateful supplication, a gold crown to wear in the public circus and, in due course, a triumph.

The hero's actual return from the East was less happy. He divorced his wife (his third) for adultery but failed to fix a marriage alliance into the heart of the senatorial establishment: young Cato was adamant that he should be kept out. Pompey's lack of talent as a speaker showed up at public meetings. Other more local business was the talk of Rome and meanwhile, the senators kept this impossible superstar at a distance. With hindsight, they should surely have accommodated him and learned to live with his glory as it faded. The trouble was that it was impossibly glorious.

In September 61 Pompey did at last hold his Eastern triumph, his third. It was a show like none before it. Conquered kings and spoils processed before the crowds, including a former 'High Priest' from Jerusalem. There was even a lynx on show, and some baboons. On the second day, Pompey entered in his jewel-covered chariot with one of his sons beside him: people alleged malevolently that he was wearing the purple cloak of Alexander himself. He made his entrance on his birthday and he displayed a symbol of the world, a globe: he had now triumphed over three separate continents, Africa (79), Spain (71) and Asia (61). Coins continued to proclaim this global message.[12]

Still on the defensive, the 'traditional' senators refused to ratify the settlements which Pompey had personally made in the East. A year after the triumph, he was being accused of really wanting to wear a royal diadem, as was proved by the white diadem of a bandage which he was wearing on his leg. In fact, the bandage was for a leg-ulcer.[13] Two years on, the 'traditional' senators were still keeping his veteran soldiers waiting to be settled on plots of land as their reward. They feared Pompey, but what exactly would this outsider now want? He had peaked so early, and yet for another nine years the senators, stiffened by Cato, would fail to repair their deliberate distance from him. Meanwhile Pompey would seek helpful friends of his own. Pompey, contemporaries concluded, was evasive and duplicitous. He was more 'a fox than a lion' in the political jungle. 'He is apt to say one thing and think another,' wrote the acute young Caelius to Cicero, 'but he is usually not clever enough to stop his real aims from showing.'[14]

THE WORLD OF CICERO

Suppose I manage to make even Caesar who is riding on the crest of the wave just now a better citizen, am I harming the state so very much? Why, even if I had no ill-wishers, even if I had everyone's goodwill (as I ought to have), there would still be as much to be said for healing unsound bits of the body politic as for amputating them. But look at the facts: the Senate has been deserted by the knights . . . our leading men think they are touching heaven with their finger tips if the bearded mullets in their fishponds are feeding out of their hands, and they neglect everything else. Don't I seem to you to be doing enough of a service if I contrive that those who have the power to do harm do not wish to do so?

Cicero, *Letters to Atticus* 2.1 (*c.* 3 June 60 BC)

LIKE POMPEY, MARCUS TULLIUS CICERO was a novelty on Rome's political scene. So far from triumphing while a non-senator, he had no senators or Roman magistrates in his family and warfare was not exactly his talent. He was born (like Marius, oddly) at Arpinum, a hill-town about eighty miles south-east of Rome in the same year as Pompey, 106 BC. He was a 'new man', with family roots in the local gentry but without a funerary mask worth dwelling on in his family's halls. Yet he has been described by an admiring modern scholar, as 'perhaps the most civilized man who has ever lived'.[1]

Nowadays, Cicero is better known for his vanity and self-obsession, his poor political judgement and his way of referring to the mass of Roman citizens as 'dregs' or 'cattle', to life in the provinces as 'insufferable tedium' and to the Greeks of his era as shifty and lightweight. But there is far more to him than these quick stereotypes: he is the Roman whom we really feel we know in these turbulent years.

Like others of his class at this time, Cicero was excellently educated, first at Rome (where he studied oratory in the grand houses and law, too, at the feet of great older experts) and then for a few years in Greece, including six months or so at Athens while he improved his Greek and his grasp of philosophy. One of his fellow students in Athens was of central importance throughout his life, Pomponius (known also, and better, as Atticus), whom Cicero, a few years his junior, had already befriended in Rome. On and off, from the early 60s BC, Cicero wrote brilliant, personal letters to Atticus, who saved them in his household, whence copies have miraculously come down to us. Atticus was a man of similar social class to Cicero, but he chose to remain a knight (*eques*) and avoid a public career. Like Cicero, he preferred the traditional establishment line in politics, but was discreet about it. He was famous for his excellent old-fashioned taste, even down to the 'period' furniture in his houses. Like Cicero, he loved books and literature and he was Cicero's mentor in the choice of furnishings and Greek works of art. Unlike Cicero, he maintained real friendships with Romans of high noble family and contrived always to slip away from political crises or to remain friends, a charming neutral, with both sides.

Unlike Atticus, Cicero was to become the outstanding Roman orator. With a typical perversity, Hadrian is said to have disagreed, preferring the bumpy Latin of the elder Cato. He was, quite simply, wrong. Oratory first made Cicero's name: in Rome's political arena, the best way for a young hopeful to make a public mark was to prosecute a superior successfully. After some early successes, Cicero embarked in August 70 on his famous prosecution of the corrupt governor Verres (it was interrupted by the days of newly offered public games which were the gift of the triumphant young consul Pompey). In August 70 the Senate's monopoly of the law courts was about to end, but Cicero's attack was a glittering success: it was backed by about eight weeks' fact-finding in Verres' province of Sicily. As a speech for the prosecution, it is a rare survivor, one of only two among Cicero's subsequent surviving speeches, but it shows similar merits to his many speeches for the defendant. Cicero could command so many different tones: a clear and concise narrative of detail or rolling rhythmical periods or hilarious wit and extreme invective. Before juries he is the master of the confiding style which attempts to lead the jurors' attention away from a case's weaker points. He remains a brilliant model for any practising barrister who happens to be widely educated. What we now read was usually polished by Cicero's hindsight for publication, and, where he is least convincing, it is because the gap between the style and Cicero's true commitment is too great. But there are political classics too, the speech in defence of feckless young Caelius with its wonderful sketches of the carefree, luxurious life of the young about Rome and the speech on behalf of Milo, a man transparently guilty of murder but defended by Cicero with brilliantly misleading logic in a court where hostile soldiers stood by to intimidate him. Cicero is often criticized as lacking courage, and he himself admitted this weakness, but he was brave when embarking, at least, on this case and brave, too, in his final year of political activity.

In his sixties, when political 'liberty' was denied to him under Julius Caesar's dominance, Cicero turned to writing theoretical works on the history and practice of oratory, of religion and of philosophy. The results are tributes to his long-amassed learning and are fundamental to our grasp of Roman intellectual life. Cicero was always inclined to a conservative position. Intellectually, he rejected the claims of divination by which individuals claimed to be able to discover the future and the will of the gods. But he was a firm upholder of the traditional civic religion which was handed down as the customs of Rome's ancestors. He was therefore overjoyed to be appointed an augur, or official Roman diviner, in 53 BC, although this public job involved the taking of omens which, intellectually, he did not believe in. Among the various types of Greek philosophy, Cicero always inclined to the sceptical style. His letters show how varied were the philosophical tastes of his Roman contemporaries, a generation for whom the language of philosophical ethics and enquiry was now a part of educated life, so different from a century earlier. Cicero's philosophical scepticism was of the old-fashioned type, at ease with his natural conservatism.

These speeches and treatises are among Cicero's claims to a civilized mind. Above all, that claim rests on his letters. They are unique survivals, written across some twenty years and sent to and from this leading Roman who was not always writing for publication. At one level they show us Cicero's tastes and lifestyle, his love of books, his views on his slaves, his family (including his beloved daughter and his irritable brother), his many houses and what they meant to him. We see him distraught with grief at his daughter's death in her early thirties,[2] his falling out with Terentia, his own wife of thirty years, writing fondly about his trusted Tiro, the slave-secretary whom he freed, or regretting the behaviour of his most recent son-in-law, Dolabella. Cicero owned no fewer than eight country houses in Italy, although farming was never one of his interests and hunting did not interest him at all. Moving between them, he had none of a country squire's attachment to one 'home', but he did appreciate the

48. Marble portrait, also posthumous, believed to represent Cicero, *c.* 40–30 BC.

solace these places offered, their woods and setting and their 'refuge' from public turmoil. But he had several houses in Rome, too, culminating in the fine house on the Palatine hill above the Forum which was such a statement of his social arrival. Its previous senatorial owner had had it designed as a mansion overlooked in the public gaze (privacy was not a priority of socially prominent figures in the world of Rome).[3] Cicero borrowed hugely in order to buy it, in an age when smart house-prices had inflated tenfold in sixty years.

The letters also show us Cicero's vacillating moods, veering between elation and despair. They show his concern for promising young protégés (which could be rather stifling), his refusal ever to be idle and his exceptionally cultivated mind. In June 59, during Caesar's controversial consulship, we find him down in his country house at Antium (Anzio), busily engaging with a projected work on geography, to be based, of course, on Hellenistic Greek masters, and fretting that the subject was too difficult to be presented attractively. We hear about his wife Terentia's forests, his access to friends' private libraries (Atticus' library was his mainstay) and his constant blend of public and scholarly life. It is the life of a very rich Roman, but it is one which is immediate and civilized to many of our tastes, whereas the lifestyle of a Pericles or a Demosthenes has left us no such letters (they never wrote them) and is lost, apart from anecdotes.

Cicero is also the one Roman father whose relationship to a daughter can be followed at some length. As 'family father', *paterfamilias*, he had her legally in his power, but he nonetheless expressed extreme affection for her as his 'haven' and 'repose' from public difficulties, a source of 'conversation and sweet ways'. When she married for the third time, aged only twenty-six, her husband was not, in fact, of Cicero's own choosing. Her opinions thus weighed with him more than law and custom might otherwise lead us to expect. But in loving her, he also, typically, loved himself. She was 'the most loving, modest and clever daughter a man ever had', and thereby 'the image of my face and speech and mind'.[4] Both the affection and the self-reflection are distinctly Cicero's, and we probably would not find them to this degree in other contemporary fathers.

But there is more to these letters than evidence of 'social life' at large. They have a wit, an oblique bearing on great public events and a superb line in caustic comments and personal jokes. Unashamedly, they revel in the failures of their contemporaries, immortalized by Cicero's gleeful nicknames, 'the Pasha' (Pompey, lord of the East), 'Little Miss Pretty' (his hated Clodius, one of whose names meant 'handsome'), 'Ox-eyes' (Clodius' promiscuous sister Clodia) and many more. They show us, like nothing else, what liberty meant in a senator's world, and they leave us secretly longing to join in. Better still, they are one man's view on events around him which he is so often interpreting as he personally wants them to be. There is a marvellous gap between Cicero's understanding, so often self-centred, and the reality which we can attribute with greater plausibility to the big fish among whom he swims. His judgement of character is often so wonderfully wrong, not least through his tendency to over-interpret his own importance to other people. Yet there are also the sharp judgements when his hopes have failed or are not at issue; these remind us that he, too, was not totally deceived.

His career had an unforgettable path, navigating the contests over 'freedom' and 'justice'. In the 60s BC he could start by swimming with the populist tide, speaking up in 66 for Pompey's extended command in the East or defending a populist tribune in court. But it was a populism tempered by professed respect for the establishment, and in 64, in an undistinguished race, the establishment backed the biddable Cicero's campaign to be a consul. He was successful for January 63.

In preparation, his younger brother Quintus had sent him a 'little note-book' on electioneering, a classic text on the strategies by which a candidate could succeed at Rome. 'Nearly every day, as you go down to the Forum,' Quintus states, 'you must repeat to yourself "I am *nouveau*; I am after a consulship; this is Rome".'[5] One should strike a balance between the cultivation of the noble and influential and attention to one's popular image, in the city, throughout Italy, and even in big households where Cicero (his brother warned) should take care that the slaves will speak well of him. Lacking family connections, Cicero did indeed take the trouble (as his brother advised) to learn about the size, location and nature of each important man's property in Italy. When he travelled by road, he was said to be capable of speaking familiarly about the owner of each estate along his route. Such people would come to Rome and prove to be especially important in 'fixing' the assemblies for elections and legislation. Quintus' handbook assumes the existence of all sorts of fascinating 'fixers', the 'distributors' (who paid bribes to blocks of potential voters), 'companionables', four groups of whom were already 'obliged' to Cicero, and 'men of outstanding influence, who have from you, or hope to have from you, control of a voting tribe or a century . . . for, in these days, experts in electioneering have worked out, with all possible keenness and resources, how to get what they want from their fellow tribesmen'.[6] Quintus' advice applied to elections, but the people who could 'fix' a voting-tribe for an election could also, surely, fix one for the separate 'tribal' assembly which passed laws. Quintus also assumed that men would fix the 'harangues', or addresses, to the people. He had one cardinal tip for his brother: do not discuss *political* matters in the streets or in a public 'harangue'. When dealing with 'the people', cultivate 'a memory for names, an ingratiating manner, constant attendance, generosity, publicity, a "fine show", a promise of advantage in the state'.[7] In classical Athens, a Pericles or Demosthenes did not lead their fellow democrats by such classic 'Italian' arts.

The year of the consulship, 63, was the very summit of Cicero's career. It was a time of acute social and political tension, much of it traceable to the effects of Sulla's reforms and the decade of reaction. Those whom Sulla had settled on farms in Italy had become beset by debt and the uncertainties of their continuing title to their land. Further up the social scale, Sulla's reforms to the Romans' political career-structure had intensified the race for high political office: ever more competitors left the starting-stalls, but less than half of them would be elected praetor, the first major obstacle to their progress. There were also the demoted senators, keen to re-emerge and regain the eminence which a 'black mark' from the censors had lost them. Specifically in 63, there were the uncertainties over the absent Pompey's intentions and the fears of popular violence in Rome (grain was still scarce and the people's 'clubs' had just been banned, in 64). First, Cicero artfully opposed a populist bill for allotting lands to yet more settlers in Italy, and then, in the autumn, he flushed out what he judged to be the seditious designs of a desperate noble, Catiline, who was heavily in debt himself after his electoral failures to win a consulship. Open rebellion was raised separately in Etruria and further plotting was uncovered in the city, including (according to Cicero) plans for arson, which certainly terrified his urban audience. Whatever the rights of Cicero's judgement, there was a real danger of murder, forcible abolition of debt and an armed coup. Conspirators were arrested, but in the Senate in December Cicero presided as consul over a fateful decision to execute the citizen-prisoners under arrest. Contrary voices were heard, especially Julius Caesar's, but the sentences went ahead although they violated the basic rights of Roman citizens to 'appeal' and, since Gaius Gracchus, to have a public trial on a capital charge before the people. It was no excuse when Cicero promptly misclassified the victims as 'public enemies'. It was also unfortunate that several of them were linked by 'friendship' to the absent Pompey.

Basking in his success nonetheless, Cicero circulated the details of his interventions in prose and in verse, in Greek and in Latin. But his moment of triumph was immediately darkened by his treatment of citizens under arrest: he had allowed the principle of 'liberty' to be infringed. Enemies attacked him as a 'tyrant', activating profound beliefs about justice and legality in the Republic. We can watch, through Cicero's letters, how the glory of his own inflation was brusquely brought down. Early in 62 he wrote to the absent Pompey, setting himself up as the great man's equal, the future adviser at his side. Pompey did not even answer.[8] In 63 Cicero had antagonized the powerful Crassus (arguably, the enmity went deep) and had also crossed the preferred path of a major rising star, young Julius Caesar. In late 62 he added the enmity of the forceful Clodius, not least by denying an alibi which Clodius wanted to plead to save himself in a scandalous cause célèbre at Rome. Having used Cicero, the nobles then stood apart from their embarrassing 'new man'. The consulship had given Cicero a seniority in the Senate, but his constant praising of his own achievements and the mess with which he became identified removed him from the centre stage.

Of the four keys to political success at Rome, Cicero had only one: he was a superb orator, but his military capacity was minimal, his finances insufficient, and his connections with noble friends and family non-existent. Nonetheless, he looked socially upwards, hoping to be taken 'up' rather than constructing a circle of similar new men and helping them to rise with him. In late 60, as new groupings formed, we can read him actually believing that Julius Caesar would be looking to him, Cicero, to reconcile great Pompey with Crassus and to help events to go more smoothly. Indeed, Julius Caesar liked Cicero: he liked his wit and his literary talent and valued his skill as a speaker. But politically he never kept him on the inside track. Pompey, too, recognized how Cicero had helped him earlier in the 60s, but the two of them were never serious friends. Crassus, basically, detested him.

For the next year, 59, these three big men agreed an ungentlemanly deal whereby they would advance each other's political needs. Cicero emerges from his letters as gloriously slow to realize the existence of this deal,[9] and, when he eventually speaks out against the three of them in fury, within hours the threat of his enemy Clodius is loosed by them against him. Neither Caesar nor Pompey would intervene to save him. In March 58 he preferred to leave Rome for a voluntary exile rather than wait for Clodius, now tribune, to prosecute him. He wandered away from the Rome which was his lifeblood, reduced to absolute misery and the possibility of suicide. In Rome, with programmatic irony, Cicero's enemy Clodius promptly demolished Cicero's proudly acquired house on the Palatine and consecrated its site as a temple to Liberty. The 'Liberty' was the people's 'freedom from' harassment, infringed by Cicero's presiding over citizens' executions in December 63.

By September 57 Cicero was back again, as Clodius' star waned and Pompey, especially, regained his nerve and realized Cicero's potential uses as an orator (Pompey was a poor speaker). But return came at a price: Cicero had promptly to speak up for Pompey's interests and once again, in 56, he was completely deceived about the three big men's intentions. He was left unaware of the renewal of their 'gentlemen's agreement' until it had happened. As a result, his ignorant stirrings of independence were quickly silenced by them yet again and he found himself obliged to co-operate, or else to risk his life; co-operation meant delivering the most humiliating speeches in defence of his former public enemies, the political friends of the dominant three. For Cicero, the one bright ray in these speeches was the occasion to hark back to his own consulship in 63: its reception was the event from which he never recovered psychologically.

Cicero's reactions to this chequered political course are the most vivid witness to the value of freedom for the psychology of a senatorial participant. It certainly did not mean the freedom of democracy, but it did mean 'freedom from' the dominance of others and 'freedom for' senators like himself to exercise authority and dignity, while retaining 'equality' among their own peer group. The artful domination by the three big men, Caesar, Pompey and Crassus, was a disaster for him, second only to exile, that fate as bad as death. In 54 he wrote to his brother: 'I am tortured, tortured by the fact that we no longer have a constitution in the state or justice in the courts. Some of my enemies I could not attack; others I have defended.' And above all, 'I am unable to give a free rein to either my opinions or my hatred. And Caesar is the only man who loves me as I wish.'[10] But this 'love' was only a love professed by Caesar in absence. Caesar (we can see) had other ambitions, and Cicero was not at the heart of them.

One resort for Cicero was to withdraw and write works of ideal political theory. From 54 onwards Cicero was engaged with writing an ideal *Republic* and books of *Laws*, works which conspicuously failed to address the realities and evils of the contemporary Republic in Rome. As a self-made man, he was the champion of the establishment view of the state: it involved the supremacy of the Senate, as opposed to the unvetted sovereignty of the people's assemblies. The Senate's decrees, he wrote, should be binding and the Senate should be 'master' of public policy: senators should also inspect the votes which the people would otherwise cast. The secret ballot was a disaster: senators should supervise voting and grant only 'the appearance of freedom' so as to preserve the 'authority' of the 'good men and true'.[11] His ideal state did leave a role for the people's tribunes, but its vague ideals of 'concord' between the senators and knights and an enlightened 'moderator' as the head of state were completely irrelevant to the real crises of his beloved Republic. The Republic's problems were rooted in the power of military commanders and their followers and the social and economic disorders which made their gangs and armies relatively easy to retain.

His other response to the dynasts' pre-eminence was to write an 'inside story' of events since the mid–60s.[12] Sadly the work is lost to us, although Cicero read bits of it aloud to Atticus and compared its tone to the most malignant of previous Greek historians, Theopompus, the contemporary of Philip and Alexander the Great. But we do know that in it he blamed both Crassus and Julius Caesar for political plottings which we would otherwise hesitate to ascribe to them: plans for a coup in 65 (Crassus, he believed, had been particularly active in this) and the backing of the desperate populist Catiline in 63. Was his book only embittered gossip, distorted by his hindsight? It is one of the books from antiquity which we would dearly like to recover, for it may well have told the truths which Cicero was afraid to state elsewhere, as well as airing yet more conspiracy theories which would be extremely entertaining to study.

In 51 BC a discontented Cicero found himself sent east to a miserable province, Cilicia, in southern Asia Minor (although Cyprus was included, together with more territory in southern Asia). Through his letters, we have our first prolonged view of a Roman governor at work abroad, applying justice to the local affairs of his province.[13] Cicero went on the customary assize-tours round the province's main towns; he issued the usual 'edict' on taking office and chose to base it, wisely, on the edict of an admired predecessor, the lawyer Scaevola. In general, he wished the Greek-speaking locals to settle their disputes between themselves, but if he found that these disputes involved Romans or foreigners or points of importance under Roman law, he would judge them on the lines of the Roman praetors' edicts at Rome. By such piecemeal decisions, the Romans' own laws on such topics as inheritance or defaulting debtors would come to apply to subjects outside Rome: there was no single act or decree imposing them.

Despite Cicero's complaints, provincial duties were a better alternative for him than political life at Rome. Cicero lived for his Republic, and pined without it, yet his life and incomparable letters were to encompass its ultimate crisis. Back in 59 BC Julius Caesar had offered Cicero a responsible post on his staff abroad so as to escape from the political storm which was then brewing round him. Even Atticus had advised him to take it. It was a typical act of graciousness, the 'clemency' which Caesar would publicize to his Roman audience. But as Cicero now observed, this 'clemency' was insidious: who was Caesar to deign to pardon the likes of us?[14] On that question, the history of 'liberty' and 'justice' would now depend.

THE RISE OF JULIUS CAESAR

I have had a visit from Cornelius–Balbus, I mean, the intimate of Julius Caesar. He assured me that Caesar will follow my advice and Pompey's in all things and will try to bring Pompey and Crassus together. This course offers the following advantages: an intimate association for me with Pompey, with Caesar too if I want it, a return to favour with my enemies, peace with the populace, tranquillity in my old age . . .

Cicero, *Letters to Atticus* 2.3 (late 60 BC)

The truth is that the present regime is the most infamous, most disgraceful and uniformly odious to all sorts and classes and ages of men that ever was, more so upon my word than I could ever have wished, let alone expected. Those 'populist' politicians have taught even quiet folk to hiss . . .

Cicero, *Letters to Atticus* 2.19, between 7 and 14 July 59 BC, on Caesar's consulship and its deal with Pompey and Crassus

JULIUS CAESAR, the most famous Roman, proved to be the most masterly populist in Roman politics. For more than twenty years he pursued this line, yet by birth and manners he was a true patrician, descended from the oldest nobility in Roman history. The founding father, Aeneas, was claimed as his family's ancestor and beyond him, the goddess Venus herself. The 'traditions' of ordinary senators were latecomers in the long view of such an ultimate aristocrat. He stands in sharp contrast to the assumed traditionalism of Cicero, the man made good.

Caesar had a proud, patrician sense of his own high worth, or *dignitas*, but, first as a consul, then ten years later as a dictator, he forced through detailed populist laws which 'traditional' senators had resisted and continued to obstruct. They ranged from curbs on extortion by provincial governors and checks on the use of violence in public life to the granting of plots of land to tens of thousands of settlers, not all of whom were veteran soldiers. There were values behind such laws, a sense of justice which made them more than personal bids for pre-eminence. Yet Caesar, the 'people's politician', ended by limiting the urban poor's right of free association in their clubs and colleges in Rome. They might be a threat to his own pre-eminence, not least during his absence from the city. Until the years of his dictatorships, he correctly relied on tribunes, the popular magistrates, to propose his legislation to the people's assemblies and to veto proposals against his interests. Yet he ended by deposing holders of the tribunate simply because their actions displeased him. Eventually he nominated Rome's magistrates himself.

Artfully, Caesar began to encourage 'open government'. In 59, as consul, he caused the business of the Senate to be published and made accessible for the first time: Hadrian, nearly two hundred years later, would be 'curator' of the published senatorial 'acts'. Those senators like Cicero who spoke contemptuously of the people as 'cattle' or the 'dregs' in the Senate house, but praised them before their assemblies, would not exactly welcome the new publications. Caesar himself spoke clearly and forcefully, dictated letters freely (even while on horseback) and became the first Roman nobleman to make a real contribution to Latin literature. For, as a general abroad, Caesar sent lucidly written 'commentaries' back from his prolonged command in Gaul. 'Avoid an unfamiliar word,' he used to say, 'as a sailor avoids the rocks.'[1] His prose works are unusually clear in structure and form, but they are also highly economical with the truth. They were composed so that a wider public in Rome, in Italy, and perhaps even in southern Gaul, could read of his prowess. Probably, they were issued year by year, but they ended in 52, long before Caesar's return to Rome. Publication of these exercises in 'spin' had important political relevance for his career at that time. These artful 'commentaries' presented a Roman Caesar who was more than the equal of Pompey the great conqueror. Whereas Pompey was glorified by Greek historians and Greek orators around him, Caesar was now glorified by his own clear Latin. Written in the third person, the commentaries use the word 'Caesar' 775 times.

In Julius Caesar, charm and ruthlessness, daring and deceit were intertwined. Above all, he proved to be a superb general. He was indifferent to personal comforts or luxuries and he was a fine horseman who could even ride fast with both hands clasped behind his back. From 58 to 50 he was the conqueror of vast territories in the West, all of which he identified as Gaul. In 55 he crossed the Channel and became the first invader of Britain, 'beyond the Ocean's limit' which had bounded Alexander the Great. Yet the British invasion failed and the conquests in Gaul went far beyond a strict interpretation of the commands which had been given to him. When these commands ended he reckoned to have caused the death in battle of no less than 1,192,000 enemies in his Gallic campaigns. Even so, civilian casualties were excluded from this total, so glorious to him, but not to us.

Caesar also showed stunning daring in further wars between 49 and 45, fought in Greece, Egypt, Asia, north Africa and Spain at places which Hadrian's peaceful touring would later encompass. However, he never published the casualties for these battles, because they were fought in a civil war against fellow Roman citizens. For, in 49, Caesar embarked on civil war inside Italy, like a 'new Hannibal', while professing the need to defend the 'liberty' of the 'Roman people', the 'sanctity of the tribunes' and, more honestly, his own 'dignity'. For nearly five years political life became subjected to the personal will of Caesar himself. He was certainly not the inevitable consequence of the times in which he lived. The Roman Republic could, indeed should, have survived him. Ultimately, he over-threw it for his own impressive 'dignity', to which all else, the populism, the inclusiveness, the much-advertised 'clemency', were secondary. He overthrew a flexible constitution which had evolved over more than four centuries, and in due course he was murdered by some sixty conspirators in Rome. But his example, and his fate, coloured the next acts in the long-running drama of the Roman Republic. These acts did then prove to be its end, a turning point for liberty.

Julius Caesar was born six years after Cicero, in the year 100 in the month which was later named July in his honour. Historians of his early years are at risk from hindsight: could contemporaries really have feared his cool ability very early in his life? Most of his historians would now postpone the 'making of Caesar' until his late thirties or forties, but contemporaries may have seen the signs much earlier. Aged (proba-bly) fifteen, Caesar was chosen to be the ceremonial Priest of Jupiter, a job for patricians only. Since the Priest was not allowed so much as to look at troops under arms, was the offer of this priesthood an early at-tempt to block this feared young noble from any public career? These years were those of Sulla's awful rise to power, and Caesar was married to the noble young daughter of Sulla's enemy, Cinna. Through his aunt, he was a nephew of the great Marius, Sulla's greatest foe. In fact, Sulla refused to let Caesar hold on to the priesthood (as if he saw no immobilizing purpose in it) but he is also said to have warned against the casually dressed young Caesar's potential. Is this story, too, only the creation of hindsight?

Caesar escaped execution and left for military service in the East. Here, hostile gossip later claimed that he became a sexual favourite of the king of Bithynia. There was nothing in it, but when Caesar was later insulted as 'womanish' he retorted brilliantly that Amazons had once ruled most of Asia and so his threat to dance on the heads of his senatorial enemies was not an empty one.[2] In 80 BC a brave exploit in the Aegean won him the 'civic crown', a very high military distinction for saving a citizen's life in battle: its oak wreath could then be worn in public and even senators would have to stand up in his presence at public games, a privilege which cannot have been lost on his high sense of dignity. He returned to Rome and gained fame, and hostility, for prosecuting a respected ex-consul for plundering his province. He then returned to the Greek East to study and let the hostility cool at Rome. Unlike the rising star, Pompey, Caesar had a quick, educated mind which was always interested in literature. But he too was a born fighter. He took a sweet, swift revenge on some pirates in the Aegean who tried to hold him to ransom. Aged twenty-six, he took troops back into Bithynia to stop defections there to Rome's great enemy, Mithridates. Already, he was acting without orders.

Back at Rome, as Sulla's reactionary settlement broke up, Caesar held fast to the alternative populist line. His aunt was the widow of the popular hero Marius, and when she died he gave a funeral speech in the Forum which dwelt on her (and therefore his) very noble descent from gods and kings. The words would eventually seem prophetic when he himself seemed to rival both these types of dangerous ancestor. People noticed him, as they did when he displayed the insignia of Marius, the long-suppressed popular hero, in his aunt's funeral procession. He even displayed Marius' trophies, long concealed, up on the Capitol. Then, later in 69, Caesar left to serve as a junior magistrate in southern Spain. Here, he went on the usual assize-tour, hearing cases. In Cádiz, he is said to have seen a statue of Alexander the Great in the town's main temple, and to have wept that he had done nothing memorable, although at his same age Alexander had already conquered the world.[3] Again, historians mostly doubt this story, but perhaps unwisely; it is a less likely story that Caesar also dreamed that he was raping his mother, signifying a wish to dominate (mother) Earth, the world. In Spain, at any rate, occasional attacks of epilepsy are specifically attested as beginning to afflict him.

At Rome, this ambitious young man was still very far indeed from global prominence. That honour went to the great all-conquering Pompey, whose exceptional command against the Mediterranean pirates had been supported by Caesar, the one senator to vote for it in 67 (a victory over the pirates would help the people by reducing the price of grain imports). Nonetheless, as an aedile (a city magistrate) in 65, it was Caesar who was the greater showman. He paid for the customary games, but added hugely to their popular appeal by offering 320 pairs of gladiators in public combat, to be dressed with silver weaponry. They were intended, he said, as a funerary honour for his dead father. But his father had died twenty years earlier and this enormous show caused an anxious Senate to 'recommend' a prompt limit on the number of gladiators which anyone could present. Like the games, the cost of Caesar's show would have been enormous. The higher reaches of a public career at Rome required huge expense, and never more so than in the intensely competitive late 60s. But Caesar borrowed hugely to pay for the costs and in the absence of glorious Pompey he borrowed from the vastly rich Crassus. Amid charges of corruption and conspiracy, the two of them were even suspected of plotting a coup in 65, so that Crassus could sort out the highly rewarding kingdom of Egypt and Caesar, still only an aedile, could serve as Crassus the dictator's second-in-command. Pompey, indeed, was absent and Egypt was certainly the great unresolved prize, whose grain and treasure would make its 'captors' uniquely powerful. Other partners were wrongly alleged later to have been in on the deal, but in 64 Cicero did hint that Crassus had been up to something.[4] We can only guess or reject the story (as most scholars do), not least because such a role for a humble aedile seems wholly incredible. But was Caesar a typical aedile?

What we do know is that he played prominent roles in the year 63, the fateful pinnacle of Cicero's career. At the start, it was Caesar who promoted a sham trial in public to warn Cicero and others about abuse of the Senate's so-called 'ultimate decree'. In December, when Cicero then abused precisely this decree against living citizens who were already under arrest, it was Caesar who spoke so forcefully in the Senate in favour of imprisoning the offenders but not killing them. Here, too, he took a populist approach in support of 'freedom', one which he, but not Cicero, would never regret. In Cicero's unpublished 'inside story', Caesar would later be roundly blamed (with Crassus) for backing Catiline in the first place and causing a near-revolution. Was this charge only the old Cicero's sour hindsight or had there once again been more to Caesar's early discredit than we know? Whatever the truth, it did not stop Caesar from two fine successes in this same year. He won the immensely prestigious 'High Priesthood' (as Pontifex Maximus he had an office, henceforward, in the heart of the Roman Forum and a house on the adjoining Sacred Way) and he was also elected to the praetorship, the next career step, for the year 62. The priesthood cost him a fortune in bribery and the praetorship began with his controversial support for the returning hero, Pompey: it did not stop Caesar gaining a command in Further Spain for 61 BC.

This provincial command did not make him by first awakening his ambition (it was surely there from his adolescence) but it was certainly crucial to his survival. On his return, a failure to pay his debts would be terminal, obliging him to become an exile. The recognized way for Romans to repay such debts was to soak a province for spoils, bribes and booty. By late 61 Caesar had done just that, by attacking enough outlying tribes in Spain, and so he could start to think of the ultimate honours, a triumph and then a consulship back in Rome. This prospect really alarmed his traditionalist contemporaries, especially Cato, the arch-conservative who would never give Caesar the benefit of any doubt. Cato therefore obliged Caesar to choose between a triumph (already voted, in principle) or standing as consul. Coolly, Caesar chose to go for the consulship, obliging Cato to compromise and try to beat him at his own game by amassing a big fund for electoral bribery and ensuring that his own reliable kinsman, Bibulus, would be elected as Caesar's fellow consul.

Both of them were duly elected for the year 59, but, unlike Bibulus, Caesar prepared for his year of office by the artful 'gentlemen's agreement' with Pompey and Crassus, a couple hitherto divided by personal enmity. Cunningly, Caesar saw they both had needs which he, as consul, could help them meet. As a major financier, Crassus needed a renegotiation of the tax-collecting contract in the province of Asia. Pompey needed two things, the ratification of the arrangements which he had personally imposed on Asia and the settlement of his veteran soldiers, who were still unrewarded from their victories in the East in the 60s. As for Caesar himself, he had a populist programme which would lead (so he hoped) to an ever greater and more profitable provincial command. Economic tension in Rome was running very high. Seeing trouble coming, surely, the senators had already allotted humdrum commands to these consuls after their year of office: not a Spain or Gaul, but 'woods and tracks' in Italy itself.

The year 59, Caesar's consulship, is a climactic moment in Roman history. Previous 'populists' had fallen prey to the same weakness, their failure to escape reprisals from 'traditionalists' either during or after their hated year of office. Caesar's plan was brutally simple: to carry Pompey and Crassus with him in a mutual balance of favours; to put laws directly to the people's assemblies, despite the Senate's opposition; to work with and through supportive tribunes who could veto such opposition; to 'fix' supportive tribunes for the following year and supportive consuls too, if possible; to be voted a major provincial command and then to leave Rome with the powers to carry it out, thus being untouchable by prosecution as he left the city. But his fellow consul, Bibulus, was flatly against him, and Caesar's 'populist' legislation would have to go straight to the people to become law, because the senators would surely never recommend it. Traditionalists, as usual, would hate the tactic.

The ensuing manoeuvres are unforgettable in Roman public and political life: the addresses to public meetings; the gangs and cliques in the Forum; the parade of 'imprisoning' the intransigent Cato, although he was a tribune; the harassment of the obstructive consul Bibulus (a bucket of dung was once poured publicly over his head). Attempted 'intercession' by other hostile tribunes was evaded by violence; it all sounds chaotic, but already in 62 even the man of principle, young Cato, had prevented a tribune from reciting an unwanted bill by having a fellow tribune jam his hand over the man's mouth. In 59 Caesar's colleague Bibulus countered by withdrawing to his house and claiming that irregularities in the heavens (observed only by him) made each possible day in the calendar unfit for the due course of public business. He also distributed posters with such scandalous attacks on Caesar that the common people crowded round to find out their fascinating contents, thereby blocking traffic in Rome's streets.

Nonetheless, sufficient laws in Caesar's programme were forced through. One, long planned, set out an eminently reasonable programme for the settlement of Pompey's veteran soldiers and other needy citizens on land in Italy. Cleverly, the proposals would not involve confiscations from any private owner. Another law lowered the Asian tax contract to suit Crassus' interests: Cato was still bitterly opposed to it. In April a second law then proposed the allotment of rich lands in Campania, behind the Bay of Naples, lands which had been first taken as 'public' after Roman victories over Hannibal in 211. It was deeply contentious. One aim was to give land to some 20,000 poor citizens in Rome and their families, part of the 'dregs', in the traditionalists' view of them, who were such a distress and a possible danger in the city. To Cicero, this fine proposal seemed an outrage.

Even as late as August good legislation was still being brought forward, especially a complex law against unchecked extortion by Roman governors abroad. But to go so far Caesar had had to play extremely hard. Not only had Cato continued to oppose him, especially on the proposed assistance to Crassus and the tax-contractors. There was a real danger that once Pompey's main needs were met he too would veer off to join the conservative senators' groupings, his more natural resting place. In the spring Pompey had married Caesar's beloved only daughter, Julia, but even a tie by marriage was very fragile. In summer 59 Caesar therefore promoted an informer (it seems) to warn the ever-nervous Pompey of a high-grade plot against his life. The final allegations included the names of almost every 'traditional' senatorial opponent, whereupon the informer was conveniently killed while in prison.[5] Cicero was surely right to see Caesar's hand behind the affair: it scared Pompey, sure enough, and so it kept the 'gentlemen's agreement' in existence. But once again, it stank.

Friendly consuls could not, after all, be fixed for the following year, but a friendly tribune (Clodius) and a provincial command were forthcoming. Overturning the Senate's earlier proposals of 'woods and tracks', Caesar obtained for himself by popular vote the far greater provinces of Cisalpine Gaul (nowadays north Italy) and Illyricum (what is now the Dalmatian coast), a promising base for conquests inland. Furthermore, they were voted for five whole years. To his great good fortune, the allotted commander for Transalpine Gaul had died in April and on news of danger from the surrounding tribes, even the senators panicked and anxiously added Transalpine Gaul to Caesar's provinces. He was, after all, a proven general for what might be a major crisis and the combined commands would certainly preoccupy him.

What had shocked senatorial conservatives so far was Caesar's sheer forcefulness, his contempt for their opposition (and themselves) and the populism of the laws for which he would now receive great public credit. The political footling of Bibulus and his obstructions were basically irrelevant but it was at least arguable that Caesar's entire legislation was technically invalid as a result: if the matter was judged in court, the senators would probably 'fix' a jury to uphold their view of 'illegality'. Meanwhile, senators had seen their old, once-famous general Lucullus forced to grovel at Caesar's feet. They were not above making a counter-proposal: could not Caesar wait and bring forward his legislation in the following year when they might no longer oppose him or even not threaten prosecution? But Caesar did not trust them and his dignity would never permit it. This time, the customary 'concord' among senators after a crisis could not be cosily reasserted.

In the first weeks of 58, following his consulship, Caesar was outside Rome's city-boundary, recruiting troops for his provincial command, but he was still accessible to the senators and daily news of politics within the city. It was imperative that attempts to undo his legislation in the new year did not succeed. In fact, Clodius (his supportive tribune) proved well up to the challenge. The incoming consuls were cleverly bought off with the offer of valuable provincial commands; populist laws continued to be brought forward, and there was even a fear that Clodius would become too powerful in his own right. Certainly Clodius had one grudge to settle, against Cicero, who (he felt) had let him down in 63 BC. As neither Pompey nor Caesar was willing to intervene, Cicero anticipated his fate by leaving the city. By mid-March Caesar, too, was off on his way to Gaul.

As he rode north, he cut a fine figure on horseback, dark-eyed, tall for a Roman and already balding. As in Spain, three years earlier, a governorship would more than restore his finances and ought to allow for no end of future bribes back in Rome. But what then? If Caesar laid down his command and re-entered Rome as a private citizen, his enemies would prosecute him at once for the 'illegalities' in his year as consul. If he wanted to become a consul yet again, how could he realize his aim when he had to wait a statutory ten years before standing and when he would surely be forced to return to Rome so as to campaign for his election in person? Pompey and Crassus would not assist him for nothing and Cato, certainly, would not go away. The consulship of 59 BC had been sensational, but it had created as many problems as it had addressed. With his armies in Gaul, proud Caesar was really out on a limb.

THE SPECTRE OF CIVIL WAR

So this is what their love affair, their scandalous union has come to—not secret backbiting, but outright war. As for my own affairs, I don't know what plan to take, and I don't doubt that the same question is going to trouble you. I have ties of obligation and friendship with these people. On the other hand, I love the cause, but hate the men.

I do not suppose that it escapes you that when there is a dispute about affairs in a community, men ought to take the more respectable side so long as the dispute is political and not conducted by force of arms. But when it comes to actual war and army-camps, then they should choose the stronger and reckon that the better course is the one which is safer.

Caelius to Cicero, *Letters to Friends* 8.14 (*c.* 8 August 50 BC)

WITHIN TWO YEARS OF FIGHTING beyond the Alps Caesar would become too successful, too quickly. In the name of Gallic 'freedom', he launched attacks on neighbouring tribes, including the Helvetii, who were preparing to migrate westwards into Gallic territory: 'all men', he wrote in his commentaries, 'have a natural keenness for liberty, and hate the condition of servitude'.[1] But then he exploited divisions among the Gauls so as to pick off their tribes separately and make them into a vast Roman province. The last thing Caesar wanted was to be recalled, mission completed. So, 'enemies' and dangers were discovered ever further afield.

In Rome, Pompey and Crassus were still pre-eminent, but there was plenty of scope for popular legislation. For the city, as Cicero's brother had described it in the mid–60s, was still 'formed from the concourse of the peoples of the world' and contained at least 750,000 inhabitants. This huge mass of citizen-freedmen, slaves and foreigners was the setting for the upper class's intense disputes about order, 'tradition' and legal propriety. As tribune in 58, Clodius had restored the common people's right to form social groups and associations, the 'colleges' which the Senate had simply declared 'contrary to the interests of the Republic' and abolished back in 64. He had also made the subsequent distribution of grain into a free monthly allotment. More than 300,000 citizens would be able to claim it, but it would be a vast burden on public funds and supply, although the allotment would sustain only one person, not an entire family. To increase funds, Clodius and others looked eastwards, not least to the rich domains of the Ptolemies in Cyprus. Clodius had an old grudge against its ruler and by a brilliant manoeuvre after Caesar's departure, forced even the principled Cato to compromise in what was needed. By proposing legislation directly to the people, he had Cato appointed to take over Cyprus from its profligate Ptolemaic prince: the appointment was Cato's publicly voted duty, so he could not refuse it. But by accepting, Cato was also accepting, indirectly, the legality of a whole chain of similarly approved legislation which he had contested, right back (some might say) to Caesar's laws in 59: 6,000 talents came in from Cyprus's resources.

Couriers and letters kept Caesar in touch. He is even said to have sent Clodius a letter approving the neat use of tribunes and an assembly-vote to compromise his rival Cato. The new settlement for Cyprus was also, usefully, a departure from Pompey's previous dealings with a Ptolemaic prince. No doubt Caesar also heard of the amazing activities of the aedile in 58 BC, Aemilius Scaurus. Scaurus, the stepson of Sulla, displayed five crocodiles and the first hippopotamus Rome had ever seen at his customary games. He then built an extraordinary theatre, three storeys high (of marble, glass and gilding), packed with gold cloth and (it was later said) 3,000 statues and room for 80,000 spectators. He even displayed the vast skeleton of a dinosaur, brought back from his service in the Near East, believing it was a monster from Greek mythology.[2] Popular life at Rome was really looking up, and like Clodius' laws these games and displays set a new standard in politicians' competition for popular prestige.

What most concerned Caesar was the duration of his command 'beyond the Alps'. In 59 it had been granted, it seems, on a yearly basis. His other command, 'this side of the Alps, and Illyricum', was secure, by contrast, for five years. There was the increasing danger that a senatorial rival with Gallic connections, Domitius Ahenobarbus, would get himself elected consul for 55 and force Caesar to be replaced. So Caesar turned again to his artful 'gentlemen's agreement'. By 56 BC both Pompey and

Crassus were wanting consulships again, to be followed by lucrative commands abroad, but neither of them was sure of the necessary popular support. Back in Rome, the free distribution of grain instituted by Clodius had been followed, predictably, by acute grain shortages. In autumn 57 Pompey had been given a commission to sort out the grain supply (with powers even 'greater' than those of other provincial governors, a fertile innovation), but the challenge was not easily met. Prices had stayed high and there were still shortages. Furthermore, the long-desired chance of intervening in Egypt had been denied to both him and Crassus. By early 56 neither man was the darling of the Roman populace and, in an atmosphere of violence and armed gangs, Pompey continued to fear for his life. When Caesar came south into Italy in spring 56, it was possible for a deal to be agreed. When he reached Ravenna in March, the first to come over was Crassus, because his ambitions were the more pressing. Then, by agreement at Lucca in mid-April, Pompey joined in the deal which was forming, for fear that his glory would be eclipsed: there would be five-year commands in the provinces for each of them, preceded by consulships for Pompey and Crassus in 55. By postponing the year's elections, they could count on support from troops whom Caesar would send to Rome for the voting and so they could keep out the rival threat of Ahenobarbus. Then, as the new consuls, Pompey and Crassus could prolong Caesar's transalpine command for another five years in spring 55, by a law taken straight to the people.

The deal worked, although Caesar's 'commentaries' never said a word about it. Previously, Caesar had even been thinking of a campaign in eastern Europe (Dacia) up to the Danube, but when his command 'beyond the Alps' was sure to be prolonged, he sought new fields in the north-west in which to exploit it. In 56 it was quite likely that he had already been planning an invasion of Britain[3] and he certainly engaged in a gratuitous slaughter of two vulnerable German tribes. On receiving the news in Rome, Cato was so disgusted that he proposed that Caesar, by ancient precedent, should be handed over to the Germans in order to divert the anger of the gods from Rome. Instead, Caesar transferred himself to Britain, briefly in 55 and again in 54, when he took an elephant with him for show. Neither campaign was much of a success. The hopes of finding gold and precious metals in Britain were ill-founded and the effect was more of a raid than a solid conquest. But the publicity was excellent: Britain was represented as 'beyond the Ocean' which had limited the ambitions of Alexander the Great. Back in Rome, Cicero had even been planning to write an epic poem on the 'glorious conquest', based on

49. Portrait head of Julius Caesar, probably posthumous, *c.* 40–30 BC.

front-line reports from his brother. The news about Britain helped to stave off the danger that Caesar's enemy Ahenobarbus would contrive to replace him in the Gallic command after the consulship which would now be available to Ahenobarbus in 54.

In the city, the summer of 54 was exceptionally hot and tension was exacerbated by continuing shortages of grain. The political setting is still a challenge to our imaginations. Rome was home to such vast numbers and the fascinating politics of the next four years include intricate bribery scandals (Ahenobarbus and his noble colleagues tried to nominate their successors in return for payment), localized bouts of violence (gangs erupted in the city, made up of soldiers, freed slaves, artisans, shopkeepers and trained gladiators) and, in 53 and 52, yet another crisis over the consulship. And yet there was no popular uprising for a change of constitution, no challenge to the total system. The main continuing question was the scope of Pompey's ambitions. After the consulship of 55 he had been allotted the provinces of Spain, a chance for glory, but since 54 he had preferred to wait with troops outside Rome's boundaries and govern Spain through subordinates. His most personal link with Caesar now ended: his wife Julia, Caesar's beloved daughter, died in childbirth. The people of Rome gave her a fine funeral, but what would Pompey now choose to do? He was, after all, becoming an old man. In 53 he lost one major competitor, then in 52 another. The first to go was the elderly Crassus, now in his late fifties, whose consulship had been followed by the granting of a command in the East against the hostile Parthians. At last, Crassus might return with the full glory of a military triumph, denied him after his actions against Spartacus in the late 70s: its absence had continued to needle the old man. In fact, he was too incompetent and was tricked into defeat by the Parthians in 53, costing him his life and most of his army.

In Rome, January 52 then saw the spectacular end of the most effective of the populists, Clodius. He was attacked on the Appian Way by a gang loyal to his conservative rival Milo, and what began as an accident ended with Clodius' brutal murder. His corpse was brought into the city, where his wife's impassioned mourning helped to incite the popular mood. Two of the tribunes added a eulogy over the dead man in the Forum, whereupon the crowd carried his corpse right into the Senate house and tried to cremate their champion on a bonfire of smashed furniture and documents. The house itself caught fire and its ashes were watched by spectators until nightfall. Meanwhile crowds rampaged in Rome and attacked anyone who was seen wearing jewels or fine clothes in the streets. There was no established police force and the one option seemed to be to call on Pompey to restore order with troops. Waiting outside the city, he had already used his power as an ex-consul inside the city in 53. Now he was voted a sole consulship, his third. It was a 'divine' one, according to an alarmed and thankful Cicero, and yet it was only two years since his last one. Caesar, by contrast, was still observing the proper ten-year interval between consulships and would not stand for election until summer 49, hoping to take up office in January 48. Meanwhile ambitious young men, new faces and those who simply relished a fight, were leaving Italy to seek promotions with Caesar in the West. Increasingly, he could reward them from his booty and so a real 'Caesarian clique' was building up outside Rome.

The crucial long-term question was whether Caesar would be allowed to stand as a candidate for a consulship while absent: if he had to return to canvass for it and lay down his power as a commander, his opponents would prosecute him inside Rome's boundaries, probably before an intimidated and bribed court. In March 52 Caesar seemed to get what he wanted: the ten tribunes, supported by Pompey, carried a law which allowed him the unusual step of a candidacy in absence. Traditionalists in the Senate were bypassed by it, but many other questions remained open: how would Caesar and Pompey coexist? Was it expected that, like Pompey, Caesar could now stand for a consulship earlier than 49, in (say) 50? If he was elected consul again, whatever would he do this time?

The answers were to mark a real rupture of the Roman Republic: why had such a crisis come? Abroad, the provinces were being ruled by individual governors with powers to do much as they wished and scope to extort huge gains from their subjects. These commands inflated their resources for competition back at Rome, but their victims, the provincials, did not bring about a crisis by rebelling against this type of rule. Nearer home, the previous bitter conflicts between senators and many of the knights and between Romans and Italians were also irrelevant: since the 70s the aftermath of the Social War and of Sulla's brief 'solution' for the jury-courts had largely settled down. In the 50s, however, Romans themselves would still think of 'luxury' as a major culprit. As consuls in 55, Pompey and Crassus, inordinately rich men, had considered introducing measures to curb it. In 51 the arch-traditionalist Cato amused the plebs by giving 'old-fashioned' games, in disapproval at recent ostentation: he offered simple wreaths, not gold, as prizes and gave small presents of food to the spectators.

We have a sense, here, of men with a traditional obsession, like the 'gypsies' or 'single mothers' of modern political rhetoric, which is diverting them from the real structural weaknesses. For, despite the years of rhetoric, luxury had marvellously proliferated. Upper-class Romans were building magnificent villas as second homes along the coastline of the Bay of Naples, supporting them on piers of concrete and adorning them with the rows of pillars and terraces which we can enjoy in later paintings of them, preserved for us at Pompeii. These attacks on nature were the work of 'Xerxes in a toga', said moralists, recalling the canal-digging of this former Persian king. Since Pompey's conquests in Asia, fine gems had reached avid Roman buyers, prompting collections of their different types. In the kitchen, specialized local delicacies were increasingly sought and identified, whether huge snails from north Africa or home-grown dormice raised in special 'dormouse-houses' (gliraria): 'they are fattened in jars which many keep even inside the villa; acorns, walnuts or chestnuts are put inside and when a cover is put on the jars they become fat in the dark.' There were even flocks of peacocks, kept for display and consumption. In classical Athens, one prominent aristocrat displayed 'Persian' peacocks, a gift from the Persian king, and sold eggs to fascinated visitors: his son was then prosecuted for treating the birds as his own. At Rome, peacocks began to be bred by the hundred in the early first century BC and, before long, a flock was reckoned to yield a small fortune of an income: 'a flock of 100' would produce a tenth of the property qualification to be an upper-class knight.

We must remember Cicero's comment: what Romans disliked was private luxury, whereas public display was munificence, and not disagreeable. It was, then, alarming to political rivals, but highly popular, when Pompey paid for a spectacular theatre in 55 BC, including a statue of himself and fourteen nations which he had conquered. Grander, even, than Scaurus' theatre three years earlier, it led up to at least four temples (including one to Victorious Venus). At its dedication, elephants and 500 lions were staged in a beastly 'hunt'. In 53 a future tribune, Curio, put up not one wooden theatre but two, built as a pair which could turn back to back, or revolve into one and become a single arena for gladiators. These luxurious displays were public, at least. What was attackable, by contrast, was the 'selfish' luxury of marble-pillared houses (the huge pillars of dark-red marble in Scaurus' hall were notorious) and when he took back the fantastically rich decoration of his theatre to adorn his own Tuscan villa, the slaves at the property are said to have set fire to it in protest at his extravagance.[4]

To us, urban poverty and suffering at Rome seem much more relevant problems. The scarcity of food and water, the appalling housing for Rome's masses were an intolerable negligence. Yet unlike the poor in many Greek cities in the age of Plato, Rome's poor did not unite and rebel for a new constitution. Poor people rioted, certainly, for Clodius, but they were rioting for a great benefactor, now lost to them. In the process the Senate house burned down, but only by accident, and there was no programme to abolish the Senate itself. There was no popular campaigning with a new ideology. One reason was that so many of the 'plebs' were still freed persons, dependent on their former masters; others were foreigners; by contrast, a hard core of Roman 'city-folk', persisting across the generations, was always much scarcer. The upper class spent lavishly in the city, and it was their spending which sustained the mass of shopkeepers and builders and even the specialists in the dreaded luxuries. Many of the plebs therefore needed the rich, and as none of them could stand up and speak in their assemblies or at political meetings, and few ever voted (and then in blocks), the 'popular' potential of the Roman constitution was wonderfully contained. At Athens, when democracy was adopted, the members of the Athenians' supreme 'senate' had been discredited by their collaboration with the previous tyranny; the exiling of other nobles by those tyrants had already taught lesser people that they could cope well enough without an aristocrat to help them along. At Rome, no such crisis had discredited the senators. Above all, in Attica the citizenry had been so much smaller; it was linked by supposed 'kinship', and was much more cohesive than the Roman citizenry now up and down Italy.

In the Italian countryside, the plight of the poor was certainly no better than in Rome, yet here too there were no 'peasants' revolts' in the 50s. Rather, more and more of the poor were being recruited, or forced, into the army for a long service abroad. Soldiers' wages, though meagre, did at least exist: the problem was that, once in the army, soldiers looked to their generals, not to any 'republican' values. What had 'the Republic' ever done for them anyway? Here, indeed, was a cause of crisis. It was not that Rome needed monarchy or 'stable government' in the late 50s because the scale of her empire had grown so big. Instead, tensions arose from the very conquests by which much of this empire was still being won. Generals rewarded their soldiers with spoils from their victories abroad and then won credit by proposals to settle them on plots of land and reward them on their return to Italy. The same generals fought on with the prolonged commands which were now being obtained by ignoring the Senate and going directly to the popular assemblies for an enabling law. A friendly tribune would then veto the proposals to recall an important general in subsequent years. The old two-headed monster, as the Roman constitution had evolved, found the limbs (the people) being used to cow what had once represented itself as the nourishing, sensible stomach (the Senate). If Polybius had lived to see it, he would have considered it proof of his theory: 'oligarchy', as morals changed, would decline into 'democracy' and then into 'monarchy'. But the 'democracy' was really no such thing.

The more the generals conquered, the more their riches grew, enabling them to pay more to their troops from their own gains. They could also pay back the massive loans through which they had bought their way to a command in the first place. In reply, senators should have increased the soldiers' pay from state funds and somehow paid publicly for their land-settlements. But even then, the sums needed would have been huge, and would have required much more than a new inheritance tax which, understandably, the rich detested.

The 'liberty' of legislation by the 'people' (few of whom actually voted) was thus manipulated to curb the 'liberty' of senators to do, and eventually say, whatever they wanted. But personal dignity, rank and esteem also exacerbated the problem. Once Pompey had set such a dazzling new standard after his conquests in Asia, his rivals could not regard themselves as his equal or superior unless they shone even more brightly. The values of their ancestors and the entire training of their careers encouraged them to compete with Pompey's new lustre. In Caesar's case, this 'dignity' was driving him to bring about the deaths of a million people in his Gallic provinces and to amass an increasingly incredible fortune. When Caesar returned to Rome he would not only be a consul. He would be able to triumph with the most astounding displays of gold, silver and booty. His debts would no longer be a problem. After plundering Gaul on an enormous scale he himself would be able to bribe and lend to people of influence at Rome, and eventually he would 'benefit' the entire city plebs. Although the plebs would never dismantle the republican system by themselves, they had acute discontents, and the man who gave all of them benefits would be almost unopposable. Meanwhile Caesar's soldiers were becoming hardened experts in warfare thanks to their years of practice at the Gauls' expense. He himself could pay them, and he would duly provide for them. If he won the consulship again, what might he not do for the urban plebs and for his troops, now his men of ten years' standing? Would he ever lay the office down? Opposition to one-man rule was the very lifeblood of republican values, and senators had certainly not become indifferent to it.

Despite the moralists' complaints, the gangs in the streets of Rome, the bribery and the fears of civil war did not signify an age of decadence. In the heart of Rome, the competition for glory was visible in the leaders' expensive public buildings. An entire new Forum was being paid for by Caesar at vast cost, rivalling the huge stone theatre which had already been paid for by Pompey. The city's architects were breaking new ground thanks to these new challenges. Above all, the years of tension were to be critical years for Latin thought and literature. Scholarship, philosophy and even the study of religious traditions blossomed under the spectre of the political crises. So did practical law. More interestingly, the superb poems of Catullus ranged from love-poetry to mythical narrative and personal invective, transcending their fine Greek models. At greater length, Lucretius' fine poem *On the Nature of Things* expressed an Epicurean philosophy of the world and society and the irrelevance to them both of the traditional gods. This masterpiece was probably composed when the crisis had just broken into open Civil War, between 49 and 48.[5] By the 50s most of the major participants in Roman political life had studied Greek thought themselves. Even Crassus had a taste for Greek philosophy, as did

Marcus Brutus, a man who had named features in his garden after features of ancient Sparta. There was also a sharpened interest in history. Works on chronology tried to interrelate Roman and Greek events and from the mid–50s onwards examples from Greek history became more prominent in Cicero's writings. Teachers (to his disgust) were even encouraging their pupils in oratory to study the historian Thucydides' horribly difficult Greek speeches.[6] When Civil War broke out, the examples of famous Greeks from the past would become even more immediate to those who became swept up in it.

Above all, there was a frankness of speech, a sharpness of wit and a magnificent scope for oratory. The wit and frankness still live for us in Cicero's letters, in sayings of Caesar or his rivals and even in letters from Cicero's lesser but educated friend, young Caelius, who favoured Caesar but wrote so vividly to Cicero on affairs at Rome in the late 50s. Here, we best catch what the 'liberty' of speech and thought really meant to such people. It is no coincidence that this age of great court-scenes, great addresses to the Senate and to popular meetings is also the supreme age of Roman oratory.

Not that the glitter was all male, either. Young Caelius was a fine dancer, but so was the remarkable lady Sempronia, whom even her critics admired for her wit, her wide reading and her personal culture.[7] No wife of a classical Athenian could have compared with such a character. She was only one of several remarkable women who are known to us in the late Republic: Clodia, the desirable sister of Clodius, was probably the inspiration for Catullus' best love-poems, while Fulvia, Sempronia's daughter, was to be the wife of three great husbands, including Clodius and then Mark Antony. Fulvia was the woman whose laments for the dead Clodius had fired a Roman crowd in the Forum. The austere ideals of the wool-working 'traditional' housewife were not to the liking of such bold spirits. They had lovers, they joked, they even advised. In autumn 52 BC, as the crisis loomed, one of the consuls was honoured with a party in which his house was turned into a brothel and two high-society ladies (one of them supposedly Fulvia, the other a former wife of Pompey) were said to have serviced the guests.[8]

For centuries, the Roman Republic had bent, regrouped and survived new tensions. It had outlived the proud Scipio, Marius even, and the ruthless conservative Sulla. The latest tensions went deep, but could it not survive both Caesar and Pompey too? Huge risks and a swathe of wonderfully unpredictable decisions would have to be taken before Caesar could ever dominate. Even then, the Republic was not dead, although

Caesar's example was essential to its subsequent extinction by his successors. Out in Gaul, while the guests in Rome enjoyed their brothel-party, Caesar was beset with difficulties. His previous Gallic conquests had turned out to be not so secure after all; he still had to pacify them and he had to establish when his provincial command would end. Was it to end in 50 or 49, and if so, precisely when in the year? Could he run on, with the help of friendly tribunes' vetoes, until he was elected consul in absence? Back in Rome, with Clodius gone, even Cicero had begun to hope that he, perhaps, might have a second consulship too. And after the crisis of Clodius' death, the elections did work again: there were consuls, noble ones, for 51 and then for 50, and for once, we hear nothing about bribery.

Through the fragmented mirror of Cicero's letters, we can follow the fascinating steps towards confrontation. In 52 Pompey was still 'friendly' to Caesar and Caesar was still said to have retained Pompey as heir to his will. By June 51 the question of a successor to Caesar in Gaul was to be raised explicitly in the Senate; on 29 September, however, it was decreed that discussions of the matter would not begin until 1 March 50. Remarks made by Pompey begin to make clear that he had a problem now with Caesar. The biggest problem, then and now, was when exactly Caesar's command would expire.

The probable answer is that there were two separate dates, one in March 49 for 'Gaul this side of the Alps and Illyricum', and one in March 50 for 'Gaul beyond the Alps'. The former, eventually, was the command which Caesar proposed he should retain, but his rivals were not allowing it. By September 50 the articulate Caelius was writing that the 'love affair' between Caesar and Pompey had broken up and that there would soon be a 'gladiatorial' fight between the two of them.[9] Nonetheless, in November the senators still voted optimistically (by 370 to 22) that both Pompey and Caesar should lay down their respective armies. Overwhelmingly, the senators simply wanted peace. But as if to stiffen Pompey, the consul of the year went out of the city and put a sword in Pompey's hands.

During persistent meetings in early January 49 the senators heard the contents of letters in which Caesar offered, arguably correctly, to retain only 'Gaul this side of the Alps and Illyricum'.[10] But the noble consul Lentulus had the motion proposed that Caesar should leave his army by a fixed date. It was then blocked by the veto of tribunes: one of them was a loyal supporter of Caesar, now in his mid-thirties, Marcus Antonius ('Mark Antony'). So on 7 January Lentulus proposed the 'ultimate decree' against the vetoing tribunes. Mark Antony and his colleagues promptly fled to Caesar, ever the 'people's friend'. Caesar was already at hand on 'this side' of the Alps and had only a few of his troops with him. But he did not hesitate. He decided to attack across the river-boundary into Italy, a frank initiation of a civil war. On 10 January he watched gladiators at exercise, bathed and dressed for dinner. Quietly, he slipped away from his guests and by a prearranged, roundabout route, reached the river Rubicon where he paused. He thought, it is said, of the enormous evils which would follow for mankind if he crossed and of the reputation of the crossing among posterity. 'The die is cast,' he said theatrically, quoting the Greek poet Menander, and then he crossed the river.[11] He had already sent a small party of armed commanders ahead of him, but he was right that his crossing was the moment to dramatize. It was also a moment for taking auspices and for religious respect: Caesar dedicated a herd of horses to the river and set them free to run where they pleased. Five years later it would be these horses, men said, who would give him a very different omen.[12]

THE FATAL DICTATOR

Here you have a man who was ambitious to be the king of the Roman people, and he achieved it. If anyone says that this desire is morally right, he is mad, for he is approving the death of the laws and liberty and is thinking that their hideous and detestable oppression is glorious.

Cicero, De Officiis 3.83 (late October 44 BC)

Utterly deplorable! According to Gaius Matius, our problems are insoluble: 'for if a man of such genius as Caesar could not find a way out, who will find one now?' In short, he was saying that everything has had it— I am inclined to agree, but he said it with glee . . .

Cicero, Letters to Atticus 14.1.1, in April 44 BC,
three weeks after Caesar's murder

AFTER CROSSING THE RUBICON, Caesar moved south with exceptional speed, helped by minimal resistance on his route through Italy. It was not so that he was profiting from coolness between the Italian towns and Rome, as if it had been persisting since the Social Wars of the 80s. Rather, he had prepared his ground. For some while he had been sending funds from Gaul to supporters who were to apply them to local sympathies in Italy, here with a benefaction, there with new buildings. Back in the autumn of 50 young Caelius had already written unforgettably to Cicero that in political conflicts men should take the more honourable course unless matters came to a fight: then they 'should take the stronger course and identify the better with the safer'.[1] In Italy, people agreed and received Caesar because they were terrified. Their only precedent for this sort of civil war was Sulla's, a dreadful one. The peasantry did not want to be conscripted to fight for Pompey and the property owners feared for their estates and 'darling villas', as Cicero acidly commented, 'and their lovely money', putting their 'fishponds' before freedom.

Caesar encouraged them by keeping up his campaign of spin. He emphasized his 'clemency' and proved it by a readiness to pardon enemies. He was the defender of 'liberty', he said, especially the 'liberty' of the Roman people's tribunes. His enemies had just harassed these tribunes with the 'ultimate decree'. Even Sulla, Caesar coolly observed, had left the tribunes a right of 'intercession' (arguably, Sulla had not left them the right of veto, but only the right to intercede against the harassment of individuals). His enemies (he said) were a minority, 'the Faction'. Caesar would have nothing to learn from modern political advisers on presentation. But he also emphasized his concern for his own 'dignity', his rank and esteem, which were driving him to stand again as consul. 'But what is dignity', Cicero aptly commented, 'if there is no honour?'[2]

If Caesar championed 'liberty of the people', Pompey championed 'liberty of the Senate'. Recently the towns of Italy had celebrated Pompey's recovery from an illness and perhaps this recent flattery misled him. In fact, they had faked it, in Cicero's view. For Pompey's hopes of support in Italy were far too optimistic. In mid-January he and many senators had to abandon Rome and head south to Brundisium where they waited until 17 March. Meanwhile, offers of compromise multiplied. If Pompey would demobilize and go off to govern in Spain, Caesar would retain only the Dalmatian coast and keep out of Italy. Pompey even offered him a second consulship and a triumph, but he refused Caesar's offers of a personal interview and did not state that he would disband his troops too. Mediators, including Cicero, had real hopes of peace, but the offers and counter-offers were yet more 'spin'. Neither side could really demobilize or climb down. Pompey's abandonment of Rome made a very bad impression, but he was said to be defending it, just as the Athenians had abandoned Athens to 'defend' it against the Persian tyranny in 480 BC. His aim was to set up in Greece and surround Caesar in Italy. He could gather help from foreign princes and squeeze away Caesar's popular support, not least by interrupting grain imports. So in mid-March he crossed by sea to regroup in north-west Greece and summon foreign help.

The Civil War imposed choices which are enduring examples in the history of all politics: their results changed world history. It caught many prominent Romans with conflicting allegiances and it tested principles which others had long professed. We can still follow them unforgettably in the surviving letters to and from Cicero who had returned to Italy in

December 50, hoping initially for the honour of a triumph for his minor victory in his minor province in the East. Events swept that hope away, and Cicero found himself being leaned on as a mediator by Caesar, who was predictably so amicable to him and others around him. Cicero was certainly no fighter, but he was still a great speaker and a senior figure who would lend respectability to Caesar's cause. It also so happened that he had borrowed hugely from Caesar to finance his houses and his career and had not yet repaid. But he refused Caesar's direct offers at interview and wrote: 'I think Caesar is not pleased with me. But I was pleased with myself, which is more than I have been for a long time.'[3] Caesar's supporters were a frightful collection of men on the make, unprincipled time-servers, the 'army of the underworld', as Cicero and his friend Atticus so wonderfully described them.[4] But the interview with Caesar ended ominously: 'if Caesar could not get my advice, he said he would take the advice of anyone he could, and stop at nothing.'[5]

He certainly did not: on reaching Rome in April 49 Caesar waited outside the city-boundary, correctly, but then crossed it and threatened to kill one of the tribunes who had, equally correctly, denied him the money in the Treasury. His next step was less expected: a quick march west to Spain, to break Pompey's possible hold on the province. He succeeded (not without trouble), returned to Rome and was appointed dictator (for a brief eleven days), and then elected consul for 48. It sounds easy, but it was not. He had repeatedly promised bonuses to his troops since reaching the Rubicon, but although he had booty in Gaul, he did not have the cash at hand with which to pay. On returning to Italy, some of his troops actually mutinied, and not for the last time, either. In Rome, there was no magistrate left to preside over an election to the consulship, so Caesar had to be made dictator in order to preside over the election of himself. He then had to cross to Greece from Brindisi in order to cope with Pompey's army. It took months to contrive a safe departure by sea and even then he was running huge risks.

In superb letters, we can watch Cicero meanwhile wavering and wondering where he could possibly go. His close friend Atticus was going to stay on in Rome, rich, uninvolved and artfully neutral. Cicero's womenfolk were there too and, so far, Caesar had not been too radical. He had not cancelled existing debts or systematically redistributed land. The land of some of his enemies had passed to some of Caesar's friends, but at least it had been auctioned or sold to them. And yet Caesar was a manifest enemy of Cicero's ideal of senatorial liberty. Should I go somewhere neutral, Cicero wondered? Should I go to Malta? Should I try Sicily or take a military command in Africa? Basically, he hated the option of war and the destruction it would bring.

On the other side, Pompey did stand for the 'liberty' of the Senate and he had done Cicero one great favour: in 57 he had helped to restore him from exile. Yet, as so often, Cicero was not entirely deceived. If Pompey returned from Greece, he would attack Italy and allow the most dreadful reprisals. In the end, Pompey too would want to dominate (though at least he was older and would last less long). Obliged by a past favour and believing in what Pompey used as spin, Cicero crossed to join him in Greece. When he eventually arrived he found Pompey's supporters there to be awful: 'their talk was so bloodthirsty I shuddered at the thought of victory.' They were already carving up their jobs for the future and 'all those great men were deep in debt. Why go on? The only good thing was the cause itself.'⁶ So Cicero resorted to his unfailing verbal wit. He made his 'disapproval of Pompey's plans obvious, but did not refrain from jokes at the foreigners who were come to help'⁷ (Pompey had called on help from 'barbarian' dynasts from Asia and even from up by the Danube). 'Cicero went round camp darkly without a smile, but he made others laugh in spite of themselves.'⁸

When Caesar eventually landed in north-west Greece he should have been defeated promptly on two occasions. Instead, the second occasion became his crucial victory near Pharsalus (in Thessaly) on 9 August 48 BC, in which his supporter Mark Antony commanded the left wing with distinction. Caesar's agents, meanwhile, had gone south to woo Athens. They had even gone through the motions of selling the obstinate Megarians as slaves and then freeing them, a sure way (still) to the neighbouring Athenians' hearts. Unprepared for defeat, Pompey fled and eventually set foot on the coast of Egypt by the eastern arm of the Nile Delta. On arrival he was killed on the advice of a Greek, a rhetor from the island of Chios. Years later, in 130, Hadrian would rediscover the simple tomb of Pompey; 'the man', Cicero wrote coolly, 'whom I knew to be honest, decent and serious'.⁹ Devious and inscrutable were also apt words for him. Hadrian cleared away the sand, restored the statues which Pompey's family had put up (and others, later, had defaced) and wrote verses for his tomb. 'How lowly a tomb . . . ', they began. Hadrian did not understand the legal and personal complexities which we have been following.

On 2 October 48 Caesar arrived, to be presented with Pompey's head which had been cut off for him. He then entered Alexandria and became involved in a fateful strife in the Ptolemaic royal house. Since the previous king's death in 51, the kingdom had been bequeathed by will to

50. Silver denarius, Rome: portrait of Julius Caesar (*obverse*) and his supposed ancestress Venus (*reverse*), 44 BC, his final year.

Rome. Caesar now settled an outstanding feud by upholding the joint rule of the previous king's young son and his slightly older daughter. As Ptolemies, this brother and sister were already married to each other, but the sister, Cleopatra, arrived in Caesar's presence, hidden in a linen bedding-sack. Aged twenty-one, she was to fascinate the thrice-married Caesar. His wife Calpurnia was back in Rome, but he was not yet a love-sated man past his prime.[10] Love now accompanied Rome's hand in Egypt.

News of the victory at Pharsalus reached Rome by October 48 and caused Caesar, the consul in absence, to be named 'dictator' for a whole year. Yet for another nine months Rome was not even to see him: was he dead? In fact, he became caught up in a savage war in Alexandria which was begun by two discontented Alexandrian Greek courtiers: during it, his troops began a fire which did irreparable damage to Alexandria's royal bookstores and libraries, perhaps Caesar's most permanent ill-effect. It was his turn, now, to depend on 'barbarian' help: Jewish soldiers arrived to help him, and in return Caesar would be a firm supporter of Jews and their status. Eventually, peace was restored and in spring 47 it does seem that he could relax by boating up the Nile with Egypt's newly secured queen, who was so sweet-voiced and accomplished in conversation. She had already become pregnant. In the summer she bore a son and called him Caesarion, a name which Caesar did not repudiate. Caesarion's birth-date and parentage continue to be questioned, but when he appears in Cicero's surviving letters in spring 44 he is not described as if his origin was disputed at the time. Julius Caesar had no other surviving children by anyone else.

Even after the death of Pompey, Caesar had to fight three more wars to assert his dominance. They are ample evidence that there was nothing inevitable about his supremacy or about the 'fall' of the Roman Republic. The first war was over quickly in July 47, a victory in Asia over Mithridates' son: it was so quick that it was here that Caesar said 'I came, I saw, I conquered' (at Zela). Then he returned to Rome, to confront yet another mutiny among troops who had been left in Italy. Here his deputy, Mark Antony, had not proved a safe pair of hands, quite apart from his carryings-on with a notorious courtesan, a woman whose presence at dinner was denounced by Cicero, a fellow guest, who was both shocked and intrigued.[11] In late December 47 Caesar was off again, this time to north Africa against another major pocket of republican resistance. Again, he ran huge risks by landing with far fewer troops against some fourteen enemy legions. After three separate victories, his constant republican opponent, Cato, killed himself. Ever the man of principle, Cato first read Plato, then took a sword and succeeded at the second attempt.

Back in Rome in spring 46 BC, news of this failed 'last stand' seemed to mark a decisive turn: Caesar was voted the first cluster of what were to proliferate as exceptional honours. A chariot and a statue with a globe were to be set up on the Capitol hill, and most remarkably an inscription on the statue was to call him 'demi-god', in the very heart of Rome. The senators, perhaps, were outrunning even Caesar's expectations. More mundanely, Caesar was voted another dictatorship, but this time for ten whole years. How was he going to rule? He was not going to legislate for a whole new system in one transforming package. He had very few changes to make to Rome's existing system of justice. Instead, laws would come out one by one, and they were to be reasonable enough. The calendar, hopelessly out of line, was to be reformed. Debts were certainly not to be cancelled (many people owed big sums to Caesar, including Cicero), but there was to be a suspension of rent, but only up to a modest limit and for one year. In Italy, debtors were finding that their security for their loans, their land, was collapsing in value in the crisis: a new ruling, therefore, obliged creditors to accept land at its pre-war value. The harsh old rules of bankruptcy were also moderated. This sort of legislation was very far from the red-blooded abolitions of debt in previous Greek history, and other populists would try to go further. In Caesar's Rome, however, the populist groups which had been the focus of Clodius in the 50s were restricted: the people's clubs and 'colleges' would not now be allowed unless they were licensed (few were) and the numbers who were eligible for grain doles were steeply cut.

Of course there were to be new settlements for veteran soldiers and also, again, for the urban poor. But they were to be settlements abroad for the most part, not on land in use in Italy: here, there were plans only to drain the Pomptine marshes and make a new fertile area available for colonists. In Caesar's new towns abroad, freedmen (unusually) would be able to hold civic office. They would pay, perhaps, for the honour, but they would also be alert to potential trade and profit, not least in sites like Corinth or Carthage, places which Caesar proposed to resettle. Caesar as city-founder is the real heir to the commercial alertness attested by some of the settlements made in Asia by Alexander the Great.

For Italy, there was the grant of citizenship to the north, 'beyond the Po'; there was even a proposal that at least one-third of the herdsmen on farms for grazing should be free-born. In the south of Italy, especially, big landowners had tended to use slaves to tend their huge herds of livestock. This practice had forced the free peasantry out of a widespread job and had also assured the landowners of a useful source of slave-recruits when-ever they needed a private gang of armed retainers. There was a broader social vision in all this legislation by Caesar, as in the detailed laws on 'clean government' or even in the recent reduction of Asia's tribute by one-third; the reduction was made possible by eliminating the hated con-tractors at Rome who used to bid for the right to collect the tribute and make a profit. It all befitted a man of the highest nobility who had served for so long outside Rome and looked back on it with a wider view. Caesar also looked down on his political rivals, people who were really rather common in comparison with his patrician self. Yet his supporters had to be honoured, too, and so the Senate was to be increased to 900 members, a vast body: many of the new intake seemed outrageous to the members from traditional families.

Of popular reactions, there was now no doubt. In Caesar's absence, with grain scarce, there had been discontent, but on his return the people were to be treated to the most amazing of all Roman triumphs, in a cele-bration of four victories at once. For four days in August 46 great proces-sions passed through Rome, including a statue of Cleopatra beside Caesar's own ancestral goddess Venus (it survived in Rome for at least two centuries). There were the usual jokes by followers in order to keep the tri-umphing general's feet on the ground, about his supposed sex with King Nicomedes (it had to be an old joke, because there had been no homosex-uality in Caesar's life then or since) or, more ominously, about Caesar as 'bad boy' and 'king'. At the games afterwards, there were animal hunts and even Rome's first sighting of a giraffe. After the concluding banquet on the fourth day, Caesar, still in slippers, was escorted from his newly planned Forum by a popular crowd and even by elephants bearing torches. It was all hugely expensive, and when a few of his soldiers protested, they were put to death: the heads of two of them were nailed up by priests on the 'royal house' in the Forum.[12] So it was as well that there were to be massive payments for the soldiers (an entire lifetime's pay) and even a payment for every single citizen. Loot from the provinces was paying for them, not least the plunder which had been collected from Spain and Asia in the Civil War of the past two years. The spending was to exceed even the final year of Alexander the Great, a tribute to Caesar's massive plundering.

More permanently, there were to be great new buildings, a temple to Mars, the biggest ever, the huge new Forum (never finished in his lifetime), a temple to mother Venus (dedicated in September), a statue of Caesar on horseback in front of it in which both Caesar and his beloved horse (now fourteen years old) were modelled in the likenesses of Alexander and the great Bucephalas. So much, at last, for Caesar's alleged tears of regret over Alexander's glory in Cadiz in 69 BC. When the Venus temple was dedicated, Caesar celebrated two evocative rituals: a 'Troy Game' on horseback for young participants, supposedly tracing back to his ancestor Aeneas, and funeral games for his daughter Julia, who had died back in 54.[13] In her honour, gladiators fought in the Forum: the 'Troy Game's' riders may perhaps have been led by a young unknown quantity, his adopted great-nephew, Octavian. Nobody could have imagined that this boy, some twenty years later, would repeat such games for himself.

Even so, for Cicero there were still flickering hopes that a republic would somehow be restored. As a dictator for a fixed term, Caesar was appointed nominally to 'settle the *res publica*' (the 'state' or the 'republic'). In the Senate, during the summer, there had been a sudden wonderful pardon for noble Marcus Marcellus, the man who as consul in 50 BC had insisted on Caesar's return from Gaul. Cicero was cheered by the event and hailed Caesar's 'justice', but a pardon, like all Caesar's power, depended on one man's 'will, or shall I say "whim"?'[14] Senators had grovelled to receive it. In fact, the beneficiary of the pardon was killed in Greece before he ever enjoyed it, and some said his death was on Caesar's orders. As Cicero makes plain at the time, Caesar was still afraid of conspirators against himself. When a mime-writer, Laberius, put a play on with the words, 'Citizens, we have lost liberty', Caesar preferred to do nothing against him.[15]

In December 46 trouble did break out, but it was in Spain, not in the Senate. Pompey had left two brave sons there and one of them, Gnaeus, led a major rebellion in Spain, forcing Caesar into one more Civil War which was probably his most dangerous. It was fought in rough terrain with difficult supplies and determined enemies. On 17 March 45 BC Caesar won decisively at Munda, although he had to rally his troops personally, jumping from his horse and shaming them into standing firm; he had really thought it was his last hour. It proved the last, instead, for Gnaeus Pompey, although the other son of Pompey, Sextus, was left at large. Caesar never imagined that Sextus would have a political future, so he left him, settled veterans in Spain and returned to Rome.

In his absence, meanwhile, it is Cicero's difficulties which we know best, not just his admirable sense of a real loss of freedom but difficulties, too, in his family. After quarrels, Cicero had divorced his long-standing wife, Terentia; he had always disliked his latest son-in-law, Dolabella, and now the bounder was putting up a statue to Cicero's blackest enemy, Clodius. In the years since returning to Italy, Cicero had been struggling to pay his beloved daughter Tullia's proper dowry (for her third marriage); he had been reduced to handing it over in instalments. Now his daughter was wanting a divorce from Dolabella anyway. Friends, meanwhile, found Cicero a second wife, Publilia, a rich young woman: his first wife said the marriage was all for sex. Then Tullia died after childbirth, throwing him into extreme grief. He had loved her so dearly; he even planned to build her a temple (not a tomb) on ground which is now near the Vatican in Rome. But Julius Caesar took the ground first. Then Cicero's second wife Publilia turned out to be a mistake, not least for the reason that she was jealous of his grief and love for his daughter. So Cicero backed quickly out of the cul-de-sac and wisely divorced her.

Through his letters we can follow identifiable stages of his extreme 'grieving process' for Tullia. We can also read a classic letter to him, sent by the politician and lawyer Sulpicius Rufus.[16] It is an extraordinary text, which is at first sight deeply moving: it expresses Sulpicius' awareness, while sailing past the coastline of Greece, of the disasters which had brought many of the old cities in Greece so low. Tullia, he reminds Cicero, was only one person, whereas these cities had lost so many. But in fact, this 'consolation' is very far from what we would nowadays expect. Sulpicius and Cicero agree that the real tragedy is the contemporary death of the Republic. Young Tullia was lucky, we read, to have died first, and the loss of the Republic is so much more regrettable than the loss of just one daughter. There could be no more vivid instance of a political Roman's priorities and the balance between male freedom and domestic loss.

Books, at least, persisted for Cicero, his honoured, beloved companions. At Rome, Caesar was planning to build the first public library (having burned down so much of Alexandria's) and to appoint the hugely learned Varro as its librarian, although Varro, Pompey's assistant, had opposed Caesar in Spain in 49. In his grief, Cicero turned to writing a spate of new books of his own, on the gods, on aspects of religion, on the history of oratory and above all on philosophy (as the creator of a new Latin vocabulary for Greek philosophy) and on the sceptical theories to which he inclined. His letters of these months remind us of his extraordinary mental range, but also of his love for his various country villas and their woods and grounds (one, even, had an area called the Academy): he had a real affinity here with the eighteenth-century English gentlemen who would so admire him. His philosophy was more encyclopedic than original, and none of it would ever have been written if he could have had the continuing thrill of a free political career, speaking, attacking and being his 'own man'. But his first philosophy dialogue, with its warnings against sex and the quest for riches, was to inflame, four centuries later, an unexpected young reader, St Augustine.

In April 45 news of the victory in Spain reached Rome. It promoted a further, crucial flood of honours. Not only was the message timed to arrive just before the city's ancient festival of the Parilia, with its links to Romulus and Rome's foundation which Caesar, therefore, could exploit. The Senate decreed that Caesar should be called 'Liberator' and a temple to Liberty should be built.[17] It is a cardinal moment in the history of freedom, for no Roman had ever been entitled 'Liberator' before. It flatteringly recalled Caesar's claims at the very start of the Civil War and ascribed 'freedom' to a man who had yet again killed honest Roman citizens in battle. His statue was even to stand on the Capitol beside the founders of the Republic. But then the 'liberated' senators went on to call him 'Father of the Fatherland', to vote him crowns, fifty days of supplications and, above all, two extreme divine honours. His ivory statue was to be wheeled in procession with those of the gods, and another statue, set in a temple, was to be inscribed 'To the Invincible God'. The inscription had strong overtones of Alexander the Great.[18] Even so, in summer 45 one shrewd noble Roman, Cicero's equal in the writing of moral philosophy, did still think that the Republic would be restored. This nobleman, Marcus Brutus, had benefited, so far, from Caesar and he was to be a praetor for the next year. Even in 45 freedom of speech still existed away from Caesar's table: in his work on oratory, Cicero had just hinted that Brutus should live up to his noble ancestors. It was a highly charged remark.

Atticus, Cicero's friend, had recently helped Brutus to construct his family tree. Brutus had then had it painted in the main room of his house, the house he called his 'Parthenon', in honour of Athens. On its wall, he could look daily at a genealogy which went back (it was said) to the two great tyrant-slayers in the earliest history of Rome.[19] One of them, also called Brutus, had killed proud King Tarquin and had then also killed his own sons for favouring Tarquin. This famous Brutus then became the first consul in the first year of the Republic which replaced kingship; his statue, long before Caesar's, had stood in honour on the Capitol. This heritage was not lost on his descendant. Brutus had represented it on coins, probably struck in 55/4 BC, with the word 'Liberty' too. Caesar was known to have had a sexual affair with Brutus' mother, but this private matter was not behind Brutus' growing discontent. The roots were political: and, as a young man, whose father was dead (killed by Pompey), Brutus had been brought up as Cato's protégé. He had philosophic interests, and in summer 45 he remarried: significantly his new wife was Porcia, the widowed daughter of the arch-republican, Cato.

While curbing political freedom, Caesar had legislated, inevitably, on that feared phantom, personal luxury. Inspectors were even said to be checking on people's dinner-parties and on food-markets and to have banned pearls and extravagant clothes. The law was not totally ignored, because we find Cicero remarking that cooks were learning to prepare new vegetarian dishes and that the obligatory new diet of roast vegetables was giving him stomach ache.[20] In October 45 Caesar did celebrate a triumph, his second, for the victories in Spain. But many resented it, as it was for victories over Romans in Civil War, not legal objects for a triumph. For the most memorable insight into what Caesar now represented, we must look to Cicero. In the festive season of mid-December 45 Caesar came to pay a 'social call' on his old friend. He arrived at Cicero's villa with about 2,000 soldiers and attendants, all of whom had to be dined too. The two of them then talked pleasantly enough over dinner, as if they were 'just human beings'.[21] But they talked not a word of politics, the lifeblood of Cicero's previous existence. Instead, they talked only of literature. It was a restriction unimaginable in their previous years together. 'But my guest', Cicero wrote afterwards, 'was not the sort to whom one says, "Do please come again when you are back". Once is enough.' At one point on the way back, he noticed, the entire troop of soldiers moved up and rode on either side of Caesar, to guard him.

At Rome, Caesar was prepared now to accept a continuing stream of honours without precedent, sacrifices on his birthday (a divine honour for kings in the Greek world), annual vows for his welfare and 'sacro-sanctity' for his person, like a tribune. He was old now, by ancient standards, and his health was not good, but nonetheless his next plan was widely recognized. It would be more of what he had always done best, military campaigning, three years of it, to win glory in the East against the Parthians, old Crassus' recent undoing. There were even rumours that he would then swing round by the Black Sea and return, a conquering champion, by the river Danube through Dacia. In cities in the Greek East, Caesar had already been given 'honours equal to those of the gods'. Other Romans before him had received these honours in the Greek world, and like Caesar they had met local kings on their travels. But unlike them, Caesar had actually brought a queen with him (Cleopatra was in the city, where she had 'diplomatic business'). Was Caesar planning to be a king (like his ancestors) and to be worshipped outright as a god with formal cult? Honours were still showering on him, perhaps purely so as to see what he would refuse. In early 44 we are told that he was voted a cult in which Antony, his fellow consul, would be his priest. His house was to have an honorary pediment like a temple; the Senate is even said to have called him 'Jupiter Julius'. Proposals for a cult of the living Caesar thus seem to be a certainty, but the ultimate horror, his willingness to take the title of king, remains uncertain. Certainly, elements of 'royalty' were proposed for him: a golden throne (but to be left empty, and in the theatre only), a golden crown (like a triumphing general). In late January crowds called out 'King!' as he returned with a solemn ovation from a festival celebration: he corrected them.[22] In mid-February 44 crowds gathered in Rome for the religious festival of the Luperci, when young men ran naked to 'touch' women with rods and assist their future fertility. While running with them, Mark Antony and others did offer Caesar a royal diadem, only to see him throw it ostentatiously away. The 'refusal', perhaps, was planned to allay traditionalists' doubts, much to the plebs' regret. But there was no doubting one thing: by mid-February 44 Caesar had accepted another 'dictatorship', his fourth, but this time it was defined as one for life. So much, then, for the Republic's future. Not unjustly, Caesar was believed to have called the Republic 'a mere name without body or form', and to have criticized Sulla for not knowing his political ABC, because Sulla had resigned the dictatorship which he had achieved.[23] There was no question, now, of Caesar restoring the senators' liberty. Here was a clear turning point.

With hindsight, various omens and warnings were remembered, but there had never been any shortage of them. Up by the Rubicon, however, the horses whom Caesar had left free were said to be refusing to eat.[24] How right the horses were: Caesar had even dismissed his bodyguards in Rome. It was not that he was courting death, surely: it was a confident sign that he was supreme. When the senators had come to honour him extravagantly, he failed (as a dictator could) to rise to greet them: deep down, he felt they were common little men, many of whom were his own creations. However, he promptly regretted his rudeness and alleged, wrongly, that he had been struck by stomach problems at the time.

The lifelong dictatorship, the imminent cult: these signs were intolerable to those senators who minded deeply about liberty. One was the impetuous Cassius, praetor for the year (with Brutus) but a proven soldier as well as a man with Epicurean philosophic interests: his ancestors, like those of Brutus, had once issued coins with the caption 'Liberty'. He was also Brutus' brother-in-law, married to his half-sister. Other men, inevitably, felt personal slights or disappointments, sustained in a system of honour which increasingly depended on Caesar's 'grace and favour'. There was also the unresolved question of kingship. It was said to be about to come up again, on the strength of a Sibylline oracle which apparently stated that Parthia could only be conquered by a 'king'.[25] On the Ides of March 44, amid routine warnings, Caesar went nonetheless to a meeting of the Senate, only to confront an insistent group of senators, among whom was Marcus Brutus. Sixty senators or so were in the plot, but no more than five or six of them could have rushed at Caesar and stabbed him, while his fellow consul Mark Antony was detained outside. Caesar's body fell, streaming blood. Twenty-three wounds were later noted on it, and the conspirators left him to lie till nightfall. It is probably only a legend that Caesar's last words were 'You too, Brutus?', but it is probably true that Brutus called out the name of the one senator whom the conspirators had excluded from the plot for fear that he was too indiscreet: Cicero! By hints, however, and in private letters, Cicero had contrived, most admirably, to protest throughout at Caesar's despotism. Now Caesar was dead, and he lay in the portico adjoining Pompey's Theatre, where the Senate had been about to meet, within yards of a statue of Pompey himself.

LIBERATION BETRAYED

As for the boy Caesar (Octavian), his natural worth and manliness are extraordinary. I only pray that I may be able to govern and hold him when he is in the full flush of honours and favour as I have done so far. That is more difficult, it is true, but still I do not despair. The young man is persuaded (most of all, through me) that our survival is his business . . .

Cicero to Marcus Brutus, *c.* 21 April 43 BC

THE EVENTS AFTER CAESAR'S MURDER are the supreme chapter in the story of freedom in ancient Rome. The days and months are wonderfully evoked for us by partisan survivors, Cicero's contemporary letters and speeches. Cicero's aims failed, but he was not always deceived. Despite moments of fear and retreat, he seldom fell below the level of events, although he was sixty-two years old. His faults were the same as always, and venially fatal: his wit and polemic against other big men's failings and his habit of seeing events as he himself wished them to be.

In Cicero's view, the golden chance was lost: as soon as Caesar lay dead, the Senate should have been called to the scene and the people summoned at once to liberty. In fact, like many tyrant-slayers in Greek history, the conspirators did nothing more: one of them hoisted a 'cap of freedom' on a spear and the corpse was left lying, 'lawfully slain' and fit only for throwing into the Tiber.[1] Instead, three slaves took it home. The surviving consul, Mark Antony, had fled, but that very evening, it seems, Antony's plans were already being feared as the 'very worst, the most treacherous'.[2] Above the Forum, noble Brutus had addressed an audience on the Capitol hill, but his speech, in Cicero's view, was too elegant and too short of fire.

When Alexander the Great died his officers faked his 'last plans' to en-sure that they were publicly rejected. When Caesar died Mark Antony took what he claimed were Caesar's plans and two days later, on the 17th, artfully urged reconciliation at a meeting of the Senate. Caesar's murder-ers, he proposed, were not to be avenged: that, at least, was a relief. Cae-sar's plans, however, and his actions, past, present and future, were all to be ratified. It was a crucial moment. So many of the senators owed their rank and prospects to Caesar's recent decisions that the measure was sure to be passed. In case they hesitated, armed soldiers, Caesar's veterans, were already present to clarify their minds. So the senators agreed. They also agreed that Caesar's body should have a funeral, a public funeral in-deed, on the urging of his father-in-law.

'Liberty', Cicero's option, was beset with difficulties. Almost all the le-gions across the world were loyal to Julius Caesar; many of his veterans were still at large, waiting to be paid off; vast spoils, booty and revenues could be dispensed from his personal sources by his political successors; Rome's common people plainly preferred Caesar to yet more 'concord' and 'liberty' for the upper classes. 'Things which Caesar would never have done or allowed', Cicero would soon remark, 'are now being brought forward from his forged "plans"', the papers which Caesar had left and which Antony now controlled and, no doubt, doctored.[3] Yet Cae-sar's armies, the money and the people's loyalties made it hard to turn the clock back as if he had not existed.

On the Ides of March, Cicero would write, they had left a fine 'ban-quet' unfinished: there were still the 'leftovers', Mark Antony. How right he proved to be: if only Antony had been killed too, the Republic really could have had a good chance of restoration. But he was not to be carved up and although Cicero wanted him killed, he was a consul still in office with an obvious technique of appeal. On 20 March he gave a taste of it. Caesar's will was opened and he was found to have left his gardens to the public and a cash sum to each citizen at Rome. It was time for Caesar's public funeral, an occasion which Cicero rightly dreaded. After the body had been brought up through the Forum with an escort of actors and singers, Antony raised the tempo by addressing the assembled people in the Forum. There are two main versions of what he said to those 'friends, Romans, countrymen', as Shakespeare memorably puts it, who lent him their ears. One, which many scholars have preferred, is that he said only a few words after a proclamation by a herald. Another, which arguably goes back to a contemporary, is more compelling and builds on what we can infer from Cicero.[4] The body on its ivory couch was set in a gilded shrine modelled on the shrine of mother Venus. After speaking of Caesar's deeds, Antony began to work with the rising emotions of the crowd (the 'pathetic praise', surely, on which Cicero comments). He chanted a lament of his own and began to weep. He held up Caesar's bloodstained toga on a spear; as feelings rose, he then displayed a wax model of Caesar's wounded corpse. Songs of lament are said to have followed from the crowd, in which Caesar himself appeared to be speaking. Evidently, Antony had mobilized actors and theatre-groups to orchestrate the occasion, people who are such an important element in crowd-scenes in Rome. This staged dialogue with the crowd caused them to erupt. Caesar's body had been supposed to be taken off to the Campus Martius, but it was carried by the people up to the Capitol, turned back by the priests and then cremated in the Forum by popular action. There was even an attempt to burn the houses of the 'Liberators'. The people's potential had been stirred, a warning to Antony's opponents.

For the moment, there was an obstacle. Caesar's plans had been upheld, but he had left the command of northern Italy to one of the men who had then murdered him (Decimus, not Marcus, Brutus) and he was believed to have booked Syria and Macedonia, two provinces with armies, for Brutus and Cassius.[5] Antony needed to alter these allotments and also to maximize his own. While he waited, Cicero began to treat Antony's aims more lightly. On 9 April he writes: 'Antony is more interested in the make-up of his dinner than in planning any mischief.'[6] Antony had even proposed that the dictatorship should be abolished for all time, a sharp comment on why Caesar had been murdered. In the same month, however, some of the plebs made moves of their own. A pillar was put up in the city in Caesar's honour and had to be demolished. Briefly, even Antony was outmanoeuvred, by the reappearance of one Amatius who had already been a thorn in Julius Caesar's side. Rumour spread that Amatius was Marius' grandson, a real populist echo of the past. Amatius probably had strong links with the 'colleges' or associations among the people of Rome, trouble-spots which Caesar had already had to regulate. He was rapidly put to death, and then Antony turned to the outstanding problem, the demobilization and settlement of Caesar's veterans in Italy.

By mid-April, however, a new presence appeared, Caesar's adopted heir by will, the eighteen-year-old Octavian who had been abroad in north-west Greece at the time of the murder. He was Caesar's favoured great-nephew, but as his great modern historian, Sir Ronald Syme, reminds us, he was by birth merely the 'grandson of a municipal banker'.[7] An unknown, unproven quantity, he was not even a senator. Yet he was to show a cool ruthlessness, a calculation and a lack of heroics which were to carry him eventually to forty-five years of supreme power. The recent stirrings among the plebs were a good omen for his prospects.

On arriving at Brindisi, in south Italy, Octavian seized one of the two most important commodities, money, and then used it to win over the other, some of Caesar's soldiers. It was a bold start, and as the young man travelled up Italy in spring 44 he stopped at the Bay of Naples and stayed in the next-door house to Cicero's. He is 'totally devoted to me', Cicero wrote at the time; 'extremely friendly and extremely respectful'.[8] But the boy was already calling himself 'Caesar', which Cicero did indeed dislike. And how could he remain a sound citizen, 'one of us', when he reached Rome? It is one of history's great meetings, the senior statesman, so often so wrong, and the most dangerous eighteen-year-old in the world. Scarcely a month later, Cicero would already be writing that he 'did not like the look of Octavian's games, nor his agents'; in mid-May Octavian was already trying to have funeral games held. The problem was that Antony was even worse. On 1 June, with further help from armed supporters, Antony 'legitimized' by a vote of the 'people' in Rome the exchange of provincial commands on which he was to rely for his power-base. He also set up a commission to distribute lands to Caesar's veterans which his brother, usefully, would head. Brutus and Cassius were insulted by their unjust treatment and prepared to leave Italy for harmless jobs abroad; Antony had taken northern Italy for himself. Cicero was left to complain that there was 'nothing planned, nothing thought out, nothing organized'. The Liberators' 'resolve had been manly, but their policies were childlike'.[9] He himself had spent these weeks giving lessons in oratory to prominent pupils, including the next year's consuls. He reproached himself for it, but he had done it nonetheless. After news of Antony's laws, he planned to leave Italy, to visit his son in Athens and to see if he was making progress in his studies abroad.

At Rome, meanwhile, Octavian moved where Antony, so far, had feared to tread. He announced that, as Caesar's heir, he would avenge Caesar's murder; he paid the cash left to each member of the urban plebs, as ordered in Caesar's will; he then tried to have Caesar's notorious golden throne brought back into public view. In late July he personally held the 'Games in Honour of Caesar's Victory' which had been denied official celebration. During them a comet burned in the sky for seven days. The Roman people hardly needed to be encouraged to think that this 'star' symbolized Caesar's divine status. Caesar and Alexander the Great are the only rulers in antiquity whose divinity was widely believed in. The young Octavian had already changed his name and was calling himself 'Caesar' too; he placed symbols of the star on coins and on a statue of Caesar which was dedicated in the Forum. The comet had overtones of a 'new age', but 'inside, he himself rejoiced in the sign of the star to which he himself would ascend'.[10] His actions put important pressure on Antony: if Caesar's loyal family-heir was making such running, surely Antony, his political 'heir', must raise the tempo too? So Antony began to claim that it was he, not Octavian, whom Caesar had adopted and to denounce the Liberators, Brutus and Cassius. In late July the two of them left Italy, but answered back in a fine, restrained letter sent on 4 August. 'We wish to see you being a great and honoured man in a free republic,' they told him. 'We are not fastening any quarrels on you; however, we value our freedom more than your friendship.'[11] Other Romans were to rank these priorities differently.

In early August Cicero set sail for Athens and his son, but the winds detained him and, fortunately, he could turn back to Rome on hearing better news. For at last, attacks on Antony's unduly Caesarian stance had begun in the Senate. Even so, Antony's biggest problem was not this opposition, but that the real Caesarian, Octavian, might steal his pre-eminence. As tension mounted between the two of them, veteran soldiers actually intervened to oblige Caesar's two heirs to sink their differences and make things up. Cicero reached Rome on 31 August, to be greeted by open hostility from Antony: once again, he was threatened with demolition of his house in Rome. But Cicero still had authority, as a speaker and a moral voice. In early September, he lent his pen to the senatorial fray, by composing the first of his fourteen powerful *Philippics* against Antony's character and conduct. By doing so, Cicero was not creating an enemy out of a possible 'moderate'. Antony had already reshuffled the provinces to take the most important for himself and he could not continue to be 'moderate' after Octavian's rival star dawned: as if to prove it, on 2 October Antony told a public meeting in Rome that the Liberators were conspirators and that Cicero had been the ringleader. Cicero still kept out of the public eye. In late October he began to write *On Moral Duties* (the *De Officiis*, or 'Offices'). It stresses that luxury is a vice (a worse one in old age), justice is the crowning virtue (it upholds private property, not socialism) and Julius Caesar was a criminal who had deserved to be killed.[12] On the strength of it, posterity has praised Cicero as a 'pagan Christian'. But the work was based on the texts of Greek Stoic philosophers. It was only written in his one last interval from life's real business, political affairs.

As for Antony, after an open challenge by Octavian in Rome he fixed next year's provinces at an illegal night-time meeting of the Senate (28 November) and then went early to the province which he had set for himself. He intended, surely, to wait and watch. But forces were gathering against him: Octavian, and the Decimus Brutus whom he was trying to remove from his province in north Italy. Seeing these allies, Cicero abandoned a low profile and prepared his case against Antony's 'tyranny'. On 20 December, in Antony's absence, he denounced him before the Senate in a speech which he regarded as the reinvigoration of a weary Senate and the Roman people's first hope of recovering their freedom.[13] There was a willing audience, but there was still a reluctance to pass the 'ultimate decree'. In speech after speech, Cicero's invective rolled on, painting Antony as a man of utter debauchery whose household was filled with male and female prostitutes and whose wife Fulvia 'sold off' public property in her private rooms. After more days of debate a state of public 'tumult' was eventually declared and by February 43 it was possible for troops to be turned against Antony in northern Italy.

However, Cicero's call for the 'Republic' had encompassed an ironic choice of ally: Octavian, the 'new Caesar'. In November this young man had already led an illegal private army and marched with troops into Rome. At a public meeting, he had gestured ominously with his right hand towards the newly erected statue of his adopted father and prayed that his own deeds would be worthy of Julius Caesar. However, his troops were not prepared to fight fellow veterans of Caesar just yet. He was 'taking the steam out of Antony neatly enough for the moment', Cicero wrote at the time, but 'may I never be saved by such a man as this'.[14] He was not, then, entirely deceived, but by January he was speaking as if safety and the Republic relied on Octavian's support. His hope, at times too rosy, was to split the Caesarian supporters by playing Julius Caesar's young heir against Antony, his consul. There were genuine differences of opinion to exploit here, even among Julius Caesar's loyal admirers, but the strategy relied on Octavian being dispensable in the longer term. On 3 January 43 not just Cicero but also the Senate in Rome voted Octavian, the young outsider, a place among their own number. They added the powers and distinctions of a praetor and the right to a consulship in only ten years' time. They were nurturing a young viper, but Cicero promised them that this young 'Caesar' 'will always be such a citizen as he is today and as we should especially wish and pray him to be'.[15]

By February 43 events seemed to be turning the Liberators' way. Brutus and Cassius had gone on to Greece and the East and were becoming established with legionary support. Antony was still trying to claim his command in northern Italy, but was caught up at Mutina (modern Modena) besieging the man (Decimus Brutus) whose provincial allotment he had overturned. In November 44 Cicero had been despondent, thinking of running away and reduced to writing a book, *On Friendship*. It was indeed an issue of the moment. But now he saw only what he wished to see, claiming 'universal consent' and wholehearted support for his plans both in Italy and among the common people. Octavian was that 'egregious young man'; he 'has entered on the affairs of the Republic in order to strengthen it, not to overturn it'.[16] Octavian was even calling him 'father'. But the 'consent' which Cicero saw around him was probably more for Caesar's young heir than for his own beloved Republic. His hope of 'liberty' rested on a man whose promotion had been highly irregular, and it required war with an ex-consul who had the backing of a 'law' of the people, voted in June. Admittedly, it had been voted under threat and with irregularities, but so had many other laws in the past twenty years.

In late April Antony's troops were defeated near Modena in a fearful battle which involved Caesar's hardened veterans on each side. There was dreadful bloodshed and, unlike Alexander the Great's veteran soldiers, Caesar's veterans would never be keen to fight each other again. Antony's remaining troops then headed northwards to the western provinces where he might hope for support. At this point, Cicero was chillingly opposed to 'clemency' or mercy. In invaluable letters, we can watch the governors of the provinces in Antony's path and the generals who were chasing him professing support to Cicero for the Republic and 'liberty'. But when the choice came those same governors wavered, lied and ended by doing deals with Antony, the 'enemy'. The cause of 'liberation' was already wavering, and Octavian was still an uncertain quantity. In early June Cicero was complaining that the Senate was no longer his 'tool' and that freedom and the Republic were being betrayed.[17] How true it was. At Modena both the consuls of the year had been killed, and in August Octavian turned round with troops and marched on Rome for the second time. He forced the Senate to elect him to a consulship in their place. He was not yet twenty years old.

As a complex summer unravelled Octavian's troops would not fight Antony's again, even if asked: their one taste of blood near Modena was still more than enough. In the East, meanwhile, Brutus and Cassius were raising huge armies of 'liberation' with looting and taxes in the provinces: the Senate proposed their command should be 'greater' than that of other governors in the East. The obvious answer for the Caesarians was to combine and take on their mutual enemies. On 27 November, near Bononia (modern Bologna), another threesome, Rome's 'triumvirate', was set up, once again for 'settling the Republic'. Antony and the new 'Caesar' included the elderly Lepidus as a noble sleeping partner, and agreed that their powers were to run for five years. Thereafter, they would in principle be renewable.

These powers have been understood by some modern theorists as the legal powers of a consul, active in Rome and Italy, combined with the legal powers of an ex-consul in the provinces. Despite their approval by a 'law', they cannot be analysed so formally. The Senate and the people's assemblies would still meet during the new arrangement; elections went on being held at Rome for various magistracies, but henceforward the three triumvirs could make or cancel laws, give personal judgements without appeal and appoint the governors of all the provinces and the consuls for the coming years. They promptly proved their paralegal, emergency status by listing, or 'proscribing', a large number of senators and Roman knights (probably 300 and 2,000 respectively) to be put to death. Sulla had set the precedent in this, but the triumvirs revived it to protect their hold on Italy while they marched eastwards against the Liberators. This dreadful terror became the subject, understandably, of many books long after the event. Some of them, perhaps, 'went a long way towards compensating for the absence of prose fiction among the Romans',[18] but there was also a real loss of life and property in Italian towns. It was not a class war, of poor against rich, but it did give old hatreds and new ambitions a free rein in the upper classes. In that sense, it was a revolution; in another, it contributed to a revolution because the winners, importantly, would not exactly be people devoted to the cause of Rome's old constitution. They had not taken power for any new system or ideology, but when one came about they would support it, so as to hang on to their gains.

Many of those named as 'proscribed' on the triumvirs' lists fled to a fourth, remarkable figurehead, outside the 'gang of three': Sextus Pompeius, the son, no less, of the great Pompey. The history of the next seven years is too often written around the dominant triumvirs only, Antony and Octavian. But this fourth man was extremely important, and we should not dismiss him as a 'pirate' adventurer. Like Octavian, he was the young son of a great man too. Like Octavian, he would soon present himself as the son of a god. In Spain in 45 BC he had survived his brother's death and Julius Caesar's victories, and by mid–44 he was negotiating for recognition. He raised a fleet on the coast of Spain and by late April 43 he had even been recognized 'as Prefect of the Fleet and the Coastline by decree of the Senate'.[19] He moved over to Sicily, increased his naval strength and became a refuge for Italian landowners and runaway slaves, the victims of the paralegal proscriptions. Sicily and Sardinia were parts of Octavian's 'territory', but Sextus soon held them both. He was now a major alternative to the new young 'Caesar', while controlling a bigger navy than any of the triumvirs. Remarkably, the contest of Pompey against Caesar was set up for a replay in this war between their sons. In Rome, Antony was occupying the great Pompey's house, but the 'pious' Sextus rightly wanted it back.

First, the proscriptions ran their course. Among the names proscribed, inevitably, was Cicero's. Even if Octavian was well disposed to him, he had said and provoked too many insults against Antony. In March 43 he had pilloried a blunt letter from Antony line by line in a scornful *Philippic*, the thirteenth, which is thus our best verbal memorial of Antony himself. Ever witty, Cicero was also said to have remarked that the 'young little fellow', Octavian his 'ally', 'must be given praises, honours—and then, the push'.[20] The story became known to Octavian.

Human to the end, Cicero was torn between flight and one last visit to Rome. Fifteen miles away from the city, at a seaside house of his own, troops caught up with him. They were directed into the grounds by one of his brother's freedmen, a man whom Cicero had once taught and educated in fine literature. Dishevelled, but calm, Cicero looked out from his litter and was killed by a centurion. His head and his right hand (perhaps both hands) were hacked off and taken up to Antony in Rome. There, they were put in the lap of Fulvia, the wife of Cicero's two great enemies, first Clodius, and then Antony. She pulled the tongue out of the skull, we are told, and stabbed it with a pin taken from her hair.[21] After a woman's revenge, the head and hands were nailed as trophies onto the Rostrum in the Forum, the very platform from which Cicero had spoken so memorably. They are terrible symbols of the loss of 'liberty'.

PART FIVE

From Republic to Empire

THE FASHION PERSISTS OF condemning and deploring the last epoch of the Roman Republic. It was turbulent, corrupt, immoral. And some speak of decadence. On the contrary, it was an era of liberty, vitality—and innovation . . . Roman life was coming to feel to the full the liberating effects of empire and prosperity. In the aftermath of the Punic Wars, cult and ritual lapsed, and law was separated from religion . . . In various other ways good sense or chicanery were able to abate or circumvent the 'ancient rigour', the 'hardness of the ancients'.

Political fraud and Augustan romanticism conspired to embellish the venerable past—with unhappy consequences for historical study ever after.

Ronald Syme, *Sallust* (1964), 16–17

THE ACT OF CREATIVE POLICY that was Augustus' abiding legacy to Rome was the bringing into being of an ideology of rule, parallel to the careful traditionalism of most of what has been spoken of so far—surprising in that it manifests itself quite early in Augustus' reign, and multifaceted, so that to describe it even summarily involves consideration of many phenomena of which the 'imperial cult' is only one. Glorification of the personality of the ruler, advertisement of his role, proclamation of his virtues, pageantry over his achievements, visual reminders of his existence, and the creation of a court and a dynasty: these are, par excellence, the things that made AD 14 different from 30 BC . . . The work known as the 'Dialogus', attributed to Tacitus, contains, through the mouth of an 'opposition' writer, a well-known expression of the view that the ending of the creative phase of, at least, Roman eloquence, was directly due to the loss of freedom. That was not the only view then, nor need it be now . . .

J. A. Crook, *The Cambridge Ancient History*, volume X
(1996, 2nd edn.), 133 and 144

ANTONY AND CLEOPATRA

Never, as those who were present tell us, was there a more pitiable sight. Smeared with blood and struggling with death, Antony was drawn up (to the window of Cleopatra's tomb), stretching his hands out to her as he dangled in the air . . . Cleopatra clung on with her hands and kept pulling up the rope, her face twisted by the strain, while those below encouraged her and shared her agony. When she had received him in this way and laid him down, she tore her robes over him, beat and tore her breasts with her hands, wiped some of his blood onto her face and kept on calling him master, husband, Commander . . .

Plutarch, *Life of Antony* 77.3–5

AFTER CICERO'S MURDER, injustice continued to be set against free-dom and 'luxury' to be cited against political rivals. Twelve memo-rable years brought the great men into conflict, Mark Antony against the young Octavian, and women into lasting fame, Antony's second wife, Oc-tavia, and once more, the Egyptian Queen Cleopatra. Lesser persons, too, had a sudden memorable chance on the stage of power, people like the childless Turia whom we know from her husband's inscription in her hon-our. She had grovelled and wept before the triumvirs to save his life, and in their household even offered that he should have a child by another woman which she would then bring up as hers (he declined).[1] In Octa-vian's circle we meet loyal 'new men' with a bright future, the urbane Maecenas, Octavian's link with the great poets of the age, and the able Agrippa, the key to so many of Octavian's military successes. Out east, we first meet Herod the Great, the future 'tyrant' in the story of Christmas. He was imposed for the first time as king of the Jews through Mark Antony's favour.

Yet these years of war and slaughter were also a fertile period for Roman literature. Great art can indeed be born in comparative anarchy. One reason was that new patrons emerged in the social shake-up and helped younger authors to break with older critics and the established canons of scholarly taste.[2] The greatest Latin poets, Virgil and Horace, began their careers now, as did the elegist Propertius: none of them came from Rome itself, as all three were Italians. There were also articulate losers, just as there had been in the age of aristocratic Greek lyric poets. One of them, the historian Sallust, developed the themes of luxury and liberty to explain political change. A former acolyte of Caesar, he had been forced out of public life and wrote an acid account of the Republic's crisis, tracing it back to Sulla and then forwards through the greed and ambition of the 'nobles'. Seen as a follower of Thucydides, Sallust had none of his intellectual depth. But his histories became a school-text for the greater mind of Tacitus and, centuries later, for St Augustine and his view of the lust for power in Roman history, as analysed in his *City of God*.

At the time the 'decisive shift' which was visible was political, not literary. In November 42 Antony and Octavian went east and defeated the almost equally enormous army of Brutus and Cassius in two battles at Philippi. Both of the Liberators, Caesar's murderers, died. It was Mark Antony who earned the military credit, whereas even Octavian's close friends had to admit that he had hidden in the marshes. Octavian was no natural soldier and he later claimed to have been kept from battle, first by an ominous dream, then by sickness. As the dominant figure, Antony retained responsibility both for Gaul and the East at this point. Octavian returned to his much smaller responsibilities, above all to Italy where he had to engage both with Sextus Pompeius' fleet off Sicily and the extremely awkward problem of overseeing the expropriation of land from up to twenty Italian towns. It involved ejecting the humble occupants in order to settle ever more of Caesar's veteran soldiers. Already, promises to the troops had multiplied, including those in cash, a reason why such vast numbers continued to fight. At Philippi, the triumvirs' army alone equalled any force maintained by Alexander the Great at his zenith: the impossible sum of 150,000 talents had already been promised in arrears and bonuses.

In the aftermath of Philippi, the protagonists' personal images developed differently. Octavian was still only in his early twenties; his portraits on his coins expressed youth and dignity, while his patron god was Apollo, the god of moral restraint and dignity, the arts and prophecy. His strongest card was his adoption by Caesar. He played it to the full by a serial change of names. First, he had called himself 'Caesar' too: then, 'Caesar, son of the divine one' (*divi filius*).[3] He claimed the further protection of Venus, the ancestral goddess of the Julii. His 'father' Julius had particularly favoured the Asian city of Aphrodisias, whose leaders had presented themselves as the special city of Venus, Caesar's divine ancestor. The city had been badly treated under the Liberators in 43/2, but the new 'Caesar' then wrote in 39 BC to affirm that he would keep it 'free' as his city in Asia. His letter was rediscovered only recently at Aphrodisias and shows that in such personal matters, the division of the East and West with Antony was not cast-iron.[4]

Antony, by contrast, took on a much more flamboyant role. After the victory at Philippi, he went down for the winter of 42/1 to Athens where he won Greek hearts by attending to intellectual debates, remaining accessible and liking to be called not just 'philhellene' but 'friend of Athens'.[5] Like Julius Caesar, he had hard words for neighbouring Megara, a sure way, since the age of Pericles, to win Athenian affection. In the following spring (41 BC) he crossed into Asia and found himself, like other powerful Romans before him, being welcomed as a god.

In 41 Antony still had responsibility in Gaul too, and so the Greek East was only one area of significance for him. At Ephesus, however, the Greeks promptly greeted him as a 'new Dionysus'. He drew a circle of Greek acolytes; perhaps there really were processions around him of men dressed as Pans and satyrs and women as wild Bacchants; in Greek eyes, Antony was as powerful as the many kings for whom these shows had been mobilized before. But there was a reciprocal willingness in Antony himself. He had been accompanied to the East by a famous courtesan, Volumnia. In the previous decade he had seen his superior officer, Gabinius, going along with such 'luxury' and the free ways of the East. As his funeral speech over Caesar showed, he also had a sense of theatre, just what his new Greek friends (including actors and mime artists) appreciated in a Hellenistic king. But Antony also had important work to do, raising yet more money and appointing new client-rulers over the adjoining hinterlands of Asia Minor. The Liberators had complicated both tasks by robbing the Greek cities and by favouring allies who could no longer be trusted. Antony had a good eye for a client king and both now and especially in 37/6 his main appointments, including Herod, proved capable and durable. If he wanted to appeal to his newly confirmed kinglets and to smooth the necessary exaction of money (nine years' tribute, to be paid in two years), it was helpful to go along with Greek honours and compliments. They helped both parties to soften the hard edges of power.

Antony also had a sharp eye for a client queen. Already in summer 41 he slept with one nominee, Queen Glaphyra, and ever fertile, fathered a child on her. Then in autumn 41 he met another, vastly more important one: Cleopatra of Egypt, who was now aged twenty-eight to Antony's forty-two and was still a crucial player in the balance of power and finance in the East. There was also something else. She had had the baby son Caesarion in 47 BC and since leaving Rome in 44 she had continued to claim that his father was Julius Caesar. The truth mattered less than the fact that she claimed it and that nobody could prove her wrong.

When summoned to Antony at Tarsus, Cleopatra arrived as befitted an eastern queen, in a golden boat under a golden canopy, with roses, it was said, strewn thickly on the floor.[6] She seemed like Aphrodite while her maids resembled Cupids: Shakespeare's magnificent lines on the occasion are based on Plutarch's well-founded ancient account. Yet again, a Roman general could not resist her. She and Antony entertained each other in turn on their boats, made love and returned for the winter to Alexandria. It was later said that when Antony bet her that she could not eat a dinner worth millions of sesterces, she took an enormous pearl and dissolved it in a cup of vinegar. She is said to have drunk it and won the bet, leaving a story which, centuries later, inspired Tiepolo's magnificent frescos in the Palazzo Labia in Venice. Octavian, meanwhile, was bogged down by a siege of Perusia (modern Perugia) in Italy and was writing coarse verses about the choice between 'screwing' jealous Fulvia (Antony's wife) or making war, not love.[7]

In Egypt, Antony as the 'new Dionysus' acquired an unforeseen aptness. Dionysus was the god whom the kings, the Ptolemies, honoured as their ancestor; he was also the consort of the goddess Isis who was sometimes equated with the Ptolemaic queen. At Alexandria, meanwhile, the art for human beings was to mix high life with low. Antony and Cleopatra excelled at it. They founded their own exotic club and called it the Inimitable Lives: we have even found an inscription for a statue-base in which a Greek, calling himself 'Parasitos' (the 'parasite'), honours Antony as a god (in 34 BC) and as 'Inimitable at Sex'.[8] Music, acting and the world of mythological models set their revels far apart from a modern wallow in drugs and debauchery. At night, in plain clothes, they would roam the streets of Alexandria among inhabitants who had always relished a witty exchange with their kings. They drank, they played dice, they hunted. Antony was not living out some stereotype of the decadent man of 'luxury', although critics pinned this label to him. Princes in the Hellenistic world were loved for luxurious display, as several Ptolemies had exemplified, especially Ptolemy IV and Cleopatra's own father. Antony had a flamboyant, theatrical streak in him, combined with the down-to-earth coarseness of a hardened soldier. He sported with the cultured attention paid to him, but then repaid it in his own uproarious style. Its models were dramatic and theatrical, with the support of myth and poetry which had surrounded Alexander's Successor kings. By the spring Cleopatra was heavily pregnant with what turned out to be twins, a boy and a girl.

There were other gains for the partners. Antony needed Egypt's loyalty, its invaluable riches and its co-operation in the eastward attacks on Parthian territory which he was probably already planning. Cleopatra wanted to be strengthened against her sister and her many enemies in Egypt; obligingly, Antony hunted them all down. But sound reasons were already only part of the story. During winter 41/0, the Parthians struck first, pressing far into Syria. If Antony had been at Antioch, on alert, would they really have come so far west? Meanwhile, back in Italy, Antony's brother Lucius and his loyal wife Fulvia had exploited the discontent which the proscriptions and veteran settlements were causing: they had declared war against Octavian in the name of 'freedom'. They had also found a natural ally, Sextus Pompeius, Pompey's son. Sextus could use his naval supremacy to squeeze the grain-supply into Italy and provoke second thoughts among the crowds in Rome about their favour for Octavian 'Caesar's' cause. Was Antony really so cut off by the winter seas in Egypt that he could not have urged his friends in the West to seize the moment, assist his family, and multiply Octavian's serious troubles as he fought a grim war round Perusia? Arguably, chances were being missed while Antony's mind was on Alexandria and passion.

When Antony did return westwards, from February 40 onwards, the cause of 'freedom' and the 'Republic' took a novel turn: its supporters attached themselves to Antony's advance. Cicero would have turned in his grave. The brave Sextus Pompeius was also looking to Antony for support, and a combined strike at Octavian in Italy might well have succeeded. But once again the two leaders' veteran soldiers refused to fight each other after their last horrible encounter up at Mutina three years before. In autumn 40, at Brundisium, Octavian and Antony met and made a pact instead. Octavian agreed to marry Scribonia, the sister, significantly, of an important senator who was the father-in-law of Sextus Pompeius. The marriage was to an older woman who had already had two husbands but it was surely an attempt to win her brother over from Sextus' camp and damage the young Pompey who had become a major player on the stage. Since the summer of 40, crucially, Antony had lost control of Gaul; he was now centred on the East, and his part of the pact was simply to marry Octavian's elegant sister, Octavia (his own wife Fulvia had died). Nothing was agreed about Cleopatra and the twins.

After the pact the two rivals went up to Rome where their welcome was far from one-sided. Sextus had damaged the city's imports of grain. Had people begun to wonder if Pompey's son was perhaps a sounder and straighter bet than Julius Caesar's heir? Both Octavian and Antony had troubles with their own officers, and in 39 BC it was as well that they sought to make terms with Sextus in the south. He was now calling himself 'son of Neptune', the sea-god, an allusion to his own sea-power and to his father Pompey's great naval victories over pirates. In late summer 39 the three of them eventually met down at Cape Misenum. Sextus was offered Sicily and other territory and promised a consulship years in advance; the slaves with him were to be freed and his veterans would be eligible for rewards. These offers would make such people much harder for Sextus to retain. When Antony and Octavian joined him for dinner on his ship, it was said that Sextus' 'pirate' captain urged him to cut the cable and leave the two rivals at his mercy so that he, Sextus, could be master of all the world.[9] Pompey's heir was more scrupulous than Caesar's, and did nothing. At Rome, meanwhile, Antony continued to own the great Pompey's house.

A pact did not solve what was now an uneasy triangle; late in 39, Octavian felt confident enough to compound it by divorcing Scribonia. Instead, he fell in love (we are told) with Livia, the wife of a noble senator who had fled to Sextus to escape the recent proscriptions. In January 38 he went on to marry her, and she would remain his wife for more than fifty years of childless marriage. At the time she was pregnant by her previous husband, but for Octavian she had another attraction: she was the granddaughter of the great Livius Drusus who had been so significant for the Italians' cause back in 91 BC. Octavian's image in Italy certainly needed to be enhanced.

As for Antony, it suited him if Sextus and Octavian now fought each other off the coast of Italy. He left Rome in October 39 (he would never see it again) and went east to Athens, from where he could visit the war which had begun against Parthia. Matters were still going his way there. In 39 and 38 his able general Ventidius won two good victories over the Parthians in the Near East. At Athens, meanwhile, the people hailed him as 'new Dionysus' and took his new wife Octavia to heart as their 'divine Benefactress'. Octavian, by contrast, turned on Sextus, hoping to eliminate him, but failed. In 37 the way forward was obvious: Antony himself should follow up in the East, attack the Parthians as directly as possible and take advantage of the quarrels which had split their royal family. Octavian, meanwhile, would be bogged down in yet more civil war with Sextus Pompeius off Italy. Success in the East would eclipse the new 'Caesar's' star, because Parthia had been Julius Caesar's last known objective. By 33, when there would be the next break in the triumvirs' five-year powers, Antony could return to Rome as the most glorious conqueror, rich with Eastern booty.

Even without his hold on Gaul, Antony was still the stronger of the two rivals. However, his infantry was not strong enough to be sure of conquering Parthia and so he needed recruits from Italy in order to maximize his chances. In summer 37 he crossed to south Italy with a huge force of 300 ships, an advantage which Octavian would envy in his own struggles against Sextus. After threatening to fight, however, Antony was obliged to negotiate and at Tarentum, the rivals agreed yet another pact: Antony would give Octavian ships to conclude the war against Sextus, while Octavian would give him troops to use against Parthia. It was to be the last pact, but its outcome was not as Antony hoped. Both the main players had war in mind, but whereas Antony gave Octavian ships, he did not receive from Octavian most of the promised troops. There was also a female dimension: Octavia had helped the pact along by mediating between her husband and her brother. In only three years of marriage Antony had already fathered two healthy daughters on her (a third, perhaps, had been short-lived). But there would now be problems for her, too. She was not to go east with him: there were the girls, perhaps a pregnancy, and all the eastern dangers, but there was promptly something else. In winter 37/6 Antony had returned to Antioch, preparing for the Parthian War, and up to him came Cleopatra, his 'Egyptian dish'. She may not have been given all the new territory she wanted, but she certainly received significant swathes of it. She also became pregnant with yet another son.

Like the Parthian venture, Cleopatra had Julius Caesar's imprint. Together, they would allow the 'new Dionysus' to counter Octavian's trump card, his name as the new 'Caesar': Cleopatra also had the little Caesarion, the son, they still said, of Julius Caesar's own blood. He also gave Cleopatra parts of Phoenicia, Syria and Judaea, rich gifts which would secure Egypt's eastern border: the Phoenician cities celebrated a new calendar era. Their twins were acknowledged; effectively, Octavia had now been repudiated. Seeing the chance and the danger, Octavian began the most overt war of spin-doctoring. He dismissed Antony as a drunk in thrall to a barbarous queen of Egypt: he would eventually even open Antony's will and allege that he planned to transfer the capital to Alexandria and be buried beside the Nile. Staid opinion in the towns of Italy might believe these shocking, but riveting, stories. At Rome, many senators were less bothered. Antony defended himself in a pamphlet 'On His Own Drunkenness'

51. The Portland Vase, (blue and white cameo-glass), probably depicting mythological Peleus and Thetis (left) and maybe Aeneas and unhappy Dido (right). Reference to Antony and Cleopatra (left) and Octavian and rejected Octavia (right) has been suggested. Perhaps *c.* 35 BC.

(sadly lost to us) and wrote an earthy letter, observing that Cleopatra was not his wife, that Octavian had all sorts of dreary little women on the side and that 'what did it matter where a man stuck his cock?'[10] Octavian was also said to have a 'pretty boy', Sarmentus, presumably a slave.

The year 36 nonetheless proved pivotal. In it, Octavian at last succeeded in defeating Sextus Pompeius at sea. The credit for the naval victory belonged to his officer Agrippa, but Octavian won popular favour by having the prisoners executed in a show at Rome. Sextus did escape but only to be put to death in the East a year later. Instead, Octavian took the 'sacrosanct' protection of a tribune both for himself and for poor Octavia who could be cleverly represented as Antony's 'abandoned' wife: he vowed the spoils of victory to a massive new temple of Apollo in Rome beside which he would place his own house, not far from the supposed ancient 'hut of Romulus'.[11] Antony, by contrast, had to cover up a campaign against Parthia which went badly wrong. After a change of direction, Antony had marched north from Syria, then east through Armenia, apparently hoping to win by a pitched battle. However, the Parthians were a mobile enemy who would keep retreating despite the loss of a fort or city. Antony was fighting a war as if it was the previous one, his campaign with Julius Caesar in the very different setting of Gaul.[12] His army was huge, about two-thirds bigger than Alexander's in western Asia, and more than 30,000 of his soldiers died on their cold, hungry retreat during winter 36/5. Antony was left to celebrate a hollow victory. In 35 he prepared to invade Armenia again, but Octavian had cleverly compromised him: he sent him troops (a mere 2,000 of those promised in 37) and his Octavia as an envoy. Antony took the troops, but forbade Octavia to meet him: he was too involved with Cleopatra. In summer 34 he did regain Armenia, but reports of his celebration were alarming. He and Cleopatra sat on golden thrones in the gymnasium in Alexandria; he gave her yet more territory and named her 'queen of kings'. He gave royal titles to their young son and daughter (called the Sun and the Moon) and, above all, he named Caesarion, now seventeen years old, the 'king of kings'.[13] What was his own role to be? Two contemporary coins suggest he kept his options open. One, very famous, is a silver denarius showing Cleopatra captioned in Latin 'queen of kings and of sons as kings': on the other royal side is Antony, uncaptioned. A separate gold coin-type, however, shows Antony with Latin titles ('commander', 'triumvir') and his young son Antyllus, born by his now dead Roman wife Fulvia. Certainly Antony had gone far with Cleopatra, to my mind in love and passion. But he had not closed off a Roman alternative or some blend, perhaps, of Roman and Cleopatran options.

At the end of 33 the triumvirs' second five-year term would expire. Back in Rome, 'Caesar' held his second consulship and was winning favour with the common people through the public works of his trusted lieutenant, Agrippa. The long-neglected drains and sewage were cleaned out in the city; Agrippa even travelled symbolically down the city's main sewer: he developed links with the chariot-racing factions in the Circus Maximus and there were plans to improve the Campus Martius, a popular open space. Nonetheless, in 32 the consuls would be Antony's men and Antony himself could return, be consul for 31 and be voted a vast personal province, with a supposed Parthian triumph behind him. Octavian had to strike back. After a bad start to 32, he boldly called 'all Italy' to swear an oath of allegiance to him. The move had echoes of a military emergency, in which a Roman leader would traditionally call for men to band together and save their cause.[14] Next, the oath was taken by the western provinces, Octavian 'Caesar's' second wing of support. He then declared war in public by re-enacting an ancient Roman rite, but cleverly declared war on Cleopatra only. Old Roman values, Italian steadiness against Egyptian corruption, the new 'Caesar's' care for his troops and for the Roman plebs: these were Octavian's public messages, but Antony still had more legions. More than three hundred senators fled Rome to join his side.

With Cleopatra and his fleet beside him, Antony eventually took up his position around Actium on the north-west coast of Greece. However, important desertions from his camp began early, probably when the newly arrived senators saw that Cleopatra was indeed at large in their camp. A first-class general could have won the war, but, as the Parthian march had shown, Antony was only second class. Octavian's fleet was allowed to cross unopposed from Italy and then to blockade Antony's smaller fleet in the bay just north of the island of Leucas. Delay induced disease, hunger and desertion in Antony's camp. The obvious tactic, a difficult one, was for Antony to try to break through at sea and escape. Cleopatra was evidently alerted (she did not simply desert) because the fleet went into battle with their sails at the ready: when the battle began on 2 September she and her sixty ships escaped through a gap in Octavian's centre. Antony quickly sailed after her. Actium is the last major sea-battle in antiquity, but although Octavian won the campaign (actually, it was Agrippa again who won it for him), there was very little fighting. Cleopatra and Antony won their objective, by escaping.

At first Antony fled to Greece and Cleopatra to Egypt. Finally the two were reunited in Alexandria, and as they waited for the follow-up, the club of 'Inimitable Lives' became refounded as 'Those about to Die Together'. Antony, the new Dionysus, even founded a shrine to the legendary Timon of Athens, the man without true friends.[15] After a brief return to Italy, Octavian arrived in Egypt in the summer of 30 BC, but Antony's offers to fight a duel were not accepted. Desertions continued apace and despite a brief flurry by the cavalry, by 1 August 30 Octavian held Alexandria. Antony wounded himself almost fatally and the greatest death scene in history began.

Detailed accounts of it were soon written by eyewitnesses, including the doctor Olympus.[16] It is probably to him that we owe the account of Cleopatra's retreat into her Mausoleum, up to whose window the dying Antony was then hauled on ropes by herself and her maids. We are not sure what he said to her, but he certainly died in her company. When the new Caesar entered, he wept over his great rival, now dead before him. It was a customary emotion on these occasions, just as Antony had once wept over the corpse of Brutus the Liberator, a fellow Roman senator. The obvious plan was to retain Cleopatra for exhibition in the triumph at Rome, but nine days later she outwitted it. Some said she had hidden poison in a hairpin, but Octavian accepted the cause was snakebite. Either in a water-jar or a basket of figs, two Egyptian asps were smuggled to her. She held one to her arm, not to her breast, and her serving-maids Iris and Charmian died beside her. Young Caesarion was caught and killed.

It is easy to say that the 'right man won', steady Octavian against flamboyant Antony. Certainly no issue of principle, no notion of greater freedom or fairer justice divided the two. It was a straight power struggle between rivals, in which respected Romans had remained on terms with both sides, men like the rich, civilized Atticus, who stayed a friend of both. Others had simply done something 'last minute' and changed sides, like Plancus or Ahenobarbus or Dellius, known as the 'circus-rider' of the Civil Wars. At Rome, on the Capitol, there was even said to have been a man with two crows on his arm, one of which he had trained to say 'Hail, Caesar, Victorious Commander', one 'Hail, Antony, Victorious Commander', as the circumstances required.[17]

Nonetheless, Antony had had his aims and a style to match them. The great campaign in the East had been a disaster, but the subsequent appointment of a friendly king in Armenia was to be a long-running Roman solution to the Parthian question. His other choices as 'friendly kings' in the East were successful too. Had Antony won, Rome would have had a very special tie with Egypt and Alexandria. Unlike Octavian, Antony had no need to compensate for military mediocrity and to seek glory by conquering in Europe. Thousands of barbarian lives might have been spared during the next fifty years, while a regeneration of the ravaged Greek cities could have been brought forward. There would also have been no shortage of heirs. Cleopatra already had two sons by the triumvir (whose paternity-rate, at least, was so much higher than Octavian's). As for the 'Augustan' poets of the future, they need not have lost their Italian voices. Patronage had won them over to Octavian in the 30s, but patronage would certainly have won them back to Antony.[18] Horace would then have been spared the need to write morally correct public poetry: there was so much for him to enjoy in Antony's less reputable entourage. Propertius retained a soft spot for it anyway,[19] and as for Virgil, his masterpiece, the *Georgics*, was already finished. Dionysus, surely, would have been much more exciting to him than his next obligatory hero, the tongue-tied Aeneas. Through Virgil's genius, Bacchus would somehow have flowered poetically at Rome. The winner would have been Ovid. The wit and the polished detachment of his poetry would have found a real centre in Rome's flamboyant couple, Antony and Cleopatra. They would have lived out his themes of love and myth, bringing his life and poetry into harmony. But members of the senatorial order still had their 'moral' values and loved 'liberty', not eastern queens: they would have had them murdered first.

THE MAKING OF THE EMPEROR

On fifty-five occasions the Senate decreed that thanksgivings should be offered to the immortal gods on account of the successes on land and sea gained by me or my legates under my auspices. The days on which thanksgivings were offered according to the decree of the Senate numbered eight hundred and ninety. In my triumphs nine kings or children of kings were led before my chariot. As I was writing this, I had been consul thirteen times and I was in the thirty-seventh year of tribunician power.

Augustus, in *The Achievements of the Divine Augustus* (*Res Gestae*), in the edition of AD 14

THE NEW 'CAESAR'S' VICTORY at Actium was represented as the welcome triumph of sober values. In fact it was followed promptly by reports of a conspiracy at Rome. The son of the third triumvir, Lepidus, is said to have had plans to assassinate Octavian and he had to be put down by Octavian's man on the spot, the obliging non-senator Maecenas.[1] The plot, if genuine, was perhaps associated with that long-running trouble, the settlement of so many veteran soldiers. After Actium it was the reason why Octavian had had to return briefly to Italy in case the protests became too serious.

After the further victory in Egypt, in August 30, the immense riches of the country were brought under Roman 'domination', as the new rule was called. After Antony's example, it was obviously too risky to entrust Egypt to a senator. Octavian chose a knight as governor, Cornelius Gallus, who had distinguished himself in the recent fighting; he was also a noted poet, which Alexandrians would like. The province was actually called 'Alexandria and Egypt' and Alexandrians were to be important in administering it. Octavian would never use the equestrian order as a whole as a counterweight to the more political Senate, but in this exceptional case he realized that a knight was a safer bet.[2] The precedent persisted and senators were banned (as were important knights) from visiting Egypt without the emperor's permission. These decisions were ratified at Rome, presumably in 30/29. Treasure in Egypt vastly increased Octavian's capacity for gifts to the Roman public. Its grain was also crucial for Rome's food-supply: after fifty years, the 'Egyptian question' was settled in one player's favour, thanks to civil war.

Having won, how was the new 'Caesar' to rule? Nobody could have imagined that he would dominate for forty-four years and that the powers which he assumed by stages would become the mainstays for those we call the 'Roman emperors' for the next three centuries. Like Augustus, all emperors would refer to their consulships, their 'tribunician power', their role as Commander (*Imperator*) of the armies. Hadrian would have a particular respect for Augustus, who was his role-model in so many ways. He had a portrait-head of Augustus on his seal-ring and he kept a bronze bust of the boy Octavian among the household gods in his bedroom. But we can see, as Hadrian perhaps could not, how Augustus' years as 'First Citizen' (*Princeps*) had been a bumpy ride. They marked a fundamental change in freedom and justice, with attempted consequences for luxury too.

In 30 and 29 one side of 'Caesar's' position was made clear to him. Ever since Alexander the Great, cities and individuals in the Greek-speaking East had become used to negotiating personally with kings and princes. They had no interest whatsoever in the arcane details of the old Roman constitution and had already regarded Roman commanders of the late Republic as personal dynasts. Octavian stepped easily into this role. He personally wrote to cities in the East and praised personal friends in them who had helped him in the recent troubles. He even referred to his wife Livia's keen efforts on behalf of the island of Samos:[3] Greeks were used to royal families and helpful queens, although royalty was anathema to Roman traditionalists. Greeks were also used to offering living rulers 'god-like honours'. The new 'Caesar' drew a cautious line here. Temples to 'Rome and Deified Julius' could be put up by Roman citizens in places like Ephesus: cult for himself while alive was un-Roman. Greeks, however, could put up temples to himself and Rome in the central cities of their provincial assemblies. Other cities would simply pay him cult outside Rome without asking permission.

When he returned to Rome in 29, the obvious first move was celebration. In mid-August Octavian held a magnificent triple triumph for three victories, those in 35–33, the win at Actium and the follow-up in Egypt. Gladiatorial shows accompanied it, always a great attraction for the people, together with magnificent gifts of money to each member of the Roman plebs and two and a half times as much to each discharged soldier. All around them grand new monuments were being built in the city, arising from Octavian—Caesar's personal exploits. His own Mausoleum was already under construction, a type of building which Hadrian would later imitate. A great temple to the Deified Julius Caesar was being finished in 29, and a huge new temple was being finished on the Palatine hill beside his house. In October 28 it would be dedicated to Apollo, his patron-god at Actium. A big arch to commemorate Actium was begun in the Forum, where columns were to be made of bronze from the prows of Cleopatra's ships. The face of Rome was being changed by its despot's career, but he could not continue in this personal style on the path of his adopted father. Prolonged dictatorship, 'kingship' or cult as a god inside Rome would be fatal. Although many of the great families of the Republic had been diminished in the Civil Wars, they had not died out. Members of them were among the senators of the moment and would be the provincial army-commanders of the future, yet some of them had hoped with Cicero for a restored Republic as recently as spring 43 BC. They had to be reconciled to a new 'order'. It was a mixed blessing that house prices were rising sharply in Rome, propelled by the spending of the captive spoils from Egypt.

Peace, at least, was a blessing, and it came at an apt moment. Since the 50s BC a new confidence had been spreading in many areas of intellectual life at Rome, as if Romans could at last measure up to the feats of the Greeks. After so much civil war, there were hopes for a return from army service to 'life on the land'. After all the devastation, there was a pride in the special qualities of Italy, potentially such a blessed country. Augustus' scholarly freedman, Hyginus, would even write a book on the origins and sites of Italian cities. In 30/29 BC these themes came together in Virgil's marvellous poem, the *Georgics*. The 'best poem by the best poet' combined praises of Italy and country living with tributes (often playful) to the new "Caesar." A virtuoso ending blended Greek myths into a new, entrancing whole. As such a poem proves, there was hope and also confidence after so much terror. It was up to the new 'Caesar' to harness them, for they underlie what he was to make into a classicizing age.

In 28 BC Octavian and his loyal 'new man' Agrippa began the process by holding the consulship together. A newly found gold coin, struck in this very year, shows Octavian seated on his chair of office, holding a scroll: the caption refers to the Restoration of Laws and Rights to the Roman People.[4] The triumvirate, therefore, was regarded as illegal and the law courts and elections, by implication, could now function normally. The swollen number of senators was reduced; the public Treasury was put back on its feet, an 'urban praetor' was appointed (to see to regular justice again in Rome) and by the end of the year, the illegal acts of the triumvirs were to be cancelled. Looted treasures were also to be returned to their temples. Meanwhile, military prowess caught the headlines. Three separate commanders celebrated personal triumphs in Rome during the summer, and it was as well that games to commemorate Actium could follow from the unmilitary 'Caesar's' own corner in September. Much more awkwardly, one of the most distinguished surviving noblemen, Licinius Crassus, claimed the highest and rarest of military honours for the feat of slaying an enemy in single combat. It was not exactly a feat which timid 'Caesar' could match, and so Crassus' request was refused. He had a fair case, but Octavian denied him with a feeble lie about past history.[5]

Nonetheless, the 'restoration' continued into the following year. Again, Octavian was consul and on 13 January 27 BC he raised in the Senate the traditional question of the allotment of provinces to the consuls. One answer, no doubt prearranged, was to offer him them all. A few days later he kindly accepted not all but many, including the important trio of Gaul, Spain and Syria, together with others which had most of the main armies. He would govern them for 'up to ten years'. He was also offered a new, solemn name: Augustus (Romulus was said to have been suggested, but Romulus had had his darker sides, including the murder of his brother and his death, on one view, at the hands of his own senators). An honorary wreath of oak-leaves was voted to adorn the entry to the new Augustus' house and an honorific shield proclaimed, and therefore defined, his special 'virtues'. Nearly twenty years before, Cicero had picked out similar virtues when pleading before Julius Caesar: valour, clemency, justice and piety.[6] It was not that Octavian had necessarily read Cicero's speech, although Atticus could have lent it to him, but these virtues had entered the 'climate of opinion'. There were precedents of a sort for his new command in the enlarged commands for the likes of Pompey under the Republic. At first, many senators may genuinely have thought of it all as restoration, especially as the other provinces were being restored to the 'people' as 'public'. Augustus then left Rome for Gaul with talk of a trip to Britain. In fact, he contented himself with a nearer edge of the world, the coast of north-west Spain (Finisterre, 'Land's End'). Perhaps not everybody expected that he would continue to be consul in the following years, but if so, he could point out that he was continuing to fight wars. In the summer of 27, in his absence, Licinius Crassus could enjoy a triumph, at least, in the city: Augustus could not deny him that honour, too, but he personally did not have to witness it on 4 July.

Despite the changed presentation, Augustus's power-base remained unchanged: like Julius Caesar the Dictator's, it was still the army, the favour of Rome's common people and a vast personal fortune. When millions of Rome's subjects abroad were looking to him as a sort of king, and many could not even have spelled a complicated word like *imperium*, why did the careful re-presentation of his power at Rome matter? It did not matter much to most of the leading families in Italy's towns. The 'Roman constitution' had never been high on their list of concerns and many of their leaders were now 'new men' who had profited mightily from the killings and proscriptions of the late 40s, the very opposite of true republican liberty. What they wanted now was peace and the absence of armies and military settlers tramping over their property. As for the people of Rome, their main concern was that somebody would feed them and attend to their security, which the Senate historically would not do. Security, however, is not the same as liberty. Rather, the important constituency for the 'restoration' was senatorial opinion, on which the supply of army-commanders, Augustus' personal safety and his legitimacy depended. Augustus' tricks here included the modern art of airing a very extreme proposal, only (mercifully) to accept something slightly less extreme. He also kept a simple profile, accessible, low-key and civil. In so many ways, he epitomized ordinariness.

Not that his position was secure. In 26 an attempt to attend to the potential problems of the 'urban mob' by appointing a Prefect of the City collapsed within seven days, no doubt through traditionalist senators' protests: there were precedents for such a job, but only if both consuls, not one, were away from Rome. In Spain, Augustus' health then went badly wrong and in the Balkans, a delicate manoeuvre went wrong too. In 24 (probably) the governor of Macedonia, a 'public province', was moved to wage war outside its boundaries. Revealingly, this illegal war had as its target a people whom the great Licinius Crassus had gained as 'clients' by his recent military prowess.[7] The action was illegal (only the Roman people had the right to make war or peace) and Augustus' tacit encouragement was suspected: it was too tempting an opportunity, a snub to Crassus yet again. Worse, there were suspicions that Augustus' young nephew, Marcellus, had urged on the offending governor. Marcellus had begun to enjoy an accelerated public career with Augustus' backing, but his advancement was not uncontroversial and, on any view, he had absolutely no business to be involved in such an order. Augustus was seriously ill, but he could see scandal coming. The year 23 began with a non-partisan noble as consul; in the spring there were real fears that Augustus would die.

The surrounding chronology is still disputed, but certainly on 1 July 23 Augustus ceremonially resigned his consulship. Instead, he took a new card, the powers of a tribune but detached from the popular office of tribune itself. The consulship could then be opened up to senatorial competitors to their satisfaction. The first holder of the honour was another non-Augustan, a man, however, whom Horace teased for his taste in slave-boys. Augustus also received the power of an ex-consul, made greater than the power of all provincial governors (he had lost this power by surrendering the consulship). Other specific powers were voted to him to 'legalize' his dealings with the Senate and people, but he could not stop the Balkan scandal playing itself out. It was arguably in early 22 that the offending governor in Macedonia was finally put on trial in Rome. In defence, he cited the advice 'now of Augustus, now of Marcellus'. It was a dreadful moment, making a nonsense of Augustus' professed 'Republic'. Augustus appeared unexpectedly in court, but let down the defendant and his defending lawyer by his answers. He was then confronted with a serious plot against his life, which was shared in by the defence lawyer whom he had betrayed. The conspirators were killed off: an informer was thoroughly rewarded. It was a real crisis.[8]

During these months Augustus might have been killed and the Republic could have been restored in earnest. Things were still very fragile. However, Augustus' new bundle of powers was certainly not a retreat from his previous legal position. Instead, they made different strengths in his power-base more prominent. The tribune's power evoked his special relations with Rome's plebs (including his power to propose laws), while his proconsular power kept him connected with the standing armies in his many provinces. It was 'greater' than that of other proconsuls, like the power voted to Pompey to cope with the grain crises of 57 BC: ironically, the Liberators (in 43 BC) had been voted the same. These powers would represent the two pillars of a Roman emperor's position for centuries. Perhaps Augustus had also been thinking during his sickness of ensuring a successor. It would be easier to give someone these powers, which were detached from any need to be elected to office. But he had also surely been planning the change for his own immediate ends in the face of a crisis which was already brewing. In the storm he would enact a shrewd withdrawal, not from his power-base, but from centre stage. The senators could have back the consulships (it would be hard for him to go on monopolizing them anyway in an age of 'peace'), but they would then learn the hard way that he was indispensable at Rome.

The sequel was severe disorder in the city. A plague, no doubt, was unforeseeable, but a severe grain shortage usefully caused Augustus to be begged to intervene: he settled it (having provoked it?) in ten days. He then left the city and went off to deal slowly with the question of Parthia in the East. In his absence, the people refused to elect two consuls for 21 BC. A constitutional impasse threatened. By 19, still in his absence, a new champion of the people's interests, Egnatius Rufus, had emerged in Rome and had to be stopped from running directly for the consulship by the 'ultimate decree', passed by the Senate and enforced by the sole consul in office. By 19 there was a continuing crisis in the city which only Augustus could solve: like Pompey in 52, he had become indispensable.

In 19 BC envoys from Rome went out to him, finding him in Greece and persuading him to nominate a new consul (he chose a noble). Augustus then returned to Italy, to his villa near Naples, where he arrived, apparently quietly, in midsummer. At Rome, an embassy of the consuls, magistrates and leading citizens was duly dispatched to meet with him. It was a cardinal moment, a further capitulation by Rome's upper orders. Augustus did not want a triumph or a big daytime welcome, but before he entered Rome again details in his formal powers did need to be sorted out. His formal power was probably able to run inside Rome already, but henceforward it was to be made visible to onlookers by being accompanied with the formal insignia of office. Manifestly, he would be seen to combine the popular powers of a tribune with his power of command greater than all consuls and ex-consuls. The ambiguity between 'Senate' and 'people' in so much of the history of the Republic was now to be seen to be resolved in one man's hands, at the request of both parties.

Instead of a triumph, Augustus opted for an altar to 'Fortune, the bringer-back'. It was false modesty, because there was no luck about his return. A separate festival, in October, was to be held just outside the city; more realistically, it was called the 'Augustalia' and became an annual event. One spectator, however, was absent: the poet Virgil whom Augustus had brought back, a sick man, from Greece. He had died in Naples, but his great epic poem, the *Aeneid*, was almost complete. It already contained lines on the official view of the past, on the decadence of Antony, the Egyptian queen (never named personally), her dreadful gods and the saving of Roman values by the victor. Yet its view of its hero,

Rome's founding father Aeneas, was more delicately shaded. If it had all been written thirty years later, there would have been even more pressure on Virgil to make Augustus' own deeds explicit. As the poem stood, it told future Romans to 'remember' that it was their role to 'spare those they subjected and to conquer utterly the proud in war'.[9] This advice was all very well, but it did not characterize the Roman of the moment, Augustus himself. He had ruthlessly killed off his opponents, he had won no glory in battle and he had cheated and outmanoeuvred the proudest men left in Rome.

MORALS AND SOCIETY

The divine Augustus banished his daughter who was shameless beyond the very limits of the word. He made public the scandals of the Emperor's household, that adulterers had been admitted in droves, that the city had been roamed through on nocturnal revels and that the very Forum and Rostrum from which her father had passed the law on adultery had been her preferred places for her debaucheries . . . from being an adulteress, she had turned to selling her person for money and had sought the right to every sort of indulgence with partners whose names she did not know.

Seneca, *On Benefits* 6.32

I myself saw in Africa someone who changed sex and became a man on the day of his marriage: Lucius Constitius, a citizen of the town of Thysdrus.

Elder Pliny, *Natural History* 7.36

AUGUSTUS' CONSERVATIVE REVOLUTION did not stop with the constitution: it also extended to religion and social and sexual behaviour. These dimensions are directly relevant to personal freedom and to what it would mean to be a prominent Roman man or woman henceforward under the Empire. They are also the context for some of the most admired poetry of the Augustan age, especially poems by Horace, Ovid and Propertius. They continued to concern each subsequent emperor, with varying responses. Under Hadrian, the senators still had to rule on vexed points of the Augustan laws on marriage and sexual relations. They also had to cope with Hadrian himself. Excelling even Augustus' concern, he was later alleged to have used army-supply officers to spy on his friends' private lives. When he intercepted letters in which a wife complained about her husband's preference for 'pleasures' and the baths, the husband, when confronted, is said to have asked Hadrian, 'Has my wife complained to you as well as to me?'[1]

Why ever had such matters become public business? The dreadful troubles of the Civil War could be traced to neglect of the gods, the collapse of ancient morality and guilt inherited from Rome's Trojan past. These facile explanations were taken up by Virgil and also by Horace and even those who did not really believe them were aware of the climate of opinion. In the 40s and 30s most of Rome's religious rites and yearly observances were not seriously in abeyance or even in sceptical decay. What had decayed, as so often in ancient cities, was the temples. Restoration of the temples was not a new idea of Augustus', either. In the 30s temple-building had been part of the competitive rivalry in Rome: even Cicero's friend, the non-political and cultured Atticus, had been urging such action.[2] But Augustus restored at least eighty-two temples. He added new ones as well, for gods connected with his own career. Like Augustus, Hadrian would also restore old temples in the city, including the magnificent Pantheon, the ancient distinction of modern Rome. He repeated the temple's great dedicatory inscription by the self-made man Agrippa, but, like so many of Augustus' restorations, his was not an exact repeat.

Augustus' religious restoration was radically new, and what made it so was his own increasing dominance. He was made a new member, like nobody else, of all Rome's priestly colleges. Cults and festivals increasingly included prayers and references to himself and his family; above all, the calendar grew to include new festival days commemorating crucial dates for 'Caesar' in the 30s and for his father Julius Caesar during his dictatorship. Time, in the restored Republic, acquired profoundly unrepublican markers. So did the religious map. The ancient Sibylline Books were moved to Augustus' new temple of Apollo, next to his house on Rome's Palatine hill. The ancient goddess of the Hearth (Vesta) received a new cult-site here, also next to his home.

'Whoever wishes to take away impious slaughter,' wrote Horace in an ode in the early 20s BC, 'if he aims to have the words "Father of cities" inscribed beneath his statues, let him dare to curb unbroken licence.'[3] The verses were suitably prophetic. From 18 BC onwards, the 'Father of the Fatherland' (as Augustus became in 2 BC) encouraged laws against 'licence' in sex and marriage. While aspiring to go back to basics, they were tendentious, intrusive and quite often hated. One answer was to evade them, but they continued to be revised and feared for centuries. In our age, the 'problems of the family' are problems of divorce and single parents, with public discussions of homosexual relations and racial integration. None of these problems was addressed in Augustan Rome.

Like the restoration of the temples, legislation on sex and the family touched a pre-existing chord. It was not only that the likes of Cicero had written of the need for Julius Caesar, as dictator, to encourage the birth of more children and to curb the 'licence' of women or that Julius had stood forward as 'prefect of morals'. On a longer view, Roman education had always been strongly based in the family and in the lessons which parents transmitted to children. For centuries, too, the censors and their reviews of Rome's upper orders had put moral standards at the centre of Roman public life. Laws, then, would rest on a strong undercurrent of custom and long-repeated examples. By now there were stories of Roman matrons who had been prosecuted in the distant past for adultery before the Roman people. Way back in 405 BC, it was alleged, a tax had been introduced on Roman bachelors. Laws against the unmarried may even have been revived in the 30s BC.[4] At that time Augustus had widely publicized the 'immorality' of 'Egyptian' Antony, a spin which Virgil enlarged on in parts of his *Aeneid*. After victory, a return to old Roman values was a natural next step for a self-styled 'restorer'. The antiquarian scholar, Varro, had recently written a book, *On the Life of the Roman People*, which gave a highly moralizing account of its ancient ideals. A 'return' to them would enhance Augustus' artful claim to be restoring ancient rights to the people. But it was only worth trying because it had a constituency. The 30s, like the 40s, had echoed to moralizing rhetoric, and they had also been a disorderly time for class-distinctions: an ex-slave was even found to have tried to stand as a praetor. Horace, himself a social nobody, had capitalized on such outrages by protesting in his poems during the 30s at jumped-up holders of prized positions.[5] The Senate, too, had grown too large, with many members of dubious merit. In 28 it had already had to be slimmed by the young 'Caesar'. Survivors were aware that there had recently been too much social confusion.

The plebs in Rome, at bottom conservatives, might also welcome this sort of restoration: it clipped upper-class excesses and few of the new legal penalties would affect them personally. There was also a marked change in the upper classes. The Civil Wars had brought more men from outlying Italy into greater prominence at Rome, 'dim characters with fantastic names'[6] whose youth had often been spent in narrow and priggish home towns. Italy was a varied place, but some of its townsmen might rally to a call of 'back to basics', like the residents of modern Idaho or

Tunbridge Wells. A reassertion of ancient dignity would appeal to new men who were newly arrived in high places; it persuaded them, Catos and Ciceros at heart, that their new eminence was indeed as sound and traditional as they had expected. Augustus may even have started to believe in his own early rhetoric as Octavian. For he too was a man from 'little Italy', from a family of petty status which lacked the breadth and assurance of Rome's great families and their awareness that 'moral dignity' was so often the limited value of those who had not been told any better. He later wrote how he had brought back 'many examples of our ancestors which were disappearing from our age'.[7]

The first major laws came in 18 BC, a year after Augustus' reception back in Italy and a year before he declared a symbolic 'new age' of his own. One target was childlessness among Roman citizens, a long-running item for social rhetoric. When addressing it, Augustus read to the Senate an ancient speech on the topic which had been delivered by the censor in 131 BC. The Civil Wars had claimed nearly twenty years' worth of Roman casualties, but there was probably a widespread feeling that Rome's legions should still be manned by Italian-born citizens only. The unmarried and the childless were now to be penalized by diminished rights to inherit property (the childless man had to surrender up to half of a legacy, although later versions of the law, perhaps as a concession, allowed him the right of free inheritance from close members of his family). Husbands with children were rewarded with the right to earlier tenure of a magistracy (one child sufficed here, including one killed in war), and various other privileges, including escape from the burdensome task of being a guardian of a child or a woman (three children were needed for this). Three children also exempted a woman from the need for her and her property to be under a guardian's control. Between couples, each child increased the capacity of a husband and wife to inherit from one another. If they were childless, they were limited to inheriting only one-tenth, and gifts between husband and wife were invalid (although a husband could buy something, for instance, and let the wife use it or regard it as acquired for her). There were also advantages for fertile freedmen and freedwomen who had recently received citizenship. Many of them were still liable to perform 'tasks' for the patrons who had freed them. Henceforward, two children, in most cases, would exempt them from these burdens. Freed persons who had several children could also exclude their patrons from a major menace, inheritance by the patron of their property on their death. This rule was most attractive to those freedmen who had gone on to make money and become rich.

In ancient Sparta, fathers of three or more children were also said to have been rewarded, but nonetheless, the male Spartiate population had declined drastically. Why would the result at Rome be any different? In the upper classes, at least, girls were already married off by their fathers when young, sometimes as young as twelve to sixteen. An early age of females at marriage is a crucial determinant of the birthrate in a pre-industrial population, but Augustus' laws did nothing directly to change it. They did, however, keep down the marriage age for ambitious men: the sooner a man married, the quicker his career would now be. There was also a very intrusive change for women later in life. Widows or divorcées were penalized if they failed to remarry promptly, within an interval which was later extended by Augustus to two years. Many women had been widowed by the recent Civil Wars and were still young, so there was quite a constituency here to bring back to family life: even in peacetime, wives, who married young, would expect to survive their husbands (childbirth permitting). The penalties were radical. It was also proposed, initially, that unmarried men should be excluded from watching the games and the theatre, but the proposal proved too much for the public's tolerance.

Only in families with property would most of the new privileges for fertility have had any relevance. There were, however, grave consequences to this insistence on big families. Knights had to own property above a fixed valuation, and, by new rules set by Augustus, so did senators. On a Roman father's death, properties were split between surviving children (there was no primogeniture), but if families were big, the property would be broken into smaller bits: those near the borderline would find their children pushed below its financial limit. Augustus' two ideals of a populous citizenry and well-defined social orders were contradictory. There was also a resentment among some of the better-off of the 'bore' (*taedium*) of bringing up brats, as we hear from the younger Pliny (*c.* AD 100), complaining about the habits of his Italian home townsmen.[8]

It is understandable, then, that members of the order of the knights at Rome protested openly before Augustus when these laws were revised in AD 9. It was all very well for Augustus to reply by publicizing his own grandson's behaviour and displaying his two young grandchildren on his lap: a prince of the imperial house was nowhere near the borderline of any social order. The display was only the latest of several of his publicity stunts in this sphere. When an old man from Faesulae (modern Fiesole, near Florence) was discovered to have sixty-one living descendants, he was brought down to Rome to make a religious sacrifice on the Capitol which was recorded in official records. The irony was that Augustus himself fathered only one daughter and no sons at all. Publicizing fertility, he himself had none of the fertility of Pompey, let alone the teeming Mark Antony. As for Hadrian, he found his wife Sabina moody and difficult and so he remained childless. The laws would have penalized him, too.

Did Roman citizens respond to Augustus' wishes by breeding faster? The recorded census figures at Rome do rise sharply after 28 BC, but the rise may only be a change in the numbers of citizens who registered, and the demographic meaning of these figures is still disputed. More obviously, there were so many obstacles and evasions to the laws, old and new. How can a law assure fertility? The important questions here are whether contraception of any effective sort was being used during marriage. Probably it was not: it was a slander that Hadrian's wife Sabina was said to boast 'that she had taken steps to make sure that she did not become pregnant by him: his children would harm the human race'.[9] In its absence, there was scope for abortion, but again we do not know whether wives in a high property class often practised it. If they did, the Augustan laws might indeed make them hesitate. Among poor families, certainly, unwanted children were exposed, especially girls, the wombs of the future (they were more expensive for fathers as they needed dowries in order to be married off). No Augustan laws addressed these age-old obstacles to a big, surviving family among people with scarce resources.

Very soon, there were to be some eloquent dodges too. Under the new laws, an engagement to marry was as effective as being married: men, therefore, were found to have betrothed themselves to baby girls whom they never intended to marry. As marriage could hasten or improve a man's career, some men married just before canvassing for a position and then unmarried as soon as they had received it. Restrictions on bequests were evaded by leaving goods 'on trust' for friends or relations to pass on to named recipients. Legal texts show Augustus upholding the validity of these 'trusts' in another context, apparently without realizing that they could also be used to outwit his laws against childlessness.[10]

The moral virtue of Roman citizens was also an old chestnut: it was a value rooted in past history, one which Augustus would take for granted. Here, he addressed all citizen-classes. Later in his reign, in 2 BC and AD 4, he curbed excessive 'manumission' (freeing) of slaves and postponed full freedom for a slave until the age of thirty. He was not concerned here with a potential slave-shortage. Tens of thousands of slaves had been taken recently during his army's wars in western Europe, with many more to come. More relevantly, some Roman slave-owners were said to be freeing slaves so that as citizens, they could claim the free corn-dole and live on it while still serving their masters as freedmen. Benefit fraud would certainly concern Augustus, but the main fear was that unworthy slaves were being given the cherished citizenship and that those who freed them were sometimes very young men, who were unable to tell good characters from bad. Once again, moral concern drove the reforms: these laws on 'quality control' persisted for the next five hundred years. Suggestively, the same year, AD 4/5, is the date of a ruling which defined the privileged citizen-class in some, perhaps all, of the towns of Egypt. Here, too, Augustus may have imposed a clearer category of 'respectable' citizenship.

The conduct of existing citizens in Rome was also addressed. On festival days old-style processions were revived for the upper orders. Distinguished young men were encouraged to ride in complex formations and to enact the 'old' game, revived by Julius Caesar and supposedly derived from Troy, Rome's parent city. Virgil's *Aeneid* obligingly traces this game back to Aeneas' funeral games for his dead father. Augustus celebrated this Troy Game 'very often', even in his new Forum, until falls and casualties obliged him to suspend it. He also revived the ancient yearly horse parade for those Roman knights who had the honour of a public horse. It was held on 15 July, but it too must have caused anxiety among men whose skills on horseback were now quite often minimal.

There was also a stress on the moral improvement of the young. In Italian towns, Augustus encouraged local 'colleges' for young men in which they were to exercise, practise with weaponry and go hunting. At Rome, boys were not allowed out to watch games or shows by night without an adult attendant. In the city centre, Augustus is even said to have ordered all citizens to wear the woolly white toga. His own daughter and granddaughters were said to have been reintroduced to the old arts of weaving and spinning. Augustus was proud of his own toga, woven in the ancient fashion. Society women were quick, however, to cut away their matronly *stola*, give it shoulder straps and wear it invitingly just above their bosoms.

Senatorial families were particularly targeted. Sons of senators had to wear the special senatorial shoe and a patterned toga: they were expected, poor boys, to wear them to senatorial meetings where they now had to watch what dragged on, as future participants. They would be penalized, too, if they married unadvisedly. From 18 BC onwards senators, their sons, grandsons and great-grandsons were to be heavily penalized if they married freedwomen, actresses or actresses' children (the stage was an ignoble and promiscuous profession). Their female descendants were to be penalized if they married a freedman. Roman laws had never penalized marriages in general between free citizens and freedmen. Nor did Augustus, though he showed his own social preference by refusing to have freedmen at his dinner table. What concerned him, rather, was his image as the upholder of senatorial dignity; hence he proposed these laws on senatorial marriages, and the ban on inferior wives or husbands marrying into this class.

However, there were ways round his obstacles. Instead of marrying, a senator could live with a freedwoman as his 'concubine', what we would call a partner. After the death of a first wife, such a 'concubine' was often preferable to the jealousies and insecurities of a second wife. Any citizen (not just a senator) was also to be penalized if he married somebody of 'ill-repute', a brothel-owner, pimp, actor or gladiator. Again, concubinage was the way round, with the advantage that gifts could be made validly to a concubine (but not to a wife) during a man's lifetime. But the option was not open to men who found themselves promoted to the Senate when already married: they were rare cases, but if they had married beneath themselves, they would have to divorce and aim higher. Again, this element of quality control over newcomers may have been Augustus' main concern.

The crowning law was a notorious law against adultery. Previously, adultery had been a private matter, to be settled by the husband or father within the Roman household. In 18 BC Augustus made it a public crime, which was to be tried in court. The scope of this law is still disputed, but much of the detail is clear enough. The most extreme case was nicely considered. If a father caught his daughter and her boyfriend in the act on family premises, he could legally kill his daughter on the spot. The threat was more rhetorical than realistic. Only if the father killed his daughter could he then kill the adulterer too ('adultery' is derived from the Latin 'to another person', *ad alterum*, not from 'adult behaviour'). Husbands' right to kill was even more restricted. If the husband caught the couple, he could not kill his wife. He could only kill her boyfriend if the offender was of ill-repute. But he could corner the bounder for up to twenty hours to extract proof of guilt from him: it could have been quite an interview.

These extreme penalties were more hypothetical than an everyday reality. Much more importantly, the husband had to divorce his wife and prosecute her within sixty days if he had caught her in the act. Even so, without a head-on discovery, it might seem that couples could agree to live privately with their affairs and do nothing. However, a third party could prosecute within another four months if no action was being taken, and the husband could be prosecuted too. The danger here was that an outsider, an angry relation perhaps, would start up a prosecution of one or the other's lover and then try to extend it as if the 'crime' had been known all along and tolerated. Even slaves could be tortured to reveal intimate details. It was a particular danger because in some cases, husbands would have been condoning a wife's affair so that they could take money or favours off her boyfriend in return. That sort of connivance was now made criminal. So was the aiding and abetting of adultery by providing a room, for instance, for the impatient couple. Similar penalties applied to men who had sex with a single woman of respectable status.

What was at stake here was not male fidelity. Like all ancient societies, Rome was highly stratified. If a man had sex with a slave-girl (or a slave-boy), a prostitute or a low-grade woman of infamy, he was not penalized at all. There was a 'double standard', one for men, and a stricter one for respectable women. Socially, this standard coexisted with a 'double classification': the lowest orders could still be penetrated without reprisals. In this light, we can make sense of Horace's poetic presentation. His public poems are explicitly in favour of the curbs on adultery (the 'staining sacrilege'[11]) and the promotion of big families. But he is also the Horace with a taste for party-girls and women with fine Greek names. The context, here, is that these women are slave-girls and mistresses in a *demi-monde*. By the double classification, they are irrelevant to matters of sound Roman family morality. Like Horace, Augustus himself had fancied a male sweetheart, evidently a boy of low servile status.[12]

To modern liberal eyes, these laws are abominable. Husbands or wives convicted of adultery lost up to half their property (and part of the wife's dowry) and were banished to an island. An adulterous wife was forbidden to remarry and, in general, the rules against widows and lovers made women's lives even less at their own discretion. Yet they were not just Augustus' idiosyncrasy. In classical Athens, after all, a husband could kill an adulterer caught in the act or humiliate him with notorious punishments (pushing a radish, penis-shaped, up his backside was an Athenian reprisal long before Romans prescribed it). There was also scope in Athens for a third party to bring a prosecution for adultery: women found guilty were banned from participating in festivals and were liable to have their clothes ripped if they did so. We now execrate the Augustan laws, but we put the Athenians' laws down to civic cohesion or fears about illegitimate citizens. The difference is that we know how, previously at Rome, this 'offence' had not been a public crime at all and that the change was hated, flouted and betrayed by those supposed to uphold it. Among the Athenians, it was not controversial. Among Romans, there was at least a context for it in recent public discourse, the sort of moralizing sounded by Cicero. He had expounded that 'if the way of life of the nobles is altered, then the customary behaviour of a state is changed'.[13] In 44 BC his invective against Antony and Fulvia had publicized what sort of behaviour in households and marriages was totally unacceptable to all 'good men and true' and how it was a risk to the functioning of the community. Not everybody took this sort of rhetoric so seriously, but it had rested on ground which Augustus now occupied too.[14]

Augustus' successor, Tiberius, had the restraint of a true Roman aristocrat: while retaining Augustus' laws, he tended to leave charges of adultery to be settled privately. In AD 19 it even emerged that a lady of good praetorian family, Vistilia, had registered herself as a prostitute in order to escape the laws altogether and continue to have her boyfriends with impunity: her aunt, by contrast, had dutifully married no less than six husbands in a row (probably, as each one died) and had given birth to seven children. Perhaps this Augustan good conduct made her niece so much more scandalous.[15] In the jaundiced view of the historian Tacitus, the law was simply motivated by the financial gains which the Treasury would make from its penalties. It was, he reasoned, part of the increased oppression of the laws, an aspect which had intensified under the emperors. Reported trials for adultery are quite rare in Tacitus' histories, but the fact remains that the laws continued to be applied and clarified in connection with the ever-growing number of Roman citizens. In AD 190 more than 3,000 prosecutions for adultery were found to be pending in Rome.[16] Legal texts confirm that Roman citizens in the provinces could be affected too.[17]

Unlike Horace, the Augustan love-poets Propertius and Ovid represent the other side to the 'crime'. They describe themselves as lovers of women who are married and not obviously from a shady *demi-monde*. Ovid's poems are more evasive, but give tips on how to pick up respectable women, while those of Propertius even dwell on the procuress, the depths of ill-repute.[18] Ovid's witty poem, the *Art of Love*, appeared in a second edition, probably in 1 BC, and if so, at a most inopportune moment. In the previous year, at the summit of his achievements, Augustus, the new 'Father of the Fatherland', had to face the fact that his own daughter Julia was guilty of flagrant adultery. It did not help that she said memorably that she only did it when pregnant: 'I only invite another pilot when the ship is full.'[19] Those who go 'back to basics' are at risk to their own households: the discovery was followed by another, that Augustus' granddaughter was guilty of the same.

The vocal opposition, the evasions and the hypocrisy in high places give the Roman legislation a deservedly bad name. There was an irony to it all. If Antony had won, it would have been quite different. 'Inimitable at sex', he would have let others get on with it unimpeded. Dead, he could at least trust to his son. In 2 BC it was this man, the young Iullus Antonius, who was held most to blame for the adultery with Augustus' daughter.

42

SPECTATOR SPORTS

Whether you win, whether you lose, we love you, Polidoxus (Renown).

**Caption for the portrait of Renown, a racehorse,
on the floor-mosaic of Pompeianus at Cirta, in Algeria**

Illustrious Fame used to sing of the lion laid low in the vast valley of Nemea, the work of Heracles.

Let ancient testimony be silent: after your shows, Caesar, we have now seen this done by a woman's hand.

**Martial, *On Spectacles* 8
(on Titus' show in the Colosseum, AD 80)**

B ESIDES ITS BUILDINGS and its new regulations, Rome under Augustus and his successors is conspicuous in history for the scale of its public entertainments. Some of them set a fashion throughout the Empire; many of them connected with the emperor's 'care' for the common people and the promotion of members of his family. They also challenged his views on morality, just as in other ways they still challenge ours.

The most civilized face of Augustan show business was the one which the Emperor Hadrian most favoured. It was the world of music and the theatre, the cultural invention of the Greeks. Italy had had its own simple tradition of farce and drama, but Greek plays became much more popular, particularly from the second century BC onwards. They were accompanied by other Greek arts: recitations of episodes from Homer, mime-acting, the declaiming of particular myths and dramatic scenes and, above all, pantomime-dancing. Pantomime was antiquity's nearest equivalent to ballet. A silent dancer, wearing silk, performed challenging roles

(Hercules in his madness being most difficult) while musicians and singers accompanied the rhythm and movement. Augustus adored the pantomime and popularized it at Rome, favouring a virtuoso dancer called Pylades who was the first to add a chorus and an orchestra.

The theatre was potentially more awkward. Mime-actors performed light sketches which were sometimes slightly risqué; prominent senators, including Mark Antony, sometimes had a mime-actress as a mistress. The top mime-actors could be impudent in public and provoke popular protests and, as a result, emperors sometimes banished the artists from Rome. But mythical tragedies could be problematic too. Augustus himself once tried to write a play about Ajax, but when Romans wrote plays on the problems of mythical Greek dynasties, the plots were not at all to his taste. By implication they reflected on his own dynastic problems.

Theatre, dance and music were the cultural Greek arts which Hadrian would also patronize. Loving Greek culture, he made them central to the Panhellenic festival which he founded in Athens in 131/2. He also approved and promoted them in provincial cities where they had remained a vigorous part of Greek civic life, as had Greek athletics, which had radiated outwards from that triumph of conservatism, the Olympic Games. At Rome, athletics had first been publicized as part of a major triumphal show in 186 BC: at the time, Greek athletes had been shown competing naked in the pentathlon. Augustus enjoyed watching Greek athletics, but never founded a festival for them in Rome itself. They became entrenched there only under the Emperor Domitian. In 86 Domitian founded Rome's first enduring Greek festival, the Capitoline Games.[1] It offered contests in music, poetry and athletics, and both male and female athletes competed for prizes. The accompanying buildings were lavish, including a stadium which is still visible as the open space of Rome's famous Piazza Navona.

A 'moral minority' disliked what so many others enjoyed. Athletes in Greek games still ran, boxed and wrestled naked, and the latter, especially, was a provocatively sexual sight: Augustus banned women from watching athletes in the city. Moralists continued to feel that such games should be banned entirely because they 'spread vice'. In the Greek cities, males also trained and wrestled naked in gymnasiums, the male clubs of the citizenry. Romans adopted gymnasiums, too, but they used them as centres for debate and fully clothed activity.

Rather inconsistently, they reserved nudity for the public baths. Baths were a Greek invention, too, but Roman patrons transformed the simple style of bath-tubs heated by charcoal braziers. Luxurious under-floor heating became a Roman hallmark and was hugely prodigal of fuel and finance. The system was given the most luxurious 'origin', being credited to the enterprising Sergius Orata when he had wanted to heat artificial oyster-beds on the Bay of Naples. In Augustus' Rome, the heated swimming pool was championed by the bon viveur, his friend Maecenas, who also introduced donkey-meat as a delicacy.[2]

Big, heated bath-houses would spread in cities all over the Roman Empire and duly became part of luxurious Roman country houses. Hadrian's huge villa had no less than three sets of them. In 33 BC, 170 small private sets of baths had been listed in the city but it was in Augustan times that heated baths became a major public amenity.[3] In 25 BC Agrippa built a big set of 'people's baths' as part of the development of the Campus Martius. Here, men and women bathed separately and there was respect for a 'Spartan'-style scalding with a hot steam bath, a rubbing with oil and a cold swim. The number of Rome's baths then multiplied fivefold during the next four centuries, leaving so-called 'Spartan' austerity far behind. In some of them, men and women bathed naked together. A dazzling array of imported marbles reflected light and colour and, under successive emperors, the scale of the places became huge. 'What is worse than Nero,' it was said, 'but what is better than Nero's baths?'[4] Soon, the answer was Titus' baths, and then the remarkable baths of Trajan, a sports-complex some 10,000 yards square which was built on the former site of a wing of Nero's 'Golden House'. Dedicated in 109, it was an architectural masterpiece of brick and concrete with a big open-air swimming pool and a huge vaulted cold bath in the shape of a cross on its main axis. The later baths of Diocletian (c. 305) were even bigger, holding up to 3,000 bathers.

Besides bathing, the most acceptable face of Augustan popular entertainment was chariot racing. It too had a long history among rich competitors at Greek festivals and it had been an early import into Rome. The historian Tacitus traced Rome's horse racing to the Greek city of Thurii in southern Italy but, as others said, it was probably an even earlier import, coming from the Etruscan cities whose nobles had loved it.[5] At Rome the sport became distinctive. The typical Roman chariot race involved seven 'laps' round two turning-posts, which were taken in an anti-clockwise direction. The main site was the Circus Maximus, where horses emerged from a Roman speciality, the starting stalls (carceres, or 'prisons'). In Greek races, many individual chariots competed (up to forty-one are attested in one race), but at Rome, competitors raced only in multiples of four, up to a maximum of twelve. One reason for these foursomes was the existence of four 'factions' at Rome, each of which was named after a colour (Blues, Greens, Reds and Whites). The factions, too, were old (probably as old as the third century BC) and in keeping with noble Romans' concern for their 'peer group', they dampened the scope for personal competition by individuals. Although factions were organized with links to socially prominent citizens, their teams no longer raced in an individual's name. In the 80s the Emperor Domitian tried to add Golds and Purples, but they did not last long. Contests between two factions, or 'colours', were held as the first big events of the day 'after the procession' and when driven by known champions they were much admired. The career of one great chariot-champion is known to us, Gaius Appuleius Diocles, who raced nearly 2,000 times. His results suggest that the early leader in a race tended to be the winner.[6]

Here, too, important popular work had been done at Rome for Octavian by Agrippa in the late 30s BC. Freedmen under his patronage can be traced in connection with the stables for chariot racing: he presented the famous silver dolphins which marked the laps in races in the Circus Maximus (they commemorated Augustus' naval victory over Sextus Pompeius in 36 BC). Augustus, in due course, allowed chariot races to be added to public celebrations of his birthday and he donated an obelisk from his Egyptian victory over Cleopatra to the centre of the Circus. The scale of these occasions was amazing. Not until Claudius did the Circus begin to have stone seating, but more than 200,000 spectators could watch the racing. The Roman crowds for horse racing are still the largest sports-crowds in world history.

In the Circus and other open spaces in the city, there were also violent blood sports. We think of gladiatorial shows before all else, but there were three other types of slaughter: bloody battles between fierce wild animals, bloody hunts between wild animals and humans, mock sea-battles, even, between teams of armed combatants. Their origins went back into the years of the Republic, but successive emperors took them to a new peak.

The most recent of these 'sports' was the mock sea-battle, a Roman speciality which had begun with Julius Caesar's spectacular display in 46 BC. By contrast, wild beast 'hunts' appear to have originated much earlier in Carthage where cruel spectacles (including crucifixion) were well established: Carthage had ready access to the teeming wild life of north Africa. Significantly, battles between wild animals first appear in Rome during the era of wars with Carthage, when elephants were shown and shot to death.[7] In 167 BC we first hear of a variation: criminals and prisoners of war were offered up to wild animals too. Quite often the participants in these 'hunts' were tied up before competing. Wild animals were tied to one another, and the criminals entered with their hands tied or were hung, just within the beasts' reach, on a stake or platform. The purely human combat of gladiators was a much older sport. It had first been staged at Rome in 264 BC, perhaps in imitation of combats in south Italy, although Romans traced it, like so much else, to the Etruscans' example (they may be right).

Augustan sports-practice, therefore, was heir to established precedent which had already been exploited massively both by Pompey and Julius Caesar. Augustus was proud of his 'blood sports' too: in 2 BC he looked back on twenty-six shows of hunting which had killed off 3,500 wild animals and eighteen gladiatorial shows which had involved 10,000 men.[8] He also built a big artificial 'lake' in Rome on which he staged his vast mock sea-battle in 2 BC. A century later his pride had been eclipsed. Between May 107 and November 109 Trajan celebrated his conquest of Dacia (modern Romania) with more than twenty weeks of blood sports, showing more than 5,500 pairs of gladiators and killing over 11,000 animals. In 119 Hadrian celebrated his own birthday with six days of slaughter which 'hunted' to death 1,000 animals (including 200 lions) in six spectacular days. The locations, too, improved. Under Augustus, the Roman shows took place in various venues in the city, including the Forum, although a stone amphitheatre was built by one of his aides. In the 70s the new Flavian dynasty built the biggest amphitheatre in Rome, what we call 'the Colosseum', with a seating capacity of up to 55,000. Apart from showing wild beast 'hunts' and gladiators, it appears to have had the capacity to be flooded for sea-battles or even (by Domitian) to be lit by night.

Rome's entertainments became a fashion throughout the Empire. The great Roman chariot races made the least impact. Although chariot racing in the Roman style was to be found in Alexandria (perhaps supported by the emperor), elsewhere there were few early copies of Rome's Circus (there is a good one, however, at Mérida in Spain). In the Greek world, horse racing had existed already for ages and so it did not need a new promotion. What really caught on were blood sports. Amphitheatres spread both east and west, whether to London (on the big Guildhall site) or Athens. The most impressive example, with important monuments and inscriptions of gladiators, was rediscovered in Córdoba in Spain in 2003. Individuals staged these shows in the Greek East, too, and Greek cities rivalled each other in the display. Above all, gladiators were associated with a province's cult of the emperor as a god. Its prestigious high priests staged these fights for eager crowds who perceived them, surely, as connected with their absent emperor. It is less clear whether Rome's mock sea-battles caught on widely. Perhaps they sometimes occurred in provincial games which commemorated Actium, Rome's last great sea-battle. At Rome, they were often staged as 'virtual history' in which teams replayed ancient contests from Greek history. Thucydides' text was much too hard to read, but his 'Peloponnesian War' found its biggest ever audience in the crowds who watched the replays, as 'Athens' was pitted against 'Sparta' in flooded Roman arenas.

This public display of violence raises distinct questions: why did people like it and why was it socially so prominent? There were certainly critics (some of whom still profited from it), and the Greeks on Rhodes refused to have gladiatorial sports at all.[9] The basic inhumanity must have been the obstacle, although we hear more about the moral outrage of 'free' people engaging in such things. However, the taste persisted, arguably because it is a latent fact of human nature. Shocked though we should be, we cannot help looking on with a thrill, like Lord Byron at a public execution, who describes himself as sympathizing with the victim but unable to hold his opera glasses steady.

The social prominence is more unusual. To say simply that Romans were brutal or sadistic is not adequate. For a start, the prominence of these games had not been uncontested. When animal hunts were first staged in the 180s BC they were banned, although the ban was probably due to the fear and envy they provoked among the donor's upper-class contemporaries.[10] Only after popular protests during the next decade were 'hunts' duly permitted. The reason for their subsequent public role is not so much 'sadism' as the particular type of political competition at Rome, where great men needed to shine before the crowd, and the Romans' military values which made this sort of display acceptable. Together, they kept 'blood sports' in the headlines. The emperors then intensified what republican Romans had already begun.

The setting of wild beasts on other wild beasts was an exotic bloody spectacle. It was not limited by concern for the animals: there was no notion of animal rights and only random sympathy for occasional piteous sights, like some distressed elephants as witnessed by Cicero. These animal shows were not official 'games' in the calendar. They were private benefactions by origin and so they came to be given as extra popular spectacles by individuals who were showing off during their military triumph. By extension, this type of game-show then became attached to the holding of magistracies: they became a magistrate's accepted bid for public favour. In Rome's distinctive culture of 'mass' and 'elite', they harnessed psycho-

52. Lavish amphitheatre mosaic, showing named hunters in the arena killing named leopards ('The Roman'; 'Luxurious'). Floor-mosaic from house of Magerius, near Thysdrus, Tunisia. Perhaps *c.* AD 260–80.

logical thrills to political competitors' lust for glory. Aspiring big men appealed to those with spectator status (and votes, seldom exercised) by promising exotic animal bloodshed which the crowds then found to be irresistible viewing. In provincial cities, such 'promises' then became the expected gesture at an earlier stage, from candidates seeking high office, even (as never at Rome) for a place on the town council. It helped if an individual had personal connections with a suitably 'animal' province. The greatest sufferer here was north Africa. On mosaics, we can see beasts being caged up and prepared for travel by ship, a complex business which, for imperial shows, might involve Roman soldiers in the catching and carting. In the magnificent later mosaic at Piazza Armerina in Sicily (*c.* AD 300), the design wittily concludes with a human hunter in a cage: the hunter is hunted, and guarded by a mythical sort of griffin.

The displays of wild beasts against criminals had a further resonance: they were public executions. Their human victims were even given a last little honour. On the night before their deaths, they were allowed a 'last supper' when the morrow's audience might come along and stare at them.[11] On the day, they might even be dressed up in purple and gold for their brief moment of 'glory'. At the sight of them, spectators might waver, albeit briefly. Sometimes, we are told, the bravery of condemned Christians made an impression on a pagan public and once, when they included naked women fresh from childbirth with 'their breasts still dripping milk' a crowd in Carthage showed its horror, and so they were taken away and dressed more decently.[12] However, the spectators were mentally distanced from the human suffering. They were watching the deaths of victims who were being 'justly' punished. These rotters (they assumed) deserved what they got, and socially they were beyond the pale.

The distance between viewers and victims was accentuated when such punishments began to be staged in imperial Rome in mythical or fantasy styles. Augustus himself had a noted Sicilian bandit executed in the Roman Forum on a replica of Mount Etna which 'erupted' and deposited the wretch among caged wild animals below. The possibilities are horribly clear in a series of epigrams by the poet Martial which celebrate the Emperor Titus' great spectacle in AD 80 for the opening of the Colosseum: they describe the re-enactment of mythological 'charades' with human victims in the Roman arena. Sex and violence could be most excitingly combined. Terracotta lamps found near the arena in Roman Athens show women having sex with animals, and so it was a small step at Rome to stage the myth of Pasiphae who squatted inside a wooden cow and had sex with her infatuation, a bull. 'What legend sings, the arena shows . . . ': 'virtual myth' became reality.[13] The mythical dimension imported elements familiar from the mime, the pantomime and theatre. The usual programme of a day's 'sport' would put the beast-hunts first in the morning, followed by the slaughter of criminals at lunchtime. A mythical staging mixed high and low culture together and livened up a repetitive midday of pure killing. It enhanced display and luxury and it distanced the viewers even further from the reality. There was nothing 'religious' about such staging, nor was it an honour for dead ancestors.

To us, the gladiators are more mysterious than the animal sports. However, most of the gladiators began as war-captives or criminals and had the status of slaves. A career in the arena gave these 'dregs' a sudden chance to win glory. Like the hunts, gladiatorial shows had never been part of the fixed calendar of games at Rome. They, too, had begun as private displays at funerals, but they then became the gift, or 'promise', of prominent men who were celebrating triumphs or bidding for yet more honours (like the young Julius Caesar, as aedile in 65). Here, the key is that many onlookers identified with the military values of the armed duels. Custom-built amphitheatres first appear in colonies of Roman veteran soldiers in Italy and the sport was then spread widely by Roman army-camps abroad. It was even said to be good for spectators to see such social inferiors being 'soldierly' and enduring wounds. Deaths did indeed occur, but they were not the essence of the show. Sometimes fighters were released with an honourable 'draw'; at other times the wounded one surrendered and the fight was stopped. We hear of prize-fighters who survived thirty fights, including a few combats which they lost. The Emperor Claudius, however, was known to be fond of a bloody finish.

Potentially, there was good money and a good career to be made here, and for the slaves or criminals there could be freedom too. In the crowds, fans went wild for particular 'stars': at Pompeii, graffiti applaud them as 'darling of the girls' or 'netter of chicks by night'.[14] For women too, 'heavy metal' and muscle could be horribly sexy: Augustus ruled that at gladiatorial shows women must sit only in the highest seats at the back. A glamour grew up around these fights, which drew free competitors into the arena too. Children played games of 'being gladiators' and there were female gladiators from time to time: at Ostia, a benefactor boasts in his inscription of being the 'first of all since Rome was founded to make women fight'.[15] Minorities, too, found a new public esteem in the arena. In 57, for a visiting Oriental prince, Nero staged the 'all-blacks', a show of north African contestants only, including women and children. It was left to Domitian to show women fighting dwarves.[16]

For Augustus and his successors, this intensified culture of the spectacle was a valuable public card. Unlike the big names of the Republic, the emperors now monopolized triumphs: they had far the greatest resources; they could show supreme 'liberality' and magnificence in shows for the plebs which nobody else could rival. Soon, the emperors had a special school for gladiators (probably beginning with Augustus). They owned gladiatorial troupes and increasingly came to predominate in staging the combats; they also dominated the chariot racing. But as 'First Citizens', they were expected to attend the shows in person. They were approved if, like Augustus or Hadrian, they took a keen interest in the events, whereas Julius Caesar, by contrast, had unwisely read his letters during the contests. Emperors were well advised to be keen, because audiences of several thousand in the theatre or 150,000 or more in the Circus Maximus would use the occasion to shout specific complaints or praises at their ruler and his family. Contemporaries did see these shows as an alternative to politics, but they were also something else. They were a dialogue between a ruler and his people whose demands were hardly very radical. The crowds usually shouted specific items of a limited, sometimes comic, scope. The occasion was one for frank speech and 'licence' in a non-political setting rather than a substitute for absent democracy. But it was also a potent reminder to foreign visitors and senatorial spectators that 'Caesar' enjoyed a relationship with the plebs which they could never possibly replicate.

The problem, for Augustus, was not so much the crowd as some of the young members of his esteemed upper orders. From the 40s BC onwards members of high society at Rome had shown a 'disgraceful' wish to appear on stage in person or even to fight in the arena. It did not help the promotion of ancestral values when Augustus' own nephew, Marcellus, allowed a Roman knight and some respectable Roman matrons to appear in the public show which he gave as a junior magistrate. Senators, knights and their families were banned from appearing as actors or gladiators, but the ban eventually proved futile. In AD 11 Augustus had to lift the ban on knights appearing as gladiators: he himself, in his old age, then sat and watched them doing it. It was still forbidden for free-born women to participate, but only if they were under twenty. Chariot racing, however, seems to have remained unregulated.

Austere Tiberius soon had the ban reinstated, but it did not last. It was so much more thrilling for young bloods to compete with a net, a sword or a trident in the arena than to uphold ancient morality in a heavy white toga. In due course, there were emperors who agreed. Caligula liked playing the gladiator, while Nero appeared on stage and drove a chariot at the races. In the 180s the ultimate shock was Commodus. Once, after fighting ostriches in the arena, he cut off their necks and advanced on the senators in their special seats, brandishing a sword in one hand and the bloodied head of a bird in the other. He gesticulated at the Senate as if their necks might be the next ones for his attention. And yet when he died there were senators who bought up his gladiatorial equipment.[17]

THE ROMAN ARMY

Total absentees	*456*
including 5 centurions	
Remainder, present	*296*
including 1 centurion	
From those:	
Sick	*15*
Wounded	*6*
Suffering from inflammation of the eyes	*10*
Total of these	*31*
Remainder, fit for active service	*265*
including 1 centurion.	

**Strength report of the First Cohort of Tungrians on
18 May (probably in the early 90s AD) at Vindolanda in
north Britain (*Tabulae Vindolandenses* 1.154)**

F OR NEARLY SIXTY YEARS Augustus' most important relationship was
not with theatre crowds: it was with the army. The soldiers had lived
through profound changes during the fall of the Republic which were crucial to the real 'Roman revolution'. Since the days of Sulla, there were so
many more of them under arms. After Julius Caesar's murder there had
been more than forty legions (each legion numbered about 5,000); the settlement of veterans remained a massive operation, inside and outside
Italy. Under Augustus, the legions reduced at first to twenty-six, but in AD
23, when we are given clear figures, there were still reckoned to be
150,000 citizen-soldiers in the legions (now numbering twenty-five) and
another 150,000 auxiliary soldiers in the important supporting units, almost all of whom were non-Romans and would receive citizenship only

on discharge. As the Empire's frontiers moved forward, these troops were being stationed ever further afield, but the sum total was still enormous.

Service, also, had been greatly increased. The age of 'triumvirs' had been characterized by long periods under arms, but after Actium those periods became official. Legionaries now had to serve for sixteen years (increased in AD 5 to twenty years) and in 13 BC a further four years 'under the standards' were added for men who had served their span. During this extra time, they were supposed to be called on only for combat with an enemy. In fact, service could drag on for up to thirty years without full discharge; in the Republic, the maximum length had been six years. Under Augustus, therefore, there was a real standing army. It was quite different from the citizen-armies which had been briefly called up in the Greek city-states, and it was far bigger than the core armies of Hellenistic kings, which were enlarged in wartime by hiring mercenaries and calling up military colonists from land-settlements. There were even localized fleets in naval bases, forming a small standing navy.

Like every emperor, Hadrian recognized the importance of this army, especially as he had to preside over its withdrawal from his predecessor's disastrous ventures in the East. Not a fighting emperor, he became a touring emperor. He gave off a military aura by addressing the troops in each province, and even sharing their diet of bread and cheese. By then (c. 120) their numbers were still bigger, as the auxiliaries and fleets had increased: up to 500,000 people were under arms, perhaps one in every 120 inhabitants of the Empire. Not until the seventeenth century, in France, would such proportions be matched again in a kingdom.

Since Augustus, each emperor was the acknowledged Commander (*Imperator*). Statues, therefore, often show emperors in military dress, and defeat of the barbarians was a major part of their image in art and poetry. They wore a wreath of laurel (signifying Victory) and at festivals, the special robe of a 'triumphing' commander. We can well see why Augustus' poor track record in combat was such a weakness. For as emperor, it was he who dealt with the army in general. It was he who fixed the pay-scales, allowances and lengths of service for each rank.[1] Until AD 6 he paid their rewards on discharge and gave the 'diplomas' for each retiring auxiliary. It was on his authority only that colonies were settled for veterans: the details of each colony's 'map' and property rights would be deposited, duly signed, in the emperor's own record office.[2] If the land for the colony was bought (sometimes it was not), it was Augustus who paid for it, a point which he emphasizes in his record of his achievements, because nobody had ever paid for so much land before. Most of the legions were in provinces which were the emperor's, not the 'public ones', and in them, his agents saw to the troops' pay.[3] In them, he alone gave out military decorations, but all veterans everywhere were 'his'. When he disbanded veterans after Actium, he gave them the full rights of Roman citizenship, the right to vote at Rome in whatever tribe they chose, exemption from all civic obligations in their local towns if they so wished, and a valuable immunity from tribute. However, veterans who settled in a colony in Spain would hardly bother about voting in Rome, while their local townsmen could no doubt make them hold local office with offers which they could not refuse. The privileges had to be asserted by their recipients, but they were not curtailed until the late second century (when they dropped to four years) and were not abolished until the third century.

Looking up to their emperor as Commander, the troops observed a calendar of Roman religious festivals and sacrifices. Probably, its form went back to Augustus' reign, although we only encounter evidence for it later, when the number of sacrifices to deified emperors and empresses had expanded. In the centre of a legionary camp, a shrine contained the legion's standards and images of the emperor and the Roman divinities (the soldiers' savings were also deposited here). Roman rituals of purification and of omen-taking were practised: we have the calendar of an auxiliary unit, of non-citizens, which included vows on 3 January for the well-being of the emperor, the eternity of the Roman Empire and sacrifices to the three great gods of the Roman Capitol.[4]

Under the Republic, refusal to serve when called had been punished by the death penalty. In the new age that sanction receded. Henceforward, service in the legions was almost always voluntary and forcible conscription was exceptional. At two moments of 'crisis', in AD 5 and 9, Augustus did resort to it; in the 60s, however, the Emperor Nero found that he could not even hold a forcible levy when he wished.[5] When levies are attested locally in the Empire, they are either levies of volunteers or levies for the non-citizen auxiliary units. Even so, the recruiting officers who conducted them were the emperor's men. About 6,000 recruits are the army's estimated yearly need, after the usual deaths and retirements, in order to maintain the legions at full strength each year. Surviving figures for the Roman census suggest that the rising citizen-population could have met that need very comfortably. It would therefore take a sudden very heavy demand for troops to make forcible enlistment a necessity. Otherwise, the emperor and his men simply saw to it. Already in AD 23 it

was quite exceptional that the Emperor Tiberius discussed army recruitment in the Senate.[6] Even the appointments to quite minor commands
came to be submitted outside the public eye to the emperor's judgement.
Quite by chance, we discover (through a poem in the 80s) that one of the
emperor's secretaries had to receive letters about cavalry commanders,
military tribunes and other subordinate officers, either so as to approve
their appointments or to assist the emperor if he wished to appoint them
himself from on high.[7]

The soldiers' tactics had become more varied during the Republic's
fall, but the basic legionary had not changed: he was still armed with a
javelin (*pilum*) to be thrown at close quarters, backed up by effective use
of the sword. He still wore open sandals with heavy nailed soles ('military boots'), a shirt of chain mail (later replaced by a breastplate of
jointed iron strips), a solid metal helmet and an oval shield or, by AD
100, one which was rectangular. In full armour, he could not swim, although swimming was one of his skills and a recommended part of his
training. In close formation, his line of shields could stand firm against
missiles; by opening out, it could let through the scythed chariots which
were launched at it without much effect by armies in Britain. There were
also stone- and arrow-shooting catapults, powered by torsion (one type,
from its 'kick', was called the wild ass). Romans copied these from the
Greek world, and stationed up to sixty machines behind each legion so
that they could begin battle with a powered barrage, shot over the legionaries' heads.

The main tactical development was the increasing use of local non-
Roman auxiliaries. By the late first century AD light-armed provincial
troops would be put in front of the traditional legionary line and would
take most of the initial battering. On the wings, squadrons of non-
Roman cavalry would shoot arrows or javelins, while riding rapidly at a
diagonal or circling on their enemy's flank. The angled cavalry charge towards the centre, the hallmark of Alexander's great victories, was not
now in fashion. Opposing cavalry tended to be skirmishers, especially in
the Near East where the Parthian horsemen would shoot scores of arrows
as they retreated.

There had always been Roman citizen cavalry too, but they had last
been used effectively in 109 BC: back in Augustan Rome, cavalrymen with
'public horses' now included people like the poet Ovid. Rome's cavalry
strength, therefore, had to be provincial and auxiliary. In the 50s and 40s
BC Julius Caesar had discovered and recruited the exceptional skill of
German and Gallic cavalry. In Spain, too, Augustus was amazed by the

fast Spanish horsemen and their skill with throwing javelins on horse-back, which he described in his autobiography. After observing such troops in Germany, Pliny the Elder wrote a manual on the art, some of which survives: it is noticeable that technical Latin cavalry-terms are often based on Spanish or Gallic words. We can still read the Emperor Hadrian's speech in north Africa, remarking on his mounted troops' fine display of this art. There were still no stirrups to hold the riders steady, but the Romans adopted a saddle, a Celtic speciality: they gave it two 'horns', or pommels, which wedged the cavalryman firmly.

One particular body of cavalrymen reached the highest honour: German horsemen, huge strapping characters whose 'amazing bodies' were first admired and recruited by Julius Caesar as his personal horseguards. On his death, these guards split between Antony and the new 'Caesar'. After victory, Augustus kept them on as his tall, magnificent bodyguards and stationed them in Rome, tactfully north of the Tiber. In 118, under Hadrian, a poem describes how one such German horseguard swam 'the wide waters of the deep Danube in full armour . . . I shot an arrow from my bow which I hit and broke with another while it hung in the air and fell back . . . Let anyone see if after me they can match my deeds.'[8] They could not, nowadays, and yet these German guards continued on and off for centuries: Augustus' successors sometimes put them under the command of a proven gladiator. They were a crucial support for the 'First Citizen'.

Even more prominent were the Commander's guards, or Praetorians. These infantry troops had first developed during the final stages of the Civil War when they had served each of the two main leaders. Highly paid and carefully selected, the Praetorians were amalgamated by the victor and numbered up to 9,000; Augustus' Praetorians came overwhelmingly from Italy. From the AD 20s they were concentrated in barracks in Rome, a most unrepublican presence, and their command, which had begun with low-key equestrians, went to some of the early Empire's most influential schemers, Sejanus under Tiberius or the odious Tigellinus who did nothing to improve the Emperor Nero's morals. They became a crucial element in every emperor's succession and survival.

The main legions were always manned with Roman citizens. However, local volunteers could quickly be given the Roman citizenship before being enrolled. Auxiliaries, by contrast, served always as non-citizens, with the prospect of citizenship only when they retired. Their units bore ethnic names, but they soon included people of mixed nationalities, a real melting pot. Wild and untamed people very seldom served in their own homeland. Britons, therefore, were sent off to serve in central Europe, while strapping Germans paraded near Scotland on Hadrian's Wall. Legionary pay was not particularly lavish and under Augustus the costs of weapons, tents and clothing were deducted. Inevitably, there were back-hand payments, too, required by centurion-soldiers to 'assure' a fellow soldier's leave. Not until AD 69 were 'back-handers' abolished (at least officially), and in due course the deductions did dwindle; the sums which were held back for tents and armour became treated as a deposit, to be released to the soldier on discharge.[9] The Praetorian guards were much more highly paid, whereas auxiliaries received less but on varying scales which sometimes amounted to as much as a legionary's wages (the exact rates are still disputed). Soldiering, as always, was the most widespread salaried career in antiquity.

The prize was the reward on discharge. Antony and Octavian had begun by trying to find plots of land of about 30 acres for each veteran soldier in Italy: after Actium, a great wave of settlement took veteran soldiers mostly into the provinces. From AD 6 a cash payment was offered instead, financed by the newly established military treasury: nonetheless, the payment was less than two-thirds as big as the ones first offered in the wars of the late 40s BC. It did not help that this treasury was partly financed by the introduction of the hated inheritance tax on Roman citizens. Bits of land continued to be offered, too (Nero even reverted to trying to offer them in Italy), but in AD 14 soldiers were complaining they were being fobbed off with bits of marshland or rough mountain.

Despite the new treasury, Augustus's reign ended with low military morale, a repeated need for levies and major mutinies on the northern frontier. The basic culprit was the old man's personal drive for wars in the north from AD 5 onwards. Hard fighting here advanced Rome to the rivers Elbe and Weser; the principal remaining enemy, Maroboduus, was classed as the 'worst since Hannibal',[10] but the attack on him required forced levies elsewhere, and these levies provoked revolts in the Balkans, especially in Illyricum. In the end, negotiations had to begin with Maroboduus. In AD 9 a German counter-attack caught the legions dispersed and off guard and inflicted a truly frightful disaster on their commander, Varus: the German hero was Arminius (whence 'Herman the German'). The reprisals were led by the future Emperor Tiberius, who revived outdated modes of discipline and imposed the harshest orders. They did not bode well for his years as emperor.

To man these campaigns, soldiers had been retained for far too long, sometimes for thirty years: the practice of 'extra time' was still widespread and resented. There had also been conscription at Rome which had brought riff-raff into the front line. The affair was all a blot on Augustus' military management, which was anyway tarnished. The old-fashioned discipline of Tiberius and his contemporaries did not help morale, either, when they came out to pull things round after some very much softer commanders.

With such specific causes, the mutinies of AD 14 were curable. Conspicuously, they did not recur, not even in the year 69 when four emperors marched against one another in succession. In 69 army pay did not even have to be increased to urge on the troops (it stayed constant until the reign of Domitian). In many provinces, meanwhile, army life settled down to peacetime routine. From military manuals and daily registers which are preserved on papyrus, we can see that it was certainly not boring.[11] There were regular exercises and an important array of civilian duties, including road-building, quarrying, mining and bridge-building. Soldiers became involved in surrounding life, even in seeing off plagues of locusts. Their commanders, inevitably, were called on to arbitrate and settle disputes, and not only disputes between soldiers. So much of what we see as 'Romanization' was the work of troops on long alert (including the aqueducts built in north Africa). Legionary camps became pools of experienced architects and engineers who could also advise on civilian projects. There was a huge volume of paperwork, to keep daily lists and details of pay: manuals urged that soldiers should, if possible, be literate, and army service was certainly an agent for promoting literacy.

Commanders of legions were senators (outside Egypt) and in a province with several legions, they were men in their mid-thirties who had already been a praetor in Rome. The linchpins of support for these amateurs were the long-serving centurions who were usually as tough as nails. The experienced 'prefects of the camp' were also particularly important here. Each legion had five experienced tribunes of equestrian rank too: the sixth tribune was a young man of senatorial birth, eighteen or nineteen years old. By comparison, he was very raw, though the commanding legate might enjoy his company. It was exceptional, the historian Tacitus noted, for these favoured young men not to lounge around and waste their posting.[12]

Even the ordinary men's diet was surprisingly varied, including quite a range of meat (much of it caught by hunting). The army, therefore, spread hunting ever further down the social ladder. The camps, meanwhile, man-ufactured the troops' armour and weapons, while their basic supplies were taken from the provincials, sometimes transported across long dis-tances. It is not clear how often they were properly paid for. A legion has been estimated to eat '2,000 tonnes' of grain a year, while the horses of a single cavalry unit needed another '635': it would have taken a very high demand by soldiers for paid local services to compensate provincials for this burden. For soldiers, however, a particular advantage of military life over civilian life was care for the sick. Hospitals are an invention of the Roman army.

In long intervals of peace, troops in these camps would inevitably 'soften', and here the Romans' long-running fear of 'luxury' came into play. A new commander or a visiting emperor would sometimes decide to tighten things up: in 121/2, Hadrian set about the troops in Germany. Beds were banned (Hadrian slept in camp on straw) and fancy dining rooms and colonnades were demolished. No doubt they had been the creations of soft officers: there was even a most interesting need to up-root their ornamental gardens. Hadrian himself undertook the hard marches, up to twenty miles in armour, which he reimposed on the le-gions. His 'discipline' was remembered for centuries by the authors of military manuals.[13] As a general practice, units were anyway moved around quite widely beyond their bases: by Hadrian's time, watchtowers had become common and outlying forts could be more than a hundred miles distant from the main camp. Military minds, meanwhile, did not forget that Hannibal's men were said to have been sapped by that winter spent among the 'luxury' of Capua, and Sulla's by the 'luxury' of Asia. So in due course, a legionary camp would be moved on and, behind it, a township would develop on its former site. Fear of luxury thus helped in-directly to urbanize Rome's subjects. The towns which grew up on for-mer camp-sites helped to 'soften' the provincials whom the hardy soldiers had been supposed to be guarding. In Britain, towns like Gloucester and Lincoln began in this way.

If soldiers had to be separated from towns, they also had to be kept away from wives. From Augustus until the third century legionaries were not allowed to marry. Existing marriages, even, were ended at the mo-ment of recruitment. Of course men could not be kept away from women. Liaisons flourished (soldiers even wrote of their 'girlfriends' and 'dar-lings'), and brothels were also kept busy, though one army-unit on the northern coast of the Black Sea can be found to have been collecting the local tax from the prostitutes. Legionaries' offspring, however, were illegitimate. In inscriptions, we find 'sons of Spurius' (soldier-bastards) and in the papyri of Roman Egypt, a conspicuous class of 'the fatherless' appear.[14] They are not orphans: they are children of legally prohibited unions, whether between Romans and Egyptians, or Roman legionaries and locals. Long before the celibate prize-fighters of the Christian monasteries, the military minds of Rome were already opposed to marriage. One advantage was that, in the case of a military disaster, nothing would need to be paid to dead soldiers' wives or families.

THE NEW AGE

*This is the oath taken by the inhabitants of Paphlagonia and the Romans
who do business among them. 'I swear by Zeus, Earth, Sun, all the gods
and goddesses and Augustus himself that I will be favourably disposed to
[Cae]sar Augustus and his children and descendants all the time of my
[life] in word and deed and thought . . . Whatever I may see or hear being
said or plotted or done against them, I will report it and I will be the enemy of the person who says or plots or does these things . . . If I do anything contrary to this [oath] . . . I pray that there may come on me, my
body and soul and life, my children and all my family and whatever is of
use to us, destruction, total destruction until the end of all my line and of
all my descendants'. . . In these same words this oath was sworn by all
the [inhabitants of the land] in the temples of Augustus throughout the local districts [of Paphlagonia] by the altars [of Augustus].*

Oath sworn in Paphlagonia, 6 March 3 BC

Augustus' first moral legislation was the prelude to his celebration
of a 'new age' in Rome. An 'ancient' oracle was conveniently cited to
support it and, on highly questionable grounds, it was calculated to fall
due in 17 BC. For three days and nights, beginning on 31 May, animal sacrifices were offered to Greek and Roman divinities under the general direction of the traditional priesthood for this occasion. The traditional items
for purification were given to the people, but it was Augustus and his heir,
the obscurely born Agrippa, who now led the proceedings. The daytime
rites were an innovation: the grim gods of the underworld were replaced
by the goddess of childbirth, mother Earth and such gods as Apollo, Diana
and Jupiter. Like so much of Augustus' professed conservatism, the apparently traditional occasion was reshaped in a new way.

On the final day, a specially commissioned hymn was sung by two fine choruses, one of twenty-seven boys, one of twenty-seven girls, all of whose parents were still living. The hymn was performed twice by these trusting young patriots, once to Apollo at the recently built temple on the Palatine hill, once to Jupiter on the Capitol, the 'father' god of the Romans. The hymn was written by the poet Horace and we can see how it goes beyond the rituals which had preceded it. It prays for the success of the recent marriage legislation (the 'decrees of the fathers on the yoking of women'); it evokes Rome's Trojan past which Virgil's great *Aeneid* had made so famous only two years before; it praises Augustus and asks for his every prayer to be heard; he is the descendant of Venus, the one (echoing Virgil) who is 'superior to the one who wages war, gentle to the fallen enemy'.[1] He rules far to the east, even being petitioned by 'proud Indians' (an Indian embassy had come to Augustus in 25 BC and agreed 'friendship' in 20).

Horace's hymn evokes the birthrate, conquest and moral values (Honour and ancient Modesty). It refers to Augustus' legendary family, the fertility of the land and Rome's future. Such a poem was quite new for this sort of occasion. It was followed by theatrical shows, chariot racing and 'hunts' of wild animals which would delight the people for another week. Among the fun, nobody, least of all Horace, could have guessed that Augustus, 'the glorious blood of Anchises and Venus', would rule for so many more years. Horace would continue to link these themes together in his *Odes*, but his praises were no truer at the end of Augustus' life than at the beginning. Prominent themes of Augustus' dominance were to be foreign campaigns (but not always conquest), organized attention to Rome and its people (but riots and natural crises still occurred) and attempts to promote his own family and assure a successor (the one coup which repeatedly eluded him). These concerns were to be the concerns of every subsequent Roman emperor.

Before celebrating the 'new age', Augustus had adopted his two grandsons, the children of his one daughter Julia and the loyal Agrippa. For once, he was surrounded by a cluster of family members, a sister, a wife and heirs. Importantly, the boys added the magic name of Caesar to their own. At the festival in 17 Augustus prayed for 'me, my house and household'[2] and over the next fifteen years, he set about marking out his two obvious successors. At a very early age, the grandsons were given magistracies; they were designated as consul years in advance (Gaius Caesar would be only twenty-one when holding this top job, usually held when about forty-two); they were tactfully presented to the armies; they were

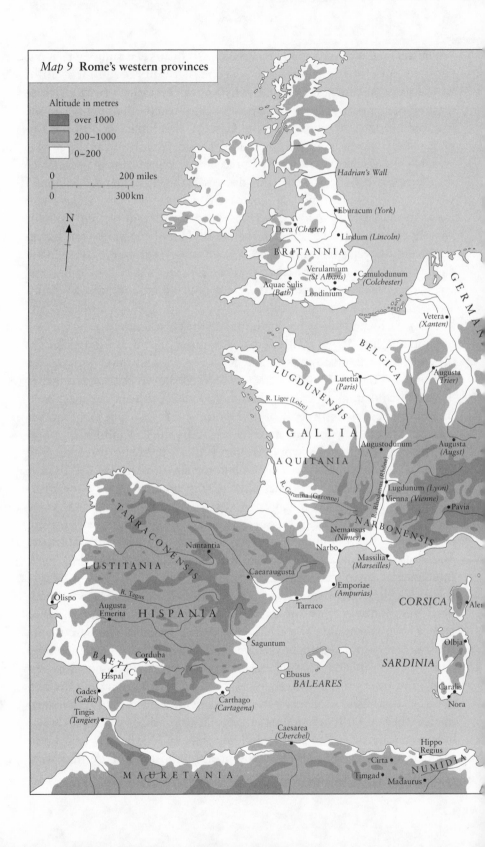

Map 9 Rome's western provinces

Altitude in metres
over 1000
200–1000
0–200

0   200 miles
0   300 km

N

Hadrian's Wall

Eburacum (York)

Deva (Chester)
Lindum (Lincoln)

BRITANNIA

Verulamium
(St Albans)   Camulodunum
Aquae Sulis   (Colchester)
(Bath)   Londinium

GERMA

Vetera
(Xanten)

BELGICA

LUGDUNENSIS   Augusta
Lutetia   (Trier)
(Paris)

R. Liger (Loire)

GALLIA   Augustodunum   Augusta
(Augst)

AQUITANIA

TARRACONENSIS   Lugdunum (Lyon)
R. Garumna (Garonne)   Vienna (Vienne)
Pavia

Nuntantia   NARBONENSIS

LUSTITANIA   Nemausus
(Nîmes)

Caearaugusta   Narbo
Massilia
(Marseilles)   CORSICA   Ale

Olispo   R. Tagus
Emporiae
Augusta   (Ampurias)
Emerita   Tarraco
HISPANIA   Olbja

Saguntum   SARDINIA

BAETICA   Corduba
Hispal   Caralis

Gades   Ebusus   Nora
(Cadiz)   Carthago   BALEARES
Tingis   (Cartagena)
(Tangier)

Caesarea
(Cherchel)
Hippo
Regius

Cirta   NUMIDIA
MAURETANIA   Timgad   Madaurus

advertised on the coinage in provincial cities. In 5 BC Gaius was made 'head of the youth', a special title which allowed him to preside over the order of Roman knights. Outside Rome, they and other family members received divine honours in provincial cities. Far inland, in western Asia, we find people in c. 3 BC swearing an oath of loyalty to Augustus, 'his children and his descendants'.[3]

There was a large unanswered question here. The troops would like to have a family successor, another 'Caesar' from the line of Julius Caesar. If the heir was adopted, as in Augustus' case, adoption did not matter to them. Such, too, was the wish of the common people of Rome, who also responded to youth and beauty. They would have loved our modern magazines and pictures of princes and princesses. But in the eyes of any thoughtful senator, the Republic was not a family affair, to be passed on by inheritance. In due course, senators would prefer to be able to elect a successor from their own number.

Between 18 and 12 BC Augustus had a junior partner whom he himself had chosen: the loyal Agrippa. It was only a sop to traditionalist opinion that his powers were formally renewable, like Augustus' own. When Agrippa inconveniently died in 12 BC Augustus pronounced a funerary eulogy over him and the speech was circulated to provincial governors: no doubt they circulated it locally in translations. There were two branches to the emerging 'dynasty': Augustus' descendants through his first wife Scribonia and their daughter Julia (the Julians), and his stepsons and descendants through his able second wife Livia (the Claudians). From these two branches, the dynasty of the next eight decades is known as the Julio-Claudians (to AD 68).

The Claudian branch began by being older and proved itself much abler. Up in the Alps, Augustus' two Claudian stepsons turned out to be far better soldiers than he could ever be. In 9 BC the younger of the two, Drusus, died; we have recently learned that his funeral was splendid and his eulogy by Augustus was circulated through the provinces too. Probably it was accompanied by moral 'encouragement' to the public: when Drusus' equally popular son died in October 19, the emperor's testimony to him was also circulated for the benefit of 'the youth of our children and descendants'.[4] 'Improvement' of the young was a part of Augustus' gratuitous programme. It impinged on the sons of senators who dressed formally and attended their fathers' meetings, or the young knights who processed on horseback. They were parts of a vision which we still recognize: set the young examples, give them public functions and try to smother independent thought.

There was also, we realize increasingly, Augustus' second wife, the redoubtable Livia: if only we had a memoir by her (she lived right on to AD 29). Wicked gossip claimed that she poisoned rivals and procured young girls for the moral Augustus and had them smuggled secretly into the house on the Palatine. Her public image was quite different, but these rumours show that it was not the Romans' only perception of her. Back in 36 BC Livia had shared the 'sacrosanctity' of a tribune with her husband: it was a most unrepublican honour for a female, but it marked her off from Antony's Eastern women. She then received other small honours and she helped to restore temples in Rome for cults which were associated with respectable women. In 7 BC she gave her name to a splendid public Portico in Rome which included colonnades with *trompe l'œil* landscape paintings and a public display of works of art (Agrippa was already said to have wanted to confiscate all private works of art and display them publicly, one reason why the Roman nobles boycotted the vulgar man's funeral). The site of Livia's Portico was significant. Previously, it had housed the enormous private mansion of the disreputable Vedius Pollio who had served Augustus in the East. He was denounced for his excessive luxury, including the bad example (men said) of throwing slaves into his pond of man-eating fish. His palace was demolished on its site and Livia publicized sober Concord (a matrimonial virtue) and a 'people's walk' where looted Greek statues were displayed. How differently she was presenting herself from the bad women of Cicero's rhetoric, from people like Antony's Fulvia whose personal greed and cruelty had been alleged so as to emphasize her husband's 'tyrannical' character.

Rhetoric then outran the restraint and consideration which these actions projected. After the death of Livia's son Drusus in 9 BC, a Roman knight even wrote a poem to console her, obsequiously, as 'the First Lady'. A spectacular recent find of inscriptions in Spain has shown us how the Senate dwelt on her virtues in an effusive response to an imperial family crisis. In AD 20 they publicly praised Livia not only for having given birth to the austere Emperor Tiberius but also for 'her many great favours to men of every rank; she could rightly and deservedly have supreme influence in what she asked from the Senate, though she used that influence sparingly'.[5] Republican traditionalists would have been horrified. Once again, this long decree was to be publicly set up for the instruction of posterity. It was to be displayed in conspicuous places in the provinces and even in the army-camps.

The moral purpose of the new age extended to buildings too. Augustus' boast in Rome was that he found the city made of brick and left it marble. Certainly, the Rome of 30 BC had had none of the planned grandeur of the great cities of the Greek East. Even its civic centre was a rambling jumble, not fit to be the showpiece of the world. There was to be much Augustan work in the city centre, and in keeping with the new moral order, sculptors and architects tended to favour a restrained classicism. The tall marble columns of the public temples were more showy, favouring the Corinthian style of capital, but admirable though the craftsmanship is, the main sculpted monuments with Augustan themes have a controlled range of allusion and form which veer to ghastly good taste. Frequently, they express ideals of his own moral and family rhetoric. The 30s BC had been a great era of political publicity in buildings, coins and literature. Augustan Rome continued its use of sculpture and architecture for a message.

As a result, the new Augustan era has one of its claims to be a 'classical' age. It is, in fact, 'classicizing', dependent on fifth- and fourth-century Greece: without it, Augustan public art would never have taken this direction. In its Roman context, this style implied dignity, authority and restraint in a way which had never been so in its original setting: 'we see in the political choice of classicism an expression of the Roman order of state.' Order, dignity and structure were also the qualities of much early Augustan literature, especially the poems of Horace and Virgil. Here, the 'new age' can claim to be 'classic', in the simple sense of first class. But its great poets, like the great oratorical prose of Cicero, had matured in the pre-Augustan age of liberty.

Apart from the classicism of the new bold stonework and the best of the new poetry, there was still the other Rome, now a teeming city of (probably) a million inhabitants, far the biggest city in the world. Social contrasts had remained amazingly extreme here. The rich lived in grand houses, but the very poor bedded down where they could; the relatively poor were crammed into tall wooden apartment blocks with thin dividing walls, the speculative landlord's dream. Narrow winding streets surrounded these hastily built and overcrowded 'vertical receptacles', while erratic supplies of water went with a total absence of public transport. Most people's Rome was both a wonder and a nightmare. It was also, of course, a slave-society. A single senator, in the 60s, owned no less than 400 slaves in his household: 'the Senate' (good men and true) would thus own about 250,000 of Rome's human beings if this senator was at all typical.[6] Perhaps two-fifths of the city's (approximate) million inhabitants were slaves, and many of the rest were ex-slaves, freed but still 'obliged' to their ex-masters. The common citizens were the plebs, but among the plebs those who were attached to the great households were not to be confused with those of the plebs who were not. For there were 'respectable' plebs, and downright 'sordid' plebs, people who begged what they could. The modern cardboard cities of refugees in Egypt or Pakistan are the nearest we can come to imagining this 'other Rome', though they lack Rome's openly accepted slavery.

This 'other Rome' had proved beyond the capacity, or concern, of Cicero's beloved Republic. Under Augustus, it took its first few steps towards health and safety. By stages, a much-needed fire brigade was introduced, the Watch or *vigiles*, whose name lives on in modern Rome's equivalent. The public water supply was vastly improved by new aqueducts and, in due course, by new overseers and public slaves to maintain it. In reply, rich families moved up to the hills above previously marshy ground and continued to develop new parks and fine palazzi there. A committee was appointed to attend to flooding from the river Tiber. The height of apartment blocks was limited to about seven storeys, no doubt to the speculators' annoyance. The grain-supply acquired a new prefect; the regular gifts of free grain to designated citizens continued (about 250,000 people were now on the list). Like the public shows, the dole did not extend 'bread and circuses' to all the free poor, because they amounted to more than half a million people. But when backed by the grain of Egypt, the general supply of grain on sale became more stable.

As one reform succeeded another, each social order in Rome began to have defined roles, and these roles were made to seem to be worth having. The Senate continued to be very busy and senators' functions multiplied, and yet ultimate power resided elsewhere, with the emperor. As time passed, therefore, it became harder to assure a quorum for senatorial meetings. Privileged knights had their annual processions; the common people, too, began to be more closely regulated. There were hundreds of thousands of them, after all, potentially a seething mass, as they had shown briefly after Caesar's murder. Augustus left them with their ancient 'tribes', all thirty-five of them, through which gifts of corn were distributed and assemblies organized. However, he continued Julius Caesar's controls. He strictly regulated their right to form 'clubs', or *collegia*, those political and social dangers in the republican city. Instead, the plebs had ever more shows to watch, but even here, they were to be regulated in a hierarchy of seating. This orderliness was only possible because the common spectators accepted it and were not rebellious against it. There was still no designated police force, although the fire-watchers did go on patrol. But Augustus had stationed soldiers in or near the city, the Praetorian guards and his German horseguards. They could always intervene in a crisis.

The obvious tactic, meanwhile, was divide and rule. In 7 BC Augustus split the city into fourteen districts under 'ward magistrates' (*vicomagistri*) who were usually freedmen. These local officials celebrated cults of the Protecting Spirits, or *Lares*, at each ward's crossroads. Previously, there had been 'august Lares': now, the same Latin words suggested the 'Lares of Augustus' (*Lares Augusti*). In cults at the crossroads, honours were also paid to the *genius* of Augustus, his 'guiding spirit'. Cults, therefore, of Augustus' own household were neatly transferred to the city's main street corners. The presiding freedmen in these cults had the robes and insignia of real magistrates, while privileged slaves served as their assistants. One surviving altar for such a cult reflects the themes of high art, showing a scene from the legend of Aeneas the founder and the honorary shield which proclaimed Augustus' 'virtues'. The self-important officials took kindly to their new function and these little local shrines persisted at Rome for centuries.

Symptomatically, stone inscriptions in honour of individuals also proliferated in the Augustan city. At the top of society, full triumphs began to be reserved for members of the imperial family only. Instead, individual senators received 'triumphal ornaments', but commemorated themselves with public inscriptions which carefully listed each of the posts in their careers. By contrast, two great monuments commemorated high points for Augustus himself. The first, the delicately sculpted Altar of Peace (*Ara Pacis*), was voted by the Senate for his return from Gaul in the summer of 13 BC. It shows a lush imagery of natural abundance and a fertile mother (probably Earth) with children. Sculpted members of the imperial family accompany figures from Rome's priesthoods, including four chief priests, veiled and preparing to sacrifice. The exact reference of the procession is disputed, but it probably records Augustus' own assumption in March 12 BC of the Supreme Priesthood (as Pontifex Maximus), which he had tactfully left in old Lepidus' hands until Lepidus' recent death.[7] The sculptures' combination of family, religion and formal togas is typically Augustan.

In 2 BC Augustus' dominance reached its climax. Again, it followed where Julius Caesar had already trod. In February he was hailed in the Senate as 'Father of the Fatherland' (like Julius Caesar), and in May, the long-awaited temple of Mars (the war god) as Avenger was completed. It overlooked his supreme monument, the 'Forum of Augustus', in the heart of the city. Beginning on 12 May, great shows publicized the opening, with gladiators and the killing of 260 lions. The entertainments were like Julius Caesar's all over again. On a newly flooded lake, mock teams of Athenians and Persians re-enacted a sea-battle fit for the old Persian Wars of 480 BC. It was a heroic prelude to the dispatch of Augustus' young grandson, Gaius, to 'triumph' in the East in his own pseudo-Persian war. Crocodile hunts then followed in the flooded Circus.

Julius Caesar had already commissioned a Forum, but Augustus' Forum of multi-coloured marble is the supreme statement of Augustan spin. Its temple of Mars commemorated the 'avenging' of Julius Caesar and the 'vengeance' (much less bloody) on the Parthians (achieved by diplomacy). It was to be the centre-point in Rome for the public giving of honours to commanders and men of military prowess: it became the standard meeting-point, in legal contracts, for people who were granted bail. On the temple, a decently sculpted Venus, goddess of the Julian family, accompanied Romulus (dressed as a shepherd) and patriotic gods such as father Tiber. Augustus' own name was carved at a focal point on the blocks directly below the pediment. Ancient Greek statuary, including two masterpieces of Alexander the Great, were displayed around the Forum. The novelties were the Forum's flanking colonnades. Like other monuments and public lists in the Augustan city, they put 'history on parade'.[8] On one side, Romulus headed an array of statues of the great triumphing Roman heroes of the past, each of whom was identified with an inscribed eulogy. On the other side stood Aeneas with his Trojan father and ancestors of the Julian family. Augustus even published an edict to announce that 'the life [of these great men] was the standard by which he wished to be weighed by the citizens as long as he lived'.[9] He even hoped that the future 'First Citizens' would be weighed likewise.

Herodotus, the first historian, would not have been surprised by the sequel. Catastrophe followed this personal climax. Within months the public adultery of his charming daughter, Julia, was alleged and then punished: did some people wonder if Augustus' adopted grandsons, her two children, were really Agrippa's children as was claimed? When she remarked 'I only invite another pilot', it was perhaps to rebut such rumours. But the cargo, too, proved short-lived. First one then the other of these grandsons died on foreign service. New and complex dynastic arrangements were needed, which ended by giving a main role to a 'Claudian', Livia's austere son Tiberius. Yet Tiberius was rumoured in 9 BC to have talked about restoring more of a 'republic' and he had already withdrawn into self-imposed exile in 6 BC, arguably so as to avoid holding the

53. Relief frieze from the shrine of the emperors, or Sebasteion, at Aphrodisias in Turkey, showing Augustus with representations of land and sea, symbolizing his power over the world, *c.* AD 60.

populist tribunician power in public. From AD 6 onwards wars on the northern frontier imposed a heavy strain on Rome's finances and on citizen-recruitment. Both were hugely resented, including the new inheritance tax on citizens, which was introduced to help pay the army's costs. There were seditious grumblings among the Roman plebs, a major fire in Rome, and years of famine in Italy. Augustus' last available grandson was banished in AD 7, and in 8 adultery was prosecuted once again, this time against Augustus' granddaughter, the younger Julia. On top of it all came the severe defeat of the legions in Germany in AD 9. It was lucky that these crises came after thirty years of domination. By now, there was, it seemed, no alternative.

What, then, was the core of the Roman revolution which could endure such continuing turbulence? From ever more parts of Italy, members of local leading families did enter the Senate and appear in the upper orders at Rome. But the revolution did not lie in this mild, ongoing enlargement of Rome's governing class. More importantly, the proscriptions and the Civil Wars had cost lives and violently transferred property: here, indeed, there had been revolutionary terror, although the political system in Italy's towns remained unchanged. With victory, there was a military and constitutional revolution of a different sort. In Italy, there were now twenty-eight new colonies of army veterans whom Augustus, like Sulla, had settled in his active lifetime, men loyal to himself on expropriated land. Elsewhere, the remaining army was now a standing army, loyal to Augustus as Commander. Politically, he held a bundle of powers which were detached from elected magistracies: what he wanted could thus be massaged through the political system at Rome. Freedom of political initiative was killed off: it became extremely hard, historians noted, to penetrate back to the truth of things. A smart new voting hall (Julius Caesar's plan) was built in Rome for the people, but the candidates who were brought before its electoral assembly were increasingly agreed in advance. Such pre-selection was introduced in AD 5, perhaps as a sop to the upper class for Augustus' dynastic arrangements of the previous year. In legislative assemblies, meanwhile, the scope for independent popular legislation or veto by a tribune had disappeared. In its place, a sense of 'dynasty' had been promoted. It is summed up by the new voting-centuries which were added to the people's electoral assembly: they were named after Gaius and Lucius, Augustus' dead grandsons. Down one side of Rome's political space, the Forum, a smart portico commemorated them too.

On a long view, the historian Polybius would have claimed that his predictive theory had proved true. The balanced 'oligarchy' of the years of the Hannibalic War had first tipped towards what Polybius, at least, might have seen as 'democracy'. In fact, it had been the use by members of the upper class of the scope for 'popular liberty' embedded in Rome's constitution. Then, as the great historian of this crisis, Peter Brunt, well puts it, their 'attempts to "restore" the powers of the people led on to monarchy, and monarchy destroyed popular freedom more completely than senatorial freedom'.[10] However, this loss of popular liberty was matched by social gains for the 'urban mob' in the city of Rome. Improved urban amenities went with new avenues of justice. As before, the elected praetors continued to preside over public courts in the city: a fourth 'panel' of jurors was added and there was no longer any concern to separate senators and knights among the jurymen. Senators would put up with this mixing because the Senate, with the consuls also, became a separate court with powers to try its own members for major crimes, including extortion: knights, therefore, were kept out of the most serious senatorial trials, and the hated 'equal liberty' was ended.

The more drastic development was the giving of justice by new officeholders. The newly appointed Prefect of the City was a senator; he dealt with cases, especially those involving the lower classes in the city, and he had the power to coerce not only slaves but those free people whose 'audacity' needed force. In due course, the Prefect of the Praetorian guard came to dispense justice too, as cases simply gravitated to such people with the authority to settle them.

The greatest such individual was the First Citizen himself. As the holder of a tribune's power, Augustus could be regarded as legally liable to receive the appeals of all Roman citizens. As early as 30 BC he is said to have been given this specific power, and in 18 BC it was probably made explicit in a law 'on public violence'. As the holder of proconsular power, he could also enquire into cases and pass sentence after an inquisition by himself. His presence, on top of the pile, was a new focus of crucial judicial importance. From the provinces, meanwhile, accusations, requests and appeals gravitated to him anyway, both in civil and criminal matters, whether from Roman citizens or not. They arrived either with embassies from distant cities, or in written form, or with patient accusers or defendants who travelled to see him. An embassy even arrived from Cnidus, theoretically a free Greek city, seeking judgement in a remarkable case against a husband and wife (now seeking refuge in Rome) and the charge that, in a recent quarrel, one party had insulted another by making a slave pour a chamber pot over his head.[11] Perhaps Augustus chose to go into the case so closely because the saga which the embassy presented to him was so extraordinary. It is a sign that pleas for justice, as always, spiralled upwards: Augustus soon had to arrange for cases both from Rome and abroad to be delegated to other parties. But like a Ptolemaic king before him, he could not escape the flood which his dominance attracted.

There was a final fearful symmetry. In 43 BC Augustus had begun by proscribing citizens to be put to death; in the difficult end to his reign, he reverted to attacks on freedom of expression. It is under Augustus that we first hear of 'dangerous' books being burned. The offence of treason against the Roman state became extended to verbal offences of libel and slander against prominent citizens. Such offences, it could be argued, insulted the moral standing of the upper class, a major theme of the new age. It was then an inevitable step to extend the offence to verbal treason against the emperor's person, whether dead or alive. This step became evident under Augustus' successor, Tiberius. When such cases for treason were heard in the Senate or in a court in the emperor's presence, the emperor's attitude during their hearing would compound the outcome of the trial.[12] Through Augustus' revolution, the upper orders had lost political freedom, while regaining civil peace and stability. But one freedom, at least, was enhanced: their freedom to prosecute each other.

PART SIX

An Imperial World

THE STRENGTH OF THE EMPIRE was derived from the devotion of its inhabitants, and that devotion was the result of gratitude for the peace which it was Rome's primary business to maintain, for the ordered government of which the monument endures in Roman Law and for that liberal attitude to the native population of which the steady extension of the Roman franchise is the most notable expression . . . The aristocracy which formed the basis of the administration at home looked for help to the aristocrats in the provinces and in a world where education among the many was as backward as the means of disseminating news and forming public opinion, the principles of democracy were neither honoured nor observed. But the age was not necessarily the worse because ability commanded esteem, nor were the ignorant necessarily the less contented for their measure of dependence on the cultured few.

Hugh Last, in *The Cambridge Ancient History*, volume XI (1936), 477

As I see it, the Roman political system facilitated a most intense and ultimately destructive economic exploitation of the great mass of the people, whether slave or free, and it made radical reform impossible. The result was that the propertied class, the men of real wealth, who had deliberately created the system for their own benefit, drained the life-blood from their world and thus destroyed Greco-Roman civilization over a large part of the empire . . . If I were in search of a metaphor to describe the great and growing concentration of wealth in the hands of the upper classes, I would not incline to anything so innocent and so automatic as drainage: I should want to think in terms of something much more purposive and deliberate—perhaps the vampire bat.

G. E. M. de Sainte Croix, *The Class Stuggle in the Ancient Greek World* (1981), 502–3

THE JULIO-CLAUDIANS

The Senate . . . hopes that all those who were soldiers in the service of our First Citizen (Tiberius) will continue to manifest loyalty and devotion to the imperial house since they know that the safety of our Empire depends on the protection of that house. The Senate believes that it belongs to their concern and duty that among those who command them at any time the greatest authority with them should belong to those who have with the most devoted loyalty honoured the name of the Caesars which gives protection to this city and to the Empire of the Roman people.

Senate's resolution on Gnaeus Piso, AD 20: lines 159–66

Tiberius was savaged in letters from the king of the Parthians, Artabanus, who accused him of parricide, murders, sloth and luxury and warned him to satisfy the intense and most deserved hatred of his fellow citizens by killing himself as soon as possible.

Suetonius, *Life of Tiberius* 66.2

IN THE SUMMER OF AD 14 the aging Augustus left Rome, never to see the city again. One of his purposes has remained highly controversial. Our main ancient sources either suggest or state that he went in the company of only one trusted senator, Paullus Fabius Maximus, to the little island of Planasia to which he had banished his last surviving grandson, the erratic Agrippa Postumus, in AD 7. On their return, first his companion Fabius Maximus, then Augustus himself died without revealing what they had been doing. The 'rumour', as it later seemed to the historian Tacitus, has sometimes been dismissed by modern scholars as a fable. But we happen to know from quite another source that both

Augustus and Fabius Maximus were unavailable in Rome in mid-May of this year. At this date, Augustus' adopted grandson, young Drusus, was being admitted to a highly prestigious Roman priesthood, the Arval Brethren. Its records show that both Augustus and Fabius Maximus voted in absence to admit him.[1] Contemporaries, then, were quite correct to say that the First Citizen, now seventy-five, and this trusted senator had been away on other business. It is immensely unlikely that both of them were suddenly ill at the time of this one priestly meeting: for that reason alone, Fabius would not have been allowed the very rare honour of voting as a senatorial member in absence. Gossip ran freely on the journey's outcome, even claiming that Augustus had changed his mind and decided to make Agrippa Postumus his successor. Fabius, it was said, had indiscreetly told his wife, thereby costing himself his life. Augustus' wife, Livia, was even alleged to have poisoned old Augustus in order to forestall his change of mind. None of this scandal is at all likely, but the journey itself should be accepted as historical. It is the last dramatic act in Augustus' long marathon of finding and keeping an heir to the new Empire.

In its wake, there was an immediate attempt to travel over to the island, rescue Agrippa Postumus and take him north to the troops. There was another attempt, two years later, to impersonate him (people did not remember what he really looked like): it was carried out by the very slave who had set out in AD 14 to ship him away and it met with considerable success among the plebs. In fact, Agrippa Postumus had been killed promptly on the first news of Augustus' death, on 19 August. The murder was organized by the discreet Sallustius Crispus, the great-nephew and adopted son, no less, of the acerbic historian Sallust. Under Roman law, Agrippa Postumus had not been disinherited when he was banished, and so he could claim a share in Augustus' inheritance. In the final months of his life Augustus went over to see him, perhaps to be sure of his unsuitability (the boy was exceptionally fond of fishing), and if so, to arrange cold-bloodedly for his removal.

Not unfittingly, the subsequent Julio-Claudian era began with a dynastic murder. There were to be so many more. The first heir was the elderly Tiberius, a tall, austere figure of a man, already in his mid-fifties. His ancestry was extremely aristocratic and he was already a proven general who was known as a severe disciplinarian. Yet he was very much a last resort, the man Augustus had had to choose. Public generosity, the popular touch and a wholehearted sense of style were not parts of his haughty nature; revealingly, he gave few public shows and exhibited no interest in those he attended. At public dinners, he was said never to have served a whole wild boar when half a one would do. He professed a wish to be the 'servant of the Senate' and to be an 'equal citizen, not the eminent First Citizen', but both wishes were unrealistic.[2] The army and the provinces now looked up to an outright emperor, whatever the niceties of the constitutional position at Rome. The First Citizen was the main source of patronage for much of the Roman upper class, and his huge finances were the essential supplement to the Public Treasury. His public spending and his jurisdiction were indispensable and, as Augustus had demonstrated by standing back between 23 and 19 BC, he was the indispensable protector and provider for the vast mass of common people at Rome. Tiberius could not behave as if he was only one member in an old-style Senate: he had asserted his succession in a manner which was very different. He had received an 'oath of allegiance', first of all from the consuls. It was then sworn in their presence by the Prefect of the Praetorian Guard and the Prefect of the Corn-supply, jobs which were Augustan innovations: they would be crucial ever after to each emperor's accession and the stability of the city crowds. Next swore the 'Senate, the soldiers and the people': the soldiery, intruding here, were a sign of the new realities.[3] This oath is telling evidence of Augustus' 'best order', as Augustus had called it. The strength of that 'order' was to be highlighted by the inadequacies of his first successors: it proved strong enough to survive them unscathed.

The recurrent lesson from Tiberius and subsequent emperors is not only that 'absolute power corrupts absolutely': it is that emperors were only as good or bad as they had been before becoming emperor. They ran true to form and never improved with the job. Each of them began his reign with a modest, judicious statement of intent, but matters soon deteriorated, partly through their own characters and weak spots, and then through complex manoeuvring for a potential successor. This process involved frequent deaths in their own families and the liquidation of yet more palace-factions and senators, as potential heirs became ever more widely scattered in branch-lines of the Julio-Claudian 'household'. As emperors married repeatedly, the number of possible heirs correspondingly increased.

In Tiberius, the Romans had someone who was cunning and inscrutable but temperamentally unsuited to populist gestures or to giving senators a clear lead. After nine years he was talking vainly of 'restoring the Republic' and giving up his job: the death of his own son disenchanted him and was followed by other bereavements. Five years later he withdrew from Rome altogether, ending up on the island of Capri where he was credited with horrible sexual orgies. In his late sixties he looked repulsive, too, bald and gaunt with blotches on his face, only partly concealed by plasters. Nonetheless, he ruled for twenty-four years, the longest reign until Hadrian's. In March 37 his death was joyfully received by the common people. The senators conspicuously refused to honour him posthumously as a god. They also annulled his will and accepted his grandson Gaius as sole heir. The decision was disastrous.

Unlike Tiberius, Gaius was only twenty-four, with no military competence whatsoever and only one minor magistracy behind him. His main appeal was that he was the son of the popular Germanicus, nephew of Tiberius. Despite fair promises, he turned out to be vicious, impossibly egocentric and mad. Some of the stories are almost too bizarre to be credible, that he promised to make his favourite horse a consul, that he ordered a big army for an invasion of Britain to pick up shells on a beach in northern France and then return home, or that he had sex with his sister and enforced an extravagant cult of her as a goddess after her death. He certainly promoted worship of himself as a god and tried to force it on the Jews and their Temple in Jerusalem: at the end of his brief reign, he was said to be dressing up as the gods and goddesses in his palace at Rome. He was even said to have split up the ancient temple of Castor and Pollux in the Roman Forum, so that an approach-road to his own 'shrine' up on the Palatine hill should push through it, with the twin gods as his 'doorkeepers': this story has some support from recent archaeology in the Forum. A soothsayer had once declared that Gaius had no more chance of becoming emperor than of riding across the Bay of Naples. To refute him, Gaius had a wooden bridge built across two points of the Bay, about three and a half miles apart, and galloped flat out across the planks while wearing what was said to be the breastplate of Alexander the Great. Gaius then held a huge drinking-party, threw some of his companions off the bridge and attacked others in a warship, leaving them to drown.

In January 41, after four ghastly years of taunting and terrorizing the senators, Gaius ordered the torture of a pretty young mime-actress during an interrogation for treason. Even he was shocked at the effect on her body. The tribune of the guard who had supervised the torture was also disgusted. When Gaius left the theatre on the Palatine hill for a lunch-break, the tribune stabbed him in a palace corridor.

The murder, on 24 January, was a cardinal chance for freedom: Gaius had no children of an age to take over. However, the senators behind the murder were divided. Should they destroy the whole beastly Julio-

Claudian family? Should they keep the system but insist on electing the next First Citizen? Should they go further and somehow restore the Republic? Like Julius Caesar's murderers, they dithered, despite their talk of restoring 'liberty' and the rule of law. The power of the palace troops then asserted itself. One of the German bodyguards found an ignored Julio-Claudian who was hiding behind a curtain in the Palace. The guards then acclaimed him as emperor and forced the divided conspirators to give in. The new emperor, Claudius, was on the face of it preposterous. Fifty years old, he drooled and could not co-ordinate his movements; he laughed uncontrollably and his voice sounded like some hoarse sea-monster. He has been plausibly diagnosed as suffering from cerebral palsy. Augustus had found him a public embarrassment and even his mother used to describe him as 'a monstrosity of a human being, one which Nature began and never finished'.[4] Claudius may have been aware of the plan to murder Gaius, but it seems he was unaware, like the participants, that the result would ever be power for himself.

Claudius began with severe disadvantages. The senators promptly declared war on him when they heard that the guards had championed him. He himself had no military experience, but he did raise the guards' wages, an effective substitute. An attempted revolt by the respected governor of Dalmatia in the following year collapsed within five days because the legions were still loyal to Claudius. In their eyes, he had a crucial quality: he was a proper household heir. He claimed a kinship with Augustus and he was grandson of Mark Antony.

Claudius went on to rule for thirteen years in a fascinating mixture of application and cruelty, over-compensation and attempted populism. To compensate for his lack of military prowess, he invaded Britain in 43: he even crossed the river Thames on an elephant. But he kept on citing his victory 'beyond the Ocean' and accepting military salutations for a campaign to the action of which he had personally contributed nothing. Perpetually at odds with the Senate, he relied excessively on the accessible freedmen in his own household. He was not creating a new 'Civil Service': he was simply turning to would-be wise advisers who were near to hand. He also had an antiquarian mind. He had written copiously during his years as a marginal figure, finishing eight books on the Carthaginians and twenty books on the Etruscans, while writing an ongoing history of Rome, unfortunately lost to us. He had even written a book on gambling with dice, one of his passions. However, he had the vanity and vengefulness of the academic *manqué*. In power, he fussed about such sillinesses as adding new letters to the alphabet; his speeches in the Senate were conceited and poorly constructed; he ordered that his long Etruscan history should be read aloud monthly in the Museum at Alexandria.

Lacking senatorial credibility, Claudius found an alternative in the responses of the Roman populace. He would sit, in popular style, on the tribunes' bench; he played up to the crowds at public shows, especially the gladiatorial ones where his taste was definitely for blood. He encouraged overdue improvements to the grain-harbour for Rome; he improved the city's aqueducts and he attended to popular shows. His displays, however, were excessive and fatuous. At Ostia, he showed off by personally fighting against a whale which had been trapped in the new harbour. On his return from Britain he boated in and out of the harbour at Ravenna in an extravagant mock floating palace.[5] He even forced through a massive plan to drain the Fucine Lake near Rome, and at the grand opening in 52 he staged an enormous sea-battle to amuse the crowds. Some 19,000 combatants were encouraged to fight, shedding blood, but the waterworks went wrong and drenched the spectators, including Claudius and his wife, who was dressed in a golden robe, like a mythical queen.

These massive displays for the crowds did nothing to endear him to the senators. They saw him as a self-willed bungler. They said that 321 knights and 35 senators were killed off by him in secret trials, and his habit of judging these cases personally in private rooms in his household was detested. Lacking senatorial friends, Claudius was recognized as a soft touch for those who had access to him, whether they were his personal doctor, prominent Gauls from the region of his birthplace Lyons or corrupt palace freedmen (who sometimes took bribes for arranging gifts of citizenship). Most memorably, there were the strong, self-willed women, a distinctive presence at court in the Julio-Claudian years.

Tiberius had lived awkwardly at Rome among two elderly imperial widows, each of whom became honoured in due course as 'Augusta'. One was Augustus' wife Livia, the great survivor. The other, also a great survivor, was Mark Antony's second daughter, Antonia: she had a beauty and an orderly style which preserved her even during long years of refusing to remarry. On Augustus' death, some had suggested honouring Livia as 'Mother of the Fatherland': it was in AD 20 that the Senate decreed and circulated praises of her for 'serving the commonwealth exceptionally, not only in giving birth to our First Citizen but also through her many great favours towards men of every rank': they also affirmed that Antonia was the stated object of their 'great admiration', 'excellent in her moral character'.[6] Republican traditionalists would have been scandalized by the reference to Livia's 'many great favours' and would have enjoyed the rumours

54. Relief frieze from the same site, showing the Emperor Claudius conquering Britannia, as his army partly did.

that she had in fact poisoned Augustus and his adopted grandsons. Eleven years later Antonia was probably quick to bring down the Emperor Tiberius' controversial favourite, Sejanus, by a well-judged letter in the interests of her terrible grandson, Gaius. However, when Gaius took power she quickly proved irritating to him and had to commit suicide.

Feminine influence on Claudius was more overt. It was not only that he lived among women at Rome who were 'gaping for gardens', in the historian Tacitus' fine phrase,[7] even to the point of pressing him for the death of a rich garden-owner so that they could take his property. Claudius' own third marriage was to the well-born and passionate Messalina (twenty years old or more at the time); she bore him a son, and then encouraged him in condemning enemies and rivals (she cited the warning dreams which were granted to herself and a freedman). In 48 she herself went too far with a younger senator, consenting to a sham 'marriage' during the grape-vintage in the absence of her ignorant husband. Claudius then took the bad advice of a freedman and married the formidable Agrippina instead. She was the sister of Gaius and thirty-three years old; disastrously, she brought a son of her own with her (born by Caesarian section). During six memorable years of new-wife syndrome the old drama of the Hellenistic royal families was played out all over again. To assure her son's succession, the new wife, Agrippina, arranged for Claudius' murder on 13 October 54. Supposedly it was done by a mushroom laced with poison, although a second dose on a feather was said to have been needed.

Agrippina's young son Nero then succeeded and proved another political disaster. Like Tiberius, he had a proud and noble ancestry, but extreme cruelty ran in its past. Members of his family had staged exceptionally bloody gladiatorial shows and one had even driven a chariot contemptuously over a member of the lower classes. After the boy's birth Nero's own father was said to have told a well-wisher that 'nothing born of me and Agrippina can be other than detestable and a public menace'.[8] He was quite right. Like Gaius, Nero had no military experience and no experience of public service. He became emperor when he was far too young, before his seventeenth birthday. For five years the combination of his mother, his tutor Seneca and his able Praetorian Prefect Burrus kept him relatively steady. Thereafter it was ever more clear that he combined vanity with irresponsibility. He expressed both in the way such people still do, by a misplaced wish to perform as an artist in public. He competed as a charioteer and worse, he sang and played the lyre. He was serious about it all, exercising with lead weights to improve his lungs and drinking the diluted dung of wild boar to help his muscles.

Between 59 and 67, his performances built up in range and publicity. In 59, he gave games to celebrate the shaving of his beard and first sang in public to the lyre, flanked by voice-coaches and a backing of 5,000 chanters and cheerleaders. In 64, he first drove in public as a charioteer. Summer 66 saw 'Golden Day', the public reception of the king of Armenia at which Nero sang and drove yet again. The natural outlet for such aspirations was Greece. In 66/7 Nero went on tour to compete at Delphi and Olympia. The rumour was that he won more than 1,800 first prizes, even for a ten-horse chariot race in which he fell off. In return he gave Olympia a new club-house for athletes, the first Roman emperor to do anything for the site.

This performing was not the fine outlet of a sympathetic 'friend of the arts'. Nero was pathologically vain and jealous: he assaulted his rivals and even had others' honorary statues destroyed. His increasing performances were accompanied by gross debauched parties, of which a river-party in 64 was particularly notorious. Nero was towed downstream on a carpeted raft, pulled by boats which were rowed by male prostitutes. On either river bank, naked females were available for sex, prostitutes and noblewomen alike. A few days later Nero married one of his male sex-

55. Gold aureus, Rome, showing Nero and his mother Agrippina, a unique double portrait of an emperor and an imperial woman, but she was a unique 'queen' mother. AD 54.

slaves. He wore a wedding veil and even squealed like a virgin bride when the wedding was apparently consummated.

Like the 'fatal charades' in Rome's arena, Nero's performances and orgies were sometimes enhanced by allusions to Greek mythology. But they are not excused or dignified by it or made into a consistent whole, as if they were being conducted by a role-playing master of 'revelry'. Egotism and cruel perversion prevailed, and the cost and extravagance ruined public funds. In 59, after all, Nero had had his mother Agrippina murdered and then publicly celebrated his 'rescue' from her plotting. His married life began relatively quietly, despite his taste for 'roving' at night with parties of friends and harassing even the better-born women in the streets. He did not care for his first wife Octavia whom he married as a child, but he compensated with a willing freedwoman. He then took a friend's wife away and married her, the lovely 'amber' haired Poppaea Sabina who was said to bathe in the milk of 500 donkeys. When she died, kicked to death by Nero, he picked the freedman who looked most like her, had him castrated and used him for sex instead. He nicknamed him 'Sporus' ('seed') and even 'Sabina' too. Throughout, his extravagance was atrocious. He was not to blame for the Great Fire which destroyed much of the city of Rome in the year 64, but his plan to build a huge Golden House for himself afterwards in the centre of the city was megalomaniac. His continuing lack of restraint and moral standards encouraged two major conspiracies against him. The second was backed by important provincial governors and proved mercifully successful. On 9 June 68 Nero anticipated events by killing himself, saying 'What an artist dies in me.' It was his final vanity.

In this Julio-Claudian household, one ancestor was taking his genetic revenge: Mark Antony. Tiberius' dangerously popular young rival, Germanicus, was Antony's grandson; so was Claudius; Gaius was Antony's great-grandson, as was Nero too. It was a dreadful time to be a senator at Rome, when the unopposable palace guards protected, and even promoted, such people as emperors. For some thirty years senators had to compromise under a mad wastrel, a cruel and susceptible spastic and a vain and self-obsessed profligate. The best place to be was in a province, away from spies and informers. Young Nero's initial 'honeymoon' period owed something to the wise counsels of the philosopher Seneca, but he was then encouraged in his natural extravagance by the odious Tigellinus. 'Obscure in parentage and debauched in early life',[9] Tigellinus was a Sicilian by birth who capitalized on his good looks and his breeding of racehorses. They were passions to which Nero was highly susceptible.

Even more than Caligula, Nero is the defining patron of the Roman orgy. Many modern historians now shy away from this aspect, regarding it as a short-lived triviality and preferring instead to study Roman administration in the provinces and the structures, or lack of them, in the impinging of Roman power on millions of provincials' lives. But the orgies are of wider significance too. For all the stress on 'traditional values' and 'Roman morals' there were senators and upper class knights who fought unashamedly in Nero's gladiatorial shows. In 59, at public games, upper class men and woman acted on the stage, not shunning indecent scenes. Nero forbade them to wear masks, but even so, ex-consuls participated and a lady in her eighties, Aelia Catella, danced in a pantomime. The infamous river party of 64 involved noblewomen in promiscuous sex with strangers, including slaves. Restraints were overturned and alarmingly people found 'licence' all too enjoyable. The upper orders had been victimised by Claudius and were deeply scared of Nero's potential cruelty. Why hold back, when they might be killed or die leaving property to be confiscated? The next thirty years are in part the history of a moral reaction, in part the story of an older generation who were trying to put an uninhibited past behind them, knowing that others at the time had been more high principled.

Luxury played an important role beside 'licence'. During the Julio-Claudian years luxury, as personal extravagance, continued to increase remorselessly with the progress of crafts and the prodigal rivalry of consumers. 'Spend now rather than be confiscated later' was one senatorial impulse; another was enhanced opportunity. It was not just that the volume of wine consumed by all classes at Rome rose sharply: a 'vigorous drinking-place culture' among urban communities in Italy has also been detected.[10] In the Julio-Claudian era we begin to have firm evidence for senatorial landowners' involvement in vine-growing. Much more extravagantly, we have evidence for their spiralling pursuit of 'luxuries', especially those in limited supply. In the Roman upper class, a personal fortune might as well be spent now, as otherwise it would be left partly to the emperor on death; legacies left by childless donors would be penalized, anyway, under Augustus' moral laws. In Tiberius' reign the prices of special luxuries, whether bronzes in pseudo-Corinthian Greek style or big mullets in the fish market, were rising so sharply that there was legislation by the emperor to control them. In 22 there were fears that Tiberius would restrict spending on anything luxurious, ranging from silver plate to dinner-parties. In fact, Tiberius wrote to the Senate that he wished that such restrictions could be effective, but that the problems were insoluble. Indeed, there was so much more now to want. Romans had discovered a taste for much that was rare, including tables made from the beautiful wood of the citrus tree, native to north Africa: the trees were wiped out as they gratified it. Craftsmen had developed the complex technique of fluorspar and of cameos in which layers of precious metals were set in glass. Like modern house-prices or salaries on Wall Street, the unchecked cost of bronzes and villas, paintings and pearls were topics of conversation at the very Roman dinner-parties which flaunted them. According to the historian Tacitus, there was also discussion of the 'effeminate' dress of rich men.[11] Female hairstyles at court were still relatively classical, but their accompaniments did become recherché. We can compare the rather simple recipe for toothpaste of the Empress Livia with the infinitely more exotic compound of Messalina, requiring mastic gum from Chios (still used in the fine local toothpaste), salt from north Africa and powdered stag's horn, which was thought to be an aphrodisiac.

Since the fourth century BC historians had so often cited luxury as a cause of defeat or disaster: in the 60s AD it did at last claim its first major victim, the Julio-Claudian household itself. Nero's hopeless extravagance was a direct cause of his overthrow and the ending of the family line. Justice, meanwhile, was more subtly corrupted by the emperors' habits. In the Senate, Tiberius had sat in on cases which included alleged slights to his own 'majesty': how could senators then be impartial in his brooding presence? Claudius heard far too many cases in private; he often refused to hear more than one side of the argument and simply imposed his own personal view. The underlying trend throughout was for officials, both at Rome and abroad, to hear cases and pass judgements in their own right. Appeals to authority thus developed a new range.

As for freedom, it had had a real chance with Gaius' murder in January 41, but the failure to secure it was revealing. It was a hundred years, on a long view, since freedom had really been rooted in the Republic, since the gentlemen's agreement between Caesar, Pompey and Crassus in 59 BC. In the face of a vast Empire, an army loyal to a dynasty and a populace fearful of senatorial rule, how ever could freedom be restored by senators who had now never even known it? Nor would that sort of freedom have been workable. Rather, the survival of the underlying imperial structures during these four grotesque emperors is evidence of their increasing strength and necessity. When the provincial governor who led the western rising against Nero declared himself to be acting for the Senate and people, the declaration led to his recognition by the Praetorian guards at Rome and then to his being empowered by the Senate as the next emperor. What senators most hoped for was a defined area of business which the Senate, if possible, should decide, while the emperor retained a restrained, moral competence in all settings. Affability and accessibility without extravagance were the crucial attributes for a good emperor.

In protest under Nero, there were senators who took a principled stand against his tyranny, partly by drawing on a veneer of ethical 'Stoic' values. Upper-class Romans were not true philosophers, but these principled ethics did at least suit the moral aspirations of new men, rising into the ruling class: they lacked the world-weary cynicism of the older intake and they wished to be principled and rather too earnest when placed in apparent honour at the centre of affairs. For other, more quizzical characters, there was always the possibility of noble and eloquent suicides, acts which were not in any way condemned by Roman religion. Seneca the philosopher cut his veins; the engaging Petronius, 'arbiter of taste',[12] compiled an exact list of Nero's sexual debaucheries with men and women and sent it to him while opening his veins and joking meanwhile with his friends. Above all, there was the example of the immensely rich senator and ex-consul, Valerius Asiaticus. By origin a Gaul, he had inherited by marriage a fine park on the Esquiline hill in Rome. 'Gaping for gardens', Claudius' wife Messalina then urged his destruction. Among all the various charges laid against him, Claudius hesitated before giving in. But he did allow Asiaticus to choose his own death. So Asiaticus exercised, dressed up and dined well. He then opened his veins, but not before he had inspected the siting of his funeral pyre. Small freedoms still remained: he ordered the pyre to be moved so that the fire would not burn his trees.[13] Claudius then confiscated the park as soon as Asiaticus was dead.

RULING THE PROVINCES

It is the most unjust thing of all for me to tighten up by my own edict what the two Augustuses, one the greatest of gods (Augustus), the other the greatest of emperors (Tiberius), have taken the utmost care to prevent, namely that anybody should make use of carts without payment. But since the indiscipline of certain people requires an immediate punishment, I have set up in the individual towns and villages a register of those services which I judge ought to be provided, with the intention of having it observed or, if it shall be neglected, of enforcing it not only with my own power but with the authority of the best of princes [Augustus], from whom I received written instructions concerning these matters.

Edict of Sextus Sotidius Strabo, legate of Galatia, soon after AD 14

And whosoever shall compel thee to go a mile, go with him twain.

Jesus, in the Gospel of Matthew 5.41

O UTSIDE ITALY, NONETHELESS, Rome's provinces are said to have viewed Augustus' new order as not unwelcome. Perceptions, as always, will have varied with social class and cultural background, but in western Asia, with the governor's encouragement, a new calendar was adopted, beginning on Augustus' birthday. From Spain to Syria, cults of emperors, both dead and alive, proliferated in varying forms. What was there to celebrate? From Augustus onwards there were certainly changes in the appointment and regulation of governors, including new procedures for trying them for extortion and (eventually) a fixed annual wage, or 'salary', for their tenure of office (the first instances of the word in this sense). Their republican predecessors had left bad memories on this score.

But what counted most to the provincials was the return of peace and the ending of all the looting, money-raising and damage done abroad in the 40s and 30s during Rome's Civil Wars. Their total population is likely to have fallen sharply in all the chaos: an Empire-wide figure of 45 million has been suggested, 25 per cent below the levels reached later after a century of peace.

This new era developed into our idea of a Roman Empire. Already under Augustus, Romans wrote of ruling 'from Ocean to Ocean': maps of this world were constructed, especially the map which Agrippa displayed publicly at Rome.[1] There were still no clear ideas of frontiers, and the basic notion of empire was still not so much a territorial one as one of obedience to Romans' commands. By Hadrian's reign the territory under Roman command would stretch from Northumberland in Britain to the Red Sea, from the coast of modern Portugal to the river Euphrates. This huge territory has never been ruled by one power since. It would also shape Hadrian's career, as he spent more than half his reign touring round more than thirty of its provinces. There were soldiers in each of them, but not every province even had a full legion. The remarkable thing is how few officials were still being sent out to govern such a huge area.

At the top of a province, both 'public' and 'imperial', the crucial figure was still the governor, who was usually a senator. A few underlings might assist him and he could always call on any local army-officers and troops: military architects in the local camps would also be helpful in carrying out major building projects. The governor had detailed instructions from the emperor, a practice which began with Augustus and which Augustus had probably extended already to both types of province. The governor's overriding duty was to preserve peace and quiet. After the 30s BC Rome's provinces were never seriously at risk to an outside invader until long after Hadrian's death. The greater danger was a rebellion by Rome's subjects or civil strife between or within the province's local communities. Most governors, then, were focused on judging and resolving local disputes. Like Cicero in his province, they visited their provinces yearly on an assize-tour, during which they dispensed justice and settled disputes in recognized assize-cities. Calls on their time were potentially very heavy: we happen to know that at least 1,406 petitions were prepared for submission to a governor in one town in Egypt on a single visit.[2]

Naturally, justice could not be done solely by one annual visitor. Local cities and communities did retain their courts in which they would try most of the civil cases. They heard criminal cases too, but usually only those without serious penalties. There were also cases heard by Roman procurators, officials who were of two different types. In imperial provinces, some of the procurators were financial officials with the duty of overseeing tax-collection. This business always provokes disputes and the procurator was likely to try such cases himself. Undesirably, he was both the prosecutor and the judge of those before him. Other procurators were the emperor's land agents: they managed lands and properties owned by the emperor in his provinces. Under Claudius, they too were confirmed in the right to try cases arising from such properties and then, near the end of his life, their judgements were made final, without the possibility of appeal.

These alternative sources of justice did help the governors' workload, but nonetheless governors were kept busy. On entering a province, a governor still published an edict which announced offences which he would particularly consider, but in the new age, the emperor's instructions might guide him. Above all, he alone could impose the death penalty (with very few exceptions). There was also the bother of civil cases which were referred back to him from the emperor. For communities and individuals would sometimes take a case directly off to the emperor, only to find that they were encouraged by him to approach their local governor with (or without) a particular recommendation. It was then quite hard for governors to apply the law, because many of these cases were not covered neatly by accepted rulings of Roman law, and Roman law did not apply to most of the provincials anyway. There was a real need for patience and discretion on a governor's part. After a preliminary hearing, he could send a case off for trial by a local court; he could also consult with local advisers before deciding. Under the Empire, he could attend to a case personally as 'inquisitor' and after investigating it in person, he could pass sentence on it. All sorts of twisted cases and allegations would be brought up for his decision and it was best if he was impartial: he was urged in law books to avoid becoming too friendly with his provincials. It was also best if he left his wife in Rome, as she might become too involved: governors were made liable for their wives' misbehaviour in their province.

This travelling circuit had formed Cicero's career as a governor in the 50s BC and, as it spread, it did bring a new source of justice to many provincials' lives. Under the Empire, from Augustus onwards, there was also the new possibility of direct appeal to the emperor himself. However, there were limitations to both processes. To present a case, a petitioner had to travel in person, gain access and, if possible, speak eloquently. As ever, this sort of justice was not realistic for the poor, especially the poor in the countryside. It was also justice at the expense of local political freedom. The Roman governors monopolized penalties which even the Athenians' classical Empire had only controlled at second hand. Offences now included many which had been created by the very existence of the Empire in the first place. From their own experience at Rome, Rome's ruling class had become very suspicious of popular associations in a city, the 'clubs' which might conceal political purposes: we thus find a governor being told to ban local fire brigades in his province's cities ('better dead than red'[3]). Subjects also became liable to charges of 'treason' for supposed insults to an emperor, his statues or property. Anonymous accusations were strongly discouraged, but these sorts of charges were a direct consequence of Empire.

So, above all, was tax. Here, Roman governors became responsible for a major Roman innovation, imposed under Augustus: the regular census of their subjects. Censuses listed individuals and property as a basis for the collection of taxes. Officials were charged with carrying them out and the details were often complex: Augustus never decreed 'that all the world should be taxed', as the Gospel of Luke puts it, but he did record his holding of separate censuses in Rome's provinces.[4] Separate officials (quaestors and procurators) then took direct responsibility for the taxes' yearly collection. They had slaves, freedmen and the possibility of using soldiers to help them, but even so they were far less numerous than the tax-collectors of a modern state.

It was not even that taxes were very much simpler than ours nowadays. Direct tax took two rather complicated forms, a tribute on land and one on persons. The details varied between provinces, but they could include taxes on slaves and rented urban property and even on movable goods, including the equipment of a farm. Occasionally they were based on the produce of a farm rather than on its extent and value. There were also important indirect taxes, including harbour-dues, and further impositions, especially for the provision of animals, supplies and labour for public transport. It is this burden to which Jesus refers in the Gospel of Matthew: 'whosoever shall compel thee to go a mile, go with him twain', an idealistic bit of advice.

Occasionally, exemptions from taxes might be granted (especially to cities after a natural disaster) but they certainly did not belong by right to holders of Roman citizenship. In the provinces, Roman citizens and their land were liable to tax like everyone else. The one privileged area was

Map 10 Rome's Empire to the East

Augusta
(Augsburg)

Carnuntum

Aquincum
(Budapest)

RAETIA   NORICUM

Pavia

Aquileia

PANNONIA

ILLYRICUM

DACIA

Drobeta

Arretium

Ancona

Salonae
(Split)

Ada

R. Danube

Perusia

ITALIA

DALMATIA

Rome

Capua

Brundisium

Tarentum

MAEDONIA

Thessalonica

Doris

THR

EPIRUS

LES

Messana

Thebes

CHI

SICILIA

Corinth

Athens

S

Agrigentum

Catana

ACHAEA

Carthage

Syracuse

Sparta

Hadrumetum

Thapsus

MELITA (MALTA)

CRE

N

Sabratha

Oea

Leptis Magna

Ptolemais

Apollonia

AFRICA

Berenice
(Benghazi)

Barca

Cyrene

Altitude in yards

over 1000

200–1000

0–200

TRIPOLITANIA

CYRENAICA

LIBYA

0   100   200   300 miles

0   100   200   300   400   500 km

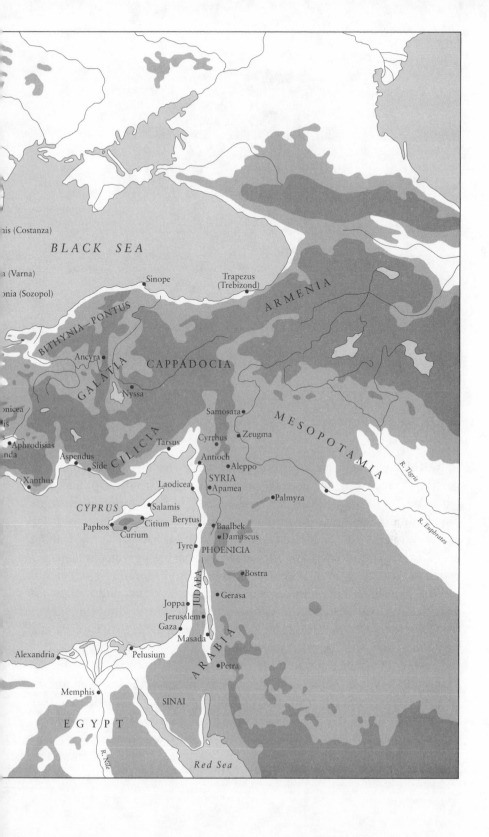

BLACK SEA

...his (Costanza)

...a (Varna)

...onia (Sozopol)

Sinope

Trapezus
(Trebizond)

ARMENIA

BITHYNIA–PONTUS

Ancyra

GALATIA

CAPPADOCIA

Nyssa

...onicea

...is

Aphrodisias

...nda

Aspendus

Side

CILICIA

Xanthus

Tarsus

Samosata

Cyrrhus

Zeugma

MESOPOTAMIA

R. Tigris

R. Euphrates

Antioch

Aleppo

SYRIA

Laodicea

Apamea

Palmyra

CYPRUS

Salamis

Paphos

Citium

Curium

Berytus

Baalbek

Damascus

Tyre

PHOENICIA

Bostra

JUDAEA

Gerasa

Joppa

Jerusalem

Gaza

Masada

ARABIA

Alexandria

Pelusium

Petra

Memphis

SINAI

EGYPT

R. Nile

Red Sea

56. Portrait of a boy, with surrounding mummy-
wrappings. Fayyum, Egypt. Reign of Trajan,
AD 98-117.

Italy, which paid indirect taxes but no tribute. Rome also benefited from a
particular type of payment: grain was taken as tax from Egypt and elsewhere and was shipped directly to the city. There, it supplied the huge
population, including those who were entitled to free distributions. If we
ask why further tax was necessary, the main answer is the big Roman
army. Taxes paid its costs, even when the tax-paying province was itself a
province without legions. Such are the injustices of Empire.

With hindsight, it might seem that the total levels of tax under Augustus
were not too burdensome: the fact is that they could be doubled and extended in the 70s. At the time, however, they were more than enough of a
load. Tax-collectors were ferocious and often used force. Conspicuously,
there were revolts in Gaul, north Africa, Britain and Judaea soon after the
imposition of direct Roman rule, and in each of them, the financial impact
was the major cause. If provincials could not pay tax in cash, collectors
were content to be paid in kind, including cattle-hides which supplied essential leather. Giving a provincial a thorough exaction was described as
'shaking him down': in newly annexed provinces, Italian moneylenders
were soon found to be profiteering from the inhabitants too.

Inevitably, there was scope for sharp practice. In Britain, governors are said to have bought up stocks of local grain and only then sold it back to the locals at a much higher price. In Gaul, Augustus' financial agent, or procurator, is said to have declared that there were fourteen months in the year, not twelve, in order to claim two more months' tax. In principle, such sharp practitioners could be accused at Rome under one of two procedures before senatorial judges. Augustus had introduced these procedures, and it is too cynical to see senators in the more serious of the two as simply acquitting their own kind. A harsh decision by the Emperor Tiberius had denied senators the right to make a valid will when found guilty of extortion. This penalty hurt an offender's family and so, with good reason, fellow senators hesitated to impose it. Such cases were thus often examined at great length. But there was a parallel intrusion of Romans on provincial lives, one which was not regulated to this limited degree. In the Athenian Empire, individual Athenians had sometimes acquired land in allied territory, a practice which came to be widely resented. In the Roman Empire, individual Romans acquired land in the provinces on a vastly greater scale. Some of it was bought or acquired after owners had defaulted on a debt but some, no doubt, was the result of offers which owners could not refuse. The emperor and his family were major beneficiaries, not least through a process of bequests by provincials. In Egypt, members of the imperial house acquired properties by the score. In north Africa in the 60s most of the land was said to be owned by no more than six hugely rich senators (not necessarily African by birth). But even so, Romans' estates abroad were still liable for tax.

How ever did the tax system work if there was not a big bureaucracy to collect it all? Part of the answer is that collection was delegated. Generally, the sums required were assessed on communities who were left to raise what was necessary. The point here is that their politically dominant class could pass most of the burden on to their inferiors. Rome thus reversed the pattern of the former Athenian Empire. Then, democracies in the allied Greek cities had voted that the rich should pay a hefty share of tribute. Under Roman rule, democracies were watered down or non-existent and so the dominant city-councillors could lessen the impact of tax on themselves. Even when they paid, the tax applied at the same rate to one and all: the poll tax was as unfair as always, and there was no surtax.

Collection was also eased by privatization. Julius Caesar had abolished the auctioning of direct taxes in a province to 'private' companies of tax-collectors at Rome: as a result, the tax imposed at Rome on Asia is said to have been reduced by a third. In the Empire, however, the cities and local communities would still use such companies locally to raise the prescribed sums on their behalf. These tax-collectors, the 'publicans' of the Gospels, guaranteed a sum in advance, but then collected much more from individuals as their profit. There was also the particular problem of indirect taxes. Their yield varied yearly with the underlying volume of business and, in order to be sure in advance of an agreed sum, Roman officials preferred to sell off, or 'farm', the right to their collection. Privatization suited the authorities but not the taxpayers.

Roman taxation built on existing practices in most provinces, but it was most people's main point of contact with Roman rule. Year in, year out, even small farmers and tenants were affected, whether or not they knew their governor's name or a single word of Greek or Latin. The emperor's image and its public prominence were less significant in his subjects' awareness of his rule, though for us this 'image' is so much more evident in the art and objects which survive. Most provinces had public cults which offered sacrifices and prayers 'for', or to, the emperors, but they were concentrated in cities, both in the city centres of provincial 'assemblies' and in individual cities with cults of their own. Statues represented emperors, often in military dress; coins carried their titles, and even the coins which were struck in provincial mints showed their images; in the third century we find the portrait of an emperor at his accession being escorted into a province's cities and being lit by candles. There was scope for ingenious exploitation in all this publicity. In the 30s AD the governor of Asia had to curb people who were already celebrating all sorts of supposed 'good news' from Rome, whether or not it existed.[5] False rumours were a chance for sharp provincials to sell 'celebratory' goods to other provincials. In Britain and Hungary, there have been finds of moulds, apparently for sacrificial cakes or buns, which were to be imprinted with stamps of the emperor shown sacrificing to the gods. The buns would be eaten by his subjects at their religious festivals.[6]

The Empire, however, did not rest on personalized cakes. There were two basic reasons for its overall stability. One was the absence of inflammable nationalism (except in troubled Judaea). There was ethnic self-consciousness in many provinces (Britain or Egypt or Germany) but it was complicated by competing cultures and, often, by bilingualism. In Syria, Greek-speakers and authors in Greek could refer to themselves as 'Syrians' and even use Aramaic or write Syriac too. But they were not acknowledging a 'Syrian nationalism' or a 'Syrian identity'.[7] Nor were Roman governors and administrators working with their subjects' eventual 'national' independence in mind, unlike some of those in the British, or even French, empires. The historian Tacitus ascribes a sturdy value for 'freedom' to faraway opponents of Roman rule and equates the adoption of Roman culture with 'slavery'. But he never argues that Rome's subjects should one day be freed.

The second, crucial support was class rule, both implicit and explicit. Rome did not 'divide and rule' between cities: the Empire encouraged cities to combine in new provincial assemblies. But she did benefit from the existing divisions between her subjects. One major reason for the loyalty of the ruling class in less civilized provinces was their explicit awareness that, without Roman power, they would return to faction and fighting among themselves. In more urbanized provinces, including the Greek East, there was a parallel advantage for the cities' upper classes: Roman rule secured them against political attack by their own lower classes. There might be the occasional food-riot, but there was no real danger of the political challenges which had propelled so much of Greek history from c. 500 to c. 80 BC. If a Greek city's popular assembly proved too turbulent, a governor would intervene and simply abolish it. Roman citizenship was given to upper-class beneficiaries in the provinces, protecting them against arbitrary harassment. Under Roman rule, meanwhile, they could pass on much of the local burden of direct tax and compete for new public honours. Democracy, as Cicero once put it, was a 'hideous monster', and now, to their relief, they had masters who agreed.

EFFECTS OF EMPIRE

There were always kingdoms and wars throughout Gaul until you sub-mitted to our laws. Although we have so often been provoked, the only thing we have imposed on you by the rights of victory is what will enable us to keep the peace ... Everything else is shared between us ... If the Romans were ever driven out—may the gods forbid!—what else will hap-pen except wars of all peoples, fighting among themselves?

Petilius Cerealis, in Tacitus, *Histories* 4.74

THE LASTING MEMORIALS OF the Roman Empire are roads and city-buildings, aqueducts and Roman law and the Latin which underlies so many European languages. Even at the time, Roman emperors were ac-claimed for their 'liberality' and the 'benefits' which their peace brought. There is an apparent unity and openness in an Empire in which a German or a Briton could become a full citizen of Rome and a man from Spain could become a senator or even, like Hadrian, an emperor. The Roman citizenship certainly spread far and wide, as did Roman laws and Latin. The most admired Latin authors in the first century AD were not often men born in Rome or even Italy: many came from Spain, such as Seneca the philosopher or Lucan the poet, Martial and his witty epigrams, and Quintilian and his teachings on how to speak and write Latin well. Al-ready in the age of Augustus, the geographer Strabo had written of the dominance of Latin, the abandonment of warlike ways and mountain strongholds and the ending of old barbarisms in southern Spain and Gaul.

A shared, educated culture allowed upper-class provincials to commu-nicate on equal terms with the existing upper class at Rome. It is from such educated people in the provinces' upper classes that the praises of Rome's 'benefits' come. There is, however, another side to this picture.

57. The Roman aqueduct at Segovia in Spain, reaching almost one hundred feet at its highest point. Built in the first century or early second century AD.

Texts for Roman readers expressed some vividly 'incorrect' stereotypes of non-Roman foreigners. Gauls were said to be big, blond, long-haired lumps who were particularly keen on homosexuality; Syrians were boastful, typical traders and over-sexed with it; in inland Spain, people were said to wash their teeth in their own urine; in Ireland, they were said to have sex in public. The 'civilizing' Romans, by contrast, brought human and animal blood sports to their subjects. The amphitheatres for both types of show were a major Roman contribution, albeit a cruel one, to the Empire's quality of life. In comparison, their language, Latin, made very little headway among civilized Greek-speakers in the traditional Greek world. Even where it did, other languages persisted, 'Celtic' in Gaul, Punic in much of north Africa or south-west Spain (the legacy of Carthage and its colonists) and Aramaic (Jesus' daily speech) in much of the Near East. Far and wide, there was more bilingualism than our barrage of surviving Greek and Latin texts might imply. Perhaps it even occurred among landowners when they returned to their country estates and liked to exchange local words with their old retainers and bailiffs.

Outside a few schools of higher learning, even such Latin as was spoken or written in the provinces was patchy or uneducated. A few phrases from important points in Virgil's *Aeneid* might be copied out, even by craftsmen in Britain, but they were probably known through writing exercises, not through a wider literary or theatrical culture. The more we find Latin outside the educated class in papyri, graffiti or other inscriptions, the less it resembles our classic rules for Latin grammar. Some of it was passed on by Italians, who had settled overseas: they had not been as well schooled as Roman orators. The style is particularly vivid in the recorded replies of Latin-speaking Christians when on trial for their lives. Many of these martyrs would fail modern examinations in Latin with spectacularly low marks.

'Liberality', at least, is evident in the Empire's surviving ruins and in the texts and inscriptions (mostly from the eloquent Greek East) which attest it. Roman emperors are thanked or commemorated for giving cities their fortified walls and aqueducts, their granaries and scores of civic buildings. Of all emperors, Hadrian was the greatest urban benefactor. He personally transformed Athens with his new library and gymnasium and temples and colonnades. His buildings elsewhere in the province revived a Greece which was generally at a low point; in north-west Asia, too, he founded a whole cluster of cities named after himself. He was amazingly generous to his own home town, Italica in western Spain. He transformed this small sleepy place into somewhere with the glamour of a capital city, giving it broad streets and walks, baths, an amphitheatre, excellent drains and a theatre. Yet as emperor he never returned to it himself. Previous emperors had done much the same to places which mattered to them (except, on the whole, the stingy Tiberius), but Hadrian's 'liberality' was on the grandest scale. He travelled more than any of them, and an imperial visit was so often the cue for a surge of new building, as we can see from the effects of Augustus' visits to southern Gaul and Spain.

What, though, was the source of this 'liberality'? Emperors might donate raw materials to beneficiaries, whether timber from forests (Hadrian owned the cedar forests of Lebanon) or fine marble from one of the highly prized quarries. Yet these local assets were ones which they had confiscated, seized or inherited at local expense. Quite often, an emperor's favour would amount to the suspension of a city's taxes for a year or two; if so, the 'liberality' was exercised with the provincials' own output. During the suspension the taxes were diverted to local public monuments, but for the mass of workers who paid most of them there was no respite.

There was another two-edged type of generosity: the giving of new lands abroad to new immigrant settlers. For the settlers, the gift was real enough. After Julius Caesar's example, Augustus had had to settle veteran soldiers in perhaps sixty new sites outside Italy, sending out more than

100,000 emigrants in all. The resulting 'colonies' were the greatest export of population since Alexander the Great's conquests. These colonists were settled as Roman citizens. They began by speaking Latin and their towns, cults and buildings tended to evoke Rome itself. Worship of the three great gods of Rome's Capitol (Jupiter, Juno and Minerva) was prominent in the colonies' major shrines, together with priests in Roman style. Nonetheless, in the Greek East the 'Roman' stamp did not usually last. Intermarriage with locals and assimilation to the strong local culture meant that colonies tended to go over to Greek in the course of time: Berytus (modern Beirut), however, remained a sturdy bastion of Latin and of Roman law in the Lebanon.

Colonies' town plans could certainly be made splendid very quickly. In southern Asia Minor, Pisidian Antioch was settled on a conspicuous hill and rapidly acquired a massive temple for worship of Augustus. It was approached through a big triple-arched gateway (dedicated to him in 2 BC) and straight streets, sculptures and other imperial buildings soon set it all off splendidly. In south-western Spain, the well-named 'Emerita' ('Time-served', for the veterans: nowadays, Mérida) was settled on the junction of two good rivers, from 25 BC onwards. Water was delivered to it by three smart new aqueducts; there were bridges, baths and, before long, an array of leisure-centres (a theatre in 16 BC and an amphitheatre for blood sports in 8 BC). The biggest success was the racecourse, or circus, which was probably built under Tiberius and was modelled on the Circus Maximus at Rome. Spain's horses were magnificent, and the races continued here for centuries, even after the end of direct Roman rule. In the forum, meanwhile, a big sculpted portico imitated the sculptures in Augustus' own great Forum at Rome.

At Pisidian Antioch in Asia, members of the Julio-Claudian family were elected as magistrates of the town in absence. It was a clever honour because like other magistrates they would be expected to give benefactions to 'their' town. Elsewhere, the Roman governor's impetus was important; it influenced the building of Emerita, as did the role of Augustus' reliable Agrippa who had campaigned nearby. On his travels, Agrippa showed a personal interest in construction: he had an Odeon built to impress the Athenians and may well have encouraged the design's huge roof-span which required sixty feet of timber. He may also have encouraged the even bigger roof, eighty feet wide, which covered the great temple of Zeus at Baalbek in Berytus' new territory where he was also active. Great feats of construction and assaults on the landscape always appealed to Romans and their architects. Hence they built great roads in Italy for

58. Roman theatre, built at Emerita Augusta (Mérida, Spain), probably with the backing of Augustus' general Agrippa. 16/5 BC.

Trajan or helped Hadrian to attack an age-old problem, the draining of Lake Copais in central Greece. The main uses of Roman roads were not for commerce or 'provincial development': they were military and governmental, for inter-communication among the governing class.

Where colonists settled, others had to leave, or keep out, because the veterans' rewards of land were not necessarily sited on virgin soil. But the colonies' showy new centres did encourage local imitation. Soon after Merida's foundation we see it in a much simpler town in Spain, Conimbriga in the north-west. Conimbriga was no colony but it lay in a metal-rich area which had no doubt attracted Italian exploiters to it before the town was developed. In the Augustan age the leading citizens of Conimbriga built baths which were served by an aqueduct, and laid out an impressive forum with a temple, colonnades and civic buildings. The Romans' new Merida was being copied by its neighbours: should we, then, reckon everywhere on provincials who 'Romanized' themselves?

Modern empires have looked back on this process as a 'blessing', like their own ideals, and ascribed to it a 'civilizing mission'. Certainly, we can point to new Roman styles and imports which travelled far beyond sites where Latin-speaking immigrants settled. Bathhouses are a widespread example, civic amenities which brought a new social style to East and West. But domestic styles changed too. Under Roman rule, people in Gaul or Britain began of their own accord to build houses in stone, not timber and thatch; they dined off smooth, shiny pottery in shapes which belonged with new table manners and new tastes. Wine took over from the pre-Roman habit of drinking almost nothing but beer. Olive oil was mass-produced for provincial use too, whether in southern Spain or inland, in what is now desert, in parts of north Africa. Salty fish sauce, an Italian speciality, became a favourite seasoning outside Italy, while the new-style houses brought new divisions of space and perhaps new daily boundaries between men and women, elders and children. In public spaces, inscriptions and statues began to honour benefactors who had become drawn into a new public exchange of gifts. In return for their own giving, such people received the gift of publicly recorded honours, granted before the new focus of a town-crowd, whether in Spain or Gaul or north Africa. This exchange also encouraged social competition by donors among themselves.

This 'Romanization' was more accurately an Italianization. The veteran soldiers, the local immigrant traders, the friends whom provincial recruits made in the army were not Romans as old Cato had imagined them. Rome's vast population was still a very mixed bunch, not purely 'Roman' now (or ever) by origin. Most of the 'Roman' colonists came from Italian towns which had themselves become Romanized during the Republic. What Romans first did to Italians, Italians then did to provincials. But the provincials were not a blank sheet of paper, either: they had their own cultures which varied from province to province. Greek and Aramaic, Hebrew and Egyptian were especially robust in the East, while Punic in south Spain and north Africa was the most robust culture in the West. Was, then, the Italianization adapted to fit the provincials' own existing lifestyle, and if so, how should we describe the process? Historians now stretch words to cover it: did Rome's subjects choose to 'acculturate' or did they 'transculturate' by developing a culture which was a mixture of old and new? Or is 'subculturation' somehow nearer the truth?

The process, surely, varied from place to place. In distant Britain, according to the historian Tacitus, it was helped along by the governor Agricola, Tacitus' own father-in-law. Agricola, he tells us, encouraged the building of 'temples, forums and houses'.[1] Archaeologically, we cannot yet weigh up this initiative, and so the current inclination is to disbelieve it, because Tacitus was writing a highly favourable book about the man involved. But in the Greek East there are scores of well-attested cases when emperors or governors did indeed encourage such buildings, and by comparison Britain was wild and only recently conquered. As in the East, military specialists from the army could be sent to help the first building-projects off to a good start. Taxes, even, might be diverted to kick-start them: within the Empire as a whole Agricola's initiative is not as unprecedented as local Western archaeologists sometimes suggest.

His son-in-law, Tacitus, described it as the softening of a warlike people by pleasures, in order to accustom them to 'peace and quiet': if Tacitus thought in this way, his father-in-law Agricola could surely have thought on these realistic lines too. The sons of the British leaders are said, surely rightly, to have been exposed very quickly to Latin education. The toga became 'frequent' and, on Tacitus' view, there was a gradual descent into seductive 'vices', encouraged by 'colonnades, baths and elegant dinners'. The 'simple Britons called it "civilization", although it was part of their slavery'.[2] Here, Tacitus uses one of his (and antiquity's) favourite contrasts, between 'free' hardy barbarians and soft 'enslaved' subjects. Yet he need not have been the only one to see 'luxury' as an aid to imperial subjection. In southern Britain, such 'slavery' to pleasure had already begun some while before Agricola arrived, as archaeology shows at London or St Albans and manifestly so at Bath. The Roman fashion for bathing was rapidly imitated by provincials: the local hot springs at Bath were already serving Roman bathers by c. AD 65, about twenty years before Agricola.

In less barbarous provinces, the governors and emperors surely gave similar encouragement for the sake of maintaining peace and quiet. There was little need for official encouragement anyway. On their own initiative, the local upper classes took swiftly to the new avenues of display and competition which Rome offered. There were new titles to be had, new privileges to be paraded. This 'status display' even underlies the most individual and immediate art-works to survive from any imperial province: the portraits on wood panels found in Egyptian mummy-burials and dating from c. AD 40 onwards. Men and women are immortalized in these lifelike portraits, as if old age did not exist, yet the representations are also status-conscious.[3] They are mostly painted on specially imported woods, lime-wood or box. Some of their women wear the up-to-date hairstyles, earrings and jewellery which we know in contemporary Italy, and yet only one of those depicted bears the names of a Roman citizen. Perhaps, like Roman funerary-masks, these portraits were displayed in funerary processions: it is attractive to connect them with the membership, or claimed membership, of the privileged Greek-speaking class in Egypt's main towns, people who had been benefited under the Empire by an exemption from paying poll tax. Their culture of portraits marked them out as distinguished people, a cut above their tax-paying inferiors.

Many of the new types of provincial display were more comfortable and much more elegant than pre-Roman life. In Augustus' lifetime the most famous symbol of rural peace, the villa, had already become widespread in southern Gaul. In Britain, its heyday was to be later, and a century or more would pass before landowners in Somerset or Gloucestershire could boast true country-house living, with mosaic floors and happy memories of their days' hunting, under the patronage (in the Cotswolds) of their special young god of the chase. It is to Romans that Britain owes so many of its 'native' trees, the cherry or the walnut. It also owes them many staples of better cooking, coriander, peaches, celery or carrots. To an educated Roman eye, the Britons' local country-house culture was probably rather curious, with its copycat buildings and a local flavour to the lifestyle. There was only one area of equal exchange. Italians, it seems, introduced the domestic cat to Gaul; provincial dogs, in turn, transformed Italians' packs of hounds. There was real progress here, people noted in the age of Hadrian, beyond the breeds of dog which had formerly been known to the Greeks.

To our age of exclusive religions, religion might seem likely to be a more contentious transplant. Religious cults of Rome and the emperor were indeed encouraged in provincial capitals, and they too became objects of extravagant competition. At Colchester in Britain, the temple of the deified Emperor Claudius was described by Tacitus both as a 'citadel of eternal domination' and also as a cause of bankruptcy among prominent Britons who 'poured out their fortunes under the guise of religion'.[4] There was no stopping their leaders' extravagance in this headlong new game of 'dynasty'. Conversely, there was no drive among the emperors or senators to civilize provincials for the sake of spreading a true religion. In Gaul and Britain, pre-Roman 'Druid' religion was actively suppressed, but only because of its barbarous aspects (probably including human sacrifice): the moral tone of cults had been a long-running Roman concern. A similar concern probably underlies Hadrian's interference with the Jews in Judaea. Beliefs, however, were not the issue: local gods, if morally innocuous, were twinned with a Graeco-Roman divinity and simply given a double name ('Mercurius Dumias'). The Roman residents and local upper classes tended to honour the god of the Graeco-Roman name only, while their inferiors preferred the explicit twinning. As so much Roman religion was concerned with worldly success and well-being, non-Roman polytheists could accommodate the new package without difficulty: they shared the same priorities.

If we take Roman law and Roman citizenship as the really important markers, there was official Roman concern to extend them, but even this concern is different from an active drive for social inclusion or a mission to civilize. Roman citizenship was traditionally bestowed in return for meritorious services; Augustus had been very sparing of it and had kept records at Rome of those few who had merited it. Even Claudius followed this principle, despite a contemporary satire on his wish to put all the Gauls and Britons into citizen-togas. One continuing road to deserving citizenship was army-service as an auxiliary; another was service as an upper-class magistrate in specially designated towns, or *municipia*. The grant of the status of *municipium* to a town under Roman rule was not automatic. Not until the 70s did the Emperor Vespasian give it to towns of Spain (probably, to the towns throughout Spain). Even there, the main reason was a calculated reward. Spain had played an important part in the recent Civil Wars and so the leaders of the towns needed a favour.

From recently discovered inscriptions, we can now better reconstruct the outlines of a guiding 'municipal law' for Spain.[5] The initial grant of municipal status gave the magistrates in these towns the right to Roman citizenship. Importantly, Roman citizenship did not exempt its recipients from the obligation of serving their home town as liturgists. They still had to give time and resources: emperors wanted to maintain vigorous local cities, on which the collection of taxes rested, and Augustus had explicitly asserted that Roman citizens still had their local obligations. So the upper classes were to pay for most of the amenities of civic life, continuing a pattern which had begun in the archaic Greek city-states and had spread as cities multiplied in the lands of Roman rule.

In classical Athens, the undertaking of liturgies had been kept separate from the holding of magistracies. Outside the older Greek city-states this distinction between benefaction and political office was not upheld, even before the Romans' conquests. It was not observed in the new *municipia*, either. In Spanish *municipia*, the magistrates were drawn only from the councillors, and the councillors were themselves drawn only from the better-off. They paid an entrance fee on joining the council, and their service was for life. They would then 'promise' benefactions or accept liturgies as magistrates. There was no question of random selection by lot or popular participation on a council in the classical Athenian style. Nor was the 'Latin right' planned to be a stage halfway on the road to full Roman citizenship for all citizens. It was an end in itself, a careful limitation of the Roman citizenship to a community's upper orders. The Roman citizenship protected such people against arbitrary violence by Roman officials and allowed them to make valid marriages with other Roman citizens. They could also make wills and enter on contracts which would be valid under Roman law before Roman officials. In return, the citizenship bound them closely to Rome's interests. It was an important part of 'class rule' in the Empire.

Nonetheless, the other citizens of these 'municipal' towns were also affected by their towns' new status. They were expected to worship Roman cults and in dealings between themselves they too were to apply Roman civil laws as 'Latins'. Those who already traded with Roman citizens would have found this provision convenient, although it was somewhat perplexing for most people. In the 70s AD there were no law books and no local law schools and a real understanding of Roman law was surely rare among most provincials, as it still is among most of us. In principle, Roman laws did affect many family matters, including inheritance and marriage, the freeing of slaves and the powers, so huge, of a Roman father over his household. But there was sure to be confusion here. Arguably, the municipal law in Spain arose from an attempt by the Emperor Domitian to regulate abuses and 'Spanish practices' in the towns in the wake of Vespasian's initial Latin grant to them. Behind these charters, there will have been more of an aspiration and an ideal than a reality realized in every matter of detail.

In the East, by contrast, this 'Latin right' was not granted to cities. The leaders of Greek civic life had their own robust culture already, and so Romans let it continue. Roman citizenship was rarer in the East, especially in those provinces without legions (legionaries were Roman citizens). Quiet and loyalty had already been secured here by supporting the existing upper classes against their lower classes, and so there was no need for yet another grant of privileges to them. Nonetheless, Roman law does turn up in the East in individual cases. In Hadrian's reign, we can find its forms in the civil petition of a Jewish woman, Babatha, some of whose papers have survived for us in a desert cave in Judaea. As Babatha wanted to press her case with a Roman governor, she appears to have found someone to draw up her Greek petition in terms which the governor might recognize from his Roman background. Other petitioners no doubt did the same, but they did so by artful choice, not legal necessity.

In the East, the most sensitive area of Roman rule was Judaea itself. Under Antony's appointee King Herod, classical civic building and 'luxury' had been lavishly advanced in this region. Herod's successors founded cities too, even up by the Sea of Galilee. Yet the results were not peace and quiet. In AD 6, ten years after Herod's death, Augustus brought Judaea under direct rule. The sequel, as usual, was a Roman census but it provoked keen opposition from particular Jews, who could cite a scriptural precedent against it. One group argued that allegiance was owed only to God: they became the Zealots (or 'dagger men', *sicarii*, in their victims' name for them), the only anti-Roman 'philosophy' to arise in the entire Empire.[6] They were the Empire's first terrorists.

During his Civil War in the East, Julius Caesar had already approached the Jews and their religion with respect. Precedents here went back to the Persian kings in the sixth century BC. From Augustus on, the emperors also paid for sacrifices in the Jerusalem Temple to be offered on their behalf. Most of the Jews were not unwilling recipients of these favours, and under Augustus favours were even confirmed for individual Jewish Diaspora communities scattered outside Judaea who were so often at risk to the citizen-bodies of Greek cities and their resentment. Under Roman rule, Jews were even exempted from the military service which they had once rendered to Alexander's Successors. Some of the Romans, meanwhile, proved susceptible to the Jews' ancient God and to the link between his cult and a code of ethics. During the first century AD several adherents to Jewish religion are traceable in high Roman society, especially among women, who were outside the most active power-structures of Roman life (where strict Judaism would have been more difficult). Women could also convert without the pain of circumcision.

Nonetheless, anti-Jewish stereotypes were still current and not only among the Greeks of Alexandria where anti-Semitism had originated. 'Politically incorrect' Roman governors of Judaea found it hard to respect the local ethnic proprieties. Uniquely, the Jews worshipped only one God and had strict prohibitions against Gentiles entering their Temple. In reply, they attracted a series of Roman taunts and insults, ranging from the bringing of military standards into Jerusalem to some rude farting by a Roman soldier at an angry Jewish crowd. Under Claudius, the province of Judaea became the plaything of imperial favourites. First, it was assigned to Herod's grandson, Agrippa I, who had assisted Claudius in his bizarre accession; then it went to Felix, the brother of the over-important freedman Pallas who had intrigued for Claudius' ill-judged marriage to Agrippina (Felix even named a city 'Agrippina' after her). Not for nothing was Paul the Christian said to have lectured Felix on 'justice, self control and the judgement to come until Felix begged him to stop'.[7] Some ten years later Nero's gorgeous wife, Poppaea, fixed the appointment of a disastrous governor of Judaea simply because she was friendly with his wife. Poppaea probably meant no mischief; she had shown herself sympathetic to a Jewish embassy and among all her personal luxury, she is said to have been sympathetic to the Jews' God. However, her choice as governor, Gessius Florus, was a tactless choice, by origin a Roman knight from a Greek city. He gratuitously enraged his subjects and helped to provoke a major Jewish War.

Florus' provocations mattered because they fell on unusually susceptible ground. Roman rule had deepened existing tensions between rich and poor in Judaea and its neighbourhood. Italian moneylenders had been active even in Galilee. As a crowded pilgrim city, Jerusalem's economy was shaky; there were acute class divisions within the priesthood and the Jews' upper classes showed a self-serving willingness to go along with Roman rule which was not to everyone's liking. Above all, Roman tactlessness impinged on an old and exclusive national cult. There was no one 'Judaism' at the time, but everyone could unite against what seemed crass Roman sacrilege against Yahweh.

In 66 the upper classes in Judaea and the senior priests tried to steer off a general uprising, but the support for it was strengthened by extremists, including the Zealots. Sacrifices for the emperor were discontinued in the Temple, and so Roman legions moved in to suppress the revolt. It took four years of hard, bloody fighting, and the later stages ended within Jerusalem, where the war became a fierce class-war of Jew against Jew as much as of Jew against Roman.

In August 70 the city fell and, as a punishment, Herod's great Temple and Jerusalem's buildings were destroyed. The loss of the Temple changed the focus of Jewish worship for ever. Whereas Jews had always made payments to their ancient shrine, now they were subjected to a special Jewish tax which was payable to Jupiter's temple at Rome. In 116/7 a second Jewish revolt broke out in the Diaspora at a time when the Emperor Trajan was fighting a war in the East. This revolt did not leave a mark on Judaea, but it did lead to the destruction of the very strong Jewish communities in Cyprus, Cyrene and above all, Egypt's Alexandria.

The final act of destruction, as we shall see, was left to Hadrian himself. He provoked a third revolt, this time within Judaea itself between 132 and 135. The results were another massive loss of Jewish lives and the conversion of Jerusalem into a Roman colony with pagan temples, a city which surviving Jews were forbidden to enter. Within one lifetime, between 70 and 135, Roman insensitivity thus obliterated the only monotheist temple (to one and only one God) in their Empire and took Judaea, literally, off the map: it was renamed 'Syria Palestina'. These measures were the ultimate acts of Romanization, but they were not imposed as rewards for services: in Roman eyes, they were deserved by uniquely unwelcome disservice. But the troubles were of Rome's own provoking, and the final solution reflects on a classicizing Roman, Hadrian, and his view of a classical world.

48

CHRISTIANITY
AND ROMAN RULE

Go to, you rich men, weep and howl for your miseries that shall come upon you. Your riches are corrupted and your garments are motheaten. Your gold and silver is cankered and the rust of them shall . . . eat your flesh as it were fire.

Epistle of 'James', 5.1–3

And when they (the members of the Areopagus council) heard of the resurrection of the dead, some mocked; and others said, 'We will hear thee again of this matter.'

Acts 17.32, on Paul in Athens

THESE CHANGING PATTERNS of Roman rule are the context for the ancient world's most influential legacy: Christianity. Its roots were Jewish, but it was shaped by the new historical environment. Jesus was born in Galilee when it was still ruled by a client king of the Romans, Herod Antipas. The tax-collectors or 'publicans' with whom he associated were Antipas' tax-collectors, not Rome's. However, even in Galilee Jesus could appeal to the text and image on a Roman coin and expect his hearers to recognize them as Caesar's. In AD 6 Judaea south of Galilee had come under direct Roman rule for the first time.

According to the Gospel of Luke, Jesus' birth coincided with a supposed 'decree from Caesar Augustus that all the world should be taxed'. Its dating places this 'decree' in AD 6 and it allegedly brought Joseph and Mary to Bethlehem where the birth of the Messiah had been prophesied in ancient texts. In fact, this supposed 'decree' could never have affected a man of Galilee, as it was a client kingdom which saw to its own taxes. The Gospel's dating is also contradictory and there is no evidence that, outside Galilee, the global 'decree' ever existed. The story of the 'first Christmas' rests on a historical impossibility.[1]

Whatever the truth of the first Easter, the Crucifixion, at least, is a historical fact, arguably datable to the year 36.[2] It was a Roman punishment and the Roman prefect was involved, Pontius Pilate, whom we also know from contemporary coins and non-Christian sources. We do not know exactly how it came about. All four Gospels differ on significant details, including the timing. Some of these details can be compared with Roman governors' procedures in other provinces, but the problem remains as to which of the Gospels' contradictory accounts, if any, is true. In the Gospel of John, a cohort of Roman troops and a Roman officer are said to have been involved in Jesus' arrest. The High Priest of the Jews and his counsellors take Jesus, already bound, to Pilate and claim that 'it is not lawful for us to put any man to death'.[3] Under direct Roman rule, most communities in the provinces had indeed lost the right to impose a capital sentence. It had passed to the Roman governor and the sensitive city of Jerusalem was surely no exception. We can at least be pretty sure that, as a Roman governor, Pilate pronounced a formal sentence from his seat of judgement (as the Gospel of John says most clearly). Also, the Cross did carry an inscribed declaration of Jesus' guilt in three separate languages. He was described as 'king of the Jews' in words which many bystanders witnessed. It was a claim which no Roman governor could tolerate.

We hear of other such 'rebels' in Roman Judaea, people who even provoked the Romans to send troops against them. Evidently, Jesus was not thought to be so dangerous as these outright rebels, and yet he was more 'rebellious' than another 'rustic' named Jesus who later went through Jerusalem during a Jewish festival in the year 62, crying out as 'a voice from the East, a voice from the West . . . a voice against Jerusalem and the Sanctuary, a voice against all the people'.[4] Prominent Jews had this man flogged and then brought him before the Roman governor, but he still went on with his lament. The governor questioned him and then released him. Unlike Jesus of Nazareth, he was not believed to be claiming to be a king. For Romans, this difference was crucial.

Jesus' preaching of this new 'kingdom' arose in a precise historical context. The beginning of direct Roman rule and taxation in AD 6 had caused the rise of the extremist Zealots with strong connections in Galilee, the people who denied that the Jewish people owed any allegiance except to God. Their terrorist movement had clear political claims, but Jesus' group looked in a different direction. Jesus chose twelve Apostles, a number which was so significant that it was promptly maintained after his death. They were twelve in order to suggest the twelve 'tribes' of a new Israel, to be based on repentance and a non-violent kingdom of love and a change of heart. Its members would be saved and honoured during the imminent end of the world when they and Jesus, it seems, would share in a heavenly banquet. The message was not at all one of violent terrorism, although this was the contemporary 'Galilaean alternative' to Rome's direct rule. When Jesus was asked what he thought of 'the Galilaeans, whose blood Pilate had mingled with their sacrifices' in Jerusalem he is said to have replied that the Galilaeans (surely terrorist suspects) were no more wicked than anyone else (their deaths, therefore, were a reward for sin) and that his questioners would all 'likewise perish' unless they repented.[5] His new kingdom, he meant, was not to be brought about by violent protests. But the insane response of extremists to the new style of Roman rule does explain Jesus' remarkable sense of urgency. His fellow Jews, he believed, were following a course which would soon lead to catastrophe, even to the destruction of Jerusalem. The verses in the Gospels in which Jesus 'prophesies' Jerusalem's fall are often considered to be the product of hindsight. Some of the details may be, but the belief in such an outcome may well be Jesus' own, even in the 30s AD. Hence his unusual hurry.

When Jesus died, only a hundred and twenty people, we are told, believed in his message. They were all of them Jews and they differed from their fellow Jews only because they believed that, in Jesus, their Messiah had come. The Jews' religious leaders would never accept that the Messiah whom so many awaited was this public menace who had been killed on their instigation by the frightful Roman punishment of crucifixion. Nonetheless, his followers remained in Jerusalem, evidently expecting an imminent end of the world. Meanwhile, some of them began to spread their news to visitors from abroad, Jews from the overseas Diaspora who had come up to Jerusalem to celebrate Passover at the Temple. It must have been particularly exciting for some of them to hear that during this great 'trip of a lifetime' they had coincided with the Messiah's arrival. The city was appallingly crowded and the Temple was not, perhaps, the simple centre of honesty and religion for which they had been hoping. Some of them, including Greek-speakers, joined the new Messianic group. Some of its leaders then scattered outside Jerusalem, bringing their message to the nearby big cities, including Caesarea and Antioch. It was in Antioch that this Messianic group was first called 'Christians', 'people of Christ', the Messiah.[6]

Jesus had not spoken Greek or visited a big Gentile city and had never preached to Gentiles. When Greeks approached those of his disciples who could speak the Greek language, Jesus is said to have responded as if it was a sign of the coming 'new age'. After his death we do not know how the new Christianity first reached Alexandria or Rome. What we do know are the missionary journeys of the Christian who did most to convert Gentiles, Paul.

Even more than that of Jesus, Paul's career was lived in the context of Roman history. Paul's father, a Jew in Tarsus, had the high privilege of Roman citizenship: one guess is that he had earned it by supplying tents to Pompey's armies in the 60s BC. Paul, an educated Jew, began as a keen persecutor of the new Christians, but then turned to preach the Christian faith in the Gentile world. Here, he travelled across to Cyprus, the home of his helper and fellow Jew, Barnabas. Once there, he impressed the Roman governor on the island, who is one more instance of a trusting Roman, impressed by the wonders of the East. He then travelled to Pisidian Antioch, one of Augustus' recent veteran-colonies in southern Asia Minor: it was the home of members of the governor of Cyprus' family, perhaps of his married daughter. Paul's first resort here was the local synagogue of the Jews, where he spoke his message in Greek. He then continued to visit points along the new network of Roman rule in the Greek East, using Roman roads and stopping in other Roman colonies like Philippi or Corinth. At Corinth, angry Jews brought him before the Roman governor of Greece, Gallio, the brother of the famous philosopher Seneca. Paul's teaching on the new Messiah was compounded by his insistence that Gentiles could join the new group as well as Jews, without their males needing to be circumcised or either sex needing to obey the Jewish law. To Gallio, the Jews' complaints against him sounded like internal quarrels in the Jews' religion. Admirably, he 'cared for none of those things' and refused to pronounce judgement.[7]

Before Paul, other Christians had already reached Rome where their teaching on the new Messiah ('Christos') provoked riots among the city's existing Jews. The reigning emperor, Claudius, had previously confronted Jewish riots in Rome and Alexandria and, probably in 49, he ordered those responsible to be expelled from the city. Before long, Paul himself became the object of a riot too. On returning to Jerusalem, he was accused of introducing a Gentile into the forbidden sanctuary of the city's Temple. He was rescued by Roman soldiers whose officer was surprised to find that Paul was a Roman citizen like himself. The citizenship protected Paul from beatings and violence without trial. His Roman captor remarked, revealingly, that he himself had paid a 'great sum' for this same privilege. Evidently he had acquired it under the Emperor Claudius. So far from 'devaluing' the citizenship, as Claudius' critics complained, the emperor had kept up the price for it, if only through his corrupt freedmen.

As a Roman citizen, Paul was able to appeal to the Roman emperor's judgement. The old right of a Roman citizen's appeal to a tribune in office in Rome had become extended to a citizen's right of appeal to the 'tribunician' emperor, even when the citizen lived abroad. Paul had been accused of treasonable teaching 'contrary to Caesar' and was sent off to Rome, presumably with a note to that effect. After another two years, his case was heard by the Emperor Nero or, more probably, the Prefect of the City. Paul was put to death, presumably on the suspicion of treacherous teaching about a new 'kingdom'. At Jerusalem, Stephen the Christian had already been lynched by Jews for asserting that the Temple was dispensable and that Jesus, a condemned criminal, was the resurrected Messiah. At Rome, the apparent treason of the Christian 'kingdom' now claimed its most famous victim.

Time then passed, and in 64, perhaps two years after Paul's conviction, the Emperor Nero needed scapegoats to divert the charge that he himself was responsible for the Great Fire of Rome. He or his advisers knew where to look, to yet more Christians, in the wake of the one whom they had recently executed. Christians were rounded up and executed as a public spectacle in the gardens of Nero's monstrous Golden House. Some of them were dressed up in the skins of wild animals, a 'fatal charade' in which they would be attacked and ripped by fierce hunting dogs. Others were crucified or set on fire and burned to death. The precedent was not lost on Rome's senators, the people who would go out in the future to govern provinces. As Paul's fate had shown, any Christians who were accused and brought before them should be put to death. There was now a Roman precedent and Gallio's fine indifference was a thing of the past.

In his lifetime Jesus had received rich presents and attended a well-to-do wedding, but riches and luxury (he said) were obstacles to his new kingdom of the coming age. The poor, he taught, were blessed: treasure should not be laid up on earth: the models for man were the heedless 'lilies of the field': it was easier for a camel to pass through the eye of a needle than for a rich man to be saved. The opposition of Christian poor to the rich is clearly stated in the Epistle ascribed to James, but it was already being subtly rephrased or ignored elsewhere. Paul's supporters and converts included some very rich members of the governing class in Gentile cities, none of whom adopted a 'lily-like' lifestyle. Unlike the

Gospels, Paul's surviving letters never discuss the 'problem of riches' or urge voluntary poverty. Among Christians, benefactions and gifts acquired a new merit, which was familiar to Jews but not to Gentiles: they were said to earn spiritual credit in heaven. Giving, therefore, became a road to salvation, while riches were considered irrelevant to true spiritual 'freedom'. The total renunciation of property, Jesus' point, remained a minority view.

The martyrdom of Christians did not arise from a real Christian threat to the Roman emperor or to Roman rule. As long as the world lasted, so would they: Paul even wrote that the Roman governors were necessary agents of God's wrath. Christians, he urged, were to submit to the 'powers that be'.[8] For Christ's kingdom was not of this world and Christian 'citizenship' lay in heaven. It was an attractive contemporary notion. The towns of the Greek and Roman world did not extend citizenship to all their free residents, quite apart from the numbers of ever-present slaves. Under Roman rule, distinctions of class and property had become even more entrenched in the political order and, as we have seen, were frankly upheld in the charters of Roman civic communities. Christian preaching bypassed these barriers as irrelevant and offered the 'real thing', for eternity. It was not even that Christians opposed slavery: Jesus was not remembered for any words on the subject and had anyway taught outside the slave-based structures of Greek and Roman cities. Paul's advice was that slaves should serve even more: in this case too, social status was irrelevant to spiritual freedom and merit.[9] This indifference to social class and slavery was one important reason why Christianity could attract members of high society right from the start; it was also a reason why bishops continued to own slaves. In Christ Jesus, Paul wrote, all were one, male and female, free and slave. But as in an army, 'unity' certainly did not entail social equality. The one worldly 'freedom' to be urged explicitly on Christians was freedom from marriage and remarriage. Jesus had spoken explicitly (and alarmingly) against divorce and had praised those who gave up sex altogether, 'eunuchs for the kingdom of heaven's sake'.[10] Paul was aware that these ideals were not for everyone, but he continued to praise celibacy, sexless living and a refusal to remarry if bereaved or divorced. Exactly the opposite ideals were being encouraged, meanwhile, by Augustus' marriage-laws which applied to all Roman citizens, including Paul himself.

While awaiting the world's elusive end, Christianity thus belittled the pursuit of luxury and promised a higher freedom in heaven. It also promised a new justice. Many pagans were quite unsure that there would be an existence beyond the grave. The end of the world was not a subject which had ever really bothered them. The world, they now heard, was the temporary province of Satan whose unsuspected agents could be exorcized or overcome by Christian specialists. It was a new explanation of evil and, for those who converted, it was a most optimistic one. It could soon point to facts of history in support. In August 70, when Roman troops destroyed the Jews' Temple in Jerusalem, God's wrath had fallen on the wicked in Jerusalem, just as the Gospel sayings predicted. Christians in Jerusalem were said to have withdrawn to safety: they were obeying a prophecy, perhaps one by Jesus, like those ascribed to him in the Gospels. In 70, therefore, the wicked had been destroyed and visibly, the just had been saved. The event was an anticipation of the Last Judgement, whose justice would dwarf all other forms of justice which had evolved so far in the classical world.

SURVIVING FOUR EMPERORS

Nothing had impelled the Gauls to believe that the end of our Empire was at hand so much as the burning of the Capitol [in Rome]. 'Once upon a time,' it was said, 'the city was captured by Gauls, but Jupiter's seat remained intact and so Roman power endured. Now, with this fatal fire, a sign has been given of heaven's anger: possession of all human affairs, it portends, will pass to peoples beyond the Alps.' Such were the prophecies of the Druids, with their empty superstition.

Tacitus, *Histories* 4.54, on AD 69–70

NERO'S DEATH IN JUNE 68 marked the end of the Julio-Claudians but it was not a prelude to the end of the world. Instead it led to a year of four consecutive emperors, civil wars between opposing units of the Roman army and the eventual triumph of Vespasian, a military man of modest Italian origins whose father had once made capital by money-lending among the Swiss. The result was a new start, based on old supports and strategies. A new dynasty was established, the Flavian family who produced three emperors and lasted for twenty-seven years. It had to negotiate the dangers which previous emperors had shown to be endemic: the need for military prowess, the temptation for the ruler to be dissolute, the need to keep the Praetorian guards sweet, the need to keep army commanders outside Italy sweet too, the importance of conciliating their source, the Senate, and the need to humour and sustain the very varied population of Rome. There was also the cardinal problem of the succession: why should a First Citizen's son succeed him?

Once again, tendentious publicity abounded during the four emperors' reigns, infecting historians who wrote under the victor. Freedom and luxury, those relative benchmarks, were prominent in the spin. The first

59. Gold aureus struck in Judaea under Titus, AD 70. Obverse, Emperor Vespasian. The reverse shows the earliest-known figure of Justice, the Romans' verdict on their sack of Jerusalem and the Temple.

emperor, Galba, was an elderly aristocrat, sagging and unmilitary to the disgust of the guards, and ugly to the disgust of the plebs. Senators saw more in him (he had no children), especially as he was the opposite of prodigal Nero. He was, however, denounced for being mean: he forced jurors in Rome to work over the cold New Year because (it was said) he would not pay for any more of them. In mid-January 69 the Praetorian Guards replaced him with Otho, one of Nero's senatorial mentors in the revelries of his youth. Otho had been married to the gorgeous Poppaea Sabina before Nero took her off him and sent him away to govern Spain. He had energy and a following among several of the armies in the provinces, but he was not a reformed character. After Nero's death he had taken on the infamous Sporus, Nero's male substitute 'Sabina'. In spring 69 he was still prepared to spend heavily on finishing Nero's Golden House. In mid-April he killed himself after he and his troops were badly defeated in north Italy by the next contender, Vitellius, who had the solid backing of the legions on the Rhine. Nonetheless, Vitellius' enemies mobilized the spectre of 'luxury' yet again to discredit their rival. He was said to have paid for a gigantic cooking-pan, cast in a special furnace, which he called the 'Shield of Minerva', like the one on the Acropolis of classical Athens. Dinners for him were said to ruin whole towns in Italy. 'Luxury' helped the winner, the Emperor Vespasian, who emphasized his own simple lifestyle as a contrast.

The flexible theme of freedom was much in evidence too. The great Russian historian, M. I. Rostovtzeff, even saw the year 68/9 as 'the protest of the provincial armies and the people of the Empire in general against the degenerate military tyranny of the successors of Augustus'.[1] It certainly began in the West as a protest, but the protest was against

Nero's particular extravagance and looting. Not all the armies or provincials responded; they lacked political leaders and there was no attempt at a new political system. What people wanted was the existing system brought back under moral restraint and a restored respect for law.

The theme of 'liberty' was voiced by army-commanders and was visible on all four emperors' coins. However, it never meant democracy or even the freedoms of the long-dead Republic. When Nero died, people in Rome wore the 'cap of liberty', as if freed from slavery. Greeks had hailed him as 'Zeus of Freedom' for freeing their province, but Roman coins now proclaimed 'Jupiter Liberator' for freeing them of their tyrant. Old Galba then proclaimed 'liberty', as did his Gallic backer Vindex, but they simply meant freedom from Nero. Galba and Verginius, another important commander, each implied that it would be for the Roman Senate and people to exercise freedom, in this case the freedom to choose the next 'First Citizen'. Vitellius proclaimed freedom, but only freedom from the Nero-like habits of Otho. Vespasian then proclaimed 'freedom' from Vitellius. It had to be 'asserted' or 'vindicated', he stated, as if the Roman people had been 'slaves' to the wrong master.[2]

The personal choice of an heir and successor was not freedom at all, but Galba and Vespasian both did it. The Praetorian guards chose Otho and nobody at Rome could stop them, either. Among these rivalries, surely the 'people of the Empire in general' had a chance to be free? Conspicuously, none took it, until the drama was nearly over and then only in a corner of north-west Europe. In early summer 69 there was a real call here to freedom from Rome and the formation of an 'Empire of the Gauls'. This campaign was led in the north-east of Gaul and among neighbouring German peoples by the well-born Civilis, a man of Germanic origin, who cut a fine figure with his one eye (like a new Hannibal, he said) and a long beard which he dyed red. Civilis was not a noble savage, but a cunning leader who knew Roman ways and tactics from his own experience of them. Others helped him, including a local prophetess, Veleda, who apparently had links with the banned lore of the Druids and prophesied success for the revolt.

The most prominent champions of it, the Batavians, had suffered particularly from Roman conscription; its officers had forced thousands of them, including young boys, into auxiliary army units which were then transferred very far from home. Civilis was to be adopted in later times by the Dutch (who presented themselves as kin of the Batavians) and became the Dutch national hero: Rembrandt even painted him for the town hall of Amsterdam.[3] But this subsequent 'nationalist' role was not true to the

Civilis of history. National consciousness was indeed behind the Batavian-Gallic uprising, but it was not inflamed into nationalism as it had been among the Jews, and it was even less unified than the Jewish revolt. More of the participants in the revolt were Germans than were Gauls and their various tribes mistrusted or hated each other already. Six Roman legions were sent to put the danger down, but even without them the revolt would have collapsed quite soon. An 'Empire of the Gauls' would have been economically isolated from Roman Britain and from Roman territories around it. People also realized that Roman power had been containing old rivalries among them and by keeping the peace it was the lesser of two evils.

The Empire's darkest year was in fact proof of its stability. The eventual winner, Vespasian, emerged from Syria and Judaea where he and Titus, one of his sons, had been leading the legions with distinction against the Jews. His formal proclamation as emperor began in Alexandria on 1 July 69, but plans had already been laid in advance. His rise was said to be backed by omens and prophecies from the gods: Vespasian consulted oracles and in Alexandria he was coaxed into a wondrous 'healing' of a blind man and a cripple who approached him on the advice of the healing god Serapis. Sceptical at first, Vespasian and his supporters capitalized on his success, a real 'royal touch'.[4] It was almost unique in the history of Roman emperors (but not of medieval kings).

Despite suffering from gout, Vespasian had promise. He was about to be sixty years old and was the first emperor since the elderly Tiberius who was a proven soldier with experience of the provinces. He had led troops very ably in the invasion of Britain in 43 where he had conquered the south-west and had taken the Isle of Wight. He was a plain blunt man who had kept a local Italian accent and he had none of Tiberius' touchiness or aristocratic pride: even his portrait-busts chose a plain 'Italian' style of realism, not the classicizing ideal look of Augustus or Nero. Unlike the other Julio-Claudians, he brought no strong-willed wife with him: he had married a humbly born Italian, Domitilla, but she was now dead. As a widower, he was living with a freedwoman, Caenis, as his 'concubine' or partner. It was amazing, but not too worrying, that way back, this same lady had been an ex-slave in the household of the great Antonia, Mark Antony's daughter. Caenis was now old and hardly likely to encourage the Mark Antony style. But she could tell old Vespasian some excellent bits of gossip in bed.

What Vespasian lacked was any other connection with his Julio-Claudian predecessors. While his supporters took Rome for him, he remained usefully out of the way. There was severe fighting in the eternal city; the very Capitol was burned and hundreds of bronze inscriptions were destroyed in an epigraphic meltdown which Vespasian then tried to repair by ordering new copies of the texts. Vespasian did not reach the city of Rome until autumn 70 and in the intervening months questions were raised about his likely manner of rule. Who would advise him? What titles would he take and would he consult the Senate or simply present them with his decisions? The upper classes wanted an emperor who would behave modestly and morally and who would not defy the law. The opponents of Nero's tyranny were not all dead and their favour for moral principles was still supported by a degree of contact with Stoic, philosophic views.

Lawyers, as usual, were more flexible than philosophers. It was arguably in early 70 that an important law was passed in Vespasian's favour which set out his powers and cited precedents (when available) from the reigns of Augustus and the Julio-Claudians (except the mad Caligula). It is not convincing to see this law as just one more example of an older practice which had already been enacted for previous emperors since AD 14.[5] Vespasian lacked his predecessors' dynastic authority. As a 'clean break' his rule needed to be spelt out and referred to the Julio-Claudian past. The philosophic minority was still pressing for a well-regulated ruler, but some of the lawyers came up with a crushing answer. The law specified anything from Vespasian's power to make treaties 'with whomsoever he wishes' to his greater role in elections: special consideration was guaranteed for 'his' candidates. No precedent (significantly) could be cited here, but henceforward, senators who wanted to be elected would be well advised to keep in with the emperor. Above all, a clause permitted Vespasian to do whatever he thought fit in the public interest 'just as was the case' (no legal right could be cited here) 'for Augustus and the others'. The face of autocracy was thus recognized by law. The legal details continued in two more clauses, one of which specified what 'Caesar Vespasian' was not bound by (citing legal precedents), another of which ratified the decisions which he had already had to take during the year 69.

This law was a very neat piece of small print. For more than a hundred years Roman lawyers would discuss it in connection with the powers of the emperor (as they still do): he was not a king, like Ptolemy and Alexander, and, lo and behold, this text did indeed relate his autocracy to law and the needs of 'the Republic'. There was something specific here for legal minds to cite and chew over. For Vespasian, the immediate advantage was that the brute facts of life had been ratified and agreed up front. The old aristocratic families, where a few able voices might have challenged him, were almost all extinct. Surviving senators included rather too many who had thrown restraint to the winds under Nero and were morally compromised by their supporting roles in his shows and orgies. The gaps in their ranks were now to be filled by lesser, newer arrivals, whose expectations of their new status would be satisfied if its role was set out and regulated. Lawyers had now defined it and the small print seemed to say that the rules were part of a tradition which went back long before these newer men arrived. Protesting philosophers were a tiresome and impractical minority. The real questions for the men in the Senate's new intake concerned who would be first to receive higher office or even the honour of a priesthood. After 71 the word 'freedom' never appeared again on Vespasian's coins.

THE NEW DYNASTY

*This statue fears no rainy winters nor the triple fire of Jupiter's lightning
. . . it will stand while earth and sky endure, while there is still a Roman
daylight. Here, in the silent night, when earthly affairs concern the gods
on high, your kin will leave the heavens and glide down and mingle their
kisses with you. Son and brother, father and sister will come down to your
embrace: your neck alone will make space for all the stars . . .*

Statius, *Silvae* 1.1.91–8,
on Domitian's bronze equestrian statue in Rome, *c.* AD 91

*It was our delight to dash those proud faces to the ground, to strike them
with the sword and savage them with the axe as if blood and agony could
follow every blow. Nobody could refrain from joy, late though our rejoic-
ing was, but everyone sought a form of revenge in seeing those statue-
bodies torn in pieces, limbs hacked to bits and those dreadful
portrait-images cast into the flames and roasted, so that from such terror
and threats, they could be transformed for the use and pleasures of
mankind.*

Pliny, *Panegyric* 52.4–5,
on the destruction of Domitian's statues in AD 93

WHEN VESPASIAN FINALLY reached Rome, nobody could dispute
the need for a new style and a new grip on the realities. After Nero
and a civil war, the finances were in a dreadful state. The grain-reserves
had almost run out; the ranks of senators had been diminished by civil
war; rivals had proclaimed 'freedom', but there had been looting by the
troops, much as during Octavian's own rise to power. The city itself was a

sorry sight. The Great Fire of 64 had been followed by yet more burning in the recent conflicts. In the middle of it all, Nero's Golden House was still standing, a gigantic affront.

Inevitably, taxes had to increase. Italy remained exempt from tribute, but existing taxes went up and new ones were soon added: there was even a new tax on the urine from public urinals (which was used for cleaning clothes, as it still was in the First World War). Vespasian, the down-to-earth Italian, had no particular fondness for Greek culture. The turbulent Alexandrians in Egypt found themselves forced to pay the poll tax for the first time and Nero's grant of tax-free 'freedom' to Greece was revoked. It was, then, particularly ingenious of the Arcadian Greeks of Tegea, down in the Peloponnese, to claim that they had uncovered ancient vessels in a sacred place, as predicted by prophets, and that the vessels were found to be carved with a face resembling Vespasian's own. So far from being 'new', they discovered, Vespasian was 'old': it was from Arcadia that the first kings of Rome were supposed to derive. No doubt these Greeks made the most of the discovery. More immediately, Vespasian could profit from the defeated Jews. As they no longer had a Temple to which they would pay regularly, they were obliged to pay a special tax in to Rome's temple of Jupiter instead. Unlike the Temple tax, it was extended to women and children and applied more widely to everyone between the ages of three and sixty. The new revenues here were significant.

Vespasian himself liked money, but disliked personal extravagance. He was a free gift, therefore, for anecdotes and amusing rumours. At his funeral, it was a neat joke when the mime-actor who was representing him in the procession (by now, a usual practice) called out to ask how much the funeral was costing. A huge sum was called out in answer, whereupon 'Vespasian' replied that he would rather be given a little bit of it and have his body thrown cheaply into the river Tiber. Exceptions comically upheld the general picture. A woman was said to have had a passion for the old man and begged to go to bed with him (after Caenis' death?). In return, she was said to have received a huge sum, enough to qualify a man as a Roman knight. The joke, surely, was that she was being paid for having ridden the emperor so ably. Vespasian was then said to have told his steward to enter the sum in his account-book, but to put it down as 'To Making Passionate Love to Vespasian'.[1] Everything had to be accounted for, including good sex after lunch.

In the provinces, particular loyalties were wooed with cheap privileges and titles (the 'Latin right' was given to Spain): financial rewards were another matter. In Rome, however, an emperor could not be entirely unremunerative. The Praetorian guards had to be rewarded, but this time they were changed, rather than bribed excessively. Those of them who were retired gradually were surely the lucky settlers in a rare phenomenon, the few colonies which Vespasian dared to found in Italy itself. In Rome, too, despite the economic squeeze, the emperor had to spend, because he could not simply hoard coins and starve society of cash in circulation. One outlet for spending was public building. Most of the city's plebs were men of all trades, whatever their particular speciality or social group: they did not depend on public building works for their daily bread, but these works gave them a very helpful extra beside the slave workers who were also engaged on them. In Rome, even during the drive for economy, Vespasian's new buildings were to be far larger than the schemes of Pericles' Athens. The building which we now call the Colosseum was put up on land from Nero's awful Golden House. Four storeys high, it was for the people, not just the emperor, as a real 'people's arena'. The expense, too, was manageable: Jews' assets helped to pay for it, the spoils taken from the victory in Judaea. Jews' assets also helped to pay for a programmatic new temple of Peace whose vast area was ten times bigger than the precinct around Augustus' famous altar to the goddess. The contents of the precinct enhanced the emperor's image.[2] The river Nile was carved as a quartz statue with sixteen children. In Egypt, an Egyptian priestess had correctly prophesied a full flood of the Nile, sixteen cubits deep (whence the sixteen children) when Vespasian visited the country at the start of his coup in 69: Vespasian's monument was alluding to his role in bringing the prophecy about. The rest of 'Peace's' decorations were antique sculptures and works of art, some of which had been looted from the Jews, others from the Greek world by Nero. There was a public message here for the people. What Nero had stolen for himself, Vespasian was now 'opening to the public' in a public temple.

Nevertheless, like Augustus, the new dynast did not go unopposed. Artfully, he sent two hated informers of the Neronian age abroad from Rome to take up governorships. However, he was then criticized by the leading philosophic voice in the city, the senator Helvidius. One likely reason for the trouble was the resort to legalized autocracy which was embodied in the new 'law' on the emperor's powers. Another, connected to it, was Vespasian's ambition for his own family. Vespasian had two sons of whom the older, Titus, had led the troops to victory in Judaea. Back in Rome, Titus was even made Prefect of the Praetorian Guard. It was a new post for a member of the imperial house to hold, but an artful one, as it limited the guards' scope for electing an emperor of their own choosing. As the reign developed, Vespasian and his family then occupied the consulship to a degree which not even Augustus had attempted. Speaking against this dynasty, the philosophic Helvidius was first exiled, then killed: it was probably in response to him that Vespasian was said to have remarked 'either my sons succeed me, or nobody', apparently on leaving the Senate. Although Vespasian founded distinguished professorships in Rome and Athens and favoured the teaching of oratory, grammar and medicine in major provincial cities, it is conspicuous that any such favour for philosophy was excluded. But versions of Helvidius' brave sayings continued to be circulated by philosophy teachers outside Rome.

Arguably, Helvidius was proved right. Vespasian's son Titus had charm, a gift for speaking and a military record, but he antagonized public opinion in the mid–70s by bringing his controversial mistress into Rome. She was a Jewish princess, Berenice, the daughter of Claudius' friend King Agrippa. When she appeared in Rome she was mocked by crowds in the theatre. It was not all a xenophobic protest: Berenice sat among the emperor's advisers, an ill-judged move which half-deserved her reputation as the 'new Cleopatra'.[3] She was then judiciously sent abroad, after a supposed conspiracy in which two very senior senators were implicated: Titus, on one view, framed the pair of them in order to get them out of the way before his own accession. He could use the charge of their involvement with Berenice to get her out of Rome too.

On 24 June 79 Vespasian died, allegedly saying 'Oh dear, I think I am becoming a god', a plain man's comment on his imminent cult. Titus took over and, most remarkably, Hadrian later stated that Titus had actually poisoned Vespasian. On the surface, Titus performed well enough for two years. He had the hated 'informers' paraded in the amphitheatre before exiling them: the next emperors repeated the spectacle. Admittedly, his brother Domitian claimed that Titus had forged his father's will. Titus had remarked that he had the talent to have been a practised forger and he may have deployed it against the two senators, the 'one crime', perhaps, which he used to say that he regretted.[4] Perhaps it was fortunate for Titus' reputation that he died so quickly, before the usual honeymoon years were over. It was less fortunate for Rome: his younger brother Domitian took over.

The change of dynasty had not supplanted the old pattern. Domitian was no better than his weaknesses before becoming emperor. In 69/70 he had been the one family member inside Rome but he had been denied any

60. Man-woman sex scene. Uncertain location. Wall painting from Pompeii, now in Naples Museum.

genuine military distinction. He resented his brother and his father and his nature was anyway suspicious and insecure. Aptly, he was looked back on as the 'bald Nero', not just because he lacked his predecessor's looks and showy hairstyle. In 83 a degree of military success in Germany gave Domitian more confidence, but what emerged was all too familiar. He began by patronizing Greek cultural pursuits and even promoted members of the philosophic clique at Rome; one reason why he favoured these things was because his father had disliked both of them. Like Nero, he promoted Greek drama, music and athletics and in 86 gave them their first full festival in the city: he founded a second festival, at his huge country villa, and included them in the programme too. There were still Roman traditionalists who disapproved of Greek athletics and gymnastics because of their links with nudity and 'disgraceful' sex between free men. Domitian's patronage, in the heart of the city, was an important counterstatement in years when the young Hadrian's tastes were forming, the great 'philhellene' of the future. But Domitian was not being idiosyncratic: Greek literature and Greek language were now the normal education, we are told, of young Romans, so much so that many 'young boys speak and learn nothing but Greek for a long while'.[5] The contrary voices were now a 'moral minority'.

Domitian then fell out with his former protégés, the philosophers, and during an insecure phase, in late 93, permitted accusations that they were fostering opposition, not least because they were writing biographies of their ancestors, 'opposition martyrs' under Nero. It was a grim time, when senators had to compromise in order to survive. There were also attacks on Christian sympathizers in high society at Rome and on those accused of the 'adoption of Jewish ways'. Modern attempts to rehabilitate Domitian are as one-sided as the wilder rumours from antiquity. On better evidence, we learn that Domitian would retire to his vast country palace (one of two) outside Rome in the Alban hills where he used to like relaxing on the lake. He was so irritable that he had to be towed in a separate boat behind an oared vessel so that he would not hear the noise of its oars in the water.[6] We can understand why his wife, a descendant of Cassius the 'Liberator', was soon found to prefer the charms of an actor. Back in Rome, Domitian was remembered for the ultimate in black humour. Senators and knights were said to have been invited at night to a dinner in a black-painted room with a black stone shaped like a tombstone behind each couch. Black-painted boys served black-painted food and the silence was only broken by Domitian who 'talked only about death and killing'.[7]

Like Nero, this bald successor kept a favourite eunuch for sex; the verses which celebrate the cutting of this eunuch's golden hair and its dedication to the gods are not the most distinguished in Latin poetry. As under Nero, the gainer was Roman architecture. In Alexandria and the East, including the desert city of Petra, there had already been a bold baroque splendour to architecture which was quite at odds with the repetitive classicism of Augustan good taste. It now had a renewed chance in Rome. The list of buildings which were restored or initiated in the city in Domitian's reign is conspicuous, but the boldest was his own great palace on the Palatine hill. Ever accessible and 'civil', Vespasian had avoided living on the hill, but Domitian's new palace was completed on it in 92 by the architectural genius, Rabirius. There were two separate parts and the rooms made a remarkable use of polygonal shapes, coloured marbles from distant quarries, light-effects, exceptional height and passages. Its nearby hippodrome was apparently more a feature of the gardens than a real racecourse. Appropriately, the vast palace-complex was sited on top of Nero's earlier building and, when a thousand senators and knights sat down to dinner in the Banqueting Hall, the spectacle was not so much black, as amazing. Under a high gilded roof, 'the tired eye scarcely reached the summit', wrote the poet Statius, 'and you would think it was the golden ceiling of the sky'.[8] The approach to the area was through a temple of ancient Jupiter. Comparisons between Domitian and Jupiter and their two palaces were favoured, but the emperor himself claimed the closest kinship with the goddess Minerva, mistress of the arts and war. There were mirrors, however, in the palace so that Domitian could always watch his own back.

Domitian's insecurity and love of 'luxury' were intolerable and like Nero he was murdered by his own palace-attendants. As he had no sons, there was scope for those in the plot to choose their own candidate. Revealingly, they chose the elderly Nerva, sixty years old, a noble patrician by birth, a respected senator and also without sons. The full Senate then approved their choice, someone who was, at last, a mature insider. It was not just that he had written admired Latin elegies in his youth. Rather, three times in the last thirty years, Nerva had been honoured highly after crises in the emperors' management of affairs. His ancestors had been lawyers and he himself probably had a knowledge of law. In 71 he had been honoured most remarkably with a consulship: perhaps it was a reward for co-ordinating work on the 'law' for Vespasian's powers in the previous year.

It is Nerva, not Titus or Vespasian, who really is the 'good' emperor. At last, senatorial contemporaries could proclaim the reconciliation of 'freedom' and the Principate. Nerva's coins publicized 'Public Freedom' and an inscription set in the 'Hall of Liberty' at Rome read, 'Liberty Restored'. Of course the system was not undone, but the popular assemblies at Rome did meet and exercise 'liberty' by passing laws. The hateful Domitian's statues were melted down and his name 'abolished' on monuments. But Domitian's appointments and rulings did have to be confirmed: too many people, including senators, had gained from them.

Besides promoting freedom, Nerva understood the importance of standing out against injustice and luxury. He corrected the harsh effects of the inheritance tax on new citizens and extreme applications of the Jewish tax on Jews and sympathizers. The accusers in tax cases in his provinces could no longer be the judges too; there were no longer to be prosecutions for slandering the emperor, and philosophy was granted public support. Spectacularly, Nerva sold off land, even clothing, in imperial ownership. He forswore 'luxury', and also directed 'liberality' towards poor people in Italy: money was set aside to buy them plots of land. It was all good policy, but the imperial system did not rest only on goodness. There were the all-important soldiers and the guards in Rome.

61. Brass sestertius from Rome, AD 96. Obverse, Nerva, the 'good' emperor; reverse, clasped hands symbolizing, optimistically, the 'concord' of the armies.

Optimistically, Nerva's coins proclaimed 'Concord of the Armies'. However, the troops still liked Domitian, who had raised their pay, and in autumn 97 the Praetorian guards forced Nerva to approve a brutal execution of Domitian's murderers. Someone more robust and military was manifestly needed. There was talk later of an outright coup but it was probably with Nerva's own agreement that he announced a soldier as his adopted heir. The choice was Trajan, a man from a colonial settlement in Spain with a distinguished military father and experience with the armies in Germany. Behind the adoption plan we can detect two senators, one of whom was Frontinus, a former governor of Britain, distinguished for his efforts in Wales, and the acknowledged authority on Rome's aqueducts.

The new pair of Nerva and 'son' might have worked very well for some years, each complementing the other. However, after three months Nerva unexpectedly died. In the footsteps of Vespasian's Flavian dynasty, he bequeathed to his successor a governing class at Rome which, inevitably, was much changed in tone and composition. Not only had prominent Greek-speakers from the East entered the Senate (Domitian's patronage had been important here, in keeping with his cultural tastes). Vespasian, from 'little Italy', had helped to replenish the Senate with yet more members from 'little Italy' too. The legal statement of his powers had been acceptable to these new men, but then Domitian had elevated himself too far above them. By defying their moral values and standards, Domitian had shown up both the strengths and limitations of what such people stood for. After his death senators were quick to dare to condemn him, but they were equally quick to justify themselves and their recent compromises. As under Nero, there was so much which was best left unsaid. As a principled dinner-guest once aptly remarked to Nerva, if the worst of Domitian's informers had still been alive, they would doubtless have been dining in their company with Nerva too.[9]

51

THE LAST DAYS OF POMPEII

If you felt the fires of love, mule-driver,
You would make more haste to see Venus.
I love a charming boy, so I beg you, goad on the mules; let's go.
You have had a drink, so let's go. Take up the reins and shake them.
Take me to Pompeii where love is sweet.

Inscribed in the peristyle courtyard of House IX.v.ii, Pompeii

THE NEW MEN PROMOTED from the towns of Italy in the 70s were credited with a new frugality and restraint, quite unlike the excess and debauchery of Nero's reign and those who had taken part despite 'traditional' Roman values. For a glimpse of small-town Italian life, we can turn to archaeology's great survivors, Pompeii and nearby Herculaneum. On 24 August 79, Mount Vesuvius erupted. A thick shower of dust and pumice rose over the surrounds, with earthquakes, flames and a cloud (said the eye-witness Pliny) shaped like the head of an umbrella pine, a type of tree still so familiar around the ruins. The cloud rose some twenty miles high and to judge from similar recent explosions of Mount St Helen's in north-west America, the explosions in Vesuvius released a force five hundred times greater than the atom bomb at Hiroshima. At Pompeii we can trace the effects in three awful stages. First of all, a shower of white pumice, some three yards deep, blocked the daylight, then grey pumice blackened streets and buildings. On the following morning, 25 August, by about 7.30 a.m., a great 'burning cloud' of hot gas rolled into the streets, suffocating and burning those who had stayed or been trapped. This very powerful ground surge was followed by the pyroclastic flow of hot liquified rock and pumice which destroyed buildings and rolled on far past the town; then 'surge' and 'flow' came in four waves of increasing ferocity until 8 a.m. They caused the death of the spectacle's most learned observer, Pliny the Elder: as his nephew's letters recall, Pliny had boated across the Bay of Naples to have a closer look. Inside the town, bodies of the dead continue to be found. They range from mules, trapped by their mangers near the millstones which they used to turn, to the young lady, dressed in jewels, whose breasts had left their imprints in the mud where she died. At Herculaneum, the surge and flow struck earlier in the morning and hit the town in six waves, running out into the sea. The town was buried even more deeply than Pompeii and not, it now seems, from the secondary effects of rain and floods. The entire disaster was massive, and we can well understand why it was a strain and expense on the Emperor Titus' first year in power.

Pompeii and Herculaneum were close to the Bay of Naples, where so many of the grandest Romans had built spectacular villas. Even at the height of the Bay's luxury (in the first century BC), neither place had been a city of the first rank; by the 70s the Bay had lost a little of its predominance. Pompeii, the better known, would have covered about 350 acres and contained a population of perhaps 8,000–12,000 in its last days. The town was laid out on a plateau of volcanic lava, the relic of a former eruption, and various types of volcanic rock had helped to build it. But the inhabitants did not know the risk they ran: Vesuvius' last eruption was more than a thousand years in the past, and the stone probably seemed harmless. Pompeii itself had grown up in layers, through clear phases of history since the sixth century BC: Etruscan (with Greeks), Samnite, colonial Roman (from 80 BC onwards) when Cicero had had one of his houses there. By AD 79 its roots, like modern London's, were at least two centuries old, and the residents continued to build and rebuild over them right until the end.

One result is that the best-preserved ancient town is in many ways still hard to understand. It never stood still, and after the fatal eruption the looting began promptly. It has been continuing ever since excavation began again in the 1740s. Fortunately, one-third of Pompeii has been reserved for future archaeology, although so much has been destroyed, sold or dispersed meanwhile.

One side of Pompeian life seems appealingly modern. There was a planned street-system to exclude wheeled traffic from areas in the town centre. There are well-preserved wine-bars with 'pub signs' of a phoenix or a peacock. There are theatres and a so-called 'sports complex' and a special market-building for fish, meat and delicacies for people doing the shopping. Many of the houses have big paintings or frescos on their walls, and there

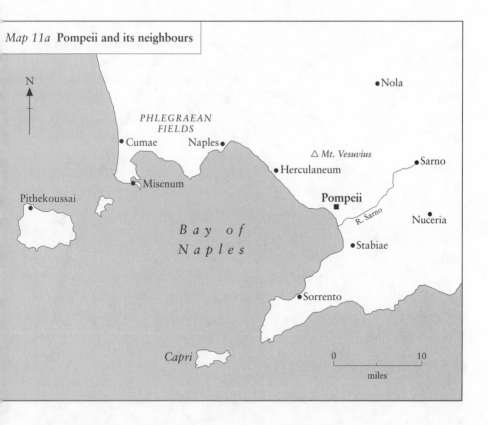

Map 11a **Pompeii and its neighbours**

was a definite cult of 'house and garden'. *Trompe l'œil* paintings seem to enlarge the gardens' space and even show exotic birds and the flowers which
grew in pots and borders, whether roses or bushes of myrtle. Owners would
eat out around a shaded table in their 'room outside': 118 pieces of silver
were found stored in one big house's basement, including a set for dinner
parties of eight people.[1] There were also graffiti and well-written inscriptions. Forty-eight graffiti of Virgil's poetry have been found (including some
in a brothel). On the street-fronts of the bars, houses and public buildings,
election-posters—some 2,800 in all—advertised support for particular candidates for civic office. About forty of these posters name women's support,
although women themselves could not vote.[2]

Through painted portraits we feel we know these people, the young
ladies with a pen to their lips and blond, classicizing features, or the men
beside them with dark eyes and a shifty sort of look. But so much of this
time warp is not our idea of a cosy town at all. Images and shrines of the
gods were all over the place, quite apart from the big formal temples on
the main forum. Slaves were essential to the households and crafts,

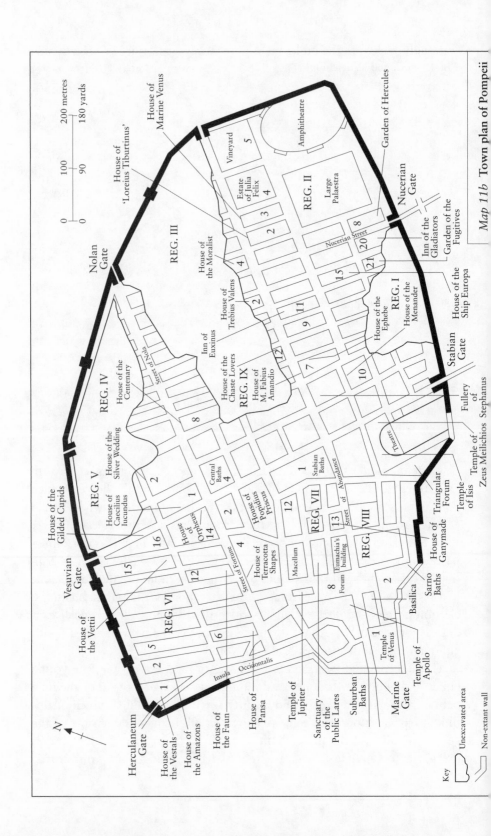

Map 11b Town plan of Pompeii

N

0   100   200 metres
0   90   180 yards

Key
Unexcavated area
Non-extant wall

House of the Gilded Cupids

Herculaneum Gate

House of the Vettii

House of the Vestals

House of the Amazons

House of the Faun

House of Pansa

Temple of Jupiter

Sanctuary of the Public Lares

Suburban Baths

Marine Gate

Temple of Apollo

Temple of Venus

Basilica

Sarno Baths

House of Ganymade

Triangular Forum

Temple of Isis

Temple of Zeus Meilichios

Fullery of Stephanus

Stabian Gate

House of the Ship Europa

House of the Menander

REG. I

Inn of the Gladiators

Garden of the Fugitives

House of the Ephebe

Nucerian Gate

Garden of Hercules

Large Palaestra

REG. II

Amphitheatre

Vineyard

Estate of Julia Felix

House of 'Loreius Tiburtinus'

House of Marine Venus

House of the Moralist

House of Trebius Valens

REG. III

Nolan Gate

REG. IV

House of the Centenary

Street of Nola

Inn of Euxinus

House of the Chaste Lovers

House of M. Fabius Amandio

REG. IX

House of the Silver Wedding

House of Caecilius Iucundus

REG. V

House of Orpheus

House of Terracotta Shapes

Street of Fortune

Central Baths

House of Popidius Priscus

Street of Abundance

Stabian Baths

REG. VII

Macellum

Eumachia's building

REG. VIII

Forum

Insula Occidontalis

REG. VI

Theatre

Nucerian Street

although the loss of the buildings' upper storeys makes it hard to visualize where many of them lived. Ex-slaves, freedmen, were also essential to the economy and the social structure. After being freed, most of them still worked for their former owners (as they did in Rome) who could thus profit 'from' business without being tied down 'to' it. There were no commercial banks (moneylending was a personal transaction) and there were no hospitals or public doctors' offices. There were brothels, but no moral 'zoning' into red-light districts. There were no street-signs, either. There are well-preserved lavatories behind discreet partitions, but two, even six, people would be accommodated on them side by side, wiping their backsides with communally provided sponges.

Despite the theatres, the main sports complex was an amphitheatre for blood sports, both human and animal: it is the earliest one to survive, dating back to the 70s BC when Pompeii's population had been changed by the arrival of Roman veteran-colonists. Gladiatorial shows are announced and applauded in many of the town's surviving graffiti: 'the girls' idol, Celadus the Thracian gladiator!'[3] Nor were the town's big houses the inward-looking centres of privacy which we now cherish. Like a Roman's, a Pompeian's home was not his castle and 'home life' was not a concept which men prized for its own sake. It is not that the Roman family was an extended family by definition, somehow sprawling in one house across generations and between siblings. It was nuclear, like ours, but it was embedded in a different set of relationships. If the head of the household, or *paterfamilias*, was an important person, he was also a patron to many dependants and 'friends' who both gave and expected favours. Every morning, a string of visitors went in and out of the house, which was itself a sort of reception centre. Many of the older, bigger houses thus gave visitors an impressive view through them from the entrance, as they looked down the straight main axis of their central rooms: this axis was supported on huge timber cross-beams, some thirty feet long.

In the last decades of the city, this type of plan was far from universal. Big houses now included workshops for craftsmen, shops or even bars adjoining the street, obscuring the 'view through'. The Latin word *familia* included household slaves, and in these work-spaces they and their owner's freedmen would be put to profitable use. Inside, in the household proper, we would be struck by the relative absence of furniture, the multi-purpose use of many of the rooms and the consequent absence of our ideas of privacy. Even the plants in the bigger gardens were often there for their economic value, not for useless gardening. In the southern sector, houses with quite large vineyards inside their plots have now been excavated, while even roses might be grown for the important industry of scent.

As the identity of so many houses' owners is still uncertain, their connections with outlying farmhouses and country villas are still uncertain too. Was Pompeii a town based on consumer-spending, where property-owners simply spent their rents and other income and consumed goods, including crops, which were only produced locally? It seems most unlikely, not just because of casual long-range imports found in the city (a pack of fine pottery from Gaul or a superb ivory statuette of a nude Indian goddess), but also because Pompeian produce is discovered so far abroad in Gaul or Spain. The town's wine was not high class, but it was widely known and widely drunk as a result: its good millstones were famous too, as was its salty fish sauce whose use is also widely attested outside the town. In the years before 79, the king of fish sauce was the freedman Umbricius Scaurus whose product was exported out into Campania: he even commemorated it in prominent mosaics in his house. Continuing excavations of the villa-farmhouses nearby confirm their role as centres of storage and production, often on an impressive scale: it was presumably not all produced for local consumption. Nor was such production 'undignified' for the town's ruling class. A big vineyard, surely a commercial one, has been found down near the amphitheatre with holes for more than 2,000 vines: the production was surely sold in the street shops and perhaps even sent outside. Prominent families in Pompeii's civic life were even remembered for giving their names to particular types of grape (the 'Holconian'). Profits from wine-growing surely mattered to them, though the workforce were their slaves and freedmen: perhaps those villa-houses with the most florid paintings of vines and grapes really were owned by keen profit-making wine-growers.[4] There must have been frequent connections between the place in town, the big house for social and political obligations, and another place in the country, a landed centre of produce. Unfortunately, the inter-connections are seldom attested by what survives. But Pompeii was excellently sited above the navigable river Sarno, with fine access to the sea. It was important to the town's outward-looking economy.

Profit did not exclude a passion for display. Hence the impressive tombs of Pompeian families extend outside the town gates along the main roads: they are most visible outside the south wall, where they are now known to run for more than a mile along the road towards Nuceria. These tomb-monuments were introduced to the locals by the Roman settlers. Some of the smarter ones commemorate whole families, even including a few of

62. Wall-painting of Terentius Neo, holding a book-scroll, and his wife, holding a stylus-pen and a folded writing-tablet. Pompeii, *c.* AD 60.

their slaves. As the tombs' public siting reminds us, life was an open-air existence, where important people wished to be seen to be important: the boasting and social competition would surprise even New Yorkers.

Culturally, the theatres in the town did matter, although mimes and pantomimes would be important in the programme. As for literary taste, the inscriptions may mislead us. The Virgil graffiti are not all evidence for bookishness or a deeply literate society. Many of them come from the opening lines of a book or poem (known through writing exercises?) and able inscribers were commissioned to write them elegantly (had the customer only heard them from others or in a theatrical recitation?). Lines from Virgil's homosexual eclogue (a pastoral poem) are particularly favoured, no doubt because of their sexual reference. One painting even parodies Aeneas and his family as dog-headed figures with huge penises.

Among the electoral posters, some, too, are rather contrived. They give ostentatious praise of a candidate who has already been elected, rather than support for a bid for electoral power. The town was headed by two magistrates (*duumviri*), with two lesser ones (the aediles), and their election was annual in March. In the last days of the town, the jobs of lesser magistrates are the ones which appear to be the most contested. The few posters which cite women's names proclaim them as supporters, or cheerleaders, but naturally not as candidates: they may sometimes even be satirical, implying that a candidate is 'fit only for women'. Candidates had to be male, free-born and elected members already of the town council (a life appointment). As the councillors had had to pay for their election (sometimes offering gladiatorial games) they, and therefore the magistrates, would be the richer citizens. But the aediles' elections, at least, were still lively: about a hundred electoral posters have been recovered from the election-campaign for one Helvius Sabinus as an aedile in what was probably the last, fateful year of 79. They have been found on most of the main streets and they allude to the usual wide range of supporters: trademen's groups, households, a woman or two and even the 'dice-throwers'. 'Are you asleep?' one poster for him says. 'Vote for Helvius Sabinus as aedile'.[5] These posters are all in Latin, but not in our classical Latin. The Bay of Naples was still multi-cultural in 79, a place where Greek was widely spoken along with Latin and the south Italian language, Oscan. All three would be heard in Pompeii, where the Oscan, which our Latin literature conceals, was still being inscribed in the first century AD.

The town was so very close to the luxurious villa life on the Bay: were Pompeii's 'last days' nonetheless indicative of steadier 'Italian values'? The last days had in fact been quite long. In 62 the town had already been badly damaged by an earthquake whose aftershocks continued into the 70s. A final phase, from 62 to 79, has been isolated by excavators, allowing us to see 'little Italy' in action during Vespasian's rise to power. In this phase, the need to repair and restore certainly did not kill off the urge to decorate, paint and fresco; houses were enlarged, and sometimes took over new plots: shops, apartments and work-spaces sometimes turned basic house-plans at an angle to their main entrance. Among all this activity, were the previous owners moving out of town and selling or developing their former urban homes for new purposes? The earthquake has been widely blamed for their departure, but so far as there was a change, it was probably longer-term, and social. Even without an earthquake, no governing class of a town remained stable in this age of early death and uncertainty. Up and down Italy, 'new blood' always had to be exploited for money, after a time in which its 'newness' could tone down. Part of the story may be that a new class of parvenus, freedmen by origin, were taking over old houses in Pompeii and showing off by over-doing them up. In several properties, there is evidence of this change, and there are also signs in this period of that designer-disaster, the 'small town garden'. Like the gardens of the Chelsea Flower Show, it crams in a jumble of scaled-down grandeur, including painted *trompe l'œil* on the walls, pergolas and third-rate sculpture. The style is not so much that of a 'villa in miniature' (big villa gardens were an agglomeration of features, anyway) as a distinctive town-garden fantasy, which often evoked quite other landscapes (woodlands, waterfalls and even Egypt and the Nile). A similar taste is visible indoors: after sixty-two new paintings proliferated in houses such as the 'House of the Tragic Poet', where they smothered the walls with episodes from Greek myths. Only some of the paintings evoke theatrical scenes which might be known from nights out in the town. Like prints and wallpapers from a modern pattern book or a newspaper special offer, most of these big panels evoke a world of culture which the owners themselves did not have to comprehend. Outside and inside, there was a taste for pretty, decorating style for its own sake.

Such redecoration was bright and, in its way, luxurious. This 'luxury' was not morally problematic. It was not that it was somehow distanced safely from its spectators by its faraway fantasy, nor was it 'acceptable' because it could be perceived as a celebration of 'abundance'.[6] The point was that, by Roman or Julio-Claudian standards, it was relatively minor luxury, and what we see at Pompeii was not a dangerous, enervating sort of luxury, one for moralists to deplore. To our eyes, the representations of 'sex' are the licentious element. However, no local protest is known about them, and not all of them belong to the town's last days, either. On doorbells, lamps or doorposts there had long been images of erect penises: there had also been sexual scenes, very explicit, on the surrounds of personal hand-mirrors and so forth. Some of them may be coarse jokes, like modern souvenirs, while others may be unfussed images of 'fertility' or apt erotica suitable for the walls of a specialized brothel. But when we find paintings of a naked woman on top of a man in the colonnade round a central peristyle garden or numbered paintings of oral sex between men and women, including foursomes, in the changing-room of a set of public baths, we cannot explain them somehow as paintings to avert the 'evil eye' and assure good fortune.[7] They are simply sexy. The changing-room scenes, above the clothes-lockers, might even (like the mirrors) have been seen by women.

Pompeian values, then, were not 'Victorian values'. But was the most blatantly coarse or erotic art in the 60s and 70s mostly displayed by a particular social class? In this era, the big House of the Vettii is famous

63. Venus in a sea-shell, pushed and pulled by cherubs, in a *trompe l'oeil* painting of the sea which thus seems to lie out beyond the adjoining garden paintings. Her hairdo was fashionable in Nero's reign. Pompeii, 60s AD.

64. Woman-man sex scene, House of the Centenary, room 43, wall painting in small bedroom of household overseer. Pompeii, AD 40–70.

538

for its painting of a man weighing an enormous penis on scales against gold coins: the Vettii were evidently freedmen. The painting of a woman having sex on top of a man in the garden colonnade was installed by the son of a moneylender who was himself the son of a freedman. Perhaps these newly rich patrons liked to show off this sort of thing, like modern bankers who buy female nudes. The vulgarity of freedmen in the Naples area is immortalized in the most remarkable prose work of this era, the *Satyricon*, written by Nero's witty and elegant courtier, Petronius. Only a fragment survives, but it tells of the adventures of three Greek companions, self-styled homosexual 'brothers' in their various sexual interrelationships. The most remarkable adventure is their dinner with the flamboyant Trimalchio and his freedmen-guests in his vulgar villa in a town which is surely the harbour-town Puteoli, also on the Bay of Naples. Petronius characterizes the freedmen-speakers by a distinctive Latin style, rich in proverbs (the mark of the uneducated) and cultural howlers. They are exaggerated characters and are only seen through his fictitious narrator, but Trimalchio's dinner artfully conjures up a showy vulgarity, a coarse love of money and extremely bad taste. The episode is a highly civilized man's satire on preposterous freedmen at large. The excruciating music, the theatricality and stage effects, the hilariously common wives (who compete over the weight of their gold bracelets) are easily imagined in embryo at an evening with Pompeii's Vettii or with fellow freedmen in the town, people like Fabius Eupor or Cornelius Tages. Some of Trimalchio's instructions for the decoration of his tomb actually match details of a known tomb which was built at Pompeii by a wife, Naevoleia Tycho, for her dead husband.

In the 60s and 70s then, freedmen were among those who were active in redecorating big houses in Pompeii. Yet they were still socially excluded from civic office (as freedmen) and the older, more restrained families at Pompeii had certainly not all vanished from the town just because the ground had started to quake. In this period, we also find the well-planned *trompe l'œil* painting of a nude 'marine Venus' in the so-called House of Venus: it was installed for the Lucretii Valentes, important citizens under Nero. The 'House of the Tragic Poet' was also redecorated for the colony's 'first citizen' (although he did then rent it out). It was not, then, that Venus and profit were attractive only to freedmen. But perhaps (a guess) it took men on the make to flaunt sex-scenes more openly on their house walls. For people in the earlier Pompeii had echoed the steadier patriotic values of Augustus' new age. The east side of its central forum had been transformed in the age of emperors: temples to their cult had been built, while the statues outside one big civic building, paid for by the prominent priestess Eumachia, showed heroes like Romulus and father Aeneas. They evoked the moral sculptures in Augustus' new programmatic Forum in Rome.

'Thrift' and 'restraint' are relative terms. To the new intake of Italians into the Roman Senate of the 70s, they meant that they were not extravagant Julio-Claudians or those senators (often provincials) who had the very biggest fortunes. By 70 there had certainly been families in Pompeii who would have adapted well to the prodigal theatricality of Nero's court. But nobody gave them the chance: none of the excavated houses belonged to someone who rose anywhere near as high as the Roman Senate. The only possible exception is Nero's beautiful Poppaea, who probably did own the huge villa at nearby Oplontis, though perhaps not the Pompeian houses which have sometimes been ascribed to her too.[8] When given scope, Pompeii's Poppaea was as luxurious as the best of them. But the trophy-wife of an emperor was exceptional. In the 60s and 70s there were plenty of others in Pompeii, perhaps the majority, who still saw themselves upholding 'traditional' values. The freedmen were only part of the story. In the colonnade of one garden-space for dining outside, verses told guests to 'divert your lascivious looks and sweet little eyes from somebody else's wife'.[9] On the Street of Abundance, the big letters of one inscription do proclaim 'Sodom and Gomorrah', perhaps as a biblical warning to Pompeians of the perils of sexual misbehaviour. But Pompeii did not collapse in a final torrent of orgies.

A NEW MAN IN ACTION

It is extraordinary how an account can be given (or seem to be given) of single days spent at Rome, but none of several days put together . . . It all seems essential on the actual day on which you did it, but if you reflect that you have done the same things every day, it seems pointless, much more so when you retreat from it all. This always happens to me when I am down at my Laurentum and I'm reading or writing something . . . The sea, the shore, they're a true and private 'seat of the Muses'; how much they inspire, how much they dictate to me . . .

Pliny, *Letters* 1.9

POMPEII AND THE Bay of Naples were by no means all of Italy. For an insight into the values of the Roman Senate's 'new intake' from much further north, we are lucky to have a priceless survival. From the 90s until 112, from Domitian to the reign of Hadrian's predecessor Trajan, we have texts which present the values of just such a new man in the Senate, the younger Pliny.

Pliny was the adopted son of the elder Pliny, his uncle, whom he admired as a famous polymath (the elder is best known to us for his long work on natural history, part of which is concerned to list 'corrupting' luxuries). The younger Pliny published nine books of his own letters, but they are not private letters like those nowadays 'made available' to modern biographers. Most of them uphold particular ways of behaving or showing discrimination. They are intended to be both examples to others and artful proofs of Pliny's own 'modesty' in action. The literary letter, like satire, is a special distinction of Latin literature, but no letters (not even Cicero's) are more elegant and more artful than those which Pliny released. They are the nearest we have to a Roman's autobiography.

A tenth book of letters was published after Pliny's death, containing letters which he had written in 111/2 during his governorship of Bithynia, a province in north-western Asia. One of his subjects there, unknown to him, was the young Antinous, Hadrian's future lover. This tenth book is uniquely valuable because it survives with replies written by or for the Emperor Trajan. They are classics of Roman government in action. Some fifty years earlier the governor of this province had been Petronius, the master of elegant wit and luxury. His letters home to Nero would have been so very different.

Justice, freedom and the perils of excessive luxury are important themes for Pliny because he was a Roman barrister, a senator, a governor and also a moralist. He presents the lifestyle of his friends, members of 'our age' whom he confesses, artfully, to favouring almost too much. Many of them come from 'Pliny country', way up in northern Italy, beyond the river Po.[1] Places like modern Brescia or Verona or Milan had not even had Roman citizenship by right in the 70s BC. Pliny presents this 'little Italy' from a priceless angle, although some of it is so undistinguished on the bigger stage. But he has a sharp eye for people worth cultivating and a happy way of picking future winners. If Hadrian had ever read the letters in his own villa, he would have found some of his own current appointees described by Pliny in an earlier, pleasant setting in their lives.

Pliny was born in 61/2, some fourteen years before Hadrian. He was too young for the worst of the Julio-Claudians and his family were not living close to Rome. His home town was Comum (modern Como), on the very frontiers of north Italy beside the dazzling beauty of its lake. In the 50s BC Julius Caesar had first put it on the Roman citizen-map. Pliny's father had already been prominent in the town, but he himself was the first in the family to rise up the ladder of a senatorial career. He was acutely aware of this honour, even noting that the great Virgil had not attained it. It relied on a very big fortune, partly his family's, partly acquired by marriage and inheritance. Like other senators, his income came mostly from land, most of which was let to tenants (a return of 6 per cent per year on capital has been inferred, not bad in decades of low inflation). Pliny also went in for money-lending, which was riskier but much more lucrative. Unlike old Cato in the 180s BC, Roman senators could now write quite openly about their involvement in usury. Any minority prejudice was long gone: this openness is one aspect of the Roman majority's frankness about money.

Pliny's career was extremely successful. In the year 100, before the age of forty, he had become a consul and in thanks, as was usual, he delivered a panegyric of the Emperor Trajan in Rome. Pliny then expanded his speech and delivered it again in three separate sessions, two hours long, before selected friends. The over-long lecture is a Roman invention: why, Pliny asks, should hearers not suffer just because they are friends? Roman reciters, like too many modern lecturers, hoped for 'feedback'. Pliny then published his enlarged *Panegyric* with a final tribute to himself.

Panegyrics were to have a lively future, typifying court-life in the later Empire, but Pliny looked backwards for his literary hero. As a new man, an orator and a public figure, he felt a special affinity with Cicero. From his teacher, the great Quintilian, he learned to imitate Cicero's style and to admire his moral example. These qualities were still socially relevant. At Rome, Pliny's rivals in the courts included amoral 'informers', people who would prosecute men of their own class on slight pretexts. They favoured blunt language and an uneducated style, whereas Pliny, the Ciceronian, was proud to present such a very different image, while not being above an opportunist prosecution himself.[2]

From the age of eighteen onwards, much of Pliny's public activity concerned cases of inheritance under Roman law. As an advocate, he was restrained by law from taking large fees. Instead, he expected 'favours' as part of the network of 'duties' which made up the mutual obligations of an important Roman's life. As in so much modern business, one good turn was expected to deserve another: Romans are closer to modern life in this respect, to the ethos of social exchanges in modern Manhattan or to 'exhibition loans' between museums, than their critics sometimes realize. Cicero was the apt model for 'duties', for 'dignity' and for law-court speeches, as he also was for Pliny's polished letters. Pliny also wrote short poems and recited them, in long batches, to his long-suffering friends. To our surprise, Cicero was helpful here also. Some of Pliny's short poems were on rather risqué subjects, but he discovered a lascivious little poem in which Cicero referred to kissing his male secretary, Tiro. The discovery of this poem helped Pliny, he claims, to overcome his own hesitations. Why, he then wrote in verse, should I not tell of my Tiro too? Some people (Pliny tells us) criticized him for writing naughty poems, but by citing Cicero, he could counter their complaint. To judge from surviving specimens, the literary level of his verses was a greater reason for concern. Pliny presents them as light amusements of his spare time, but he also claims that Greeks were learning Latin in order to enjoy them. They can only have been disappointed.

As an adult in the Senate, Pliny was more in his element. Like Cicero, he spoke out against corrupt provincial governors, but his audience was more patient than in the old days. Since Augustus, cases of extortion would be heard in the Senate and advocates might speak on one case for five hours or more. Pliny took part in several long cases, including twisted ones brought by Bithynians, and this was one reason why Trajan later sent him to sort out this province. Yet a senator's horizons had changed so much since Cicero, as Pliny, his admirer, exemplifies. There was none of Cicero's free political struggle, played out before senators and the people. Young senators still became tribunes of the people, but the emperors held the enhanced tribunician power. A main concern for holders of the job was simply whether to continue practising as a barrister while holding it, the modern Member of Parliament's dilemma. As for elections, the thrilling manipulations of Cicero's times had vanished. Elections to high office were largely prearranged before being put before the Senate. Pliny, the new member, was particularly distressed by the other members' habit of writing obscenities on the ballot papers which were distributed for their assent.[3] It was one of their few liberties in the matter. The prearranged choices were then read out to the people in the Campus Martius.

At best, senators could publicize the values by which an emperor would be publicly assessed. In this light, Pliny's *Panegyric* on Trajan is not just tedious flattery. It sets up 'modesty' and 'moderation' as values for Trajan, the 'most excellent'; it even dwells on 'liberty'. Significantly, it is not the 'liberty' of Cicero's early years. Pliny acclaims Trajan for being a consul 'as if he was only a consul' and for showing care for equity and the law.[4] But as Trajan himself is the 'maker of consuls', it is equitable that he should stand out above them and 'teach' them. This 'liberty' depends on another's grace and whim, exactly what Cicero had detested about Julius Caesar. As Pliny's own letters observe, everything now is 'under the decision of one man': he has undertaken the 'cares and labours of all' on behalf of 'the common good'. A few things flow down to us from that 'most benevolent fountain' but they come in a 'salubrious blend'.[5] Or so a senator could simply hope. In this age of monarchy senators were expected to acclaim their First Citizen in fine phrases, like the backing to a singer. 'Trust us, trust yourself,' they chanted, or 'Oh, how fortunate we are'... In reply, said Pliny, Trajan shed tears.[6] Under Augustus, eulogies of members of the imperial family had been circulated 'for posterity' through the provinces, where we still rediscover them. Under Trajan, for the first time, acclamations of the Senate were inscribed and circulated likewise for posterity's benefit. Perhaps they will turn up too, for our moral good.

In a slave-society, where senators owned thousands of disposable human beings, this loss of liberty may seem rather marginal. It was also a loss for males only, the only political sex. But it affected what the articulate male class wrote and what they spoke: the political distance since Cicero (let alone Pericles) affects the culture which Romans left behind for posterity, the turgid epic poems (though some now over-estimate them) and the verbose, evasive rhetoric. Despite the cult, among some Romans, of a 'Stoic' inner freedom from passion and emotion, an educated Roman could no longer truly be his 'own man'. Romans had liberties, but they did not have liberty constrained only by their free consent. This change affected their feelings and self-respect, and it put them in moral predicaments which we still recognize, not least in our modern 'People's Republics' and our memories of the 'Iron Curtain' years. Since 96 both Nerva and Trajan, Pliny said, had brought back 'freedom'. But it was a relative concept: the point was that under Domitian the despotism had been so much worse.

Here, Pliny's published letters parade a particularly interesting alternative. They stress a particular set of friendships which he cultivated with the families of a philosophically minded coterie in Rome. They were direct descendants of the 'Stoic' opposition to Nero and the brave Helvidius who had spoken out under Vespasian. 'Thunderbolts', Pliny tells us, had been falling all around him during the time of Domitian's worst tyranny, but he himself had risked protecting a philosopher in the city. However, Pliny was a praetor-magistrate under Domitian, and his year of office was almost certainly 93. At that time members of this philosophical group had been arrested and executed and their biographies of former brave martyrs under Nero were ordered to be burned. As praetor, Pliny may well have helped to carry out the burning. Assiduously, he presents himself later as a friend of the families, but he discreetly fails to emphasize that after his praetorship he went on to another distinguished office during Domitian's reign.

Of all our surviving Latin authors, it is the poet Ovid who lived longest under Augustus, but eighty years later it is Pliny, not Ovid, who best conforms to Augustus' 'vision' of Roman society. Like Augustus himself, Pliny was profoundly unmilitary: he makes no mention of the military prowess of some of his correspondents. His crowning honour, he tells us, was a Roman priesthood, the proud job of augur which Cicero, too, had held. His one Augustan failing was his total lack of children, but not for want of trying: he was married three times, with wives who miscarried. Like Cicero, Pliny went out for a while to govern a second-rank province, Bithynia, but here too his role was shaped by Augustus' legacy. While abroad, freedom and justice were directly his business, but both were exercised in a changed imperial context.

Pliny had already had experience of the Bithynians as an advocate at Rome; even among Romans of the new generation his Greek was exceptionally good (he had written a Greek play when aged fourteen); Trajan was wise to choose him for a Greek-speaking province which had recently emerged as chaotic. Like Cicero, Pliny travelled round the cities of his province on a yearly assize-tour, but unlike Cicero he had been chosen by an emperor. Like all other governors in this period, he arrived with written instructions from the emperor, but unusually for his province he was to be its first imperial legate, the 'emperor's man', sent to sort it out. In you, Trajan reminds Pliny, the provincials can see my own care for them.[7] No such higher authority had existed for Cicero and his friends. Like Cicero, Pliny was aware of the glorious free past of the great cities of Greece, but his letters show the tightened checks which now intruded on the locals' civic freedom. He is required to inspect the cities' financial accounts; he has been ordered to ban clubs and societies in the cities for fear that they will promote popular trouble. It is Pliny, then, who bans local fire brigades, putting social peace before safety. Trajan's answers are often respectful of local practice, more so than Pliny himself, but only within these strict constraints. They are much tighter constraints than those applied by Cicero, let alone by kings or governors in the previous history of Greek Asia. The years from 96 to 138 blend into the age which Edward Gibbon declared to be the happiest in human history. But as in Rome, so in civic life in the Greek-speaking world, there had been a real loss of liberty. It is enshrined for us, a moral lesson, in the gap between Pliny's letters and their models, Cicero's marvellous correspondence, which had immortalized the turning point of an age of true liberty for his class.

In return, Pliny's Greek-speaking subjects presented him with all manner of local bad practice, including slaves in the Roman army, a total illegality. There were also those hardy perennials, a devious philosopher who was claiming tax privileges or some poorly run building projects and the embezzlement of funds by local city councillors: Cicero, too, had confronted all manner of local financial fraud. But again and again Pliny writes for Trajan's advice on the smallest matters or to make the slightest proposals. Cicero had had no emperor to consider: governors in his lifetime were more concerned to restore their personal finances at the provincials' expense. One reason why Pliny wrote so often, and sometimes so irritatingly, was surely to cover his own tracks. Like his predecessors, he might be prosecuted by the provincials on leaving office, under the procedures Augustus had formalized.

A PAGAN AND CHRISTIANS

Meanwhile, this is the method I have followed with those who were de-
nounced to me as Christians. I interrogated them whether they were
Christians. If they confessed that they were, I interrogated them a second
and third time, threatening them with capital punishment. Those who
persevered I ordered to be taken away. For I did not doubt, whatever it
was that they were confessing, that their contumacy and inflexible obsti-
nacy ought to be punished.

Pliny to Trajan, *Letters* 10.96

D URING A TOUR of his province Pliny was confronted with people
who were most unusually obstinate: they refused to worship the
gods. They were brought to him for punishment; he gave them every
chance by questioning them three times; if they persisted in their 'madness', he ordered them to be taken away and executed. A few of them had
the Roman citizenship which protected them against physical punishment
by a governor abroad. Correctly, Pliny sent the citizens off to Rome for
trial, illustrating the value of the privilege.[1]

Their 'madness' was Christianity. When yet more Christians were denounced to Pliny (he appeared to be receptive), some of them denied the
charge. So Pliny devised a test. Would they call on the gods? Would they
pray to an image of Trajan and offer incense and wine? Would they curse
Christ? Some of them then stated that they had once been Christians but
had given the practice up. They passed Pliny's test, but were these ex-
Christians guilty of crimes committed in their Christian past? On their
own account of their 'madness', they had behaved while Christians in a
moral, if misguided, way. In order to be sure, Pliny tortured two female
Christian 'ministers', who were evidently deaconesses, not women priests.

He found only a 'wicked and immoderate superstition', not the lurid tales of group-sex and cannibalism which others ascribed to the sect.

Pliny's encounter is extremely important because it left him uncertain and in need of advice from the emperor. Trajan's answer then set guidelines which were observed not only by Hadrian, but by subsequent emperors until the mid-third century. The Christians were not an unknown problem to important Romans. After Paul's trial Christians had continued to be sentenced in Rome, even in the dark year 93 when Pliny had been a judicial magistrate, or praetor.[2] He had not been present personally at such trials, but nonetheless he knew what to do with a stubborn Christian believer. There were well-known precedents by now and such people were 'godless'. As a result they might provoke the anger of the gods; they were not being asked to do much, only to offer the gods a pinch of incense, but if they refused they should be killed. The really awkward problems were the ex-Christians. After his enquiries, Pliny was strongly inclined to let them off, and so he wrote to Trajan, encouraging him to agree. Trajan replied that existing Christians were not to be 'hunted'; anonymous denunciations must not be received; lapsed Christians, the nub of Pliny's problems, must indeed be left alone. This answer limited the dangers for the Church. In the words of a modern atheist historian, the Romans' prosecution of the Christians was to be a matter of 'too little and too late'.

The legal grounds of Pliny's actions have been endlessly debated, but there was also a wider conflict of values. If the poor suffering deaconesses had read Pliny's nine books of published letters, what would they have made of the values which these presented so artfully? They would have disliked Pliny's indecent verses, especially those on his 'Tiro' and male loves: their Apostle Paul had implied that such sexual acts were a cause of earthquakes. They would also have disliked his respect for suicide. Like other Roman contemporaries, Pliny admired suicide if it was a reasoned end to a life which had become impaired by extreme sickness or old age.[3] To Christians, suicide was a sin against God's gift of life: suicides would long be denied Christian burial.

Unlike most Christian members, Pliny was extremely rich, a Roman senator who had inherited or married into at least six properties in Italy. Nonetheless, he wrote very often of his gifts and help to others. He bestowed civic and cultural gifts on his home town, Comum: he gave it a set of baths and their decoration (but not their maintenance), a temple and a third of the cost of a schoolteacher for Comum's children. This teacher was Comum's first ever after the primary stage (the parents, even then, were to contribute the other two-thirds of the cost, but they could at least select the teacher themselves). Pliny also gave favours to friends, even to his old nanny, and he set aside a capital sum whose revenue would support no fewer than 175 children at Comum (they were poor children, but they would be citizen-soldiers and mothers for the future). Despite three marriages, Pliny had no children himself to be his heirs.

Pliny's gifts were part of a widespread donor culture among the rich on which civic life depended throughout the Empire. In Pliny's case, the gifts were not self-interested bids for power. He was locally very prominent already. Rather, he gave for the ideals of culture and civic life which he himself upheld. His letters then publicized his gifts. The deaconesses, by contrast, would have told him to give indiscriminately to the poor, because the poor were blessed by God. Gifts (they believed) were not just for deserving friends or local townsmen. Gifts could earn their donor spiritual treasure in heaven, an idea which Pliny never entertained. Gifts should also be made discreetly, not trumpeted abroad in letters and honorary inscriptions.

Pliny also had hundreds and hundreds of slaves, at least five hundred (to judge from his will) and no doubt many more. Here, the deaconesses would be less bothered: Paul had told slaves to 'serve the more' and Christian slave-owning had continued. It was rather fine when Pliny described how he did not interfere in the capacity of his ex-slaves to make wills and bequests: few Roman masters were so restrained, preferring to take 'legacies' back for themselves. Pliny was quite unlike the bad slave-owners in his class, men like the frightful Macedo, whose slaves (Pliny described) had murdered him by his bathing pool. Pliny stood for a kinder style, but with a sharp eye, too, on the masters' safety and the interests which kindness served. The changes in Roman laws for sick or old slaves since Claudius' reign had had similar prudential concerns: they arose from the underlying fear of a slave-war and their concern was to assure the slave-masters' survival and 'interests'.

There was also something fine about Pliny's family values. It was good to read him telling others to criticize their own faults first (taking out the 'beam' in their own eye, just as Jesus had preached): it was particularly good to read him saying the same to an all-powerful Roman father about his erring son. Paul, too, had told fathers not to be harsh to their children 'in case they should despair'. Pliny's praises of his wife were most intriguing. Calpurnia was his third wife (two having died) and was very much younger than himself. The deaconesses would like to read how Pliny claimed to have formed her manners and literary tastes: Christian wives,

Paul had said, must submit to their husbands. But it was boastful of him to publicize what loyalty Calpurnia was showing.[4] She read Pliny's works repeatedly (Pliny tells us) and even learned them by heart. When he spoke in court she would send messengers to and fro to hear how his speech was being received. She would wait anxiously behind a curtain while Pliny recited his own works in public; she 'drinks in greedily the praises of myself'. Calpurnia even set his awful verses to music and sang them to the lyre. The coarse songs to boys were not, one assumes, in Calpurnia's songbook.

To Christians, this mousy submissiveness was also a virtue. The problem, simply, was Pliny, its self-centred end. What Calpurnia stood for were the virtues of 'little Italy': shrewdness, frugality and, as Pliny writes to tell her aunt, 'she loves me'.[5] Pliny has therefore been upheld as the first person in European literature to 'blend together the role of husband and lover'. Cicero in fact precedes him (in his early years of marriage only), but in both men the strongest love is love of himself. Yet Calpurnia existed in a social setting which Christians accepted too. Women of her class (like many rich Christian women) would often be married by the age of sixteen; they could not prosecute a case in their own right in court; paternalist laws protected them from lending money to just any person who appealed to them. A similar paternalism remained strong in the laws of the later Christian Empire.

In Christian society, a girl might opt out as a virgin, or be vowed to virginity by her parents. In Pliny's world, there were no lifelong virgins. There was, however, no alternative route to female 'freedom'. Since the 'licence' of the Julio-Claudian years the women of Rome's Stoic philosophic cliques were now the most likely to join in an intelligent discussion or to show resolve in a public crisis. Elsewhere, Pliny could not credit that a woman might have literary skills. When one Roman lady wrote witty letters in old-fashioned Latin, Pliny assumed that her husband must have written them himself or taught his wife how to do it. In Christian churches, too, women were certainly not expected to teach or publish or even to send and receive letters (which might be billets-doux).

In upper-class circles, nonetheless, Christianity soon found female converts: heresy was even thought to be particularly attractive to females. Pliny's social world could have helped the deaconesses to see why. In a rich household, there was almost nothing for the lady to do all day. Slaves looked after her husband; in the evenings he had male guests and listened to music or yet more recitations, but not to anything so limited as conversation à deux over dinner. Pliny likes to describe the exemplary retirement routines of unusually active old men. These 'keep-fit' gentlemen read and exercise but even when they go for a drive they rarely take their wife with them. The female of a grand household might end up passing her day by playing board-games.[6] In an intended comment on the changes in 'luxury' between the generations, Pliny describes how one distinguished grand-mother amused herself by keeping a troupe of pantomime-dancers in her household. She always sent her upright young grandson away, of course, before he could watch the troupe performing. Her raffish tastes, Pliny says, were not those of 'our age'. Although she maintained them when in her late seventies, she had taken them up long before, in days when Nero was still young.[7] After Pliny, in the absence of such fun, one alternative for such a bored person would be the Church.

Repeatedly, Pliny commended simplicity, the values of little Italy up near Comum, away from corrupting Rome. Here there was an emphasis which the first Christians had not yet cultivated. 'Simplicity' meant coun-try life, in charmed settings whose peace and quiet were upheld as blessed escapes from business down in Rome. Here a man could rest and write in peace, away from the bother of clients and the dependants whom he pro-fessed to find so tiresome. Here he could hunt wild boar in the woods (Pliny was keener on this sport than his throw-away remarks at first im-ply). Here, too, he could lay out a garden. The early Christian contribu-tion to garden history is precisely zero, but Pliny is our great spokesman for the Italian ideals of villa life.

By the beautiful lake at Como, he had two particular villas, one by the lakeside called Comedy, one on a hill overlooking it called Tragedy. They were named not for alternating moods, but for the beloved theatrical world. Comedy was low-lying, like the flat shoes of a comic actor, whereas Tragedy was perched high up, like the high heels of the tragic ac-tor's boots. Pliny also had another villa on the coast just south of Rome, where Aeneas' Trojans were alleged to have landed and where senators had country bolt-holes within a twenty-mile range of the city. On the bor-ders of modern Tuscany and Umbria (just north of Città di Castello and south of San Sepolcro), Pliny had yet another villa, fanned by a cool breeze in summer. His description of it is the most influential letter to have survived from the Roman world: it can now be matched with ar-chaeologists' continuing excavations of the site at San Giustino.[8]

Behind Pliny's country homes stretched some three hundred years of Roman experience in smart villa life. Cicero had already loved his various houses and, like contemporaries, kept a keen eye on possible buys: he was never one to have two homes when as many as eight might do. In country settings, villas were low and spreading buildings, usually without the tall eighteenth-century symmetry of our Georgian homes. Pliny's villas extended at odd angles and we need to remember that his stylish letter is not concerned to describe their full extent. He says nothing about the site's former owners and builders (archaeologists can now point to Granius Marcellus before Pliny). He says nothing about their slaves' quarters or kitchens or the probable use (as at Pompeii) of his garden porticoes for storing the fields' important crops: the 'productive' buildings have begun to be known through recent archaeology. He emphasizes other aspects. Like so many prominent Romans, Pliny liked the challenge of an assault on nature. Like many country gentlemen ever since, he designed his garden and bits of his villa himself. When he dwells on this part of his villas' charms, he is aware, correctly, that he is breaking new literary ground. For the first time in world literature, hunting, gardening and country-house design appear as life's heavenly trinity, a non-Christian Paradise on earth.

Pliny's Tuscan garden had a terrace and colonnades, clipped box hedging and enclosed courtyards with fountains. Its special distinction was a 'hippodrome outside', a miniature version of Rome's racecourse, the Circus, perhaps in imitation of Domitian's hippodrome on Rome's Palatine hill. It was shaded by surrounding cypress trees and was wittily planted with the staple plants of so many Italian gardens since: clipped box, fruit trees, laurels, plane trees (up whose trunks ivy climbed) and glistening acanthus whose leaves seemed 'smooth' to Pliny's eyes. There was no racing in such a 'hippodrome' and, to our taste, the planting was rather spotty. But the evergreens (not yews) were clipped into shapes and letters, including the initials of family-members and working gardeners. At one end, fine marble pillars shaded an area for dining, where male and female guests, as always at Rome, reclined on couches. Water ran merrily through the mock hippodrome and fed the fountains and a marble basin beside the dinner-guests, in which the dishes were floated during meals. In the early sixteenth century Pliny's letter on his garden was rediscovered and shown to Raphael, who used it as the backbone for his most influential garden, the Villa Madama in Rome.[9] Viewed from the house, the supporting countryside seemed to Pliny to be like a painting, while the meadow was 'jewelled' with flowers. These ways of viewing landscape would also have a long history in garden design.

Pliny's praises of rural simplicity, his home and villa life were not unusual in the era. We find them in contemporary poems, especially those of his friend Martial. Martial, too, had prospered under Domitian, but he then left Rome in the new era of the late 90s and kept his praises of

65. A reconstruction of Pliny's Villa at Laurentum, one of many, based on Pliny's own Letter. By L.-P. Haudebourt, in 1838, after visiting the area in 1815–16.

country living for his years of retirement back in Spain.[10] He had delighted Pliny by comparing him with Cicero. There was a real similarity of themes in the two friends' writings: Martial's coarse epigrams suggest what Pliny is likely to have written in some of his risqué verses.

The Christians' green landscape, by contrast, was Paradise, waiting in the world to come. Villa life was way beyond most of their membership's social status; however, Pliny's views on public shows would be very congenial to their taste. The deaconesses would have agreed with his moral dislike of pantomime-dancing and the 'corruptions' of naked Greek athletics. Pliny also found chariot racing 'boring', though there were many keen Christian fans of the sport who would long disagree over this.[11] His views on rank and class were also quite Church-compatible. For Pliny, 'equality' was proportional to an individual's social standing: it varied for each of us according to our rank. Spiritually, the Gospels took a contrary view, but although Christians were said to be 'one' in Christ Jesus, 'unity' did not entail worldly equality. Distinctions of worldly class persisted, therefore, among Christian believers: they were irrelevant, merely, to the life to come.

Here, the deaconesses would have found Pliny very under-informed. The one route to immortality, in his view, was literary work. He could entertain the idea of ghosts, but he had no expectations of a life after death: his uncle even considered the afterlife a fable which restrained old people from a noble death by suicide. Bodily resurrection would have seemed completely absurd to both of them. Unlike the brave deaconesses, Pliny was certainly not cut out for martyrdom, either. Like many other Christians, he would have lapsed when investigated and would have sought forgiveness later. But as a writer-up of others' martyrdoms, he would have been second to none, even among authors in the early Church.

In Pliny's values, there was one glaring absentee: humility. He professed 'modesty', but it was not the same thing, least of all when he used it to set off his own unfailing virtues. For Christians, but not for Pliny, humility belonged with something else, with the need for redemption as humans created by God.

Three centuries later, in a Christian Empire, the Christian Augustine would withdraw to just such a villa in 'little Italy', near Milan, in the wake of his conversion from sex and worldly ambition. In marbled homes like Pliny's, there were bishops meanwhile who shared many of Pliny's tastes, the hunting, the landscape, the rural ease. There were even those who wrote scurrilous verses and built grandly with rare stones.[12] Far into the Middle Ages, one part of the future lay in a blend of Pliny's values with a flexible Christian faith.

REGIME CHANGE,
HOME AND AWAY

Then Trajan came down to the very Ocean and when he learned about its nature and saw a boat sailing to India, he said, 'I would certainly have crossed to the Indians as well, if I was still a young man.' For he started to think about the Indians, and to bless Alexander . . . He used to say that he had gone even further than Alexander and he wrote this to the Senate, though he could not even retain what had been subdued. Among much else, he was granted triumphs for as many nations as he wished: because of the number which he kept on writing about to them, the senators were unable to understand some of them or even name them properly.

Cassius Dio, on Trajan in Mesopotamia,
Epitome of his *Histories* 68.29

'YOUR ONLY RELAXATION', Pliny assured the Emperor Trajan in his speech as consul, 'is to range through forests, beat out wild animals from their lairs, scale immense mountain ridges and set foot on awesome rocks.'[1] With Trajan, the man from Spain, hunting returned as the active sport of an ancient ruler. 'For him, the sweat of catching and finding is equal': unlike 'hunters' in the Roman arena, Trajan went after free-range prey, a passion which was shared by his successor Hadrian. For the events of Trajan's reign bring us, at last, to Hadrian's own times and to stories which he knew much better than we can. When Trajan took power, Hadrian was aged twenty-two.

Trajan (ruling 98–117) was styled the 'most excellent', but to us, as to Hadrian, he presents a mixed picture. On the one hand, he showed civility, or moderation, in his dealings with the Senate and the upper class. Sound judgement also shows in many of his answers to Pliny's fussing letters from his province. On the other hand, there was a decided intemperance. Trajan drank heavily (he even took to beer): Hadrian admits in his autobiography how he, too, had to drink heavily with Trajan on campaign. Like Hadrian, Trajan was conspicuously keen on sex with young men. They included actors and the young son of an Eastern dynast who danced for him by the Euphrates and was teased about his gold earrings. The major legacies of Trajan's reign were two vast military invasions and the most massive building projects in Rome. The buildings endured for centuries (Trajan's Column is still a landmark in Rome), but the invasions proved more difficult. Their most positive effect (fostered by Hadrian) was to discredit Roman attempts at military expansion for another fifty years.

Trajan's wars have a decidedly modern ring to them. Rome was the dominant military superpower and any defeats of her were temporary setbacks, always duly avenged. Trajan himself was a Roman 'natural' for aggression. He was a military man, but unlike his father he had yet to win a significant victory. The groundwork for one was probably laid during his first eighteen months and then, from spring 101 to December 102, Trajan took a huge army into Dacia in eastern Europe (in part, modern Romania). In the mid–50s BC, Julius Caesar had toyed with suppressing the Dacian 'threat'. Trajan now made the long-planned suppression a reality. There was a previous Roman defeat to avenge here (under Domitian), and as Trajan advanced, the Dacians had no option but to send him an ultimatum. As a sign of their uncouthness, they sent 'long-haired' envoys; their barbarian allies even sent an enormous mushroom, inscribed with a message in Latin. In the course of their advance, the Romans built a huge bridge over the Danube, so strong that its pillars are still standing. Many lives were then lost until the most prominent Dacian king, Decebalus, agreed to surrender all his siege-equipment and weapons of destruction, to demolish his forts and not to shelter deserters from Rome. In return, Rome would help him with subsidies.

Inevitably, reports then came that Decebalus was rebuilding his forts and luring military experts over from the Roman sector. In June 105 Trajan attacked yet again, with about 100,000 men and the aim of annexation. Eventually Decebalus killed himself, and his corpse was decapitated in the Roman camp.[2] A wide expanse of Dacia became a Roman province for the first time.

As so often, conquest was the prime source of growth for an ancient economy. Dacia produced vast quantities of slaves and spoils and gave access to metals including new gold-mines. Back in Rome, the recent

a) Dacian prisoners before Trajan outside a Roman camp.

66. Scenes from Trajan's Column at Rome, dedicated in AD 113 to commemorate Trajan's Dacian Wars (in modern Romania).

b) Roman soldiers lock shields in the 'tortoise'-testudo formation against a Dacian fort.

c) The Dacians' leader Decebalus kills himself by a tree as Roman cavalry attack him.

d) Victory inscribes a shield with Trajan's successes for posterity.

557

economic weakness was reversed (the Roman coinage had just been de-based) and so Trajan could afford to build in style. Within Rome, there-fore, his reign is the summation of the despotism of a 'First Citizen'. Although Hadrian would add big temples to Rome, neither he nor his im-mediate successors built any more secular buildings. From Trajan on-wards, the job had been done: rulers could now travel for years outside the city of Rome without needing to 'benefit' its people in this particular way.

Since Vespasian's coup, the senatorial class had acquiesced in the em-perors' legality: 'you bid us be free', as Pliny told Trajan. Lawyers did not question the limits on this 'freedom' or the right, historically, by which the emperors' 'bidding' was being exercised. There were reasons for this significant silence. In Italy, nobody was being 'imposed on' to pay new taxes or conscripted to fight wars. Taxation and conscription are the acts by which rulers do most to raise questions of their subjects' rights and lib-erties. Neither occurred in this period in imperial Rome.

Instead, the eternal city wore prominent marks of its subservience: it had grown to be punctuated by so many dynastic buildings, by temples to deified members of Vespasian's dynasty and by the emperors' personal fo-rums, each of them built since Julius Caesar's own. Trajan's wife, sister, niece and great-niece would all be commemorated at Rome; there was the predictable concern to adjust Roman opinion to a new 'dynasty'. The im-perial women's elaborate new hairstyles certainly made them unmistak-able. Trajan's sister Marciana favoured tight spiralling curls in rows leading to a big nest of hair at the back of the head. These time-consuming styles even required wire frames underneath as supports. In more durable materials, coins and inscribed titles, buildings and posthumous cults were deployed to publicize a family image. Remains of them are the ancient ruins which are nowadays the most conspicuous in the city of Rome's cen-tre. But once again the 'other Rome', the people both 'sordid' and 'well connected', were not unwilling spectators of this public programme. There were proven ingredients for winning their support: the food-supply, blood sports and (when possible) baths. Trajan excelled in all three, the summation of the process which we have followed from Augustus on-wards. He was rightly looked back on as the ruler whose 'popularity with the people nobody has excelled and few have equalled'.

Fortunately, he had an architectural genius to hand, the Greek-speaking Apollodorus of Damascus. Like Sinan, the great architect of the Ottoman Turks, Apollodorus had been a military engineer: it was he who had de-signed the big Danube bridge. On the coast near Rome, an improved har-bour was built to cater for the safety of the city's imported grain, but in

Rome itself, the wonder was Trajan's Forum. It was enough to take a visitor's breath away even three centuries later. The Forum took some of its proportions from Vespasian's temple of Peace. Like that temple, it included two library spaces (one library for Greek, one for Latin, in the Roman fashion) but Trajan's two libraries were much bigger, holding some 20,000 scrolls in all. There were fine colonnades with sculpted Dacian prisoners; there was a big statue of Trajan on horseback; above all, there was a massive hall in which to dispense justice. The form of these halls, or basilicas, would later influence the first big Christian churches.

At the far end stood Trajan's Column whose sculpted panels (155 in all) are our most vivid evidence of the Roman army in action. Their subject is the Dacian campaign. They show Roman troops laying bridges over rivers, deploying siege-machinery (the frames of the catapults were changed from wood to metal under Trajan) and attacking Dacian women who were themselves torturing Dacian prisoners. At the top, much-discussed scenes show men, women and children on the move with their animals. Are they Roman settlers arriving in the new province or (more probably) Dacians being expelled? Either way, the scene is one of new-style 'direct rule' by Rome.

Trajan also commissioned a nearby market, one of modern Rome's most conspicuous ruins: its brilliant use of changing levels is also due to Apollodorus' genius. After a fire on the Esquiline, he paid the overdue last rites to what remained there of Nero's preposterous Golden House and built an enormous set of public baths on top of its remaining West Wing, burying Nero's array of dining-rooms and concrete dome under a building of public utility. It was a good, popular move, and in 109 his 'blood sports' to celebrate the Dacian conquests were on an unsurpassed scale. Yet he was still not content. In the Near East, Rome's direct rule had already been extended to the Red Sea by the annexation (in 106) of Petra and its accompanying 'Arabian' (Nabataean) kingdom in modern Jordan. In 113, a year after his Forum's opening, Trajan set off eastwards, accompanied by Hadrian, to settle the one elusive old score in this sector: a conquest of Rome's Parthian neighbours, at least along the river Euphrates. They halted at Antioch in north Syria and up on the Jebel Aqra, the great pagan mountain of the gods which towers above the city, Trajan dedicated spoils from Dacia in the hope of winning divine favour for the coming campaign.[3]

'Regime change' was now to be extended to the Near East. In 114 Trajan invaded Armenia with a huge army and refused to accept a climb-down by its ruling prince. This poor fellow had been appointed by the

Parthian king, but without the usual Roman approval. When he sought it, Trajan took over Armenia as a province instead. To protect it, he then headed south and invaded Mesopotamia (modern Iraq) in another extension of 'direct rule'. He crossed the river Euphrates, imposed 'regime change' on the local princes and even crossed the river Tigris. Babylon was taken and Trajan then travelled down and captured the Parthian capital of Ctesiphon. It seemed an amazing success. The people of Mesopotamia, the historian Sallust had written (c. 40 BC), are 'unbridled in sexual lust, in both sexes': Trajan sampled one sex, at least (the male).[4] He also sailed victoriously on the river Euphrates in a boat whose sails displayed his name in gold letters. It was the peak of Roman conquest in the East, making Mark Antony's failures and Nero's hesitations seem paltry by comparison.

In antiquity, historians credited Trajan with a nostalgia for Alexander the Great and even with thoughts of conquest as far as India. Perhaps Trajan really did wish to visit the house in Babylon where Alexander had died and to pay sacrifice in it: who would not? However, Trajan was over sixty, and he was certainly no Alexander. The chronology of his three-year campaign in Mesopotamia is a key to his intentions, but it has often been misunderstood.[5] After the first year's successes in Armenia, he had gone back to his base at Antioch for winter 114/5 and was lucky to survive a shattering earthquake there. In 115 he had his year of conquest through territory which is now Iraq. After taking Ctesiphon, he wrote tactfully back to the Senate for approval, just as he had asked for their approval in settling Dacia. He had had enough, he said, and the solution was now to put a client king on Ctesiphon's throne: 'this country' (our Iraq) 'is so immeasurably vast and separated from Rome by such an incalculable distance that we cannot administer it.'[6] By early 116, the Senate received his letter and had time to write back from Rome and agree. There was no 'Alexander-mania' in these plans.

However, Trajan's entire conquests then blew up around him. In spring 116 the trouble began with the Jews. Their revolts spread from Libya (Cyrene) through Cyprus and Egypt, encouraged by fellow Jews who were fleeing from the conquered Parthian sector. The Near East was thrown into revolt. Armenia was attacked and had to be partly given away and Trajan's Mesopotamian conquests rose in rebellion. In 116 Trajan spent a hot summer there besieging the strongly walled city of Hatra. He was lucky that the defendants just missed his conspicuous grey head as he rode past without a helmet. To cap it all, Dacia broke into war again.

67. Bronze portrait head of Hadrian, second quarter of the second century AD.

These upheavals cost thousands of lives, especially in the large Jewish population on Cyprus and the yet bigger Jewish communities in Egypt. There was even a glimpse of the end of the world. Down in southern Mesopotamia, war among the 'angels of the north' was seen at this time in a vision by one Elchasai, evidently a Christian member of a strict Baptist community. Elchasai's concerns were very different to Trajan's. What he saw was a vision of an angel and a (female) Holy Spirit who were promising one last forgiveness of sins to Christian sinners: this 'sin', to a pagan outsider, would have seemed like a condition created by their foolish Christian faith. Then the world as Trajan knew it would end. Elchasai wrote up his vision in a book which survived to inspire another Christian visionary in this region more than a century later, Mani. Mani's post-Christian 'Gospel of Light' survived for many centuries and was called Manichaeism by its many enemies.[7]

There was to be no such second chance for Trajan. He left Hadrian with the armies in Syria and in 117 withdrew westwards. In early August he was declared ill, and he died in Cilicia on the southern coast of Turkey, aged sixty-two. It was a potentially chaotic moment, with so many rebellions still in progress around him. Who was to succeed him? Hadrian was nearby and, as he had been named consul already for the following year, he was a natural choice. But had he yet been chosen formally? On 9 August Hadrian could claim receipt of documents in Syria which conveniently 'proved' his adoption. On 11 August news then came to him, even more conveniently, that Trajan was dead. Later historians wrote of Trajan's sickness and described symptoms which suggest a heart attack. But there were other strong possibilities. On 12 August Trajan's intimate palace-secretary Phaedimus died too, the man who had once been Trajan's official 'taster' of foods and his personal butler. Only after many years were Phaedimus' ashes conveyed back to Rome: had there been a wish not to draw too much attention to the emperor's taster's death? Later in the century, the senatorial historian Dio was told firmly by his father that Hadrian had never been adopted by Trajan at all, that his death had been concealed for a while by those close to him and that the letter informing the Senate of Hadrian's 'adoption' was actually signed by Trajan's wife, Plotina. Was the cause of death sickness, or was Trajan poisoned along with Phaedimus the butler? Scandal later alleged that Hadrian had bribed Trajan's freedmen and had had sex with his boy-favourites in the hope of assuring his own succession. What we do know is that Hadrian promptly withdrew from Trajan's 'conquests' in Mesopotamia.

The truth of his predecessor's death remains buried with Hadrian. It is an ironic silence because the distinction of this period is not military but historical: it saw two Latin accounts of the imperial past, both of which are classics for our understanding of the Roman emperors. One of them is also a work of genius which sets freedom, luxury and justice among its prominent themes. Significantly, neither of their authors risked writing the history of Trajan's reign itself.

PRESENTING THE PAST

I strongly predict—and my prediction does not mislead me—that your histories will be immortal: so, all the more (I will admit it, candidly) I want to be included in them . . .

Pliny to Tacitus, *Letters* 7.33

FROM AUGUSTUS TO Hadrian, the Roman 'First Citizens' live on for us as individuals. The reason for this afterlife is only marginally their archaeological remains; their sculptures and buildings spread such lies by presenting their patrons only as they wished to be seen. Until Domitian, the emperors live so vividly because they are described in texts, in the biographies of Suetonius and the penetrating histories of Tacitus.

Both of these authors ranked among Pliny's friends. Suetonius was the younger of the two and benefited from Pliny's patronage: Pliny exercised 'suffrage' for him by writing and asking for favours on his behalf. Significantly, the word 'suffrage' now applied to intercession, not (as formerly) to the free exercise of a Roman citizen's vote.[1] Tacitus, by contrast, needed none of Pliny's suffrage. His formidable learning was recognized early. Hence, in 88 he was appointed one of the Roman priests who oversaw foreign cults, of which Christianity would have been one. Tacitus was a fine orator and was a consul three years before Pliny. Pliny published eleven letters to him in order to show proof of a friendship which would dignify himself. Like Pliny, Tacitus loved hunting, but he also had a style, an insight and a capacity for judgement which Pliny, his good friend, lacked.

Suetonius was of equestrian rank. Perhaps his family hailed from north Africa. He was never a senator, but he held three literary posts in the emperor's household, including the job of librarian, and travelled

68. Portrait of a woman, with fine pearl and red-
stone earrings: mummy portrait from Hadrian's
new foundation of Antinoopolis, AD 130s.

very interestingly. He was with Pliny in Bithynia and later he was with
Hadrian in Britain. In 122 his career came to a halt there. Later gossip
alleged that he had been 'too familiar' in Britain with Hadrian's disgruntled wife, Sabina.

Suetonius' most famous surviving works are his *Lives of the Caesars*
which included, revealingly, a *Life* of Julius Caesar: Suetonius did not
avoid describing the life of the real founder of 'the Empire'. The strengths
of the best of his *Lives* are their vivid details and their use (in the case of
Augustus' *Life*) of the emperor's own letters and autobiography. Through
anecdotes, they bring out each emperor's fondness for 'luxury' and they
observe each man's practice of giving justice. They are interested in astrol-
ogy and in most of the emperors' revealing fondness for it. They are also
our best sources for each emperor's origins and physical appearance. The

best emperors, in Suetonius' view, were Augustus and Vespasian, the two obvious choices.

Suetonius' *Lives* became a model for later biographers, especially for the important life of the post-Roman 'emperor' Charlemagne, written by Einhard (*c.* AD 850). However, their understanding and their accuracy are limited. The further Suetonius went on, the weaker the *Lives* become: perhaps, after his dismissal in Britain, research became harder. He is at his best with anecdotes, especially when reporting stories contemporary with himself. Did Nero really dress himself up in animal skins, have himself let out of a cage and then attack the private parts of men and women who were tied to stakes, before being sexually gratified by a freedman whom he had married? Such was the gossip fifty years later. Suetonius also insisted that he had discovered from 'quite a few people' that Nero was convinced that nobody was chaste in any part of his body, and that everyone concealed this fact.[2] His researches are evidence, at least, for people's later attitudes to Julio-Claudian debauchery.

What he ignores is the cardinal issue of liberty. Here, we have to look to his greater contemporary, Tacitus. Whereas Suetonius was only an equestrian and a functionary in the emperor's service, Tacitus was a senator and a consul, ranks for which 'liberty' was a living issue. Pliny was already aware that Tacitus was the real genius of his age, the one with whom he would do well to be associated. Like Pliny, Tacitus was not born in Rome. Almost certainly, he came from southern Gaul, perhaps from Vasio (modern Vaison). The south of Gaul was heavily Italianized, however, and was no more 'provincial' than north Italy. Tacitus' career rose quickly to a consulship and then to the grand provincial governorship of Asia: the rise was even more rapid and the result more distinguished than Pliny's own. Born in *c.* 58, Tacitus' progress has now been confirmed in more detail by renewed study of what appears to be part of his funerary inscription, found in Rome.[3]

Like Pliny, Tacitus had prospered as a senator under Domitian, but he was explicit about the compromises which were imposed on him at that time. As a senator, he knew the relevance of hypocrisy and fraudulence in human nature. 'Liberty' was a cardinal value to him, but he also fraternized with contemporaries 'who knew too much to be hopeful'.[4] He wrote variously, on oratory (where he diagnosed correctly the connection between great oratory and a free political context) and on his father-in-law, Agricola, the governor of Britain (Tacitus gave fine words on 'freedom' to a northern Caledonian chieftain). He was not at all blind to provincial life. He wrote good things on the Gauls (though nothing on Spain). He also wrote a remarkable text on Germany, where his father had served and where he himself had also, probably, spent part of his career. Liberty, he wrote, is beloved by Germans, but discipline is not. Germans are prone to strong emotions, and their priests are more powerful than their kings. There is real thought and observation here and he is not inventing his Germans simply by crediting them with the converse of Rome's own vices. The text has been called 'the most dangerous ever written'; it became extremely important for Germans' later independence from the Roman Catholic Church and more recently, for the Nazis' pathological 'German' nationalism. A high-level operation was mounted by Hitler's SS to seize the main manuscript of Tacitus' *Germania* from its Italian owners, but fortunately it was frustrated.[5]

Tacitus was shocked, like many, by the later years of Domitian. It was this experience, not the brusque 'adoption' of Trajan, which did most to shape his historical interpretation. His two masterpieces are the *Histories*, which run from 69 until Domitian's reign, and then later, the *Annals*, which run from Augustus' death until Nero's. Unfortunately, neither has survived intact, but their style, human insight and penetration are the classics of Roman history-writing.

As a 'new man' in the Senate, Tacitus' social views were certainly not liberal. He had no faith in the political wisdom of the mob and no respect, either, for men and women on the make or take. He was similarly prejudiced against Greeks and Jews. He did, however, endorse the inclusive policy of Rome towards its subjects: he revised a speech by the Emperor Claudius so as to make the merits of this inclusion explicit (as a provincial, he had benefited from it). But as a new man at Rome, he liked episodes of old-style robustness, whether in battle or religion or diplomacy. The very form of his *Annals* was old-world: he followed the year-by-year arrangement of the earliest Roman historians, a form which had existed long before the emperors transformed the nature of the state.

Tacitus' supreme gift is to see the gap between profession and reality and the need for constant distrust of the devious 'spin' and professed morality of one-man rule. Tacitus did do research by reading the 'acts' of previous senatorial meetings, and perhaps he did it in the spacious rooms of Trajan's new library in Rome. Brilliantly, he appreciated the oratorical style of individual emperors and their eras, while also seeing through the abundant official deceptions and euphemisms about events.

The recent find of the inscribed official response of the Senate to events in Tiberius' family in AD 20 confirms, in essentials, the penetration of Tacitus' own version and its mistrust of the clouds of rhetoric around these happenings.

Theoretical constitutions, Tacitus remarks, are hard to realize and very quick to fail. Unlike Cicero, he did not waste time on ideal republics nor did he praise, like Thucydides, a 'moderate blend' of opposing classes. There is a wonderfully truculent sarcasm in Tacitus' judgement. He is not an incurable pessimist, but he is always wry about events and about what their participants were hiding. In him, posterity found the supreme historian of absolute rule, both how to sustain it and how to react to it. For despite Tacitus' sarcasm and his sense of what had been lost, he was also prepared to serve under a despot (like his friend Pliny). While regretting lost liberty, he advocated the middle path in politics and hoped that chance or destiny would bring some ruler who might be better than the worst. In the 30s BC Sallust had acidly described the Republic's loss of freedom: Tacitus, heir to Sallust's style, described the effects of that loss, but not the ways in which to reverse it.

In due course, his stress on liberty and 'moderate' accommodation with a ruler intrigued Edward Gibbon and left a profound mark on his *Decline and Fall of the Roman Empire*: conversely, Tacitus was abhorred by the fraudulent Napoleon. His greatest age of influence was the seventeenth century. He showed readers of that age how to react under despotism and how to cherish a contrary notion of 'freedom'. He also addressed their concerns about the many court 'favourites' whom contemporary rulers in England and Europe were promoting so wantonly. Tacitus had seen both the rulers' need for favourites and the favourites' foibles, exemplifying them in his descriptions of Tiberius' hated Sejanus or Claudius' assertive freedmen.[6] But he also described how despots induce servility, how freedom becomes artful subservience and how justice is distorted by informers and 'sneaks'. This picture of the Romans' predicament was powerfully received by English lawyers and political gentlemen when confronted with the vanities of James I and the luxurious demands of his successor, Charles I. At Rome, lawyers had obsequiously found precedents and a context for autocracy; in England, by contrast, lawyers trained in the classics upheld the conception of 'liberty' whose loss, they found, had been so poignantly described by Tacitus. And yet Tacitus saw that full liberty was impossible in the existing Roman system and that other values now mattered since the republican days of Cicero's youth.

69. Reconstruction of Trajan's Library in Rome where the historian Tacitus may have worked (reconstruction by G. Gorski).

To us, his insights are still highly relevant in our age of one-party rule, of 'spin' and 'favourites' and 'democracies' emptied of the word's real content. His works still guide a real understanding of the Roman Empire, rather than pseudo-bureaucratic studies of its 'structures'. For one major reason why the flavour of each decade was so different was because of the people whom Tacitus grasped so brilliantly at its centre—the crafty, malign Tiberius, the foolish and pedantic Claudius, the depraved Nero. To complain that Tacitus focused on court politics, not on the social and regional diversity which appeals more to many modern historians, is to miss the value of what he gives us. The emperors' characters did have profound consequences throughout society. The intertwined personalities of their females were also significant for structures and events. The Messalinas and Agrippinas are distinctive facts of the Julio-Claudian era, and only those who have no awareness of high-society women in such contexts are likely to mistake their portraits as mere rhetoric or a male-prejudiced stereotype.

His *Histories*, describing events from 69 to 96, were the first of the long works to be finished, with their brilliant sense of the soldiers' varying reactions and the differing styles of the crowds who participated in the year of Four Emperors (AD 69). The *Annals*, from 14 to 68, followed next. The date of the *Annals*' completion continues to be disputed, but the clear sign is that they too were composed entirely in the reign of Trajan. Their terse, mordant style needed no long gestation: Sallust and Cicero had been the staples of Tacitus' education as a young man. He was not writing them with one eye on Hadrian and the controversial early years of Hadrian's reign: the work had already been finished under Trajan. Perhaps it was the appearance of each of Tacitus' masterpieces which prompted Suetonius to attempt his own *Lives* of past rulers, beginning, however, with the life of Julius Caesar, whom Tacitus did not discuss.

Like Suetonius and Pliny, Tacitus considered Christianity to be a 'pernicious superstition'. He observed, however, that people pitied those Christians whom Nero martyred on a false charge. Suetonius, by contrast, thought that Nero had been right. For Tacitus, rule by a 'First Citizen' was an evil, but in some ways an inevitable evil. By being moderate, 'civil' and law-abiding, the ruler could mitigate the evil, but the loser would always be sturdy liberty. Aspects of this liberty could still be defended, especially the liberty of free speech: speakers in Tacitus' *Annals* put the decisive case against repressive censorship, a case which Tacitus himself endorses. So, too, laws (he realizes) will never succeed in confining luxury: the standards of luxury simply change and evolve, with the passing of time. Yet neither his own nor his speakers' conception of liberty is our idea of democratic freedom. They were Romans, after all, and they were senators. When the crafty Tiberius sat in on trials and expressed his own wishes concerning them, his conduct was regrettable to Tacitus, even when Tiberius' preferred verdicts were the true and just ones. For Tiberius was undermining a different liberty: the freedom of senators to exert influence on others' behalf, even if, as true Romans, they used that influence most unfairly.

HADRIAN: A RETROSPECTIVE

*That joke of his in the baths became famous. Once, he saw a veteran sol-
dier whom he had known during his military service, and the man was
rubbing his back and the rest of his body against the wall. So he asked
him why he had given himself over to its marbles in order to be rubbed
down, and when he heard that he was doing it because he did not have a
slave, he gave the man both some slaves and the cost of their maintenance. But on another day, a number of old men started to rub themselves
against the wall so as to provoke the emperor's generosity. But he ordered
them to be summoned and then to rub each other down in turn.*

Spartianus, *Life of Hadrian* 17.6–7

THE RIGHTS OF HADRIAN's accession were questionable, but he was
quick to undo his predecessor's mistakes. Trajan's attempted conquests in the Middle East were abandoned. Then his conquests in eastern
Europe were scaled down and reorganized. Hadrian quoted old Cato in
support: 'they must have their freedom because they cannot be protected.'[1] At least the remark gave his decision a 'traditional' precedent.

More to the point, Hadrian had close personal ties with the prefect of
the Praetorian guards, the elderly Acilius Attianus, who came from the
same home town and had been his guardian as a young man. Back in
Rome, four senior senators, all of them ex-consuls, were put to death on
Attianus' orders. While the shock subsided it was as well that Hadrian
could travel slowly through the Greek East and not return to Rome for
several months. On his arrival, he insisted in a speech to the Senate that
the four men had not been killed on his orders. In his autobiography, at
the end of his life, he stated again that he regretted these four executions.
But by now they were a pattern, as was the guards' involvement, which

marked the loss of liberty since the fall of the Republic and the 'classical' age of Augustus' rule.

It was, then, instead of conquering that Hadrian took up touring and inspecting on the Empire-wide journeys with which this book began. From northern Britain to Egypt, he visited his provinces and made himself known to his troops. Nobody who saw or heard him could have missed the differences from his predecessor Trajan. Hadrian chose to have a beard, a short trim one, but it came to be seen as a deliberate sign of his passion for Greek culture. Although beards were the particular fashion of Greek-speaking philosophers, Hadrian himself was not a real intellectual. Unlike Trajan he did have an informed mind but he liked to show it off at intellectuals' expense. He did not like abstract ideas and reasoning and he had no theoretical views on politics and society: his preferred 'philosophy' was the least intellectual, Epicureanism. Instead, he had a wide range of learning, and his passion for antiquarian details was supported by his wide travels. He also had a taste for writing poetry and a keen interest in architecture and design. When he tried to interfere with plans of the architect Apollodorus, the master is said to have told him to confine himself to drawing 'still lives', not buildings.[2] But Hadrian was certainly a 'man of taste'.

In this taste, the two worlds of this book, the classical Greek and the Roman, came closely together. Hadrian's love of Greek culture is evident in his patronage, his favours for Greek cities (especially Athens) and his personal romantic life. Trajan's patronage had already helped Greek-speakers from the East into the Roman Senate, but they tended to be dynasts and men from grandiose local families. The Greek senators in Hadrian's reign were abler men from educated and lettered Greek families: they were the sort of people he liked. For the city of Athens, Hadrian had enormous respect. Before his accession he had spent a year in the city and served as its senior magistrate; it became the centre of his new Greek synod, the Panhellenion; it received such notable buildings that its town-centre was transformed. As emperor, he approved a new structure for its council, the august Areopagus; wearing Greek dress, he presided over the city's great theatrical festival, the Dionysia, and he was initiated into the Mysteries.

His love-life was more remarkable than any ruler's since Alexander the Great. Trajan had had sexual affairs with males, but mostly (it was said) with boys in the army-camp or on his staff: Hadrian, by contrast, had a grand passion which was lived out in the Greek style and involved that un-Roman object, a free-born young man. In Pliny's former province in

70. Relief of Hadrian's beloved Antinous,
deified, from near Lanuvium in Italy.

north-west Asia, Hadrian encountered the young Antinous and fell madly
in love. They hunted together; they travelled, but in October 130 young
Antinous died in Egypt, drowned in the river Nile. For want of evidence
the circumstances remain obscure. It is probably only gossip that Antinous had voluntarily killed himself as a votive offering for Hadrian's own
poor health. But the effects of his loss are visible far and wide. Not only
did Hadrian found a town near the Nile in his lover's honour: prominent
citizens of this new Antinoopolis enjoyed an array of rare civic privileges
and exemptions.[3] He encouraged the worship of his dead lover as a 'new
Osiris', the Egyptian god of rebirth. He promoted worship of Antinous in
towns throughout his Empire. Images of him, therefore, have been discovered far beyond Egypt. Whereas Alexander promoted cult of the dead
Hephaestion as a hero, Hadrian promoted the dead Antinous as a god,

the most positive religious policy of any Roman emperor until the Christians' dominance.

Hadrian's love of Greek culture was classicizing because it imitated a classical model but was pursued without the political context of a classical Greek city-state. It also proved to be less flexible. In sculpture, Hadrian's classicizing taste is still most evident. He favoured statues of white marble, not just for his beloved Antinous, and patronized many sculptors from the big city-centres of Greek western Asia, giving a new prominence to classicism in sculpture at Rome. There was also a rigidity in his cultural tolerance. From Homer onwards, one classical Greek inclination had been to understand foreign non-Greeks as being more like their Greek 'kinsmen' than they really were. Even so, the best-known Greek travellers, Herodotus or Alexander the Great, had not been cultural relativists for whom all customs everywhere were equally valid. Herodotus had been disgusted by the alleged prostitution of Babylonian women, Alexander by the Iranians' very non-Greek habit of exposing their dead to wild birds and dogs: he banned the practice. But for Hadrian, the classicizing Greekling, the boundaries of cultural tolerance were much more tightly drawn. His classicizing world-view could not accommodate the Jews.

We still do not have enough evidence to be sure of the origins of his major war against the Jews in Judaea (from 132 to 135). Unlike a truly classical Greek, he was heir to a tradition of anti-Semitism, passed on in literature since its Greek originators in Alexandria, especially since the second century BC. The year of Antinous' death (130) does show signs of being a turning point in Hadrian's own behaviour. Ancient sources do connect the major uprising among the Jews with Hadrian's decision, while in the Near East, to ban circumcision (a classicizing Greekling would find it an offensive habit). He even planned to turn Jerusalem into a classicizing city with pagan temples and to name it Aelia (after himself) Capitolina (after the Romans' great Jupiter of the Capitol hill). The result was a bitter rebellion, led in Judaea by Bar Kochva ('son of a star') which cost the lives of hundreds of thousands of Jews during more than three years. From the Jews' own coins, we learn that the 'redemption' and 'freedom' of Israel were publicly proclaimed: Bar Kochva was probably seen as a Messiah.[4] Hadrian had to send for one of his best generals, all the way from Britain, in order to defeat what was evidently a massive challenge. Only then did he have his way, turning Jerusalem into a pagan city and banning the surviving Jews from entering it. 'What has Athens to do with Jerusalem?' the early Christian author Tertullian was soon to ask, challenging the link between classical Greek culture and Christianity.[5] For Hadrian, the answer was simple: intolerance, and total destruction.

Like Alexander the Great and his Successors, Hadrian was also a passionate hunter, the sport which he most enjoyed in life. In north-west Asia, he founded a city to commemorate his killing of a she-bear in the wild; in Egypt, he and darling Antinous killed a lion. At Rome, eight round sculpted reliefs portrayed Hadrian's great hunting moments on a building which was probably begun as a special hunting-monument.[6] But Hadrian was not just being philhellenic: hunting was part of a wider culture which cannot be split into 'Greek' or 'Roman' elements. It had already been championed by Trajan, another man from that paradise for the sport, Spain. Hadrian would surely have enjoyed it in Italy long before going east. The long days which he spent on it helped to shape his varied unintellectual gifts: his notable endurance on horseback in all weathers and his conspicuous openness to the company of his fellow men.[7]

These manners linked him commendably to the difficult question of 'luxury'. As an emperor, Hadrian had the power and the money to gratify almost any personal taste, but nonetheless he cultivated the civility which befitted a 'good emperor'. In the city of Rome, on his travels and especially in front of his troops, he showed a popular plainness and openness. This accessibility had been a virtue in Greek tradition, but it was as a Roman soldier and traveller and, above all, as a hunter that Hadrian maintained it as his style. He was said to be the 'most self-proclaimed lover of the plebs':[8] he would receive petitioners while in the bath; he would even bathe with the plebs in the public baths, no doubt in Trajan's vast new establishment in Rome. In the army-camps, too, he set a personal example of austerity and disdain for comfort. He consumed the cheese, bacon and coarse wine which belonged in a proper soldier's diet. He avoided soft bedding, restoring standards of military discipline which were still being cited long after him.

In Homer's poems, our starting point, luxury was admired unreservedly as the splendour of the heroes' palaces and the fairytale kings whom wandering Odysseus met. It first became problematic for the early Greek aristocrats who feared it as a source of disruptive competition from the seventh century BC onwards. Philosophers then idealized 'austerity' against the 'softness' of luxurious Asia and its kings, a view which the puritanical Plato supported. After Alexander, nonetheless, the Greek kings, especially those in Egypt, exploited 'luxury' as part of their royal image and their fantasy 'world apart'. There was so much more now worldwide for them to want, acquire and display.

At Rome, these attitudes converged and became one of straightforward disapproval. Opposition to monarchy had been rooted in the Republic and its ruling class from its very origins: royal luxury was out of the question. In the ideal peer group of free senators, 'luxury' was morally disreputable and socially disruptive. Together, this heritage persisted after the ending of Cicero's world and was maintained in the early Empire and its increasingly unclassical culture: it belonged with the emperor's public image of restoration and moral 'back-to-basics'. So Hadrian, too, limited expenses on public banquets to the 'levels prescribed by ancient laws'. But public munificence had not been a bad sort of luxury: Hadrian also gave public beast-shows and days of human blood sports, setting a scale which made even Julius Caesar's seem limited. To enhance his marginal links with the previous dynasty, he built vast public monuments to family members, including women, and a big Mausoleum in Rome (the modern Castel Sant'Angelo), outdoing even Augustus. In Trajan's honour, he even had all the seats in the theatre washed with the most expensive of floral extracts, oil from the saffron-crocus, a gift which would have needed whole hillsides of these flowers to meet the demand. And in later life he withdrew more and more to his enormous villa at Tibur (modern Tivoli), which had no less than three sets of heated baths and a canal named after the notoriously luxurious Canopus, the waterway which ran beside Egypt's Alexandria. The visible, sprawling ruins of this villa are less than half of its probable extent: the rest still waits to be excavated.

'Luxury' had always promoted a gap between practice and public profession. By Hadrian's reign, it connected with changes in the scope of 'justice' and 'freedom'. In our collection of Roman legal opinions, Hadrian's own rulings survive identifiably; so does a collection, probably authentic, of the 'opinions' which he gave in answer to requests. In the history of Roman law, it is Hadrian who patronized a codification of the long-running edict of the annual praetors and saw that it was published in an agreed form.[9] Much of our inscribed record of his reign around the Empire is the record of his judging and deciding petitions and local disputes. In Italy, he even appointed four ex-consuls to judge cases submitted to them. When hearing cases himself, Hadrian was particularly remembered for including specialized experts in law as his advisers.

This body of advice, writings and tribunals may seem very far removed from the giving of justice in the distant world of Homer and Hesiod. In the Roman Empire, judges were literate; textbooks and copies of previous rulings existed; complex distinctions of procedure and civil law underlay what Hadrian decided. Yet in another way the distance travelled was no longer so very large. As in the Homeric world, justice was being rendered by an individual's inquisition, which was not subject to the decisions of a jury. This change in the structure of jurisdiction had re-entered the classical world with the rise of King Philip and the age of monarchy. The randomly selected juries of classical democratic Athens were no longer the main type of public adjudication. There was also another telling change. In Hadrian's reign a frank distinction between the 'more respectable' and the 'more humble' begins to be stated, for the first time in Roman legal texts.[10] The 'more respectable' included army-veterans, but also those with the rank (to be paid for) of city-councillor, let alone the Roman knights and senators. The 'more humble' extended down to property-less vagrants and below. For the same crimes, these two social orders were now to be liable to different punishments: there was to be no flogging, no torture for respectable citizens, and no beheading, crucifixion or deportation, either. Previously, protection from these extreme penalties had been linked to possession of Roman citizenship and was founded on that cardinal principle of Roman liberty, the right to 'call out' or appeal. Now a 'humble' Roman citizen was liable to the most brutal penalties like any one else of low status, as if his citizenship carried no privilege. Respectable persons were protected because they were respectable, whether citizens or not.

Hadrian did not initiate this distinction, but in his reign there began to be explicitly 'one penalty for the rich, one for the poor'. This development had older roots in Roman practice, and the punishment of lower-class citizens in Cicero's Rome may also have been as savage as it now became. But the distinction was now in writing, and to many Romans (including Pliny) it was not even unjust. For 'fair justice', such people thought, was proportional, varying according to the class and worth of the recipient. Homer's Odysseus, speaking moderately to his fellow nobles and thumping the lower classes with his sceptre, is no longer very far away.

This frank calibration of justice by social status devalued Roman citizenship and went with a change in the scope of freedom. In Homer's poems, 'freedom' had been freedom from enslavement or conquest, individual or collective. In classical Athens, it became the freedom of democracy, the freedom of the male citizens 'to do whatever they decide', with accompanying notions of their personal 'freedom from' undue influence. In the Roman Republic, founded by ending a monarchy, 'freedom

71. Replica statue of a beardless warrior, probably a Greek hero, not a war god, by the 'Canopus' canal, Hadrian's villa at Tivoli, *c.* AD 135.

from' one-man rule was historically a very strong value, together with the popular notion of a freedom which was 'freedom from' harassment by social superiors and the senators' notions of 'freedom for' their senatorial order to say or do what it wanted. Under the emperors' rule, freedom, as the opposite to slavery, was still prized in Rome's slave-society, as it had been prized everywhere else in the classical world. But from the years of Augustus' dominance onwards, only 'traces' (as Tacitus stressed) remained of the senators' particular 'freedom', and throughout the Empire, the 'freedom' of cities and popular assemblies had become a matter only of degree. Under Hadrian, his beloved Athens was still called a 'free city', but it honoured him, the emperor, as an Olympian god. On the Greek island of Lesbos, inscriptions honoured Hadrian as a 'liberator' while also paying him divine honours.[11] The former 'freedom' of Athens and Sparta, so Pliny observed, was now only a 'shadow': in general, Roman rule had curbed or abolished democracies and popular rule in the Greek subject-cities. At Rome, meanwhile, the 'resolutions' of the Senate had acquired the force of law, because they communicated the emperor's own considered wish or even, in due course, the very words of his speech. In AD 129 the consuls 'brought forward a bill, based on a paper of Imperator Caesar Hadrian Augustus, son of Trajan Parthicus, grandson of the deified Nerva, greatest First Citizen, father of the state, on 3 March . . . '.[12] The result passed into our Roman law-books. The 'First Citizen', who initiated it, was himself now 'released from the laws', a status which was justified (for legal minds) by the law which had set out the Emperor Vespasian's powers.

'Liberty' of speech and decision, as Cicero had known it, was now dead. While in Greece, in his mid-twenties, Hadrian had been one of the many hearers of a noted teacher, Epictetus.[13] Epictetus was himself the ex-slave of a freedman in the emperor's household: he discoursed on freedom, justice and moderation to large audiences, people who were mostly drawn from the respectable young men of cities in the Greek-speaking world. Epictetus taught the doctrine of Stoic philosophers which had been formulated in the decade after Alexander and was known, too, to Cicero and his contemporaries. For Epictetus, 'freedom' was an individual's reasoned control of his desires and passions. A rich man, torn by fears and wants, was therefore as much, even more, of a 'slave' as any slave in the real world. Epictetus' surviving teachings never even mention his own experience of slavery in his youth. Rather, with first-hand illustrations, he spoke of the court-life around a Roman emperor as 'futile' slavery.

In the classical Greek world, the freedom which had belonged with the greatest cultural expression was the freedom of democratic citizens, the political freedom of a male majority which was limited only by decisions to which they themselves consented. In Hadrian's world, freedom had become only a freedom from bad, cruel emperors or the unpolitical 'freedom' of an individual's control over his desires. From an admired teacher, Epictetus, Hadrian had heard what Pericles or Alexander never heard from theirs, that a public career at the centre of power was a dangerous, disturbing vanity and that its public honours were futile.

As a many-sided man, Hadrian would not have forgotten this view of the world which he dominated. But it was only one view, in a mind which entertained so many others. At his huge villa at Tibur, Hadrian could walk through monuments named after great places in the classical Greek world: there was a Lyceum and an Academy, places where Socrates, Plato and Aristotle had taught, a Tempe where the Muses had once played, and a Prytaneum, where the free councillors of Greek democracies had typically dined and attended to public business. In the gardens of his villa, Hadrian even had a so-called 'underworld', a representation of Hades: it is probably still to be seen in some of the underground tunnels on the site. His own tastes in philosophy were for the Epicurean school, for whom the fear of death was an unwarranted 'disturbance' and the tales of an afterlife only fables for the superstitious masses.

From his provinces, Hadrian had already answered requests about the persecution of a most 'wicked superstition', the beliefs held by members of the Christian churches. Hadrian's answers continued to insist that trials must involve individual prosecutors, people who would bring formal charges in public against these Christians. Contrary to the wishes of some leading provincials, he thus insisted that the persecution of Christians must be a formal process, to be publicly pursued with rules. By his judgements, his letters and his edicts, it was Hadrian who now made the laws by which justice was done. As emperor, he was freed from the laws; as an educated man, he was personally free from fears of the underworld. Nonetheless, in a famous poem, he addressed consolatory words to his 'little soul', a future wanderer in a chilly and humourless afterlife. Long centuries of change in the scope of justice, freedom and luxury lay behind Hadrian's outlook from his villa garden. But he had no idea that the Christians, whose harassment he regulated, would then overturn this world by antiquity's greatest realignment of freedom and justice: the 'underworld' would no longer be a garden-designer's fancy.

NOTES

HADRIAN AND THE CLASSICAL WORLD

1. Aulus Gellius, 19.8.5.

2. J. M. C. Toynbee, *The Hadrianic School: A Chapter in the History of Greek Art* (1934).

3. A. Spawforth, S. Walker, in *Journal of Roman Studies* (1985), 78–104, and (1986), 88–105, are still the fundamental studies.

4. *Corpus Inscriptionum Latinarum*, 12.1122.

5. Josephus, *Jewish War* 2.385.

6. *Historia Augusta*, Life of Hadrian 12.6.

7. Tertullian, *Apology* 5.7.

8. William J. Macdonald, John A. Pinto, *Hadrian's Villa and Its Legacy* (1995).

9. R. Syme, *Fictional History Old and New: Hadrian* (1986, lecture), 20–21: 'the notion that Hadrian, if anything, was an Epicurean may engender disquiet or annoyance.' So far, it has not.

10. Sophocles, *Antigone* 821.

11. F. D. Harvey, in *Classica et Mediaevalia* (1965), 101–46.

12. Mary T. Boatwright, *Hadrian and the Cities of the Roman Empire* (2000), an excellent study whose bibliography is important for this book.

13. Naphtali Lewis, in *Greek, Roman and Byzantine Studies* (1991), 267–80, with the history of the scholarly debate over authenticity.

14. G. Daux, in *Bulletin de Correspondance Hellénique* (1970), 609–18, and in *Ancient Macedonia II*, Institute for Balkan Studies number 155 (1977), 320–23.

CHAPTER 1. HOMERIC EPIC

1. L. Godart, A. Sacconi, in *Comptes Rendus de L'Académie des Inscriptions et Belles Lettres* (1998), 889–906, and (2001), 527–46.

2. S. Mitchell, in *Journal of Roman Studies* (1990), 184–5, translating lines 40ff. of C. Julius Demosthenes' inscription at Oenoanda (AD 124).

3. Homer, *Iliad* 6.528 and *Odyssey* 17.323.

4. Homer, *Iliad* 2.270.

5. Ibid. 16.384–92.

6. Ibid. 18.507–8.

Chapter 2. The Greeks' Settlements

1. M. H. Hansen, in M. H. Hansen (ed.), *A Comparative Study of Thirty City-state Cultures* (2000), 142–86, at 146.

2. W. D. Niemeier, in *Aegaeum* (1999), 141–55.

3. J. D. Hawkins, in *Anatolian Studies* (2000), 1–31.

4. Plutarch, *Greek Questions* 11.

5. Pliny, *Natural History* 19.10–11.

6. S. Amigues, in *Revue Archéologique* (1988), 227.

7. S. Amigues, in *Journal des Savants* (2004), 191–226, contesting the recently revived identification with *Cachrys ferulacea*.

8. Diodorus, 13.81.5 and 83.3.

9. T. J. Dunbabin, *The Western Greeks* (1948), 77 and 365.

10. P. A. Hansen (ed.), *Carmina Epigraphica Graeca*, Volume I (1983), number 400: Robert Parker kindly cited this for me.

11. J. Reynolds, in *Journal of Roman Studies* (1978), 113, lines 2–12, and, for the local side to it, see A. J. Spawforth and Susan Walker, ibid. (1986), 98–101, a fascinating study.

Chapter 3. Aristocrats

1. Hesiod, *Theogony* 80–93 and *Works and Days* 39.

2. Aristotle, *Politics* 1306A 15–20.

3. Homer, *Iliad* 3.222.

4. O. Murray, in *Apoikia: scritti in onore di Giorgio Buchner*, AION n.s. 1 (1994), 47–54, for this dating.

5. M. Vickers, *Greek Symposia* (Joint Association of Classical Teachers, London, n.d.).

6. L. Foxhall, in Lynette G. Mitchell and P. J. Rhodes (eds.), *The Development of the Polis in Archaic Greece* (1997), 130, gives calculations, perhaps on the high end of the scale.

7. Jacob Burckhardt, *The Greeks and Greek Civilization*, abridged and translated by Sheila Stern (1998), 179. I incline to his view, which is still controversial.

8. H. W. Pleket, in Peter Garnsey, Keith Hopkins and C. R. Whittaker (eds.), *Trade in the Ancient Economy* (1983), 131–44, the model which essentially I follow on this vexed question throughout this book.

Chapter 4. The Immortal Gods

1. Homer, *Iliad* 23.75–6 and 100.

2. Homeric *Hymn to Apollo* 189–93.

3. Erich Csapo, *Theories of Mythology* (2005), 165–71.

4. Robert Parker, in J. Boardman, J. Griffin and O. Murray (eds.), *The Oxford History of the Classical World* (1986), 266.

5. Homer, *Odyssey* 11.241–4.

6. Ibid. 11.251 and Homeric *Hymn to Aphrodite* 286–9, with P. Maas, *Kleine Schriften* (1973), 66–7, implying the gods make love only to virgins. But Helen's mother Leda was not one.

7. Prices from Attic data only, in M. H. Jameson, in *Proceedings of the Cambridge Philological Society*, supplementary volume 14 (1988), 91.

8. Hesiod, *Theogony* 418–52 with M. L. West's *Commentary* (1971 edn.), 276–91.

9. Homeric *Hymn to Apollo* 390–end, with the remarkable study by W. G. Forrest, in *Bulletin de Correspondance Hellénique* (1956), 33–52.

10. Adrienne Mayor, in *Archaeology* 28 (1999), 32–40.

11. W. G. Forrest, in *Historia* (1959), 174.

CHAPTER 5. TYRANTS AND LAWGIVERS

1. Hesiod, *Works and Days* 225–37.

2. Chester G. Starr, *The Origins of Greek Civilization* (1962), part III, for the phrase I reapply here.

3. *Anthologia Palatina* 14.93.

4. Solon F36 (West).

5. Solon F4 (West), line 18.

6. Solon F36 (West).

7. R. F. Willetts, *The Law Code of Gortyn* (1967), with a possible translation; A. L. Di Lello-Finuoli, in D. Musti (ed.), *La transizione dal Miceneo all'Arcaismo . . . Roma, 14–19 Marzo, 1988* (1991), 215–30; K. R. Kristensen, in *Classica et Medievalia* (1994), 5–26.

8. E. Lévy, in P. Brulé and J. Oulken (eds.), *Esclavage, guerre, économie en Grèce ancienne: Hommages à Yvon Garlan* (1997), 25–41, is fundamental here.

9. Aristotle, *Athenaion Politeia* 7.3–4; on the (non-numerical) classes, see (correctly) G. E. M. de Sainte Croix, *Athenian Democratic Origins* (2004), 5–72; I must stress that the '300' and '200' measures for hippeis and zeugites are only an Aristotelian guess (*eulogotera*) and are not historical. *Zeugitai*, like (e.g.) *boarii* in early medieval law-codes, owned oxen; hippeis owned horses. It is unfortunate that these Aristotelian guesses are too often taken as key 'statistical' sources for the archaic state's economy and land-holdings.

10. Pausanias, 6.4.8.

11. Aelian, *Varia Historia* 2.29.

CHAPTER 6. SPARTA

1. J. Reynolds, in *Journal of Roman Studies* (1978), 113, lines 39–43; Paul Cartledge and Antony Spawforth, *Hellenistic and Roman Sparta* (1992 edn.), 113.

2. A. Andrewes, *Probouleusis: Sparta's Contribution to the Technique of Government* (1954).

3. Plutarch, *Greek Questions* 4, with G. Grote, *A History of Greece*, volume II (1888, revised edn.), 266 and note 2 for the relevance of it at 'Laconian' Cnidus.

4. Homer, *Odyssey* 17.487; A. Andrewes, in *Classical Quarterly* (1938), 89–91.

5. Terpander in Plutarch, *Life of Lycurgus* 21.4.

6. Mucianus, cited in Pliny, *Natural History* 19.12.

CHAPTER 7. THE EASTERN GREEKS

1. Homeric *Hymn to Apollo* 146–55.

2. Herodotus, 2.152.4.

3. Sappho F 39 (Diehl), with (independently of mine) the fine observations by John Raven, *Plants and Plant Lore in Ancient Greece* (2000), 9.

4. J. D. P. Bolton, *Aristeas* (1962), a brilliant study, although his pp. 8–10 take a more cautious view of Longinus, *On the Sublime* 10.4 (his F7, p. 208).

5. Text of the Oath in Loeb Library, *Hippocrates*, volume I, translated by W. H. S. Jones (1933), 298, with Vivian Nutton, *Hippocratic Morality and Modern Medicine*, in *Entretiens de la Fondation Hardt*, volume XLIII (1997), 31–63.

6. Athenaeus, *Deipnosophistae* 12.541A, Ps.-Aristotle, *De Mirabilibus* 96 and the brilliant study by J. Heurgon, *Scripta Varia* (1986), 299.

7. Herodotus, 1.164.3.

CHAPTER 8. TOWARDS DEMOCRACY

1. Herodotus, 1.152.3.

2. P. A. Cartledge, *Agesilaos* (1987), 10–11.

3. A. Andrewes, *The Greek Tyrants* (1956), chapter VI, for this fine phrase.

4. Herodotus, 5.72.2, with P. J. Rhodes, *Ancient Democracy and Modern Ideology* (2003), 112–13 and notes 17 and 19.

5. Mogens H. Hansen, *The Athenian Democracy in the Age of Demosthenes* (1991), 220.

6. Herodotus, 5.78.1; E. Badian (ed.), *Ancient Society and Institutions: Studies Presented to V. Ehrenberg* (1966), 115.

7. Herodotus, 5.73.3.

CHAPTER 9. THE PERSIAN WARS

1. Herodotus, 1.212–14.

2. Ibid. 1.153.1–2.

3. Section 8 of the Naqsh-i-Rustam DN-b text, as rendered in P. Briant, *From Cyrus to Alexander*, translated by Peter T. Daniels (2002), 212.

4. J. S. Morrison, J. F. Coates and N. B. Rankov, *The Athenian Trireme* (2000, rev. edn.), 250 and 252.

5. Herodotus, 6.112.3.

6. V. D. Hanson, *The Western Way of War* (1989), 158 and 175, also now in Hans van Wees, *Greek Warfare* (2004), 184.

7. Homer, *Iliad* 2.872.

8. Found by M. H. Jameson and concisely discussed in R. Meiggs and D. M. Lewis, *A Selection of Greek Historical Inscriptions* (1988 edn.), number 23.

9. R. Étienne and M. Piérart, in *Bulletin de Correspondance Hellénique* (1975), 51.

10. Deborah Boedeker and David Sider (eds.), *The New Simonides* (1996).

11. Angelos P. Matthaiou, in Peter Derow and Robert Parker (eds.), *Herodotus and His World* (2003), 190–202.

12. Herodotus, 8.83.

CHAPTER 10. THE WESTERN GREEKS

1. Pindar, *Pythian* 1.75.

2. *Historia Augusta*, Life of Hadrian 13.3.

3. Ps.-Plato, *Seventh Letter* 326B.

4. Pindar, *Olympian* 5.13–14.

5. T. J. Dunbabin, *The Western Greeks* (1948), p. vii.

6. F. Cordano, *Le tessere pubbliche dal tempio di Atena a Camarina* (1992); O. Murray, in Mogens H. Hansen (ed.), *The Polis as an Urban Centre and as a Political Community: Acts of the Copenhagen Polis Centre*, volume IV (1997), 493–504.

7. Michael H. Jameson, David R. Jordan and Roy D. Kotansky, *A Lex Sacra from Selinous* (1993).

8. Pindar, F106 (Maehler): I owe this to P. J. Wilson.

9. Herodotus, 7.164.1.

10. A. Giovannini, 'Le Sel et la fortune de Rome', in *Athenaeum* (1985), 373–87, a brilliant study.

11. Livy, 3.31.8, with R.M. Ogilvie, *A Commentary on Livy, Books 1–5* (1965), 449–50, for the variants and a sceptical view.

CHAPTER 11. CONQUEST AND EMPIRE

1. Herodotus, 5.92 on *isokratia*.

2. Pindar, *Pythian* 7.18–19.

3. Herodotus, 8.124.3.

4. Pliny, *Natural History* 18.144.

5. Thucydides, 2.65.2 is important here; A. G. Geddes, in *Classical Quarterly* (1987), 307–31, for the problematic question of dress.

6. Thucydides, 2.63.2 and 3.37.2.

CHAPTER 12. A CHANGING GREEK CULTURAL WORLD

1. Hippocrates, *Epidemics* 1.1; Jean Pouilloux, *Recherches sur l'histoire et les cultes de Thasos*, volume I (1954), 249–50 is crucial for the dating, but I identify the mention of the 'new wall' with Thasos' new wall built by the 460s, and I keep Polygnotus and therefore 'Antiphon, son of Critoboulus' up in the 460s too. I acknowledge many discussions of this rare point with the late D. M. Lewis, who agreed.

2. Herodotus, 3.80.3.

3. J. S. Morrison, J. F. Coates and N. B. Rankov, *The Athenian Trireme* (2000), 238.

4. Athenaeus, 14.619A, with Walter Scheidel, in *Greece and Rome* (1996), 1.

5. Ps.-Demosthenes, 59.122.

6. Ps.-Xenophon, *Constitution of the Athenians* 3.2 and 3.8.

7. David Harvey and John Wilkins, *The Rivals of Aristophanes* (2000).

8. Alberto Cesare Cassio, in *Classical Quarterly* (1985), 38–42.

CHAPTER 13. PERICLES AND ATHENS

1. H. L. Hudson-Williams, in *Classical Quarterly* (1951), 68–73, on 'pamphlets'; Harvey Yunis (ed.), *Written Texts and the Rise of Literate Culture in Ancient Greece* (2003), has all the bibliography.

2. Thucydides, 2.65.9.

3. Ion, in Plutarch, *Life of Pericles* 5.3.

4. Plato, *Menexenus*, with the comic Callias F15 (Kock), for this sort of joke.

5. Plutarch, *Life of Pericles* 24.9.

6. Ibid. 8.7.

7. Glenn R. Bugh, *The Horsemen of Athens* (1988), 52–78.

8. Thucydides, 2.41.4.

9. J. M. Mansfield, '*The Robe of Athena and the Panathenaic Peplos*' (Dissertation, Univ. of California, Berkeley 1985), supplementing D. M. Lewis, *Selected Papers in Greek and Near Eastern History* (1997), 131–2.

10. Aeneas Tacticus, 31.24.

11. Thucydides, 2.40.2.

12. Plutarch, *Life of Pericles* 3.5 and 13.5, with Anthony J. Podlecki, *Perikles and His Circle* (1998), 172, citing A. L. Robkin for the view I, too, have always preferred.

CHAPTER 14. THE PELOPONNESIAN WAR

1. M. H. Jameson, in R. G. Osborne and S. Hornblower (eds.), *Ritual, Finance and Politics* (1994), 307.

2. Thucydides, 3.36.6; 5.16.1; 8.73.3; 8.97.2.

3. Xenophon, *Hellenica* 2.3.39; Thucydides, 7.86.5.

4. Thucydides, 1.22.3.

5. Thucydides, 2.27.1, whereas Herodotus, 6.91.1, adduces a religious explanation.

CHAPTER 15. SOCRATES

1. Diogenes Laertius, 2.40; on the sense of '*theous nomizein*', I confess to preferring J. Tate, in *Classical Review* (1936), 3 and (1937), 3.

2. Xenophon, *Symposium* 2.10.

3. Aristophanes, *Clouds* 1506–9.

4. Plutarch, *Life of Pericles* 32.2 with L. Woodbury, in *Phoenix* (1981), 295 and M. Ostwald, *From Popular Sovereignty to the Sovereignty of Law* (1986), 528–31.

5. Xenophon, *Symposium* 8.2.

CHAPTER 16. FIGHTING FOR FREEDOM AND JUSTICE

1. Plutarch, *Life of Lysander* 30.3–5.

2. Diodorus, 15.54.3; Xenophon, *Hellenica* 6.4.7; Plutarch, *Life of Pelopidas* 20.4–21.1; Plutarch, *Moralia* 856F; Pausanias, 9.13.5.

3. K. J. Dover, *Greek Homosexuality* (1978), 190–94.

4. Xenophon, *Hellenica* 7.5.27.

CHAPTER 17. WOMEN AND CHILDREN

1. John M. Oakley, in Jenifer Neils and John H. Oakley, *Coming of Age in Ancient Greece: Images of Childhood from the Classical Past* (2003), 174, and catalogue 115, on pp. 162 and 174.

2. Aeschines, 3.77–8.

3. D. Ogden, *Greek Bastardy* (1996), 199–203.

4. Plato Comicus F143 and F188, with James Davidson, *Courtesans and Fishcakes* (1998), 118.

5. L. Llewellyn-Jones, *Aphrodite's Tortoise* (2003), is important here, citing (p. 62) Heracleides Criticus, 1.18; compare *Tanagra, mythe et archéologie*, Louvre catalogue 15 September 2003–5 January 2004 (Paris, 2003), which is excellent, especially number 101 from Athens (a veiled prostitute?).

6. *Supplementum Epigraphicum Graecum*, volume XV (1958), 384 and J. M. Hannick, in *Antiquité Classique* (1976), 133–48.

7. Justin, *Epitome* 7.5.4–9.

CHAPTER 18. PHILIP OF MACEDON

1. Arrian, *Indica* 18.6–7; on Aristotle's view, note the case advanced by P. A. Brunt, *Studies in Greek History and Thought* (1993), 334–6.

2. E. Voutiras, *Revue des Études Grecques* (1996), 678, with *Supplementum Epigraphicum Graecum*, volume XLVI (1996), 776, and volume XLIX (1999), 759.

3. Arrian, *Anabasis* 1.10.1, and Diodorus, 17.16.3, which I accept, differing from A. B. Bosworth, *Commentary on Arrian's History of Alexander*, volume I (1980), 97, who credits Arrian with an 'error'.

4. Plutarch, *Life of Alexander* 39.2–3.

5. M. W. Dickie, in *Zeitschrift für Papyrologie und Epigraphik*, 109 (1995), 81–6 and L. Rossi, ibid. 112 (1996), 59; Poseidippus F44 (ed. Austin–Bastiniani).

6. Ps.-Demosthenes, 17.15.

7. Plutarch, *Moralia* 179 C–D.

CHAPTER 19. THE TWO PHILOSOPHERS

1. Plato, *Republic* 558C; the entire section, starting at 555B, is brilliantly malign.

2. Plato, *Laws* 636B–D4; 836B8–C7; 836D9–E4; 841D4–5; G. E. M. de Sainte Croix used to lecture with great force on Plato as the first attested 'Greek homophobe', citing the *Laws*, including *Laws* 636C5 which applies, too, to 'lesbians'.

3. *Laws* 907E–910D; for 'corrective' punishment, T. J. Saunders, *Plato's Penal Code: Tradition, Controversy and Reform in Greek Penology* (1991) is a fine study.

4. Aristotle, *Meteorologica* 1.352A30, F13 (Rose), F25 (Rose), *Metaphysics* 1074 B1–14.

5. Aristotle, *History of Animals* 523A18 and *Generation of Animals* 736A11–12.

6. Aristotle, *Politics* 1254A20, explicitly appealing to 'ta gignomena' as proof that slaves exist: 'natural slavery' is not just a theoretical construct of his thinking. P. A. Brunt, *Studies in Greek History and Thought* (1993), 343–88, is the definitive study on this issue.

7. Aristotle, *Politics* 1260A12.

8. To the texts in Brunt, *Studies in Greek History and Thought*, 288–90, a sceptical view, we can add on Cotys' death, Philostratus, *Life of Apollonius* 7.2 and on Clearchus', Justin, *Epitome* 16.5.12–13, Philodemus, *Index Academicorum* 6.13 (Dorandi) and the fiction in I. Düring, *Chion of Heraclea* (1951). Memnon 434F1 (Jacoby) says Clearchus himself had 'heard Plato'.

9. Aristotle F668 (Rose).

10. Aristotle, *On the Heavens* 297A3–8.

11. Duris, in Athenaeus 12.542D; Diogenes Laertius, 5.75 (the statues); William W. Fortenbaugh and Eckart Schütrumpf, *Demetrius of Phaleron*, texts and translation (2000).

12. Diogenes Laertius, 5.38; C. Habicht, *Athens from Alexander to Antony* (1997), 73, and the fine study in his *Athen in Hellenisticher Zeit: Gesammelte Aufsätze* (1994), 231–47.

CHAPTER 20. FOURTH-CENTURY ATHENIANS

1. Jacob Burckhardt, *The Greeks and Greek Civilization*, abridged and translated by Sheila Stern (1998), 289–90.

2. Ps.-Demosthenes, 50.26.

3. G. E. M. de Sainte Croix, *Origins of the Peloponnesian War* (1972), 371–6.

4. S. Lewis, *News and Society in the Greek Polis* (1996), 102–15.

5. D. M. Lewis, *Selected Papers in Greek and Near Eastern History* (1997), 212–29.

6. J. K. Davies, in *Journal of Hellenic Studies* (1967), 33–40.

7. W. K. Pritchett, *The Greek State at War*, part V (1991), 473–85, is essential here.

8. I disagree with D. M. MacDowell, in *Classical Quarterly* (1986), 438–49 (an important paper), and incline more (but not wholly) to A. H. M. Jones, *Athenian Democracy* (1957), 28–9.

9. W. G. Arnott, in *Bulletin of the Institute of Classical Studies* (1959), 78–9.

10. Theophrastus, *Characters* 4.11, 21.5, and R. J. Lane Fox, in *Proceedings of the Cambridge Philological Society* (1996), 147, and notes 210–13.

11. Theophrastus, *Characters* 23.2, with Lane Fox, op. cit. (note 10), 147 and note 208.

12. K. Hallof and C. Habicht, in *Mitteilungen der deutschen Archäologischen Institut (Athenische Abteilung)*, 110 (1995), 273–303; *Supplementum Epigraphicum Graecum*, volume XLV (1995), 300–306.

13. Xenophon, *Ways and Means* 1.1.

14. Demosthenes, 10.36–45.

CHAPTER 21. ALEXANDER THE GREAT

1. Herodotus, 6.69.2–3; Plutarch, *Life of Lysander* 26.1; Plutarch, *Moralia* 338B. Aristander (Alexander's own *mantis*) is named in Origen, *Against Celsus* 7.8, a neglected and important citation.

2. Arrian, *Anabasis* 6.19.4.

3. Nearchus, *Indica* 40.8.

4. P. J. Rhodes and R. G. Osborne, *Greek Historical Inscriptions 404–323 BC* (2000), 433.

5. Duris, in Athenaeus, *Deipnosophistae* 4.155C.

6. Arrian, *Anabasis* 7.26.1.

CHAPTER 22. ALEXANDER'S EARLY SUCCESSORS

1. Abraham J. Sachs and Hermann Hunger, *Astronomical Diaries and Related Texts from Babylonia*, volume I (1988), 207.

2. Plutarch, *Moralia* 180D; I owe an 'empire of the best' to Guy Rogers of Wellesley College.

3. Arrian, *Anabasis* 7.12.4.

4. Diodorus, 18.4.4.

5. Plutarch, *Life of Demosthenes* 31.5.

6. W. W. Tarn, *Antigonus Gonatas* (1913), 18.

7. Libanius, *Oration* 49.12; earlier, Herodian, 4.8.9.

8. E. J. Bickermann, in E. Yarshater (ed.), *The Cambridge History of Iran*, volume III (1) (1983), 7, a brilliant overview.

9. H. W. Parke, *The Oracles of Apollo in Asia Minor* (1985), 44–55, and L. Robert, in *Bulletin de Correspondance Hellénique* (1984), 167–72.

10. Theocritus, *Idyll* 14.61.

Chapter 23. Life in the Big Cities

1. W. W. Tarn, *Antigonus Gonatas* (1913), 185 and note 60, for all the evidence.

2. P. Leriche, in *Bulletin d'Études Orientales* (2000), 99–125.

3. Diodorus, 18.70.1.

4. E. E. Rice, *The Grand Procession of Ptolemy Philadelphus* (1983) for the details; D. J. Thompson, in Leon Mooren (ed.), *Politics, Administration and Society . . . Studia Hellenistica*, 36 (2000), 365–88, particularly on the dating problem.

5. D. B. Thompson, *Troy: The Terracotta Figurines of the Hellenistic Period* (1963), 46.

6. J. D. Lerner, in *Zeitschrift für Papyrologie und Epigraphik*, 142 (2003), 45, for the papyrus and the full bibliography.

7. Dorothy Burr Thompson, *Ptolemaic Oinochoai and Portraits in Faience* (1973), 78, a superb study.

8. A controversial view, for which I can now cite the full study of P. F. Mittag, in *Historia* (2003), 162–208.

9. W. Clarysse, in L. Mooren (ed.), op. cit. (n. 4), 29–43 for these visits.

10. Maryline Parca, in L. Mooren (ed.), *Le Rôle et le statut de la femme . . .* , Studia Hellenistica 37 (2002), 283–96, for similar aggressive cases concerning women.

Chapter 24. Taxes and Technologies

1. M. I. Finley, in *Economic History Review* (1965), 35.

2. Plutarch, *Life of Marcellus* 17.5–8.

3. Seneca, *Letters* 90.25.

4. Pliny, *Natural History* 15.57.

5. P. M. Fraser, *Ptolemaic Alexandria*, Volume I (1972), 150.

6. Antipater, in *Greek (Palatine) Anthology* 9.418.

7. G. Raepsaet, in *Annales*, 50 (1995), 911–42.

Chapter 25. The New World

1. J. B. Connelly, in T. Fahd (ed.), *L'Arabie préislamique et son environnement historique et culturel* (1989), 145–58, especially 149–51.

2. Theophrastus, *'History' of Plants* 8.4.5.

3. Pytheas, F7A lines 16–20 (H. J. Mette).

4. Hippolochus' *Letter*, in Athenaeus 4.128C–130D, a marvellous text which Athenaeus already quotes as a rarely known one.

5. Theophrastus, *Hist. Plant.* 5.8.1–3, on 'Italy' and the 'land of the Latins', not fully considered by P. M. Fraser, in S. Hornblower (ed.), *Greek Historiography* (1994), 182–5; for Italy, note 2.8.1, 4.5.6 (Italia pasa); 3.17.8 (Lipari isles) and so on.

6. Theophrastus, *Hist. Plant.* 7.11.4.

7. P. M. Fraser, in *Afghan Studies*, 3–4 (1982) 53, where 'Alexandreusin en astois' (obviously acceptable wording for a verse-dedication, not a civic decree) should, *pace* Fraser, be restored.

8. Diodorus, 1.74; P. M. Fraser, *Ptolemaic Alexandria*, volume I (1972), 502: 'that is the voice of the anti-democratic Greek as it may be heard at any time in the fifth and fourth centuries BC.'

9. I suspect the 'Callaneus' in the Milesian 'parapegma' (Diels–Rehm no. 456A) really is our 'Calanos': text in Liba Taub, *Ancient Meteorology* (2003), 248.

10. Aristobulus, in Strabo, 15.1.62, amplified by Onesicritus, in Strabo, 15.1.30 and then Diodorus, 19.33; I differ from A. B. Bosworth, *Legacy of Alexander* (2002), 181–4.

11. Edict 13, in Beni Mahab Barun, *Inscriptions of Asoka* (1990, 2nd edn.).

12. Heraclides Ponticus, 840F23 (Jacoby) with Fraser, op. cit. (note 5), 186–7.

Chapter 26. Rome Reaches Out

1. A. Erskine, *Troy between Greece and Rome* (2001), 131–56, with 149 note 81.

2. J. G. Pedley, *Paestum* (1990), 120–25; E. Dench, *From Barbarians to New Men* (1995), 64–6; M. W. Frederiksen, *Dialoghi di archeologia* (1968), 3–23.

3. Aristotle, in Plutarch, *Life of Camillus* 22.3; T. J. Cornell, *The Beginnings of Rome* (1995), 315–18, for variants; N. Horsfall, in *Classical Journal* (1981), 298–311.

4. Diodorus, 14.93.4.

5. Pliny, *Natural History* 34.26, with Dench, *From Barbarians*, 62, notes 142–3.

6. Polybius, 3.22; Diodorus, 16.69.1 and Livy, 7.27.2; Livy, 9.43.12; I accept all three and put Polybius' second treaty in the 340s; for the debate, Cornell, *Beginnings of Rome*, 210–14.

7. Duris, 76 (Jacoby) F 56.

8. David Potter, in Harriet I. Flower (ed.), *The Cambridge Companion to the Roman Republic* (2004), 66–88 is a very important rethink of these issues.

9. M. H. Crawford, *Roman Statutes*, volume II (1996), 579–703.

10. A. W. Lintott, in *Aufstieg und Niedergang der Römischen Welt*, volume I.ii (1972), 226–67.

11. Livy, 3.26.8.

12. N. M. Horsfall, in J. N. Bremmer and N. M. Horsfall, *Roman Myth and Mythology* (1987), 68.

13. M. W. Frederiksen, *Campania* (1984), 183–9.

14. Appian, *Samnitica* 3.7.2; Cassius Dio, 9.F39.5–10.

15. Appian, *Samnitica* 3.7.1 where I side with M. Cary, in *Journal of Philology* (1920), 165–70 against P. Wuilleumier, *Tarente* (1939), 87, 95, 102 in an excellent Treatment.

Chapter 27. The Peace of the Gods

1. J. P. V. D. Balsdon, *Romans and Aliens* (1979), 30–58, at 33, in a fine treatment.

2. Cicero, *Pro Flacco* 9.14; *Pro Sestio* 141.

3. Polybius, 6.53, with Harriet I. Flower, *Ancestor Masks and Aristocratic Power in Roman Culture* (1996).

4. Virgil, *Georgics* 4.276.

5. M. W. Frederiksen, *Campania* (1984), 200 note 53 for the problem; Livy, 8.9–11; H. W. Versnel, in *Le Sacrifice dans l'antiquité*, Entretiens de la Fondation Hardt, volume XXVII (1981), 135–94.

6. Polybius, 12.41.1; Plutarch, *Roman Questions* 97; Festus 190 L; W. Warde Fowler, *The Roman Festivals* (1899), 241–50.

7. Ovid, *Fasti* 5.331; Valerius Maximus, 2.10.8, for young Cato's reaction; Warde Fowler, *Roman Festivals*, 91–5.

8. Servius, on Virgil, *Aeneid* 9.52.

CHAPTER 28. LIBERATION IN THE SOUTH

1. Plutarch, *Life of Pyrrhus* 19.6–7, with P. Lévèque, *Pyrrhos* (1957), 355 note 7 and in general 345–56.

2. Florus, 1.13.9, with H. H. Scullard, *The Elephant in the Greek and Roman World* (1973), 110, on the story's credentials.

3. Plutarch, *Life of Pyrrhus* 21.14.

4. Ibid. 23.8.

5. Diodorus, 23.1.4.

6. Hanno the Carthaginian, *Periplus*, with introduction and notes by Al. Oikonomides and M. C. J. Miller (1995, 3rd edn.).

7. Lawrence E. Stager, in H. G. Niemeyer, *Phönizier im Westen* (1982), 155–65: W. Huss, *Geschichte der Karthager* (1985), 532–42; Diodorus, 20.14.4–7; Plutarch, *Moralia* 171D.

8. C. Sempronius Tuditanus, F5 (Peter), for the legend; Diodorus, 24.12, for the torturing.

9. Polybius, 3.11, with F. W. Walbank, *Commentary*, volume I (1957).

10. Livy, 21.18.13–14.

CHAPTER 29. HANNIBAL AND ROME

1. V. D. Hanson, 'Cannae', in R. Cowley (ed.), *The Experience of War* (1992), with Gregory Daly, *Cannae: The Experience of Battle in the Second Punic War* (2002), 156–201.

2. Polybius, 3.78.1.

3. Ibid. 3.88.1.

4. Pliny, *Natural History* 3.103, with Justin, *Epitome* 32.4.11.

5. Livy, 22.51.

6. Livy, 21.62.3 and 22.1.8–15.

7. Michael Koortbojian, in *Journal of Roman Studies* (2002), 33–48.

8. Livy, 27.37, and M. Beard, J. North and S. R. F. Price, *Religions of Rome*, volume I (1998), 82.

9. M. W. Frederiksen, *Campania* (1984), 243–50.

10. Tim Cornell, in Tim Cornell, Boris Rankov and Philip Sabin (eds.), *The Second Punic War: A Reappraisal* (1996), 97–117.

11. Seneca, *Epistle* 86.4–6.

12. Suetonius, *Life of Domitian* 10.

Chapter 30. Diplomacy and Dominance

1. Polybius, 5.104.

2. Appian, *Illyrica* 7, P. S. Derow, in *Phoenix* (1973), 118–34, for its value.

3. R. K. Sherk, *Rome and the Greek East to the Death of Augustus* (1988), number 2, the text; Polybius, 9.39.1–5 for reactions to it.

4. Plutarch, *Life of Flamininus* 10.6 ff.

5. E. T. Salmon, *Roman Colonization under the Republic* (1969), 95–112.

6. A. Erskine, in *Mediterraneo antico: economie, società, culture*, 3.1 (2000), 165–82, an excellent study.

7. P. J. Rhodes and D. M. Lewis, *The Decrees of the Greek States* (1997), 531–49 is now fundamental on the changes in inscribed decrees.

8. Polybius, 3.4.12, with F. W. Walbank, *Polybius* (1972), 174–81, arguing however that the 'troubled times' began *c.* 152 BC.

9. Polybius, 30.15; for a subsequent (and differently based) 'change for the worse', Polybius, 6.57.5 and 31.25.6.

10. John Briscoe, in *Journal of Roman Studies* (1964), 66–77.

Chapter 31. Luxury and Licence

1. A good overview by Matthew Leigh, in Oliver Taplin (ed.), *Literature in the Greek and Roman Worlds: A New Perspective* (2000), 288–310.

2. O. Skutsch, *The Annals of Quintus Ennius* (1985), the basic study.

3. Polybius, 30.22.

4. G. Clemente, in A. Giardina and A. Schiavone (eds.), *Società romana e produzione schiavistica*, volume I (1981), 1–14, a very good survey; M. Coundry, in *Chroniques italiennes*, 54 (1997), 9–20, for history up to Tiberius.

5. Cato, in Festus 350 L.

6. Plutarch, *Life of Cato* 51; also, 2.1–3; 20.2–4.

7. Ibid. 21.8.

8. Cato, in Cicero, *De Officiis* 2.89; Cato, preface to *On Agriculture*.

9. Cato, in Aulus Gellius, *Attic Nights* 6.3.7: I owe the emphasis on 'ill-gotten gains' to discussion with T. J. Cornell.

10. Cato, in Pliny, *Natural History* 29.14.

11. Plutarch, *Life of Cato* 27.

12. Polybius, 30.18.

13. Ibid. 29.4 and 30.5.

14. 2 Maccabees, 5.11–6.2, with the important reconsideration by F. Millar, in *Journal of Jewish Studies* (1978), 1–21.

15. 2 Maccabees, 7.9 ff.

16. Polybius, 3.4.12.

17. Polybius, 12.25 E, with F. W. Walbank, *Commentary* and his *Polybius* (1992), 66–96.

18. A. Erskine, in *Mediterraneo antico: economie, società, culture*, 3.1 (2000), 165–82, an excellent study of this too.

19. Polybius, 10.15.4–6.

20. Polybius, 31, 25.3–8; on Romans and money, A. Erskine, in F. Cairns (ed.), *Papers of Leeds 'International' Latin Seminar* (1996), 1.

21. F. W. Walbank, *Polybius* (1972), 130–56 and his *Polybius, Rome and the Hellenistic World* (2002), 277–92 for further thoughts.

CHAPTER 32. TURBULENCE AT HOME AND ABROAD

1. Sallust, *Catiline* 10.

2. M. Pobjoy, in E. Herring and Kathryn Lomas (eds.), *The Emergence of State Identity in Italy in the First Millennium* (2000), 187–247.

3. Plutarch, *Life of Tiberius Gracchus* 14.1, 19.2; Florus, 2.14.7; C. Gracchus, Fragment 62 (Malcovati).

4. Diodorus, 37.9.

5. A. N. Sherwin-White, in *Journal of Roman Studies* (1982), 28, part of a very important study.

6. Plutarch, *Life of Sulla* 38.3; Appian, *Civil War* 1.106.

CHAPTER 33. POMPEY'S TRIUMPHS

1. Stressed by F. G. B. Millar, *The Crowd in Rome in the Late Republic* (1998), 204–26, and his *The Roman Republic in Political Thought* (2002), 19.

2. A. W. Lintott, in *Journal of Roman Studies* (1998), 1–16, moving between the two concepts.

3. Sallust, *The Histories*, ed. P. McGushin, volume II (1994), 27–31.

4. Macrobius, *Sat.* 3.13.10; Varro, *De Re Rustica* 3.6.6.

5. Plutarch, *Life of Lucullus* 39.2–41; Pliny, *Natural History* 15.102; P. Grimal, *Les Jardins romains* (1984 edn.), 128–30.

6. Plutarch, *Life of Pompey* 2.6.

7. Helvius Mancia, in Valerius Maximus, 6.2.8.

8. Cicero, *De Imperio* 41–2.

9. A. N. Sherwin-White, *Roman Foreign Policy in the East* (1984), 186–234, for the detailed results.

10. Plutarch, *Life of Pompey* 14.6; Pliny, *Natural History* 8.4.

11. Cicero, *Ad Atticum* 2.1.8.

12. S. Weinstock, *Divus Julius* (1971), 43, and Cicero, *Pro Sestio* 129.

13. Valerius Maximus, 6.2.7 and Ammianus, 17.11.4.

14. Julian, *The Caesars*, Loeb Library, volume II (1913), ed. W. C. Wright, 384 for the 'lion'; Caelius, in Cicero, *Ad Familiares* 8.1.3; compare Cicero, *Ad Atticum* 4.9, Another Classic.

CHAPTER 34. THE WORLD OF CICERO

1. J. P. V. D. Balsdon, in T. A. Dorey (ed), *Cicero* (1965), 171–214, at 205, in a brilliant appreciation of the man.

2. S. Treggiari, in *Transactions of the American Philological Association* (1998), 11–23.

3. Ibid. 1–7; E. Rawson, in M. I. Finley (ed.), *Studies in Roman Property* (1976), 85–101, a fine study on Cicero's properties; S. Treggiari, *Roman Social History* (2002), 74–108, on 'privacy'.

4. Ibid. 49–73; Cicero, *Ad Familiares* 4.6.

5. *Commentariolum Petitionis*, 1.2.

6. Ibid. 5.18.

7. Ibid. 11.1.

8. Cicero, *Ad Familiares* 5.7; Scholia Bobiensia 167 (Strangl).

9. Cicero, *Ad Atticum* 2.3.3–4, with the very useful debate and discussion by A. M. Ward, B. A. Marshall and many others in *Liverpool Classical Monthly*, 3.6 (1978), 147–75.

10. Cicero, *Ad Quintum Fratrem* 3.2.4.

11. Cicero, *De Legibus* 3.28 and 3.34–9, especially 39.

12. E. Rawson, in *Liverpool Classical Monthly*, 7.8 (1982), 121–4, a very good study of this tantalizing subject.

13. S. Treggiari, *Selection and Translation of Cicero's Cilician Letters* (1996, 2nd edn.).

14. Cicero, *Ad Atticum* 8.16.2; compare 8.9.4.

CHAPTER 35. THE RISE OF JULIUS CAESAR

1. Aulus Gellius, 1.10.4.

2. Suetonius, *Life of Caesar* 22.2–3.

3. Plutarch, *Life of Caesar* 11.4.

4. Asconius, *In Toga Candida* 71, on which I agree with E. Rawson, in *Liverpool Classical Monthly*, 7.8 (1982), 123.

5. L. R. Taylor, in *Historia* (1950), 45–51, is still a basic study: Cicero, *Ad Atticum* 2.24.

CHAPTER 36. THE SPECTRE OF CIVIL WAR

1. Caesar, *Gallic War* 3.10.

2. Pliny, *Natural History* 9.11; 36.114–15, for the theatre.

3. B. M. Levick, in Kathryn Welch and Anton Powell (eds.), *Julius Caesar as Artful Reporter* (1998), 61–84.

4. Pliny, *Natural History* 36.116, on Curio; 36.115 on Scaurus' villa.

5. G. O. Hutchinson, in *Classical Quarterly* (2001), 150–62.

6. Cicero, *De Oratore* 30–1; A. C. Dionisiotti, in *Journal of Roman Studies* (1988), 35–49, on Nepos and comparative history, especially 38–9, an excellent study.

7. Sallust, *Catiline* 25, with R. Syme, *Sallust* (1964), 133–5.

8. Valerius Maximus, 9.1.8.

9. Cicero, *Ad Familiares* 8.14.

10. Suetonius, *Life of Caesar* 29.2; Appian, *Civil War* 2.32; Plutarch, *Life of Caesar* 31.

11. Ibid. 32.8.

12. Suetonius, *Life of Caesar* 81.2.

CHAPTER 37. THE FATAL DICTATOR

1. Cicero, *Ad Familiares* 8.14.3.

2. Cicero, *Ad Atticum* 7.11.1.

3. Ibid. 9.18.1.

4. Ibid. 9.10.7 and 9.18.2.

5. Ibid. 9.18.3.

6. Cicero, *Ad Familiares* 7.3.2.

7. Plutarch, *Life of Pompey* 38.2–3.

8. Dio, 42.14.3–4.

9. *Anthologia Palatina* 9.402; Cicero, *Ad Atticum* 11.6.7.

10. For context, E. E. Rice, *Cleopatra* (1999), 46–71, a very clear survey.

11. Cicero, *Ad Atticum* 10.10.5.

12. Dio, 43.23.3; S. Weinstock, *Divus Julius* (1971), 76–9.

13. Dio, 43.23.6 and Suetonius, *Life of Caesar* 39.2; Weinstock, *Divus Julius*, 88–90.

14. Cicero, *Ad Familiares* 9.16.3.

15. Macrobius, *Saturnalia* 2.7.4; Cicero, *Ad Familiares* 12.18.2.

16. Ibid. 4.5.

17. Dio, 43.44.1, with Weinstock, *Divus Julius*, 133–45.

18. Cicero, *Ad Atticum* 12.43.3 and 13.28.3, with S. Weinstock, in *Harvard Theological Review* (1957), 212.

19. Cicero, *Ad Atticum* 13.40.1; Nepos, *Atticus* 18.3.

20. Cicero, *Ad Familiares* 7.26.2.

21. Ibid. 13.52, a classic letter.

22. Dio, 44.10.1–3; I disagree with Weinstock, *Divus Julius*, 330, that it was a pre-planned 'advent' as a king.

23. Suetonius, *Life of Caesar* 77.1.

24. Ibid. 81.2: I cannot, sadly, accept 'ubertimque flere'.

25. Suetonius, *Life of Caesar* 79.3; Cicero, *De Divinatione* 2.110; Dio, 44.15.3; Appian, *Civil War* 2.110.

CHAPTER 38. LIBERATION BETRAYED

1. Appian, *Civil War* 2.118–19; Suetonius, *Life of Caesar* 82.3–4; Appian, *Civil War* 2.134.

2. Cicero, *Ad Familiares* 11.1.1: the dating is famously disputed, some delaying this letter until 20 March.

3. Cicero, *Ad Atticum* 14.13.6.

4. Against Suetonius, 84.2, I set Cicero, *Ad Atticum* 14.10, 14.11, 14.22 and *Philippic* 2.91, pointing to more. Surely Appian, *Civil War* 2.144–7, is usable evidence of what did go on.

5. Appian, *Civil War* 3.2.

6. Cicero, *Ad Atticum* 14.3.

7. R. Syme, *Augustan Aristocracy* (1986), 39, with Suetonius, *Life of Augustus* 2.3.

8. Cicero, *Ad Atticum* 14.11.2 ('mihi totus deditus': in Shackleton-Bailey's view, Loeb Library, volume IV, 164 note 2, 'Atticus would know better than to take this at face value'. I wonder). Compare 14.12.2 ('perhonorifice').

9. Cicero, *Ad Atticum* 15.4.2.

10. Suetonius, *Life of Caesar* 88 and Pliny, *Natural History* 2.94 with S. Weinstock, *Divus Julius* (1971), 370–71.

11. Cicero, *Ad Familiares* 11.3, a very fine letter.

12. Cicero, *De Officiis* 3.83; compare 2.23–9 and especially 2.84.

13. Cicero, *Ad Familiares* 10.20.2.

14. Cicero, *Ad Atticum* 16.15.3; compare 16.14.1, but also 16.11.6, a classic.

15. Cicero, *Philippic* 5.50, another classic.

16. Cicero, *Ad Familiares* 10.28.3; *Philippic* 5.50.

17. Cicero, *Ad Familiares* 11.14 and 12.30.2.

18. R. Syme, *The Roman Revolution* (1939), 190, note 6.

19. Kathryn Welch, in Anton Powell and Kathryn Welch (eds.), *Sextus Pompeius* (2002), 1–30.

20. Cicero, *Ad Familiares* 11.20.1.

21. Plutarch, *Life of Cicero* 47–8 for his last hours; on Fulvia, Dio, 47.8.4–5.

Chapter 39. Antony and Cleopatra

1. Nicholas Horsfall, in *Bulletin of the Institute of Classical Studies* (1983), 85–98; E. K. Wifstrand, *The So-called Laudatio Turiae* (1976).

2. R. G. M. Nisbet, in his *Collected Papers on Latin Literature* (1995), 390–413, a brilliant study of 'the Survivors'.

3. R. Syme, in *Historia* (1958), 172–88.

4. Joyce Reynolds, *Aphrodisias and Rome* (1982), 438, with numbers 6, 10 and 12.

5. Plutarch, *Life of Antony* 23.2–3.

6. Ibid. 26, and Socrates of Rhodes, FGH 192 F1 (Jacoby).

7. Martial, *Epigrams* 11.20; the pearl story, Pliny, *Natural History* 9.120–21 and Macrobius, *Saturnalia* 3.17.15.

8. P. M. Fraser, in *Journal of Roman Studies* (1957), 71–4.

9. Plutarch, *Life of Antony* 23.5–8 with C. B. R. Pelling, *Commentary* (1988), 205.

10. K. Scott, in *Classical Philology* (1929), 133–41, on 'On Drunkenness'; Suetonius, *Life of Augustus* 69.2, on sex; on Sarmentus, Plutarch, *Life of Antony* 59.4 with Craig A. Williams, *Roman Homosexuality* (1999), 275.

11. T. P. Wiseman, in *Classical Quarterly* (1982), 475–6, and his *Roman Studies* (1987), 172.

12. A. N. Sherwin-White, *Roman Foreign Policy in the East* (1984), 307–21.

13. Plutarch, *Life of Antony* 36.3–5 and Dio, 49.32, with Pelling, *Commentary*, 217–20.

14. J. Linderski, in *Journal of Roman Studies* (1984), 74–80.

15. Plutarch, *Life of Antony* 71.4; on Timon, Strabo, 17.794 and Plutarch, *Life of Antony* 69.6–7 and 70.

16. Ibid. 76.5–78.4.

17. Macrobius, *Saturnalia* 2.4.28–9, brought to notice by F. Millar, *The Emperor in the Roman World* (1977), 135.

18. On the poets' earlier attitudes, note Virgil, *Eclogue* 9, with M. Winterbottom, in *Greece and Rome* (1976), 55–8; Horace, *Epodes* 6 and 16 with the remarkable study by Nisbet, *Collected Papers*, 161–81, and Propertius 1.21 with Gordon Williams, *Tradition and Originality in Roman Poetry* (1968), 172–81.

19. Jasper Griffin, in *Journal of Roman Studies* (1977), 17–26.

Chapter 40. The Making of the Emperor

1. Velleius, 2.88; Livy, *Periochae* CCXIII; Dio, 54.15.4.

2. I differ on this from P. A. Brunt, in *Journal of Roman Studies* (1983), 61–2.

3. Joyce Reynolds, *Aphrodisias and Rome* (1982), 104, number 13.

4. J. Rich and J. Williams, *Numismatic Chronicle* (1999), 169–214.

5. Livy, 4.20.7 with R.M. Ogilvie, *Commentary on Livy Books 1–5* (1965), *ad loc.*

6. S. Weinstock, *Divus Julius* (1971), 228–43, a fine study.

7. B. M. Levick, in *Greece and Rome* (1975), 156–63, especially the important note 10.

8. I opt for a trial in 22 BC, because it seems to occur when Marcellus is dead and therefore not called to give evidence; on Castricius the informer, D. Stockton, in *Historia* (1965), 27.

9. Virgil, *Aeneid* 6.851–3.

Chapter 41. Morals and Society

1. *Historia Augusta*, Life of Hadrian 11.6–7.

2. Nepos, *Atticus* 20.3.

3. Horace, *Odes* 3.24.25–30.

4. The suggestion of E. Badian, in *Philologus* (1985), 82–98.

5. Horace, *Epodes* 4; Dio, 48.34.5 and 48.43.3.

6. R. Syme, *The Roman Revolution* (1939), 361; Florus, 2.6.6 on 'municipalia prodigia', of which there are many.

7. Augustus, *Res Gestae* 8.5.

8. Pliny, *Letters* 1.8.11.

9. *Epitome de Caesaribus*, 14.8.

10. P. A. Brunt, *Italian Manpower* (1971), with Gaius, *Institutes* 2.286.

11. Horace, *Odes* 4.5.22.

12. Craig A. Williams, *Roman Homosexuality* (1999), 275, note 115; S. Treggiari, *Roman Freedmen During the Late Republic* (1969), 271–2.

13. Cicero, *De Legibus* 3.30–2.

14. S. Treggiari, in *Ancient History Bulletin* (1994), 86–98, for this connection.

15. Tacitus, *Annals* 2.85, with Pliny, *Natural History* 7.39, and R. Syme, *Roman Papers*, volume II (1979), 805–24, esp. 811 and R. Syme, *Augustan Aristocracy* (1986), 74.

16. Dio, 77.16.4 with F. Millar, *A Study of Cassius Dio* (1964), 204–7.

17. S. Riccobono, *Fontes Iuris Romani . . .* , volume III, numbers 2 and 4.

18. K. Sara Myers, in *Journal of Roman Studies* (1996), 1–20.

19. Macrobius, *Saturnalia* 2.5.9.

Chapter 42. Spectator Sports

1. L. Robert, *Comptes Rendus de L'Académie des Inscriptions et Belles Lettres* (1970), 6–11.

2. Pliny, *Natural History* 8.170; on the heated pool, Dio, 55.7.6.

3. Pliny, *Natural History* 36.121.

4. Ibid. 9.168 on Sergius Orata; Martial, *Epigrams* 7.34.

5. Tacitus, *Annals* 14.21.

6. H. Dessau (ed), *Inscriptiones Latinae Selectae*, 5287, with David S. Potter, in D. S. Potter and D. J. Mattingly (eds.), *Life, Death and Entertainment in the Roman Empire* (1998), 296, on Diocles.

7. In 252 BC; Pliny, *Natural History* 8.6.17.

8. Augustus, *Res Gestae* 22 and 23.

9. L. Robert, *Les Gladiateurs dans l'orient grec* (1940), 248: 'ce n'est pas le seul trait original de la fière et virile république de Rhodes.'

10. Livy, 39.22.2; 41.27.6; 44.18.8.

11. Plutarch, *Moralia* 1099B; *Martyrdom of Perpetua* 17.2–3, with G. Ville, *La Gladiature dans l'occident des origines à la mort de Domitian* (1981), 363.

12. *Martyrdom of Perpetua* 20.2.

13. Martial, *On Spectacles* 6, in Loeb Library edition of Martial, *Epigrams* 1 (1993), notes and translation by D. R. Shackleton Bailey.

14. Celadus, in Dessau, *Inscriptiones Latinae Selectae*, 5142A and B, with Robert, *Les Gladiateurs*, 302 on his name; 5142C, on 'puparum nocturnarum'.

15. M. Cébeillac-Gervasoni and F. Zevi, in *Mélanges de l'École Française à Rome* (1976), 612.

16. Dio, 67.8.4.

17. S. Riccobono.

CHAPTER 43. THE ROMAN ARMY

1. Suetonius, *Life of Augustus* 49.

2. Hyginus, in *Corpus Agrimensorum Romanorum*, ed. C. Thulin, volume I (1913), 165–6; O. A. W. Dilke, *The Roman Land Surveyors* (1971), 113–14.

3. Strabo, 3.4.20.

4. M. Beard, J. North and S. R. F. Price (eds.), *Religions of Rome*, volume I (1998), 324–8, and volume II (1998), 71–6.

5. Suetonius, *Life of Nero* 44.1; I disagree with P. A. Brunt, in *Scripta Classica Israelica* (1974), 80; a 'levy' (*dilectus*) is either of auxiliaries or of volunteers (Tacitus, *Histories* 3.58, is a good example).

6. Tacitus, *Annals* 4.4.2, and Suetonius, *Life of Tiberius* 30, where M. W. Frederiksen pointed out to me the force of 'etiam' ('even').

7. Statius, *Silvae* 5.1.94–5.

8. H. Dessau (ed.), *Inscriptiones Latinae Selectae*, 2558, with the fine study of M. P. Speidel, in *Ancient Society* (1991), 277–82, and his *Riding for Caesar* (1994), 46.

9. Tacitus, *Annals* 1.17, and J. F. Gilliam, in *Bonner Jahrbücher* (1967), 233–43, especially 238.

10. Suetonius, *Life of Tiberius* 16.

11. R. W. Davies, in *Aufstieg und Niedergang der Römischen Welt*, volume II.i (1974), 301–34, an excellent survey.

12. Tacitus, *Agricola* 5.1–2, with Brian Campbell, in *Journal of Roman Studies* (1975), 18–19.

13. *Historia Augusta*, Life of Hadrian 10.4–5.

14. H. C. Youtie, in J. Bingen, G. Cambier and G. Nachtergael (eds.), *Le Monde grec . . . : Hommages à Claire Préaux* (1975), 723, a brilliant study.

CHAPTER 44. THE NEW AGE

1. Horace, *Carmen Saeculare* 50–51, with 56; M. Beard, J. North and S. R. F. Price, *Religions of Rome*, volume I (1998), 201–6, and volume II (1998), 140–44.

2. Ibid. 140.

3. R. K. Sherk, *The Roman Empire: Augustus to Hadrian* (1988), number 15, line 10.

4. Ibid., number 36, page 66, lines 15ff.

5. M. T. Griffin, in *Journal of Roman Studies* (1997), 252, lines 115–20.

6. Tacitus, *Annals* 14.43.

7. G. W. Bowersock, in Kurt A. Raaflaub and Mark Toher (eds.), *Between Republic and Empire* (1990), 380–94.

8. Fergus Millar, in *Greece and Rome* (1988), 48–51; W. Eck, in F. Millar and E. Segal (eds.), *Caesar Augustus* (1984), 129–67.

9. Suetonius, *Life of Augustus* 31.5.

10. P. A. Brunt, *The Fall of the Roman Republic* (1988), 350.

11. R. K. Sherk, *Rome and the Greek East to the Death of Augustus* (1984), number 133.

12. Tacitus, *Annals* 1.75.1–2; D. C. Feeney, in Anton Powell (ed.), *Roman Poetry and Propaganda in the Age of Augustus* (1992), 1.

CHAPTER 45. THE JULIO-CLAUDIANS

1. H. Dessau (ed.), *Inscriptiones Latinae Selectae*, 5026; I owe this to C. E. Stevens. It was not adduced by R. Syme; J. Scheid, *Les Frères Arvales* (1975), 87, does cite it, and R. Syme, *The Augustan Aristocracy* (1986), 415, then dismisses it, quite unconvincingly.

2. Velleius, 2.124.2; Suetonius, *Life of Tiberius* 30.

3. Tacitus, *Annals* 1.7.

4. Suetonius, *Life of Claudius* 3.2.

5. Pliny, *Natural History* 3.119.

6. M. T. Griffin, in *Journal of Roman Studies* (1997), 252, lines 115 ff.

7. Tacitus, *Annals* 11.1.1.

8. Suetonius, *Life of Nero* 6.2 and Dio, 61.2.3.

9. Tacitus, *Histories* 1.72.

10. N. Purcell, in *Journal of Roman Studies* (1985), 14.

11. Tacitus, *Annals* 3.53.5 and 2.33.1 (silks).

12. Tacitus, *Annals* 16.18.

13. Ibid. 11.3.

CHAPTER 46. RULING THE PROVINCES

1. C. Nicolet, *Space, Geography and Politics in the Early Roman Empire* (1991).

2. *Oxyrhynchus Papyrus* 2131; *Papyrus Yale* 61; Naphtali Lewis, *Life in Egypt under Roman Rule* (1983), 190.

3. B. M. Levick, in *Greece and Rome* (1979), 120.

4. E. Schuerer, *A History of the Jewish People*, volume I (1973, rev. edn. by F. G. B. Millar and G. Vermes), 399–427; R. J. Lane Fox, *The Unauthorized Version* (1991), 27–34.

5. L. Robert, *Laodicée du Lycos*, volume I (1969), 274, a fine study.

6. G. C. Boon, *Antiquaries Journal* (1958), 237–40; Richard Gordon, in Mary Beard and John North (eds.), *Pagan Priests* (1990), 217.

7. J. L. Lightfoot (ed.), *Lucian: On the Syrian Goddess* (2003), 200–207.

CHAPTER 47. EFFECTS OF EMPIRE

1. Tacitus, *Agricola* 21.1.

2. Ibid. 21.2.

3. Susan Walker (ed.), *Ancient Faces: Mummy Portraits from Roman Egypt* (2000, rev. edn.).

4. Tacitus, *Annals* 14.31.

5. A. T. Fear, *Rome and Baetica* (1996), 131–69.

6. I incline to M. Stern, in M. Avi-Yonah and Z. Baras (eds.), *Society and Religion in the Second Temple Period* (1977), 263–301; note also M. Smith, in *Harvard Theological Review* (1971), 1–19; 'Zealots' occur first in Josephus, *The Jewish War* 4.161; for other views, Martin Goodman, *The Ruling Class of Judaea* (1987), 93–6, 219–21.

7. The city 'Agrippina' is in E. Schuerer, *A History of the Jewish People*, volume I (1973, rev. edn. by F. G. B. Millar and G. Vermes), 461, note 20; Acts of the Apostles 24.25.

CHAPTER 48. CHRISTIANITY AND ROMAN RULE

1. E. Schuerer, *A History of the Jewish People*, volume I (1973, rev. edn. by F. G. B. Millar and G. Vermes), 399–427; R. J. Lane Fox, *The Unauthorized Version* (1991), 27–34.

2. N. Kokkinos, in J. Vardman and E. M. Yamauchi (eds.), *Chronos, Kairos, Christos: Studies in Honor of Jack Finegan* (1989), 133, is still the important study.

3. John 18.31, and the cardinal study by E. J. Bickerman, in his *Studies in Jewish and Christian History*, volume III (1986), 82 with Lane Fox, *Unauthorized Version* (1991), 283–310.

4. Josephus, *The Jewish War* 6.300–309; E. Rivkin, *What Crucified Jesus?* (1986).

5. Luke 13.1–5.

6. Acts of the Apostles 11.26 with the still-penetrating study of Elias J. Bickerman, in *Harvard Theological Review* (1949), 109–24.

7. Acts of the Apostles 18.17; on Paul and Pisidian Antioch, W. Ramsay, in *Journal of Roman Studies* (1926), 201.

8. Romans 13.1–5.

9. 1 Corinthians 7.21; Ephesians 6.5.

10. Matthew 19.12.

CHAPTER 49. SURVIVING FOUR EMPERORS

1. M. I. Rostovtzeff, *The Social and Economic History of the Roman Empire*, volume I (1957, rev. edn. by P. M. Fraser), 86.

2. T. E. J. Wiedemann, in Alan K. Bowman *et al.* (eds.), *Cambridge Ancient History*, volume X (1996), 256–7; Pliny, *Natural History* 20.100.

3. Rhiannon Ash, in *Omnibus*, 45 (2003), 11–13.

4. A. Henrichs, in *Zeitschrift für Papyrologie und Epigraphik*, 3 (1968), 51–80, and Barbara Levick, *Vespasian* (1999), 227, note 9.

5. Translated in Robert K. Sherk, *The Roman Empire: Augustus to Hadrian* (1988), 82–3, with the important study of P. A. Brunt, in *Journal of Roman Studies* (1977), 95–116, with which I disagree.

CHAPTER 50. THE NEW DYNASTY

1. Suetonius, *Life of Vespasian* 22.

2. R. Darwall-Smith, *Emperors and Architecture: A Study of Flavian Rome* (1996), 55–68, an excellent discussion.

3. Barbara Levick, *Vespasian* (1999), 194; Quintilian, *Institutes* 4.1.19.

4. Suetonius, *Life of Titus* 10.2.

5. Quintilian, *Institutes* 1.1.12.

6. Pliny, *Panegyric* 82.1–3.

7. Dio, 67.9.1–5.

8. Statius, *Silvae* 4.2.30–1.

9. Pliny, *Letters* 4.22.5–6.

CHAPTER 51. THE LAST DAYS OF POMPEII

1. Kenneth S. Painter, *The Insula of the Menander at Pompeii*, volume IV: *The Silver Treasure* (2001).

2. Liisa Savunen, in Richard Hawley and Barbara Levick (eds.), *Women in Antiquity: New Assessments* (1995), 194–206, for the evidence, at least.

3. H. Dessau (ed.), *Inscriptiones Latinae Selectae*, 5145.

4. R. C. Carrington, in *Journal of Roman Studies* (1931), 110–30, an excellent study: 'Pompeii and its vicinity was no garden city or suburb, but the scene of an intense industrial activity' (130).

5. *Corpus Inscriptionum Latinarum*, IV.2993t.

6. I differ from Paul Zanker, *Pompeii: Public and Private Life* (1998, English transl.), 23–4.

7. J. R. Clarke, in D. Fredrick (ed.), *The Roman Gaze: Vision, Power and the Body* (2002), 149–81, suggests the scenes were comic; J. R. Clarke, *Looking at Lovemaking: Constructions of Sexuality in Roman Art* (1998), 212–40.

8. Lorenzo Fergola and Mario Pagano, *Oplontis* (1998), 19 and 85, for the 'Poppaea' possibility (I incline to it); P. Castren, *Ordo Populusque Pompeianus* (1963, 2nd edn.), 209 for the evidence for the family in Pompeii.

9. *Corpus Inscriptionum Latinarum*, IV.7698B, from the 'House of the Moralist', III.iv.2–3.

CHAPTER 52. A NEW MAN IN ACTION

1. R. Syme, *Roman Papers*, volume VII (1991), 621, and index, 695, for the phrase.

2. M. Winterbottom, in *Journal of Roman Studies* (1970), 90–97.

3. Pliny, *Letters* 4.25.1–2.

4. Pliny, *Panegyric* 76.6; 65.1; 80.

5. Pliny, *Letters* 3.20.12.

6. Pliny, *Panegyric* 74.2 with 73.4 and 2.8.

7. Pliny, *Letters* 10.18.

CHAPTER 53. A PAGAN AND CHRISTIANS

1. Pliny, *Letters*, 10.96.

2. R. J. Lane Fox, *Pagans and Christians* (1986), 433 and 751 note 37.

3. Pliny, *Letters* 1.12 and 1.22.8–10; M. T. Griffin, in *Greece and Rome* (1986), 64–77 and 192–202.

4. Pliny, *Letters* 4.19.

5. Ibid. 4.19.2.

6. Ibid. 7.24.5.

7. Ibid. 7.24.3 and 6.

8. Ibid. 5.6 with P. Barconi and Jose Uroz Saez, *La Villa di Plinio . . .* (1999).

9. David R. Coffin, *The Villa in the Life of Renaissance Rome* (1979), 248; also 266–7, on Pliny's impact on the Villa Trivulziana, near Salone.

10. Martial, *Epigrams* 12.18, 12.31, 12.57.

11. Pliny, *Letters* 9.6; contrast Pope Damasus, in John Matthews, *The Roman Empire of Ammianus* (1989), 422.

12. Hagith Sirvan, *Ausonius of Bordeaux* (1993), an excellent introduction; G. P. O'Daly, 'Cassiciacum', in C. Mayer (ed.), *Augustinus-Lexikon*, volume I (1986–94), 771–82, for the happy life.

CHAPTER 54. REGIME CHANGE, HOME AND AWAY

1. Pliny, *Panegyric* 81.1 and 3.
2. M. P. Speidel, *Roman Army Studies*, volume I (1984), 173 and 408.
3. *Anthologia Palatina*, 6.332; Arrian, *Parthica* F 85 (Jacoby).
4. Sallust, *Histories* 4.78.
5. The crucial point is the death of Pedo, consul for 115, replaced in that year by a suffect; John Malalas is wrong to date his death by earthquake to 13 December 115, wrongly followed by F. A. Lepper, *Trajan's Parthian War* (1949), 54 and 99, as already observed by Isobel Henderson, in *Journal of Roman Studies* (1949), 121–4. Coins support an earlier date for the earthquake: *British Museum Catalogue*, volume III.100. The correct dating is now revived by Anthony R. Birley too, *Hadrian: The Restless Emperor* (1997), 324 note 13.
6. John Malalas, *Chronicle* 11.6 (274), which then mentions Arrian's account of 'the war', the source, I suspect, of the letter to the Senate in the previous sentence.
7. Samuel N. C. Lieu, *Manichaeism in Mesopotamia and the Roman East* (1994), 84–7; G. Luttikhuizen, *The Revelation of Elchasai* . . . (1985).

CHAPTER 55. PRESENTING THE PAST

1. G. E. M. de Sainte Croix, in *British Journal of Sociology* (1954), 33–48, a brilliant study.
2. Suetonius, *Life of Nero* 29.
3. *Corpus Inscriptionum Latinum*, VI.1574, with the very good discussion by Anthony R. Birley, in *Historia* (2000), 230–47.
4. R. Syme, *Ten Studies in Tacitus* (1970), 1–10 and 119–40.
5. Good description in Simon Schama, *Landscape and Memory* (1996).
6. J. H. Elliott and L. W. B. Brockliss, *The World of the Favourite* (1999), especially 2 and 300.

HADRIAN: A RETROSPECTIVE

1. *Historia Augusta*, Life of Hadrian 5.3.
2. Dio, 69.4.2.
3. H. I. Bell, in *Journal of Roman Studies* (1940), 133–47.
4. B. Isaac and A. Oppenheimer, in *Journal of Jewish Studies* (1985), 33–60.
5. Tertullian, *Apology* 46 and *On the Prescription of Heretics* 7.
6. Mary Boatwright, *Hadrian and the City of Rome* (1987), 190.
7. I emphasize this as an antidote to 'Hadrian the intellectual', the theme of R. Syme, *Roman Papers*, volume VI (1991), 103.
8. *Historia Augusta*, Hadrian 7.6, 20.1 and 20.8: 'plebis iactantissimus amator'.
9. For the skills of Salvius Julianus, see H. Dessau (ed.), *Inscriptiones Latinae Selectae*, 8973, and R. Syme, in *Bonner Historia Augusta Colloquium 1986–9* (1991), 201–17.

10. Peter Garnsey, *Social Status and Legal Privilege in the Roman Empire* (1970), with *Digest* 48.19.15, 48.28.13 and 18.21.2; very importantly reviewed by P. A. Brunt, in *Journal of Roman Studies* (1972), 166–70.

11. *Inscriptiones Graecae ad Res Romanas Pertinentes*, volume IV (1927), number 84; also 85–7.

12. *Digest*, 5.3.20.

13. F. Millar, in *Journal of Roman Studies* (1965), 141–60, and P. A. Brunt, in *Athenaeum* (1977), 19–48, two notable studies of the context.

SELECT BIBLIOGRAPHY

I list a few of the books and articles which are most relevant to each chapter; these cite many other sources which I have often absorbed. Space has obliged me to be selective, but the numbered notes and the bibliography should direct readers to the sources and discussions of the main issues in my text. The latest *Oxford Classical Dictionary*, revised by S. Hornblower and A. J. Spawforth (1996), is an invaluable first stop on topics and individuals, with excellent short entries. Throughout, I would refer to *The Cambridge Ancient History*, volumes III.2–XI (1982–2000) in its second, updated edition. Many of its chapters should be the next resort for those wanting more. Many other one- or two-volume surveys of the classical world, or parts of it, exist. John Boardman, Jasper Griffin and Oswyn Murray (eds.), *The Oxford History of the Classical World* (1986) has many good chapters and retains its value. Paul Cartledge (ed.), *Cambridge Illustrated History of Ancient Greece* (1998) gives particular space to the material world and the labourers, on which I have said less. Greg Woolf, *Cambridge Illustrated History of the Roman World* (2003) is now its thematic companion volume. Nigel Spivey and Michael Squire, *Panorama of the Classical World* (2004) is a thematic survey with many more illustrations. Charles Freeman, *Egypt, Greece and Rome* (2004) is a good one-volume survey including non-classical worlds. Many have been interested by Mary Beard and John Henderson, *Classics: A Very Short Introduction* (1995). *The Very Short Introduction to Ancient Warfare*, by Harry Sidebottom (2004) is outstandingly good.

The best general work of art history on the Greek side is Martin Robertson, *A History of Greek Art*, volumes 1 and 2 (1972). Nothing quite so good exists in English on the Roman side, but Paul Zanker, *The Power of Images in The Age of Augustus* (1988) has made a big impression. Sculpture is fully surveyed by W. Fuchs, *Skulptur der Griechen* (1993, 3rd edn.), the fullest one-volume guide, with many photographs. B. S. Ridgway, *The Archaic Style in Greek Sculpture* (1993), *Fourth-century Styles in Greek Sculpture* (1997) and *Hellenistic Sculpture*, volumes I–III (1990–2002) are all excellent guides. J. G. Pedley, *Greek Art and Archaeology* (2002, 3rd edn.) is another, with J. Boardman's very many books especially his *The Diffusion of Classical Art in Antiquity* (1994). There are now two outstandingly good archaeological guidebooks in English, expert but accessible: Amanda Claridge, *Rome: An Oxford Archaeological Guide* (1998) and Antony Spawforth and Christopher Mee, *Greece: An Oxford Archaeological Guide* (2001) which is outstandingly helpful, a major guide to visible Greek 'material culture'.

Several publishers now run series on the periods or key themes of ancient history. The Cambridge University Press 'key themes' are accessible and compact, of which Keith Bradley, *Slavery and Society at Rome* (1994), Peter Garnsey, *Food and Society in Classical Antiquity* (1999) and Jean Andreau, *Banking and Business in the Roman World* (1999) are particularly helpful on themes I compress here. Routledge publish an excellent series which fills out what I condense: Robin Osborne, *Greece in the Making, 1200–479 BC* (1996); Simon Hornblower, *The Greek World after Alexander, 323–30 BC* (2000); T. J. Cornell, *The Beginnings of Rome, c. 1000–264 BC* (1995); Martin Goodman, *The Roman World, 44 BC–AD 180* (1997). Fontana have published an excellent series of shorter interpretative studies which are also highly recommended: Oswyn Murray, *Early Greece* (1993); J. K. Davies, *Democracy and Classical Greece* (1993); F. W. Walbank, *The Hellenistic World* (1992 edn.); Michael Crawford, *The Roman Republic* (1978); Colin Wells, *The Roman Empire* (1992). They are the best short introductions to these periods. Blackwells have begun a bigger series of 'Companions', of which Andrew Erskine (ed.), *A Companion to the Hellenistic World* (2003) is exceptionally good, with other promising volumes to follow. P. J. Rhodes, *A History of the Classical Greek World, 478–323 BC* (2005) will be the basic survey of this complex period.

After a Fontana volume, then a Routledge one and a 'Companion', I recommend strongly the collections of important articles from Edinburgh University Press, of which P. J. Rhodes (ed.), *Athenian Democracy* (2004), Michael Whitby (ed.), *Sparta* (2001), Walter Scheidel and Sitta von Reden (eds.), *The Ancient Economy* (2002), Mark Golden and Peter Toohey (eds.), *Sex and Difference in Greece and Rome* (2003) and Clifford Ando (ed.), *Roman Religion* (2003) are particularly relevant and well chosen.

Older volumes retain their exceptional value, of which I recommend especially L. H. Jeffery, *The Archaic States of Greece* (1976), E. R. Dodds, *The Greeks and the Irrational* (1951); A. Andrewes, *The Greeks* (1967); W. G. Forrest, *The Emergence of Greek Democracy* (1968); W. W. Tarn and G. T. Griffith, *Hellenistic Civilization* (1952); E. J. Bickerman, *The Jews in the Greek Age* (1988), a masterpiece, P. A. Brunt, *Social Conflicts in the Roman Republic* (1971) and J. P. V. D. Balsdon, *Life and Leisure at Rome* (1969), still not surpassed.

On my three main themes, I should mention on freedom Kurt Raaflaub, *The Discovery of Freedom in Ancient Greece* (2004), from which I have sometimes carefully diverged, and P. A. Brunt, *The Fall of the Roman Republic* (1988), 281–350, with C. Wirszubski, *Libertas as a Political Idea at Rome during the Late Republic and Early Principate* (1950), importantly reviewed by A. Momigliano in *Journal of Roman Studies* (1951), 144–53. Paul A. Rahe, *Republics Ancient and Modern*, volume I (1994), is important and challenging. The changing administration of justice is a topic of such increasing complexity that I am aware I have often compressed it. D. M. MacDowell, *Spartan Law* (1986) and *The Law in Classical Athens* (1978) are accessible, with the old, but not unprofitable, survey of R. J. Bonner and G. Smith, *The Administration of Justice from Homer to Aristotle*, volumes I–II (1930–8). For Rome, John A. Crook, *Law and Life of Rome* (1967) retains its value, with Alan Watson, *Rome of the XII Tables* (1975) on the earlier period, and the good survey-chapters by Duncan Cloud and John Crook in *Cambridge Ancient History*, volume IX (1994), 498–563 and Bruce W. Frier, ibid., volume X (1996), 959–79.

On luxury, A. Dalby, *Empire of Pleasures* (2000) lists much that was local, as do D. Braund and J. Wilkins, (eds.), *Athenaeus and His World* (2000), with L. Foxhall, in N. Fisher and H. van Wees, *Archaic Greece: New Approaches and New Evidence* (1998), 295–309, James Davidson, *Courtesans and Fishcakes* (1998), J. Tondriau, in *Revue des Études Anciennes* (1948), 49–52, on the Ptolemies, and A. Passerini, in *Studi italiani di filologia classica* (1934), 35–56. R. Bernhardt, *Luxuskritik und Aufwandsbeschränkungen in der Griechischen Welt* (2003) is important. For Rome, the bibliography to Chapter 30, 'Luxury and Licence', gives good starting points.

Of course, the ancient sources, including inscriptions, remain fundamental throughout, of which the main authors are all translated in the Penguin Classics series or, with facing original texts, in the Loeb Library series whose two volumes on Arrian by P. A. Brunt and those on Cicero's Letters and Martial's Epigrams by D. R. Shackleton Bailey are major scholarly commentaries in their own right.

HADRIAN AND THE CLASSICAL WORLD

Elizabeth Speller, *Following Hadrian: A Second-Century Journey through the Roman Empire* (2002) is a good account, while Anthony R. Birley, *Hadrian: The Restless Emperor* (1997) is an excellent factual study; Mary T. Boatwright, *Hadrian and the Italian Cities* (1989), *Hadrian and the City of Rome* (1987) and *Hadrian and the Cities of the Roman Empire* (2000) are indispensable sources too. R. Syme's many studies are also an important resource, now available in his *Roman Papers* II.617–28; III.1303–15 and 1436–46; IV.94–114 and 295–324; V.546–78; VI.103–14, 157–81, 346–57, 398–408. W. L. MacDonald and John A. Pinto, *Hadrian's Villa and Its Legacy* (1995) is particularly strong on the architecture; David Breeze and Brian Dobson, *Hadrian's Wall* (2000, 4th edn.), for Britain; A. J. Spawforth and S. Walker, in *Journal of Roman Studies* (1985), 78–104, is still a brilliant study of Hadrian and Athens; J. M. C. Toynbee, *The Hadrianic School: A Chapter in the History of Greek Art* (1934) is unsurpassed, still. On the term 'classic', see now P. R. Hardie, 'Classicism' in *Oxford Classical Dictionary* (1996, 3rd edn.), 336, to which add Tonio Hölscher, *The Language of Images in Roman Art* (2004, English translation). R. Lambert, *Beloved and God: The Story of Antinous and Hadrian* (1984) is worth serious engagement. L. Robert, in *Bulletin de Correspondance Hellénique* (1978), 437–52, is brilliant on Hadrian the Hunter in Asia Minor.

CHAPTER 1. HOMERIC EPIC

Jasper Griffin, *Homer on Life and Death* (1980) is a classic; Jasper Griffin, *Homer: The Odyssey* (1987), a good short guide. J. B. Hainsworth, *The Idea of Epic* (1991), on composition. Douglas L. Cairns, *Oxford Readings in Homer's Iliad* (2001), a good selection of essays; Robert Fowler (ed.), *The Cambridge Companion to Homer* (2004), the latest of many such. The best commentaries are the three-volume *A Commentary on Homer's Odyssey*, translated and republished by the Clarendon Press, Oxford (1985–93) and the six-volume *The Iliad: A Commentary*, under the general editorship of G. S. Kirk, from Cambridge (1985–93). J.-P. Crielaard (ed.), *Homeric Questions* (1995), 201–89, on eighth-century dating. Barbara Graziosi, *Inventing Homer: The Early Reception of Epic* (2002), on the 'biography' of Homer. On the trial scene in *Iliad* 18, H. J. Wolff, in *Traditio* (1946), 31–87, is still a starting point.

CHAPTER 2. THE GREEKS' SETTLEMENTS

On the *polis*, M. H. Hansen, in *Historia* (2003), 257–82, summarizes his group's researches since 1993; John Boardman, *The Greeks Overseas: Their Early Colonies and Trade* (4th edn., 1999) is fundamental; R. Osborne, *Greece in the Making, 1200–479 BC* (1996), 19–136, and especially I. Lemos, *The Protogeometric Aegean: The Archaeology of the Late Eleventh and Tenth Centuries BC* (2002), for the 'dark' ages. M. Popham, in Gocha R. Tsetskhladze and F. de Angelis (eds.), *The Archaeology of Greek Colonization* (1994), 11–34, summarizes work at Lefkandi in Euboea; M. A. Aubet, *The Phoenicians and the West: Politics, Colonies and Trade* (1996 edn.). On Greekness, see especially R. Fowler, 'Genealogical Thinking: Hesiod's Catalogue and the Creation of the Hellenes', in *Proceedings of the Cambridge Philological Society*, 44 (1998), 1–20. G. R. Tsetskhladze and A.M. Snodgrass (eds.), *Greek Settlements in the Eastern Mediterranean and the Black Sea* (2002). Otar Lordkipanidze, *Phasis: The River and City in Colchis* (2000). L. Robert, in

Bulletin de Correspondance Hellénique (1978), 535–8, is brilliant on wine-growing at Koumi in Euboea; Günter Kopcke, in Erica Ehrenberg (ed.), *Leaving No Stones Unturned* . . . (2002), 109–18, on the pottery fragments found in Galilee; D. Ridgway, *The First Western Greeks* (1992), on work at Ischia; W. Burkert, *The Orientalizing Revolution* (1992) provokes thought; Irad Malkin, in Peter Derow and Robert Parker (eds.), *Herodotus and His World* (2003), 153–70, opposes, as I do, the incorrect notion that settlements were unofficial in every case, and that all written evidence for their nature and organization should be regarded as later folk tale or adjusted 'legend'. On Acragas, Sybaris and everything Western, T. J. Dunbabin, *The Western Greeks* (1948), especially pages 75–83 and 305–25.

CHAPTER 3. ARISTOCRATS

Jacob Burckhardt, *The Greeks and Greek Civilization*, abridged and translated by Sheila Stern (1998), 160–213, a classic study, though best read in German as the translation is abbreviated. Walter Donlan, *The Aristocratic Ideal in Ancient Greece* (1980) is a good modern survey, now updated with his selected papers (1999) in a reissue. Robert Parker, *Athenian Religion: A History* (1996), chapters 2–3, 5 and pages 284–327 show the detail and problems of *genê* in our best-known city-state; F. Bourriot, *Recherches sur la nature du genos* (1976) is not a definitive treatment by any means. R. Lane Fox, in R. Brock and S. Hodkinson (eds.), *Alternatives to Athens* (2000), 35–51, on Theognis' arch-aristocratic outlook; I have to say I am quite unconvinced, as Theognis would be, by H. van Wees, ibid., pages 52–67, and the attempt to reclassify him as a mafioso, one among many; Theognis, lines 183–8 are eugenic, as Xenophon, in *Stobaeus Florilegium* 88.14 was aware, though arguing for a new interpretation. The 'aristocracy' cannot be taken out of early Greek ('eupatrid') history. Nigel Spivey, *The Ancient Olympics* (2004) is now an excellent guide to athletic matters; O. Murray (ed.), *Sympotica: A Symposium on the Symposium* (1990), on the parties; on hunting, R. Lane Fox, in J. B. Salmon and Graham Shipley (eds.), *Human Landscapes in Classical Antiquity* (1996) 119–53; K. J. Dover, *Greek Homosexuality* (1978), 49–135, is basic, but with the important critique by James Davidson, in *Past and Present* (2001), 3–51. Sitta von Reden, *Exchange in Ancient Greece* (1995), 1–78, on gifts; Paul Cartledge, in Peter Garnsey, Keith Hopkins and C. R. Whittaker (eds.), *Trade in the Ancient Economy* (1983), 1–15, on trade and politics; Philip de Souza, in Nick Fisher and Hans van Wees, *Archaic Greece* (1998), 271–94, discusses, less optimistically, the problems of early naval warfare.

CHAPTER 4. THE IMMORTAL GODS

Mary Lefkowitz, *Greek Gods, Human Lives: What We Can Learn from the Myths* (2003) also sees the lasting force of this aspect of Greeks' imagination; Jan N. Bremmer, *The Rise and Fall of the Afterlife* (2002), with N. J. Richardson, in P. E. Easterling and J. V. Muir (eds.), *Greek Religion and Society* (1985), 50–66. Simon Price, *Religions of the Ancient Greeks* (1999); W. Burkert, *Greek Religion: Archaic and Classical* (1985) is the classic handbook; A. D. Nock, *Essays on Religion and the Ancient World*, ed. Z. Stewart, volumes I and II (1972) are classics; so is R. C. T. Parker, *Athenian Religion: A History* (1996), with his 'Gods Cruel and Kind' in C. Pelling (ed.), *Greek Tragedy and the Historian* (1997), 143–60. W. H. D. Rouse, *Greek Votive Offerings* (1902). F. Graf, 'Dionysian and Orphic Eschatology: New Texts and Old Questions', in T. H. Carpenter and C. A. Faraone (eds.),

Masks of Dionysos (1993), 239–58, marks a new start. J. Gould, *Myth, Ritual, Memory and Exchange* (2001), 269–82, and E. Csapo, in *Phoenix* (1997), 253–95, are both good on Dionysus; R. Lane Fox, *Pagans and Christians* (1986), 102–67, on the presence of the gods; H. W. Parke, *Greek Oracles* (1967), *The Oracles of Zeus* (1967) and *The Oracles of Apollo in Asia Minor* (1983), with Robert Parker, in P. Cartledge and F. D. Harvey, *Crux: Essays Presented to G. E. M. de Sainte Croix* (1985), 298–326.

Chapter 5. Tyrants and Lawgivers

A. Andrewes, *The Greek Tyrants* (1974 edn.); H. W. Pleket, 'The Archaic Tyrannis', in *Talanta I* (1969), 19–61; J. B. Salmon, 'Political Hoplites', in *Journal of Hellenic Studies* (1977), 84–101; J. B. Salmon, *Wealthy Corinth* (1984), 186–230, and Graham Shipley, *A History of Samos* (1987), 69–102, for two good surveys of major tyrannies; Hermann J. Kienast, 'Topography and Architecture of the Archaic Heraion at Samos', in Maria Stamatopoulou and Marina Yeroulanou (eds.), *Excavating Classical Culture* (2002), 311–26, is important. On Solon, A. Andrewes, in *Cambridge Ancient History*, volume III.3 (1982), 375–91 and P. J. Rhodes, *A Commentary on the Aristotelian Athenaion Politeia* (1993 edn.), 118–78, are superior to studies written since, most of which they refute; O. Murray, in Paul Cartledge, Paul Millett and Stephen Todd (eds.), *Nomos: Essays in Athenian Law, Politics and Society* (1990), 139–146, adds value; A. Zimmern, *The Greek Commonwealth* (1911), 125–38, on 'fair play', with the classic study of W. G. Forrest, *Bulletin de Correspondance Hellénique* (1956), 33–52, whose long-shots I still want to believe; R. F. Willetts, *The Law Code of Gortyn* (1967) translates the great text on which I side with Edmond Lévy, 'La Cohérence du code de Gortyne', in Edmond Lévy (ed.), *La Codification des lois dans l'antiquité* (2000), 185–214; G. E. M. de Sainte Croix, *Athenian Democratic Origins* (2004) is magnificently right about the property classes (pages 5–72), wrong on the 'zeugite' (page 50) and vigorously wrong, but wary, about *'hektemoroi'* ('sixth-part payers') as essentially debtors (pages 109–27). The entire collection is a classic.

Chapter 6. Sparta

W. G. Forrest, *A History of Sparta* (1980 edn.); M. Whitby (ed.), *Sparta* (2002); Paul Cartledge, *The Spartans: An Epic History* (2002) and *Spartan Reflections* (2001); Anton Powell and Stephen Hodkinson (eds.), *Sparta beyond the Mirage* (2002); Anton Powell (ed.), *Classical Sparta: Techniques behind Her Success* (1989) is a fine collection, especially the essays on laughter, on drink and the promotion of harmony and a very penetrating study of Spartan religion by Robert Parker. Alcman's bewitching, and partially intelligible, *Partheneion* is most recently discussed by G. O. Hutchinson, *Greek Lyric Poetry* (2001); G. Devereux, in *Classical Quarterly* (1965), 176–84, is excellent on the horses; Daniel Ogden, in *Journal of Hellenic Studies* (1994), 85–91, is an excellent guide to the Great Rhetra's problems; Nino Luraghi and Susan Alcock (eds.), *Helots and Their Masters* (2003), on an ill-attested subject; Robin Osborne, 'The Spartan Exception?', in Marja C. Vink (ed.), *Debating Dark Ages* (1996–7), 19–23, for a clear summary of archaeological evidence.

Chapter 7. the Eastern Greeks

John M. Cook, *The Greeks in Ionia and the East* (1960) and G. L. Huxley, *The Early Ionians* (1966) are full of detail; Graham Shipley, *A History of Samos* (1983) and C. Roebuck and H. Kyrieleis, in J. Boardman and C. E. Vaphopoulou-Richardson (eds.), *Chios* (1984), 81–8 and 187–204, are excellent island studies; Ellen Greene (ed.), *Re-reading Sappho: Contemporary Approaches* (1996), especially chapters 7 and 8. Edward Hussey, *The Presocratics* (1996 edn.) is very clear; Jonathan Barnes, *Early Greek Philosophy* (2001, revised edn.) and *The Presocratic Philosophers* (1999) are fuller; Alan M. Greaves, *Miletos: A History* (2002), not displacing the older and wilder Adelaide G. Dunham, *The History of Miletus Down to the Anabasis of Alexander* (1919); R. M. Cook and Pierre Dupont, *East Greek Pottery* (2002). Thomas Braun, 'Hecataeus' Knowledge of the Western Mediterranean', in Kathryn Lomas (ed.), *Greek Identity in the Western Mediterranean* (2004), 287–348, a very important study; Robert Leighton, *Tarquinia: An Etruscan City* (2004) with Sybille Haynes, *Etruscan Civilization: A Cultural History* (2000), an excellent overview, and her well-based novel about Etruscan life, *The Augur's Daughter* (1987).

Chapter 8. Towards Democracy

I. Malkin, *Myth and Territory in the Spartan Mediterranean* (1994); W. G. Forrest, *A History of Sparta* (1968), 69–95, a classic; Adrienne Mayor, *The First Fossil Hunters* (2000), a brilliant study of 'bones'; Martin Ostwald, *Autonomia: Its Genesis and Early History* (1982), with which I have disagreed; R. J. Lane Fox and also O. Murray, in John T. A. Koumoulides, *The Good Idea: Democracy and Ancient Greece* (1995) on Cleisthenes, and Orlando Patterson, *Freedom In The Making of Western Culture* (1991) with which I disagree; W. G. Forrest, *The Emergence of Greek Democracy* (1963) is the classic study still, with the very important essay by A. Andrewes, in *Classical Quarterly* (1977), 241–8 and by H. T. Wade-Gery, *Essays in Greek History* (1958), 135–54, a still-inspiring collection; D. M. Lewis, in *Historia* (1963), 22–40, is the classic on the infrastructure; P. J. Rhodes (ed.), *Athenian Democracy* (2004) is a good selection of papers; G. E. M. de Sainte Croix, *Athenian Democratic Origins* (2004), 180–214, excellent on ostracism; Mogens H. Hansen, *The Athenian Democracy in the Age of Demosthenes* (1991; revised edn., 1999), on institutions; J. K. Davies, in Peter Derow and Robert Parker, *Herodotus and His World* (2003), 319–36, on sixth-century state development; D. Mertens, in *Bolletino d'arte* (1982), 1–57, on Metapontum; Eric W. Robinson, *The First Democracies* (1997), for rival 'firsts' for which I do not accept the evidence.

Chapter 9. The Persian Wars

P. Briant, *From Cyrus to Alexander: A History of the Persian Empire*, translated by Peter T. Daniels (2002), is a massive survey, with strong interpretations; E. J. Bickerman, in *Journal of Biblical Literature* (1945–6), 249–75, is classic on Cyrus and the Jews; O. Murray, in *Cambridge Ancient History*, volume IV (1988), 461–90, J. L. Myres, in *Palestine Exploration Quarterly* (1953), 8–22, a brilliant essay, and W. G. Forrest, in *International History Review* (1979), 311–25, another: all discuss the Revolt in Asia Minor; A. R. Burn, *Persia and the Greeks: The Defence of the West* (1984, 2nd edn.) is best on the wars; Philip de Souza, *The Greek and Persian Wars, 499–386 BC* (2003) gives a simple overview; N. G. L. Hammond and J. P. Barron in *Cambridge Ancient History*, volume IV (1988), 461–90 and

592–622, are excellent on detail; D. B. Thompson, in *The Aegean and the Near East: Studies Presented to Hatty Goldman* (1956), 281–91 is classic on the Persian spoils in Athens; E. Hall, *Inventing the Barbarian: Greek Self-Definition through Tragedy* (1989) is valid for vase painting and drama at Athens only; Margaret C. Miller, *Athens and Persia in the Fifth Century* BC (1997) elaborates on the Persians' impact.

CHAPTER 10. THE WESTERN GREEKS

E. A. Freeman, *A History of Sicily*, volume II (1891), 49–222, is still unsurpassed; Georges Vallet, in *Pindare: Huit exposés*, Entretiens Fondation Hardt XXXI (1984), 285–327, is also a tour de force, especially Pindar as 'témoin oculaire' of erupting Etna, Pindar in (male) love while others were at war at Marathon (page 312: 'oui, Pindare a aimé ce jeune homme sage et bon, ami des Muses': Thrasybulus of Agrigentum) and then Pindar confronted with unpredictable democracy (pages 316–17), with the brilliant study by W. S. Barrett, in *Journal of Hellenic Studies* (1973), 23–35. On Pindar and the afterlife, Hugh Lloyd-Jones, ibid. (1984), 245–83 is also excellent. J. G. Pedley, *Paestum: Greeks and Romans in Southern Italy* (1990) is a fine survey of a fine site; J. J. Coulton, *Greek Architects at Work* (1977), 82–8 and 141–4, on temple-building; M. W. Frederiksen, *Campania* (1984), 85–133, on Greeks in Italy and Etruria; on early Rome, T. J. Cornell, *The Beginnings of Rome* (1995), chapters 3–11, although I certainly do not accept that 'Etruscan Rome' was a 'myth'; Christopher J. Smith, *Early Rome and Latium* (1996), for Rome's surrounds; A. Grandazzi, *The Foundation of Rome: Myth and History* (1997), for more of the former than the latter; Alan Watson, *Rome of the XII Tables: Persons and Property* (1975) is an enjoyable study, with A. W. Lintott, *The Constitution of the Roman Republic* (1999), 27–146, a magisterial survey. For the Tables themselves, M. H. Crawford, *Roman Statutes*, volume II (1996), 555–722, a fine study.

CHAPTER 11. CONQUEST AND EMPIRE

P. J. Rhodes, *The Athenian Empire* (1985) gives an excellent survey; R. Meiggs, *The Athenian Empire* (1975) is classic, especially chapters 11–23 and pages 413–589; I confess to disbelieving in a 'Delian League', to rejecting the superfluous activities of Aristides, mythologized in Aristotle, *Athenaion Politeia* 23.4–5, and therefore to accepting the lucid view of A. Giovannini and G. Gottlieb, in *Sitzungsberichte der Heidelberger Akademie der Wissenschaften: Phil.-Hist. Klasse* (1980), 7–45 which torpedoes much modern debate. P. J. Stylianou, *The Age of the Kingdoms* (1989), 428–58, is a good view from Cyprus outwards; W. G. Forrest, in *Classical Quarterly* (1960), 232–41, is a classic, on the 'two groups' of Athenians. J. K. Davies, *Democracy and Classical Greece* (1993, 2nd edn.), chapters 4, 5 and 6, is particularly clear. S. Brenne and P. Siewert, *Ostrakismos-Testimonien* (2002–in progress) publishes the excellent new range of ostraka, while G. E. M. de Sainte Croix, *Athenian Democratic Origins* (2004), 180–214, explains the institution; M. Ostwald, *From Popular Sovereignty to the Sovereignty of Law* (1986), 28–83, on constitutional change at Athens; G. E. M. de Sainte Croix, in *Historia* (1954–5), 1–40, is still the best study of the 'character' of the Empire, after decades of debate and criticism; D. M. Lewis, *Selected Papers in Greek and Near Eastern History* (1997) 9–21, on the 'first' war; Jeffrey M. Hurwit, *The Athenian Acropolis* (1999), 138–245, on its changing face. E. A. Freeman, *The History of Sicily*, volume II (1891), 222–429, is still unsurpassed on the West.

CHAPTER 12. A CHANGING GREEK CULTURAL WORLD

Deborah Boedeker and Kurt A. Raaflaub (eds.), *Democracy, Empire and the Arts in Fifth Century Athens* (1998); T. B. L. Webster, *Athenian Culture and Society* (1973) is still valuable; Martin Robertson, *A History of Greek Art*, volume I (1972), 292–362, and his *The Art of Vase Painting in Classical Athens* (1992) are classic on the classical age; James Whitley, *The Archaeology of Ancient Greece* (2001), 269–94, finds 'defining the "classical" an elusive task', by contrast. Terence Irwin, *Classical Thought* (1989) is very clear and E. R. Dodds, *The Greeks and the Irrational* (1951), 179–206, and *The Ancient Concept of Progress* (1973), 1–25, are unarguably classics, perhaps even for J. Whitley. R. Netz, *The Shaping of Deduction in Early Greek Mathematics* (1999) is very important. On Herodotus, John Gould, *Herodotus* (1989) with Thomas Harrison, *Divinity and History* (2000), a helpful study, Rosalind Thomas, *Herodotus in Context* (2000) from whom I differ. R. L. Fowler, in *Journal of Hellenic Studies* (1996), 62–87, inclines against a Herodotus who is 'first' on the historical scene. W. G. Forrest, in *Phoenix* (1984), 1–11, is very important on Herodotus' politics. W. K. Pritchett, *The Liar School of Herodotus* (1993) is vigorous and pages 150–59 address the chariot-group at Athens and Herodotus' visit, a reason why, perhaps too specifically, I put him in Athens in 438/7, before (on usual dating) the new Propylaea; the ancients think of a visit in 446/5, perhaps only as a synchronism with the Thirty Years Peace. Margaret C. Miller, in *American Journal of Archaeology* (1999), 223–54, memorably discusses the scenes of cross-dressing. J. Gould, in *Journal of Hellenic Studies* (1980), 38–55, is a basic study on Athenian women, with Roger Just, *Women in Ancient Law and Life* (1989), essays in Ian McAuslan and Peter Walcot, *Women in Antiquity* (1996) and much else. R. Osborne, in *Past and Present* (1997), 3–33, points to a change in the representation of women, albeit in our surviving evidence; I hesitate to link it as he does to the citizenship law, on which see G. E. M. de Sainte Croix, *Athenian Democratic Origins* (2004), 233–53. On Sculpture, Andreas Scholl, *Die Korenhalle des Erechtheion* (1998), with J. B. Connelly, in *American Journal of Archaeology* (1996), 53–80, brilliantly controversial and not yet refuted by critics; Stefano d'Ayala Valva, in *Antike Kunst* (1996), 5–13, is very important, with W. Fuchs, Torsten Mattern, ed., *Munus . . . für Hans Wiegart* (2000) 111–2 identifying Erichthonios in the Frieze's procession. A. W. Pickard-Cambridge, *The Dramatic Festivals of Athens* (1988, revised edn.), 263–78, is still basic on the audience; on tragedy and 'political ideas', S. Goldhill, in Christopher Rowe and Malcolm Schofield (eds.), *Cambridge History of Greek and Roman Political Thought* (2000), 60–88, for a clear survey, but see Jasper Griffin, in *Classical Quarterly* (1998), 39–61. I wrote this chapter before the publication of P. J. Rhodes, in *Journal of Hellenic Studies* (2003), 104–19, which is very important. Eric Segal (ed.), *Oxford Readings in Aristophanes* (1996) and Malcolm Heath, *Political Comedy in Aristophanes* (1987) provoke thought; W. G. Forrest, in *Klio* (1970), 107–16, is important for the context, surely, of *Knights*; Nan Dunbar, *Aristophanes' Birds* (1994) is a brilliant commentary.

CHAPTER 13. PERICLES AND ATHENS

Plutarch's *Life of Pericles* is edited by Frank J. Frost (1980); Anthony J. Podlecki, *Perikles and His Circle* (1998) and *An Age of Glory: Athens in the Time of Pericles* (1975); A. W. Gomme, *Historical Commentary on Thucydides*, volumes 1 and 2, for noble observations on Thucydides, 1.140–44, 2.35–46 and 2.60–64. Jeffrey M. Hurwit, *The Acropolis in the Age of Pericles* (2004).

CHAPTER 14. THE PELOPONNESIAN WAR

D. M. Lewis, in *Cambridge Ancient History*, volume V (1992), 370–432, and A. Andrewes, ibid. (1992), 433–98, are now the best surveys; V. D. Hanson, *Why the West Has Won: Carnage and Culture from Salamis to Vietnam* (2001) is enjoyably controversial; H. van Wees, *Greek Warfare: Myths and Realities* (2004), especially chapters 12 onwards. On Thucydides, G. E. M. de Sainte Croix, *Origins of the Peloponnesian War* (1972), 5–34, is a classic, as is the rest of the book; Tim Rood, *Thucydides: Narrative and Explanation* (1998) is important; A. Andrewes and K. J. Dover, *Commentary on Thucydides*, volumes IV and V (1981), are also fundamental, although we disagree about Thucydides 8.97.2. The latest commentary in progress is S. Hornblower, *A Commentary on Thucydides* (1991–6, so far). On a Spartan's brutality, Sherry Lee Bassett, in *Ancient History Bulletin* (2001), 1–13; compare S. Hornblower, in Hans van Wees, *War and Violence in Ancient Greece* (2000), 57–82, on their canes, and Clifford Hindley, in *Classical Quarterly* (1994), 347–66, on their sex-lives. For a memorable view of the war's impact, Gilbert Murray, in *Journal of Hellenic Studies* (1944), 1–9; for one which is more factually based, Barry Strauss, *Athens after the Peloponnesian War: Class, Faction and Policy, 403–386 BC* (1987).

CHAPTER 15. SOCRATES

C. C. W. Taylor, *Socrates* (1998) is an excellent short guide; Gregory Vlastos, *Socrates* (1991) is a fuller, vigorous study; R. C. T. Parker, *Athenian Religion: A History* (1996), 152–218, is very important, with E. R. Dodds, *The Greeks and the Irrational* (1951), 179–206, a classic. W. G. Forrest, in *Yale Classical Studies* (1975), 37–52, is still the outstanding study of the 'generation gap', though composed in 1968 whose *événements* are audible in it; M. Ostwald, *From Popular Sovereignty to the Sovereignty of Law* (1986), 537–50, studies the personnel very interestingly. Paula Gottlieb, in *Classical Quarterly* (1992), 278–9, is important on irony; Thomas C. Brickhouse and Nicholas D. Smith, *The Trial and Execution of Socrates* (2002) collects sources and discussions, including the pungent one by I. F. Stone, *The Trial of Socrates* (1997); James A. Coliaso, *Socrates against the Athenians* (2001) and Malcolm Schofield, in T. P. Wiseman (ed.), *Classics in Progress* (2002), 263–84, on Socrates and the lot. Paul Zanker, *The Mask of Socrates* (1995, English translation) is a fine study of the later portraitures.

CHAPTER 16. FIGHTING FOR FREEDOM AND JUSTICE

S. Hornblower, *The Greek World, 479–323 BC* (2002, 3rd edn.), 210–60, is an excellent guide through the complex events; J. K. Davies, *Democracy and Classical Greece* (1993, 2nd edn.), 134–260, is an interpretative survey; N. G. L. Hammond, *A History of Greece to 322 BC* (1967), 466–520, and especially pages 663–5 on army-numbers in the main states; P. Carlier, *Le IVème siècle avant J.-C.: Approches historiographiques* (1996). J. Roy, in Roger Brock and Stephen Hodkinson (eds.), *Alternatives to Athens* (2000), 308–26, is important on Arcadia, with Frank W. Walbank, *Selected Papers* (1985), chapters 1 and 2, on Greek nationality and Greek 'federalism'; Alexander Fuks, *Social Conflict in Ancient Greece* (1984), with A. W. Lintott, *Violence, Civil Strife and Revolution in the Classical City* (1982), chapters 6 and 7; M. N. Tod, *International Arbitration among the Greeks* (1913) is still valuable.

CHAPTER 17. WOMEN AND CHILDREN

Jenifer Neils and John H. Oakley, *Coming of Age in Ancient Greece: Images of Childhood from the Classical Past* (2003), with excellent illustrations; Mark Golden, *Children and Childhood in Classical Athens* (1990); Mark Golden, in *Greece and Rome* (1988), 152–62, on whether the ancients cared when children died. On abortion, K. Kapparis, *Abortion in the Ancient World* (2002); D. Ogden, *Greek Bastardy* (1996); J.-M. Hannick, 'Droit de cité et mariages mixtes', in *L'Antiquité classique* (1976), 133–48; Mary R. Lefkowitz and Maureen A. Fant, *Women's Life in Greece and Rome: A Sourcebook* (1992); Ellen D. Reeder, *Pandora: Women in Classical Greece* (1995); Helen King, *Hippocrates' Woman: Reading the Female Body in Ancient Greece* (1998) is excellent on medical fantasies; James Davidson, *Courtesans and Fishcakes* (1998), 73–212, on prostitution and sex; Sian Lewis, *The Athenian Woman* (2002), very good on the iconography; Pierre Brulé, *Women of Ancient Greece* (2003, English translation), a thoughtful study; Debra Hamel, *Trying Neaira* (2003) is an excellent, clear read. On education, H. I. Marrou, *Histoire de L'éducation dans L'antiquité* (1965, revised edn.) is classic. Matthew Dillon, *Girls and Women in Classical Greek Religion* (2002), with the excellent study of R. G. Osborne, in *Classical Quarterly* (1993), 392–405. On King Philip's family, Kate Mortensen, in *Ancient History Bulletin* (1992), 156–71.

CHAPTER 18. PHILIP OF MACEDON

The evidence for Philip and his predecessors is admirably assembled by N. G. L. Hammond and G. T. Griffith, *A History of Macedonia*, volume II (1979), 113–722, with very lengthy discourse. There are short biographies by G. L. Cawkwell, *Philip of Macedon* (1978) and a remarkable construct by N. G. L. Hammond, *Philip of Macedon* (1994), a eulogy; on Macedonian Greek, M. B. Hatzopoulos, in *Atti XI Congresso Internazionale di Epigrafia Greca e Latina*, volume I (1999), 257–73, and Supplementum Epigraphicum Graecum XLIX (1999) numbers 656–7; René Ginouvès, *Macedonia from Philip II to the Roman Conquest* (1993) gives a good idea of finds in Macedon, up to that date; M. B. Hatzopoulos and Louisa D. Loukopoulos (eds.), *Philip of Macedon* (1981) includes good essays by G. T. Griffith on Philip as a general and M. Andronicos (the hero of this subject) on the Royal Tombs at Aigai; M. Andronicos, *Vergina: The Royal Tombs and the Ancient City* (1989) and *Vergina II: The Tomb of Persephone* (1994) are stunning, with A. N. J. W. Prag, J. H. Musgrave and R. A. H. Neave, in *Journal of Hellenic Studies* (1984), 60–78; attempts to attribute Tomb II to Philip III continue on unconvincing grounds and are increasingly behind the evidence now available on site; O. Palagia, in E. J. Baynham and A. B. Bosworth, *Alexander the Great in Fact and Fiction* (2000), 189–200, is a recent example.

CHAPTER 19. THE TWO PHILOSOPHERS

The bibliography is vast here: two good very short introductions are R. M. Hare, *Plato* (1982) and Jonathan Barnes, *Aristotle* (1982); Bernard Williams, *Plato: The Invention of Philosophy* (1998) is very clear; Julia Annas, *An Introduction to Plato's Republic* (1981), T. H. Irwin, *Plato's Ethics* (1995) and R. B. Rutherford, *The Art of Plato* (1995) are a good trio, on accessible topics; Gail Fine (ed.), *Plato 1 and 2* (1999) gives an excellent selection of studies, with a fine introduction and bibliographies; R. Kraut (ed.), *The Cambridge Companion to Plato* (1992) is also excellent; David Sedley, in T. Calvo and L.

Brisson (eds.), *Interpreting the Timaeus and Critias* (1997), 327–39, on 'likeness to God', with the superb study by A. J. Festugière, *La Révélation de L'Hermès Trismégiste*, volumes I–IV (1949–54), a profound classic. P. A. Brunt, *Studies in Greek History and Thought* (1993), 242–344, is magisterial on the laws, the letters and Plato's pupils. Julia Annas and Robin Waterfield (eds.), *Plato's Statesman* (1995); M. M. Markle, in *Journal of Hellenic Studies* (1976), 80–99, on Speusippus. On Aristotle, W. D. Ross, *Aristotle* (1923) is slightly easier than J. L. Ackrill, *Aristotle the Philosopher* (1981), an excellent study; J. O. Urmson, *Aristotle's Ethics* (1988) is clear; Jonathan Barnes (ed.), *The Cambridge Companion to Aristotle* (1995); on women, Robert Mayhew, *The Female in Aristotle's Biology* (2004) is a good, short rethink; on democracy, A. W. Lintott, in *Classical Quarterly* (1992), 114–28, is excellent.

Chapter 20. Fourth-Century Athenians

A. H. M. Jones, *Athenian Democracy* (1957), chapters 1–2, is still a starting point. On slavery, G. E. M. de Sainte Croix, *The Class Struggle in the Ancient Greek World* (1981), 112–204: on religion, R. C. T. Parker, *Athenian Religion: A History* (1996) 218–55; on citizenship, D. Ogden, *Greek Bastardy* (1996), 166–88; on Apollodorus, R. J. Bonner, *Lawyers and Litigants in Ancient Athens* (1927) and J. Trevett, *Apollodorus Son of Pasion* (1992); on Aeschines, R. J. Lane Fox, in S. Hornblower, and R. G. Osborne (eds.), *Ritual, Finance and Politics* (1994), 135–55; on drinking, James Davidson, *Courtesans and Fishcakes* (1998), 36–73; on cockfights, Nan Dunbar, *Aristophanes' Birds* (1995) 158; on the Tanagras, the excellent Louvre catalogue, *'Tanagras'* (2003); on the art, Martin Robertson, *History of Greek Art*, volume 1 (1972), 363–444; on theatre, Pat Easterling, in A. H. Sommerstein, S. Halliwell *et al.* (eds.), *Tragedy, Comedy and the Polis* (1993), 559–69, and Gregory W. Dobrov (ed.), *Beyond Aristophanes* (1995), especially pages 1–46; on Menander, T. B. L. Webster, *An Introduction to Menander* (1990); on lawmaking, P. J. Rhodes, in *Classical Quarterly* (1985), 55–60; also P. J. Rhodes, in *Journal of Hellenic Studies* (1986), 132–144, and M. M. Markle III, in *Ancient Society* (1990), 149–66, on participation; on taxes, P. J. Rhodes, in *American Journal of Ancient History* (1982), 1; on display, D. M. MacDowell (ed.), *Demosthenes against Meidias* (1990); on silver-mines, R. J. Hopper, in *Annual of British School at Athens* (1968), 293–326; Paul Millett, *Lending and Borrowing in Ancient Athens* (1991), though I do not share the Finley–de Sainte Croix notion of maritime loans as 'insurance'; R. G. Osborne, in *Chiron* (1988), 279–323, is important on leasing and also in John Rich and Andrew Wallace-Hadrill, *City and Country in the Ancient World* (1991), 119–46, on the decidedly non-subsistence economy of the rich in Attica; Jack Cargill, *The Second Athenian League* (1981) is an English treatment; on sycophants, D. Harvey, in P. Cartledge *et al.* (eds.), *Nomos* (1990), 103–22; on feuds, P. J. Rhodes, in P. Cartledge *et al.* (eds.), *Kosmos* (1998), 144–67. Walter Eder (ed.), *Athenische Demokratie im 4. Jahrhundert v. Chr. . . .* (1995) has several good essays; on the navy, G. L. Cawkwell, in *Classical Quarterly* (1984), 334–45, is important. On Demosthenes, A. W. Pickard-Cambridge, *Demosthenes* (1914) is still the best English 'life'; J. C. Trevett, in *Historia* (1999), 184–202, is important on his foreign policy.

Chapter 21. Alexander the Great

Ulrich Wilcken, *Alexander the Great* (1932) is the best short study; R. Lane Fox, *Alexander the Great* (1973) and A. B. Bosworth, *Conquest and Empire* (1988) are biographical and thematic respectively; A. B. Bosworth's lifelong *Historical Commentary on Arrian's History of Alexander* (1980–) is a fundamental resource; P. A. Brunt, *Arrian*, volumes I–II (1976–83; Loeb Library) is a translation with excellent notes and studies, a major contribution; J. R. Hamilton, *Plutarch, Alexander: A Commentary* (1969) is a guide to the problems in the best short 'life' of Alexander; J. E. Atkinson, *A Commentary on Q. Curtius Rufus' Historiae Alexandri Magni* (1980–) is valuable. J. Roisman (ed.), *Brill's Companion to Alexander the Great* (2003) is a good recent range of articles. Recent significant contributions, each provoking thought and dissent, are Georges Le Rider, *Alexander le grand: Monnaies, finance et politique* (2003), Pierre Briant, *Histoire de l'empire perse* (1996), 713–892, and P. M. Fraser, *Cities of Alexander the Great* (1996), a masterpiece of related scholarship, but on its main topic, compare N. G. L. Hammond, in *Greek, Roman and Byzantine Studies* (1998), 243–69, for much that it left out, not always rightly.

Chapter 22. Alexander's Early Successors

The best presentation is still Edouard Will, *Histoire politique du monde hellénistique*, volume I (1979, 2nd edn.), 1–120; F. Schachermeyr, *Alexander in Babylon* (1970) repays careful thought; biographies of the Successors include R. Billows, *Antigonus the One-Eyed and the Hellenistic State* (1997), John D. Grainger, *Seleukos Nikator* (1990) and especially Helen Lund, *Lysimachus* (1992); Pierre Briant, *Rois, tributs et paysans* (1982), 13–94, on Eumenes; A. B. Bosworth, *The Legacy of Alexander* (2002), a valuable collection; A. B. Bosworth and E. J. Baynham, *Alexander the Great in Fact and Fiction* (2000), 207–41, is thought-provoking on Alexander's so-called 'Will'; E. Badian, in *Harvard Studies in Classical Philology* (1967), 183–204, on the 'Plans' and in W. Will and J. Heinrichs (eds.), *Zu Alexander dem Grossen: Festschrift Gerhard Wirth*, volume I (1987), 605–25, on his 'ring'; Elizabeth D. Carney, *Women and Monarchy in Macedonia* (2000); Daniel Ogden, *Polygamy, Prostitutes and Death* (1999) and Jim Roy, in Lin Foxhall and John Salmon (eds.), *When Men Were Men* (1998), 111–35, with differing views on polygamy. E. J. Bickerman, *Religions and Politics in the Hellenistic and Roman Periods* (1985), 489–522, is a classic, on the Seleucids and the Achaemenids.

Chapter 23. Life in the Big Cities

P. M. Fraser, *Ptolemaic Alexandria*, volumes 1–3 (1972) is the fundamental study; Christian Jacob and François de Polignac, *Alexandria: The Third Century* BC (2000, English translation) is more slight; J.-Y. Empereur, *Alexandria Rediscovered* (1998) and *Alexandria: Past, Present and Future* (2002) include very recent discoveries, as does the different project of Franck Goddio, *Alexandria: The Submerged Royal Quarters* (1998) and *Alexandria: The Submerged Canopic Region* (2004); Judith McKenzie, in *Journal of Roman Archaeology* (2003), 35–63, is an excellent survey of the evidence; P. Leriche, in J.-L. Huot, *La Ville neuve: Une idée de l'antiquité* (1994), 109–25, is an important survey; Günther Hölbl, *A History of the Ptolemaic Empire* (2001) makes the royal family accessible in English. Paul Bernard, Olivier Guillaume, Henri Paul Francfort, Pierre Leriche and others present aspects of the, sadly interrupted, excavations of Ai Khanum in Afghanistan in *Fouilles d'Ai Khanum* (1973 onwards); E. E. Rice, *The Grand Procession of Ptolemy Philadelphus* (1983); O. Murray, 'Hellenistic Royal Symposia', in P. Bilde (ed.), *Aspects of Hellenistic Kingship* (1996), 15–27, is important; G. E. R. Lloyd, *Greek Science after Aristotle* (1973) is still a good overview; H. von Staden, *Herophilus: The Art of Medicine in Early Alexandria* (1989) is a major advance, with V. Nutton, *Ancient Medicine* (2004) on Erasistratus; Lionel Casson, *Libraries in the Ancient World* (2001) is an excellent short survey. G. O. Hutchinson, *Hellenistic Poetry* (1988) is acute and appreciative; R. L. Hunter and M. Fantuzzi, *Tradition and Innovation in Hellenistic Poetry* (2004) are up-to-date guides. Collections by Paul Cartledge, P. Garnsey and E. Gruen (eds.), *Hellenistic Constructs . . .* (1997) and Peter Green (ed.), *Hellenistic History and Culture* (1993) show what is going on in English publications. W. W. Tarn, with G. T. Griffith, *Hellenistic Civilization* (1952, 3rd edn.) is unsurpassed as a vigorous read.

Chapter 24. Taxes and Technologies

C. Préaux, *L'Économie Royale des Lagides* (1939) is still basic, with the renewed study of J. Bingen, *Le Papyrus Revenue Laws: Tradition grecque et adaptation hellénistique* (1978); J. G. Manning, *Land and Power in Ptolemaic Egypt* (2003) uses non-Greek evidence well; Georges Le Rider, *Alexandre Le Grand: Monnaie, finances et politique* (2003), 214–65; D. J. Thompson, in P. A. Cartledge, P. Garnsey and E. Gruen (eds.), *Hellenistic Constructs . . .* (1997), 242–57, is an important survey. On technology, a minimalist view is given by M. I. Finley, in *Economic History Review* (1965), 29–45 and rather vigorously attacked by Kevin Greene, in *Economic History Review* (2000), 29–59, not always convincingly; his bibliography is very valuable. O. Wikander, *Exploitation of Water-power or Technological Stagnation?* (1984) is important; so is Michael J. T. Lewis, *Millstone and Hammer: The Origins of Water Power* (1997), 20–58, on the Alexandrian texts; Andrew Wilson in *Journal of Roman Studies* (2002), 1–32, another vigorous revisionist of Finley's views; Paul Millett, a Finley follower, denies 'growth' in D. J. Mattingly and J. Salmon (eds.), *Economies Beyond Agriculture in the Classical World* (2000), 17–48; R. B. Hitchner, 'The Advantages of Wealth and Luxury', in J. Manning and I. Morris (eds.), *The Ancient Economy: Evidence and Models* (2002) tries to reassert it: K. D. White, *Greek and Roman Technology* (1984) is still a valuable survey; Sir Desmond Lee, in *Greece and Rome* (1973), 65–77 and 180–192, is good on the 'non-industrial' ancient world. P. M. Fraser, *Ptolemaic Alexandria I* (1972), 132–88, on Alexandrian trade, and 425–434 (applied sciences, but not the 'toys', unfortunately: 426).

Chapter 25. The New World

L. Robert, 'De Delphes à l'Oxus', in *Comptes-Rendus de L'Académie des Inscriptions et Belles Lettres* (1968), 416–57, is a 'classic'; Barry W. Cunliffe, *The Extraordinary Voyage of Pytheas the Greek* (2002) is a readable account but concludes, as I do not, that Pytheas went to Iceland; I. Pimouguet-Pédarres and F. Delrieux, *L'Anatolie, la Syrie, l'égypte . . .* (2003) collects excellent articles, comments and bibliography, which I presuppose; Claire Préaux, *Le Monde hellénistique: La grèce et l'orient*, volumes 1–2 (1978), is an outstanding survey, with invaluable bibliographies; E. J. Bickerman, *The Jews in the Greek Age* (1988) is a classic, even among his works. On spreading Greek, D. J. Thompson, in A. K. Bowman and G. Woolf (eds.), *Literacy and Power* (1994), 67–83, is very important. C. Habicht, *Athens from Alexander to Antony* (1997) opens up a fragmented subject, with his important *Hellenistic Athens and Her Philosophers* (1988, English translation). E. R. Bevan, *Stoics and Sceptics* (1913) is still worth reading, as is A. J. Festugière, *Epicurus and His Gods* (1969, English translation); A. A. Long, *Hellenistic Philosophy* (1986, 2nd edn.); W. Capelle, 'Der Garten des Theophrast', in Wolfgang Müller (ed.), *Festschrift für Felix*

Zucker (1954), 47–82, is more sympathetic than J. E. Raven, *Plants and Plant Lore in Ancient Greece* (2000); on Zenon, Claude Orrieux, *Les Papyrus de Zenon . . .* (1983) and *Zenon de Caunos, Parepidemos* (1985) are excellent studies, with X. Durand, *Des grecs en Palestine au III siècle: Le dossier syrien de Zénon de Caunos* (1997). On a great geographer, P. M. Fraser, 'Eratosthenes of Cyrene', in *Proceedings of the British Academy* (1970), 176–207; on ethnography, Albrecht Dihle, 'Zur Hellenistischen Ethnographie', in *Grecs et Barbares*, Entretiens Fondation Hardt VIII (1965), 205–39, is excellent; so is A. Momigliano, *Alien Wisdom: The Limits of Hellenization* (1975). On Hecataeus, O. Murray, in *Journal of Egyptian Studies* (1970), 141, and J. Dillery, in *Historia* (1998), 255–75. On India, Pascal Charvet and Fabrizia Baldissera, *Arrien: Le voyage en Inde d'Alexandre le grand* (2002) has an excellent bibliography; K. Karttunen, *India in Early Greek Literature* (1989); W. W. Tarn, *The Greeks in Bactria and India* (1951, 2nd edn.) is a superb read whose ingenuities deserve, and require, a lifetime of correction. P. Brulé, 'Enquête démographique sur la famille grecque antique', in *Revue des Études Anciennes* (1990), 233–58, repays careful thought; on other lines, R. van Bremen, in Andrew Erskine (ed.), *A Companion to the Hellenistic World* (2003), 313–30, part of an excellent collection.

CHAPTER 26. ROME REACHES OUT

T. J. Cornell, *The Beginnings of Rome* (1995), chapters 7–15, takes a thoughtfully positive line on the evidence; Andrew Erskine, *Troy between Greece and Rome* (2001) is very well written; A. W. Lintott, *The Constitution of the Roman Republic* (1999) is an excellent guide through a great jungle; Fergus Millar, *The Roman Republic in Political Thought* (2002) is a fine complement; M. W. Frederiksen, *Campania* (1984), chapters 8, 9, 10 are very important on Rome's expansion. Kurt A. Raaflaub (ed.), *Social Struggles in Archaic Rome* (1986); on the army reforms, David Potter, in Harriet I. Flower (ed.), *The Cambridge Companion to the Roman Republic* (2004), 66–88, is very important; N. Purcell, in David Braund and Christopher Gill (eds.), *Myth, History and Culture in Republican Rome* (2003), 12–40, on foreign contacts; Tim Cornell, ibid. (2003), 73–97, on Coriolanus; J. H. C. Williams, *Beyond the Rubicon: Romans and Gauls in Republican Italy* (2001), on the Gallic question; Hanneke Wilson, *Wine and Words* (2003), 55–73, on women and wine; N. Purcell, in *Cambridge Ancient History*, volume VI (1994), 381–403 on South Italy and T. J. Cornell, ibid. volume VIII.2 (1989), 351–419; on Tarentum, G. C. Brauer Jun., *Taras: Its History and Coinage* (1983) with P. Wuilleumier, *Tarente, des origines à la conquête romaine* (1939), a classic, J. Heurgon, *The Rise of Rome to 264 BC* (1973, English translation) is still excellent.

CHAPTER 27. THE PEACE OF THE GODS

Translated texts and discussions are now available in M. Beard, J. North and S. R. F. Price, *Religions of Rome*, volumes 1–2 (1998), giving an accessible history and excellent bibliographies; R. M. Ogilvie, *The Romans and Their Gods* (1969) is still valuable and John Scheid, *An Introduction to Roman Religion* (2003, English translation) is excellent; Clifford Ando (ed.), *Roman Religion* (2003) is a good selection of important articles; W. Warde Fowler, *The Roman Festivals of the Period of the Republic* (1899) is still important; T. P. Wiseman, in Bettina Bergmann and Christine Kondoleon, *The Art of Ancient Spectacle* (1999), 195–204, discusses the Floralia; T. P. Wiseman, *The Myths of Rome* (2004) is a great synthesis. Edward Bispham and Christopher Smith (eds.), *Religion in Archaic and*

Republican Rome and Italy (2000) includes papers on Italy outside Rome, which I have compressed, or had to omit. J. A. North, *Roman Religion* (2000) is a 'New Survey' which takes the subject forward through the centuries, with good bibliographies too.

CHAPTER 28. LIBERATION IN THE SOUTH

J. Heurgon, *The Rise of Rome to 284* BC (1973, English translation) is an excellent survey; Pierre Lévêque, *Pyrrhos* (1957) is the classic starting point; Jane Hornblower, *Hieronymus of Cardia* (1981) is excellent on one major historian, and A. Momigliano, *Essays in Ancient and Modern Historiography* (1977) is a classic on Timaeus; David Asheri, in *Scripta Classica Israelica* (1991), 52–89, on Timaeus' synchronisms; J. F. Lazenby, *The First Punic War* (1996) is a military history and Y. Le Bohec, *Histoire militaire des guerres puniques* (2003) is another; Werner Huss, *Karthago* (1995) is fundamental for Carthage.

CHAPTER 29. HANNIBAL AND ROME

S. Lancel, *Hannibal, 247–182* BC (1998, English translation) is the best up-to-date general study; Tim Cornell, Boris Rankov and Philip Sabin (eds.), *The Second Punic War: A Reappraisal* (1996) is a very good selection of essays. The sources pose problems, recently reviewed by Briggs L. Twyman, in *Athenaeum* (1987), 67, and R. T. Ridley, 'Livy and the Hannibalic War', in C. Bruun (ed.), *The Roman Middle Republic: Politics, Religion and Historiography* (2000, Acta Instituti Romani Finlandiae, 23), 13–40; on coins, E. S. G. Robinson, in *Numismatic Chronicle* (1964), 37–64. On warfare, Philip Sabin, 'The Roman Face of Battle', in *Journal of Roman Studies* (2000), 1–17 and once again, H. H. Scullard, *The Elephant in the Greco-Roman World* (1974), 146–77. Gregory Daly, *Cannae: The Experience of Battle in the Second Punic War* (2002) is vivid. On the war's impact in Italy, Andrew Erskine, in *Hermes* (1993), 58–62; W. V. Harris, *Rome in Etruria and Umbria* (1971), 131–43, and the very different views of two magnificent works, A. J. Toynbee, *Hannibal's Legacy*, volumes I–II (1965) and P. A. Brunt, *Italian Manpower, 225* BC–AD *14* (1987, 2nd edn.), 269–88. Here, my views are closer to those of T. J. Cornell, 'Hannibal's Legacy: The Effects of the Hannibalic War on Italy', in Tim Cornell, Boris Rankov and Philip Sabin (eds.), *The Second Punic War: A Reappraisal* (1996), 97–117.

CHAPTER 30. DIPLOMACY AND DOMINANCE

Peter Derow, in Andrew Erskine (ed.), *A Companion to the Hellenistic World* (2003), 51–70, is an excellent overview, based on years of reconsideration; W. V. Harris, *War and Imperialism in Republican Rome* (1979), 68–130 and 200–44; J. S. Richardson, *Hispaniae: Spain and the Developments of Roman Imperialism, 218–82* BC (1986) and *The Romans in Spain* (1996). On particular episodes, P. S. Derow, 'Polybius, Rome and the East', in *Journal of Roman Studies* (1979), 1–15; A. Meadows, 'Greek and Roman Diplomacy on the Eve of the Second Macedonian War', in *Historia* (1993), 40–60; J. J. Walsh, 'Flamininus and the Propaganda of Liberation', in *Historia* (1996), 344–63; F. W. Walbank, 'The Causes of the Third Macedonian War: Recent Views', in *Ancient Macedonia II . . .* (Thessaloniki, Institute for Balkan Studies, 1977), 81–94; N. Purcell, 'On the Sacking of Carthage and Corinth', in D. Innes, H. Hine and C. Pelling (eds.), *Ethics and Rhetoric:*

Classical Essays for Donald Russell on His Seventy-fifth Birthday (1995), 133–48. On dealings with kings, John T. Ma, *Antiochus III and the Cities of Western Asia Minor* (1999) and E. Badian, in J. Harmatta (ed.), *Proceedings of the VIIth Congress of the International Federation of the Societies of Classical Studies* (1984), 397. On Roman motivation, John Rich, 'Fear, Greed and Glory', in J. Rich and G. Shipley (eds.), *War and Society in the Roman World* (1993), 38–68, A Ziolkowski, 'Urbs Direpta, or How the Romans Sacked Cities', ibid. (1993), 69–91. On third-century Greece, Graham Shipley, *The Greek World after Alexander, 323–30 BC* (1999), 108–152; F. W. Walbank, 'An Experiment In Greek Union', in *Proceedings of the Classical Association* (1970), 13–27 and his 'The Causes of Greek Decline', in *Journal of Hellenic Studies* (1944), 10–20; G. E. M. de Sainte Croix, *The Class Struggle in the Ancient Greek World* (1981), 344–50 and 518–37, with John Briscoe, in *Past and Present* (1967), 1–20 and J. J. Walsh, in *Classical Quarterly* (2000), 300–3. On the 'destruction of democracy', P. J. Rhodes and D. M. Lewis, *The Decrees of the Greek States* (1997), 542–50.

CHAPTER 31. LUXURY AND LICENCE

Erich S. Gruen, *Culture and National Identity in Republican Rome* (1992) is an excellent survey of Greek–Roman interrelations; Jean-Louis Ferrary, *Philhellénisme et impérialisme* (1988) is extremely important for the relations of power; Matthew Leigh, *Comedy and the Rise of Rome* (2004), on the dramas; E. Baltrusch, *Regimen Morum* (1989) is full of detail; A. G. Clemente, in A. Giardina and A. Schiavone (eds.), *Società romana e produzione schiavistica*, volume I (1981), 1–12, is the best short survey of sumptuary law; E. Gabba, *Del buon uso della richezza* (1988) is longer. On Cato, A. E. Astin, *Cato the Censor* (1978) is a narrative, with all the evidence; Jonathan C. Edmondson, in Bettina Bergmann and Christine Kondoleon, *The Art of Ancient Spectacle* (1999), 77–96, is excellent on the shows in the East and at Rome in the 160s BC. Erich S. Gruen, *Heritage and Hellenism* (2002), on culture-clashes in Judaea. On Polybius, P. S. Derow, in T. James Luce, *Ancient Writers: Greece and Rome*, volume I (1982), 525–40, is a very penetrating introduction. F. W. Walbank, *Polybius* (1972) is essential, with the subsequent survey to 2000 and some fascinating essays in his *Polybius, Rome and the Hellenistic World* (2002). His three-volume *Commentary on Polybius* (1957–79) is the outstanding such work by a living scholar on Greek history.

CHAPTER 32. TURBULENCE AT HOME AND ABROAD

Much is compressed, or omitted, in this chapter, but the period is excellently served in the revised *Cambridge Ancient History*, volume IX (1994), especially chapters 2–6, pages 498–563, on public and private law (a particularly compressed element in my 'story') and chapter 15 (administration of the Empire). The sources are collected invaluably by A. H. J. Greenidge and A. M. Clay, *Sources of Roman History, 133–70 BC* (1986, 2nd edn.). On individual careers, A. E. Astin, *Scipio Aemilianus* (1967); David Stockton, *The Gracchi* (1979); T. Carney, *A Biography of C. Marius* (1970, 2nd edn.); E. Badian, *Lucius Sulla: The Deadly Reformer*, Todd Memorial Lecture (1970); Arthur Keaveney, *Sulla: The Last Republican* (1982) and J. P. V. D. Balsdon, 'Sulla Felix', in *Journal of Roman Studies* (1951), 1–10. On particular aspects, A. N. Sherwin-White, 'The Political Ideas of C. Gracchus', in *Journal of Roman Studies* (1982), 18–31 and P. A. Brunt, *The Fall of the Roman Republic* (1988), chapters 2–4 are exceptionally important; also, J. S. Richardson, in *Journal of Roman Studies*

(1987), 1–12, on extortion; A. W. Lintott, *Judicial Reform and Land Reform in the Roman Republic* (1992), 10–33, and 44–50; E. Gabba, *Republican Rome, the Army and the Allies* (1976), chapters 1 and 2. Robert Morstein Kallet-Marx, *Hegemony to Empire* (1995) is excellent on Rome's 'empire' to 62 BC. M. H. Crawford (ed.), *Roman Statutes I* (1996), numbers 1, 2, 12 and 14, gives excellent commentaries on four major documents.

CHAPTER 33. POMPEY'S TRIUMPHS

Pat Southern, *Pompey the Great* (2002) is a lively popular introduction; Robin Seager, *Pompey the Great* (2003, revised edn.) is a scholarly study of political factions and detail. F. G. B. Millar, *The Crowd in Rome in the Late Republic* (1998), chapters 2–4, takes a clear and vigorous line, though the main 'democratic' emphasis is not followed in my chapter, on which see M. Jehne (ed.), 'Demokratie in Rom?', in *Historia Einzelschrift*, 96 (1995), for full critiques. For questions linked to aristocratic competition, see the exchanges of view by Nathan Rosenstein, Callie Williamson, John North and W. V. Harris, in *Classical Philology* (1990), 255–98. For Rome, the East and Mithridates, A. N. Sherwin-White, *Roman Foreign Policy in the East* (1984), 149–270. On Pompey and public shows, Richard C. Beacham, *Spectacle Entertainments of Early Imperial Rome* (1999), 49–74.

CHAPTER 34. THE WORLD OF CICERO

J. P. V. D. Balsdon, 'Cicero the Man', in T. A. Dorey (ed.), *Cicero* (1965), 171–214, remains an outstanding study; Elizabeth Rawson, *Cicero: A Portrait* (1983, 2nd edn.) is a many-sided study, while David Stockton, *Cicero: A Political Biography* (1971) is good on its chosen ground. L. R. Taylor, *Party Politics in the Age of Caesar* (1968) is excellent, especially chapter III ('Delivering the Vote') and chapter V ('The Criminal Courts and the Rise of a New Man'). D. R. Shackleton Bailey (ed.), *Cicero's Letters to Atticus*, volume I (1965), 3–58, is a superb study of Atticus and Cicero; Miriam T. Griffin, 'Philosophical Badinage in Cicero's Letters To His Friends', in J. G. F. Powell (ed.), *Cicero the Philosopher: Twelve Papers* (1995), 325–46, catches a wider world. The editions of D. R. Shackleton Bailey, including the recent Loeb Library texts and translations of Cicero's Letters, are acknowledged masterpieces. S. Treggiari, *Roman Social History* (2002), 49–73, is an exemplary study of how they can be used for nonpolitical topics; Susan Treggiari, *Roman Marriage* (1991), 127–38, 414–27 and chapter 13 ('Divorce') guides us through marriage and Cicero; Susan Treggiari, *Roman Freedmen during the Late Republic* (1969), 252–64, on Cicero's freedmen, including Tiro; S. Weinstock, in *Journal of Roman Studies* (1961), 209–10, underlies my view of Cicero and 'religion'.

CHAPTER 35. THE RISE OF JULIUS CAESAR

J. P. V. D. Balsdon, *Julius Caesar and Rome* (1967) is an excellent brief introduction; Matthias Gelzer, *Caesar* (1968) is the basic fully documented account; Christian Meier, *Caesar* (1995, English translation) is more abstract, but is notably reviewed by E. Badian in *Gnomon* (1990), 22–39, whose own brief survey in the *Oxford Classical Dictionary* (1996, 3rd edn.), 780–2, is important. Kathryn Welch, Anton Powell and Jonathan Barlow (eds.), *Julius Caesar as Artful Reporter* (1998) has much of value on Caesar's style and 'spin'. On

Cato, L. R. Taylor, *Party Politics in the Age of Caesar* (1968), 119–39. On land allotment, P. A. Brunt, *The Fall of the Roman Republic* (1988), 240–88, is a classic; on debt and financing, M. W. Frederiksen, 'Caesar, Cicero and the Problem of Debt', in *Journal of Roman Studies* (1966), 128–41, is another. J. Sabben Clare, *Caesar and Roman Politics, 60–50 BC* (1971), 1–49, translates much of the main evidence very helpfully. P. A. Brunt, *Italian Manpower* (1987, 2nd edn.), 312–19, discusses Caesar's agrarian laws. On public speaking, Andrew J. E. Bell, 'Cicero and the Spectacle of Power', in *Journal of Roman Studies* (1997), 1–22, and the very important study by R. Morstein-Marx, *Mass Oratory and Political Power in the Late Roman Republic* (2004).

CHAPTER 36. THE SPECTRE OF CIVIL WAR

T. P. Wiseman, 'Caesar, Pompey and Rome, 59–50 BC,' in *Cambridge Ancient History*, volume IX (1994), 368–423, gives an intelligible narrative; P. A. Brunt, *The Fall of the Roman Republic* (1988), chapter 1 is masterly and chapter 6 ('*Libertas* in the Republic') is fundamental at this point; David Stockton, 'Cicero and the Ager Campanus', in *Transactions of the American Philological Society* (1962), 471–89, is an outstanding study of 57–56 BC and much more besides; A. W. Lintott, 'P. Clodius Pulcher–Felix Catilina', in *Greece and Rome* (1967), 157–69, and 'Cicero and Milo', in *Journal of Roman Studies* (1974), 62–78, help to explain two leading 'populists', together with A. W. Lintott, *Violence in Republican Rome* (1999, 2nd edn.), especially pages 67–88. On living conditions, P. A. Brunt, 'The Roman Mob', in M. I. Finley (ed.), *Studies in Ancient Society* (1974), 74–102, is fundamental, with A. Scobie, in *Klio* (1986), 399–443. Emily A. Hemelrijk, *Matrona Docta* (1999) is good on educated women, in the late Republic and in the Empire. J. F. Drinkwater, *Roman Gaul* (1983), 5–20, briefly summarizes Caesar's Gallic years; Elizabeth Rawson, *Roman Culture and Society* (1991), 416–26, is very interesting on Crassus senior and junior; G. R. Stanton, in *Historia* (2003), 67–94, studies 'why did Caesar cross the Rubicon?'

CHAPTER 37. THE FATAL DICTATOR

S. Weinstock, *Divus Julius* (1971), 133–345, is the outstanding study still, in my judgement, with I. Gradel, *Emperor Worship and Roman Religion* (2002), 54–72. Elizabeth Rawson, *Roman Culture and Society* (1991), 169–88 on the 'kingship', and pages 488–507, especially, on Cassius, with David Sedley, in *Journal of Roman Studies* (1997), 41–53; Stephen G. Chrissanthos, in *Journal of Roman Studies* (2001), 63–71, on money; M. W. Frederiksen, in *Journal of Roman Studies* (1966), 128–41 on debt, with G. E. M. de Sainte Croix, *The Class Struggle in the Ancient Greek World* (1981), 166 and notes 60–63. P. A. Brunt, in *Journal of Roman Studies* (1986), 12–32, on Cicero's dilemma; R. B. Ulrich, in *American Journal of Archaeology* (1993), 49–80, on the new Forum; C. Habicht, *Cicero the Politician* (1990), chapter 6, on Cicero; Z. Yavetz, *Caesar and His Public Image* (1983), 101–6, on Caesar's legislation; Tenney Frank, *An Economic Survey of Ancient Rome*, volume I (1933), 316–18, on the colonies, and pages 333–42 on funding, is still excellent. J. P. V. D. Balsdon, in *Historia* (1958), 80–94, a classic on the Ides and motives, though not the last word.

Chapter 38. Liberation Betrayed

R. Syme, *The Roman Revolution* (1939; revised edn., 1951) is a classic, but I am one of those who find it a very difficult read. Henriette van der Blom, in *Classica et Mediaevalia* (2003), 287–320, is now an excellent and much clearer account of Cicero in 44–43 BC; compare Elizabeth Rawson, *Cicero* (1975), 260–98. The new emphasis of importance is on Sextus Pompeius, in Anton Powell and Kathryn Welch (eds.), *Sextus Pompeius* (2002); on the Liberators, Elizabeth Rawson, *Roman Culture and Society* (1991), 488–507; Lawrence Keppie, *The Making of the Roman Army* (1984), 112–21, 199–204; S. Weinstock, *Divus Julius* (1971), 346–47 is masterly here too. T. N. Mitchell, *Cicero the Senior Statesman* (1991), chapter 7, is well documented; R. Syme, *Sallust* (1964) is an important study.

Chapter 39. Antony and Cleopatra

R. Syme, *The Roman Revolution* (1939; revised edn., 1951), chapters XII to XXI, a classic, but reductionist; Pat Southern, *Mark Antony* (1998) is a simple start on Antony; Ellen Rice, *Cleopatra* (1999), likewise. Major changes since Syme's book include awareness of the 'fourth man', in Anton Powell and Kathryn Welch (eds.), *Sextus Pompeius* (2002) and much more work on monuments and publicity. Paul Zanker, *The Power of Images in the Age of Augustus* (1988), 5–78, a fine study, with the excellent article of K. Scott, in *Memoirs of the American Academy at Rome* (1933), 7–49; the good survey of 36–28 BC by Fergus Millar, in *La Révolution romaine après Ronald Syme*, Entretiens Fondation Hardt XLVI (1999), 1–38, with the others in the volume, especially John Scheid, pages 39–72, on religion. Syme's contribution is reconsidered by H. Galsterer and Z. Yavetz, in Kurt A Raaflaub and Mark Toher (eds.), *Between Republic and Empire* (1990), 1–41. The marriage of Antony and Cleopatra and Cleopatra's death raise questions too, beyond Syme's book: John Whitehorne, *Cleopatras* (1994), especially pages 186–96, and Duane W. Roller, *The World of Juba II and Kleopatra Selene* (2003), an excellent study. Jacob Isager, *Foundation and Destruction of Nicopolis and Northeastern Greece* (2001), for one aftermath; Joyce Reynolds, *Aphrodisias and Rome* (1982) for the important documents.

Chapter 40. The Making of the Emperor

W. K. Lacey, *Augustus and the Principate: The Evolution of the System* (1996) is a very useful collection of studies; P. A. Brunt, in *La rivoluzione romana*, Biblioteca de Labeo, 6 (1982), 236–44 is best on 27 BC; D. Stockton, in *Historia* (1965), 18–40, adopts 23 BC for the trial which I have put now in 22 BC; P. A. Brunt and J. M. Moore, *Res Gestae Divi Augusti* (1967) with translation and excellent commentary, especially on 19 BC; A. H. M. Jones, *Studies in Roman Government and Law* (1960), 1–17 is a lucid basis for much since written in dialogue with it; M. T. Griffin, in Loveday Alexander (ed.), *Images of Empire* (1991), 19–46, questions the overtones of the 'tribunician' side to 23 BC. A. Wallace-Hadrill, in *Journal of Roman Studies* (1982), 32–48, on the emperor's many-sided image; P. A. Brunt, in *Classical Quarterly* (1984), 423–44, on the Senate's continuing functions, if not power.

CHAPTER 41. MORALS AND SOCIETY

M. Beard, J. North and S. R. F. Price, *Religions of Rome*, volume I (1998), 114–210, is an excellent, questioning survey, with J. Liebeschuetz, *Continuity and Change in Roman Religion* (1979), chapter 2; P. A. Brunt, *Italian Manpower* (1971), 558–66, is important; Catherine Edwards, *The Politics of Immorality in Ancient Rome* (1983) gives the context very well; S. Treggiari, *Roman Marriage* (1991) is a classic, especially pages 60–80, 277–98 and 450–61. J. A. Crook, *Law and Life of Rome* (1967), 99–118, especially on the rather varied implications of the changes in 'manus' marriage; Beryl Rawson (ed.), *The Family in Ancient Rome* (1986) is still a fine collection throughout, including J. A. Crook on the (later) wariness about women making loans (pages 83–92); Beryl Rawson, *Marriages, Divorce and Children in Ancient Rome* (1991) is also excellent, especially chapters 1–5; Jane F. Gardner, *Women in Roman Law and Society* (1995, 2nd edn.) is a fundamental guide; Susan Dixon, *Childhood, Class and Kin* (2001) is relevant too. Jasper Griffin, in *Journal of Roman Studies* (1976), 87, and R. G. M. Nisbet, ibid. (1987), 184–90, debate the poets and their context; Peter Green, *Classical Bearings* (1989), 210–22 is excellent on Ovid's exile. A. M. Duff, *Freedmen in the Early Roman Empire* (1928), 12–35 and 72–88 and K. R. Bradley, *Slaves and Masters in the Roman Empire* (1984) untangle the laws on slaves very well.

CHAPTER 42. SPECTATOR SPORTS

D. S. Potter and D. J. Mattingly (eds.), *Life, Death and Entertainment in the Roman Empire* (1998) is an excellent collection to which I owe much. Richard C. Beacham, *Spectacle Entertainments of Early Imperial Rome* (1999) is excellent, with good bibliographies. K. M. Coleman, in *Journal of Roman Studies* (1990), 44–73, and (1993), 48–74, are excellent studies; R. E. Fantham, in *Classical World* (1989), 153–63, on mimes; on pantomime, E. J. Jory, in *Bulletin of the Institute of Classical Studies* (1981), 147–61, and in W. J. Slater (ed.), *Roman Theatre and Society* (1996), 1–28, a valuable collection throughout; C. P. Jones, in W. J. Slater (ed.), *Dining in a Classical Context* (1991), 185–98, on theatre over dinner; Garrett G. Fagan, *Bathing in Public in the Roman World* (1999), with translated texts; J. H. Humphrey, *Roman Circuses: Arenas for Chariot Racing* (1986) is invaluable; Eckart Köhne and Cornelia Ewigleben, *Gladiators and Caesars* (2000) is very vivid; Adriano La Regina (ed.), *Sangue e arena* (2001) is outstandingly good; David Potter, in Martin M. Winkler (ed.), *Gladiator: Film and History* (2004) gives an excellent account of gladiators' careers; Donald G. Kyle, *Spectacles of Death in the Roman Amphitheatre* (1998), full of explanatory theories too; D. C. Bomgardner, *The Story of the Roman Amphitheater* (2000), a social history; Keith Hopkins, *Death and Renewal* (1983), chapter 1; Bettina Bergmann and Christine Kondoleon (eds.), *The Art of Ancient Spectacle* (1999), an excellent collection; B. M. Levick, in *Journal of Roman Studies* (1983), 97–115, is the classic study of official reactions, and Elizabeth Rawson, *Roman Culture and Society* (1991), 508–45 of theatre-regulations and the Lex Julia; Kathleen M. Coleman, in Kathleen Lomas and Tim Cornell (eds.), *Bread and Circuses* (2002), 61–88, on the location of Augustan shows.

CHAPTER 43. THE ROMAN ARMY

J. J. Wilkins (ed.), *Documenting the Roman Army: Essays in Honour of Margaret Roxan* (2003, Bulletin of the Institute of Classical Studies) is an excellent collection of essays, especially W. Eck on the emperor's role in issuing 'diplomas'; L. R. Keppie, *The Making of the Roman Army* (1984), 132–216, is excellent on the change from Civil War to the age of Augustus; J. B. Campbell, *The Emperor and the Roman Army, 31 BC–AD 235* (1984), 17–242 and 300–316, is basic on the emperor's role and the giving of privileges; G. R. Watson, *The Roman Soldier* (1969) is lively and P. Connolly, *The Roman Army* (1975) is by an author who is interested in reconstructing the realities; G. Webster, *The Roman Imperial Army* (1985, 3rd edn.); Brian Campbell, *The Roman Army, 31 BC–AD 337* (1994) is a very good sourcebook; Harry Sidebottom, *Ancient Warfare: A Very Short Introduction* (2004) is outstandingly good, with a very good bibliography. I incline to the studies by M. P. Speidel, *Riding for Caesar* (1994) and Ann Hyland, *Equus: The Horse in the Roman World* (1990), especially on saddles and harness. Jonathan Roth, *The Logistics of the Roman Army* (1999) is of wide relevance; T. J. Cornell, in J. Rich and G. Shipley (eds.), *War and Society in the Roman World* (1993), 139–70, surveys Roman military expansion in the early imperial age; J. N. Adams, in *Journal of Roman Studies* (1994), 87–112 and ibid. (1999), 109–34, two fascinating studies of soldiers' Latin in north Africa.

CHAPTER 44. THE NEW AGE

M. Beard, J. North and S. R. F. Price (eds.), *Religions of Rome*, volume I (1998), 182–210, on rites and temples; D. C. Feeney, *Literature and Religion at Rome* (1998), 28–38; A. D. Nock, *Essays on Religion and the Ancient World*, volume I (1972), 16–25 and 348–56. Greg Rowe, *Princes and Political Culture* (2003), especially pages 102–24 on Pisa and elsewhere; Beth Severy, *Augustus and the Family at the Birth of the Roman Empire* (2003) is excellent; N. Purcell, in *Proceedings of the Cambridge Philological Society* (1986), 78–105, and M. Boudreau Flory, in *Historia* (1984), 309–330, are important on Livia; N. Horsfall, *The Culture of the Roman Plebs* (2003); P. Zanker, *The Power of Images in the Age of Augustus* (1988), 79–297, extremely readable; Kurt A. Raaflaub and Mark Toher (eds.), *Between Republic and Empire* (1990), especially T. J. Luce, pages 123–38, B. A. Kellner, pages 276–307, and K. Raaflaub, pages 428–54; F. G. B. Millar and E. Segal (eds.), *Caesar Augustus: Seven Aspects* (1984), especially Millar, pages 37–60, and W. Eck, pages 129–68, in an excellent collection; A. H. M. Jones, *Criminal Courts of the Roman Republic and Principate* (1972); F. G. B. Millar, *The Emperor in the Roman World* (1977), 363–550, on embassies and justice; A. W. Lintott, *Imperium Romanum* (1993), 115–20.

CHAPTER 45. THE JULIO-CLAUDIANS

T. P. Wiseman, *Roman Studies: Literary and Historical* (1987) cautions that, strictly, there was no Julio-Claudian 'dynasty', but the Julian *gens* and the imperial *domus*, so that Claudius is strictly an interloper: pages 96 and 376–7. Thorough biographies now guide us through all the issues: Barbara Levick, *Tiberius the Politician* (1999, 2nd edn.); G. P. Baker, *Tiberius Caesar: Emperor of Rome* (2001, reissue) is vivid; A. A. Barrett, *Caligula: The*

Corruption of Power (1993); Barbara Levick, *Claudius* (1993); Miriam Griffin, *Nero: The End of a Dynasty* (1984); Edward Champlin, *Nero* (2003); Jas Elsner and Jamie Masters (eds.), *Reflections of Nero* (1994), on the culture and legacy. On their settings, Clemens Krause, *Villa Jovis: Die Residenz der Tiberius auf Capri* (2003) is excellent, with A. F. Stewart, in *Journal of Roman Studies* (1977), 76–94; Elisabeth Segala and Ida Sciortino, *Domus Aurea* (1999), on Nero's awful House. On two of the women, Nikos Kokkinos, *Antonia Augusta: Portrait of a Great Roman Lady* (2002), updated for new evidence; Anthony Barrett, *Agrippina* (1996). Greg Rowe, *Princes and Political Culture: The New Tiberian Senatorial Decrees* (2002) discusses the remarkable new finds of inscriptions. Doreen Innes and Barbara Levick, in *Omnibus II* (1989), 17–19, on empresses' toothpaste.

CHAPTER 46. RULING THE PROVINCES

Barbara Levick, *The Government of the Roman Empire* (2000, 2nd edn.) is an outstanding commentary on major texts in translation; P. A. Brunt, *Roman Imperial Themes* (1990) is now the classic study, especially chapters 4 (on which I differ, somewhat), 6, 8, 10, 11, 12 and 14–18; A. H. M. Jones, *The Roman Economy*, edited by P. A. Brunt (1974), chapters 1, 2 and 8 are also fundamental; Andrew Lintott, *Imperium Romanum* (1993) is an excellent synthesis; S. R. F. Price, *Rituals and Power* (1984), chapters 3–8, on cults of the empires in the Greek East. J. A. Crook, *Law and Life of Rome* (1967), chapters 2, 3 and 8 are still valuable; Stephen Mitchell, *Anatolia: Land, Men and Gods in Asia Minor*, volume I (1993), is an exemplary study of Asia Minor's provinces; Alan K. Bowman, *Egypt after the Pharaohs* (1986) and Naphtali Lewis, *Life in Egypt under Roman Rule* (1983) are excellent introductions to the best-documented area; C. R. Whittaker, *Frontiers of the Roman Empire* (1994) is a series of social and economic studies; F. G. B. Millar, *The Roman Empire and its Neighbours* (1981, 2nd edn.) is a good collection on the world beyond.

CHAPTER 47. EFFECTS OF EMPIRE

R. MacMullen, *Romanization in the Time of Augustus* (2000) is a very good survey; on benefactions, Stephen Mitchell, in *Harvard Studies in Classical Philology* (1987), 333–66, a very valuable study; P. A. Brunt, *Roman Imperial Themes* (1990), 267–81, and also pages 282–7 and 517–31 on Judaea are fundamental; *Cambridge Ancient History*, volume XI (2000, 2nd edn.), 444–678, is full of important material; Stephen Mitchell and Marc Waelkens, *Pisidian Antioch: The Site and Its Monuments* (1998) is excellent; on the West, T. F. Blagg and Martin Millett, *The Early Roman Empire in the West* (2002), especially Jonathan C. Edmondson, pages 169–73 on Conimbriga, and Nicola Mackie, pages 179–93 on 'epigraphic' honours and urban consciousness. A. T. Fear, *Rome and Baetica* (1996) is excellent on municipal law in Spain, with J. Gonzalez, in *Journal of Roman Studies* (1986), 147–243, and Alan Rodger, ibid. (1991), 74–90, and (1996), 61–73, on the recent Irni law. Peter Salway, *Roman Britain* (1981) and M. D. Goodman, *The Ruling Class of Judaea* (1987). Tessa Rajak, *Josephus: The Historian and His Society* (2002, 2nd edn.) is excellent on a historian I regret having omitted as not fully 'classical'. J. N. Adams, in *Journal of Roman Studies* (1995), 86–134 is excellent on the Latin found at Hadrian's Wall, a comfort to those in Britain whose Latin is still no better.

Chapter 48. Christianity and Roman Rule

E. P. Sanders, *The Historical Figure of Jesus* (1993) is an excellent methodical study; Gerd Theissen and Annette Merz, *The Historical Jesus* (1998, English translation), 125–280, gives a full survey; Paula Frederiksen, *From Jesus to Christ* (1988), the next stage; G. B. Caird, *The Apostolic Age* (1955) is still valuable; 'Christmas', was refuted by E. Schuerer, in *A History of the Jewish People*, volume I (1973, revised edn. by F. G. B. Millar and G. Vermes), 399–427; R. J. Lane Fox, *The Unauthorized Version* (1991), 27–36, 200–11, 243–51 and 283–310, and *Pagans and Christians* (1986), 265–335; G. E. M. de Sainte Croix, in D. Baker (ed.), *Studies in Church History*, volume 12 (1975), 1–38, vigorously criticizes Christian attitudes to property and slavery, and in *Past and Present* (1963), 6–38, he gives the classic account of Christian persecution; Wayne A. Meeks, *The First Urban Christians: The Social World of the Apostle Paul* (1983); M. Goodman, *Mission and Conversion* (1994) provokes thought; Henry Chadwick, *The Early Church* (1993, 2nd edn.) is the best one-volume history.

Chapter 49. Survivng Four Emperors

Kenneth Wellesley, *The Year of the Four Emperors* (2000, 3rd edn.) is the fullest modern account; early chapters in Barbara Levick, *Vespasian* (1999) are also fundamental, with full bibliography; on Vespasian's law, I differ from the very important study of P. A. Brunt, in *Journal of Roman Studies* (1977), 95–116; P. A. Brunt, *Papers of the British School at Rome* (1975), 7–35 is the classic study of philosophers and Stoics.

Chapter 50. The New Dynasty

Barbara Levick, *Vespasian* (1999) is the fundamental guide, with full notes and bibliography; Pat Southern, *Domitian: Tragic Tyrant* (1997) is one readable guide, especially on the later years; also, Brian W. Jones, *The Emperor Domitian* (1992); John D. Grainger, *Nerva and the Roman Succession Crisis of AD 96–99* (2001) discusses Nerva's reign too; A. J. Boyle and W. J. Dominik, *Flavian Rome: Culture, Image, Text* (2003) range widely over arts and culture; R. Darwall-Smith, *Emperors and Architecture: A Study of Flavian Rome* (1996); Paul Zanker, in Alan K. Bowman and Hannah M. Cotton (eds.), *Representations of Empire* (2002), 105–30, an overview of Domitian's palace in Rome.

Chapter 51. The Last Days of Pompeii

English readers are much better served now, with Paul Zanker, *Pompeii: Public and Private Life* (1998); Alison E. Cooley and M. G. C. Cooley, *Pompeii: A Sourcebook* (2004) which is now invaluable, with Alison E. Cooley, *Pompeii: Guide to the Lost City* (2000). Salvatore Nappo, *Pompeii* (2000) is the best popular guide; James L. Franklin, *Pompeiis Difficile Est . . .* (2001) is a very good epigraphic study; Antonio D'Ambrosio, *Women and Beauty in Pompeii* (2001) is short but interesting; W. F. Jashemski and Frederick G. Meyer (eds.), *The Natural History of Pompeii* (2002) has much new evidence, as does Annamaria Ciarallo, *Gardens of Pompeii* (2000); John R. Clarke, *Roman Sex: 100 BC–AD 250* (2003) puts Pompeian erotica in a wider context; Sara Bon and R. Jones, *Sequence and Space in*

Pompeii (1997) and T. McGran and P. Carafa (eds.), *Pompeian Brothels: Pompeii's Ancient History . . .* (2002) are two good essay collections. There is much else, but J. J. Deiss, *Herculaneum: A City Returns to the Sun* (1968) is the main English book given solely to Pompeii's important neighbour.

Chapter 52. A New Man in Action

A. N. Sherwin-White, *The Letters of Pliny* (1966) is a superb commentary; the Bithynian letters are revisited by his pupil, Wynne Williams, *Pliny: Correspondence with Trajan from Bithynia* (1990); R. Syme, *Roman Papers*, volume VII (1991), is more narrowly focused on prosopography; Richard Duncan-Jones, *The Economy of the Roman Empire* (1974), 17–32, is excellent on Pliny's finances. C. P. Jones, *The Roman World of Dio Chrysostom* (1978) is a fine study of Bithynia through another contemporary's texts; Christian Marek, *Pontus Et Bithynia* (2003) is a brilliantly illustrated local study; J. P. Sullivan, *Martial: The Unexpected Classic* (1991) with D. R. Shackleton Bailey, *Martial: Epigrams*, volumes I–III (1993, Loeb Library) which is masterly. Samuel Dill, *Roman Society from Nero to Marcus Aurelius* (1905, 2nd edn.), 141–286, is still unsurpassed in general range.

Chapter 53. A Pagan and Christians

Much that I discuss here is implicit in R. J. Lane Fox, *Pagans and Christians* (1986) and the valuable review-article of P. R. L. Brown, in *Philosophical Books*, 43 (2002), 185–208, together with his *The Body and Society* (1989) and *Poverty and Leadership in the Later Roman Empire* (2002). On suicide, see M. T. Griffin, in *Greece and Rome* (1986), 64–77 and 192–202; on gardens, the best English guide is Linda Farrar, *Ancient Roman Gardens* (2000), with the legacy well illustrated in Patrick Bowe, *Gardens of the Roman World* (2004).

Chapter 54. Regime Change, Home and Away

Julian Bennett, *Trajan* (1997) gathers together recent work excellently and allows me to refer simply to its bibliography on the matters in (and outside) my text; F. A. Lepper and S. S. Frere, *Trajan's Column* (1988) have excellent discussions of the Dacian War and many related issues, but should be read with M. Wilson Jones, in *Journal of Roman Archaeology* (1993), 23–38 and the very important revisions of Amanda Claridge, ibid. (1993), 5–22, attributing to Hadrian a major role in the monument, a view which I have hesitated over, simply because it is controversial, as James E. Packer shows, in *Journal of Roman Archaeology* (1994), 163–82. James E. Packer, *The Forum of Trajan in Rome* (2001, paperback) gives a briefer version of his masterwork on this subject; Lionel Casson, *Libraries in the Ancient World* (2001) puts the library in context. There is much in Annette Nünnerich-Asmus, *Traian: Ein Kaiser der Superlative am Beginn einer Umbruchzeit?* (2002). Anthony R. Birley, *Hadrian: The Restless Emperor* (1997), 35–77 is helpful, and in *Journal of Roman Studies* (1990), 115–26, discusses the Parthian War, but I remain firm about the chronology I adopt here, noting that it is also adopted by Birley, *Hadrian*, 71–3.

Chapter 55. Presenting the Past

Andrew Wallace-Hadrill, *Suetonius* (1995, 2nd edn.) and R. Syme, *Roman Papers*, volume III (1984), 1251–75, on biography; R. Syme, *Ten Studies in Tacitus* (1970) is more accessible than his *Tacitus* (1958) whose Hadrianic date for the *Annals* I reject; Syme, *Roman Papers* volume III pages 1014–42, *IV* (1988), 199–222, and *VI* (1991), 43–54, are all penetrating; Ronald Mellor, *Tacitus* (1993) and R. Martin, *Tacitus* (1981) are clear and helpful; J. B. Rives, *Tacitus: Germania* (1999) translates it; R. M. Ogilvie and I. Richmond (eds.), *Taciti Agricola* (1967) gives excellent notes and introduction; T. D. Barnes, in *Harvard Studies in Classical Philology* (1986), 225–64, is perceptive on the *Dialogues*; M. T. Griffin, in *Scripta Classica Israelica* (1999), 139–58, is excellent on Pliny and Tacitus; also in I. Malkin and Z. W. Rubensohn, *Leaders and Masses in the Roman World* (1995), 33–58, on Tacitus and Tiberius and in *Classical Quarterly* (1982), 404–16, on Tacitus, the Lyons Tablet and his provincial view.

COMMENTARY ON
THE ILLUSTRATIONS

1. Gold aureus from Rome, AD 134–8; obverse, a portrait of Hadrian; reverse, a personification of Egypt (Heberden Coin Room, Ashmolean Museum, Oxford)

2. Tondo, originally from a Hadrianic monument commemorating great hunting moments in his reign, set at Rome. Moved under the later Emperor Constantine, after AD 312, to adorn the Arch of Constantine in Rome. The lion killed here was in the Western Desert in Egypt in September AD 130. A verbose poem by a contemporary poet describes it as terrorizing the area and, when hunted, attacking Antinous on his horse but being killed by Hadrian himself and then stamped on by Antinous' steed. Here, Hadrian is second left (later, recut to resemble Constantine) and many believe, others dispute, that Antinous is at the far left, with his foot on the lion's head. If so, he looks unlike his boyish 'divine' portraits, spread after his death soon after the hunt (Arch of Constantine, Rome: author's photograph)

3. Black-figure amphora of the Tyrrhenian Group, c. 540 BC, showing a pentathlete in action (British Museum, London)

4. Older male, sexually aroused, fondles a young boy, who has slight down on his cheeks but no pubic hair: under age, certainly, so perhaps pre-pubic paidophilia, and definitely not 'ephebophilia', sex with older adolescents. The cup is now in Oxford, but it is not showing a 'teacher' sexually harassing a 'pupil'. A sponge and a strigil are behind the older man, signifying a gym or wrestling space: the boy has a net or bag, possibly for 'gym' gear. It represents a sexual advance in a sports-arena: as the male owner of the cup drank the last of the wine, this sex-scene appeared, a 'tondo' at the bottom of the cup. Red-figure tondo; Brygos Painter, c. 480 BC (Ashmolean Museum, Oxford)

5. Black-figure *lekythos*, or oil flask, showing a hunter with his spears and hound: Edinburgh Painter, Athens c. 510–500 BC (Vienna, Kunsthistorisches Museum: Photo: AKG Images, London)

6. Red-figure mixing-bowl, or *krater*, showing a symposion during which a slave-girl plays music for the male diners on their couches. On the right the diner is pouring watered wine into a cup, *phiale*, from a drinking-horn, *rhyton*, which ends in the forepart of a horse. Fourth century BC (Kunsthistorisches Museum, Vienna)

7. Marble statue from the acropolis in Sparta of a god or hero, bearded but not moustached. Probably one of a group on a Spartan temple: misunderstood as the famous Spartan warrior, Leonidas, when discovered in 1925 (Archaeological Museum of Sparta. Photo: Deutsches Archäologisches Institut-Athens)

8. Bronze figurine of a Spartan girl, detached from the rim of a bronze vessel. Her dress is cut away from the shoulder, Spartan style, and held up at the knee, suggesting that she is not an athlete running in a lady's race (in honour of Hera) but a dancer, though female Spartan dancers were said often to dance naked (British Museum)

9. Modern colour reconstruction of the so-called 'Peplos Korê', or 'Maiden in a Robe', one of several such statues dedicated in Athenian dress for upper-class Athenian women, perhaps often to commemorate their role as a 'priestess' in an important cult. She may have held a pomegranate, symbol of fertility in other contexts, in her outstretched hand. Most Greek marble statues were brightly painted in this way, refuting their 'austere' or 'marmoreal' reputation. Original *c.* 530 BC, from Athens (Photo and reconstruction: Museum of Classical Archaeology, Cambridge)

10. Colour reconstruction of the grave-stele of Aristion, by Aristocles. Aristion's name is inscribed on its own, with no father's name: perhaps he was a recent arrival in Attica, possibly the famous sculptor Aristion from Paros. Original *c.* 510 BC, found at Marathon in Attica. (Photo: V. Brinkmann, Staatliche Antikensammlungen und Glyptothek, Munich)

11. Footsoldiers of Persian king, wearing pointed hats, with ear-flaps, in Scythian style: limestone relief from palaces at Persepolis, fourth century BC (Vorderasiatisches Museum, Berlin)

12. Painting on the inner surface of the coffin-lid of the 'Tomb of the Diver', found in 1968 about a mile south of Paestum. Four other paintings of scenes from a symposium decorated the inner sides: the young boy dives, holding his head awkwardly, from a plinth of uncertain significance. Like the symposium scenes, the scene surely refers to worldly life, perhaps to something in the dead man's earlier life, rather than symbolizing his dive out into the 'unknown' space of the underworld, a favoured but fanciful interpretation. Painting on white stucco surface (Paestum Museum. Photo: © author)

13. Small terracotta plaque, one of many dedicated at the sanctuary of Persephone at Locri, in the Greek West, now Calabria in S. Italy. Probably the plaques were fixed on trees. In my view the young woman is putting away the folded cloth, not taking it out. The front of the chest is decorated with a panel of the goddess Athena killing a giant (Enceladus?) and another of a man leading off a woman, apparently willingly, by taking her right wrist. The allusion is possibly to an 'abduction' for marriage: the scene with the giant suggests, but only to some, that 'violence' is involved in male-female marriage. The lady is also thought to be preparing for marriage, perhaps packing up in her parental home. In my view, the young woman is already married, and enjoying it all, with symbols of her household role, including the cloth (a blanket) and the mirror and the wool-basket of a 'good wife' above her head. Just as the virgin Athena laid low a giant, so she, a virgin, thunderstruck her man whom she followed, taken willingly by the hand. If so, the plaque is dedicated by a woman in gratitude, not in preparation. *c.* 470–450 BC (Museo Archeologico Nazionale di Reggio Calabria)

14. Attic red-figure cup by the Cage painter, showing a youth, wreathed, so perhaps not a slave, filling his *kylix*, or drinking cup, with watered wine from the mixing bowl at a symposium, *c.* 490 BC (Musée du Louvre, Paris)

15. The upper half of one of the 'Riace bronzes', Warrior A, displayed since recovery in 1980, in Reggio di Calabria. Certainly a hero, he survived with his teeth and original eye-balls, a masterpiece. On one view, he and Warrior B were two of the ten heroes, eponyms of the Athenian democracy's tribes, made by the great Pheidias and dedicated at Delphi *c.* 460 BC. Others champion an artist from Argos, citing the (inconclusive) evidence of the type of earth used in the statue's filling. Many others remain safely agnostic. But he is a great work, plundered from Greece and shipped west before being wrecked (and saved on the seabed) near Locri in S. Italy (Museo Archeologico Nazionale di Reggio Calabria)

16. Attic black-figure tondo, painted inside a drinking-cup and showing a slave, contemptibly ugly, with ankles chained: he puts stones into a basket. As the drinker emptied the wine, he would see this contemptible figure at the bottom of his cup, and be amused. Attic black-figure tondo, *c.* 490–80 BC (Rijksmuseum van Oudheiden, Leiden)

17. Marble relief showing a pensive Athena in front of what is probably a grave monument, rather than a boundary marker. It might be inscribed with the names of Athenian casualties, recently dead in war, *c.* 460 BC (Acropolis Museum, Athens)

18. Fine marble Attic funerary-relief, perhaps of 431/0 BC, showing a dismounted Athenian cavalryman, holding his horse's reins in one hand and raising his sword in the other to kill his fallen enemy. The victim and the killer gaze at each other in a 'frozen' classic moment, of great power. The left of the relief shows hilly landscape, perhaps in Attica itself. The encounter may, then, belong in the first battle, a cavalry one, of the Peloponnesian War, described in Thucydides 2.22.2. If so, the victim may be a Theban and the Athenian cavalryman commemorated here will have been one of the beneficiaries of Pericles' Funeral Oration, the defining classical speech (Villa Albani, Rome. Photo: Hirmer Verlag)

19. Grave monument of Sosias and Kephisodorus whose names are inscribed above, from the left to beyond centre. It seems, then, that these two are the two left-hand figures, the left one wearing a priestly robe, the other hoplite armour and a pointed helmet, shaking hands with a third hoplite on the right. Are they the only dead men, one of whom takes a fond farewell of a fellow hoplite? Or, less plausibly, are all three dead? They fell in the Peloponnesian War: c. 410 BC (Antikensammlungen, Berlin)

20. Attic red-figure jug, or *pelike*, showing a baby learning to crawl, c. 430–520 BC (British Museum, London)

21. White-ground *lekythos*, or oil-flask showing a lady musician, with the caption 'Helicon', mountain of the Muses. She plays to a second lady, round the flask, who appears to gesture to the music. The implication, perhaps, is that the dead Athenian lady honoured by this flask is 'like a Muse': certainly, well-born Athenian women learned music. Achilles Painter, c. 440 BC (Antikensammlungen, Munich)

22. The 'Lady in Blue', a terracotta Tanagra figurine found with four others in a tomb just north of Tanagra in central Greece in the early 1870s when thousands of local tombs, some with these figurines, were excavated. The 'Tanagras' seemed to give an intimate glimpse of ancient Greek life and were a sensation, especially in France of the 1870s for whose public many copies, and clever fakes, were mass-produced. The Tanagran ladies were hailed as the 'Parisiennes' of their day, apparently exemplifying the grace and innate elegance of true Parisian ladies. The figurines' original purpose is uncertain, some now considering them to be 'dolls'. Their style, at times echoing marble sculpture, probably began in Athens, being imitated in Thebes (before 335 BC, when Alexander destroyed it) and then in nearby Tanagra. 'Tanagras' were widely exported, early to Macedon and then out eastwards as far as eastern Iran for Alexander's settlers in Asia who wanted such figurines from home. French critics named several, this one being 'La Dame en Bleu'. She preserves her blue and pink paint and some of the gold leaf, rare and precious, for her robe and the edge of her fan. Her robe, covered head and fan suggest that (like some Parisiennes) she is a courtesan. Tanagra, Greece, c. 330–300 BC (Musée du Louvre, Paris)

23. Wall painting from the big cist 'Tomb of Persephone' at Vergina (Aigai), the Macedonian royal centre, a few yards south-east of King Philip's tomb. The god Pluto ascends to his chariot, with his left foot still free, carrying a distraught Persephone off to the underworld. Beyond her, a female, perhaps her friend Kyane, is shown distressed. Beneath the chariot are flowers, like those Persephone was gathering in the meadow. The couple are also shown painted on the back of the marble throne in the tomb ascribed to King Philip's mother Eurydice, also at Vergina (c. 340 BC). The artist sketched freely, with visible revisions, before painting this four-colour masterpiece: he may be the famous Nicomachus. Dated c. 340 BC (Vergina [Aigai]: Photo: courtesy of Professor C. Paliadeli)

24. Detail from the façade painting on the Tomb of Philip at Vergina (Aigai), showing the face of the man identified as Alexander c. 336/5 BC (Photo: Professor C. Paliadeli)

25. Detail from the tomb façade painting on the Tomb of Philip at Vergina showing King Philip II on horseback, c. 336/5 BC (Photo: Professor C. Paliadeli)

26. Modern reconstruction by G. Miltsakakis of the original hunt painting, found on the façade of King Philip II's tomb at Vergina (Aigai). The scene is an expressive masterpiece, perhaps not true to one single day's hunting. The figure of the prancing horse, directly over the door,

is surely Alexander, centrally placed as the new king who paid for the scene. The dogs have been remarked for their exceptional jaws and fierce breeding. On the right, the older Philip (conforming to his coin portraits) attacks a lion, still at large in Macedon (a previous king had shown a lion pierced by a broken spear on his coinage). We are in Macedon, not Asia, and Philip hunts with younger lads, the Royal Pages whom he instituted. Alexander has brought down a boar, behind him, and now gallops to the lion: for the pose, compare our 34. The implausible notion that the Tomb contained the later Philip III, Alexander's half-witted half-brother (died 317 BC), is refuted by, among much else, the extreme implausibility of a painting on his tomb with Alexander himself at the centre and his absence (as a half-wit) from any such scene of hunting in person. Dated, therefore, 336/5 BC, the year of Philip II's murder, by a Greek master, possibly Aristides, whose use of a bare tree, the prancing horse and (possibly) these faces was paralleled in other near-contemporary paintings for Macedonians (Photo: Professor C. Paliadeli)

27. Grave stele of Thraseas and Euandria, husband and wife. She sits while he fondly clasps her hand and the head of a girl, surely a slave, looks on, pensively. A married Athenian scene, with a domestic onlooker, but we do not know which of the two had died. Athens, c. 350 BC (Antikensammlungen, Berlin)

28. Copy of the portrait-statue by Polyeuctus of the great Athenian orator and democrat Demosthenes, which was set up by admiring democrats in Athens in 280–79 BC, forty years after his death. It stood in the Agora near the Altar of the Twelve Gods. In the original, his hands were clasped simply, without a scroll. The style is admirably classical, in a 'severe' style, and the face and the position of the hands are apt for the expression of grief: the great Demosthenes, then, is mourning the city's loss of freedom to King Philip, and was put up in 280 on the proposal of his nephew Demochares at a time of renewed patriotic and democratic fervour against Macedon. The last great classical Greek statue, looking back to a classical hero, but made in a post-classical age (Ny Carlsberg Glyptothek)

29. Byzantine wall painting from the church of St Thomas at Kastoria in the north-west of Alexander's Macedon, showing the great king with King Porus of India, whose elephants he conquered but whose person he greatly honoured, King Cyrus, founder of the Persian Empire and King Nebuchadnezzar of Babylon, each of them two centuries older than Alexander. Great Alexander and the kings of these three Eastern empires meet here for the Last Judgement. Late Byzantine, fourteenth century AD (Photo: J. L. Lightfoot)

30. Three sections of the painted frieze above the doorway of a Macedonian tomb, discovered in 1994, at Agios Athanasios (probably ancient Chalastra) about twelve miles west of Thessalonica in Macedonia. Our middle register shows the frieze's centre, six men reclining at a symposion on bright cushions, listening to one woman (surprisingly, clothed) who plays the double *aulos*, like our oboe, while another, to the right, sits and plays a stringed *kithara*. A three-legged table is set with after-dinner dessert and the second male diner holds a drinking-horn, or *rhyton*, which ends in an 'oriental' griffin. Our upper register is the left of the frieze, showing three garlanded revellers on horseback, with others on foot carrying torches and a silver vessel for a drinking-party, similar to known examples, including one found in King Philip's tomb at Aigai. Our lower register shows eight Macedonian warriors, in military dress with shields typical of the Macedonian infantry. On either side of the door (not shown) a tall young Macedonian leans against a sarissa-spear, mourning the dead man inside. Despite the presence of a coin of Phillip II the tomb is currently dated to c. 320 BC. This splendid painting appeared in time for the size of its shields and its plumed helmets to be a starting point for the designers of Oliver Stone's epic *Alexander* film (2004), in which the comfortable lace-up cavalry boots, hand-made in Italy, resembled these Macedonians' own. So did the revels during filming. (Greek Archaeological Service; M. Tsimbidou-Avloniti, excavator)

31. Cast of a Roman copy of a contemporary marble portrait of Demetrius the Besieger, the most handsome and most flamboyant of Alexander's Successors. Born in 336 BC, the year of Alexander's accession, he was son of Antigonus the one-eyed and is sculpted here with small

bull's horns in his hair, attributes of the god Dionysus with whom he liked to be compared. He also wears a narrow diadem, symbol of royalty for Alexander's Successors since 306/5 BC. Cast, from Copenhagen Glyptotek (Photo: Professor Marianne Bergmann)

32. Cast of a Roman bronze portrait bust of Seleucus I, commander of Alexander's Royal Shield-bearers, then a Successor King in Asia (he wears the royal diadem here) and founder of the Seleucid dynasty to which Antiochus III in figure 11.4 belonged. From the Villa of the Papyri, Herculaneum, Roman copy *c.* 50 BC of a lost marble original. Cast from Copenhagen Glyptotek (Photo: Professor Marianne Bergmann)

33. Silver plate, 25 cms in diameter, with gilded figures, found carefully buried in a city-temple on the site at Ai Khanum, Afghanistan. A goddess is driven by a winged Victory in a chariot pulled by lions, attended by a priest behind, with parasol, and driven to a high stepped altar where a second priest waits, making an offering. A youthful Sun, the moon and a star are in the sky. The goddess wears a turreted headdress and is currently, but uncertainly, identified as the Greek Cybele coming down from her mountains, shown behind. However she may be Syrian, or local. The chariot is of near Eastern style, as are the altar and the priest's pointed hat, but the Victory and the youthful Sun are certainly Greek. A similar plate has now been found just to the west, at Takht-i-Sangin (see 36), implying a local craftsman, not an import from Seleucid Syria. This fine plate survived the wars of the 1980s and 1990s and is still in Afghanistan (Photo: Délégation Archélogique Française en Afghanistan, courtesy of Professor Paul Bernard)

34. Modern drawing to reconstruct a major Macedonian hunting scene, known in a mosaic copy, perhaps *c.* 150 BC, which survives in the Piazza Vittoria, Palermo. The original painting showed a hunt in Asia, confirmed by the vegetation on the right side: perhaps it is a famous hunt in Syria, in 332/1 BC. The mounted huntsman, rescuing the fallen warrior from a lion, replicates the pose of the figure to be identified as Alexander in figure 20.1. The fallen warrior was, arguably, identified with Lysimachus, one of Alexander's Bodyguards and an eventual Successor in western Asia. To the right, a participant in Oriental dress runs away from a hunted boar: he chickens out symptomatically, so unlike the brave Macedonian 'lion kings'. The original is similar to parts of the Vergina hunt painting and probably comes from the same circle, or artist, at an uncertain date, but surely in Alexander's own lifetime, close to the memorable lion-hunting of 332/1 BC (Reconstruction, drawing and photo by William Wootton)

35. South façade of the court of Tomb I in Moustapha Pasha necropolis, Alexandria, Egypt, with a reconstructed altar in front and traces of fine painting, including Macedonian cavalrymen pouring libations with one hand and ladies standing between. Probably *c.* 280–260 BC, Alexandria (Photo: Professor Marianne Bergmann)

36. The most remote Ionic Greek column-capital yet known: locally carved for the big temple-portico of the largely Asiatic-style temple to the river Oxus at Takht-i-Sangin where the Oxus and Waksh rivers meet. The capital recalls details of late fourth–third century BC Ionic capitals back in Ionia, but the site is on the Oxus's northern bank, in Tadjikistan. After Alexander, perhaps *c.* 300–280 BC under Seleucus (Photo: Délégation Archéologique Française en Afghanistan: R. Besenval)

37. Aerial view of the Greek city-site on the Oxus, in modern Afghanistan, at Ai Khanum. The site in the plain contained Greek inscriptions, fragments of Greek sculpture (including a big horse statue, with a wild animal-skin shown as its horse-blanket: ridden by a king, no doubt), a big Greek gymnasium, a palace, and a theatre set in the hillside. It was then plundered and devastated during the wars of the 1980s and 1990s. But the 'acropolis' was never excavated, nor a mound less than a mile up river: the site may thus be a foundation of Alexander in 329–7 BC, subsequently enlarged and flourishing until *c.* 130 BC (D. A. F. A., courtesy of Professor Paul Bernard)

38. Painting of drunken Silenus, Dionysus' companion on his revels, set on a marble funeral-bed in a Macedonian Tomb, excavated at Potidaea in south-east Macedonia. He holds a drinking-horn, or *rhyton*, ending in an 'oriental' griffin, like the Macedonian diners in our figure 34.

Late fourth century BC (Excavator: Dr. Costas Sismanidis: photo courtesy of Professor D. Pandermalis)

39. Big Corinthian column-capitals excavated at Ai Khanum, the Greek city on the Oxus and Kokcha rivers in northern Afghanistan, probably an Alexandria, subsequently enlarged. Reused as the main city-site was pillaged and ruined during the wars of the 1980s and 1990s: they now support the roof of a nearby modern tea-house (Photo: Délégation Archélogique Française en Afghanistan: R. Besenval)

40. Foot of a colossal Greek acrolith statue, surely of a god, *c.* 250–150 BC, from the Greek city at Ai Khanum, Afghanistan (Délégation Archéologique Française en Afghanistan, courtesy of Prof. Paul Bernard)

41. Ptolemy I, silver tetradrachm, *c.* 310–305 BC. Head of Alexander (Heberden Coin Room, Ashmolean Museum, Oxford)

42. Indo-Greek silver tetradrachm, *c.* 170–145 BC. Bust of Eucratides (Heberden Coin Room, Ashmolean Museum, Oxford)

43. Indo-Greek silver tetradrachm, 160–145 BC. Bust of Menander (Heberden Coin Room, Ashmolean Museum, Oxford)

44. Silver tetradrachm from Sardis, *c.* 213–190 BC. Head of Antiochus III (Heberden Coin Room, Ashmolean Museum, Oxford)

45. Silver denarius from Rome, 113 or 112 BC, showing voting scenes. On the left, a supervisor (the *custos*) gives a voting tablet to a voter who will mark it, walk up to a wooden 'bridge' and follow the man (right) who is putting his tablet into an urn. Both voters wear the required toga and above, the letter 'P' signifies a tribe. This voting one by one is at an assembly to pass laws for which a 'secret' ballot was relatively recent, and special to Rome. In 119 BC, the 'bridges' had been narrowed, as proposed by Marius when tribune, so as to stop intimidation of individual voters. The moneyer who issued this coin, Licinius Nerva, may be a partisan of Marius, celebrating the reform (Heberden Coin Room, Ashmolean Museum, Oxford)

46. Silver denarius from Rome, 82 BC, showing Sulla on the reverse triumphing in a four-horse chariot. Significantly, the coin was issued before Sulla actually celebrated a triumph for his victory over Mithridates in Asia. In 82 BC, he invaded Italy and marched on Rome in open civil war. The triumph began only on January 27, 81 BC (Heberden Coin Room, Ashmolean Museum, Oxford)

47. Imperial Roman copy of a marble portrait head of Pompey, combining the realism of small eyes and expression with a hairstyle recalling the great Alexander with whom Pompey was at times, optimistically, compared (Ny Carlsberg Glyptotek, Copenhagen)

48. Marble portrait generally assumed to represent Cicero, 30s BC (Galleria degli Uffizi, Florence)

49. Portrait head of Julius Caesar, probably posthumous: *c.* 40–30 BC (Vatican Museum, Rome)

50. Silver denarius, Rome, 44 BC. On obverse, a portrait of Julius Caesar, dictator, in the year of his murder. On reverse, his 'ancestor', the goddess Venus (Heberden Coin Room, Ashmolean Museum, Oxford)

51. The Portland Vase, brilliantly crafted blue and white cameo-glass. The uncaptioned figures have attracted many interpretations, of which the mythological ones are most likely. In our left-hand picture, the seated lady, holding a sea-monster, may be Thetis, goddess of the sea, watched pensively by the sea-god Poseidon, shown in a famous pose based on his statue by Lysippus, Alexander's favoured sculptor. She draws fondly to her the nearly naked Peleus whom she will marry. A 'Cupid' with a flaming torch leads him on. The tree above may be a myrtle, although it has been compared with a budding peach, erotically more apt. Our right-hand picture is more disputed. I suggest a (slightly) regretful Aeneas, looking to the distressed Dido whom he has 'reluctantly' abandoned. She sits on a heap of marble plaques, possibly symbolizing a 'broken home', and her torch of 'love' is lowered. She will kill herself on a bonfire, perhaps implied

here. To the far right, Venus, Aeneas' mother, looks on with a sceptre. The tree is probably a fig tree, symbolizing barrenness. On the one side, then, the vase shows love leading to marriage, and to the future child Achilles. On the other side, love is abandoned and instead Aeneas will found a new home in Italy. As the supposed ancestors of Julius Caesar, Venus (and Aeneas) were Octavian's ancestors. So, there may be a hint of Octavian-Augustus in the choice of themes. There is now a theory that on the left, the figures are Mark Antony, a seated Cleopatra, and Anton (a Heracles-figure and a supposed ancestor of Antony). On the right, Octavian is suggested as looking at his poor sister Octavia, Antony's abandoned wife, while Venus and her sceptre assure him all will be well. The problems here are that Cleopatra is not naturally associated with a sea-monster (although she came by ship to meet Antony) nor with Poseidon, certainly the figure to her right. A half-naked pose for Octavia would also be surprising. The figures are surely mythological, not historical. Any reference to Octavian-Augustus is partial, and indirect, although the vase was made between *c.* 35 and 10 BC (British Museum, London)

52. Amphitheatre mosaic from a house floor at Smirat in Tunisia (north of ancient Thysdrus): it is antiquity's supreme combination of text and image. A company of professional animal-hunters called the 'Telegonii' are shown fighting under the patronage of Dionysus, with Diana, goddess of the hunt, also in the mosaic. Each is captioned with their tough professional name ('the Mamertine') and each has just killed one of four leopards, individually named too ('the Roman' and 'Luxurious'): these two of the leopards are garlanded with ivy, Dionysus' plant. The inscription is a classic, recording how the herald in the arena called on 'my Lords', the local big-wigs, to pay 500 denarii to each hunter as the reward for each dead leopard. The crowd then started a chanted acclamation, to encourage a possible donor. 'By your example, may future donors learn how to give a show! Let past donors hear! From where has such a show ever come? When has there been one like this? (*Quando tale*). You will be giving a show like the quaestors at Rome . . . The day will be yours'. . . Then, the great moment occurred . . . 'Magerius is donating! This is what it means to have money! This is what it is to be powerful! This is it—here and now! Night is here! By your gift, they've taken their leave with bags of money.' The mosaic shows four moneybags but specifies each one was of 1,000 denarii: Magerius doubled the huntsmen's reward. Above all, Magerius had the scene, the very words of the herald and the crowd, the moneybags, the names (of the leopards, the hunters and his own) laid out in mosaic, naturally in his own house for future visitors' instruction. It is the pearl of all hunt-mosaics, though later than Hadrian, perhaps *c.* AD 260–80: Magerius' like, however, existed earlier, and still does (Sousse Museum, Tunisia)

53. Relief frieze from upper storey of the portico leading to the shrine of the Roman emperors, the Sebasteion at Aphrodisias in modern Turkey, showing Augustus with symbolic representations of land and sea, symbolizing his world-wide power. *c.* 60 AD (Photo: M. Ali Dü(enci, courtesy of Professor R. R. R. Smith)

54. Relief frieze from same location, showing the Emperor Claudius conquering Britannia, as his army partly did in his presence in AD 43 (Photo: M. Ali Düğenci, courtesy of Professor R. R. R. Smith)

55. Gold coin showing Nero and his mother Agrippina, face to face on the obverse. A unique placing for an imperial woman, but in December 54 (the coin's date), Agrippina was a unique 'queen mother'. Her titles are on this side of the coin, whereas Nero's are only on the reverse. In the next year (55) the portraits are shown side by side and the titles swap sides, no doubt by order of Nero (British Museum, London)

56. Portrait of a boy, surrounded by the original mummy-wrappings which held his picture onto the mummy-case. From the Fayyum, Egypt. Reign of Trajan, AD 98–117 (British Museum, London)

57. The huge aqueduct at Segovia in Spain, on which an inscription refers to 'restoration' by Trajan's orders in AD 98, undertaken by local magistrates. So, an aqueduct existed earlier and was then improved (Photo: J. L. Lightfoot)

58. Roman theatre at Emerita (now Mérida) in Spain, founded by Augustus as a colony-city for his retired soldiers (*emeriti*). Datable to 16/15 BC, with the patronage of his general Agrippa, and subsequently further decorated. Emerita quickly became a showpiece, with loads of marble, including a Forum (later decorated to imitate Augustus' own at Rome), big temples and an amphitheatre for blood-sports (Photo: J. L. Lightfoot)

59. Gold aureus from Judaea, AD 70, found at Finstock, West Oxfordshire, UK in the 1850s and only recently recognized. Obverse, Vespasian, the new Emperor. Reverse, a personification of Justice, the first known. She expresses the Roman view of their 'just' sack of Jerusalem and its Temple. Struck under Titus, Vespasian's son and the commander in Judaea (Heberden Coin Room, Ashmolean Museum, Oxford)

60. Male–Female sex scene, uncertain location, wall painting. AD 40–70, Pompeii (Museo Archeologico, Naples; photo, Giovanni Battista)

61. Brass sestertius from Rome, AD 96, with a portrait of the 'good' Emperor Nerva on the obverse. The reverse shows clapsed hands symbolising, optimistically, the 'concord' of the armies (Heberden Coin Room, Ashmolean Museum, Oxford)

62. Wall painting of Terentius Neo, holding a book-scroll, and his wife, holding a stylus-pen and a folded writing-tablet. Pompeii, House vii.2.6, c. 60 AD. Terentius Neo's common features remind us that literacy was not the art, or pretension, only of an upper class at Pompeii (Photo: AKG Images, London)

63. Wall painting from the portico on the far side of the peristyle garden of the House of Marine Venus in a Shell, at Pompeii. Venus is drawn by a cherub on a dolphin and pushed by another cherub across the sea: the scene seems to have been painted by different hands, of which the artist for her head is best. Venus was a patron-goddess of Pompeii and here, her hairstyle follows a fashion in Nero's reign at Rome. The *trompe l'œil* style makes her and the sea seem to float beyond the adjoining wall paintings of enclosed gardens, at least when viewed from the peristyle's entrance way. AD 60s (Photo: J. L. Lightfoot)

64. Female–male sex scene from House of the Centenary, Room 43. Sited above the recessed bed in the small 'slave-quarters' room of the supervisor of the household: not, then, in a main room in this house, which was eventually owned by an aedile of the town. c. AD 49–70, Pompeii (Photo: Giovanni Battista)

65. A reconstruction of Pliny's Villa at Laurentum, one of many, based on Pliny's own Letter, a major text in the history of landscape gardening. Louis-Pierre Haudebourt prided himself on his Latin and classical allusions; he visited Pompeii in 1815–16, was a respected architect in Paris and in 1838, published plans, imagined interior and exterior views and this general impression of Pliny's villa, with a learned commentary between himself and an imaginary architect used by Pliny, one Mustius. From L. P. Haudebourt, Le Laurentin, Maison de Campagne de Pline Le Jeune (Paris, 1838)

66. Scenes from the Column of Trajan in his Forum at Rome, dedicated in AD 112/3 to commemorate his campaigns against the Dacians (modern Romania)

a) Dacian prisoners are brought before the emperor Trajan outside a Roman camp

b) Roman soldiers lock their shields together in the 'tortoise' (*testudo*) formation as they attack a Dacian fortress

c) The Dacian's leader, Decebalus, kills himself near a tree as the Roman cavalry attacks him

d) Victory inscribes a shield, recording Trajan's successes for posterity (Photos: Deutsches Archäologisches Institut, Rome)

67. Bronze portrait head of Hadrian, second quarter of second century AD (Museo Nazionale, Rome)

68. Portrait of a woman, with fashionable pearl and red-stone earrings and unusual highlighting, suggesting a tear-drop in her left eye. Found at Antinoopolis, Hadrian's new city for his dead male lover. She will have been one of the first batch of settlers, keen to show her social status. AD 130s (Arthur M. Sackler Museum, Harvard University)

69. Modern reconstruction of the south-westerly of the two chambers which made up the Library of Trajan in his Forum at Rome, dedicated in AD 112–3. Between these two facing chambers stood his Column in its portico: on one side, able to be closed by grilles, each chamber opened out onto it. Two storeys high, this chamber was about 30 yards by 20 yards, a stairway leading to the upper gallery. Each side-wall had seven upper and seven lower niches for scrolls in 'bookcases', set away from the wall to avoid damp. The floor was paved in grey granite from Egypt with strips of yellow marble from north Africa. The walls of brick-faced concrete were covered with a layer of multicoloured marble from western Asia. The white marble statue at the far end was surely of Trajan. Perhaps the historian Tacitus worked here among the 10,000 rolls which each chamber held (Reconstruction by G. Gorski)

70. Marble relief of the deified Antinous from near Lanuvium, Italy, represented in the style of the nature-god Silvanus. Signed by Antonianos from Aphrodisias, now in Turkey and a great seat of marble sculpture (from Istituto dei Fondi Rustici, now Banco Nazionale, Rome)

71. Replica statue from the grounds of Hadrian's villa at Tivoli, representing a classical Greek warrior whose bronze original has not survived. The warrior is beardless, and therefore unlikely to represent the war god Ares. He is probably a semi-divine hero: his pose and weaponry have suggested that he may represent one of the Athenians' ten tribal heroes, sculpted by the great Pheidias and dedicated at Delphi c. 460 BC. A similar origin has been upheld for the fine 'Riace Bronze' warrior, (our number 15), who held a shield and also a spear (now lost). But unlike the Roman who stole an original from Greece, and then lost it off Riace at sea, Hadrian patronized a replica by a contemporary sculptor, thus respecting the 'classical' original. His replica stands by the long canal in his garden, known as 'Canopus' after the celebrated canal by Alexandria in Egypt, well known for its luxury. So, Hadrian combined 'luxury' and respect for the classical world, a fitting climax to our illustrations. Hadrian's villa, Tivoli, c. AD 135 (Photo: © Macduff Everton/CORBIS)

INDEX